THE CRICKETERS' WHO'S WHO 1992

THE CRICKETERS' WHO'S WHO 1992

compiled and edited by
IAIN SPROAT

Foreword by
MARK NICHOLAS

Statistics by
RICHARD LOCKWOOD

Portraits photographed or researched by
BILL SMITH

Lennard Publishing

LENNARD PUBLISHING
a division of Lennard Associates Limited
Mackerye End, Harpenden
Herts AL5 5DR

Published in association with
The Cricketers' Who's Who Limited

First published in Great Britain 1992

British Library Cataloguing in Publication
is available

ISBN 1 85291 107 7

Typeset in Times
Cover design by Cooper Wilson

Cover photographs and acknowledgements
(*clockwise from top left*)
Dean Jones (*Chris Cole, AllSport*)
Durham University ground (*Chris Cole, AllSport*)
John Glendenen (*Durham CCC*)
David Graveney (*Chris Cole, AllSport*)
Darren Blenkiron (*Durham CCC*)

Reproduced, printed and bound by
Butler and Tanner Limited, Frome and London

PREFACE

The cricketers listed in this volume include all those who played for a first-class county at least once last season in any form of cricket. All statistics are complete to the end of the last English season. Figures about 1000 runs and 50 wickets in a season refer to matches in England only. All first-class figures this year include figures for Test matches which are also extracted and listed separately. One-day 100s and 50s are for the English domestic competitions and all One-Day Internationals, home and abroad. The Refuge figures include both League and Cup matches.

The following abbreviations apply: *means not out; All First – all first-class matches; 1-day Int – One-Day Internationals; Refuge – Refuge Assurance League/Cup; NatWest – NatWest Trophy; B&H – Benson & Hedges Cup. The figures for batting and bowling averages refer to the full first-class English list for 1991, followed in brackets by the 1990 figures. Inclusion in the batting averages depends on a minimum of six completed innings, and an average of at least 10 runs; a bowler has to have taken at least 10 wickets. The same qualification has been used for compiling the bowlers' strike rate.

Readers will notice certain occasional differences in the way the same kind of information is presented. This is because I have usually tried to follow the way in which the cricketers themselves have provided the relevant information.

Each year in *The Cricketers' Who's Who,* in addition to those cricketers who are playing during the current season, I also include the biographical and career details of those who played in the previous season but retired at the end of it. The purpose of this is to have, on the record, the full and final cricketing achievements of every player when his career has ended.

A book of this complexity and detail has to be prepared several months in advance of the cricket season, and occasionally there are recent changes in a player's circumstances which cannot be included in time. Many examples of facts and statistics which can quickly become outdated in the period between the actual compilation of the book and its publication, months later, will spring to the reader's mind, and I ask him or her to make the necessary commonsense allowance and adjustments.

Iain Sproat
February 1992

FOREWORD

Glory days; the West Indies are held at home, two Tests each. They are matched punch for punch by a combative English team, who also comfortably win the one-day internationals. A route march through New Zealand continues unabated (at the time of writing anyway – should put the mockers on it!) and the World Cup lies waiting: a pot of gold at the end of an optimistic rainbow.

Glory days indeed. The four consecutive Test victories (remember the efficient demolition of Sri Lanka) were chiselled from dependable, positive batting, tidy seam bowling and the cunning of a London ragamuffin, Philip Tufnell – the cockney imp with the guts to flight the ball and the native trickery of a Bishen Bedi. Suddenly England have the world's most potent finger-spinner. They have a single-minded captain, a man who is rapidly becoming the most influential cricketer of his time, and a team of no little style and application.

The road ahead appears clear. To work hard is *the* ethic, bowl straight and bat long. But is it? Is our domestic game healthy? And on what sort of diet are our spectators being fed?

The 1992 season is upon us. By the time these words are consumed that World Cup will have been decided, as will the World Series Cup, as will many other one-day internationals all over the Southern Hemisphere. England, long-time conservationists of 'trad' cricket have succumbed to a further two (making five in all) one-dayers against Pakistan this summer and the Sunday League continues in all its shame, unsponsored (at the time of writing), unloved by its participants, ridiculed by its press and barely spoken for by its governing body.

This surfeit of cheap one-day cricket, though understandable in its origina-tion, is damaging. We are foul of the Costa del Sol syndrome – commercialize and expand. The boom time is here, so sell and listen to the tills chatter, as studs do on concrete, with high energy takings and no regard for style or charm. One-day cricket is McDonald's hamburger. Easy to get, moorish at first but in danger of becoming indigestible. It has set a standard with which a generation has grown older. It is not a standard that is easy to break down. Any parent will tell you that.

When 60-over cricket was first integrated into our domestic system it was a much needed injection of funk. The Championship was sterile. A change was as good as a rest. 1963 saw the first Gillette Cup and wow, how good it tasted. New interest, full houses and a climax in September – as good a day out as any in the sporting calendar – that thrilled cricket's rejuvenated populace. Us kids were dizzy with excitement as Dexter and Alley; Lloyd and Bond; 'Dolly' , Hughes and Asif improvised, chipped and slogged their way into the hearts of a nation. The audiences whistled the tunes of the players as they rid themselves of shackles imposed by declarations and draws, bonus points and boredom. But this innocent complement to 'the real thing' is rapidly becoming a monster, so dominant and all-consuming that the game's life blood, the refined skills first learnt at grass-root level, is now sorely threatened.

While this one-day takeover has continued apace the County Championship has also moved its goalposts. Out has gone the 'sticky dog' and pitches, since 1981, have become fully covered to allow stroke-makers their stuff and sponsors maximum value from their input. The 'sticky dog ', a dry pitch that got sodden by rain and half dried again in the sun, was a spinner's dream as the ball bit into the crusty surface and spat at batting gloves. This was the sort of pitch on which Laker and Underwood bowled out the Australians – what fun! You dare not choose a team without a tweaker or two.

Not now, for the lifeless surfaces negate our embryonic Lakers. In addition heavy bats, ludicrous field settings and a 'limited over' line and length prevail.

This is a nonsense, we know it, and we are slow to change. The spinner is not the only victim as dead pitches take their toll on the fast men, whose pace and bounce is sterilized. The enthusiasm of attack is quickly swopped for the meanness of defence.

Under these circumstances the three-day game is often a sham. Stalemate on the last morning ensures give-away runs so that mutually agreeable targets are reached and declarations may be set for the afternoon. These 'agreed declarations' revive the players from their dreary state of impasse and the spectator is then given some cricket that is competitive and frequently compelling, if contrived. So where are we? We are back at McDonald's that is where.

Within the current structure of domestic cricket, three areas need examining. How much limited-overs cricket should we play? How can the Championship become more exciting and exhilarating for all its contributors – players, spectators, sponsors alike – and on what surfaces should it be played?

40-over cricket must be exorcized – three limited-overs competitions is too many anyway. For one thing the players are drained by excessive travelling and one competition less would allow time for recuperation and consequently a fresher more committed attitude to each new match.

Sunday is the crucial revenue day and therefore should be a day which television cannot afford to miss. A 50-over league of 17 matches (under the eye of Benson & Hedges perhaps) would allow counties enough matches to maximize income from both out-grounds and headquarters. Effectively this competition would replace the Sunday League and substitute the existing 55-over competition. In order to allow the sponsor his head the top eight teams would play off at the quarter-final stage with the top four in the league rewarded with a home draw. This way, counties who start the season indifferently will always have 8th place, and a prospective final, to challenge for.

To attract further revenue the sponsor's name should be emblazoned on the shirtfront and the player's name and number on his back (recognising a player under a crash helmet is a tricky business). It would be possible to accommodate coloured clothing, in pastel shades, or simply to have piping on sleeves and trousers to encourage merchandising.

One or two rule changes might recharge interest. As in Australia only two players would be allowed outside the 'circle' for the first 20 overs, and two must be in catching positions, i.e. slip fielders or within 15 yards of the stumps. This would ensure stroke-play early in the innings but also wicket-taking with the new ball. Tactically, the game would be less transparent than at present and we might not have to wait quite so long for the real thrills and spills.

Bowlers may be allowed full run-ups, though I favour an experiment of 25 yards: (a) to ensure that the game is played within reasonable television hours (six ought to be plenty) and (b) to see whether the faster bowlers can generate rhythm and pace from this distance. Certainly Hadlee, Akram, Garner and Marshall of recent experts have bowled convincingly from shorter runs.

This competition is the money-maker; nothing should stop the quest for income from this new, exciting 'Weekend League'. I say weekend because I suspect it will be difficult to play the whole competition, league and play-offs, before mid-September. As long as every available Sunday is catered for, Saturdays could be used when there is a lull in the Championship.

The NatWest Trophy would stay as it is – mind you I'd have sponsor's names and players names and numbers, etc. on those shirts too. This would maximize the strengths of the one-day game without strangling its excitement or colour. More importantly we are dictating the style of the cricket and creating fresh impetus for both players and spectators.

It may be more complicated to adjust the County Championship. Uncovered pitches are in some way more desirable. On an uncertain surface nimble footwork and a delicate touch are at a premium. Knowledge of back-foot play is essential as the spiteful delivery will wound the committed front-footer. The bowler also has to think carefully: If his length is a fraction short the ball will sit up and beg and the batsman is primed for counter attack. A full length is essential to encourage risky strokes on so tacky a surface. The spinner and swinger hold sway.

Sometimes, of course, the surface becomes unreasonable, even dangerous. Today, danger is negated by exceptional protective equipment, equipment that may truly have a part to play against Waqar on a wet one! One last unproven thought about opening pitches to the elements: will the grass grow better if it is not suffocated quite so often? Will not the good pitch be even better if sun, rain and wind are allowed to work their natural mystique?

With that off my chest, I shall play 'devil's advocate' and explore the other side of the coin. There are two acceptable reasons not to play on uncovered pitches. The first is that it would be ludicrous for our Test players to prepare for international matches on surfaces different from those used at Test level, particularly as we are doing all in our power to ensure a successful England team. The second is the debt we owe to sponsors. Corporate hospitality accounts for a huge percentage of each county's budget. I doubt whether marketing directors will re-book if their clients fail to see a ball bowled due to an overnight thunderstorm.

If we are to continue with the three-day Championship there must be some leeway in the preparation of pitches. After the 1989 season there was an outcry against green, damp, 'doctored' surfaces. The ball had a large rope-like seam and journeymen medium-pacers were creating havoc as destructive as a Shackleton or Cartwright might have done. Naturally, we don't want to return to such farce. Neither, however, do we wish for stagnant cricket and last day fiascos.

The seam on the ball has already been successfully minimized and swing-bowling is having a slow but welcome resurgence. With careful monitoring so as to ensure that pitches are not 'unfit' for first-class cricket, it may now be prudent, indeed entertaining, to allow some home advantage. Balance between bat and ball is essential – in fact it is the very art in preparing a pitch. To go to Middlesex and find a dry 'turner', or to Manchester and see a grassier 'seamer' may not be so daft. Some of the charm of our county game is in its idiosyncrasies. No pitch, however, should *start* damp. This tendency must be repulsed as it weighs the odds too heavily in favour of the winner of the toss.

The answer may be to play 17 four-day matches on dry, hard, undoctored pitches. The TCCB should govern the groundsmen and, if necessary, employ them, so that each surface is prepared to the Board's satisfaction. Since the surface is the key to the contest, control by the central authority can be no bad thing.

A four-day match favours the stronger team. There is no hiding place for the meek and 110-over days mean that virtually as much cricket is played as in a Test match.

I have one last idea to spice things up a little, whether in the three-day or the four-day game. Under current laws the bowler may follow through no further than four feet down the pitch in a line six inches either side of the stumps. Should he go further than four feet on this line he is roughing an area in which the spinner may land the ball with some relish. For this crime he will be warned twice and then banned from bowling for the remainder of the innings. Why?

Why, you might ask: in order to unearth another Tufnell or two I suggest that we extend this area to five feet and lessen the distance either side of the stumps to three inches. We should then see more tactical seam bowling from close to, and wide of, the stumps and from over and around the wicket. This would surely rough things up for 'Tuffers' and his clan. Suddenly that last afternoon declaration may have some real significance, for who will give away runs only to chase them again on a disordered, rough surface.

The law will need changing of course, which will prompt some tutt-tutting at HQ but then who would be bothered by such changes if some of cricket's charm and variety is recovered by the beloved spinner, the most lamented soul in the modern game.

MARK NICHOLAS
Bangkok, Thailand
February 1992

THE QUIZ

Throughout this book there are 200 quiz questions.

The answers can be found on page 602.

Where the questions relate to players topping their county first-class averages the averages referred to are those for the Britannic Assurance Championship and not all first-class matches.

ADAMS, C. J. Derbyshire

Name: Christopher John Adams
Role: Right-hand bat, right-arm
medium pace bowler, slip and out fielder
Born: 6 May 1970, Whitwell, Derbyshire
Height: 6ft **Weight:** 13st 5lbs
Nickname: Grizzly
County debut: 1988
1st-Class 50s scored: 7
1st-Class 100s scored: 4
1st-Class catches: 51
One-Day 50s: 3
Place in batting averages: 104th av. 31.40
(1990 157th av. 31.06)
Parents: John and Elyned
Marital status: Engaged to Samantha
Family links with cricket: Brother David
played 2nd XI cricket for Derbyshire and
Gloucestershire. Father played for Yorkshire
Schools and uncle played for Essex 2nd XI.

Education: Chesterfield Grammar School and Repton College
Qualifications: 6 O-levels, NCA Coaching Certificate
Careers outside cricket: Salesman, shop assistant, woodcutter, driver...
Off-season: Playing and coaching abroad
Cricketing habits: 'I like to be at the ground at least $2^1/_2$ hours before play starts.'
Overseas tours: Barbados with Repton School, 1986
Overseas teams played for: Takapuna, New Zealand 1987-88, Te Puke, New Zealand
1989-90
Cricketers particularly admired: 'All the great players – Ian Botham in particular, Alan
Hill for his preparation game and his do or die attitude and Mohammad Azharuddin (Azzy)
simply the best around today.'
Other sports followed: Football (Southend and Arsenal), golf, rally driving and most
other sports
Injuries: Missed one game in 1991 with bursitis (fluid on the knee)
Relaxations: 'Relaxing on the settee in front of the tele. Enjoying a pint in my local, The
Mallet and Chisel, and going to the cinema.
Extras: 'Beat Richard Hutton's 25-year-old record for most runs scored in a season at
Repton. Represented ESCA at U15 and U19 levels, MCC Schools U19 and Young England
in 1989. Took two catches fielding as 12th man for England v India at Old Trafford in
1990.'
Opinions on cricket: 'I believe that four-day cricket is a must. With the introduction of
Durham it seems sense to me that 17 four-day games, playing each county once, is a far
better system than the present one. Coloured clothing would be great and anything else that

13

would promote the game and bring in more spectators – especially at sunny Derby.'
Best batting: 134 Derbyshire v Cambridge University, Fenner's 1991
Best bowling: 4-29 Derbyshire v Lancashire, Derby 1991

1991 Season

	M	Inns	NO	Runs	HS	Avge	100s	50s	Ct	St	O	M	Runs	Wkts	Avge	Best	5wI	10wM
Test																		
All First	15	24	2	691	134	31.40	2	1	15	-	19.4	3	59	6	9.83	4-29	-	-
1-day Int																		
NatWest																		
B&H	4	3	1	18	16 *	9.00	-	-	1	-	1	0	3	0	-		-	-
Refuge	15	13	2	375	71	34.09	-	2	4	-								

Career Performances

	M	Inns	NO	Runs	HS	Avge	100s	50s	Ct	St	Balls	Runs	Wkts	Avge	Best	5wI	10wM
Test																	
All First	46	70	7	1905	134	30.23	4	7	51	-	202	115	8	14.37	4-29	-	-
1-day Int																	
NatWest	2	1	0	0	0	0.00	-	-	1	-							
B&H	8	7	2	98	44	19.60	-	-	3	-	6	3	0	-		-	-
Refuge	37	32	9	665	71	28.91	-	3	12	-							

AFFORD, J. A.   Nottinghamshire

Name: John Andrew Afford
Role: Slow left-arm bowler, right-hand bat and 'hopeless fielder'
Born: 12 May 1964, Crowland, Peterborough
Height: 6ft 1^{1}/$_{2}$in **Weight:** 13st
Nickname: Aff, Des
County debut: 1984
County cap: 1990
50 wickets in a season: 2
1st-Class 5 w. in innings: 7
1st-Class 10 w. in match: 1
1st-Class catches: 32
Place in bowling averages: 63rd av. 31.87 (1990 114th av. 46.28)
Strike rate: 70.57 (career 72.21)
Parents: Jill
Wife and date of marriage: Lynn, 1 October 1988

Children: Lily Meagan, 1 June 1991
Education: Spalding Grammar School; Stamford College for Further Education
Qualifications: 5 O-levels, NCA coaching certificate
Overseas tours: England A to Kenya/Zimbabwe 1989-90
Overseas teams played for: Upper Hutt, Taita and Petone, all in Wellington, New Zealand between 1984 and 1991.
Cricketers particularly admired: Richard Hadlee, Clive Rice and Andy Pick – 'he can't leave it alone'. Anyone who bowls a lot
Other sports followed: Football – Peterborough United FC
Injuries: 'Bad knee all season. Thigh strain – missed one game, bad attitude – missed one game.'
Relaxations: 'Now our house is finished I tend to lie on the sofa watching TV.'
Extras: Hat-trick against Leics 2nd XI in 1989, also took 100 wickets in that season, 47 in 2nd XI and 53 in 1st XI
Opinions on cricket: 'Why is it that if a pitch offers too much assistance to the bowler the pitch inspector is called in and the clubs are terrified of repercussions but when, as in the case of Notts v Surrey at The Oval, 7 wickets fall in 3 days this is regarded as a good pitch! Perhaps it is *too* good.'
Best batting: 22* Nottinghamshire v Leicestershire, Trent Bridge 1989
Best bowling: 6-81 Nottinghamshire v Kent, Trent Bridge 1986

1991 Season

	M	Inns	NO	Runs	HS	Avge	100s	50s	Ct	St	O	M	Runs	Wkts	Avge	Best	5wI	10wM
Test																		
All First	19	12	4	42	13	5.25	-	-	10	-	670.3	207	1817	57	31.87	4-44	-	-
1-day Int																		
NatWest	2	0	0	0	0	-	-	-	-	-	23	5	78	1	78.00	1-40	-	
B&H	1	0	0	0	0	-	-	-	-	-	11	0	43	1	43.00	1-43	-	
Refuge																		

Career Performances

	M	Inns	NO	Runs	HS	Avge	100s	50s	Ct	St	Balls	Runs	Wkts	Avge	Best	5wI	10wM
Test																	
All First	97	82	35	166	22 *	3.53	-	-	32	-	17693	8301	245	33.88	6-81	7	1
1-day Int																	
NatWest	5	2	2	2	2 *	-	-	-	-	-	348	164	5	32.80	3-32	-	
B&H	11	1	1	1	1 *	-	-	-	1	-	708	458	12	38.16	4-38	-	
Refuge	15	3	2	0	0 *	0.00	-	-	5	-	552	474	10	47.40	2-39	-	

ALIKHAN, R. I. Surrey

Name: Rehan Iqbal Alikhan
Role: Right-hand bat, right-arm medium bowler
Born: 28 December 1962, London
Height: 6ft 2in **Weight:** 13st
Nickname: Tiger, Prince, Munch
County debut: 1986 (Sussex), 1989 (Surrey)
1000 runs in a season: 1
1st-Class 50s scored: 30
1st-class 100s scored: 2
1st-Class catches: 54
One-Day 50s: 2
Place in batting averages: 94th av. 32.96 (1990 44th av. 51.85)
Parents: Akbar and Farida
Wife and date of marriage: Janine, 8 December 1991
Family links with cricket: Father played at university and at club level
Education: King's College School, Wimbledon
Qualifications: 8 O-levels, 2 A-levels
Career outside cricket: Insurance broker
Off-season: 'Getting married in Australia and working at my game.'
Overseas tours: CCC tour to Kenya 1986, Surrey pre-season tour to Dubai 1989, 1990
Overseas teams played for: Mossman Middle Harbour, Sydney 1982-84, Pakistan International Airlines 1986-87, Claremont Nedlands, Perth 1987-91
Cricketers particularly admired: Imran Khan, Viv Richards, Sunil Gavaskar
Other sports followed: All ball sports
Injuries: Played with a broken finger for one month last season
Relaxations: 'I enjoy spending time in the West Indies with my fiancee, drinking and dining with friends and watching videos with Nenee.'
Extras: Released by Sussex at end of 1988 season. Surrey 2nd XI Player of the Year 1989. Scored first first-class 100 in 1990. 'I played nearly a full season for the first time (in 1991) and managed 1000 runs also for the first time.'
Opinions on cricket: 'Four-day cricket will result in the best side always winning; preparing players for Test cricket, will give players a rest between games thus enhancing their performances and will mean that batsmen like myself (the more sedate players of the game) will last longer in the game. Also, a fast bowler should be allowed to bowl as many bouncers as he likes, thus providing a complete test for batsmen and also resulting in success for batsmen that are not frightened, or ill-equipped to play against fast bowling.'
Best batting: 138 Surrey v Essex, The Oval 1990
Best bowling: 2-19 Sussex v West Indians, Hove 1988

16

1991 Season

	M	Inns	NO	Runs	HS	Avge	100s	50s	Ct	St	O	M	Runs	Wkts	Avge	Best	5wI	10wM
Test																		
All First	19	34	2	1055	96 *	32.96	-	8	10	-	5	0	43	2	21.50	2-43	-	-
1-day Int																		
NatWest																		
B&H																		
Refuge																		

Career Performances

	M	Inns	NO	Runs	HS	Avge	100s	50s	Ct	St	Balls	Runs	Wkts	Avge	Best	5wI	10wM
Test																	
All First	99	170	14	4482	138	28.73	2	30	54	-	347	274	7	39.14	2-19	-	-
1-day Int																	
NatWest	8	8	1	125	41	17.85	-	-	2	-							
B&H	3	3	0	137	71	45.66	-	2	1	-							
Refuge	12	8	2	72	23	12.00	-	-	-	-	54	47	0	-		-	-

ALLEYNE, M. W.   Gloucestershire

Name: Mark Wayne Alleyne
Role: Right-hand bat, right-arm medium bowler, cover fielder, occasional wicket-keeper
Born: 23 May 1968, Tottenham
Height: 5ft 10½in **Weight:** 12st 10lbs
Nickname: Boo-Boo
County debut: 1986
County cap: 1990
1000 runs in a season: 1
1st-Class 50s scored: 21
1st-Class 100s scored: 5
1st-Class 200s scored: 1
1st-Class catches: 80
1st-Class stumpings: 2
One-day 50s: 2
Place in batting averages: 101st av. 32.02 (1990 105th av. 40.66)
Place in bowling averages: 123rd av. 43.09 (1990 9th av. 24.43)
Strike rate: 78.63 (career 68.20)
Parents: Euclid Clevis and Hyacinth Cordeilla

Marital status: Single
Family links with cricket: Brother played for Gloucestershire 2nd XI and Middlesex YCs. Father played club cricket in Barbados and England
Education: Harrison College, Barbados and Cardinal Pole School, E. London
Qualifications: 6 O-levels, NCA senior coaching award, and volleyball coaching certificate
Overseas tours: England YC to Sri Lanka 1987 and Australia 1988
Cricketers particularly admired: Gordon Greenidge, Viv Richards
Other sports followed: Football, volleyball, athletics
Relaxations: Watching films and sport; listening to music
Extras: Youngest player to score a century for Gloucestershire. In 1990 also became the youngest to score a double hundred for the county. Graduate of Haringey Cricket College
Best batting: 256 Gloucestershire v Northamptonshire, Northampton 1990
Best bowling: 4-48 Gloucestershire v Glamorgan, Bristol 1988

1991 Season

	M	Inns	NO	Runs	HS	Avge	100s	50s	Ct	St	O	M	Runs	Wkts	Avge	Best	5wI	10wM
Test																		
All First	25	40	5	1121	165	32.02	1	6	12	1	144.1	27	474	11	43.09	3-35	-	-
1-day Int																		
NatWest	2	2	0	48	45	24.00	-	-	-	-								
B&H	4	3	0	7	6	2.33	-	-	2	-	15	0	67	1	67.00	1-24	-	
Refuge	15	14	2	409	76 *	34.08	-	2	1	-	65	1	344	10	34.40	2-19	-	

Career Performances

	M	Inns	NO	Runs	HS	Avge	100s	50s	Ct	St	Balls	Runs	Wkts	Avge	Best	5wI	10wM
Test																	
All First	102	158	22	4017	256	29.53	5	21	80	2	3274	2003	48	41.72	4-48	-	-
1-day Int																	
NatWest	14	10	4	68	45	11.33	-	-	5	-	378	258	8	32.25	5-30	1	
B&H	20	15	3	182	36	15.16	-	-	6	-	642	490	21	23.33	5-27	1	
Refuge	81	68	22	1231	76 *	26.76	-	2	24	-	2273	1938	67	28.92	3-25	-	

1. Who succeeded Viv Richards as captain of the West Indies in 1991?

2. Who is the Yorkshire captain for the 1992 season?

ALLOTT, P. J. W. Lancashire

Name: Paul John Walter Allott
Role: Right-hand bat, right-arm
fast-medium bowler
Born: 14 September 1956, Altrincham,
Cheshire
Height: 6ft 4in **Weight:** 15st
Nickname: Walt
County debut: 1978
County cap: 1981
Benefit: 1990 (£109,617)
Test debut: 1981
Tests: 13
One-Day Internationals: 13
50 wickets in a season: 5
1st-Class 50s scored: 10
1st-Class 5 w. in innings: 30
1st-Class catches: 136
Place in batting averages: 254th av. 10.50
Place in bowling averages: 100th av. 36.85
(1990 102nd av. 40.55)
Strike rate: 82.35 (career 59.70)
Parents: John Norman and Lillian Patricia
Wife and date of marriage: Helen, 27 October 1979
Children: Ben and Susie
Family links with cricket: Father was dedicated club cricketer for twenty years with
Ashley CC and is now a selector, administrator and junior organiser with Bowdon CC
Education: Altrincham Grammar School; Bede College, Durham
Qualifications: Qualified teacher and cricket coach
Overseas tours: With England to India 1981-82; India and Australia 1984-85
Cricketers particularly admired: Dennis Lillee
Injuries: Groin and back strains
Relaxations: Playing golf, watching all sports, listening to music, eating out, photography
Extras: Played football as goalkeeper for Cheshire schoolboys
Opinions on cricket: 'Too varied to be contained in one paragraph!'
Best batting: 88 Lancashire v Hampshire, Southampton 1987
Best bowling: 8-48 Lancashire v Northamptonshire, Northampton 1981

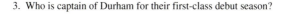

3. Who is captain of Durham for their first-class debut season?

4. Who topped the first-class bowling averages last season for Yorkshire?

1991 Season

	M	Inns	NO	Runs	HS	Avge	100s	50s	Ct	St	O	M	Runs	Wkts	Avge	Best	5wI	10wM
Test																		
All First	9	8	2	63	26	10.50	-	-	6	-	192.1	49	516	14	36.85	4-56	-	-
1-day Int																		
NatWest	1	1	0	2	2	2.00	-	-	-	-	12	3	48	0	-		-	-
B&H	7	2	0	10	10	5.00	-	-	5	-	74	17	200	11	18.18	4-23	-	
Refuge	17	5	5	20	10 *	-	-	-	2	-	121	8	481	11	43.72	2-30	-	

Career Performances

	M	Inns	NO	Runs	HS	Avge	100s	50s	Ct	St	Balls	Runs	Wkts	Avge	Best	5wI	10wM
Test	13	18	3	213	52 *	14.20	-	1	4	-	2225	1084	26	41.69	6-61	1	-
All First	245	262	64	3360	88	16.97	-	10	136	-	38927	16665	652	25.56	8-48	30	-
1-day Int	13	6	1	15	8	3.00	-	-	2	-	819	552	15	36.80	3-41	-	
NatWest	26	13	5	67	19 *	8.37	-	-	4	-	1668	811	47	17.25	4-28	-	
B&H	59	24	7	163	23 *	9.58	-	-	18	-	3242	1650	71	23.23	4-23	-	
Refuge	161	65	33	556	43	17.37	-	-	28	-	6612	4314	153	28.19	4-28	-	

AMBROSE, C. E. L.   Northamptonshire

Name: Curtly Elconn Lynwall Ambrose
Role: Left-hand bat, right-arm fast bowler;
'like the gully area'
Born: 21 September 1963, Antigua
Height: 6ft 7in **Weight:** 14st 4lbs
Nickname: Ambie
County debut: 1989
County cap: 1990
Test debut: 1987-88
Tests: 33
One-Day Internationals: 46
50 wickets in a season: 4
1st-Class 50s scored: 3
1st-Class 5 w. in innings: 18
1st-Class 10 w. in match: 3
1st-Class catches: 20
Place in batting averages: (1990 248th
av. 15.61)
Place in bowling averages: 2nd av. 17.03
(1990 6th av. 23.16)
Strike rate: 45.88 (career 51.22)
Parents: Jasper (deceased) and Hillie

Marital status: Single
Family links with cricket: Brother used to play club cricket and got trials for Antigua. Cousin Rolston Otto plays for Antigua and Leeward Islands
Education: Swetes Primary School; All Saints Secondary School
Qualifications: 3 O-levels, 3 A-levels, qualified carpenter
Off-season: Touring Pakistan and Australia with West Indies, then playing cricket in the Caribbean and returning to Australia for the World Cup
Overseas tours: West Indies to England 1988; Australia 1988-89; India for Nehru Cup 1989-90; Pakistan 1990-91; England 1991; Pakistan 1991-92; Australia for Benson & Hedges World Series and World Cup 1991-92
Overseas teams played for: Leeward Islands
Cricketers particularly admired: 'David Gower, Richard Hadlee, and of course my West Indian colleagues.'
Other sports followed: Basketball and tennis – 'Boris Becker is my favourite player.'
Relaxations: Listening to music, relaxing on the beach, going to the cinema
Extras: A basketball player who only began playing cricket seriously at age 17. Took a wicket with his first ball on Championship debut for Northamptonshire against Glamorgan in 1989. Figures of 8 for 45 are the best in Tests for West Indies v England
Opinions on cricket: 'Too many games played in county cricket. The wickets are too slow so do not encourage the bowlers a lot. It should be an even contest.'
Best batting: 59 West Indians v Sussex, Hove 1988
Best bowling: 8-45 West Indies v England, Bridgetown 1989-90

1991 Season

	M	Inns	NO	Runs	HS	Avge	100s	50s	Ct	St	O	M	Runs	Wkts	Avge	Best	5wI	10wM
Test	5	7	0	37	17	5.28	-	-	-	-	249	68	560	28	20.00	6-52	2	-
All First	10	8	1	53	17	7.57	-	-	1	-	390	122	869	51	17.03	6-52	3	-
1-day Int	3	3	3	32	21 *	-	-	-	-	-	30	5	101	3	33.66	2-36	-	
NatWest																		
B&H																		
Refuge																		

Career Performances

	M	Inns	NO	Runs	HS	Avge	100s	50s	Ct	St	Balls	Runs	Wkts	Avge	Best	5wI	10wM
Test	33	49	8	501	53	12.22	-	1	6	-	7855	3240	140	23.14	8-45	5	1
All First	89	115	26	1360	59	15.28	-	3	20	-	18133	7745	354	21.87	8-45	18	3
1-day Int	46	25	15	176	26 *	17.60	-	-	14	-	2519	1518	79	19.21	5-17	2	
NatWest	8	3	0	70	48	23.33	-	-	4	-	528	227	10	22.70	3-31	-	
B&H	5	4	3	51	17 *	51.00	-	-	3	-	330	166	10	16.60	3-19	-	
Refuge	12	6	1	23	13 *	4.60	-	-	1	-	507	285	10	28.50	3-15	-	

ANDREW, S. J. W.   Essex

Name: Stephen Jon Walter Andrew
Role: Right-hand bat, right-arm
medium bowler
Born: 27 January 1966, London
Height: 6ft 3in **Weight:** 14st
Nickname: Rip, Chinny, His Chinness,
Le Grand Chien, G.O.S.
County debut: 1984 (Hants), 1990 (Essex)
1st-Class 5 w. in innings: 5
1st-Class catches: 21
Place in batting averages: (1990 258th
av. 13.22)
Place in bowling averages: 58th av. 31.44
(1990 105th av. 41.23)
Strike rate: 55.74 (career 57.10)
Parents: Jon and Victoria
Marital status: Single
Education: Hordle House Prep. School;
Milton Abbey Public School
Qualifications: 3 O-levels
Off-season: 'Abroad somewhere.'
Overseas tours: Young England to West Indies 1985
Overseas teams played for: Pirates, Durban 1983-84; S.A.P., Durban 1984-86; Manly,
Sydney 1987-88; Pinetown, Durban 1988-89; Taita, Wellington 1990-91
Cricketers particularly admired: Dennis Lillee
Other sports followed: Interested in most sports
Relaxations: Music, videos, films, books, playing golf, sleeping, drinking
Opinions on cricket: 'I think the balance between bat and ball has swayed too much to the
batsman's favour. Keep wickets white but bring back the '89 ball to give the bowler a
chance at least to swing it.'
Best batting: 35 Essex v Northamptonshire, Chelmsford 1990
Best bowling: 7-92 Hampshire v Gloucestershire, Southampton 1987

1991 Season

	M	Inns	NO	Runs	HS	Avge	100s	50s	Ct	St	O	M	Runs	Wkts	Avge	Best	5wI	10wM
Test																		
All First	15	9	2	30	13	4.28	-	-	5	-	399.3	74	1352	43	31.44	4-38	-	-
1-day Int																		
NatWest																		
B&H																		
Refuge	8	3	1	14	8	7.00	-	-	-	-	49	3	253	8	31.62	3-33	-	

Career Performances

	M	Inns	NO	Runs	HS	Avge	100s	50s	Ct	St	Balls	Runs	Wkts	Avge	Best	5wI	10wM
Test																	
All First	90	57	27	254	35	8.46	-	-	21	-	13476	7500	236	31.78	7-92	5	-
1-day Int																	
NatWest	6	1	1	0	0 *	-	-	-	2	-	372	219	7	31.28	2-34	-	
B&H	11	3	3	5	4 *	-	-	-	1	-	654	363	20	18.15	5-24	1	
Refuge	30	5	2	20	8	6.66	-	-	2	-	1173	1009	22	45.86	4-50	-	

AQIB JAVED Hampshire

Name: Aqib Javed
Role: Right-hand bat, right-hand fast bowler
Born: 5 August 1972
Height: 5ft 11in **Weight:** 12st 8lbs
County debut: 1991
Test debut: 1988-89
Tests: 5
One-Day Internationals: 35
50 wickets in a season: 1
1st-Class 5 w. in innings: 3
1st-Class 10 w. in match:
1st-Class catches: 4
Place in bowling averages: 57th av. 31.24
Strike rate: 57.75 (career 70.27)
Parents: Abdul Jabbar
Marital status: Single
Education: Government School, Sheikhupura
Qualifications: 'Student of Fine Art'
Off-season: Playing cricket in Pakistan and
going to Australia for the World Cup
Career outside cricket: Department manager in Pakistan automobile company
Overseas tours: Pakistan U19 to Australia 1987-88; Australia and New Zealand 1988-89;
Sharjah Cup 1989-90; India, Nehru Cup 1989-90; Australia 1989-90; New Zealand 1989-
90; Sharjah Cup 1990-91; West Indies 1990-91; Sharjah Cup 1991-92; Australia for World
Cup 1991-92
Cricketers particularly admired: Imran Khan
Other sports followed: Football and tennis
Relaxations: Music
Opinions on cricket: 'Cricket is a funny game.'
Best batting: 32* PACO v PIA, Lahore 1989-90
Best bowling: 6-91 Hampshire v Nottinghamshire, Trent Bridge 1991

1991 Season

	M	Inns	NO	Runs	HS	Avge	100s	50s	Ct	St	O	M	Runs	Wkts	Avge	Best	5wI	10wM
Test																		
All First	18	12	8	25	15 *	6.25	-	-	-	-	510.1	84	1656	53	31.24	6-91	3	-
1-day Int																		
NatWest	5	0	0	0	0	-	-	-	2	-	52.5	4	213	8	26.62	4-51	-	
B&H	5	2	1	3	3	3.00	-	-	-	-	53	6	208	9	23.11	3-43	-	
Refuge	12	2	2	5	4 *	-	-	-	1	-	92.1	4	423	10	42.30	3-50	-	

Career Performances

	M	Inns	NO	Runs	HS	Avge	100s	50s	Ct	St	Balls	Runs	Wkts	Avge	Best	5wI	10wM
Test	5	5	1	11	7	2.75	-	-	1	-	1075	502	10	50.20	3-57	-	-
All First	35	30	13	131	32 *	7.70	-	-	4	-	5692	2943	81	36.33	6-91	3	-
1-day Int	35	8	5	3	1 *	1.00	-	-	8	-	1740	1221	34	35.91	3-28	-	
NatWest	5	0	0	0	0	-	-	-	2	-	317	213	8	26.62	4-51	-	
B&H	5	2	1	3	3	3.00	-	-	-	-	318	208	9	23.11	3-43	-	
Refuge	12	2	2	5	4 *	-	-	-	1	-	553	423	10	42.30	3-50	-	

ASIF DIN, M.   Warwickshire

Name: Mohamed Asif Din
Role: Right-hand bat, leg-spin bowler
Born: 21 September 1960, Kampala, Uganda
Height: 5ft 9in **Weight:** 10st 7lbs
Nickname: Gunga 'and many others'
County debut: 1981
County cap: 1987
1000 runs in a season: 2
1st-Class 50s scored: 38
1st-Class 100s scored: 8
1st-Class 5 w. in innings: 1
1st-Class catches: 107
One-Day 50s: 18
One-Day 100s: 5
Place in batting averages: 147th av. 26.34
(1990 180th av. 27.82)
Place in bowling averages: (1990 145th
av. 63.50)
Strike rate: (career 87.90)
Parents: Jamiz and Mumtaz
Wife and date of marriage: Ahmerin, 27 September 1987
Children: Zahra, 18 October 1990

Family links with cricket: Brothers Khalid and Abid play in Birmingham League
Education: Ladywood Comprehensive School, Birmingham
Qualifications: CSEs and O-levels
Off-season: Play and work for Stumps Indoor Cricket Centre
Cricketers particularly admired: Zaheer Abbas, Majid Khan
Injuries: Back trouble early in the season and a broken finger
Other sports followed: American football, basketball
Relaxations: Fishing and shooting
Opinions on cricket: 'Too much cricket. Would like to see 17 four-day matches.'
Best batting: 158* Warwickshire v Cambridge University, Fenner's 1988
Best bowling: 5-100 Warwickshire v Glamorgan, Edgbaston 1982

1991 Season

	M	Inns	NO	Runs	HS	Avge	100s	50s	Ct	St	O	M	Runs	Wkts	Avge	Best	5wl	10wM
Test																		
All First	15	27	1	685	140	26.34	2	1	9	-	53	9	206	2	103.00	1-37	-	-
1-day Int																		
NatWest	3	2	0	61	44	30.50	-	-	-	-	3	0	10	0	-		-	-
B&H	4	4	0	291	137	72.75	1	1	-	-								
Refuge	11	11	2	330	101 *	36.66	1	1	3	-								

Career Performances

	M	Inns	NO	Runs	HS	Avge	100s	50s	Ct	St	Balls	Runs	Wkts	Avge	Best	5wl	10wM
Test																	
All First	196	321	43	8244	158 *	29.65	8	38	107	-	6153	4162	70	59.45	5-100	1	-
1-day Int																	
NatWest	26	23	7	645	94 *	40.31	-	3	6	-	139	88	7	12.57	5-40	1	
B&H	37	34	4	1049	137	34.96	2	4	4	-	66	62	1	62.00	1-26	-	
Refuge	139	125	22	3013	113	29.25	3	11	24	-	171	182	4	45.50	1-11	-	

5. Why was 1919 a memorable season for Derbyshire?

6. Who is Director of Cricket at Durham?

7. Who topped the first-class batting averages last season for Essex?

8. Who is the 1992 captain of Lancashire?

ATHERTON, M. A. Lancashire

Name: Michael Andrew Atherton
Role: Right-hand bat, leg-break bowler
Born: 23 March 1968, Manchester
Height: 6ft **Weight:** 12st 6lbs
Nickname: Athers, Dread, Iron, Ice
County debut: 1987
County cap: 1989
Test debut: 1989
Tests: 18
One-Day Internationals: 10
1000 runs in a season: 4
1st-Class 50s scored: 27
1st-Class 100s scored: 21
1st-Class 5 w. in innings: 3
1st-Class catches: 84
One-Day 50s: 16
One-Day 100s: 1
Place in batting averages: 53rd av. 41.00
(1990 9th av. 71.25)

Place in bowling averages: (1990 34th av. 31.06)
Strike rate: (career 82.03)
Parents: Alan and Wendy
Marital status: Single
Family links with cricket: Father and brother both play league cricket
Education: Briscoe Lane Primary, Manchester GS; Downing College, Cambridge
Qualifications: 10 O-levels, 3 A-levels; BA (Hons) (Cantab)
Off-season: 'Trying to get fit after a spinal fusion operation. Otherwise watching Manchester United to their first Championship for 23 years.'
Overseas tours: Young England to Sri Lanka 1987 and Australia 1988; England A to Zimbabwe 1989-90; England to Australia and New Zealand 1990-91
Cricketers particularly admired: 'Many, especially in the Lancashire dressing room – Gehan Mendis, Neil Fairbrother and Wasim Akram – all exciting, often brilliant, cricketers.'
Other sports followed: Golf, rugby and most sports except racing, darts and snooker
Injuries: Stress fracture of the lower back
Relaxations: Reading (Heller, Kundera, Barnes etc), music, golf
Extras: In 1987 was first player to score 1000 runs in his debut season since Paul Parker in 1976. Youngest Lancastrian to score a Test century (151 v NZ at Trent Bridge in 1990); second Lancastrian to score a Test century at Old Trafford (138 v India in 1990). First captained England U19 aged 16. Selected for England tour to New Zealand and also England A tour to Bermuda and West Indies but ruled out of both through injury
Opinions on cricket: 'The present system of three/four-day cricket does not work. There should be a reduced amount of cricket with either all four-day cricket on dry, covered

wickets encouraging pace/spin alike, or all three-day cricket on uncovered wickets.'
Best batting: 191 Lancashire v Surrey, The Oval 1990
Best bowling: 6-78 Lancashire v Nottinghamshire, Trent Bridge 1990

1991 Season

	M	Inns	NO	Runs	HS	Avge	100s	50s	Ct	St	O	M	Runs	Wkts	Avge	Best	5wI	10wM
Test	5	9	0	79	32	8.77	-	-	3	-								
All First	14	23	3	820	138	41.00	3	2	9	-								
1-day Int	3	3	1	168	74	84.00	-	2	-	-								
NatWest	1	1	0	38	38	38.00	-	-	-	-								
B&H	7	7	0	282	91	40.28	-	3	3	-								
Refuge	9	9	1	171	48	21.37	-	-	5	-								

Career Performances

	M	Inns	NO	Runs	HS	Avge	100s	50s	Ct	St	Balls	Runs	Wkts	Avge	Best	5wI	10wM
Test	18	34	1	1166	151	35.33	3	7	15	-	366	282	1	282.00	1-60	-	-
All First	102	174	20	6826	191	44.32	21	27	84	-	8368	4323	102	42.38	6-78	3	-
1-day Int	10	10	1	335	74	37.22	-	3	3	-							
NatWest	7	7	1	229	55	38.16	-	1	4	-	120	71	4	17.75	2-15	-	
B&H	26	26	2	901	91	37.54	-	8	13	-	198	168	7	24.00	4-42	-	
Refuge	22	22	2	658	111	32.90	1	4	10	-	174	190	5	38.00	3-33	-	

ATHEY, C. W. J.   Gloucestershire

Name: Charles William Jeffrey Athey
Role: Right-hand bat, right-arm medium bowler
Born: 27 September 1957, Middlesbrough
Height: 5ft 10in **Weight:** 12st
Nickname: Bumper, Wingnut, Ath
County debut: 1976 (Yorks), 1984 (Gloucs)
County cap: 1980 (Yorks), 1985 (Gloucs)
Benefit: 1990
Test debut: 1980
Tests: 23
One-Day Internationals: 31
1000 runs in a season: 9
1st-Class 50s scored: 95
1st-Class 100s scored: 40
1st-Class catches: 350
1st-Class stumpings: 2
One-Day 50s: 67

One-Day 100s: 8
Place in batting averages: 40th av. 44.76 (1990 43rd av. 52.64)
Parents: Peter and Maree
Wife and date of marriage: Janet Linda, 9 October 1982
Family links with cricket: 'Father played league cricket in North Yorkshire and South Durham League for twenty-nine years, twenty-five of them with Middlesbrough. President of Middlesbrough CC since 1975. Brother-in-law Colin Cook played for Middlesex, other brother-in-law (Martin) plays in Thames Valley League. Father-in-law deeply involved in Middlesex Youth cricket.'
Education: Linthorpe Junior School; Stainsby Secondary School; Acklam Hall High School
Qualifications: 4 O-levels, some CSEs, NCA coaching certificate
Off-season: Staying in Bristol
Overseas tours: England U19 to West Indies 1976; England to West Indies 1980-81; Australia 1986-87; Pakistan, Australia and New Zealand 1987-88; England B to Sri Lanka 1985-86; unofficial English XI to South Africa 1989-90
Cricketers particularly admired: Gordon Greenidge, Malcolm Marshall, Chris Smith
Other sports followed: Most sports
Relaxations: Music, good films, good food
Extras: Played for Teesside County Schools U16 at age 12. Played for Yorkshire Colts 1974. Played football for Middlesbrough Schools U16 and Junior XI. Offered but declined apprenticeship terms with Middlesbrough FC. Captain of Gloucestershire in 1989
Opinions on cricket: 'Should play four-day cricket, playing each county once. Over-rate fines are not realistic.'
Best batting: 184 England B v Sri Lanka XI, Galle 1985-86
Best bowling: 3-3 Gloucestershire v Hampshire, Bristol 1985

1991 Season

	M	Inns	NO	Runs	HS	Avge	100s	50s	Ct	St	O	M	Runs	Wkts	Avge	Best	5wI	10wM
Test																		
All First	25	40	6	1522	127	44.76	5	9	18	-	66	10	189	2	94.50	1-18	-	-
1-day Int																		
NatWest	2	2	1	123	76	123.00	-	1	-	-								
B&H	4	4	1	108	81	36.00	-	1	2	-								
Refuge	15	15	1	352	85	25.14	-	2	8	-	14	0	79	2	39.50	2-18	-	

Career Performances

	M	Inns	NO	Runs	HS	Avge	100s	50s	Ct	St	Balls	Runs	Wkts	Avge	Best	5wI	10wM
Test	23	41	1	919	123	22.97	1	4	13	-							
All First	367	607	62	19107	184	35.05	40	95	350	2	3970	2155	43	50.11	3-3	-	-
1-day Int	31	30	3	848	142 *	31.40	2	4	16	-	6	10	0	-	-	-	
NatWest	36	35	7	1214	115	43.35	1	9	20	-	133	120	1	120.00	1-18	-	
B&H	63	59	9	1799	95	35.98	-	15	32	-	340	242	12	20.16	4-48	-	
Refuge	204	194	16	5953	121 *	33.44	5	39	78	-	706	660	24	27.50	5-35	1	

AUSTIN, I. D. Lancashire

Name: Ian David Austin
Role: Left-hand bat, right-arm medium bowler
Born: 30 May 1966, Haslingden, Lancs
Height: 5ft 10in **Weight:** 14st 7lbs
Nickname: Oscar, Bully
County debut: 1986
County cap: 1990
1st-Class 100s scored: 1
1st-Class 50s scored: 4
1st-Class 5 w. in innings: 1
1st-Class catches: 7
One-Day 50s: 2
Place in batting averages: 149th av. 26.25 (1990 161st av. 30.66)
Place in bowling averages: 142nd av. 65.58 (1990 135th av. 55.16)
Strike rate: 118.66 (career 78.10)
Parents: Jack and Ursula
Family links with cricket: Father opened batting for Haslingden CC
Education: Haslingden High School
Qualifications: 3 O-levels; NCA coaching certificate
Off-season: Playing for Maroochydore CC, Queensland
Cricketers particularly admired: Ian Botham, Clive Lloyd
Overseas tours: England U19 to Bermuda 1985; Lancashire to Jamaica 1987 & 1988, Zimbabwe 1989, Tasmania and Western Australia 1990 & 1991
Other sports followed: Football, golf
Injuries: Thigh and groin strains
Relaxations: Listening to music, playing golf
Extras: Holds amateur Lancashire League record for highest individual score (147*). Broke Lancashire CCC record for most wickets in the Sunday league.
Opinions on cricket: 'Get rid of over-rate fines or bring down the over rate. Play 3 x 2-hour sessions'
Best batting: 101* Lancashire v Yorkshire, Scarborough 1991
Best bowling: 5-79 Lancashire v Surrey, The Oval 1988

---

9. Who were the 1991 county champions?

10. Who won the 1991 NatWest Trophy?

1991 Season

	M	Inns	NO	Runs	HS	Avge	100s	50s	Ct	St	O	M	Runs	Wkts	Avge	Best	5wI	10wM
Test																		
All First	12	16	4	315	101 *	26.25	1	1	4	-	237.2	42	787	12	65.58	3-58	-	-
1-day Int																		
NatWest	2	1	0	2	2	2.00	-	-	-	-	21	1	105	1	105.00	1-46	-	
B&H	7	2	0	29	22	14.50	-	-	1	-	72	2	319	6	53.16	2-50	-	
Refuge	18	7	2	83	48	16.60	-	-	3	-	124.3	3	660	29	22.75	5-56	1	

Career Performances

	M	Inns	NO	Runs	HS	Avge	100s	50s	Ct	St	Balls	Runs	Wkts	Avge	Best	5wI	10wM
Test																	
All First	43	56	15	1019	101 *	24.85	1	4	7	-	5155	2397	66	36.31	5-79	1	-
1-day Int																	
NatWest	8	3	1	25	13 *	12.50	-	-	1	-	516	360	8	45.00	3-36	-	
B&H	19	11	4	228	80	32.57	-	2	3	-	1122	760	20	38.00	4-25	-	
Refuge	69	38	16	322	48	14.63	-	-	13	-	2750	2284	80	28.55	5-56	1	

AYLING, J. R.   Hampshire

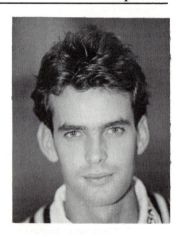

Name: Jonathan Richard Ayling
Role: Right-hand bat, right-arm medium bowler
Born: 13 June 1967, Portsmouth
Height: 6ft 5in **Weight:** 13st 7lbs
Nickname: Victor, Kitty
County debut: 1988
County cap: 1991
1st-Class 50s scored: 9
1st-Class catches: 10
One-Day 50s: 1
Place in batting averages: 69th av. 46.00
Place in bowling averages: 15th av. 23.80 (1990 133rd av. 52.00)
Strike rate: 50.68 (career 59.61)
Parents: Christopher and Mary
Marital status: Single
Education: Portsmouth Grammar School
Qualifications: 8 O-levels, 1 A-level
Overseas clubs played for: Pinelands, Cape Town
Cricketers particularly admired: Malcolm Marshall, Robin Smith, Paul Terry, Cardigan Connor

Other sports followed: Athletics, soccer, rugby union, snooker
Injuries: Knee reconstruction operation in 1989.
Relaxations: 'Good food, good music, good company.'
Extras: Wicket with first ball in first-class cricket; missed all of 1989 season with a serious knee injury. One of only four players to play in two Lord's finals for Hampshire
Opinions on cricket: 'An alternative to the present benefit system should exist: regardless of whether he has had ten years' capped service a player should be rewarded financially at the end of his first-team career. This would prevent capped players 'hanging on' simply to gain a benefit and would promote younger and more ambitious players.'
Best batting: 88* Hampshire v Lancashire, Liverpool 1988
Best bowling: 4-47 Hampshire v Surrey, The Oval 1991

1991 Season

	M	Inns	NO	Runs	HS	Avge	100s	50s	Ct	St	O	M	Runs	Wkts	Avge	Best	5wI	10wM
Test																		
All First	10	14	3	321	58	29.18	-	2	3	-	211.1	49	595	25	23.80	4-47	-	-
1-day Int																		
NatWest	3	1	1	18	18 *	-	-	-	2	-	36	0	151	4	37.75	2-39	-	
B&H	4	3	2	10	5 *	10.00	-	-	2	-	42	0	186	4	46.50	2-56	-	
Refuge	13	12	3	206	56	22.88	-	1	4	-	91	2	512	14	36.57	3-25	-	

Career Performances

	M	Inns	NO	Runs	HS	Avge	100s	50s	Ct	St	Balls	Runs	Wkts	Avge	Best	5wI	10wM
Test																	
All First	38	58	10	1400	88 *	29.16	-	9	10	-	4948	2265	83	27.28	4-47	-	-
1-day Int																	
NatWest	11	8	4	105	29	26.25	-	-	4	-	768	502	16	31.37	3-30	-	
B&H	9	5	2	25	14	8.33	-	-	2	-	498	348	10	34.80	2-22	-	
Refuge	42	32	10	518	56	23.54	-	1	6	-	1674	1391	44	31.61	4-37	-	

11. Who topped the first-class batting averages last season for Glamorgan?

12. Who won the Benson & Hedges Cup in 1991?

13. Who were the last-ever Refuge League champions?

14. Which former England Test cricketer retired as Worcestershire's coach at the end of last season?

AYMES, A. N.   Hampshire

Name: Adrian Nigel Aymes
Role: Right-hand bat, wicket-keeper
Born: 4 June 1964, Southampton
Height: 6ft **Weight:** 13st
Nickname: Les, Adi, Aymser
County debut: 1987
County cap: 1991
1st-Class 50s scored: 6
1st-Class catches: 51 (career 74)
1st -Class stumpings: 2 (career 5)
Place in batting averages: 135th av. 28.00
Parents: Michael and Barbara
Marital status: Engaged to Marie
Education: Shirley Middle; Bellemoor
Secondary; Hill College
Qualifications: 4 O-levels, 1 A-level
Career outside cricket: Working for a
building company
Off-season: Keeping fit, working,
playing football

Overseas tours: Hampshire XI to the Isle of Wight
Cricketers particularly admired: Any wicket-keeper, especially Bob Taylor and Alan
Knott. Jimmy Cook and Gordon Greenidge
Other sports followed: Football, American and Australian Rules football, martial arts
Injuries: Bad back at times and twisted knee ligaments
Relaxations: All sport and watching videos
Extras: Half century on debut v Surrey; equalled club record of 6 catches in an innings and
10 in a match
Opinions on cricket: 'More result wickets would bring in the crowds. Some kind of night
cricket would also bring in the public.'
Best batting: 75* Hampshire v Glamorgan, Pontypridd 1990

1991 Season

	M	Inns	NO	Runs	HS	Avge	100s	50s	Ct	St	O	M	Runs	Wkts	Avge	Best	5wI	10wM
Test																		
All First	24	30	7	644	53	28.00	-	2	51	2								
1-day Int																		
NatWest	5	1	0	2	2	2.00	-	-	6	1								
B&H	5	2	0	12	10	6.00	-	-	4	4								
Refuge	13	11	7	169	33*	42.25	-	-	13	3								

Career Performances

	M	Inns	NO	Runs	HS	Avge	100s	50s	Ct	St	Balls	Runs	Wkts	Avge	Best	5wI	10wM
Test																	
All First	32	40	12	1043	75 *	37.25	-	6	74	5							
1-day Int																	
NatWest	5	1	0	2	2	2.00	-	-	6	1							
B&H	5	2	0	12	10	6.00	-	-	4	4							
Refuge	16	12	8	184	33 *	46.00	-	-	15	4							

AZHARUDDIN, M. Derbyshire

Name: Mohammad Azharuddin
Role: Right-hand bat, leg-break bowler
Born: 8 January 1963, Hyderabad, India
Height: 5ft 11in
Nickname: Azzy
County debut: 1991
County cap: 1991
Test debut: 1984-85
Tests: 41
One-Day Internationals: 112
1000 runs in a season: 1
1st-Class 50s scored: 46
1st-Class 100s scored: 30
1st-Class 200s scored: 2
1st-Class catches: 104
One-Day 50s: 14
One-Day 100s: 3
Place in batting averages: 13th av. 59.29
Education: Nizam College;
Osmania University
Off-season: Captaining India in Australia

Overseas tours: Young India to Zimbabwe 1984; India to Sri Lanka 1985-86; England 1986; West Indies 1988-89; Pakistan 1989-90; New Zealand 1989-90; England 1990; Australia 1991-92
Overseas teams played for: Hyderabad 1981-91 and South Zone
Extras: First appointed captain of India for the tour to New Zealand 1989-90. Scored a century in his first three Tests (against England 1984-85). One of *Wisden*'s Five Cricketers of the Year 1990. Broke the record for the fastest century in limited-over internationals in December 1988, reaching three figures off 62 deliveries against New Zealand at Baroda
Best batting: 226 South Zone v East Zone, Jamadoba 1983-84
Best bowling: 2-33 Hyderabad v Andhra, Hyderabad 1987-88

1991 Season

	M	Inns	NO	Runs	HS	Avge	100s	50s	Ct	St	O	M	Runs	Wkts	Avge	Best	5wI	10wM
Test																		
All First	22	39	5	2016	212	59.29	7	10	24	-	86.4	18	252	3	84.00	1-35	-	
1-day Int																		
NatWest																		
B&H	4	4	1	125	44 *	41.66	-	-	4	-	16	0	58	1	58.00	1-17	-	
Refuge	15	14	2	371	73	30.91	-	2	6	-	0.5	0	5	0	-	-	-	

Career Performances

	M	Inns	NO	Runs	HS	Avge	100s	50s	Ct	St	Balls	Runs	Wkts	Avge	Best	5wI	10wM
Test	41	61	3	2976	199	51.31	10	10	32	-	6	8	0	-	-	-	
All First	121	184	23	9038	226	56.13	30	46	104	-	937	533	7	76.14	2-33	-	
1-day Int	112	101	21	2829	108 *	35.36	3	12	42	-	540	468	12	39.00	3-19	-	
NatWest																	
B&H	4	4	1	125	44 *	41.66	-	-	4	-	96	58	1	58.00	1-17	-	
Refuge	15	14	2	371	73	30.91	-	2	6	-	5	5	0	-	-	-	

BABINGTON, A. M.   Gloucestershire

Name: Andrew Mark Babington
Role: Left-hand bat, right-arm
fast-medium bowler
Born: 22 July 1963, London
Height: 6ft 2in **Weight:** 13st
Nickname: Vinny Jones, Oscar, Gypsy Bob
County debut: 1986 (Sussex)
1991 (Gloucestershire)
1st-Class 50s scored: 1
1st-Class 5 w. in innings: 2
1st-Class catches: 28
Place in batting averages: 235th av. 13.53
Place in bowling averages: 91st av. 35.40
Strike rate: 69.07 (career 67.08)
Parents: Roy and Maureen
Marital status: Divorced
Family links with cricket: Father and
brother played club cricket.
Education: Reigate Grammar School;
Borough Road PE College
Qualifications: 5 O-levels, 2 A-levels; NCA coaching certificate; Member of Institute of
Legal Executives; holds consumer credit licence to work in the insurance industry

Career outside cricket: Working for mortgage/insurance brokers
Off-season: Abroad
Overseas tours: Surrey YCs to Australia 1980; Gloucestershire to Kenya 1991
Cricketers particularly admired: Dennis Lillee, John Snow, David Smith, Martin Lee
Other sports followed: Motor racing, boxing, fishing, shooting, football
Injuries: Groin and stomach muscle injury
Relaxations: 'Driving, drinking and eating out, snooker, fishing, golf. Spending time in the Cherry Tree pub in Faygate and visiting friends.
Extras: Took hat-trick (3rd, 4th & 5th Championship wickets) v Gloucestershire in 1986. Scored maiden 1st-class 50 of 28 balls (5 sixes) v Sussex at Cheltenham 1991
Opinions on cricket: '17 x four-day games; better standard of balls now that pitches are OK; coloured clothing on Sundays; 1-day competitions to be played early in the season and midweek so that we can have one rest day a week. Please let us always play same side on Sunday as in the Championship to cut down on travelling.'
Best batting: 58 Gloucestershire v Sussex, Cheltenham 1991
Best bowling: 5-37 Sussex v Lancashire, Liverpool 1989

1991 Season

	M	Inns	NO	Runs	HS	Avge	100s	50s	Ct	St	O	M	Runs	Wkts	Avge	Best	5wI	10wM
Test																		
All First	18	20	7	176	58	13.53	-	1	7	-	483.3	79	1487	42	35.40	4-33	-	-
1-day Int																		
NatWest	1	0	0	0	0	-	-	-	-	-	6	0	17	0	-		-	-
B&H	4	3	1	13	8	6.50	-	-	1	-	40	9	111	3	37.00	2-49	-	
Refuge	13	5	1	27	11	6.75	-	-	3	-	88.4	3	426	14	30.42	4-53	-	

Career Performances

	M	Inns	NO	Runs	HS	Avge	100s	50s	Ct	St	Balls	Runs	Wkts	Avge	Best	5wI	10wM
Test																	
All First	78	81	33	400	58	8.33	-	1	28	-	11874	6158	177	34.79	5-37	2	-
1-day Int																	
NatWest	8	2	2	4	4 *	-	-	-	3	-	420	297	11	27.00	3-53	-	
B&H	15	7	3	28	9	7.00	-	-	2	-	872	534	22	24.27	4-29	-	
Refuge	57	13	4	29	11	3.22	-	-	14	-	2164	1701	48	35.43	4-48	-	

15. Who took his 1000th first-class wicket playing for Yorkshire v Lancashire last season?

16. Which county won both the Minor Counties Championship and their knock-out competition last season?

Name: Robert John Bailey
Role: Right-hand bat, off-break bowler, county vice-captain
Born: 28 October 1963, Biddulph, Stoke-on-Trent
Height: 6ft 3in **Weight:** 14st
Nickname: Bailers, Nose Bag ('I eat a lot!')
County debut: 1982
County cap: 1985
Test debut: 1988
Tests: 4
One-Day Internationals: 4
1000 runs in a season: 8
1st-Class 50s scored: 64
1st-Class 100s scored: 27
1st-Class 200s scored: 3
1st-Class catches: 144
One-Day 50s: 35
One-Day 100s: 6

Place in batting averages: 58th av. 39.48 (1990 17th av. 64.09)
Place in bowling averages: 104th av. 38.09 (1990 134th av. 54.90)
Strike rate: 66.81 (career 75.52)
Parents: Marie, father deceased
Wife and date of marriage: Rachel, 11 April 1987
Children: Harry John, 7 March 1991
Family links with cricket: Father played in North Staffordshire League for thirty years for Knypersley and Minor Counties cricket for Staffordshire as wicket-keeper
Education: Biddulph High School
Qualifications: 6 CSEs, 1 O-level, NCA senior coach
Off-season: Working on promotions and marketing for N.C.C.C.
Overseas tours: England to Sharjah 1985 and 1987; West Indies 1989-90
Injuries: 'Missed two weeks after colliding with a boundary board in the NatWest quarter-final at Northampton – ironically it was the NatWest board I went into!'
Other sports followed: Football (Stoke City and Coventry City)
Relaxations: Listening to music
Extras: Played for Young England v Young Australia 1983. Selected for cancelled tour of India 1988-89. Youngest Northamptonshire player to score 10,000 runs
Opinions on cricket: 'NatWest finals are becoming a farce with early starts in September. Sixty overs is far too long – why are we the only country in the world to play so many overs?'
Best batting: 224* Northamptonshire v Glamorgan, Swansea 1986

Best bowling: 3-27 Northamptonshire v Glamorgan, Wellingborough 1988

1991 Season

	M	Inns	NO	Runs	HS	Avge	100s	50s	Ct	St	O	M	Runs	Wkts	Avge	Best	5wI	10wM
Test																		
All First	21	36	5	1224	117	39.48	1	11	10	-	122.3	16	419	11	38.09	3-44	-	-
1-day Int																		
NatWest	4	4	1	253	145	84.33	1	1	-	-	2	0	3	1	3.00	1-3	-	
B&H	5	5	0	184	75	36.80	-	2	1	-								
Refuge	14	13	1	388	99	32.33	-	2	3	-	4	0	37	0	-	-	-	-

Career Performances

	M	Inns	NO	Runs	HS	Avge	100s	50s	Ct	St	Balls	Runs	Wkts	Avge	Best	5wI	10wM
Test	4	8	0	119	43	14.87	-	-	-	-							
All First	209	349	53	12071	224 *	40.78	27	64	144	-	3474	2037	46	44.28	3-27	-	-
1-day Int	4	4	2	137	43 *	68.50	-	-	1	-	36	25	0	-	-	-	-
NatWest	26	26	7	806	145	42.42	1	4	4	-	108	74	6	12.33	3-47	-	-
B&H	39	36	3	1408	134	42.66	1	11	7	-	60	29	1	29.00	1-22	-	-
Refuge	119	114	14	3530	125 *	35.30	4	20	28	-	151	196	4	49.00	3-23	-	

BAINBRIDGE, P.   Durham

Name: Philip Bainbridge
Role: Right-hand bat, right-arm medium bowler
Born: 16 April 1958, Stoke-on-Trent
Height: 5ft 9¹/₂in **Weight:** 12st 7lbs
Nickname: Bains, Robbo
County debut: 1977 (Gloucestershire)
County cap: 1981
Benefit: 1989
1000 runs in a season: 8
1st-Class 50s scored: 69
1st-Class 100s scored: 22
1st-Class 5 w. in innings: 7
1st-Class catches: 110
One-Day 50s: 21
One-Day 100s: 1
Strike rate: (career 72.86)
Parents: Leonard George and Lilian Rose
Wife and date of marriage: Barbara, 22 September 1979

Children: Neil, 11 January 1984; Laura, 15 January 1985
Family links with cricket: Cousin, Stephen Wilkinson, played for Somerset
Education: Hanley High School; Stoke-on-Trent Sixth Form College; Borough Road College of Education
Qualifications: 9 O-levels, 2 A-levels, BEd
Career outside cricket: Partner in corporate hospitality company and sports tour operators – Rhodes Leisure, Bristol
Off-season: 'Working in the business.'
Overseas tours: British Colleges to W. Indies 1978; Eng. Counties XI to Zimbabwe 1985
Cricketers particularly admired: Mike Procter
Other sports followed: All sports, particularly rugby union. 'Followed England all the way through to the final – well played, lads!'
Relaxations: 'Golf, listening to music, playing and watching all sports, and coaching Thornbury Rugby Club mini rugby U9s for whom my son plays.'
Extras: Played for four 2nd XIs in 1976 – Gloucestershire, Derbyshire, Northamptonshire and Warwickshire. Played for Young England v Australia 1977. Scored first century for Stoke-on-Trent aged 14. One of *Wisden's* Five Cricketers of the Year, 1985. Joined Durham for their first season in first-class cricket after 14 seasons with Gloucestershire. Played for Leyland CC as professional in 1991 – they won the Northern League.
Opinions on cricket: 'Too much cricket, and even more being played next year with Durham joining (although I think this is excellent for cricket apart from the fact that I have joined them). I favour a four-day Championship with everyone playing each other once, alternatively home and away. I welcome the introduction of coloured clothing on Sundays, and of course the re-introduction of South Africa to cricket and other sports.'
Best batting: 169 Gloucestershire v Yorkshire, Cheltenham 1988
Best bowling: 8-53 Gloucestershire v Somerset, Bristol 1986

1991 Season

	M	Inns	NO	Runs	HS	Avge	100s	50s	Ct	St	O	M	Runs	Wkts	Avge	Best	5wl	10wM
Test																		
All First																		
1-day Int																		
NatWest	1	1	0	27	27	27.00	-	-	-	-	12	0	42	0	-		-	-
B&H																		
Refuge																		

Career Performances

	M	Inns	NO	Runs	HS	Avge	100s	50s	Ct	St	Balls	Runs	Wkts	Avge	Best	5wl	10wM
Test																	
All First	257	424	60	12353	169	33.93	22	69	110	-	19893	9985	273	36.57	8-53	7	-
1-day Int																	
NatWest	26	22	3	637	89	33.52	-	6	4	-	1501	849	27	31.44	3-49	-	-
B&H	46	42	9	967	96	29.30	-	6	16	-	2133	1265	38	33.28	3-21	-	
Refuge	163	144	25	2531	106 *	21.26	1	9	33	-	5596	4754	159	29.89	5-22	1	

BAKKER, P.-J. Hampshire

Name: Paul-Jan Bakker
Role: Right-hand bat, right-arm medium
bowler, fine-leg and mid-off/mid-on fielder
Born: 19 August 1957, Vlaardingen,
Holland
Height: 6ft 1in **Weight:** 14st (very up
and down)
Nickname: Nip, Peach, Dutchie
County debut: 1986
County cap: 1989
50 wickets in a season: 1
1st-Class 5 w. in innings: 7
1st-Class catches: 9
Place in bowling averages: 69th av. 32.75
(1990 87th av. 38.89)
Strike rate: 71.85 (career 57.98)
Parents: Hubertus Antonius Bakker and
Wilhelmina Hendrika Bakker-Goos
Marital status: Single

Family links with cricket: 'Father is scorer for Quick CC, my club in the Hague.'
Education: 1ᵉ VCL and Hugo de Groot College, The Hague, Holland
Qualifications: 'We have a different school system but finished my HAVO schooling.'
Ski-instructor
Career outside cricket: Ski holidays/ ski touring and ski lessons in Switzerland
Off-season: Holiday in Saint Maarten (Dutch West Indies) and Anguilla, followed by
skiing in Switzerland.
Overseas tours: Several tours to England with Dutch clubs and with Holland national side,
including ICC Trophy 1986; MCC to USA 1989-90; Namibia 1990-91
Overseas teams played for: Quick, The Hague 1965-85; Green Point, Cape Town 1981-
86; Flamingo Touring Club 1986-91
Cricketers particularly admired: 'Malcolm Marshall – best bowler I've ever seen (but
he can't beat me at golf!) and Michael Holding – the most beautifully balanced run-up'
Other sports followed: Formula One motor racing, skiing, golf and most other sports
Injuries: 'A damaged knee that ruled me out for about seven weeks. Couldn't use the left
arm properly because there was no strength due to lack of impulses from that nerve.'
Relaxations: Golf – but is it relaxation when you double-bogey a par 3. Winter sports are
most relaxing, especially the end of a day's skiing
Extras: First ever Dutch player to play professional cricket. Played for Holland in 1986
and 1990 ICC Trophy competitions. 'To be invited for the Crickethon at Wembley was a
big thrill, especially being the only "European" in the side.'
Opinions on cricket: 'The balance between bat and ball has been improved but I would
like to see the return of the "old" ball on the wickets we play on now. I think the schedule

is a bit hectic at times. The only option is less cricket and a four-day Championship. But money seems to rule everything nowadays so that change won't materialise.'

Best batting: 22 Hampshire v Yorkshire, Southampton 1989
Best bowling: 7-31 Hampshire v Kent, Bournemouth 1987

1991 Season

	M	Inns	NO	Runs	HS	Avge	100s	50s	Ct	St	O	M	Runs	Wkts	Avge	Best	5wI	10wM
Test																		
All First	10	6	2	17	6*	4.25	-	-	2	-	239.3	65	655	20	32.75	4-66	-	-
1-day Int																		
NatWest	1	0	0	0	0	-	-	-	-	-	4	1	15	0	-	-	-	
B&H	4	2	0	11	7	5.50	-	-	1	-	44	6	146	4	36.50	2-37	-	
Refuge	5	1	0	4	4	4.00	-	-	-	-	40	2	186	4	46.50	2-36	-	

Career Performances

	M	Inns	NO	Runs	HS	Avge	100s	50s	Ct	St	Balls	Runs	Wkts	Avge	Best	5wI	10wM
Test																	
All First	63	47	18	264	22	9.10	-	-	9	-	10553	4965	182	27.28	7-31	7	-
1-day Int																	
NatWest	11	3	1	7	3*	3.50	-	-	-	-	688	378	11	34.36	3-34	-	
B&H	10	2	0	11	7	5.50	-	-	1	-	648	332	10	33.20	2-19	-	
Refuge	37	10	8	26	9	13.00	-	-	3	-	1573	1159	54	21.46	5-17	2	

BALL, M. C. J. Gloucestershire

Name: Martyn Charles John Ball
Role: Right-hand bat, off-spin bowler, slip fielder
Born: 26 April 1970, Bristol
Height: 5ft 9in **Weight:** 11st 8lbs
Nickname: Benny
County debut: 1988
1st-Class 5 w. in innings: 1
1st-Class catches: 17
Place in batting averages: 249th av. 11.77
Place in bowling averages: 53rd av. 30.63
Strike rate: 58.73 (career 62.42)
Parents: Kenneth Charles and Pamela Wendy
Wife and date of marriage: Mona, 28 September 1991
Children: Kristina, 9 May 1990

Education: King Edmund Secondary School, Yate; Bath College of Further Education
Qualifications: 6 O-levels, 2 AO-levels, 3 A-levels
Off-season: Driving a baker's van
Overseas teams played for:
North Melbourne 1988-89; Old Hararians Zimbabwe) 1990-91
Cricketers most admired: Ian Botham, Vic Marks, David Graveney
Other sports followed: All sports except show-jumping and synchronised swimming
Injuries: Cracked thumb early last season
Relaxations: Following Manchester City FC, listening to music and watching a movie while sprawled flat out on the sofa.
Extras: Played for Young England against New Zealand in 1989
Opinions on cricket: 'Four-day cricket on good pitches with a good seamed ball please. Coloured clothing in all one-day games. Lunch and tea intervals should be extended.'
Best batting: 28 Gloucestershire v Surrey, Guildford 1991
Best bowling: 5-128 Gloucestershire v Kent, Canterbury 1991

1991 Season

	M	Inns	NO	Runs	HS	Avge	100s	50s	Ct	St	O	M	Runs	Wkts	Avge	Best	5wI	10wM
Test																		
All First	6	9	0	106	28	11.77	-	-	8	-	186	36	582	19	30.63	5-128	1	-
1-day Int																		
NatWest																		
B&H																		
Refuge	8	5	1	14	5	3.50	-	-	3	-	34.5	0	174	0	-	-	-	-

Career Performances

	M	Inns	NO	Runs	HS	Avge	100s	50s	Ct	St	Balls	Runs	Wkts	Avge	Best	5wI	10wM
Test																	
All First	20	23	3	178	28	8.90	-	-	17	-	2622	1377	42	32.78	5-128	1	-
1-day Int																	
NatWest	1	0	0	0	0	-	-	-	-	-	72	42	3	14.00	3-42	-	
B&H	2	0	0	0	0	-	-	-	-	-	60	68	0	-	-	-	
Refuge	13	7	1	19	5	3.16	-	-	5	-	353	309	1	309.00	1-17	-	

17. Who came top of the first-class batting averages in England last season?

18. Who came top of the first-class bowling averages in England last season?

BAPTISTE, E. A. E. Northamptonshire

Name: Eldine Ashworth Elderfield Baptiste
Role: Right-hand bat, right-arm
fast bowler
Born: 12 March 1960, Antigua
Height: 5ft 11in **Weight:** 12st
Nickname: Bapo, Soca
County debut: 1983 (Kent)
1991 (Northamptonshire)
County cap: 1983 (Kent)
Test debut: 1983-84
Tests: 10
One-Day Internationals: 43
50 wickets in a season: 1
1st-Class 50s scored: 31
1st-Class 5 w. in innings: 21
1st-Class 10 w. in match: 3
1st-Class catches: 85
Place in batting averages: 134th av. 28.04
Place in bowling averages: 42nd av. 28.86
Strike rate: 63.52 (career 53.93)
Parents: Samuel and Gertrude

Marital status: Single
Children: Forbes, 30 December 1981; Quamé, 15 June 1982
Family links with cricket: Father played club cricket in Antigua.
Education: Liberta Primary School; All Saints Secondary School
Career outside cricket: Coaching in the Sport and Education Department
Off-season: 'Relax in the sea after a hard season.'
Overseas tours: Young Antiguans to England 1979; Young West Indies to England 1984; West Indies to India 1983-84 & 1987-88; Australia 1984-85; Zimbabwe 1986-87; Pakistan 1987-88
Overseas teams played for: Geelong City 1985-86; Tasmania University 1986-87
Cricketers particularly admired: Alan Fordham, Andy Roberts, Guy Yearwood
Other sports followed: Football, boxing, tennis, golf, athletics
Injuries: Out for six weeks with right leg muscle strains
Relaxations: Listening to music
Opinions on cricket: 'Too many new laws are killing the game. The County Championship should be all four-day matches because this would make better Test cricketers for the future.'
Best batting: 136* Kent v Yorkshire, Sheffield 1983
Best bowling: 8-76 Kent v Warwickshire, Edgbaston 1987

1991 Season

	M	Inns	NO	Runs	HS	Avge	100s	50s	Ct	St	O	M	Runs	Wkts	Avge	Best	5wI	10wM
Test																		
All First	18	22	1	589	80	28.04	-	4	9	-	529.2	122	1443	50	28.86	7-95	3	-
1-day Int																		
NatWest	4	3	1	51	34	25.50	-	-	1	-	42	4	171	9	19.00	4-27	-	
B&H	4	3	1	28	15 *	14.00	-	-	-	-	31.1	5	118	1	118.00	1-30	-	
Refuge	11	11	4	83	15 *	11.85	-	-	2	-	81.1	5	340	6	56.66	2-25	-	

Career Performances

	M	Inns	NO	Runs	HS	Avge	100s	50s	Ct	St	Balls	Runs	Wkts	Avge	Best	5wI	10wM
Test	10	11	1	233	87 *	23.30	-	1	2	-	1362	563	16	35.18	3-31	-	-
All First	173	242	31	5907	136 *	27.99	3	31	85	-	26642	12672	494	25.65	8-76	21	3
1-day Int	43	16	4	184	31	15.33	-	-	14	-	2214	1510	36	41.94	2-10	-	
NatWest	16	13	2	129	34	11.72	-	-	7	-	1014	595	23	25.87	5-20	1	
B&H	23	20	6	228	43 *	16.28	-	-	8	-	1237	762	23	33.13	5-30	1	
Refuge	74	63	10	885	60	16.69	-	5	22	-	2968	2229	79	28.21	4-22	-	

BARNES, S. N.   Gloucestershire

Name: Stuart Neil Barnes
Role: Right-hand bat, right-arm medium-fast bowler
Born: 27 June 1970, Bath
Height: 6ft 1in **Weight:** 12st 7lbs
Nickname: Digger, Digs
County debut: 1989 (one-day), 1990 (1st-class)
1st-Class catches: 3
Place in bowling averages: (1990 77th av. 37.62)
Strike rate: (career 82.12)
Parents: Hedley George and Georgina
Marital status: Single
Family links with cricket: 'Father plays village cricket for Dunkerton CC. Brother Darren represents the county.'
Education: Fosse Way Junior and Beechen Cliff School, Bath
Qualifications: CSEs
Career outside cricket: 'Worked in Barclays Bank, Bath, for three years before having a six-week trial in 1989.'

Cricketers particularly admired: Ian Botham, Richard Hadlee
Other sports followed: Football, rugby
Relaxations: Watching sport on TV, listening to music
Extras: Released by Gloucestershire at the end of the 1991 season
Best batting: 12* Gloucestershire v Indians, Bristol 1990
Best bowling: 4-51 Gloucestershire v Cambridge University, Fenner's 1990

1991 Season

	M	Inns	NO	Runs	HS	Avge	100s	50s	Ct	St	O	M	Runs	Wkts	Avge	Best	5wI	10wM
Test																		
All First	1	1	1	0	0*	-	-	-	-	-	12	4	23	0	-	-	-	-
1-day Int																		
NatWest																		
B&H																		
Refuge	1	0	0	0	0	-	-	-	-	-	8	0	33	1	33.00	1-33	-	

Career Performances

	M	Inns	NO	Runs	HS	Avge	100s	50s	Ct	St	Balls	Runs	Wkts	Avge	Best	5wI	10wM
Test																	
All First	11	10	3	23	12*	3.28	-	-	3	-	1314	625	16	39.06	4-51	-	-
1-day Int																	
NatWest	2	1	0	0	0	0.00	-	-	1	-	108	93	1	93.00	1-64	-	
B&H																	
Refuge	8	2	2	11	11*	-	-	-	3	-	342	298	8	37.25	3-39	-	

BARNETT, A. A.   Lancashire

Name: Alex Anthony Barnett
Role: Right-hand bat, slow left-arm bowler
Born: 11 September 1970. Malaga, Spain
Height: 6ft **Weight:** 12st
Nickname: Bung, Barny
County debut: 1991
1st-Class catches: 0
Place in bowling averages: 72nd av. 32.90
Strike rate: 64.60 (career 80.80)
Parents: Michael and Patricia
Marital status: Single
Family links with cricket: Great uncle, Charlie J. Barnett was opening batsman for Gloucestershire and England.
Education: Primrose Hill Primary, William Ellis Secondary
Qualifications: 'Not many Os, no As, no degrees.'

Career outside cricket: 'Professional out-of-work cricketer'
Off-season: 'Looking for employment.'
Overseas tours: England U19 to Australia 1990
Cricketers particularly admired: Don Wilson, Des Haynes, Clive Radley, Mike Gatting
Other sports followed: Boxing
Injuries: Problems with right shoulder
Relaxations: Reading, listening to music
Extras: First-class debut aged 17. Hit first first-class ball for four (between 1st and 2nd slip). Joined Lancashire from Middlesex on a one-year contract at the end of the 1991 season
Opinions on cricket: 'Cricket should be played more positively, which should reduce the increasing amount of artificially

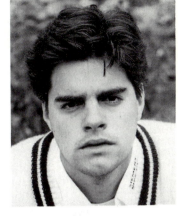

manufactured run-chases. The LBW law concerning the ball pitching outside the leg stump is ridiculous and unfair to left-arm bowlers – spinners or seamers.'
Best batting: 11* Middlesex v Surrey, The Oval 1991
Best bowling: 4-119 Middlesex v Derbyshire, Lord's 1991

1991 Season

	M	Inns	NO	Runs	HS	Avge	100s	50s	Ct	St	O	M	Runs	Wkts	Avge	Best	5wI	10wM
Test																		
All First	2	2	2	12	11 *	-	-	-	-	-	107.4	23	329	10	32.90	4-119	-	-
1-day Int																		
NatWest																		
B&H																		
Refuge																		

Career Performances

	M	Inns	NO	Runs	HS	Avge	100s	50s	Ct	St	Balls	Runs	Wkts	Avge	Best	5wI	10wM
Test																	
All First	3	3	2	22	11 *	22.00	-	-	-	-	808	394	10	39.40	4-119	-	-
1-day Int																	
NatWest																	
B&H																	
Refuge																	

BARNETT, K. J.   Derbyshire

Name: Kim John Barnett
Role: Right-hand bat, leg-break
bowler, county captain
Born: 17 July 1960, Stoke-on-Trent
Height: 6ft 1in **Weight:** 13st 7lbs
County debut: 1979
County cap: 1982
Test debut: 1988
Tests: 4
One-Day Internationals: 1
1000 runs in a season: 9
1st-Class 50s scored: 94
1st-Class 100s scored: 34
1st-Class 200s scored: 2
1st-Class 5 w. in innings: 2
1st-Class catches: 211
One-Day 50s: 44
One-Day 100s: 9
Place in batting averages: 67th av. 37.81
(1990 49th av. 49.93)
Place in bowling averages: 20th av. 24.80 (1990 26th av. 29.11)
Strike rate: 63.35 (career 77.33)
Parents: Derek and Doreen
Marital status: Single
Children: Michael Nicholas, 24 April 1990
Education: Leek High School, Staffs
Qualifications: 7 O-levels
Overseas tours: With England Schools to India 1977; Young England to Australia 1978-79; England B to Sri Lanka 1986 (vice-captain); unofficial English XI to South Africa 1989-90
Overseas teams played for: Boland 1982-83, 1984-85, 1987-88
Cricketers particularly admired: Gordon Greenidge, Richard Hadlee
Other sports followed: Horse racing
Relaxations: Watching racing on TV, eating and sleeping
Extras: Played for Northamptonshire 2nd XI when aged 15, Staffordshire and Warwickshire 2nd XI. Became youngest captain of a first-class county when appointed in 1983. Banned from Test cricket after joining tour to South Africa
Opinions on cricket: 'It's time pitches were created to provide a decent balance between bat and ball instead of flat, slow, nothing wickets which only produce boredom for everyone concerned. County cricket should be left to run itself with variation in pitches around the country. County cricket should not be blamed for failure at Test level. Maybe Test pitches should be more like county pitches and not too much in favour of the bat.'

Best batting: 239* Derbyshire v Leicestershire, Leicester 1988
Best bowling: 6-28 Derbyshire v Glamorgan, Chesterfield 1991

1991 Season

	M	Inns	NO	Runs	HS	Avge	100s	50s	Ct	St	O	M	Runs	Wkts	Avge	Best	5wI	10wM
Test																		
All First	24	39	2	1399	217	37.81	2	9	25	-	211.1	47	496	20	24.80	6-28	1	-
1-day Int																		
NatWest																		
B&H	4	4	0	256	102	64.00	1	2	3	-	29	4	97	3	32.33	1-28	-	
Refuge	14	14	4	289	60 *	28.90	-	1	6	-	24	0	105	4	26.25	2-40	-	

Career Performances

	M	Inns	NO	Runs	HS	Avge	100s	50s	Ct	St	Balls	Runs	Wkts	Avge	Best	5wI	10wM
Test	4	7	0	207	80	29.57	-	2	1	-	36	32	0	-	-	-	-
All First	314	504	42	17225	239 *	37.28	34	94	211	-	10286	5074	133	38.15	6-28	2	-
1-day Int	1	1	0	84	84	84.00	-	1	-	-							
NatWest	25	25	2	798	88	34.69	-	6	10	-	178	107	11	9.72	6-24	1	
B&H	59	50	2	1674	115	34.87	3	12	19	-	234	139	5	27.80	1-10	-	
Refuge	186	178	27	5217	131 *	34.55	6	26	64	-	659	585	16	36.56	3-39	-	

BARTLETT, R. J.   Somerset

Name: Richard James Bartlett
Role: Right-hand bat, off-spin bowler
Born: 8 October 1966, Ash Priors, Somerset
Height: 5ft 9in **Weight:** 12st 7lbs
Nickname: Pumpy
County debut: 1986
1st-Class 50s scored: 6
1st-Class 100s scored: 2
1st-Class catches: 30
One-Day 50s: 8
Place in batting averages: 120th av. 29.50
Parents: Richard and Barbara
Family links with cricket: 'Dad used to play club cricket but now umpires in the Somerset League.'
Education: Taunton School
Qualifications: 8 O-levels, 3 A-levels
Cricketers particularly admired:
Jimmy Cook, Steve Waugh, Adrian Jones,

Trevor Gard, Viv Richards
Other sports followed: Golf, hockey (county U21 player) and most others
Relaxations: Music, socialising, playing golf
Extras: First Somerset player to score a century on first-class debut since Harold Gimblett. Represented England Schools and England Young Cricketers. Rapid Cricketline 2nd XI Player of the Season 1990
Opinions on cricket: 'Cricket is now loaded in the favour of batsmen due to the changes to the pitches and ball. To even this out we should revert to the old ball and keep the wickets as they were in 1990.... but it's a great game when you're doing well!'
Best batting: 117* Somerset v Oxford University, The Parks 1986
Best bowling: 1-9 Somerset v Glamorgan, Taunton 1988

1991 Season

	M	Inns	NO	Runs	HS	Avge	100s	50s	Ct	St	O	M	Runs	Wkts	Avge	Best	5wI	10wM
Test																		
All First	5	7	1	177	71	29.50	-	1	3	-								
1-day Int																		
NatWest																		
B&H	2	2	0	28	14	14.00	-	-	1	-								
Refuge	7	7	0	98	34	14.00	-	-	1	-								

Career Performances

	M	Inns	NO	Runs	HS	Avge	100s	50s	Ct	St	Balls	Runs	Wkts	Avge	Best	5wI	10wM
Test																	
All First	43	69	6	1504	117 *	23.87	2	6	30	-	180	145	4	36.25	1-9	-	-
1-day Int																	
NatWest	3	3	1	147	85	73.50	-	2	1	-							
B&H	9	9	1	108	36	13.50	-	-	3	-							
Refuge	38	38	1	885	55	23.91	-	6	20	-							

19. Which county won the Minor Counties Western Division championship last season?

20. Which former England player plays League cricket for Soothill?

BARWICK, S. R. Glamorgan

Name: Stephen Royston Barwick
Role: Right-hand bat, right-arm
medium bowler
Born: 6 September 1960, Neath
Height: 6ft 2in **Weight:** 13st
Nickname: Bas
County debut: 1981
County cap: 1987
50 wickets in a season: 2
1st-Class 5 w. in innings: 9
1st-Class 10 w. in match: 1
1st-Class catches: 31
Place in bowling averages: 34th av. 27.39
Parents: Margaret and Roy
Wife and date of marriage: Margaret,
12 December 1987
Children: Michael Warrren,
25 September 1990
Family links with cricket: 'My Uncle
David played for Glamorgan 2nd XI.'
Education: Cwrt Sart Comprehensive, Dwr-y-Felin Comprehensive
Qualifications: 'Commerce, human biology, mathematics, English.'
Career outside cricket: Ex-steel worker
Overseas teams played for: Benoni, South Africa
Cricketers particularly admired: Ian Botham, Richard Hadlee
Other sports followed: Football and rugby
Injuries: Broken finger
Relaxations: 'Spending time with my little boy, sea fishing and the odd pint or two.'
Opinions on cricket: 'I think there should be more four-day cricket. And I hope that coloured clothing takes off this year.'
Best batting: 30 Glamorgan v Hampshire, Bournemouth 1988
Best bowling: 8-42 Glamorgan v Worcestershire, Worcester 1983

1991 Season

	M	Inns	NO	Runs	HS	Avge	100s	50s	Ct	St	O	M	Runs	Wkts	Avge	Best	5wI	10wM
Test																		
All First	12	10	1	64	24 *	7.11	-	-	1	-	317.5	86	767	28	27.39	4-46	-	-
1-day Int																		
NatWest	3	1	0	3	3	3.00	-	-	-	-	33	0	153	5	30.60	2-51	-	
B&H	4	2	2	5	4 *	-	-	-	3	-	39	4	175	4	43.75	2-61	-	
Refuge	15	8	4	23	8	5.75	-	-	3	-	81.1	0	441	12	36.75	3-30	-	

Career Performances

	M	Inns	NO	Runs	HS	Avge	100s	50s	Ct	St	Balls	Runs	Wkts	Avge	Best	5wI	10wM
Test																	
All First	155	147	58	693	30	7.78	-	-	31	-	24238	11304	342	33.05	8-42	9	1
1-day Int																	
NatWest	16	7	3	21	6	5.25	-	-	2	-	826	432	23	18.78	4-14	-	
B&H	36	21	12	75	18	8.33	-	-	8	-	1935	1242	44	28.22	4-11	-	
Refuge	107	37	23	179	48 *	12.78	-	-	13	-	3956	3064	99	30.94	4-23	-	

BASE, S. J. Derbyshire

Name: Simon John Base
Role: Right-hand bat, right-arm medium bowler
Born: 2 January 1960, Maidstone
Height: 6ft 3in **Weight:** 14st
Nickname: Basey, Bok
County debut: 1986 (Glamorgan), 1988 (Derbys)
County cap: 1990
50 wickets in a season: 1
1st-Class 50s: 2
1st-Class 5 w. in innings: 10
1st-Class 10 w. in match: 1
1st-Class catches: 42
Place in batting averages: 252nd av. 10.78 (1990 225th av. 19.54)
Place in bowling averages: 102nd av. 37.33 (1990 97th av. 50.05)
Strike rate: 72.27 (career 52.08)
Parents: Christine and Peter
Wife and date of marriage: Louise Ann, 23 September 1989
Family links with cricket: Grandfather played
Education: Fish Hoek Primary School, Fish Hoek High School, Cape Town, South Africa
Qualifications: High School, School Certificate Matriculation. Refrigeration and air conditioning technician
Career outside cricket: Hall-Thermotank in South Africa as a technician and S.A. Sea Products, G.S.P.K. Electronics in North Yorkshire, England
Off-season: Playing for Border in South Africa
Overseas teams played for: Western Province B 1982-83; Boland 1986-89; Border 1989-91
Cricketers particularly admired: Eddie Barlow, Graham Gooch, Graeme Pollock

Other sports followed: Golf, tennis, snooker, all sports

Relaxations: Windsurfing, golf, reading science fiction, watching films, music

Extras: Suspended from first-class cricket for ten weeks during 1988 season for a supposed breach of contract, joining Derbyshire when he was still said to be contracted to Glamorgan. The TCCB fined Derbyshire £2000. Banned from playing Test cricket for continuing to play in South Africa

Opinions on cricket: 'I feel that politics should not interfere with international sport at any level.'

Best batting: 58 Derbyshire v Yorkshire, Chesterfield 1990

Best bowling: 7-60 Derbyshire v Yorkshire, Chesterfield 1989

1991 Season

	M	Inns	NO	Runs	HS	Avge	100s	50s	Ct	St	O	M	Runs	Wkts	Avge	Best	5wI	10wM
Test																		
All First	15	18	4	151	36	10.78	-	-	14	-	433.4	69	1344	36	37.33	4-34	-	-
1-day Int																		
NatWest																		
B&H	4	2	0	8	7	4.00	-	-	-	-	36	4	134	3	44.66	2-40	-	
Refuge	15	7	0	21	12	3.00	-	-	5	-	104.5	4	474	18	26.33	4-14	-	

Career Performances

	M	Inns	NO	Runs	HS	Avge	100s	50s	Ct	St	Balls	Runs	Wkts	Avge	Best	5wI	10wM
Test																	
All First	96	119	31	1076	58	12.22	-	2	42	-	15713	8300	297	27.94	7-60	10	1
1-day Int																	
NatWest	2	2	0	6	4	3.00	-	-	1	-	90	61	2	30.50	2-49	-	
B&H	15	9	3	53	15 *	8.83	-	-	-	-	870	629	15	41.93	3-33	-	
Refuge	60	24	4	75	19	3.75	-	-	16	-	2457	1869	74	25.25	4-14	-	

21. What is the title of Peter Roebuck's history of Somerset cricket, published last season?

22. Which county wicket-keeper claimed the most victims last season?

23. Who topped the first-class batting averages for Derbyshire last season?

BASTIEN, S.   Glamorgan

Name: Steven Bastien
Role: Right-hand bat, right-arm
fast-medium bowler, outfielder
Born: 13 March 1963, Stepney
Height: 6ft 1in **Weight:** 13st
Nickname: Bassie
County debut: 1988
1st-Class 5 w. in innings: 4
1st-Class catches: 3
Place in bowling averages: 128th av. 46.50
(1990 31st av. 30.43)
Strike rate: 97.18 (career 67.85)
Parents: Anthony and Francisca
Marital status: Single
Children: Linden Kieron,
20 December 1990
Family links with cricket: Brother Roger
plays in the Essex League
Education: St Mary's Academy School,
Dominica; St Bonaventure School, London
Qualifications: 3 CSEs; NCA coaching certificate; carpentry and CCPR course
Cricketers particularly admired: Viv Richards, David Gower, Robin Smith, Michael
Holding, Malcolm Marshall
Other sports followed: Football, boxing, basketball, athletics
Injuries: Side strain and Achilles tendon trouble
Relaxations: Listening to reggae, soul and calypso music
Extras: Took five wickets on first-class debut in 1988. Member of Haringey Cricket
College
Opinions on cricket: 'There is still too much three-day cricket. I think we should have
more four-day games instead, because there is a better chance of getting a result.'
Best batting: 36* Glamorgan v Warwickshire, Edgbaston 1988
Best bowling: 6-75 Glamorgan v Worcestershire, Worcester 1990

1991 Season

	M	Inns	NO	Runs	HS	Avge	100s	50s	Ct	St	O	M	Runs	Wkts	Avge	Best	5wI	10wM
Test																		
All First	13	6	3	26	22*	8.66	-	-	1	-	356.2	99	1023	22	46.50	5-39	1	-
1-day Int																		
NatWest																		
B&H																		
Refuge	3	0	0	0	0	-	-	-	-	-	14	0	79	2	39.50	2-42	-	

Career Performances

	M	Inns	NO	Runs	HS	Avge	100s	50s	Ct	St	Balls	Runs	Wkts	Avge	Best	5wI	10wM
Test																	
All First	34	23	10	131	36 *	10.07	-	-	3	-	5225	2761	77	35.85	6-75	4	-
1-day Int																	
NatWest																	
B&H	2	1	0	7	7	7.00	-	-	-	-	66	64	0	-	-	-	
Refuge	7	1	0	1	1	1.00	-	-	1	-	198	165	3	55.00	2-42	-	

BATTY, J. D. Yorkshire

Name: Jeremy David Batty
Role: Right-hand bat, off-spin bowler, cover fielder
Born: 15 May 1971, Bradford
Height: 6ft 1in **Weight:** 11st 10lbs
Nickname: Bullfrog, Sniper, Nora
County debut: 1989
1st-Class 5 w. in innings: 2
1st-Class catches: 11
Place in batting averages: 203rd av. 18.36
Place in bowling averages: 88th av. 35.09
(1990 141st av. 60.16)
Strike rate: 67.26 (career 70.70)
Parents: David and Rosemary
Marital status: Single
Family links with cricket: Father took over 1000 wickets in the Bradford League.

Education: Parkside Middle School, Bingley Grammar School, Horsforth College
Qualifications: 5 O-levels; BTec: Diploma in Leisure Studies; coaching certificate
Off-season: Coaching
Overseas tours: England Young Cricketers to Australia 1989-90
Overseas teams played for: Sunrise 1989-90, Country Districts 1990-91 (both Zimbabwe)
Cricketers particularly admired: Phil Carrick, John Emburey, Ian Botham, Mike Gatting
Other sports followed: Rugby league, rugby union, football
Relaxations: Drink, food, music and movies
Extras: Took five wickets on first-class debut v Lancashire in 1989
Opinions on cricket: 'There should be more razzmatazz on a Sunday to get younger people involved, and more effort by clubs to find employment for players in off-seasons.'
Best batting: 51 Yorkshire v Sri Lankans, Headingley 1991
Best bowling: 6-48 Yorkshire v Nottinghamshire, Worksop 1991

1991 Season

	M	Inns	NO	Runs	HS	Avge	100s	50s	Ct	St	O	M	Runs	Wkts	Avge	Best	5wI	10wM
Test																		
All First	18	17	6	202	51	18.36	-	1	7	-	459.4	106	1439	41	35.09	6-48	1	-
1-day Int																		
NatWest	1	1	0	4	4	4.00	-	-	-	-	6	2	17	1	17.00	1-17	-	
B&H	3	0	0	0	0	-	-	-	-	-	22	3	75	1	75.00	1-34	-	
Refuge	11	4	2	27	13 *	13.50	-	-	6	-	77	4	376	12	31.33	4-33	-	

Career Performances

	M	Inns	NO	Runs	HS	Avge	100s	50s	Ct	St	Balls	Runs	Wkts	Avge	Best	5wI	10wM
Test																	
All First	26	24	9	236	51	15.73	-	1	11	-	4313	2354	61	38.59	6-48	2	-
1-day Int																	
NatWest	1	1	0	4	4	4.00	-	-	-	-	36	17	1	17.00	1-17	-	
B&H	3	0	0	0	0	-	-	-	-	-	132	75	1	75.00	1-34	-	
Refuge	11	4	2	27	13 *	13.50	-	-	6	-	462	376	12	31.33	4-33	-	

BEAL, D. Somerset

Name: David Beal
Role: Right-hand bat, right-arm medium bowler
Born: 17 July 1966, Butleigh, nr Glastonbury
Height: 6ft 1in **Weight:** 13st
County debut: 1991
1st-class catches: 1
Parents: Keith and Delia
Wife: Rebecca Anne
Children: Joshua Francis, 18 June 1991
Family links with cricket: Father plays for Glastonbury.
Education: Crispin School, Street
Career outside cricket: Working for father's sheepskin business
Overseas teams played for: Waneroo, Perth
Cricketers particularly admired: Viv Richards, Malcolm Marshall, Dennis Lillee
Other sports followed: Football
Injuries: Bad back
Relaxations: 'Watching my son grow up.'

Opinions on cricket: 'There must be a stop to this declaration bowling.'
Best batting: 1 Somerset v Sussex, Hove 1991
Best bowling: 1-37 Somerset v Essex, Southend 1991

1991 Season

	M	Inns	NO	Runs	HS	Avge	100s	50s	Ct	St	O	M	Runs	Wkts	Avge	Best	5wI	10wM
Test																		
All First	3	2	0	1	1	0.50	-	-	1	-	71	6	320	3	106.66	1-37	-	-
1-day Int																		
NatWest	1	1	0	0	0	0.00	-	-	-	-	2	0	12	0	-	-	-	-
B&H	2	2	1	1	1	1.00	-	-	-	-	16	1	114	3	38.00	2-63	-	
Refuge	3	0	0	0	0	-	-	-	1	-	8	0	40	2	20.00	2-40	-	

Career Performances

	M	Inns	NO	Runs	HS	Avge	100s	50s	Ct	St	Balls	Runs	Wkts	Avge	Best	5wI	10wM
Test																	
All First	3	2	0	1	1	0.50	-	-	1	-	426	320	3	106.66	1-37	-	-
1-day Int																	
NatWest	1	1	0	0	0	0.00	-	-	-	-	12	12	0	-	-	-	-
B&H	2	2	1	1	1	1.00	-	-	-	-	96	114	3	38.00	2-63	-	
Refuge	3	0	0	0	0	-	-	-	1	-	48	40	2	20.00	2-40	-	

BELL, R. M. Gloucestershire

Name: Robert Malcolm Bell
Role: Right-hand bat, right-arm medium bowler and outfielder
Born: 26 February 1969, St Mary's, Isles of Scilly
Height: 6ft 6in
Nickname: Belly, Archy, Tinker
County debut: 1990
1st-class catches: 0
Marital status: Engaged to Chantal
Family links with cricket: Father played for his school, brother used to play for Cornwall Schools
Education: St Mary's Primary, Isles of Scilly; Truro School
Qualifications: Completed sports management course at college, qualified coach

Career outside cricket: 'Worked on the Kent groundstaff and take a very big interest in the preparation of wickets and grounds.'
Off-season: Coaching and playing in South Africa
Overseas teams played for: Avendale, Cape Town 1987-92
Cricketers particularly admired: Bob Woolmer, Bob Willis, Dennis Lillee and Ed Milburn
Other sports followed: 'Enjoy watching rugby and snooker but hate horse racing.'
Injuries: Strained left hamstring in the early part of last season
Relaxations: 'Enjoy discussing my bowling with county colleague Stuart Barnes, plus spending some time at the bar with Tim Hancock.'
Extras: Played for Kent 2nd XI in 1989 and for Cornwall in the Minor Counties Championship in 1990. Released by Gloucestershire at the end of the 1991 season
Opinions on cricket: 'With the continuation of flat pitches the ball must be changed to help the bowlers. All Championship matches should be four-day, with less 1-day cricket. With the B&H and NatWest there is no need for the Sunday league. Players need more time between matches.'
Best batting: 0* Gloucestershire v Worcestershire, Worcester 1990
Best bowling: 2-38 Gloucestershire v Worcestershire, Worcester 1990

1991 Season

	M	Inns	NO	Runs	HS	Avge	100s	50s	Ct	St	O	M	Runs	Wkts	Avge	Best	5wl	10wM
Test																		
All First	1	0	0	0	0	-	-	-	-	-	5	2	9	0	-	-	-	-
1-day Int																		
NatWest																		
B&H																		
Refuge																		

Career Performances

	M	Inns	NO	Runs	HS	Avge	100s	50s	Ct	St	Balls	Runs	Wkts	Avge	Best	5wl	10wM
Test																	
All First	3	2	1	0	0 *	0.00	-	-	-	-	294	123	3	41.00	2-38	-	-
1-day Int																	
NatWest																	
B&H																	
Refuge	1	0	0	0	0	-	-	-	-	-	24	38	0	-	-	-

24. Who hit the highest individual first-class score last season, and what was the score?

BENJAMIN, J. E.   Surrey

Name: Joseph Emmanuel Benjamin
Role: Right-hand bat, right-arm
fast-medium bowler
Born: 2 February 1961, St Kitts, West Indies
Height: 6ft 1in **Weight:** 12st
Nickname: Boggy
County debut: 1988 (Warwickshire)
1st-Class 5 w. in innings: 4
1st-Class catches: 7
Place in batting averages: (1990 187th
av. 26.85)
Place in bowling averages: (1990 8th
av. 28.02)
Strike rate: (career 61.79)
Parents: Henry and Judith
Marital status: Single
Education: Cayon High School, St Kitts;
Mount Pleasant, Highgate, Birmingham
Qualifications: 4 O-levels
Off-season: 'Playing as little cricket as I can.'
Cricketers particularly admired: 'All bowlers above dibbly dobs pace.'
Other sports followed: Mud-wrestling
Relaxations: Music, going to the movies, concerts etc
Extras: Released by Warwickshire at the end of the 1991 season and signed up by Surrey
for 1992
Opinions on cricket: 'There should be more four-day games. In three-day matches, when
the opposition cannot get the batting side out they tend to put the joke bowlers on just to
make a game of it. Whereas in four-day games you have lots of time to bowl the opposition
out and get more results which are fair.'
Best batting: 41 Warwickshire v Surrey, The Oval 1990
Best bowling: 5-29 Warwickshire v Cambridge University, Fenner's 1990

1991 Season

	M	Inns	NO	Runs	HS	Avge	100s	50s	Ct	St	O	M	Runs	Wkts	Avge	Best	5wI	10wM
Test																		
All First	3	4	0	12	11	3.00	-	-	1	-	76.4	11	257	7	36.71	2-62	-	-
1-day Int																		
NatWest																		
B&H																		
Refuge	9	3	1	14	12*	7.00	-	-	6	-	58	0	262	9	29.11	3-33	-	

Career Performances

	M	Inns	NO	Runs	HS	Avge	100s	50s	Ct	St	Balls	Runs	Wkts	Avge	Best	5wI	10wM
Test																	
All First	25	22	8	225	41	16.07	-	-	7	-	3955	2020	64	31.56	5-29	4	-
1-day Int																	
NatWest	4	4	2	27	19	13.50	-	-	1	-	222	151	3	50.33	2-37	-	
B&H	2	1	0	20	20	20.00	-	-	1	-	132	72	3	24.00	2-32	-	
Refuge	22	11	6	88	24	17.60	-	-	7	-	918	653	20	32.65	3-33	-	

BENSON, J. D. R. Leicestershire

Name: Justin David Ramsay Benson
Role: Right-hand bat, right-arm medium bowler
Born: 1 March 1967, Dublin
Height: 6ft 3in **Weight:** 15st
Nickname: Rambo, Archie, Baldy
County debut: 1988
1st-Class 50s scored: 4
1st-Class 100s scored: 2
1st-Class catches: 22
One-Day 50s: 2
Place in batting averages: 79th av. 35.72 (1990 133rd av. 34.52)
Parents: Malcolm and Liz
Marital status: Single
Family links with cricket: Father is a qualified first-class umpire and was a 'mean left-arm spinner'

Education: The Leys School, Cambridge; St Faith's; Cambridge College of Further Education
Qualifications: 10 O-levels
Off-season: Playing in South Africa
Overseas teams played for: Club cricket in Cape Town and Bloemfontein, South Africa
Cricketers particularly admired: Gustav van Heerden, Robert Stenner, Warren Peterson
Other sports followed: Most sports on TV
Injuries: Knee trouble which lasted 3 months, and 2 weeks lost with a broken finger
Relaxations: Keeping fit and eating at expensive restaurants
Extras: Scored 85 and won the Man of the Match award for Cambridgeshire in his first NatWest Trophy match in 1986
Opinions on cricket: 'About time South Africa were let back into international sport.'
Best batting: 133* Leicestershire v Hampshire, Bournemouth 1991

Best bowling: 1-18 Leicestershire v Warwickshire, Leicester 1991

1991 Season

	M	Inns	NO	Runs	HS	Avge	100s	50s	Ct	St	O	M	Runs	Wkts	Avge	Best	5wI	10wM
Test																		
All First	9	12	1	393	133 *	35.72	1	1	9	-	35.1	7	145	1	145.00	1-18	-	-
1-day Int																		
NatWest																		
B&H	3	3	1	36	27	18.00	-	-	-	-	7	0	39	1	39.00	1-10	-	
Refuge	11	9	2	136	42	19.42	-	-	5	-	67	0	354	14	25.28	3-37	-	

Career Performances

	M	Inns	NO	Runs	HS	Avge	100s	50s	Ct	St	Balls	Runs	Wkts	Avge	Best	5wI	10wM
Test																	
All First	32	48	7	1231	133 *	30.02	2	4	22	-	507	346	3	115.33	1-18	-	-
1-day Int																	
NatWest	2	2	0	96	85	48.00	-	1	-	-	13	13	0	-	-	-	-
B&H	6	6	2	117	43	29.25	-	-	1	-	42	39	1	39.00	1-10	-	
Refuge	40	34	9	575	67	23.00	-	1	13	-	546	512	20	25.60	3-37	-	

BENSON, M. R.   Kent

Name: Mark Richard Benson
Role: Left-hand bat, off-break bowler, county captain
Born: 6 July 1958, Shoreham, Sussex
Height: 5ft 9¹/₂in **Weight:** 12st 7lbs
Nickname: Benny
County debut: 1980
County cap: 1981
Benefit: 1991
Test debut: 1986
Tests: 1
One-Day Internationals: 1
1000 runs in a season: 10
1st-Class 50s scored: 82
1st-Class 100s scored: 38
1st-Class 200s scored: 1
1st-Class catches: 105
One-Day 50s: 38
One-Day 100s: 4
Place in batting averages: 29th av. 47.46 (1990 55th av. 48.79)

Parents: Frank and Judy
Wife and date of marriage: Sarah, 20 September 1986
Children: Laurence Mark Edward, 16 October 1987
Family links with cricket: Father played for Ghana, sister Tina is Marketing Manager for Kent CCC
Education: Sutton Valence School
Qualifications: O and A-levels and 1 S-level. Qualified tennis coach
Career outside cricket: Marketing assistant with Shell UK Oil; financial adviser
Cricketers particularly admired: Malcolm Marshall, Jimmy Cook, Chris Tavare
Other sports followed: Football, horse racing
Relaxations: Windsurfing, tennis, golf and bowls
Extras: Scored 1000 runs in first full season. Record for most runs in career and season at Sutton Valence School. Appointed Kent captain at end of 1990 season
Opinions on cricket: 'The Championship should be four-day cricket, with each county playing each other once.'
Best batting: 257 Kent v Hampshire, Southampton 1991
Best bowling: 2-55 Kent v Surrey, Dartford 1986

1991 Season

	M	Inns	NO	Runs	HS	Avge	100s	50s	Ct	St	O	M	Runs	Wkts	Avge	Best	5wI	10wM
Test																		
All First	20	30	2	1329	257	47.46	4	6	9	-	13	0	44	0	-	-	-	-
1-day Int																		
NatWest	2	2	0	35	21	17.50	-	-	-	-								
B&H	5	5	0	228	76	45.60	-	3	-	-								
Refuge	14	14	0	422	84	30.14	-	3	6	-								

Career Performances

	M	Inns	NO	Runs	HS	Avge	100s	50s	Ct	St	Balls	Runs	Wkts	Avge	Best	5wI	10wM
Test	1	2	0	51	30	25.50	-	-	-	-							
All First	227	384	29	14553	257	40.99	38	82	105	-	449	468	4	117.00	2-55	-	-
1-day Int	1	1	0	24	24	24.00	-	-	-	-							
NatWest	26	26	1	874	113 *	34.96	1	5	7	-							
B&H	50	49	6	1735	118	40.34	3	11	5	-							
Refuge	119	113	1	3145	97	28.08	-	22	34	-							

25. Who topped the first-class bowling averages for Derbyshire last season?

26. Who was the youngest ever Test captain?

BENT, P.   Worcestershire

Name: Paul Bent
Role: Right-hand bat, off-break bowler
Born: 1 May 1965, Worcester
Height: 6ft **Weight:** 13st
Nickname: Benty, Bodell
County debut: 1985
1st-Class 50s scored: 6
1st-Class 100s scored: 2
1st-Class catches: 4
Place in batting averages: 164th av. 24.00
(1990 173rd av. 28.83)
Parents: Emily and Roy
Wife and date of marriage: Lynne,
29 September 1990
Family links with cricket: Brother plays
local club cricket, as did father-in-law
Education: Worcester Royal Grammar
School

Qualifications: 7 O-levels, 2 A-levels;
senior award coach
Off-season: 'Looking for a job, which is the same as last year and the five years before
that.'
Overseas teams played for: Birkenhead, Auckland 1985-88; S.A.P., Pretoria 1988-89
Cricketers particularly admired: Graeme Hick, Tim Curtis, Tom Moody, Geoff Boycott
Other sports followed: Supports West Bromwich Albion
Injuries: Damaged cheekbone, chipped bone on index finger
Relaxations: Art history, forensic science and gardening
Extras: Hat-trick v Leicestershire 2nd XI, 1988. Fielded as 12th man for England v India
in 1986 while on Lord's ground staff. Released by Worcestershire at the end of the 1991
season
Opinions on cricket: 'I would like to see a minimum wage level from day one of a contract,
not after two years. I would also like to see the TCCB listen more to players' views before
implementing new rules.'
Best batting: 144 Worcestershire v Kent, Worcester 1989

---

27. Who has played the longest Test innings at Lords?

28. Which player won four England caps, two while with Hampshire,
two during his time with Northamptonshire?

	M	Inns	NO	Runs	HS	Avge	100s	50s	Ct	St	O	M	Runs	Wkts	Avge	Best	5wl	10wM
Test																		
All First	8	13	1	288	100 *	24.00	1	1	3	-	3	1	5	0	-	-	-	-
1-day Int																		
NatWest																		
B&H																		
Refuge																		

Career Performances

	M	Inns	NO	Runs	HS	Avge	100s	50s	Ct	St	Balls	Runs	Wkts	Avge	Best	5wl	10wM
Test																	
All First	32	54	2	1289	144	24.78	2	6	4	-	18	5	0	-	-	-	-
1-day Int																	
NatWest																	
B&H																	
Refuge	3	3	0	51	36	17.00	-	-	3	-							

BERRY, P. J.   Durham

Name: Philip John Berry
Role: Right-hand bat, off-break bowler
Born: 28 December 1966, Saltburn
Height: 6ft **Weight:** 12st
Nickname: Chuck, Goose, Charlie, TCT
County debut: 1986 (Yorkshire)
1st-Class catches: 6
Parents: John and Beryl
Marital status: Single
Family links with cricket: Brother used to play league cricket for Saltburn
Education: Saltscar Comprehensive School; Longlands College of FE
Qualifications: 1 O-level, City & Guilds passes in Recreational and Leisure Services
Career outside cricket: 'Worked with my father on Redcar racecourse.'
Off-season: 'Working on the racecourse, picking out plenty of winners and going to the races elsewhere.'
Overseas tours: NCA to Bermuda for U19 International Youth Tournament 1985
Cricketers particularly admired: Brian Bainbridge, the local league cricketer who

taught me everything when I played at Middlesbrough, John Emburey, David Gower
Other sports followed: Horse racing, rugby union, Middlesbrough FC and for a laugh my brother's Sunday morning football team – plus any other sport on TV
Relaxations: 'Reading autobiographies or Dick Francis racing stories, watching TV, crosswords, eating.'
Opinions on cricket: 'I still don't think that clubs do enough for players during the winter, to help find jobs or positions overseas. It seems that once the last game is over it is "Goodbye, see you all next April".'
Best batting: 31* Yorkshire v Northamptonshire, Headingley 1990
Best bowling: 2-35 Yorkshire v Cambridge University, Fenner's 1988

1991 Season (did not make any first-class or one-day appearances)

Career Performances

	M	Inns	NO	Runs	HS	Avge	100s	50s	Ct	St	Balls	Runs	Wkts	Avge	Best	5wl	10wM
Test																	
All First	7	7	6	76	31*	76.00	-	-	6	-	815	401	7	57.28	2-35	-	-
1-day Int																	
NatWest																	
B&H	1	-	-	-	-	-	-	-	-	-	30	28	0	-		-	-
Refuge																	

BEVINS, S. R. Worcestershire

Name: Stuart Roy Bevins
Role: Right-hand bat, wicket-keeper
Born: 8 March 1967, Solihull
Height: 5ft 6½in **Weight:** 10st 5lbs
Nickname: Tot
County debut: 1989
1st-Class catches: 18
Parents: Roy and Gwen
Marital status: Single
Family links with cricket: 'Grandad and father played club cricket. Brother Martyn has played for Warwickshire U19, English Schools and Worcestershire 2nd XI.'
Education: Solihull School; Solihull College of Technology
Qualifications: 5 O-levels; Diploma in Business Studies
Cricketers particularly admired: Alan

Knott, Rodney Marsh, Richard Hadlee, Ian Botham
Other sports followed: Hockey, football, golf. Warwickshire U21 hockey player
Relaxations: Eating out and playing golf
Opinions on cricket: 'I think the cricketing public are far too eager to criticise county players when they are struggling for form. With so much cricket being crammed into a season, in addition to all the travelling, it is inevitable that players will become weary occasionally.'
Best batting: 10 Worcestershire v New Zealand, Worcester 1990

1991 Season

	M	Inns	NO	Runs	HS	Avge	100s	50s	Ct	St	O	M	Runs	Wkts	Avge	Best	5wl	10wM
Test																		
All First	2	1	0	6	6	6.00	-	-	5	-								
1-day Int																		
NatWest																		
B&H																		
Refuge	2	0	0	0	0	-	-	-	-	-								

Career Performances

	M	Inns	NO	Runs	HS	Avge	100s	50s	Ct	St	Balls	Runs	Wkts	Avge	Best	5wl	10wM
Test																	
All First	6	6	2	34	10	8.50	-	-	18	-							
1-day Int																	
NatWest																	
B&H	2	1	1	0	0*	-	-	-	2	1							
Refuge	4	0	0	0	0	-	-	-	4	1							

BICKNELL, D. J.   Surrey

Name: Darren John Bicknell
Role: Left-hand opening bat, left-arm bowler, gully fielder
Born: 24 June 1967, Guildford
Height: 6ft 4$\frac{1}{2}$in **Weight:** 14st
Nickname: Denzil, Denz
County debut: 1987
County cap: 1990
1000 runs in a season: 3
1st-Class 50s scored: 27
1st-Class 100s scored: 15
1st-Class catches: 39
One-Day 50s: 6
One-Day 100s: 2

Place in batting averages: 30th av. 47.20
(1990 12th av. 69.31)
Parents: Vic and Valerie
Marital status: Engaged to Rebecca
Family links with cricket: Brother Martin
'is fairly well known'; younger brother
Stuart is a keen cricketer and assistant
groundsman at Guildford; father is a
qualified umpire
Education: Robert Haining County
Secondary; Guildford County College of
Technology
Qualifications: 2 O-levels, 5 CSEs,
City and Guilds qualification in
Recreation and Leisure Management
Off-season: Touring with England A
Overseas tours: Surrey to Sharjah 1988
& 1989; England A to Zimbabwe and
Kenya 1989-90; Pakistan 1990-91;
Bermuda and West Indies 1991-92

Cricketers particularly admired: Waqar
Younis, Robin Smith and Graham Gooch
Other sports followed: 'I watch Aldershot FC and also follow the fortunes of West Ham.'
Injuries: 'Sore shins! How a batsman can get them I've no idea!'
Relaxations: 'Eating out, and lazing around the house.'
Extras: Shares county record third wicket stand of 413 with David Ward v Kent at
Canterbury in 1990 – both made career bests
Opinions on cricket: 'Too much cricket. Four-day cricket is a must: the best teams must
surely come out on top. There was also a much better balance between bat and ball this year.
All 2nd team cricket should be played on first-class grounds with first-class pitches and
facilities.'
Best batting: 186 Surrey v Kent, Canterbury 1990
Best bowling: 2-62 Surrey v Northamptonshire, Northampton 1991

1991 Season

	M	Inns	NO	Runs	HS	Avge	100s	50s	Ct	St	O	M	Runs	Wkts	Avge	Best	5wI	10wM
Test																		
All First	24	42	2	1888	151	47.20	5	9	11	-	5.3	0	62	2	31.00	2-62	-	-
1-day Int																		
NatWest	4	4	0	89	28	22.25	-	-	-	-								
B&H	4	4	0	108	53	27.00	-	1	1	-								
Refuge	9	9	0	260	68	28.88	-	2	3	-								

Career Performances

	M	Inns	NO	Runs	HS	Avge	100s	50s	Ct	St	Balls	Runs	Wkts	Avge	Best	5wI	10wM
Test																	
All First	93	162	17	5819	186	40.13	15	28	39	-	199	175	3	58.33	2-62	-	-
1-day Int																	
NatWest	8	8	1	284	135 *	40.57	1	-	-	-							
B&H	12	12	0	372	119	31.00	1	2	3	-							
Refuge	23	22	1	570	75	27.14	-	4	5	-							

BICKNELL, M. P. Surrey

Name: Martin Paul Bicknell
Role: Right-hand bat, right-arm
fast-medium bowler
Born: 14 January 1969, Guildford
Height: 6ft 4in **Weight:** 14st
Nickname: Bickers, Spandau
County debut: 1986
County cap: 1989
50 wickets in a season: 3
1st-Class 50s scored: 2
1st-Class 5 w. in innings: 9
1st-Class catches: 31
Place in batting averages: 207th av. 17.33
(1990 113th av. 38.75)
Place in bowling averages: 38th av. 27.91
(1990 14th av. 27.26)
Strike rate: 62.77 (career 58.41)
Parents: Vic and Valerie
Marital status: Single
Family links with cricket: Brother Darren
'occasional cricketer'; father is qualified umpire and younger brother Stuart also plays
Education: Robert Haining County Secondary
Qualifications: 2 O-levels, 5 CSEs
Off-season: Touring with England A
Overseas tours: England YC to Sri Lanka 1986-87 and Australia 1987-88; England A to
Zimbabwe and Kenya 1989-90; England to Australia 1990-91; England A to Bermuda and
West Indies
Cricketers particularly admired: Richard Hadlee, Dennis Lillee, Ian Botham
Other sports followed: 'Leeds United, and generally most sports.'
Injuries: Recurring hamstring problem, neck spasm
Relaxations: Golf, snooker, videos. and 'listening to Tony Murphy's theories on cricket.'

Extras: Youngest player to play for Surrey since David Smith. His figures of 9 for 45 were the best for the county for thirty years. One of four players on standby as reserves for England's World Cup squad 1992

Opinions on cricket: 'Four-day cricket is wanted by all players and makes for better cricket. Hopefully then we will need fewer declarations and the better team will generally win. At the moment we often get to the last day and it becomes a one-day game to get a result.'

Best batting: 63 Surrey v Lancashire, Old Trafford 1991

Best bowling: 9-45 Surrey v Cambridge University, Fenner's 1988

1991 Season

	M	Inns	NO	Runs	HS	Avge	100s	50s	Ct	St	O	M	Runs	Wkts	Avge	Best	5wI	10wM
Test																		
All First	15	22	4	312	63	17.33	-	1	3	-	470.5	118	1256	45	27.91	7-52	1	-
1-day Int																		
NatWest	4	2	1	70	66 *	70.00	-	1	-	-	39.3	2	135	5	27.00	2-45	-	
B&H	4	3	0	17	7	5.66	-	-	-	-	41	2	158	5	31.60	3-28	-	
Refuge	7	4	2	50	20 *	25.00	-	-	2	-	51	1	239	7	34.14	3-36	-	

Career Performances

	M	Inns	NO	Runs	HS	Avge	100s	50s	Ct	St	Balls	Runs	Wkts	Avge	Best	5wI	10wM
Test																	
All First	100	107	32	1116	63	14.88	-	2	31	-	18227	8475	312	27.16	9-45	9	-
1-day Int	7	6	2	96	31 *	24.00	-	-	2	-	413	347	13	26.69	3-55	-	
NatWest	18	9	5	81	66 *	20.25	-	1	8	-	1131	619	22	28.13	4-49	-	
B&H	17	11	2	81	27 *	9.00	-	-	7	-	1019	668	28	23.85	3-28	-	
Refuge	62	21	11	123	20 *	12.30	-	-	19	-	2546	1745	60	29.08	4-14	-	

29. Who topped the first-class bowling averages for Essex last season?

30. Who were the last-placed county in the Britannic Assurance Championship last season?

31. Who finished last in the Refuge League last season?

BISHOP, I. R.   Derbyshire

Name: Ian Raphael Bishop
Role: Right-hand bat, right-arm fast bowler
Born: 24 October 1967, Port of Spain, Trinidad, West Indies
Height: 6ft 5¹/₂in **Weight:** 15st 10lbs
Nickname: Bish
County debut: 1989
County cap: 1990
Test debut: 1988-89
Tests: 8
One-Day Internationals: 26
50 wickets in a season: 1
1st-Class 100s scored: 1
1st-Class 5 w. in innings: 14
1st-Class 10 w. in match: 1
1st-Class catches: 13
Place in batting averages: (1990 181st av. 27.75)
Place in bowling averages: (1990 1st av. 19.05)

Strike rate: (career 44.29)
Parents: Randolph and Recalda
Marital status: Single
Family links with cricket: Uncle played for Young West Indies against England U20 in the Caribbean 1984-85
Education: Belmont Primary and Belmont Secondary Schools
Qualifications: 2 O-levels
Overseas tours: West Indies to England 1988; Australia 1988-89; India for Nehru Cup 1989-90; Pakistan 1990-91; Pakistan and Australia 1991-92
Overseas teams played for: Trinidad & Tobago
Cricketers particularly admired: Malcolm Marshall, Michael Holding, Gordon Greenidge
Other sports followed: Athletics, soccer, basketball
Relaxations: Watching television, reading sports magazines and theological books
Extras: Played for Northumberland club Tynedale in 1987. Top of 1990 bowling averages. 'I am a born-again Christian.'
Opinions on cricket: 'I think wickets at county level should be well-prepared to encourage bowlers and batters to learn their trade thoroughly. The present fining for slow over-rates is ridiculous.'
Best batting: 103* Derbyshire v Yorkshire, Scarborough 1990
Best bowling: 6-39 West Indians v Kent, Canterbury 1988

1991 Season

	M	Inns	NO	Runs	HS	Avge	100s	50s	Ct	St	O	M	Runs	Wkts	Avge	Best	5wI	10wM
Test																		
All First	1	0	0	0	0	-	-	-	-	-	17	3	58	2	29.00	2-58	-	-
1-day Int																		
NatWest																			
B&H																			
Refuge																			

Career Performances

	M	Inns	NO	Runs	HS	Avge	100s	50s	Ct	St	Balls	Runs	Wkts	Avge	Best	5wI	10wM
Test	8	12	6	124	30 *	20.66	-	-	1	-	1795	790	37	21.35	6-87	2	-
All First	68	94	30	954	103 *	14.90	1	-	13	-	11574	5542	261	21.17	6-39	14	1
1-day Int	26	11	7	73	33 *	18.25	-	-	7	-	1339	858	46	18.65	5-27	1	
NatWest																	
B&H																	
Refuge	1	1	1	16	16 *	-	-	-	-	-		48	51	1	51.00	1-51	-

BLAKEY, R. J.   Yorkshire

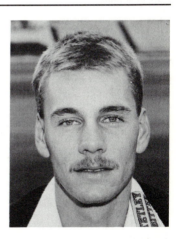

Name: Richard John Blakey
Role: Right-hand bat, wicket-keeper
Born: 15 January 1967, Huddersfield
Height: 5ft 10in **Weight:** 11st 3lbs
Nickname: Dick, Pugh
County debut: 1985
County cap: 1987
1000 runs in a season: 3
1st-Class 50s scored: 32
1st-Class 100s scored: 7
1st-Class 200s scored: 2
1st-Class catches: 205
1st-Class stumpings: 18
One-Day 50s: 18
One-Day 100s: 2
Place in batting averages: 151st av. 26.13
(1990 164th av. 30.38)
Parents: Brian and Pauline
Wife and date of marriage: Michelle,
28 September 1991
Family links with cricket: Father played local cricket
Education: Woodhouse Primary; Rastrick Grammar School

Qualifications: 4 O-levels, NCA coaching certificate
Overseas tours: Young England to West Indies 1985; England A to Zimbabwe and Kenya 1989-90; Pakistan 1990-91
Overseas teams played for: Waverley, Sydney 1986-89; Mt Waverley, Sydney 1988-89
Cricketers particularly admired: Keith Fletcher, Alan Knott, Peter Hartley, Phil Carrick, Martyn Moxon
Other sports followed: Football (Leeds United FC) and golf
Relaxations: Squash, aerobics, eating out
Extras: Established himself in Huddersfield League. Made record 2nd XI score – 273* v Northamptonshire 1986. Yorkshire's Young Player of the Year 1989
Opinions on cricket: 'Too much cricket is played which lowers the standard. I am in favour of coloured gear for Sundays to attract a younger audience.'
Best batting: 221 England A v Zimbabwe, Bulawayo 1989-90
Best bowling: 1-68 Yorkshire v Nottinghamshire, Sheffield 1986

1991 Season

	M	Inns	NO	Runs	HS	Avge	100s	50s	Ct	St	O	M	Runs	Wkts	Avge	Best	5wI	10wM
Test																		
All First	24	38	2	941	196	26.13	1	6	40	5								
1-day Int																		
NatWest	1	1	0	0	0	0.00	-	-	-	-								
B&H	6	6	1	113	39	22.60	-	-	11	-								
Refuge	15	15	2	490	130 *	37.69	1	2	18	1								

Career Performances

	M	Inns	NO	Runs	HS	Avge	100s	50s	Ct	St	Balls	Runs	Wkts	Avge	Best	5wI	10wM
Test																	
All First	135	220	26	6110	221	31.49	7	32	205	18	63	68	1	68.00	1-68	-	-
1-day Int																	
NatWest	10	7	1	78	22	13.00	-	-	13	1							
B&H	24	21	3	570	79	31.66	-	5	16	-							
Refuge	53	52	10	1849	130 *	44.02	2	13	39	3							

BLENKIRON, D. A.   Durham

Name: Darren Andrew Blenkiron
Role: Left-hand bat
Born: 4 February 1974, Solihull
Height: 5ft 10in **Weight:** 11st
Nickname: Pitbull
One-Day 50s: 1
Parents: Bill and Margaret

Marital status: Single
Family links with cricket: Father played for Warwickshire and MCC
Education: Bishop Barrington Comprehensive, Bishop Auckland
Off-season: Indoor nets and touring with England U19
Overseas tours: England U18 to Canada; England U19 to Pakistan
Cricketers particularly admired:
'Ian Botham, David Gower, Graeme Hick, Geoff Cook and my father.'
Other sports followed: Football, boxing and athletics
Relaxations: Music, watching videos and socialising
Extras: Was one of the first players to sign for Durham. Played for England U19 in the home series against Australia 1991

Opinions on cricket: 'Fines should be introduced for slow over rates and players should be given one or two days rest per week. The umpires should be more strict and be strong enough in character to warn bowlers about intimidating the batsman. They should have the power to either take the bowler off or send him off the field during play.'

1991 Season

	M	Inns	NO	Runs	HS	Avge	100s	50s	Ct	St	O	M	Runs	Wkts	Avge	Best	5wI	10wM
Test																		
All First																		
1-day Int																		
NatWest	1	1	0	56	56	56.00	-	1	-	-								
B&H																		
Refuge																		

Career Performances

	M	Inns	NO	Runs	HS	Avge	100s	50s	Ct	St	Balls	Runs	Wkts	Avge	Best	5wI	10wM
Test																	
All First																	
1-day Int																	
NatWest	1	1	0	56	56	56.00	-	1	-	-							
B&H																	
Refuge																	

BOILING, J. Surrey

Name: James Boiling
Role: Right-hand bat, right-arm off-spin
bowler, gully fielder
Born: 8 April 1968, New Delhi
Height: 6ft 2in **Weight:** 13st 2lbs
Nickname: Roger (Rabbit),
Capt Mainwaring
County debut: 1988
1st-Class catches: 8
Place in bowling averages: 119th av. 42.08
Strike rate: 90.75 (career 92.88)
Parents: Graham and Geraldine
Marital status: Single
Family links with cricket: 'Father gives me
a lift to matches, mother washes my whites.'
Education: Rutlish School, Merton;
Durham University
Qualifications: 10 O-levels, 3 A-levels,
BA (Hons) in History, NCA Senior
Coaching Award

Career outside cricket: Journalist, stand-up comedian
Off-season: 'Playing and coaching for Bionics CC, Harare. Putting the finishing touches
to my thesis *Cricket's Place in Society*.'
Overseas tours: England YCs to Youth World Cup in Australia, 1988
Cricketers particularly admired: 'Matthew Fleming for his refreshing approach to the
game, Rehan Alikhan for his dedication and bravery.'
Other sports followed: Rowing, hang-gliding
Relaxations: Catching up with old friends, watching old episodes of 'Monty Python' and
'Vic Reeves' Big Night Out', listening to Van Morrison and sharing a bottle of Chateauneuf
du Pape with Graham Thorpe
Extras: Won Gold Award for 8-3-9-3 analysis against Surrey for Combined Universities
in 1990. Believed to be the first player to win a Gold Award against his own county.
Opinions on cricket: 'I am sure that the majority of professional cricketers would benefit
from more regular and logical programme of fixtures. During the summer it is not
uncommon to have 15 days solid cricket followed by perhaps six or seven days without a
match. Perhaps if a typical week's cricket consisted of a four-day fixture, a 1-day game and
2 days free either for practice or for benefit matches, then it would be easier to cope with
the stresses and strains of what is an arduous season. I would also be an advocate of a mid-
season break of perhaps a week or ten days, not only to re-charge the batteries, but also to
ensure some time can be spent catching up on our lives outside cricket. I am certain that
players and spectators alike would return with renewed interest after a short summer
break.'

Best batting: 16 Surrey v Middlesex, The Oval 1991
Best bowling: 4-157 Surrey v Lancashire, Old Trafford 1991

1991 Season

	M	Inns	NO	Runs	HS	Avge	100s	50s	Ct	St	O	M	Runs	Wkts	Avge	Best	5wI	10wM
Test																		
All First	5	7	1	22	16	3.66	-	-	7	-	181.3	44	505	12	42.08	4-157	-	-
1-day Int																		
NatWest	4	2	0	29	22	14.50	-	-	3	-	48	4	165	3	55.00	2-22	-	
B&H	2	2	1	10	7	10.00	-	-	-	-	20	0	81	2	40.50	1-38	-	
Refuge	9	4	2	20	12 *	10.00	-	-	-	-	60	0	312	8	39.00	2-24	-	

Career Performances

	M	Inns	NO	Runs	HS	Avge	100s	50s	Ct	St	Balls	Runs	Wkts	Avge	Best	5wI	10wM
Test																	
All First	9	13	4	60	16	6.66	-	-	8	-	1579	707	17	41.58	4-157	-	-
1-day Int																	
NatWest	4	2	0	29	22	14.50	-	-	3	-	288	165	3	55.00	2-22	-	
B&H	15	10	7	32	9 *	10.66	-	-	7	-	850	592	13	45.53	3-9	-	
Refuge	9	4	2	20	12 *	10.00	-	-	-	-	360	312	8	39.00	2-24	-	

BOON, T. J.   Leicestershire

Name: Timothy James Boon
Role: Right-hand bat, right-arm medium bowler
Born: 1 November 1961, Doncaster, South Yorkshire
Height: 5ft 11 1/2in **Weight:** 12st 3lbs
Nickname: Ted Moon, Cod
County debut: 1980
County cap: 1986
1000 runs in a season: 6
1st-Class 50s scored: 49
1st-Class 100s scored: 10
1st-Class catches: 91
One-Day 50s: 12
One-Day 100s: 1
Place in batting averages: 106th av. 31.18 (1990 123rd av. 37.53)
Parents: Jeffrey and Elizabeth
Marital status: Single

Family links with cricket: Father played club cricket
Education: Mill Lane Primary; Edlington Comprehensive. Three months at Doncaster Art School
Qualifications: 1 A-level, 6 O-levels. Coaching qualifications
Overseas tours: England YC to West Indies 1980
Cricketers particularly admired: 'Those who make the most of their ability.'
Other sports followed: 'Enjoy playing and watching all sports.'
Relaxations: Sleeping, barbecue in garden, dining out
Extras: Captain England YC v West Indies 1980 and v India 1981; missed 1985 season due to broken leg sustained in a car crash in South Africa the previous winter
Best batting: 144 Leicestershire v Gloucestershire, Leicester 1984
Best bowling: 3-40 Leicestershire v Yorkshire, Leicester 1986

1991 Season

	M	Inns	NO	Runs	HS	Avge	100s	50s	Ct	St	O	M	Runs	Wkts	Avge	Best	5wI	10wM
Test																		
All First	22	40	2	1185	108	31.18	2	6	11	-	10	3	21	1	21.00	1-11	-	-
1-day Int																		
NatWest	2	2	1	90	76 *	90.00	-	1	1	-								
B&H	3	2	0	119	103	59.50	1	-	1	-								
Refuge	6	6	0	173	68	28.83	-	2	-	-								

Career Performances

	M	Inns	NO	Runs	HS	Avge	100s	50s	Ct	St	Balls	Runs	Wkts	Avge	Best	5wI	10wM
Test																	
All First	184	309	36	8669	144	31.75	10	49	91	-	445	350	7	50.00	3-40	-	-
1-day Int																	
NatWest	12	10	4	205	76 *	34.16	-	1	4	-	6	2	0	-		-	-
B&H	24	21	5	588	103	36.75	1	3	4	-							
Refuge	92	80	10	1643	97	23.47	-	8	19	-	12	14	0	-		-	-

BOOTH, P. A.   Warwickshire

Name: Paul Anthony Booth
Role: Left-hand bat, left-arm spin bowler
Born: 5 September 1965, Huddersfield
Height: 6ft **Weight:** 11st 7lbs
Nickname: Boot, Lynford
County debut: 1982 (Yorks), 1990 (Warwicks)
1st-Class 50s scored: 3
1st-Class 5 w. in innings: 1
1st-Class catches: 15

Place in batting averages: 237th av. 13.46
(1990 238th av.17.14)
Place in bowling averages: 107th av. 38.33
(1990 127th av. 48.92)
Strike rate: 75.38 (career 102.71)
Parents: Colin and Margaret
Wife and date of marriage: Beverley,
13 October 1990
Family links with cricket: Father played
local cricket for over 30 years
Education: Meltham C of E; Honley High
School
Qualifications: 2 O-levels (maths and
woodwork); coaching certificate
Career outside cricket: Postman, labourer
Off-season: Training and running, trying to
build up speed
Overseas tours: England U19 to the
West Indies 1984-85
Cricketers particularly admired: Ray Illingworth, Derek Underwood
Other sports followed: Football (Leeds United)
Relaxations: Playing football and golf
Extras: Yorkshire debut aged 17 years 3 days. Released by Yorkshire at end of 1989 season
Opinions on cricket: 'Championship should be 17 four-day matches.'
Best batting: 62 Warwickshire v Somerset, Taunton 1991
Best bowling: 5-98 Yorkshire v Lancashire, Old Trafford 1988

1991 Season

	M	Inns	NO	Runs	HS	Avge	100s	50s	Ct	St	O	M	Runs	Wkts	Avge	Best	5wI	10wM
Test																		
All First	10	13	0	175	62	13.46	-	1	5	-	226.1	47	690	18	38.33	4-103	-	-
1-day Int																		
NatWest	1	0	0	0	0	-	-	-	-	-								
B&H	3	2	1	15	11	15.00	-	-	3	-	13	0	81	1	81.00	1-35	-	
Refuge																		

Career Performances

	M	Inns	NO	Runs	HS	Avge	100s	50s	Ct	St	Balls	Runs	Wkts	Avge	Best	5wI	10wM
Test																	
All First	43	58	11	608	62	12.93	-	3	15	-	6779	2843	66	43.07	5-98	1	-
1-day Int																	
NatWest	2	1	1	6	6 *	-	-	-	-	-	66	33	0	-	-	-	
B&H	7	5	2	34	13 *	11.33	-	-	4	-	240	200	5	40.00	2-28	-	
Refuge	4	0	0	0	0	-	-	-	1	-	144	146	3	48.66	1-33	-	

BOTHAM, I. T.   Durham

Name: Ian Terence Botham
Role: Right-hand bat, right-arm
fast-medium bowler, slip fielder
Born: 24 November 1955, Heswall,
Cheshire
Height: 6ft 2in **Weight:** 15st 5lbs
Nickname: Guy, Both, Beefy
County debut: 1974 (Som), 1987 (Worcs)
County cap: 1976 (Som), 1987 (Worcs)
Benefit: 1984 (£90,822)
Test debut: 1977
Tests: 99
One-Day Internationals: 99
1000 runs in a season: 4
50 wickets in a season: 7
1st-Class 50s scored: 90
1st-Class 100s scored: 36
1st-Class 200s scored: 2
1st-Class 5 w. in innings: 59
1st-Class 10 w. in match: 8
1st-Class catches: 336
One-Day 50s: 35
One-Day 100s: 7
Place in batting averages: 45th av. 43.61 (1990 131st av. 35.00)
Place in bowling averages: 19th av. 24.47 (1990 28th av. 29.23)
Strike rate: 47.88 (career 53.30)
Parents: Les and Marie
Wife and date of marriage: Kathryn, 31 January 1976
Children: Liam James, 26 August 1977; Sarah Lianne, 3 February 1979; Rebecca Kate, 13 November 1985
Family links with cricket: Father played for Navy and Fleet Air Arm; mother played for VAD nursing staff; son Liam already a very promising all-rounder
Education: Millford Junior School; Buckler's Mead Secondary School, Yeovil
Overseas tours: England to Pakistan and New Zealand 1977-78; Australia 1978-79; Australia and India 1979-80; West Indies 1980-81; India 1981-82; Australia and New Zealand 1982-83; West Indies 1985-86; Australia 1986-87; New Zealand 1991-92
Cricketers particularly admired: Viv Richards, David Gower, Allan Border, Andy Roberts ('the fastest bowler I ever faced')
Off-season: Appearing in pantomine. Captain of celebrity team in the BBC quiz show 'A Question of Sport.' Touring with England.
Other sports followed: Rugby, football, American sports, 'virtually anything'
Relaxations: Golf, shooting, fishing (salmon and trout), flying

Extras: England captain for twelve Tests between 1980 and 1981. Played for Somerset 2nd XI 1971. On MCC staff 1972-73. Took five Australian wickets on his first day in Test cricket aged 21. One of *Wisden's* Five Cricketers of the Year, 1977. Best man at Viv Richards's wedding in Antigua in March 1981. Subject of 'This is Your Life' television programme in November 1981 and voted BBC TV Sports Review Sporting Personality of 1981 following his exploits against Australia. Scored 200 in 272 minutes for England v India at The Oval in 1982, third fastest Test double century by an Englishman, after Walter Hammond and Denis Compton. His published books include *High, Wide and Handsome,* an account of his record-breaking 1985 season; *It Sort of Clicks*, in collaboration with Peter Roebuck, and *Cricket My Way* with Jack Bannister. First cricketer since W.G. Grace to have painting commissioned by National Portrait Gallery. Captain of Somerset 1984-85. Holds record for having scored 1000 runs and taken 100 wickets in fewest Test matches. First player to score a century and take eight wickets in an innings in a Test match, v Pakistan at Lord's in 1978. Most sixes in a first-class season in 1985. Left Somerset at the beginning of 1987 to join Worcestershire after Somerset had decided not to renew the contracts of Richards and Garner. Missed nearly all 1988 season with back injury. Appeared on 'Desert Island Discs' in November 1989, when his choice of music ranged from The Beatles to Beethoven. The one book he wanted was an encyclopedia of fish, and his luxury was a fishing rod. Raised over £1,000,000 for Leukaemia Research with a series of fund-raising walks. Left Worcestershire at the end of 1991 season to join Durham
Opinions on cricket: 'The Comprehensive (school) system is a disgrace. How can we bring our youngsters on when there are 3000 kids in one school, and no facilities for cricket. When I was a lad we would stay on after school, being taught how to play by an experienced cricket master. Now the kids are just not being given the chance.'
Best batting: 228 Somerset v Gloucestershire, Taunton 1980
Best bowling: 8-34 England v Pakistan, Lord's 1978

1991 Season

	M	Inns	NO	Runs	HS	Avge	100s	50s	Ct	St	O	M	Runs	Wkts	Avge	Best	5wI	10wM
Test	2	3	1	57	31	28.50	-	-	5	-	43	13	108	4	27.00	2-40	-	-
All First	13	21	3	785	161	43.61	2	4	12	-	351.1	73	1077	44	24.47	7-54	3	-
1-day Int	1	1	0	8	8	8.00	-	-	-	-	11	2	45	4	11.25	4-45	-	
NatWest	1	1	0	27	27	27.00	-	-	1	-	10	0	39	0	-	-	-	
B&H	6	5	3	88	35 *	44.00	-	-	1	-	63	14	174	8	21.75	3-11	-	
Refuge	12	10	3	249	58	35.57	-	1	3	-	80.3	2	493	12	41.08	3-21	-	

Career Performances

	M	Inns	NO	Runs	HS	Avge	100s	50s	Ct	St	Balls	Runs	Wkts	Avge	Best	5wI	10wM
Test	99	157	6	5176	208	34.27	14	22	117	-	21539	10741	380	28.26	8-34	27	4
All First	373	573	43	18254	228	34.44	36	90	336	-	60128	30126	1128	26.70	8-34	59	8
1-day Int	99	90	12	1738	72	22.28	-	7	30	-	5335	3556	122	29.14	4-45	-	
NatWest	42	34	8	1092	101	42.00	1	7	20	-	2578	1538	59	26.06	5-51	1	-
B&H	82	68	11	1522	138 *	26.70	2	2	50	-	4648	2648	127	20.85	5-41	1	
Refuge	186	170	26	4582	175 *	31.81	4	19	75	-	7253	5560	234	23.76	5-27	1	

BOWLER, P. D. Derbyshire

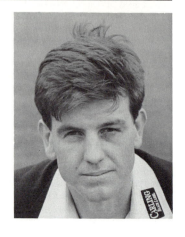

Name: Peter Duncan Bowler
Role: Right-hand opening bat,
off-spinner, occasional wicket-keeper
Born: 30 July 1963, Plymouth
Height: 6ft 1in **Weight:** 13st 7lbs
Nickname: Croc
County debut: 1986 (Leics), 1988
(Derbys)
County cap: 1989
1000 runs in a season: 4
1st-Class 50s scored: 38
1st-Class 100s scored: 12
1st-Class 200s scored: 1
1st-Class catches: 69
1st-Class stumpings: 1
One-Day 50s: 18
One-Day 100s: 2
Place in batting averages: 80th av. 35.56
(1990 96th av. 42.00)
Parents: Peter and Etta
Marital status: Single
Education: Daramalan College, Canberra, Australia
Qualifications: Australian Year 12 certificate
Career outside cricket: Has worked for BBC Radio as a sports journalist on occasions
Off-season: Playing in Australia
Cricketers particularly admired: Greg Chappell, Rick McCosker
Other sports followed: Rugby union and most ball sports
Relaxations: Sport in general – family and friends
Extras: First Leicestershire player to score a first-class hundred on debut (100 not out v
Hampshire 1986). Moved to Derbyshire at end of 1987 season and scored a hundred on his
debut v Cambridge University in 1988
Opinions on cricket: 'Leave individual counties and players to get the balance between
bat and ball right. 17 four-day games, playing each county once, is long overdue. Four-day
cricket sorts the good sides from the bad, it's proper cricket. My bowling average has been
badly affected due to contrived situations, rising from 80 per wicket to nearly 100!'
Best batting: 210 Derbyshire v Kent, Chesterfield 1990
Best bowling: 3-41 Derbyshire v Leicestershire, Leicester 1991

---

32. Which player scored a century in his only first-class
game in 1991?

1991 Season

	M	Inns	NO	Runs	HS	Avge	100s	50s	Ct	St	O	M	Runs	Wkts	Avge	Best	5wI	10wM
Test																		
All First	24	44	3	1458	104 *	35.56	2	11	15	-	114	20	464	9	51.55	3-41	-	-
1-day Int																		
NatWest																		
B&H	4	4	0	141	100	35.25	1	-	6	-								
Refuge	13	13	1	396	77	33.00	-	2	8	-	5.2	0	31	3	10.33	3-31	-	

Career Performances

	M	Inns	NO	Runs	HS	Avge	100s	50s	Ct	St	Balls	Runs	Wkts	Avge	Best	5wI	10wM
Test																	
All First	104	185	15	6212	210	36.54	12	38	69	1	2145	1357	20	67.85	3-41	-	-
1-day Int																	
NatWest	7	7	0	98	46	14.00	-	-	3	-	18	14	0	-	-	-	-
B&H	19	18	0	637	109	35.38	2	4	13	1	246	125	4	31.25	1-15	-	
Refuge	72	69	5	1866	77	29.15	-	14	37	1	224	216	7	30.85	3-31	-	

BRIERS, M. P.   Durham

Name: Mark Paul Briers
Role: Right-hand bat, leg-spin bowler
Born: 21 April 1968, Kegworth
Height: 5ft 11in **Weight:** 11st 5lbs
Nickname: The Duke, Wong
Parents: Graham and Mary
Marital Status: Single - 'but looking!'
Education: Shepshed Hindleys
Qualifications: Plumbing and Heating Certificates
Off-season: Coaching abroad
Overseas teams played for: South African Police, Pretoria; Manaia, New Zealand and Taranaki Province
Cricketers particularly admired: Ian Botham, Richard Stemp
Other sports followed: 'Golf, soccer, rugby – most sports.'
Injuries: 'Brain failure on the field!'
Extras: Played in friendly one-day matches in 1991 against Surrey, Sri Lanka and Victoria

No appearance in first-class cricket or in any one-day competition

BRIERS, N. E.   Leicestershire

Name: Nigel Edwin Briers
Role: Right-hand opening bat, right-arm
medium bowler, county captain
Born: 15 January 1955, Leicester
Height: 6ft **Weight:** 12st 8lbs
Nickname: Kudu
County debut: 1971
County cap: 1981
Benefit: 1990
1000 runs in a season: 8
1st-Class 50s scored: 75
1st-Class 100s scored: 23
1st-Class 200s scored: 1
1st-Class catches: 132
One-Day 50s: 32
One-Day 100s: 3
Place in batting averages: 60th av. 39.07
(1990 50th av. 49.90)
Parents: Leonard Arthur Roger and
Eveline

Wife and date of marriage: Suzanne Mary Tudor, 3 September 1977
Children: Michael Edward Tudor, 25 March 1983; Andrew James Tudor, 30 June 1986
Family links with cricket: Father was captain and wicket-keeper of Narborough and
Littlethorpe CC in the South Leicestershire League for fifteen years and mother was scorer.
Father was also captain of South Leicestershire Representative XI and played for the Royal
Marines in the same team as Trevor Bailey. Cousin, Norman Briers, played once for
Leicestershire in 1967
Education: Lutterworth Grammar School; Borough Road College
Qualifications: Qualified teacher (Cert Ed), BEd (Hons), MCC Advanced Cricket Coach
Career outside cricket: Teaching at Ludgrove School
Off-season: Teaching PE and History at Ludgrove School and captaining the MCC tour
to the Leeward Islands
Overseas tours: Derrick Robins tour to South America 1979; MCC to the Far East 1981;
Leicestershire to Zimbabwe, Holland, Jersey and Guernsey; MCC to the Virgin and
Leeward Islands 1991-92
Cricketers particularly admired: Ray Illingworth, Richard Hadlee, Geoff Boycott,
Barry Richards
Other sports followed: Rugby (Leicester Tigers) and football (Leicester City)
Extras: Youngest player ever to appear for Leicestershire (aged 16 years 104 days). Shares
record with Roger Tolchard for highest fifth wicket stand of 233 v Somerset, 1979.
Appointed county captain in 1990. Captained MCC on 1991-92 tour of the Virgin and
Leeward Islands

Best batting: 201* Leicestershire v Warwickshire, Edgbaston 1983
Best bowling: 4-29 Leicestershire v Derbyshire, Leicester 1985

1991 Season

	M	Inns	NO	Runs	HS	Avge	100s	50s	Ct	St	O	M	Runs	Wkts	Avge	Best	5wI	10wM
Test																		
All First	24	43	5	1485	160	39.07	4	7	19	-								
1-day Int																		
NatWest	2	2	0	38	29	19.00	-	-	-	-								
B&H	4	4	0	103	46	25.75	-	-	4	-								
Refuge	15	15	0	352	48	23.46	-	-	5	-								

Career Performances

	M	Inns	NO	Runs	HS	Avge	100s	50s	Ct	St	Balls	Runs	Wkts	Avge	Best	5wI	10wM
Test																	
All First	311	505	49	14605	201 *	32.02	23	75	132	-	2047	988	32	30.87	4-29	-	-
1-day Int																	
NatWest	28	28	2	479	59	18.42	-	1	6	-	84	75	6	12.50	2-6	-	
B&H	49	44	3	794	93 *	19.36	-	3	15	-	330	266	3	88.66	1-26	-	
Refuge	185	182	23	4989	119 *	31.37	3	28	44	-	482	384	10	38.40	3-29	-	

BROAD, B. C.   Nottinghamshire

Name: Brian Christopher Broad
Role: Left-hand bat, right-arm medium bowler
Born: 29 September 1957, Bristol
Height: 6ft 4in **Weight:** 14st 7lbs
Nickname: Walter, Broadie
County debut: 1979 (Gloucs), 1984 (Notts)
County cap: 1981 (Gloucs), 1984 (Notts)
Test debut: 1984
Tests: 25
One-Day Internationals: 34
1000 runs in a season: 9
1st-Class 50s scored: 95
1st-Class 100s scored: 42
1st-class 200s scored: 1
1st-Class catches: 167
One-Day 50s: 59

One-Day 100s: 10
Place in batting averages: 24th av. 49.68 (1990 37th av. 54.29
Parents: Nancy and Kenneth
Wife and date of marriage: Carole Ann, 14 July 1979
Children: Gemma Joanne, 14 January 1984; Stuart Christopher John, 24 June 1986
Family links with cricket: Father and grandfather both played local cricket. Father member of Gloucestershire Committee until retired
Education: Colston's School, Bristol; St Paul's College, Cheltenham
Qualifications: 5 O-levels, NCA advanced coach
Career outside cricket: Runs his own furniture import business
Off-season: Running business and watching rugby
Overseas tours: English Counties to Zimbabwe 1985; England to Australia 1986-87; Pakistan, Australia and New Zealand 1987-88; Unofficial English team to South Africa 1989-90
Overseas teams played for: Orange Free State 1985-86 (captain)
Cricketers particularly admired: Graham Gooch, Richard Hadlee, Clive Rice
Other sports followed: Rugby
Relaxations: 'Playing any sport, spending time with my family.'
Extras: Struck down by osteomyelitis at age 15. First played adult cricket for Downend CC, where W. G. Grace learnt to play; played with Allan Border in Gloucestershire 2nd XI. Published autobiography *Home Thoughts from Abroad* in 1987 after he had hit three centuries in a row in Test series v Australia, 1986-87. Banned from Test cricket for five years for joining tour to South Africa. Passed 2000 runs in a season for the first time and made his first double hundred in 1990
Opinions on cricket: 'I would have loved playing as an amateur. I am an unashamed traditionalist.'
Best batting: 227* Nottinghamshire v Kent, Tunbridge Wells 1990
Best bowling: 2-14 Gloucestershire v West Indians, Bristol 1980

1991 Season

	M	Inns	NO	Runs	HS	Avge	100s	50s	Ct	St	O	M	Runs	Wkts	Avge	Best	5wI	10wM
Test																		
All First	21	38	3	1739	166	49.68	5	7	9	-								
1-day Int																		
NatWest	3	3	0	83	38	27.66	-	-	-	-								
B&H	4	4	1	140	108 *	46.66	1	-	-	-								
Refuge	16	16	3	647	108	49.76	2	4	6	-								

33. Which county won the 2nd XI Championship last season?

Career Performances

	M	Inns	NO	Runs	HS	Avge	100s	50s	Ct	St	Balls	Runs	Wkts	Avge	Best	5wI	10wM
Test	25	44	2	1661	162	39.54	6	6	10	-	6	4	0	-	-	-	-
All First	297	530	35	19107	227 *	38.60	42	95	167	-	1625	1036	16	64.75	2-14	-	-
1-day Int	34	34	0	1361	106	40.02	1	11	10	-	6	6	0	-	-	-	
NatWest	30	30	0	1098	115	36.60	1	10	8	-							
B&H	57	56	3	1682	122	31.73	3	8	14	-	348	308	6	51.33	2-73	-	
Refuge	155	153	10	4951	108	34.62	5	30	41	-	669	602	19	31.68	3-46	-	

BROADHURST, M. Yorkshire

Name: Mark Broadhurst
Role: Right-hand (lower order) bat, right-arm fast-medium bowler
Born: 20 June 1974, Barnsley
Height: 6ft **Weight:** 11st 5lbs
Nickname: Broady, Stanley, Ditherer, Gibby
County debut: 1991
1st-Class catches: 0
Parents: Robert and Pamela
Marital status: Single
Family links with cricket: Father played local league cricket for Ward Green
Education: Worsborough Common Junior School; Kingstone Comprehensive
Qualifications: 8 GCSEs, City and Guilds qualification in Leisure and Recreation
Off-season: Participating in the Poundstretcher Challenge Fitness Programme
Overseas tours: England U19 to New Zealand 1990-91; NCA YC to Canada 1991
Cricketers particularly admired: Dennis Lillee, Richard Hadlee, Michael Holding, Malcolm Marshall, Arnie Sidebottom, Steve Oldham
Other sports followed: Football, golf, athletics
Injuries: Groin injury, weakened left back muscle towards the end of the season.
Relaxations: 'I enjoy watching cricket videos, listening to music and reading.'
Extras: Selected for England U19 squad aged 16. Made first class debut for Yorkshire at age 16 becoming the third youngest in Yorkshire history. Contributor to Wombwell Cricket Society's 12th Man magazine. Played for England U19 v Australia 1991. Selected for England U19 tour to Pakistan 1991-92 but forced to drop out through back injury
Opinions on cricket: 'Not enough cricket played in Comprehensive schools. I think the Bull Development of Excellence scheme offers great opportunities for young players,

giving such as myself a chance to compete in international matches at home and abroad.'
Best batting: 1 Yorkshire v Sri Lanka, Headingley 1991
Best bowling: 3-61 Yorkshire v Oxford University, The Parks 1991

1991 Season

	M	Inns	NO	Runs	HS	Avge	100s	50s	Ct	St	O	M	Runs	Wkts	Avge	Best	5wI	10wM
Test																		
All First	2	1	0	1	1	1.00	-	-	-	-	38	7	130	6	21.66	3-61	-	-
1-day Int																		
NatWest																		
B&H																		
Refuge	1	0	0	0	0	-	-	-	-	-	8	0	27	0	-		-	-

Career Performances

	M	Inns	NO	Runs	HS	Avge	100s	50s	Ct	St	Balls		Runs	Wkts	Avge	Best	5wI	10wM
Test																		
All First	2	1	0	1	1	1.00	-	-	-	-	228		130	6	21.66	3-61	-	-
1-day Int																		
NatWest																		
B&H																		
Refuge	1	0	0	0	0	-	-	-	-	-	48		27	0	-		-	-

BROADLEY, V. J. P. Nottinghamshire

Name: Vaughan John Pascal Broadley
Role: Right-hand bat, right-arm fast-medium bowler
Born: 4 April 1972, Sutton-in-Ashfield
Height: 6ft 2in **Weight:** 11st
Nickname: Fruity, Bully
County debut: 1991
1st-Class catches: 0
Parents: Stuart and Susan
Marital status: Single
Family links with cricket: Father plays club cricket
Education: Dukeries Comprehensive and Sixth Form College; Sheffield University
Qualifications: 8 GCSEs, 4 A-levels (Grade As)
Off-season: Studying at Sheffield University for Maths degree

Cricketers particularly admired: Richard Hadlee, Ian Botham
Other sports followed: Horse racing (on TV) and indoor cricket
Injuries: Split webbing between first finger and thumb on first-class debut
Relaxations: Solving mathematical problems, playing cricket (indoor and out)
Opinions on cricket: 'Less three/four-day cricket should be played on Saturdays. Only one-day cricket should be played at the weekend, to increase interest in the game.'
Best batting: 6 Nottinghamshire v Derbyshire, Derby 1991
Best bowling: 1-92 Nottinghamshire v Derbyshire, Derby 1991

1991 Season

	M	Inns	NO	Runs	HS	Avge	100s	50s	Ct	St	O	M	Runs	Wkts	Avge	Best	5wI	10wM
Test																		
All First	1	1	0	6	6	6.00	-	-	-	-	32	6	111	1	111.00	1-92	-	-
1-day Int																		
NatWest																		
B&H																		
Refuge																		

Career Performances

	M	Inns	NO	Runs	HS	Avge	100s	50s	Ct	St	Balls	Runs	Wkts	Avge	Best	5wI	10wM
Test																	
All First	1	1	0	6	6	6.00	-	-	-	-	192	111	1	111.00	1-92	-	-
1-day Int																	
NatWest																	
B&H																	
Refuge																	

34. Who topped the first-class bowling averages for Glamorgan last season?

35. Who hit the most sixes last season in first-class games? What was his total?

36. Who were the only two bowlers to take over 100 first-class wickets last season?

BROWN, A. D. Surrey

Name: Alistair Duncan Brown
Role: Right-hand bat, occasional leg-spin bowler and occasional wicket-keeper
Born: 11 February 1970, Beckenham
Height: 5ft 10in **Weight:** 12st
Nickname: Lordy
County debut: 1991 (one-day)
Parents: Robert and Ann
Marital status: Single
Family links with cricket: 'Father played for Surrey Young Amateurs 1953-54, mother does my washing and ironing.'
Education: Cumnor House Prep School; Caterham School
Qualifications: 5 O-levels
Career outside cricket: Works for Skandia Life Assurance Co
Off-season: as above
Overseas teams played for: North Perth, Western Australia 1988-90
Cricketers particularly admired: Ian Botham, David Ward, David Gower, Viv Richards
Other sports followed: Golf, snooker, tennis, football
Injuries: Needed three stitches in left elbow following collision with a boundary board in Refuge match at Worcester
Relaxations: Golf, music and three-card brag
Extras: The Cricket Society All-Rounder of the Year Award winner 1986.
Opinions on cricket: 'Covered wickets and 1989-style seam on the ball.'

1991 Season

	M	Inns	NO	Runs	HS	Avge	100s	50s	Ct	St	O	M	Runs	Wkts	Avge	Best	5wI	10wM
Test																		
All First																			
1-day Int																			
NatWest																			
B&H	1	1	0	37	37	37.00	-	-	-	-								
Refuge	7	6	0	133	45	22.16	-	-	-	-								

> 37. Which English wicket-keeper last season equalled Wally Grout's world record for 8 catches in one innings set 32 years ago?

Career Performances

	M	Inns	NO	Runs	HS	Avge	100s	50s	Ct	St	Balls	Runs	Wkts	Avge	Best	5wI	10wM
Test																	
All First																		
1-day Int																		
NatWest																		
B&H	1	1	0	37	37	37.00	-	-	-	-							
Refuge	11	10	0	247	56	24.70	-	1	4	-							

BROWN, A. M. Derbyshire

Name: Andrew Mark Brown
Role: Left-hand opening bat, right-arm
medium bowler, occasional wicket-keeper
Born: 6 November 1964, Heanor, Derbys
Height: 5ft 9in **Weight:** 10st 7lbs
Nickname: Brownie
County debut: 1985
1st-Class 50s scored: 3
1st-Class 100s scored: 1
1st-Class catches: 12
Parents: John and Marion
Marital status: Single
Family links with cricket: 'Father is
Youth Coaching Organiser for Derbyshire;
brother Stephen played for Derbyshire
youth teams; sister Helen also plays.'
Education: Langley Mill Junior School;
Aldercar Comprehensive School;
South-East Derbyshire College of PE
Qualifications: 8 O-levels, 1 A-level; coaching certificate
Off-season: Playing and coaching in South Africa
Overseas teams played for: Pukekohe Metro and Counties, New Zealand 1983-84; Old
Boys, Hastings and Hawkes Bay 1984-86; Kia Toa University and Manawatu 1987-90
Cricketers particularly admired: John Wright, Bob Taylor
Other sports followed: Football (Nottingham Forest)
Injuries: Broken left thumb (again) – out for 4 weeks from June 6th
Relaxations: 'Lying on beaches and attempting to surf.'
Extras: 'Born 100 yards away from where I made my first senior appearance for
Derbyshire. Hold world record for opening partnership without either batsman scoring a
hundred (246) with Neil Weighman (ex-Notts), 94* and 96* respectively.'
Opinions on cricket: '2nd XI pitches should be of a similar standard to those used for 1st-

class matches. Bowlers get too much help from over responsive pitches and batsman looking for form, or trying to make their way in the game, are at a disadvantage.'
Best batting: 139* Derbyshire v Northamptonshire, Chesterfield 1990

1991 Season

	M	Inns	NO	Runs	HS	Avge	100s	50s	Ct	St	O	M	Runs	Wkts	Avge	Best	5wI	10wM
Test																		
All First	1	1	0	3	3	3.00	-	-	-	-								
1-day Int																		
NatWest																		
B&H																		
Refuge																		

Career Performances

	M	Inns	NO	Runs	HS	Avge	100s	50s	Ct	St	Balls	Runs	Wkts	Avge	Best	5wI	10wM
Test																	
All First	15	23	3	671	139 *	33.55	1	3	12	-							
1-day Int																	
NatWest																	
B&H																	
Refuge	3	1	1	2	2 *	-	-	-	-	1			-				

BROWN, D.R. Warwickshire

Name: Douglas Robert Brown
Role: Right-hand bat, right-arm fast-medium bowler
Born: 29 October 1969, Stirling
Height: 6ft 2in **Weight:** 13st 7lbs
Nickname: Fergie, Ramsey, Haggis, Moose
County debut: 1991 (one-day)
Parents: Alastair and Janette
Marital status: Single
Family links with cricket: Both grandfathers played club cricket
Education: Alloa Academy, West London Institute of Higher Education (Borough Road College)
Qualifications: 9 O-grades, 5 Higher Grades; qualified trampoline and rugby league coach

Career outside cricket: PE teacher
Off-season: 'In order of priority – working on my game and getting ready for next season and completing my final year of my BEd degree.'
Overseas tours: Scotland XI to Pakistan 1989
Cricketers particularly admired: Omar Henry, Tim Munton, Richard Hadlee
Other sports followed: Football (Alloa Athletic), golf – 'everything except horse racing.'
Injuries: Damaged muscle tissue in right shoulder, sore Achilles tendon
Relaxations: 'Spending time at home with my parents, eating out with my girlfriend, listening to soul music, watching sport.'
Extras: Played football at Hampden Park for Scotland U18
Opinions on cricket: 'If young cricketers are to learn their trade in the 2ndXI in readiness for first-class cricket, then surely the balls which are used and the pitches which are played on should be the same as are used in first-class cricket.'

1991 Season

	M	Inns	NO	Runs	HS	Avge	100s	50s	Ct	St	O	M	Runs	Wkts	Avge	Best	5wI	10wM
Test																		
All First	1	-	-	-	-	-	-	-	-	-	6	0	35	1	35.00	1-35	-	-
1-day Int																		
NatWest																		
B&H																		
Refuge																		

Career Performances

	M	Inns	NO	Runs	HS	Avge	100s	50s	Ct	St	Balls	Runs	Wkts	Avge	Best	5wI	10wM
Test																	
All First	1	-	-	-	-	-	-	-	-	-	36	35	1	35.00	1-35	-	-
1-day Int																	
NatWest																	
B&H																	
Refuge																	

38. Who topped the first-class bowling averages for Gloucestershire last season?

39. For which two first-class counties did former England Test wicket-keeper, Paul Downton, play?

40. In which season was Mike Brearley's last Test series?

BROWN, G.K.   Durham

Name: Gary Kevin Brown
Role: Right-hand opening bat, off-spin bowler
Born: 16 June 1965, Welling, Kent
Height: 5ft 10in **Weight:** 13st 7lbs
Nickname: Browny, Barry
County debut: 1986 (Middlesex)
1st-Class 50s scored: 1
1st-Class 100s scored: 1
One-Day 50s: 1
1st-Class catches: 2
Parents: Kenneth William and Margaret Sonia
Marital status: Single
Family links with cricket: Brother Keith plays for Middlesex; father played club cricket and is a qualified umpire
Education: Chace Comprehensive, Enfield
Qualifications: 3 O-levels; qualified cricket coach
Career outside cricket: Cricket coach at McEwans Cricket Centre, Houghton-le-Spring
Off-season: as above
Overseas teams played for: Marist CC, New Zealand 1985-89
Cricketers particularly admired: All players who have reached Test level
Other sports followed: Most sports
Relaxations: 'Spending time with family, playing golf occasionally, pint down the local.'
Extras: Was on the Middlesex staff before moving to Durham. Plays first-class rugby for Durham City RFC
Opinions on cricket: 'More four-day cricket, less overseas players.'
Best batting: 103 Minor Counties v India, Trowbridge 1990
Best bowling: 1-39 Minor Counties v India, Trowbridge 1990

1991 Season

	M	Inns	NO	Runs	HS	Avge	100s	50s	Ct	St	O	M	Runs	Wkts	Avge	Best	5wI	10wM
Test																		
All First																		
1-day Int																		
NatWest																		
B&H	4	4	0	107	82	26.75	-	1	2		-							
Refuge																		

Career Performances

	M	Inns	NO	Runs	HS	Avge	100s	50s	Ct	St	Balls	Runs	Wkts	Avge	Best	5wI	10wM
Test																	
All First	2	4	1	209	103	69.66	1	1	2	-	54	39	1	39.00	1-39	-	-
1-day Int																	
NatWest	2	2	0	66	42	33.00	-	-	-	-							
B&H	12	12	0	298	82	24.83	-	1	4	-	6	8	0	-		-	-
Refuge																	

BROWN, K. R. Middlesex

Name: Keith Robert Brown
Role: Right-hand bat, wicket-keeper
Born: 18 March 1963, Edmonton
Height: 5ft 11in **Weight:** 13st 7lbs
Nickname: Browny, Scarface, Stally
County debut: 1984
County cap: 1990
1000 runs in a season: 2
1st-Class 50s scored: 28
1st-Class 100s scored: 9
1st-class 200s scored: 1
1st-Class catches: 141
One-Day 50s: 7
One-Day 100s: 2
Place in batting averages: 87th av. 33.82
(1990 39th av. 53.75)
Parents: Kenneth William and Margaret
Sonia
Wife and date of marriage: Marie, 3 November 1984
Children: Zachary, 24 February 1987; Rosanna, 18 December 1989
Family links with cricket: Brother Gary was on Middlesex staff for three years and now
plays for Durham. Father is a qualified umpire
Education: Chace Comprehensive School, Enfield
Qualifications: French O-level; NCA Senior Coaching Award
Jobs outside cricket: Plasterer, PE instructor, Coach
Off-season: Playing and coaching in New Zealand
Overseas tours: NCA Youth tour to Denmark; Middlesex pre-season tours to La Manga
and Portugal
Overseas teams played for: Sydney University, Australia

Cricketers particularly admired: Clive Radley and Derek Randall
Other sports followed: Rugby, boxing, most other sports apart from motor racing
Relaxations: 'Enjoy relaxing with family, walking pet dog and finishing with a couple of pints in local.'
Extras: Had promising boxing career but gave it up in order to concentrate on cricket. Picked to play rugby for Essex
Opinions on cricket: 'None that would make any difference!.'
Best batting: 200* Middlesex v Nottinghamshire, Lord's 1990
Best bowling: 2-7 Middlesex v Gloucestershire, Bristol 1987

1991 Season

	M	Inns	NO	Runs	HS	Avge	100s	50s	Ct	St	O	M	Runs	Wkts	Avge	Best	5wl	10wM
Test																		
All First	24	41	6	1184	143 *	33.82	1	6	36	-	5.5	1	33	1	33.00	1-17	-	-
1-day Int																		
NatWest	2	2	0	57	49	28.50	-	-	1	-	1	0	8	0	-		-	-
B&H	4	4	1	57	25	19.00	-	-	1	-								
Refuge	15	15	4	359	81 *	32.63	-	2	4	-	0.2	0	2	0	-		-	-

Career Performances

	M	Inns	NO	Runs	HS	Avge	100s	50s	Ct	St	Balls	Runs	Wkts	Avge	Best	5wl	10wM
Test																	
All First	111	175	29	5283	200 *	36.18	9	28	141	-	231	162	5	32.40	2-7	-	-
1-day Int																	
NatWest	11	9	2	269	103 *	38.42	1	-	3	-	6	8	0	-		-	-
B&H	15	14	2	283	56	23.58	-	1	4	-	6	0	0	-		-	-
Refuge	69	60	14	1315	102	28.58	1	6	24	1	28	29	0	-		-	-

BROWN, S. J. E.   Durham

Name: Simon John Emmerson Brown
Role: Right-hand bat, left-arm medium pace bowler, gully fielder
Born: 29 June 1969, Cleadon Village, Sunderland
Height: 6ft 3in **Weight:** 13st
Nickname: Chubby
County debut: 1987 (Northamptonshire)
1st-Class catches: 5
Parents: Ernest and Doreen
Marital status: Single
Education: Boldon Comprehensive, Tyne & Wear; South Tyneside College
Qualifications: 5 O-levels, qualified electrician

Career outside cricket: Electrician
Off-season: Working as a self-employed electrician
Overseas tours: England YC to Sri Lanka 1987; Australia for Youth World Cup 1988
Overseas teams played for: Marist, Christchurch, New Zealand
Cricketers particularly admired: John Lever, Dennis Lillee, Richard Hadlee, Ian Botham
Other sports followed: Basketball and football
Relaxations: Playing basketball, football and most sports
Extras: Offered basketball scholarship in America
Opinions on cricket: 'Too much cricket is played during the season. Players should be rested more often.'

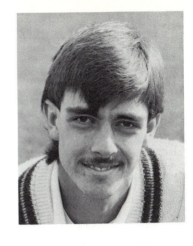

Best batting: 25* Northamptonshire v Gloucestershire, Northampton 1988
Best bowling: 3-20 Northamptonshire v Oxford University, The Parks 1988

1991 Season

	M	Inns	NO	Runs	HS	Avge	100s	50s	Ct	St	O	M	Runs	Wkts	Avge	Best	5wl	10wM
Test																		
All First																		
1-day Int																		
NatWest	1	1	1	7	7 *	-	-	-	-	-	12	1	73	1	73.00	1-73	-	
B&H																		
Refuge																		

Career Performances

	M	Inns	NO	Runs	HS	Avge	100s	50s	Ct	St	Balls	Runs	Wkts	Avge	Best	5wl	10wM
Test																	
All First	15	14	6	70	25 *	8.75	-	-	5	-	1728	814	25	32.56	3-20	-	-
1-day Int																	
NatWest	1	1	1	7	7 *	-	-	-	-	-	72	73	1	73.00	1-73	-	
B&H	1	0	0	0	0	-	-	-	-	-	42	33	0	-	-	-	
Refuge	13	3	1	4	3 *	2.00	-	-	-	-	501	467	13	35.92	3-26	-	

BULLEN, C.K. Surrey

Name: Christopher Keith Bullen
Role: Right-hand bat, off-break bowler, slip/gully fielder
Born: 5 November 1962, Clapham
Height: 6ft 5¹/₂in **Weight:** 14st 8lbs
Nickname: CB, Bullo
County debut: 1985
County cap: 1990
1st-Class 50s scored: 4
1st-Class 5 w. in innings: 1
1st-Class catches: 30
Parents: Keith Thomas and Joan
Marital status: Single
Family links with cricket: 'Parents are avid supporters but father's claims of playing at a high standard are unfounded. Cousin David from Cornwall is a rising star.'

Education: Glenbrook Primary, Chaucer Middle, Rutlish School
Qualifications: 6 O-levels; qualified cricket coach
Off-season: Coaching in schools for the Surrey development staff and looking for a new county. Playing football for Malden Vale
Overseas tours: Surrey Schools to Australia 1980-81; Surrey to Lanzarote 1991
Overseas teams played for: Claremont Cottesloe, Perth, Western Australia 1984-86
Cricketers particularly admired: Jim Laker, Eddie Hemmings, Chris Brown, Anthony Wreford, John Gerard, Matt Bland
Other sports followed: Soccer, golf, rugby, American football
Injuries: Sore shin, bruised fingers
Relaxations: Golf, watching videos, clothes shopping
Extras: Spare time spent playing for Wimbledon CC and Rutlishian CC. Played for Young England v Young West Indies in Test series at home in 1982. Released by Surrey at the end of 1991 season
Opinions on cricket: 'More first-class umpires so that there can be two in charge of 2nd XI games. English registration given too easily.'
Best batting: 65 Surrey v Pakistanis, The Oval 1987
Best bowling: 6-119 Surrey v Middlesex, Lord's 1987

---

41. When did Ian Botham resign as captain of Somerset?

1991 Season

	M	Inns	NO	Runs	HS	Avge	100s	50s	Ct	St	O	M	Runs	Wkts	Avge	Best	5wI	10wM
Test																		
All First	1	1	1	37	37 *	-	-	-	4	-	17	2	48	4	12.00	4-48	-	-
1-day Int																		
NatWest																		
B&H	2	2	0	16	16	8.00	-	-	2	-	13	0	58	1	58.00	1-29	-	
Refuge	6	4	4	40	22 *	-	-	-	2	-	14	0	83	3	27.66	3-38	-	

Career Performances

	M	Inns	NO	Runs	HS	Avge	100s	50s	Ct	St	Balls	Runs	Wkts	Avge	Best	5wI	10wM
Test																	
All First	30	35	7	663	65	23.67	-	4	30	-	2393	1078	38	28.36	6-119	1	
1-day Int																	
NatWest	11	8	4	154	93 *	38.50	-	1	5	-	768	420	8	52.50	2-55	-	
B&H	18	11	5	168	35 *	28.00	-	-	13	-	995	637	15	42.46	2-14	-	
Refuge	73	39	20	344	28 *	18.10	-	-	42	-	2582	2055	67	30.67	5-31	1	

BUNTING, R. A.   Sussex

Name: Rodney Alan Bunting
Role: Right-hand bat, right-arm
fast-medium bowler
Born: 25 April 1965, King's Lynn
Height: 6ft 5in **Weight:** 13st 10lbs
Nickname: Tiddler
County debut: 1988
1st-Class 50s scored: 2
1st-Class 5 w. in innings: 3
1st-Class catches: 5
Place in batting averages: (1990 273rd
av. 10.62)
Place in bowling averages: (1990 131st
av. 50.53)
Strike rate: (career 64.37)
Parents: Geoffrey Thomas and Frances
Wife and date of marriage: Christine
Antoinette, 7 March 1986
Children: Jonathan Charles, 16
September 1986
Family links with cricket: Two elder brothers played county schools cricket and both
parents very interested followers of cricket

Education: King Edward VII Grammar School
Qualifications: 6 O-levels
Cricketers particularly admired: Bob Willis, Mike Hendrick
Other sports followed: Soccer, American football, golf
Relaxations: 'Crosswords, enjoying being with my family.'
Extras: After six years in the game, won first title with Sussex 2nd XI in 1990. Retired at the end of the 1991 season
Opinions on cricket: 'If bowlers have to bowl with a reduced-seam ball, why not reduce the width of the batsman's bat? Fair's fair!'
Best batting: 73 Sussex v Warwickshire, Hove 1989
Best bowling: 5-44 Sussex v Warwickshire, Hove 1988

1991 Season

	M	Inns	NO	Runs	HS	Avge	100s	50s	Ct	St	O	M	Runs	Wkts	Avge	Best	5wI	10wM
Test																		
All First	4	4	3	106	51 *	106.00	-	1	1	-	62.2	7	260	8	32.50	4-99	-	-
1-day Int																		
NatWest																		
B&H	2	2	2	3	2 *	-	-	-	1	-	17	1	75	1	75.00	1-34	-	
Refuge	4	3	2	3	2 *	3.00	-	-	-	-	24.3	0	137	8	17.12	4-35	-	

Career Performances

	M	Inns	NO	Runs	HS	Avge	100s	50s	Ct	St	Balls	Runs	Wkts	Avge	Best	5wI	10wM
Test																	
All First	38	40	14	366	73	14.07	-	2	5	-	5150	3047	80	38.08	5-44	3	-
1-day Int																	
NatWest	1	1	0	6	6	6.00	-	-	-	-	30	30	1	30.00	1-30	-	
B&H	8	4	3	3	2 *	3.00	-	-	4	-	438	330	8	41.25	2-43	-	
Refuge	8	4	3	8	5 *	8.00	-	-	-	-	201	198	10	19.80	4-35	-	

42. In what year did Mike Gatting receive the OBE?

43. Who topped the first-class bowling averages for Hampshire last season?

44. Whom did Graham Gooch first replace as England's captain?

BURNS, M.   Warwickshire

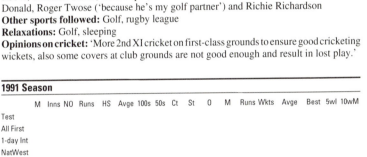

Name: Michael Burns
Role: Right-hand bat, wicket-keeper
Born: 6 February 1969, Barrow-in-Furness
Height: 6ft **Weight:** 13st 7lbs
Nickname: George, Red Hot
County debut: 1991
Parents: Bob and Linda, stepfather Stan
Marital status: Single
Education: Walney Comprehensive
Qualifications: Served apprenticeship as
a fitter at USEL in Barrow
Career outside cricket: Works in family
fruit and veg business
Off-season: Coaching in South Africa
Overseas teams played for: Somerset East,
South Africa 1991-92
Cricketers particularly admired: Dermot
Reeve, Dominic Ostler, Keith Piper, Allan
Donald, Roger Twose ('because he's my golf partner') and Richie Richardson
Other sports followed: Golf, rugby league
Relaxations: Golf, sleeping
Opinions on cricket: 'More 2nd XI cricket on first-class grounds to ensure good cricketing
wickets, also some covers at club grounds are not good enough and result in lost play.'

1991 Season

	M	Inns	NO	Runs	HS	Avge	100s	50s	Ct	St	O	M	Runs	Wkts	Avge	Best	5wI	10wM
Test																		
All First																		
1-day Int																		
NatWest																		
B&H	1	1	0	3	3	3.00	-	-	-	-								
Refuge																		

Career Performances

	M	Inns	NO	Runs	HS	Avge	100s	50s	Ct	St	Balls	Runs	Wkts	Avge	Best	5wI	10wM
Test																	
All First																	
1-day Int																	
NatWest																	
B&H	1	1	0	3	3	3.00	-	-	-	-							
Refuge																	

BURNS, N. D. Somerset

Name: Neil David Burns
Role: Left-hand bat, wicket-keeper
Born: 19 September 1965, Chelmsford
Height: 5ft 10in **Weight:** 11st 7lbs
Nickname: Burnsie, Ernie, George
County debut: 1986 (Essex),
1987 (Somerset)
County cap: 1987 (Somerset)
1st-Class 50s scored: 20
1st-Class 100s scored: 4
1st-Class catches: 237
1st-Class stumpings: 25
One-Day 50s: 4
Place in batting averages: 109th av. 31.07
(1990 109th av. 39.62)
Parents: Roy and Marie
Wife and date of marriage: Susan,
26 September 1987

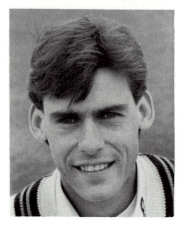

Family links with cricket: Father
Roy played club cricket for Finchley CC; brother Ian captained Essex U19 and plays for
Stock Exchange CC and MCC
Education: Mildmay Junior and Moulsham High School
Qualifications: 6 O-levels, advanced cricket coach
Career outside cricket: Director of NBC Ltd, a sports promotion and management
company; cricket coach
Off-season: 'Working on behalf of the National Holiday Fund for Sick and disabled and
Disabled Children; coaching; playing and coaching in South Africa.'
Overseas tours: England YC to West Indies 1985; Essex to Barbados 1986; Christians in
Sport to India 1990
Overseas teams played for: Northerns/Goodwood, Cape Town 1984-88; Western Province
B 1985-86
Cricketers particularly admired: Alan Knott, Bob Taylor, Rod Marsh, Graham Gooch,
Allan Border, Graeme Pollock, Jimmy Cook and many others who have performed at the
highest level over a long period of time.
Other sports followed: 'Will play/watch most sports but particularly soccer, squash and
golf.'
Relaxations: 'Photography, majority of music, relaxing at home, watching or playing
sport.'
Extras: Former schoolboy footballer with Tottenham Hotspur FC and Orient FC. Joined
Somerset in 1987 after spending four years at Essex. Signed further four-year contract in
1989. Once took eight stumpings in match v Kent 2nd XI at Dartford in 1984. Once took
a hat-trick of stumpings off Nasser Hussain's leg-breaks for Essex U11 v Berkshire U11

Scored maiden first-class 100 against old county at Chelmsford in 1988

Opinions on cricket: '17 four-day Championship has to be the best and fairest competition, avoiding too much joke-bowling and contrived run-chases which cause cynicism. Sunday league to be jazzed up for 1992 is a step in the right direction to make it more attractive to a wider audience. Possibly one hour earlier starting time now that the Sunday league throws up more regularly venues that are different to Saturday/Monday venues. This may also help spectators who have families, offering them an extra hour for their return journey. Most of them are in the ground by lunchtime anyway. As professionals we must play a greater role in ensuring that one-day matches are completed, when weather has not intervened, in one day through quicker over-rates, fewer changes of gloves, unscheduled drinks etc. We must avoid repeats of the Surrey v Northants NatWest semi-final.'

Best batting: 166 Somerset v Gloucestershire, Taunton 1990

1991 Season

	M	Inns	NO	Runs	HS	Avge	100s	50s	Ct	St	O	M	Runs	Wkts	Avge	Best	5wI	10wM
Test																		
All First	23	34	8	808	108	31.07	1	4	35	8								
1-day Int																		
NatWest	3	3	1	11	5 *	5.50	-	-	2	-								
B&H	4	4	1	110	43 *	36.66	-	-	1	1								
Refuge	15	13	4	235	52 *	26.11	-	2	12	6								

Career Performances

	M	Inns	NO	Runs	HS	Avge	100s	50s	Ct	St	Balls	Runs	Wkts	Avge	Best	5wI	10wM
Test																	
All First	121	178	38	4098	166	29.27	4	20	237	25	3	8	0	-	-	-	-
1-day Int																	
NatWest	10	8	3	75	25 *	15.00	-	-	8	3							
B&H	25	18	6	341	51	28.41	-	1	23	5							
Refuge	77	61	15	844	58	18.34	-	3	73	16							

45. Whose cricketing autobiography is called *Hitting Across the Line*?

46. Who won the 1991 Red Stripe Cup, and who captained the team?

BUTCHER, A. R.   Glamorgan

Name: Alan Raymond Butcher
Role: Left-hand bat, slow left-arm
or medium pace bowler,
county captain
Born: 7 January 1954, Croydon
Height: 5ft 8in **Weight:** 11st 7lbs
Nickname: Butch, Budgie
County debut: 1972 (Surrey),
1987 (Glamorgan)
County cap: 1975 (Surrey),
1987 (Glamorgan)
Benefit: 1985
Test debut: 1979
Tests: 1
One-Day Internationals: 1
1000 runs in a season: 12
1st-Class 50s scored: 122
1st-Class 100s scored: 46
1st-Class 200s scored: 1
1st-Class 5 w. in innings: 1
1st-Class catches: 183
One-Day 50s: 55
One-Day 100s: 6
Place in batting averages: 39th av. 45.32 (1990 24th av. 58.77)
Parents: Raymond and Jackie
Wife and date of marriage: Elaine, 27 September 1972
Children: Mark, Gary, Lisa
Family links with cricket: Brother Martin played for MCC Young Professionals. Brother Ian played for Leicestershire and Gloucestershire. Son Mark made his Surrey debut in 1991 and played against his father at The Oval
Qualifications: 5 O-levels, 1 A-level
Other sports followed: Football
Relaxations: Most sport, rock music, reading
Extras: Released by Surrey at end of 1986 season. Joined Glamorgan in 1987. First Englishman to score 1000 runs in both 1989 and 1990. Appointed captain of Glamorgan during 1989 after Hugh Morris resigned in mid-season
Best batting: 216* Surrey v Cambridge University, Fenner's 1980
Best bowling: 6-48 Surrey v Hampshire, Guildford 1972

---

47. Which spin bowler has taken the most Test wickets?

1991 Season

	M	Inns	NO	Runs	HS	Avge	100s	50s	Ct	St	O	M	Runs	Wkts	Avge	Best	5wI	10wM
Test																		
All First	23	39	2	1677	147	45.32	4	13	13	-	2	1	1	0	-	-	-	-
1-day Int																		
NatWest	3	3	0	87	70	29.00	-	1	2	-								
B&H	4	4	0	279	127	69.75	1	2	1	-	3	0	16	0	-	-	-	
Refuge	11	11	1	329	77	32.90	-	3	3	-	5.1	0	36	0	-	-	-	

Career Performances

	M	Inns	NO	Runs	HS	Avge	100s	50s	Ct	St	Balls	Runs	Wkts	Avge	Best	5wI	10wM
Test	1	2	0	34	20	17.00	-	-	-	-	12	9	0	-	-	-	-
All First	398	679	59	22543	216 *	36.36	46	122	183	-	10008	5433	141	38.53	6-48	1	-
1-day Int	1	1	0	14	14	14.00	-	-	-	-							
NatWest	38	36	4	1083	104 *	33.84	1	5	12	-	404	249	5	49.80	1-27	-	
B&H	79	74	4	1982	127	28.31	1	15	22	-	1125	603	27	22.33	4-36	-	
Refuge	234	223	26	5478	113 *	27.80	4	35	51	-	2073	1556	38	40.94	5-19	1	

BUTCHER, M. A. Surrey

Name: Mark Alan Butcher
Role: Left-hand opening bat, right-arm medium bowler
Born: 23 August 1972, Croydon
Height: 5ft 11in **Weight:** 11st
Nickname: Butch, Ralph
County debut: 1991
Parents: Alan and Elaine
Marital status: Single
Family links with cricket: Father captains Glamorgan
Education: Cumnor House School, Trinity School and Archbishop Tenison's, Croydon
Qualifications: 5 O-levels
Off-season: 'Taking driving test, training and nets – and hopefully earning enough money to survive on.'
Overseas tours: England U19 to New Zealand 1990-91
Cricketers particularly admired: David Gower, Michael Holding
Other sports followed: Football, gymnastics
Injuries: Damaged knee ligaments

Relaxations: Music, reading, films

Extras: Youngest player on the Surrey staff. Played his first game for Surrey against his father's Glamorgan in the Refuge League at The Oval, the first ever match of any sort between first-class counties in which a father and son have been in opposition

Opinions on cricket: 'The new rule on bouncers will make the game artificial for batsmen and bowlers alike.'

1991 Season

	M	Inns	NO	Runs	HS	Avge	100s	50s	Ct	St	O	M	Runs	Wkts	Avge	Best	5wI	10wM
Test																		
All First																		
1-day Int																		
NatWest																		
B&H																		
Refuge	1	1	1	48	48 *	-	-	-	-	-	3	0	16	0	-		-	-

Career Performances

	M	Inns	NO	Runs	HS	Avge	100s	50s	Ct	St	Balls		Runs	Wkts	Avge	Best	5wI	10wM
Test																		
All First																		
1-day Int																		
NatWest																		
B&H																		
Refuge	1	1	1	48	48 *	-	-	-	-	-	18		16	0	-		-	-

48. Which England batsman holds the highest Test average?

49. Which player topped the Kent first-class bowling averages last season?

50. Which county captain caddied at the Asian Golf Classic in Bangkok in February 1992?

BUTLER, K.A.   Essex

Name: Keith Andrew Butler
Role: Right-hand bat
Born: 20 January 1971, Camden Town
Height: 5ft 8in **Weight:** 11st
Nickname: Billy
County debut: 1991
Parents: John and Kath
Marital status: Single
Education: Dagenham Priory Comprehensive
Qualifications: 2 O-levels, coaching certificate
Career outside cricket: Air freight clerk
Off-season: 'Getting fit after operation.'
Overseas tours: Young England to Australia 1989-90
Overseas teams played for: East Torrens, Adelaide 1989-90
Cricketers particularly admired: Graham Gooch, Ian Botham, Viv Richards, Giles Ecclestone
Other sports followed: Football, golf
Injuries: Double stress fracture of lower back
Relaxations: 'Music, going to the pub, watching Guy Lovell at fielding practice.'
Best batting: 10* Essex v Cambridge University, Fenner's 1989

1991 Season

	M	Inns	NO	Runs	HS	Avge	100s	50s	Ct	St	O	M	Runs	Wkts	Avge	Best	5wI	10wM
Test																		
All First																		
1-day Int																		
NatWest																		
B&H																		
Refuge	2	1	0	1	1	1.00	-	-	1	-								

Career Performances

	M	Inns	NO	Runs	HS	Avge	100s	50s	Ct	St	Balls	Runs	Wkts	Avge	Best	5wI	10wM
Test																	
All First	1	1	1	10	10 *	-	-	-	-	-							
1-day Int																	
NatWest																	
B&H																	
Refuge	3	1	0	1	1	1.00	-	-	1	-	6	5	0	-		-	-

BYAS, D.   Yorkshire

Name: David Byas
Role: Left-hand bat (No 3), right-arm
medium bowler
Born: 26 August 1963, Kilham
Height: 6ft 4in **Weight:** 14st 7lbs
Nickname: Bingo, Gadgett
County debut: 1986
County cap: 1991
1000 runs in a season: 1
1st-Class 50s scored: 16
1st-Class 100s scored: 7
1st-Class catches: 69
One-Day 50s: 6
Place in batting averages: 43rd av. 44.48
(1990 176th av. 28.16)
Parents: Richard and Anne
Wife and date of marriage: Rachael
Elizabeth, 27 October 1990
Family links with cricket: Father plays
in local league
Education: Scarborough College
Qualifications: 1 O-level (Engineering)
Career outside cricket: Partner in family farm
Off-season: Farming
Overseas teams played for: Papetoetoe, Auckland 1989
Cricketers particularly admired: David Gower, Viv Richards, Ian Botham
Other sports followed: Hockey, motor racing
Relaxations: 'Playing hockey for Welton, shooting and eating out with my wife Rachael.'
Extras: Youngest captain (aged 21) of Scarborough CC in 1985
Best batting: 153 Yorkshire v Nottinghamshire, Worksop 1991
Best bowling: 3-55 Yorkshire v Derbyshire, Chesterfield 1990

1991 Season

	M	Inns	NO	Runs	HS	Avge	100s	50s	Ct	St	O	M	Runs	Wkts	Avge	Best	5wI	10wM
Test																		
All First	24	41	6	1557	153	44.48	5	2	21	-	9	2	14	0	-		-	-	-	-
1-day Int																		
NatWest	1	1	0	2	2	2.00	-	-	-	-								
B&H	6	6	0	207	92	34.50	-	2	-	-								
Refuge	16	16	4	369	74 *	30.75	-	2	3	-								

Career Performances

	M	Inns	NO	Runs	HS	Avge	100s	50s	Ct	St	Balls	Runs	Wkts	Avge	Best	5wI	10wM
Test																	
All First	78	129	13	3697	153	31.87	7	16	69	-	948	612	10	61.20	3-55	-	-
1-day Int																	
NatWest	6	4	0	77	54	19.25	-	1	4	-	18	23	1	23.00	1-23	-	
B&H	14	12	1	299	92	27.18	-	2	2	-	283	155	5	31.00	2-38	-	
Refuge	59	57	13	1132	74 *	25.72	-	3	10	-	523	445	19	23.42	3-19	-	

CADDICK, A. R. Somerset

Name: Andrew Richard Caddick
Role: Right-hand bat, right-arm
fast-medium bowler
Born: 21 November 1968, Christchurch,
New Zealand
Height: 6ft 5in **Weight:** 13st 7lbs
Nickname: Kiwi, Sky, Bean
County debut: 1991
1st-Class catches: 1
Parents: Christopher and Audrey
Marital status: Single
Education: Papanui High School,
Christchurch
Qualifications: University entrance,
qualified plasterer and tiler
Off-season: Labouring, training
Overseas tours: New Zealand U19 to
England 1988; Youth World Cup in
Australia 1987-88
Cricketers particularly admired:
Dennis Lillee, Richard Hadlee, Jimmy Cook
Other sports followed: Football, rugby
Relaxations: Music, TV, videos, the beach, water-skiing, scuba-diving, squash, badminton,
walking, skiing
Extras: Played for Middlesex 2nd XI 1988-89, joined Somerset 1989. Qualifies for
England in April 1992. Rapid Cricketline Player of the Year 1991
Opinions on cricket: 'For a bowler it's a very hard game.'
Best batting: 0 Somerset v West Indies, Taunton 1991
Best bowling: 2-40 Somerset v Sri Lanka, Taunton 1991

1991 Season

	M	Inns	NO	Runs	HS	Avge	100s	50s	Ct	St	O	M	Runs	Wkts	Avge	Best	5wI	10wM
Test																		
All First	2	1	0	0	0	0.00	-	-	1	-	64.5	13	251	5	50.20	2-40	-	-
1-day Int																		
NatWest																		
B&H																		
Refuge																		

Career Performances

	M	Inns	NO	Runs	HS	Avge	100s	50s	Ct	St	Balls	Runs	Wkts	Avge	Best	5wI	10wM
Test																	
All First	2	1	0	0	0	0.00	-	-	1	-	389	251	5	50.20	2-40	-	-
1-day Int																	
NatWest																	
B&H																	
Refuge																	

CAIRNS, C. L.   Nottinghamshire

Name: Christopher Lance Cairns
Role: Right-hand bat, right-arm
fast-medium bowler
Born: 13 June 1970, Picton, New Zealand
Height: 6ft 2in **Weight:** 14st
Nickname: Sheep
County debut: 1988
Test debut: 1990-91
Tests: 2
One-Day Internationals: 2
1st-Class 50s scored: 4
1st-Class 100s scored: 1
1st-Class 5 w. in innings: 2
1st-Class 10 w. in match: 1
Ist-Class catches: 13
Parents: Lance and Sue
Family links with cricket: Father played
for New Zealand, uncle played first-class
cricket in New Zealand
Education: Christchurch Boys' High School, New Zealand
Qualifications: 5th and 6th form certificates
Marital status: Single

Off-season: Playing for New Zealand
Overseas tours: New Zealand Youth XI to Australia for Youth World Cup 1988
Cricketers particularly admired: Mick Newell, Richard Hadlee, Dennis Lillee
Other sports followed: Most sports
Opinions on cricket: 'Great game.'
Best batting: 110 Northern Districts v Auckland, Hamilton 1988-89
Best bowling: 7-39 Canterbury v Central Districts, Napier 1990-91

1991 Season (did not make any first-class or one-day appearance)

Career Performances

	M	Inns	NO	Runs	HS	Avge	100s	50s	Ct	St	Balls	Runs	Wkts	Avge	Best	5wl	10wM
Test	2	3	0	46	28	15.33	-	-	2	-	426	271	9	30.11	5.75	1	-
All First-	30	36	6	799	110	26.63	1	4	13	-	4743	2773	89	31.15	7.39	2	1
1-day Int	2	2	0	11	6	5.50	-	-	2	-	114	96	6	16.00	4-55	-	
NatWest																	
B&H																	
Refuge	2	2	0	8	4	4.00	-	-	1	-	78	68	2	34.00	2.38	-	-

CANN, M. J.   Glamorgan

Name: Michael James Cann
Role: Left-hand bat, off-break bowler
Born: 4 July 1965, Cardiff
Height: 5ft 9in **Weight:** 12st
Nickname: Tin, Canny
County debut: 1986
1st-Class 50s scored: 7
1st-Class 100s scored: 3
1st-Class catches: 17
Place in batting averages: (1990 218th av. 20.60)
Parents: Leslie and Catherine
Wife's name and date of marriage: Jacqui, 6 May 1991
Education: St Illtyd's College, Cardiff; Swansea University
Qualifications: 10 O-levels, 3 A-levels, Degree in Biochemistry, senior NCA coach
Career outside cricket: 'None at present but I am about to find one.'
Off-season: Playing for Griqualand West in South Africa

Overseas tours: Glamorgan pre-season tour to Barbados 1989
Overseas teams played for: Orange Free State B 1989-90; Griqualand West 1990-92
Cricketers particularly admired: 'Everyone who plays the game from club level to Test level.'
Other sports followed: Football (Cardiff City) and most sports
Injuries: 'Manic depression about being released.'
Relaxations: General socialising. Drinking Cape wines with my wife Jacqui
Extras: Represented Combined Universities in B & H Cup 1987. Released by Glamorgan at the end of 1991 season
Opinions on cricket: 'All cricketers who play the game have opinions on cricket which are usually valid, up-to-date and well worth listening to, so why doesn't the TCCB listen to them! I feel I was good enough to have played longer.'
Best batting: 141 Griqualand West v Boland, Stellenbosch 1990-91
Best bowling: 3-30 Glamorgan v Middlesex, Abergavenny 1989

1991 Season

	M	Inns	NO	Runs	HS	Avge	100s	50s	Ct	St	O	M	Runs	Wkts	Avge	Best	5wI	10wM
Test																		
All First	1	1	1	29	29 *	-	-	-	1	-	8	0	37	0	-		-	-
1-day Int																		
NatWest																		
B&H																		
Refuge	2	2	0	4	2	2.00	-	-	-	-								

Career Performances

	M	Inns	NO	Runs	HS	Avge	100s	50s	Ct	St	Balls	Runs	Wkts	Avge	Best	5wI	10wM
Test																	
All First	45	71	6	1916	141	29.47	4	8	17	-	2045	1226	19	64.52	3-30	-	-
1-day Int																	
NatWest	2	2	1	4	2 *	4.00	-	-	1	-	66	40	3	13.33	3-40	-	
B&H	8	6	2	97	46	24.25	-	-	2	-	162	127	2	63.50	1-1	-	
Refuge	6	5	0	10	5	2.00	-	-	1	-							

51. Which county captain played against his son in a Refuge League match last season?

52. Who is the 1992 captain of Gloucestershire?

CAPEL, D. J.   Northamptonshire

Name: David John Capel
Role: Right-hand bat, right-arm
fast-medium bowler, all-rounder
Born: 6 July 1963, Northampton
Height: 5ft 11in **Weight:** 12st
Nickname: Capes, Fiery, Riocha
County debut: 1981
County cap: 1986
Test debut: 1987
Tests: 15
One-Day Internationals: 23
1000 runs in a season: 3
50 wickets in a season: 3
1st-Class 50s scored: 57
1st-Class 100s scored: 11
1st-Class 5 w. in innings: 11
1st-Class catches: 110
One-Day 50s: 17
One-Day 100s: 3
Place in batting averages: 153rd av. 25.54 (1990 63rd av. 47.47)
Place in bowling averages: 111th av. 40.25 (1990 21st av. 28.44)
Strike rate: 82.32 (career 62.45)
Parents: John and Janet
Wife and date of marriage: Debbie, 21 September 1985
Children: Jenny, 21 October 1987
Family links with cricket: Father and brother Andrew both captained their local league
sides
Education: Roade Primary and Roade Comprehensive School
Qualifications: 3 O-levels, 4 CSEs, NCA coaching certificate
Off-season: Playing overseas
Overseas tours: England to Sharjah 1986; Pakistan, New Zealand and Australia 1987-88;
India for Nehru Cup and West Indies 1989-90
Overseas teams played for: Eastern Province 1985-87
Cricketers particularly admired: 'Numerous, for various reasons: Sobers, Richards and
Botham (ability), Gooch and Wessels (professionalism), Clive Lloyd and Geoff Cook
(gentlemen), Lillee (bowling, character, great man), Rice and Hadlee (great all-rounders),
Boycott (dedication and knowledge).'
Other sports followed: 'Golf, local rugby and soccer teams.'
Relaxations: Golf, family days, barbecues at home.
Extras: Only second Northampton-born man to play for England
Opinions on cricket: 'The contest between bat and ball should be as even as possible and,
ideally, variety is essential. Flat batting pitches make for plenty of runs and attractive

strokes, but the game could get a bit stereotyped with the same brown pitches producing record-breaking run-feasts. It would be a more interesting proposition going from a turning pitch to a seamer and then to a flat one, etc., each game bringing a fresh set of circumstances to work out and to test the technique of individual players and the strength in depth of sides. As long as pitches are not dangerous for the batsmen, and pace and bounce are even, lateral movement is what makes for a test of skill – whether it is spin, seam or swing – and is where, I believe, the art of the game lies. Demands on county cricketers are high: 16 or 17 four-day games and 2 rather than 3 one-day competitions (50-overs a side) would give players more time to build up for and wind down from games and to train properly. This would make for far better first-class cricket and more keenly contested one-day matches – to the benefit of both players and spectators.'

Best batting: 134 Eastern Province v Western Province, Port Elizabeth 1986-87
Best bowling: 7-46 Northamptonshire v Yorkshire, Northampton 1987

1991 Season

	M	Inns	NO	Runs	HS	Avge	100s	50s	Ct	St	O	M	Runs	Wkts	Avge	Best	5wI	10wM
Test																		
All First	22	33	2	792	100	25.54	1	7	10	-	383.1	83	1127	28	40.25	4-83	-	-
1-day Int																		
NatWest	4	3	0	7	6	2.33	-	-	-	-	14	0	50	3	16.66	3-26	-	
B&H	5	5	0	102	42	20.40	-	-	-	-	40.4	3	147	5	29.40	4-37	-	
Refuge	16	15	3	360	77 *	30.00	-	2	3	-	80	1	400	17	23.52	3-30	-	

Career Performances

	M	Inns	NO	Runs	HS	Avge	100s	50s	Ct	St	Balls	Runs	Wkts	Avge	Best	5wI	10wM
Test	15	25	1	374	98	15.58	-	2	6	-	2000	1064	21	50.66	3-88	-	-
All First	238	360	54	9176	134	29.98	11	57	110	-	24415	13136	391	33.59	7-46	11	-
1-day Int	23	19	2	327	50 *	19.23	-	1	6	-	1038	805	17	47.35	3-38	-	
NatWest	27	24	7	710	101	41.76	1	3	6	-	1063	712	21	33.90	3-26	-	
B&H	40	34	5	611	97	21.06	-	1	8	-	1822	1076	45	23.91	4-29	-	
Refuge	125	114	24	2696	121	29.95	2	12	25	-	3615	2846	91	31.27	4-30	-	

CARRICK, P. Yorkshire

Name: Phillip Carrick
Role: Right-hand bat, slow left-arm bowler
Born: 16 July 1952, Leeds
Height: 6ft **Weight:** 14st
Nickname: Fergie
County debut: 1970
County cap: 1976
Benefit: 1985

50 wickets in a season: 11
1st-Class 50s scored: 41
1st-Class 100s scored: 3
1st-Class 5 w. in innings: 45
1st-Class 10 w. in match: 5
1st-Class catches: 189
One-Day 50s: 2
Place in batting averages: 126th av 28.78
(1990 193rd av. 25.75)
Place in bowling averages: 40th av. 28.65
(1990 52nd av. 34.13)
Strike rate: 68.98 (career 72.03)
Parents: Arthur (deceased) and Ivy
Wife and date of marriage: Elspeth,
2 April 1977
Children: Emma Elizabeth, 6 May 1980;
Philippa Louise, 11 January 1982
Family links with cricket: Father and
brother useful league players
Education: Bramley CS, Intake CS, Park Lane College of Further Education
Qualifications: 2 O-levels, 8 CSEs, NCA coaching certificate
Jobs outside cricket: Partner in promotional products business
Off-season: Working for Parker Carrick
Overseas tours: Derrick Robins XI to South Africa 1976; Far East 1977; MCC to Namibia
1991
Overseas teams played for: Eastern Province 1976-77; Northern Transvaal 1982-83
Cricketers particularly admired: Graeme Pollock, Gary Sobers
Other sports followed: Rugby League and golf
Injuries: 'Old age!'
Relaxations: Golf. 'Watching my daughters with their ponies.'
Extras: Yorkshire captain 1987-1989. Won B & H Cup in first season
Best batting: 131* Yorkshire v Northamptonshire, Northampton 1980
Best bowling: 8-33 Yorkshire v Cambridge University, Fenner's 1973

1991 Season

	M	Inns	NO	Runs	HS	Avge	100s	50s	Ct	St	O	M	Runs	Wkts	Avge	Best	5wl	10wM
Test																		
All First	21	32	9	662	67	28.78	-	4	3	-	701.2	231	1748	61	28.65	5-13	2	-
1-day Int																		
NatWest	1	1	0	12	12	12.00	-	-	-	-	6	1	18	0	-	-	-	-
B&H	3	2	0	9	7	4.50	-	-	2	-	32	1	106	5	21.20	3-22	-	
Refuge	10	7	4	89	25	29.66	-	-	2	-	74	2	276	19	14.52	5-22	2	

Career Performances

	M	Inns	NO	Runs	HS	Avge	100s	50s	Ct	St	Balls	Runs	Wkts	Avge	Best	5wI	10wM
Test																	
All First	421	541	97	9987	131 *	22.49	3	41	189	-	73761	30626	1024	29.90	8-33	45	5
1-day Int																	
NatWest	30	22	3	320	54	16.84	-	1	6	-	1518	676	23	29.39	3-8	-	
B&H	56	34	5	306	53	10.55	-	1	8	-	2715	1478	40	36.95	3-22	-	
Refuge	199	137	40	1455	48 *	15.00	-	-	49	-	6192	4622	159	29.06	5-22	2	

CHAPMAN, C. A. Yorkshire

Name: Colin Anthony Chapman
Role: Right-hand bat, wicket-keeper
Born: 8 June 1971, Bradford
Height: 5ft 8in **Weight:** 11st 7lbs
Nickname: Humpy, Turtle, Chappy
County debut: 1990
1st-Class catches: 2
Parents: Mick and Joyce
Marital status: Single
Education: Nabwood Middle;
Beckfoot Grammar; Bradford & Ilkley
Community College
Qualifications: 5 O-levels; BTec Diploma
in Graphic Design, coaching certificate
Career outside cricket: Working in
graphics
Off season: 'Relaxation; enjoying my first
Christmas at home for two years.'
Overseas teams played for: Waitamata,
Auckland 1989-91
Cricketers particularly admired: Phil Carrick, Alan Knott
Other sports followed: 'Anything slightly interesting.'
Relaxations: 'Spending a few hours at the pub.'
Opinions on cricket: 'Would like to see league (club) cricket played to a two-day format
with two innings per team and bonus points. For up-and-coming cricketers the one-day
game in the leagues is nothing like anything else they might play in. Since school cricket
is a joke youngsters are growing up playing in and around the leagues meaning that there
are too many one-day cricketers around.'
Best batting: 20 Yorkshire v Middlesex, Uxbridge 1990

1991 Season

	M	Inns	NO	Runs	HS	Avge	100s	50s	Ct	St	O	M	Runs	Wkts	Avge	Best	5wI	10wM
Test																		
All First																		
1-day Int																		
NatWest																		
B&H																		
Refuge	2	2	0	3	2	1.50	-	-	-	-								

Career Performances

	M	Inns	NO	Runs	HS	Avge	100s	50s	Ct	St	Balls	Runs	Wkts	Avge	Best	5wI	10wM
Test																		
All First	2	4	0	47	20	11.75	-	-	2	-								
1-day Int																		
NatWest																		
B&H																		
Refuge	4	3	1	39	36 *	19.50	-	-	1	-								

CHILDS, J. H. Essex

Name: John Henry Childs
Role: Left-hand bat, slow left-arm bowler
Born: 15 August 1951, Plymouth
Height: 6ft **Weight:** 12st 6lbs
Nickname: Charlie
County debut: 1975 (Gloucs), 1985 (Essex)
County cap: 1977 (Gloucs), 1986 (Essex)
Testimonial: 1985
Test debut: 1988
Tests: 2
50 wickets in a season: 6
1st-Class 5 w. in innings: 42
1st-Class 10 w. in match: 8
1st-Class catches: 98
Place in batting averages: 225th av. 15.00
(1990 269th av. 11.18)
Place in bowling averages: 45th av. 29.33
(1990 140th av. 58.88)
Strike rate: 69.33 (career 70.05)
Parents: Sydney and Barbara (both deceased)
Wife and date of marriage: Jane Anne, 11 November 1978
Children: Lee Robert, 28 November 1980; Scott Alexander, 21 August 1984

113

Education: Audley Park Secondary Modern, Torquay
Qualifications: Advanced cricket coach
Off-season: Working for Essex CCC marketing department
Cricketers particularly admired: Gary Sobers, Mike Procter
Relaxations: 'Watching rugby, decorating at home, walking on moors and beaches, enjoying my family.'
Extras: Played for Devon 1973-74. Released by Gloucestershire at end of 1984 and joined Essex. One of *Wisden's* Five Cricketers of the Year, 1986. Selected for England's cancelled tour to India 1988-89
Best batting: 41* Essex v Middlesex, Lord's 1991
Best bowling: 9-56 Gloucestershire v Somerset, Bristol 1981

1991 Season

	M	Inns	NO	Runs	HS	Avge	100s	50s	Ct	St	O	M	Runs	Wkts	Avge	Best	5wI	10wM
Test																		
All First	22	15	7	120	41 *	15.00	-	-	6	-	751.1	248	1907	65	29.33	6-61	4	-
1-day Int																		
NatWest	1	0	0	0	0	-	-	-	-	-	-	11.4	4	43	2	21.50	2-43	-
B&H																		
Refuge	2	0	0	0	0	-	-	-	-	-	16	1	62	3	20.66	2-35	-

Career Performances

	M	Inns	NO	Runs	HS	Avge	100s	50s	Ct	St	Balls	Runs	Wkts	Avge	Best	5wI	10wM
Test	2	4	4	2	2 *	-	-	-	1	-	516	183	3	61.00	1-13	-	-
All First	304	273	128	1281	41 *	8.83	-	-	98	-	54150	23273	773	30.10	9-56	42	8
1-day Int																	
NatWest	9	4	3	22	14 *	22.00	-	-	-	-	574	327	10	32.70	2-15	-
B&H	23	7	5	25	10	12.50	-	-	6	-	1272	688	21	32.76	3-36	-
Refuge	75	27	16	103	16 *	9.36	-	-	11	-	2851	2137	56	38.16	4-15	-

CLEAL, M. W.   Somerset

Name: Matthew William Cleal
Role: Right-hand bat, right-arm medium bowler
Born: 23 July 1969, Yeovil
Height: 6ft 3in **Weight:** 14st
Nickname: Hog – 'because I hogged the batting *and* bowling at school'
County debut: 1988
1st-Class catches: 4
Strike rate: (career 60.84)
Parents: Michael Gordon and Diana
Family links with cricket: Father played schools cricket for Somerset

Education: Parcroft Junior; Preston Comprehensive, Yeovil
Career outside cricket:
'Groundsman, painter, delivery man - you name it, I've done it!'
Off-season: Playing a lot of golf
Overseas teams played for: Wanganui, New Zealand 1988-89
Cricketers particularly admired: Richard Hadlee, Waqar Younis, Malcolm Marshall
Other sports followed: Golf and football (Bristol Rovers FC)
Injuries: 'Bad back, injured shoulder – bad year for injuries.'
Extras: Bowler of the Tournament in 7 Nations International Youth Festival in Belfast, 1987: Somerset Young Player of the Year 1988; 'my best bowling figures are still from my first game.' Released by Somerset at the end of 1991 season

Opinions on cricket: 'I think we should change the ways in which we try to develop young pace bowlers. Too many young bowlers do not reach their full potential. Too much bowling in the wrong way causes bad injuries (eg stress fractures). I think we should take a tip from the Australians and their teaching methods.'
Best batting: 30 Somerset v Leicestershire, Taunton 1989
Best bowling: 4-41 Somerset v West Indies, Taunton 1988

1991 Season

	M	Inns	NO	Runs	HS	Avge	100s	50s	Ct	St	O	M	Runs	Wkts	Avge	Best	5wI	10wM
Test																		
All First																		
1-day Int																		
NatWest																		
B&H	2	1	0	18	18	18.00	-	-	-	-	10	0	55	0	-		-	-
Refuge																		

Career Performances

	M	Inns	NO	Runs	HS	Avge	100s	50s	Ct	St	Balls	Runs	Wkts	Avge	Best	5wI	10wM
Test																	
All First	15	19	1	165	30	9.16	-	-	4	-	1582	909	26	34.96	4-41	-	
1-day Int																	
NatWest	2	2	1	28	25	28.00	-	-	-	-	120	86	2	43.00	1-42	-	-
B&H	2	1	0	18	18	18.00	-	-	-	-	60	55	0	-	-	-	-
Refuge	13	8	4	57	15	14.25	-	-	1	-	354	322	3	107.33	1-14	-	

CONNOR, C. A.   Hampshire

Name: Cardigan Adolphus Connor
Role: Right-hand bat, right-arm
fast-medium bowler
Born: 24 March 1961, Anguilla
Height: 5ft 10in **Weight:** 11st 4lbs
Nickname: Cardi, CC
County debut: 1984
County cap: 1988
50 wickets in a season: 3
1st-Class 5 w. in innings: 9
1st-Class 10 w. in match: 1
1st-Class catches: 42
Place in batting averages: (1990 200th
av.24.66)
Place in bowling averages: 108th av. 38.41
(1990 80th av. 38.06)
Strike rate: 68.82 (career 62.54)
Parents: Ethleen Snagg
Marital status: Single
Education: The Valley Secondary
School, Anguilla; Langley College
Qualifications: Engineer
Cricketers particularly admired: Viv Richards, Richard Hadlee
Other sports followed: American football, athletics and most others
Relaxations: Keeping fit and playing golf
Extras: Played for Buckinghamshire in Minor Counties before joining Hampshire. First
Anguillan-born player to appear in the County Championship
Best batting: 46 Hampshire v Derbyshire, Portsmouth 1990
Best bowling: 7-31 Hampshire v Gloucestershire, Portsmouth 1989

1991 Season

	M	Inns	NO	Runs	HS	Avge	100s	50s	Ct	St	O	M	Runs	Wkts	Avge	Best	5wl	10wM
Test																		
All First	16	16	0	148	30	9.25	-	-	3	-	390	69	1306	34	38.41	4-49	-	-
1-day Int																		
NatWest	5	0	0	0	0	-	-	-	2	-	51.1	6	182	15	12.13	4-29	-	
B&H	5	2	0	3	3	1.50	-	-	3	-	55	4	272	10	27.20	3-54	-	
Refuge	14	4	1	28	18	9.33	-	-	2	-	103.3	1	481	18	26.72	4-29	-	

Career Performances

	M	Inns	NO	Runs	HS	Avge	100s	50s	Ct	St	Balls	Runs	Wkts	Avge	Best	5wI	10wM
Test																	
All First	144	116	33	762	46	9.18	-	-	42	-	23330	11940	373	32.01	7-31	9	1
1-day Int																	
NatWest	22	4	2	28	13	14.00	-	-	7	-	1408	882	41	21.51	4-29	-	
B&H	32	8	4	19	5 *	4.75	-	-	7	-	1840	1252	52	24.07	4-19	-	
Refuge	111	25	12	120	19	9.23	-	-	19	-	4774	3517	140	25.12	4-11	-	

COOK, G. Durham

Name: Geoffrey Cook
Role: Right-hand bat, slow left-arm bowler
Born: 9 October 1951, Middlesbrough, Yorkshire
Height: 6ft **Weight:** 12st 10lbs
Nickname: Geoff
County debut: 1971(Northamptonshire)
County cap: 1975 (Northamptonshire)
Benefit: 1985
Test debut: 1981-82
Tests: 7
One-Day Internationals: 6
1000 runs in a season: 12
1st-Class 50s scored: 112
1st-Class 100s scored: 37
1st-Class 200s scored: 1
1st-Class catches: 419
1st-Class stumpings: 3
One-Day 50s: 51
One-Day 100s: 4
Place in batting averages: (1990 191st av. 26.09)
Parents: Harry and Helen
Wife and date of marriage: Judith, 22 November 1975
Children: Anna, 21 May 1980
Family links with cricket: Father and brother David very keen club cricketers. Father very involved in running cricket in Middlesbrough
Education: Middlesbrough High School
Qualifications: 6 O-levels, 1 A-level
Off-season: Preparing Durham for their first season in the County Championship
Overseas tours: England to India and Sri Lanka 1981-82, Australia 1982-83
Overseas teams played for: Eastern Province 1978-81

Cricketers particularly admired: Clive Rice
Relaxations: Walking, reading, crosswords
Extras: 'Great believer in organised recreation for young people. Would enjoy time and scope to carry my beliefs through.' Northants captain from 1981 to 1988. Secretary of Cricketers' Association. Retired at end of 1990 season and worked on the promotion of Durham's claim to first-class status. Subsequently appointed the county's Director of Cricket.
Best batting: 203 Northamptonshire v Yorkshire, Scarborough 1988
Best bowling: 3-47 England XI v South Australia, Adelaide 1982-83

1991 Season

	M	Inns	NO	Runs	HS	Avge	100s	50s	Ct	St	O	M	Runs	Wkts	Avge	Best	5wI	10wM
Test																		
All First																		
1-day Int																		
NatWest	1	1	0	13	13	13.00	-	-	-	-								
B&H																		
Refuge																		

Career Performances

	M	Inns	NO	Runs	HS	Avge	100s	50s	Ct	St	Balls	Runs	Wkts	Avge	Best	5wI	10wM
Test	7	13	0	203	66	15.61	-	2	9	-	42	27	0	-	-	-	-
All First	460	793	65	23277	203	31.97	37	112	419	3	1238	806	15	53.73	3-47	-	-
1-day Int	6	6	0	106	32	17.66	-	-	2	-							
NatWest	43	43	2	1533	130	37.39	3	11	24	-							
B&H	78	71	6	1915	108	29.46	1	11	30	-							
Refuge	238	221	20	4783	98	23.79	-	29	94	-	12	10	0	-		-	-

COOK, N. G. B.   Northamptonshire

Name: Nicholas Grant Billson Cook
Role: Right-hand bat, slowleft-arm bowler
Born: 17 June 1956, Leicester
Height: 6ft **Weight:** 12st 8lbs
Nickname: Beast, Rag'ead
County debut: 1978 (Leics), 1986 (Northants)
County cap: 1982 (Leics), 1987 (Northants)
Test debut: 1983
Tests: 15
One-Day Internationals: 3
50 wickets in a season: 8
1st-Class 50s scored: 4

1st-Class 5 w. in innings: 30
1st-Class 10 w. in match: 3
1st-Class catches: 188
Place in batting averages: 250th av. 11.40
(1990 260th av. 13.00)
Place in bowling averages: 93rd av. 35.50
(1990 50th av. 34.10)
Strike rate: 72.10 (career 73.06)
Parents: Peter and Cynthia
Wife and date of marriage: Sian,
20th September 1991
Family links with cricket: Father
played club cricket
Education: Stokes Croft Junior;
Lutterworth High; Lutterworth Upper
Qualifications: 7 O-levels, 1 A-level,
advanced cricket coach
Off-season: 'Another knee operation
and recovering from the operation,

followed by tours to the Leeward Islands (Feb-March) and South Africa (March-April).'
Overseas tours: England to New Zealand and Pakistan 1983-84; Pakistan 1987-88; India for Nehru Trophy 1989-90; English Counties XI to Zimbabwe 1984-85; England B to Sri Lanka 1985-86
Other sports followed: Soccer (especially Leicester City), rugby, horse racing
Injuries: 'Pulled hamstring – May; jumper's knee – all season!'
Relaxations: Crosswords, reading (especially Wilbur Smith), good comedy programmes, good food
Extras: Played for ESCA 1975. Played for Young England v Young West Indies 1975. Left Leicestershire to join Northamptonshire in 1986
Opinions on cricket: 'Should be 17 four-day games. Sunday league should be divided into two leagues playing 50-over cricket with top two qualifying for play-offs and final. A 60-over competition should remain but it must be played earlier in the season, thus avoiding farce of semi-final and final being played in near darkness.'
Best batting: 75 Leicestershire v Somerset, Taunton 1980
Best bowling: 7-63 Leicestershire v Somerset, Taunton 1982

1991 Season

	M	Inns	NO	Runs	HS	Avge	100s	50s	Ct	St	O	M	Runs	Wkts	Avge	Best	5wI	10wM
Test																		
All First	18	15	5	114	29	11.40	-	-	10	-	336.3	79	994	28	35.50	4-74	-	-
1-day Int																		
NatWest	1	0	0	0	0	-	-	-	2	-	12	0	35	1	35.00	1-35	-	
B&H	3	2	0	1	1	0.50	-	-	1	-	26	2	77	1	77.00	1-21	-	
Refuge	5	2	1	23	17 *	23.00	-	-	1	-	17	0	80	0	-	-	-	-

Career Performances

	M	Inns	NO	Runs	HS	Avge	100s	50s	Ct	St	Balls	Runs	Wkts	Avge	Best	5wI	10wM
Test	15	25	4	179	31	8.52	-	-	5	-	4172	1689	52	32.48	6-65	4	1
All First	320	333	88	2871	75	11.71	-	4	188	-	59618	23441	816	28.72	7-63	30	3
1-day Int	3	0	0	0	0	-	-	-	2	-	144	95	5	19.00	2-18	-	
NatWest	19	7	2	42	13	8.40	-	-	7	-	1312	726	22	33.00	4-24	-	
B&H	33	15	5	128	23	12.80	-	-	10	-	1705	1012	21	48.19	3-35	-	
Refuge	100	40	19	208	17 *	9.90	-	-	32	-	3785	2826	89	31.75	3-20	-	

COOK, S. J. Somerset

Name: Stephen James Cook
Role: Right-hand bat
Born: 31 July 1953, Johannesburg
Height: 6ft 3in **Weight:** 14st
Nickname: Mutley
County debut: 1989
County cap: 1989
1000 runs in a season: 3
1st-Class 50s scored: 79
1st-Class 100s scored: 55
1st-Class 200s scored: 3
1st-Class 300s scored: 1
1st-Class catches: 132
One-Day 50s: 16
One-Day 100s: 8
Place in batting averages: 2nd av. 81.02
(1990 7th av. 76.70)
Parents: Denzil Chesney and Nancy
Harding
Wife and date of marriage: Linsey, 11 April 1981
Children: Stephen Craig, 29 November 1982; Ryan Lyall, 2 October 1985
Family links with cricket: Father played local club cricket
Education: Rosebank Primary and Hyde Park High Schools; Witwatersrand University;
Johannesburg College of Education
Qualifications: Matric Pass; TTHD from Johannesburg College of Education
Career outside cricket: School teacher; Manager of Cricket Affairs at Rand Afrikaans
University
Off-season: Playing for Transvaal
Overseas tours: South Africa to India 1991
Overseas teams played for: Transvaal 1972-1990; South Africa 1982-1990
Cricketers particularly admired: Barry Richards, Clive Rice, Vince van der Bijl,

Graeme Pollock, Kevin McKenzie, Henry Fotheringham
Other sports followed: Golf, football, rugby, tennis, athletics
Relaxations: Quiet meal and a glass of wine with family and friends
Extras: 'Scored 114 against England on my debut in unofficial Tests in 1981-82.' Captain of South African team v Mike Gatting's English team in 1989-90. First batsman to reach 1000 first-class runs in both 1989 and 1990. One of *Wisden's* Five Cricketers of the Year, 1990. His 313* is the highest score by a South African in county cricket. Highest run aggregate (902) for a Sunday League season in 1990. Came to England as manager of South African Schools side in 1983, 1988. Retired from county cricket at the end of 1991 season.
Opinions on cricket: 'I would like to see more four-day cricket.'
Best batting: 313* Somerset v Glamorgan, Cardiff 1990
Best bowling: 2-25 Somerset v Derbyshire, Chesterfield 1990

1991 Season

	M	Inns	NO	Runs	HS	Avge	100s	50s	Ct	St	O	M	Runs	Wkts	Avge	Best	5wI	10wM
Test																		
All First	24	42	8	2755	210 *	81.02	11	8	16	-	4	0	26	0	-	-	-	-
1-day Int																		
NatWest	3	3	0	56	35	18.66	-	-	-	-								
B&H	4	4	0	213	76	53.25	-	2	1	-								
Refuge	15	15	1	546	129 *	39.00	1	3	4	-								

Career Performances

	M	Inns	NO	Runs	HS	Avge	100s	50s	Ct	St	Balls	Runs	Wkts	Avge	Best	5wI	10wM
Test																	
All First	239	421	49	18696	313 *	50.25	55	79	132	-	144	107	3	35.66	2-25	-	-
1-day Int																	
NatWest	7	7	0	177	45	25.28	-	-	3	-							
B&H	16	16	0	854	177	53.37	1	7	6	-							
Refuge	47	47	4	2004	136 *	46.60	7	9	17	-							

53. Which player topped the batting averages in the Britannic Assurance County Championship last season?

54. What was remarkable about Roly Jenkins' bowling for Worcester v Surrey at Worcester in 1949?

COOPER, K. E.   Nottinghamshire

Name: Kevin Edwin Cooper
Role: Left-hand bat, right-arm
fast-medium bowler
Born: 27 December 1957,
Sutton-in-Ashfield
Height: 6ft **Weight:** 12st 4lbs
Nickname: Henry
County debut: 1976
County cap: 1980
Benefit: 1990
50 wickets in a season: 8
1st-Class 5 w. in innings: 25
1st-Class 10 w. in match: 1
1st-Class catches: 85
Place in batting averages: 266th av. 11.35
(1989 246th av. 11.95)
Place in bowling averages: (1990 103rd
av. 40.79)
Strike rate: (career 60.66)
Parents: Gerald Edwin and Margaret
Wife and date of marriage: Linda Carol, 14 February 1981
Children: Kelly Louise, 8 April 1982; Tara Amy, 22 November 1984
Family links with cricket: Father played local cricket
Off-season: Working in cricket development for Nottinghamshire CCC
Cricketers particularly admired: John Snow
Injuries: Missed most of 1991 season with double stress fracture of 4th vertebra, had bone graft and operation to insert two screws into fractures
Relaxations: Golf, clay pigeon shooting
Extras: In 1974 took 10-6 in one innings for Hucknall Ramblers against Sutton College in the Mansfield and District League. First bowler to 50 first-class wickets in 1988 season
Best batting: 46 Nottinghamshire v Middlesex, Trent Bridge 1985
Best bowling: 8-44 Nottinghamshire v Middlesex, Lord's 1984

1991 Season

	M	Inns	NO	Runs	HS	Avge	100s	50s	Ct	St	O	M	Runs	Wkts	Avge	Best	5wI	10wM
Test																		
All First	1	0	0	0	0	-	-	-	-	-	17	3	54	1	54.00	1-54	-	-
1-day Int																		
NatWest																		
B&H	3	1	0	0	0	0.00	-	-	-	-	31	5	103	2	51.50	1-27	-	
Refuge	7	2	2	4	4 *	-	-	-	-	-	50	3	200	3	66.66	1-20	-	

Career Performances

	M	Inns	NO	Runs	HS	Avge	100s	50s	Ct	St	Balls	Runs	Wkts	Avge	Best	5wl	10wM
Test																	
All First	271	279	67	2139	46	10.09	-	-	85	-	42766	19269	705	27.33	8-44	25	1
1-day Int																	
NatWest	23	8	1	45	11	6.42	-	-	6	-	1568	717	34	21.08	4-49	-	
B&H	63	22	13	118	25 *	13.11	-	-	12	-	3667	2035	71	28.66	4-9	-	
Refuge	160	55	18	250	31	6.75	-	-	26	-	6766	4925	138	35.68	4-25	-	

CORK, D. G. Derbyshire

Name: Dominic Gerald Cork
Role: Right-hand bat, right-arm medium-fast bowler
Born: 7 August 1971, Newcastle-under-Lyme, Staffordshire
Nickname: Corky, Snafflers, Son of Base, Phantom, Golden, Young Dermot
Height: 6ft 2¹/₂in **Weight:** 13st
County debut: 1990
50 wickets in a season: 1
1st-Class 5 w. in innings: 1
1st-Class 10 w. in match: 1
1st-Class catches: 9
Place in batting averages: 188th av. 21.15
Place in bowling averages: 27th av. 25.61
Strike rate: 52.05 (career 54.25)
Parents: Gerald and Mary
Marital status: Single
Family links with cricket: Father and two brothers all play in North Staffs and South Cheshire League
Education: St Joseph's College, Stoke-on-Trent
Off-season: Playing cricket overseas
Overseas tours: England YCs to Australia 1989-90; England A to Bermuda and West Indies 1991-92
Overseas teams played for: East Shirley CC, Christchurch, New Zealand
Cricketers particularly admired: Richard Hadlee, Ian Botham, Kim Barnett, Phil Russell. Alan Hill, Bernie Maher, Alan Warner
Other sports followed: Football (Stoke City and Port Vale) and racing (horses and greyhounds)
Relaxations: Listening to music and socialising after the close of play
Extras: Scored a century as nightwatchman for England U19 in the third match v Pakistan

at Taunton. Took a wicket in first over in first-class cricket v New Zealand at Derby. First played cricket for Betley CC in the North Staffordshire and South Cheshire League. Played Minor Counties cricket for Staffordshire in 1989 and 1990. Played for England A in 1991– his first season of first-class cricket. The Cricket Association Young Player of 1991
Opinions on cricket: 'I feel that county wickets should always be hard and bouncy with a tinge of green, allowing bowlers to keep interest and to encourage batsmen to play shots.'
Best batting: 44 Derbyshire v Nottinghamshire, Derby 1991
Best bowling: 8-53 Derbyshire v Essex, Derby 1991

1991 Season

	M	Inns	NO	Runs	HS	Avge	100s	50s	Ct	St	O	M	Runs	Wkts	Avge	Best	5wI	10wM
Test																		
All First	18	28	8	423	44	21.15	-	-	9	-	494.3	84	1460	57	25.61	8-53	1	1
1-day Int																		
NatWest																		
B&H																		
Refuge	9	5	0	83	30	16.60	-	-	4	-	62	3	291	11	26.45	3-45	-	

Career Performances

	M	Inns	NO	Runs	HS	Avge	100s	50s	Ct	St	Balls	Runs	Wkts	Avge	Best	5wl	10wM
Test																	
All First	20	30	9	432	44	20.57	-	-	9	-	3201	1583	59	26.83	8-53	1	1
1-day Int																	
NatWest																	
B&H																	
Refuge	9	5	0	83	30	16.60	-	-	4	-	372	291	11	26.45	3-45	-	

COTTEY, P. A.   Glamorgan

Name: Phillip Anthony Cottey
Role: Right-hand opening bat, right-arm off-spin bowler, cover fielder
Born: 2 June 1966, Swansea
Height: 5ft 5in **Weight:** 10st 7lbs
County debut: 1986
Nickname: Cotts, Lofty
1000 runs in season: 1
1st-Class 50s scored: 10
1st-Class 100s scored: 3
1st-Class catches: 31
One-Day 50s: 3
Place in batting averages: 173rd av. 23.00 (1990 143rd av. 33.36)
Parents: Bernard and Ruth

Marital status: Engaged to Gail
Family links with cricket: Father
played for Swansea CC
Education: Bishopston Comprehensive
School, Swansea
Qualifications: 9 O-levels
Off-season: Coaching in South Africa
Overseas tours: Glamorgan pre-season
tours to La Manga, Barbados, Trinidad
and Zimbabwe
Overseas teams played for: Penrith,
Sydney 1986-88; Benoni, Johannesburg
1989-90
Cricketers particularly admired: Ian
Botham, Viv Richards
Other sports followed: Soccer, golf, rugby
Relaxations: 'Golf, running,
weight-training, being a lager lout.'
Extras: Left school at 16 to play for

Swansea City FC for three years as a professional. 3 Welsh Youth caps (1 as captain)
Opinions on cricket: 'I still think that 17 four-day games would make for a fairer
Championship.'
Best batting: 156 Glamorgan v Oxford University, The Parks 1990
Best bowling: 1-49 Glamorgan v Warwickshire, Swansea 1990

1991 Season

	M	Inns	NO	Runs	HS	Avge	100s	50s	Ct	St	O	M	Runs	Wkts	Avge	Best	5wI	10wM
Test																		
All First	14	20	7	299	55	23.00	-	1	9	-								
1-day Int																		
NatWest	2	2	1	13	10	13.00	-	-	-	-								
B&H																			
Refuge	7	7	3	233	92 *	58.25	-	1	1	-								

Career Performances

	M	Inns	NO	Runs	HS	Avge	100s	50s	Ct	St	Balls	Runs	Wkts	Avge	Best	5wI	10wM
Test																	
All First	63	101	17	2253	156	26.82	3	12	31	-	114	122	1	122.00	1-49	-	-
1-day Int																	
NatWest	4	4	2	42	27	21.00	-	-	1	-							
B&H	7	7	0	107	68	15.28	-	1	1	-							
Refuge	27	22	5	469	92 *	27.58	-	2	7	-							

COWANS, N. G.   Middlesex

Name: Norman George Cowans
Role: Right-hand bat, right-arm
fast bowler
Born: 17 April 1961, Enfield St Mary,
Jamaica
Height: 6ft 3in **Weight:** 14st 7lbs
Nickname: Flash, George, Seed
County debut: 1980
County cap: 1984
Test debut: 1982-83
Tests: 19
One-Day Internationals: 23
50 wickets in a season: 6
1st-Class 50s scored: 1
1st-Class 5 w. in innings: 23
1st-Class 10 w. in match: 1
1st-Class catches: 59
Place in batting averages: 255th av. 10.33
(1990 261st av. 12.70)
Place in bowling averages: 80th av. 34.09
(1990 38th av. 31.97)

Strike rate: 73.93 (career 49.02)
Parents: Gloria and Ivan
Children: Kimberley, 27 December 1983
Education: Park High Secondary, Stanmore, Middlesex
Qualifications: Qualified coach
Off-season: Working in the City for Whittingdale Holdings Ltd
Overseas tours: England YCs to Australia 1979; England to Australia and New Zealand 1982-83; New Zealand and Pakistan 1983-84; India and Australia 1984-85
England B to Sri Lanka 1985-86
Cricketers particularly admired: Viv Richards, Malcolm Marshall
Other sports followed: Football (Arsenal FC), athletics, boxing
Relaxations: Fishing, photography, travelling, being with friends, listening to reggae and soul music
Extras: Played for England YC. Won athletics championships in sprinting and javelin throwing and was a squash and real tennis professional. Played thirteen Tests for England before being awarded his Middlesex cap
Opinions on cricket: 'The county programme is far too intense, and I think that 17 four-day games would be a much better system for producing quality players.'
Best batting: 66 Middlesex v Surrey, Lord's 1984
Best bowling: 6-31 Middlesex v Leicestershire, Leicester 1985

1991 Season

	M	Inns	NO	Runs	HS	Avge	100s	50s	Ct	St	O	M	Runs	Wkts	Avge	Best	5wI	10wM
Test																		
All First	23	29	11	186	35	10.33	-	-	5	-	542.1	144	1500	44	34.09	4-42	-	-
1-day Int																		
NatWest	2	2	0	10	10	5.00	-	-	1	-	18	1	61	5	12.20	4-51	-	
B&H	3	2	1	5	5	5.00	-	-	1	-	33	2	130	8	16.25	3-39	-	
Refuge	13	5	2	14	5 *	4.66	-	-	-	-	98.5	7	425	18	23.61	6-9	1	

Career Performances

	M	Inns	NO	Runs	HS	Avge	100s	50s	Ct	St	Balls	Runs	Wkts	Avge	Best	5wI	10wM
Test	19	29	7	175	36	7.95	-	-	9	-	3452	2003	51	39.27	6-77	2	-
All First	220	228	61	1531	66	9.16	-	1	59	-	30398	15232	620	24.56	6-31	23	1
1-day Int	23	8	3	13	4 *	2.60	-	-	5	-	1282	913	23	39.69	3-44	-	
NatWest	32	12	2	43	12 *	4.30	-	-	9	-	1864	1018	47	21.66	4-24	-	
B&H	32	15	6	50	12	5.55	-	-	6	-	1861	1027	47	21.85	4-33	-	
Refuge	94	32	12	160	27	8.00	-	-	13	-	3985	2682	102	26.29	6-9	1	

COWDREY, C. S.   Kent

Name: Christopher Stuart Cowdrey
Role: Right-hand bat, right-arm medium bowler
Born: 20 October 1957, Farnborough, Kent
Height: 6ft **Weight:** 14st
Nickname: Cow, Woody
County debut: 1977
County cap: 1979
Benefit: 1989 (£146,287)
Test debut: 1984-85
Tests: 6
One-Day Internationals: 3
1000 runs in a season: 4
1st-Class 50s scored: 57
1st-Class 100s scored: 21
1st-Class 5 w. in innings: 2
1st-Class catches: 290
One-Day 50s: 41
One-Day 100s: 2
Place in batting averages: (1990 104th av. 40.72)
Parents: Michael Colin and Penelope Susan

Wife and date of marriage: Christel, 1 January 1989
Family links with cricket: Grandfather, Stuart Chiesman, on Kent Committee, twelve years as Chairman. Pavilion on Kent's ground at Canterbury named after him. Father played for Kent and England, brother Graham made Kent debut 1984
Education: Wellesley House, Broadstairs; Tonbridge School
Career outside cricket: Director of Ten Tenths Travel. Consultant to Stuart Canvas Products
Overseas tours: Captained England YC to West Indies 1976; England to India and Australia 1984-85; Unofficial English XI to South Africa 1989-90
Cricketers particularly admired: David Gower
Other sports followed: All sports
Extras: Played for Kent 2nd XI at age 15. County vice-captain 1984 and appointed captain in 1985. Captained England for one Test v West Indies in 1988; injury kept him out of next Test and was not selected again. Banned from Test cricket for joining tour to South Africa in 1989-90. Resigned from Kent captaincy at end of 1990 season. David Gower was best man at his wedding. Published autobiography, *Good Enough?*, 1986. Released by Kent at end of 1991 season
Best batting: 159 Kent v Surrey, Canterbury 1985
Best bowling: 5-46 Kent v Hampshire, Canterbury 1986

1991 Season

	M	Inns	NO	Runs	HS	Avge	100s	50s	Ct	St	O	M	Runs	Wkts	Avge	Best	5wI	10wM
Test																		
All First	3	4	0	154	97	38.50	-	1	1	-								
1-day Int																		
NatWest	1	1	0	0	0	0.00	-	-	1	-								
B&H	5	5	1	97	57*	24.25	-	1	4	-	5	1	17	2	8.50	2-17	-	
Refuge	7	6	1	154	45	30.80	-	-	4	-	3	0	37	0	-	-	-	

Career Performances

	M	Inns	NO	Runs	HS	Avge	100s	50s	Ct	St	Balls	Runs	Wkts	Avge	Best	5wI	10wM
Test	6	8	1	101	38	14.42	-	-	5	-	399	309	4	77.25	2-65	-	-
All First	297	451	68	12202	159	31.85	21	57	290	-	14524	7962	200	39.81	5-46	2	-
1-day Int	3	3	1	51	46*	25.50	-	-	-	-	52	55	2	27.50	1-3	-	
NatWest	34	31	6	841	122*	33.64	1	8	14	-	1026	628	22	28.54	4-36	-	
B&H	70	63	10	1574	114	29.69	1	10	27	-	2086	1490	47	31.70	4-14	-	
Refuge	205	185	29	4103	95	26.30	-	23	59	-	4040	3354	117	28.66	5-28	1	

COWDREY, G. R.   Kent

Name: Graham Robert Cowdrey
Role: Right-hand bat, right-arm
medium bowler, slip/cover fielder
Born: 27 June 1964,
Farnborough, Kent
Height: 5ft 10in **Weight:** 14st
Nickname: Van, Cow
County debut: 1984
County cap: 1988
1000 runs in season: 2
1st-Class 50s scored: 26
1st-Class 100s scored: 8
1st-Class catches: 60
One-Day 50s: 10
One-Day 100s: 1
Place in batting averages: 59th av. 39.16
(1990 61st av. 47.75)
Parents: Michael Colin and
Penelope Susan
Marital status: Single

Family links with cricket: Father (M.C.) and brother (C.S.)played for, and captained, Kent and England
Education: Wellesley House, Broadstairs; Tonbridge School; Durham University
Qualifications: 8 O-levels, 3 A-levels, qualified electrician
Off-season: 'Working for Zenith Cricket Company and touring with Fred Rumsey's XI in Barbados.
Overseas tours: Christians in Sport to India 1986 and 1990
Overseas teams played for: Avendale, Cape Town 1983-84; Mossman, Sydney 1985-86; Randwick, Sydney 1986-87
Cricketers particularly admired: Chris Cowdrey, Steve Marsh, John Inverarity, Justin Bairmian
Other sports followed: Horse racing, golf, tennis, soccer – all sports
Relaxations: Reading, theatre, and live music. 'I have seen Van Morrison 95 times in concert. Allergic to pubs.'
Extras: Played for England YC. Made 1000 runs for Kent 2nd XI first season on staff, and broke 2nd XI record with 1300 runs in 26 innings in 1985.
Opinions on cricket: 'Fitness, although very important, is becoming over-hyped within cricket. More time should be spent on technique and a thorough mental approach to the game.'
Best batting: 145 Kent v Essex, Chelmsford 1988
Best bowling: 1-5 Kent v Warwickshire, Edgbaston 1988

1991 Season

	M	Inns	NO	Runs	HS	Avge	100s	50s	Ct	St	O	M	Runs	Wkts	Avge	Best	5wI	10wM
Test																		
All First	22	34	4	1175	114	39.16	3	5	17	-	2	1	6	0	-		-	-	-
1-day Int																		
NatWest	2	2	1	25	25 *	25.00	-	-	-	-	4	0	19	0	-		-	-
B&H	5	5	1	111	70 *	27.75	-	1	1	-								
Refuge	15	14	0	327	80	23.35	-	2	9	-								

Career Performances

	M	Inns	NO	Runs	HS	Avge	100s	50s	Ct	St	Balls	Runs	Wkts	Avge	Best	5wI	10wM
Test																	
All First	103	162	21	4718	145	33.46	8	26	60	-	799	536	9	59.55	1-5	-	-
1-day Int																	
NatWest	12	9	3	173	37	28.83	-	-	1	-	267	126	6	21.00	2-19	-	
B&H	26	23	3	585	70 *	29.25	-	5	10	-	112	62	2	31.00	1-8	-	
Refuge	79	73	12	1531	102 *	25.09	1	5	28	-	576	441	21	21.00	4-15	-	

COX, R. M. F.   Hampshire

Name: Rupert Michael Fiennes Cox
Role: Left-hand bat, off-break bowler
Born: 20 August 1967, Guildford
Height: 5ft 8in **Weight:** 11st 5lbs
Nickname: Coxy, Ucca and MC
County debut: 1990
1st-Class 100s scored: 1
1st-Class catches: 4
Parents: Mike and Jo
Marital status: Single
Family links with cricket: Father
played for MCC and Hampshire Hogs
Education: Cheam Prep School and
Bradfield College
Qualifications: 8 O-levels, 2 A-levels
Career outside cricket: School sports
master and 'a minor dabble in sports
journalism'
Off-season: Playing and coaching abroad
Cricketers particularly admired: Geoffrey Boycott, Robin Smith and Ian Turner (for his
placid temperament)
Other sports followed: Golf and football

Injuries: Ankle ligament injury
Relaxations: 'Taking life gently with friends – and being happy'
Extras: Scored century in second first-class match
Opinions on cricket: 'Too much cricket is being played which makes it hard to enjoy all the cricket days of summer – but, more important, in mid-summer it is often impossible to spend any length of time working on your technique.'
Best batting: 104* Hampshire v Worcestershire, Worcester 1990

1991 Season

	M	Inns	NO	Runs	HS	Avge	100s	50s	Ct	St	O	M	Runs	Wkts	Avge	Best	5wI	10wM
Test																		
All First	2	2	0	41	26	20.50	-	-	1	-								
1-day Int																		
NatWest																		
B&H																		
Refuge	2	2	0	15	13	7.50	-	-	1	-								

Career Performances

	M	Inns	NO	Runs	HS	Avge	100s	50s	Ct	St	Balls	Runs	Wkts	Avge	Best	5wI	10wM
Test																	
All First	6	9	2	261	104 *	37.28	1	-	4	-	6	1	0	-	-	-	-
1-day Int																	
NatWest																	
B&H																	
Refuge	3	3	1	17	13	8.50	-	-	1	-							

55. Who has taken 100 first-class wickets in a season most times, and how many times has he done it?

56. Whose recent autobiography is entitled *The Alderman's Tale*?

CRAWLEY, J. P. — Lancashire

Name: John Paul Crawley
Role: Right-hand bat, occasional wicket-keeper
Born: 21 September 1971, Malden, Essex
Height: 6ft 1in **Weight:** 13st
Nickname: Creeps, Jonty, Flid
County debut: 1990
1st-Class 50s scored: 9
1st-Class 50s scored: 1
1st-Class catches: 14
Place in batting averages: 33rd av. 47.16
Parents: Frank and Jean
Marital status: Single
Family links with cricket: Father played in Manchester Association; brother Mark played for Lancashire before moving to Notts; other brother Peter plays for Warrington and Scottish Universities; godfather umpires in Manchester Association
Education: Manchester Grammar School and Trinity College, Cambridge
Qualifications: 10 O-levels, 3 A-levels, 2 S-levels
Off-season: At University
Overseas tours: England U19 to Australia 1989-90; New Zealand 1990-91
Cricketers particularly admired: Michael Atherton, Neil Fairbrother, Graeme Hick, Graham Gooch, Robin Smith, Allan Lamb
Other sports followed: Soccer (Man Utd), golf
Relaxations: 'Golf, soccer, squash, listening to music, any sports really.'
Extras: Captained England U19 to New Zealand 1990-91 and played for England U19 in three home series v New Zealand 1989, Pakistan 1990 and Australia (as captain) 1991
Opinions on cricket: 'Tea-break not long enough; cricket is not commercial enough; not enough money in cricket; there is too much played at a high level.'
Best batting: 130 Lancashire v Surrey, Old Trafford 1991

1991 Season

	M	Inns	NO	Runs	HS	Avge	100s	50s	Ct	St	O	M	Runs	Wkts	Avge	Best	5wI	10wM
Test																		
All First	12	20	2	849	130	47.16	1	8	13	-	2	0	14	0	-	-	-	-
1-day Int																		
NatWest																			
B&H	4	4	0	58	40	14.50	-	-	1	-								
Refuge																			

Career Performances

	M	Inns	NO	Runs	HS	Avge	100s	50s	Ct	St	Balls	Runs	Wkts	Avge	Best	5wI	10wM
Test																	
All First	15	23	3	952	130	47.60	1	9	14	-	12	14	0	-	-	-	-
1-day Int																	
NatWest																	
B&H	4	4	0	58	40	14.50	-	-	1	-							
Refuge																	

CRAWLEY, M. A.   Nottinghamshire

Name: Mark Andrew Crawley
Role: Right-hand bat, right-arm medium bowler, slip fielder
Born: 16 December 1967, Newton-le-Willows
Height: 6ft 3½in **Weight:** 13st 8lbs
Nickname: Creeps, Flat-cap-whippet, Perch
County debut: 1990 (Lancashire), 1991 (Nottinghamshire)
1st-Class 50s scored: 8
1st-Class 50s scored: 4
1st-Class catches: 31
Place in batting averages: 115th av. 30.22
Place in bowling averages: 120th av. 42.09
Strike rate: 96.45 (career 104.81)
Parents: Frank and Jean
Wife and date of marriage: Natasha, 27 December 1991
Family links with cricket: Father and uncle both excellent league players; brother John plays for Lancashire; other brother Peter plays for Warrington CC, Cheshire and Scottish Universities
Education: Manchester Grammar School and Oxford University
Qualifications: 10 O-levels, 3 A-levels, BA (Hons) in Chemistry, Special Diploma in Social Studies
Off-season: Working in Nottingham
Overseas tours: North of England U19 to Bermuda 1985; Young England to Sri Lanka 1987; Oxbridge to Holland 1987
Overseas teams played for: University of New South Wales, Sydney 1990-91

Cricketers particularly admired: Dennis Lillee, Jeff Thomson, David Gower, Jim Robson
Other sports followed: Soccer (Man Utd), golf, American football, rugby
Injuries: Broken finger which had to be pinned – missed 6 weeks
Relaxations: Soccer, golf, squash and playing most sports. Reading, crosswords
Extras: Third Notts player to score a century on his first-class debut
Opinions on cricket: 'Four-day cricket is becoming a must to prevent contrived results. The ball and pitches were just about right in 1991 for a Championship of 17 four-day games.'
Best batting: 140 Oxford University v Cambridge University, Lord's 1987
Best Bowling 6-96 Oxford University v Glamorgan, The Parks 1990

1991 Season

	M	Inns	NO	Runs	HS	Avge	100s	50s	Ct	St	O	M	Runs	Wkts	Avge	Best	5wI	10wM
Test																		
All First	11	13	4	272	112	30.22	1	-	14	-	176.5	53	463	11	42.09	3-21	-	-
1-day Int																		
NatWest	2	2	2	109	74 *	-	-	1	-	-	13	1	29	4	7.25	4-26	-	
B&H	3	3	1	74	58	37.00	-	1	-	-	17	0	82	1	82.00	1-44	-	
Refuge	11	8	2	121	47 *	20.16	-	-	3	-	46	1	232	8	29.00	2-13	-	

Career Performances

	M	Inns	NO	Runs	HS	Avge	100s	50s	Ct	St	Balls	Runs	Wkts	Avge	Best	5wI	10wM
Test																	
All First	37	50	10	1603	140	40.07	4	8	31	-	3983	2035	38	53.55	6-92	1	-
1-day Int																	
NatWest	2	2	2	109	74 *	-	-	1	-	-	78	29	4	7.25	4-26	-	
B&H	14	13	2	268	58	24.36	-	2	4	-	728	436	7	62.28	2-72	-	
Refuge	11	8	2	121	47 *	20.16	-	-	3	-	276	232	8	29.00	2-13	-	

CROFT, R. D. B. Glamorgan

Name: Robert Damien Bale Croft
Role: Right-hand bat, off-spinner
Born: 25 May 1970, Swansea
Height: 5ft 11in **Weight:** 11st 5lbs
Nickname: Crofty
County debut: 1989
1st-Class 50s scored: 5
1st-Class 5 w. in innings: 1
1st-Class catches: 18
Place in batting averages: 226th av. 15.00 (1990 80th av. 44.80)

Place in bowling averages: 136th
av. 50.78 (1990 121st av. 47.67)
Strike rate: 111.21 (career 106.58)
Parents: Malcolm and Susan
Family links with cricket: Father
played local league cricket
Education: St John Lloyd
Comprehensive; West Glamorgan Institute
of Higher Education
Qualifications: 9 O-levels; OND
Business Studies; HND Business
Studies; NCA senior coaching certificate
Off-season: Touring with England A
Overseas tours: England A to Bermuda
and West Indies 1991-92
Other sports followed: Rugby, soccer
Relaxations: Shooting, fishing
Extras: Captained England South to
victory in International Youth

Tournament 1989; also voted Player of the Tournament
Best batting: 91* Glamorgan v Worcestershire, Abergavenny 1990
Best bowling: 5-62 Glamorgan v Warwickshire, Swansea 1991

1991 Season

	M	Inns	NO	Runs	HS	Avge	100s	50s	Ct	St	O	M	Runs	Wkts	Avge	Best	5wI	10wM
Test																		
All First	25	27	4	345	50	15.00	-	1	12	-	704.2	168	1930	38	50.78	5-62	1	-
1-day Int																		
NatWest	2	1	0	13	13	13.00	-	-	-	-	17	0	46	2	23.00	2-28	-	
B&H	1	1	0	0	0	0.00	-	-	-	-	9	0	49	2	24.50	2-49	-	
Refuge	10	6	0	35	19	5.83	-	-	3	-	69	2	333	10	33.30	2-30	-	

Career Performances

	M	Inns	NO	Runs	HS	Avge	100s	50s	Ct	St	Balls	Runs	Wkts	Avge	Best	5wI	10wM
Test																	
All First	47	63	17	1213	91 *	26.37	-	5	18	-	7461	3796	70	54.22	5-62	1	-
1-day Int																	
NatWest	3	2	0	39	26	19.50	-	-	-	-	162	90	2	45.00	2-28	-	
B&H	1	1	0	0	0	0.00	-	-	-	-	54	49	2	24.50	2-49	-	
Refuge	14	10	1	88	31	9.77	-	-	5	-	588	492	11	44.72	2-30	-	

CURRAN, K. M.   Northamptonshire

Name: Kevin Malcolm Curran
Role: Right-hand bat, right-arm
fast-medium bowler
Born: 7 September 1959,
Rusape, Rhodesia
Height: 6ft 2in **Weight:** 14st
Nickname: KC
County debut: 1985 (Gloucs)
1991 (Northamptonshire)
County cap: 1985 (Gloucs)
One-Day Internationals: 11
1000 runs in a season: 5
50 wickets in a season: 3
1st-Class 50s scored: 37
1st-Class 100s scored: 18
1st-Class 5 w. in innings: 11
1st-Class 10 w. in match: 4
1st-Class catches: 108
One-Day 50s: 21

Place in batting averages: 85th av. 34.50 (1990 47th av. 50.68)
Place in bowling averages: 22nd av. 25.08 (1990 32nd av. 30.64)
Strike rate: 54.54 (career 49.20)
Parents: Kevin and Sylvia
Marital status: Single
Family links with cricket: Father played for Rhodesia 1947-54. Cousin Patrick Curran
played for Rhodesia 1975
Education: Marandellas High School, Zimbabwe
Qualifications: 6 O-levels, 2 M-levels
Career outside cricket: Tobacco buyer/farmer
Off-season: Playing for Natal
Overseas tours: Zimbabwe to Sri Lanka 1982 and 1984; England 1982 and for World Cup
1983; Pakistan and India for World Cup 1987
Overseas teams played for: Zimbabwe and Natal 1988-90
Other sports followed: Rugby Union
Relaxations: 'Game fishing, especially along the North Natal coast, the Mozambique
coast, and Magaruque Island.'
Extras: First player to take a Sunday League hat-trick, and score a 50 in the same match,
Gloucestershire v Warwickshire, Edgbaston 1989. Released by Gloucestershire at end of
1990 after he had completed the season's double of 1000 runs and 50 wickets. Chose to
join Northamptonshire for the 1991 season after he had been approached by several
counties
Opinions on cricket: 'Four-day cricket would be good idea for the 1992 Championship.'

Best batting: 144* Gloucestershire v Sussex, Bristol 1990
Best bowling: 7-54 Natal v Transvaal, Johannesburg 1988-89

1991 Season

	M	Inns	NO	Runs	HS	Avge	100s	50s	Ct	St	O	M	Runs	Wkts	Avge	Best	5wI	10wM
Test																		
All First	21	31	7	828	89 *	34.50	-	6	11	-	436.2	110	1204	48	25.08	5-60	1	-
1-day Int																		
NatWest	4	3	2	77	38	77.00	-	-	-	-	32	3	140	1	140.00	1-61	-	
B&H	2	2	0	26	26	13.00	-	-	-	-	6	0	36	0	-	-	-	
Refuge	13	12	4	236	61 *	29.50	-	1	2	-	77.1	2	384	16	24.00	3-24	-	

Career Performances

	M	Inns	NO	Runs	HS	Avge	100s	50s	Ct	St	Balls	Runs	Wkts	Avge	Best	5wI	10wM
Test																	
All First	189	290	52	8711	144 *	36.60	18	37	108	-	17665	9213	359	25.66	7-47	11	4
1-day Int	11	11	0	287	73	26.09	-	2	1	-	506	398	9	44.22	3-65	-	
NatWest	21	19	4	448	58 *	29.86	-	2	3	-	965	545	15	36.33	4-34	-	
B&H	28	24	6	567	57	31.50	-	3	5	-	1291	813	35	23.22	4-41	-	
Refuge	100	97	20	2381	92	30.92	-	14	18	-	2894	2294	97	23.64	5-15	1	

CURTIS, T. S.   Worcestershire

Name: Timothy Stephen Curtis
Role: Right-hand bat, leg-break bowler,
county captain
Born: 15 January 1960, Chislehurst, Kent
Height: 5ft 11in **Weight:** 12st 5lbs
Nickname: TC, Duracell, Professor
County debut: 1979
County cap: 1984
Test debut: 1988
Tests: 5
1000 runs in a season: 8
1st-Class 50s scored: 75
1st-Class 100s: 23
1st-Class 200s: 1
1st-Class catches: 124
One-Day 50s: 54
One-Day 100s: 4
Place in batting averages: 41st av. 44.67
(1990 32nd av. 55.83)

Parents: Bruce and Betty
Wife and date of marriage: Philippa, 21 September 1985
Children: Jennifer May, 9 February 1991
Family links with cricket: Father played good club cricket in Bristol and Stafford
Education: The Royal Grammar School, Worcester; Durham University; Cambridge University
Qualifications: 12 O-levels, 4 A-levels, BA (Hons) in English, PCGE in English and Games
Off-season: Teaching
Overseas tours: NCA U19 tour of Canada 1979
Other sports followed: Rugby, tennis, squash, golf
Injuries: 'Innumerable bruises!'
Extras: Captained Durham University to UAU Championship. Chairman of the Cricketers' Association. Appointed county captain for 1992 season
Opinions on cricket: '17 four-day matches would seem to be the best combination for Championship cricket, with one-day competitions taking place at the weekends. This would reduce the amount of cricket played and place a greater emphasis on the quality.'
Best batting: 248 Worcestershire v Somerset, Taunton 1991
Best bowling: 2-17 Worcestershire v Oxford University, The Parks 1991

1991 Season

	M	Inns	NO	Runs	HS	Avge	100s	50s	Ct	St	O	M	Runs	Wkts	Avge	Best	5wI	10wM
Test																		
All First	25	40	3	1653	248	44.67	3	9	15	-	28	3	112	2	56.00	2-17	-	-
1-day Int																		
NatWest	2	1	0	34	34	34.00	-	-	-	-								
B&H	7	7	0	163	53	23.28	-	1	3	-								
Refuge	18	17	4	816	88 *	62.76	-	9	10	-								

Career Performances

	M	Inns	NO	Runs	HS	Avge	100s	50s	Ct	St	Balls	Runs	Wkts	Avge	Best	5wI	10wM
Test	5	9	0	140	41	15.55	-	-	3	-	18	7	0	-	-	-	-
All First	226	382	49	13482	248	40.48	23	75	124	-	782	541	9	60.11	2-17	-	-
1-day Int																	
NatWest	27	26	3	1158	120	50.34	2	8	7	-	24	15	2	7.50	1-6	-	
B&H	41	41	3	1178	97	31.00	-	10	7	-	2	4	0	-	-	-	
Refuge	123	120	19	4414	124	43.70	2	36	36	-							

57. For which South African team does Kepler Wessels play?

DALE, A.   Glamorgan

Name: Adrian Dale
Role: Right-hand bat, right-arm medium bowler
Born: 24 October 1968, Germiston, South Africa
Height: 6ft **Weight:** 11st 8lbs
Nickname: Arthur, Emma
County debut: 1989
1st-Class 50s scored: 6
1st-Class 100s scored: 1
1st-Class catches: 15
One-Day 50s: 3
Place in batting averages: 51st av. 41.38 (1990 245th av. 16.35)
Parents: John and Maureen
Marital status: Single
Family links with cricket: Father played for Glamorgan 2nd XI and Chepstow CC

Education: Pembroke Primary, Chepstow Comprehensive and Swansea University
Qualifications: 9 O-levels, 3 A-levels, BA (Hons) in Economics
Off-season: Playing and coaching in New Zealand
Overseas tours: Welsh Schools to Australia 1986-87; Combined Universities to Barbados 1989
Overseas teams played for: Bionics, Zimbabwe 1990-91
Cricketers particularly admired: Ian Botham, Michael Holding
Other sports followed: Football (Arsenal FC) and athletics
Injuries: Slight muscle injury in lower back – missed two weeks
Relaxations: 'Eating out, crosswords, bottles of wine, videos, sleeping.'
Extras: Played in successful Combined Universities sides of 1989 and 1990. Only batsman to score two half-centuries against the West Indies tourists in the same match in 1991. Took a wicket with his first delivery at Lord's.
Opinions on cricket: 'Too much cricket, along with travelling, makes it difficult to prepare mentally and physically for each game. As there is so little time off, the only place to iron out faults is "in the middle" which is surely the worst place to do so.'
Best batting: 140 Glamorgan v Gloucestershire, Abergavenny 1991
Best bowling: 3-21 Glamorgan v Indians, Swansea 1990

---

58. Who captained South Africa in their first official international game in twenty-one years in November 1991?

1991 Season

	M	Inns	NO	Runs	HS	Avge	100s	50s	Ct	St	O	M	Runs	Wkts	Avge	Best	5wI	10wM
Test																		
All First	17	26	5	869	140	41.38	1	5	8	-	120.1	24	436	9	48.44	2-33	-	-
1-day Int																		
NatWest	3	2	0	101	86	50.50	-	1	2	-	30	2	115	1	115.00	1-42	-	
B&H	1	1	0	19	19	19.00	-	-	-	-	4	0	30	0	-	-	-	
Refuge	14	11	2	213	56	23.66	-	1	6	-	72	1	430	13	33.07	3-44	-	

Career Performances

	M	Inns	NO	Runs	HS	Avge	100s	50s	Ct	St	Balls	Runs	Wkts	Avge	Best	5wI	10wM
Test																	
All First	31	50	7	1350	140	31.39	2	6	15	-	1495	903	18	50.16	3-21	-	-
1-day Int																	
NatWest	7	5	1	118	86	29.50	-	1	2	-	352	227	5	45.40	2-32	-	
B&H	10	9	1	124	40	15.50	-	-	2	-	432	291	9	32.33	3-24	-	
Refuge	32	25	5	465	67 *	23.25	-	2	10	-	984	970	27	35.92	3-35	-	

DALEY, J.A. Durham

Name: James Arthur Daley
Role: Right-hand bat
Born: 24 September 1973, Sunderland
Height: 5ft 10in **Weight:** 11st 10lbs
Parents: William and Christine
Marital status: Single
Education: Hetton Comprehensive
Qualifications: 4 GCSEs
Off-season: Overseas
Overseas tours: Durham to Zimbabwe, 1991-92
Cricketers particularly admired: 'Robin Smith and Mark Ramprakash for their cool temperament and remarkable ability.'
Other sports followed: Most sports
Relaxations: Watching TV
Extras: Scored three centuries in 1991 for MCC Young Cricketers at Lord's.
Opinions on cricket: 'Cricket is a great game for travelling and meeting people.'

Career performances – no appearance in first-class cricket or one-day competition

DAVIES, M.   Gloucestershire

Name: Mark Davies
Role: Right-hand bat, slow left-arm
bowler
Born: 18 April 1969, Neath
Height: 5ft 8in **Weight:** 11st 2lb
Nickname: Sparky, Billy
County debut: 1990 (Glamorgan)
Parents: Peter Holbrook and Dorothy
Marital status: Single
Family links with cricket: Brother is club
opening bat and has represented the
South Wales Cricket Association
Education: Cwrt Sart Comprehensive;
Neath Tertiary College
Qualifications: 6 O-levels; BTec ONC in
Science; NCA 1st & 2nd level coaching
awards
Career outside cricket: Production
technician in biotechnology firm
Overseas tours: Sponsored by The Cricketers' Club of London to tour Barbados with Fred
Rumsey's XI
Overseas teams played for: Newcastle City, New South Wales 1990-91
Cricketers particularly admired: Malcolm Marshall, Bishen Bedi, John Steele
Other sports followed: All contact sport, especially rigby union
Injuries: Split webbing on right hand
Relaxations: Indian food, 'picking up other players' bats'
Extras: Was on the MCC goundstaff in 1987. Glamorgan 2nd XI Player of the Year 1991.
Released by Glamorgan at the end of the 1991 season and signed to play for Gloucestershire
in 1992, on a two-year contract
Best batting: 5* Glamorgan v Oxford University, The Parks 1990

1991 Season – no first team appearance for Glamorgan

Career Performances

	M	Inns	NO	Runs	HS	Avge	100s	50s	Ct	St	Balls	Runs	Wkts	Avge	Best	5wI	10wM
Test																	
All First	1	1	1	5	5 *	-	-	-	-	-	48	16	0	-		-	-
1-day Int																	
NatWest																	
B&H																	
Refuge																	

DAVIS, R. P. Kent

Name: Richard Peter Davis
Role: Right-hand bat, slow left-arm bowler
Born: 18 March 1966, Westbook, Margate
Height: 6ft 4in **Weight:** 14st
Nickname: Dicky
County debut: 1986
County cap: 1990
50 wickets in season: 1
1st-Class 50s scored: 3
1st-Class 5 w. in innings: 6
1st-Class 10 w. in match: 1
1st-Class catches: 60
Place in batting averages: 206th av. 17.40 (1990 236th av. 17.37)
Place in bowling averages: 116th av. 41.37 (1990 88th av. 38.95)
Strike rate: 83.24 (career 84.87)
Parents: Brian and Sylvia
Wife and date of marriage: Samantha Jane, 3 March 1990
Family links with cricket: Father played club cricket and is an NCA coach; father-in-law Colin Tomlin helps with England's fitness training
Education: King Ethelbert's School, Birchington; Thanet Technical College, Broadstairs
Qualifications: 8 CSEs; NCA coaching certificate
Career outside cricket: Carpentry, general labouring, coaching
Off-season: 'Coaching and working at my game.'
Overseas tours: Kent Schools to Canada 1983
Overseas teams played for: Hutt Districts, New Zealand 1986-88
Cricketers particularly admired: Derek Underwood, Graham Gooch; and Geoff Arnold and Norman Gifford for their coaching achievements
Other sports followed: Football, badminton, tennis, local athletics
Relaxations: 'Spending time with my wife, Sam, going to the pictures and eating out.'
Opinions on cricket: 'I would like to see the Championship consist of 17 four-day games, played on good wickets, and better practice facilities at all grounds.'
Best batting: 67 Kent v Hampshire, Southampton 1989
Best bowling: 6-40 Kent v Cambridge University, Fenner's 1990

---

59. Which three men have captained Worcestershire for ten seasons?

1991 Season

	M	Inns	NO	Runs	HS	Avge	100s	50s	Ct	St	O	M	Runs	Wkts	Avge	Best	5wI	10wM
Test																		
All First	20	26	4	383	44	17.40	-	-	23	-	513.2	133	1531	37	41.37	4-81	-	-
1-day Int																		
NatWest	2	1	0	2	2	2.00	-	-	1	-	20	4	56	2	28.00	1-22	-	
B&H	1	1	0	1	1	1.00	-	-	-	-	11	1	62	0	-	-	-	
Refuge	14	11	5	108	40 *	18.00	-	-	7	-	105	5	485	15	32.33	3-33	-	

Career Performances

	M	Inns	NO	Runs	HS	Avge	100s	50s	Ct	St	Balls	Runs	Wkts	Avge	Best	5wI	10wM
Test																	
All First	92	112	26	1308	67	15.20	-	3	83	-	17484	8401	206	40.78	6-40	6	1
1-day Int																	
NatWest	9	4	1	15	12	5.00	-	-	5	-	501	243	10	24.30	3-19	-	
B&H	9	3	2	1	1	1.00	-	-	1	-	511	383	6	63.83	2-33	-	
Refuge	62	26	10	166	40 *	10.37	-	-	22	-	2330	1779	66	26.95	5-52	1	

DAWSON, R.I.   Gloucestershire

Name: Robert Ian Dawson
Role: Right-hand bat, right-arm medium bowler
Born: 29 March 1970, Exmouth, Devon
Height: 5ft 11in **Weight:** 12st
Nickname: Daws
County debut: 1991 (one-day)
Parents: Barry and Shirley
Marital status: Single
Family links with cricket: Father and brother both played club cricket
Education: Millfield School; Newcastle Polytechnic
Qualifications: 8 O-levels, 3 A-levels
Cricketers particularly admired: Ian Botham, David Gower, Viv Richards
Other sports folowed: Football and rugby
Relaxations: Watching most sports and 'a night out with my mates'
Extras: His NatWest appearances have all been for Devon , for whom he has played since 1988. He made his only appearances for Gloucestershire in the Seeboard Trophy matches at Hove in 1991

	M	Inns	NO	Runs	HS	Avge	100s	50s	Ct	St	O	M	Runs	Wkts	Avge	Best	5wI	10wM
Test																		
All First																		
1-day Int																		
NatWest	1	1	0	13	13	13.00	-	-	-	-								
B&H																		
Refuge																		

Career Performances

	M	Inns	NO	Runs	HS	Avge	100s	50s	Ct	St	Balls	Runs	Wkts	Avge	Best	5wI	10wM
Test																	
All First																	
1-day Int																	
NatWest	2	2	0	13	13	6.50	-	-	-	-	24	37	1	37.00	1-37	-	
B&H																	
Refuge																	

DEFREITAS, P. A. J.   Lancashire

Name: Phillip Anthony Jason DeFreitas
Role: Right-hand bat, right-arm
fast bowler
Born: 18 February 1966, Scotts Head,
Dominica
Height: 6ft **Weight:** 13st 7lbs
Nickname: Daffy, Lunchy
County debut: 1985 (Leics), 1989 (Lancs)
County cap: 1986 (Leics), 1989 (Lancs)
Test debut: 1986-87
Tests: 26
One-Day Internationals: 62
50 wickets in a season: 5
1st-Class 50s scored: 19
1st-Class 100s scored: 4
1st-Class 5 w. in innings: 26
1st-Class 10 w. in match: 2
1st-Class catches: 42
One-Day 50s: 3

Place in batting averages: 190th av. 20.79 (1990 112th av. 38.82)
Place in bowling averages: 18th av. 24.38 (1990 63rd av. 36.00)
Strike rate: 54.01 (career 55.51)

Parents: Sybil and Martin
Wife and date of marriage: Nicola, 10 December 1990
Children: Alexandra Elizabeth Jane, 5 August 1991
Family links with cricket: Father played in the Windward Islands. All six brothers play
Education: Willesden High School
Qualifications: 2 O-levels
Career outside cricket: 'Full-time dad!'
Off-season: Touring with England
Overseas tours: Young England to West Indies 1985; England to Australia 1986-87; Pakistan, Australia and New Zealand 1987-88; India and West Indies 1989-90; Australia 1990-91; New Zealand 1991-92
Overseas teams played for: Port Adelaide, South Australia 1985; Mossman, Sydney 1988
Cricketers particularly admired: Ian Botham, Graham Gooch, Geoff Boycott, Mike Gatting
Other sports followed: Football (Manchester City) and rugby league (Warrington)
Injuries: Broken big toe, sinusitis
Relaxations: 'Golf, gardening, visiting stately homes, spending spare time with wife and daughter Alexandra.'
Extras: Left Leicestershire and joined Lancashire at end of 1988 season. Originally agreed to join unofficial English tour of South Africa 1989-90, but withdrew under pressure. Man of the match in 1990 NatWest Trophy final.
Opinions on cricket: 'Pyjama cricket more interesting for children on a Sunday. New rule allowing only one bouncer per over not a good idea.'
Best batting: 113 Leicestershire v Nottinghamshire, Worksop 1988
Best bowling: 7-21 Lancashire v Middlesex, Lord's 1989

1991 Season

	M	Inns	NO	Runs	HS	Avge	100s	50s	Ct	St	O	M	Runs	Wkts	Avge	Best	5wI	10wM
Test	6	9	1	135	55 *	16.87	-	1	1	-	233.5	71	572	30	19.06	7-70	1	-
All First	18	26	2	499	60	20.79	-	3	2	-	657.1	173	1780	73	24.38	7-70	3	-
1-day Int	3	1	0	8	8	8.00	-	-	4	-	33	7	98	3	32.66	2-26	-	
NatWest	2	2	1	17	11	17.00	-	-	1	-	22	5	62	0	-	-	-	
B&H	7	2	0	31	19	15.50	-	-	5	-	73.1	13	235	14	16.78	4-15	-	
Refuge	11	9	3	105	41 *	17.50	-	-	1	-	84	5	369	12	30.75	3-27	-	

Career Performances

	M	Inns	NO	Runs	HS	Avge	100s	50s	Ct	St	Balls	Runs	Wkts	Avge	Best	5wI	10wM
Test	26	40	3	513	55 *	13.86	-	1	6	-	5634	2603	78	33.37	7-70	3	-
All First	149	206	22	3961	113	21.52	4	19	42	-	27589	13384	497	26.93	7-21	26	2
1-day Int	62	44	17	473	49 *	17.51	-	-	16	-	3533	2303	71	32.43	4-35	-	
NatWest	18	12	3	186	69	20.66	-	1	1	-	1118	551	29	19.00	5-13	3	
B&H	31	19	4	346	75 *	23.06	-	2	8	-	1848	1016	49	20.73	4-13	-	
Refuge	83	59	11	626	41 *	13.04	-	-	11	-	3271	2545	97	26.23	4-20	-	

DE LA PENA, J. M.   Gloucestershire

Name: Jason Michael de la Pena
Role: Right-hand bat, right-arm
fast-medium bowler, fine-leg/mid-off or
mid-on
Born: 16 September 1972, London
Height: 6ft 4in **Weight:** 13st
Nickname: Ronnie, Chewy, Ping-pong,
Stingray
County debut: 1991
1st-Class catches: 0
Parents: Michael and Jacqueline
Marital status: Single
Education: Lambrook Prep School, Ascot;
Stowe School; Cheltenham Burnside
Sixth Form College
Qualifications: 9 GCSEs, 2 A-levels
Off-season: Playing cricket in Tasmania
Overseas tours: Gloucestershire to
Namibia 1990; Kenya 1991

Cricketers particularly admired: Michael Holding, Andy Roberts, Jack Russell, Imran
Khan, Mike 'Pasty' Harris, Dennis Lillee, John Hampshire
Other sports followed: Golf, tennis, surfing – all ball sports
Injuries: Sore shins, needing shin splints
Relaxations: 'Meeting non-cricket-playing friends in the pub after a week of intense
cricket. Travelling to far-off places, staying at home with girlfriend Emma.'
Extras: Member of the England U19 squad against Australia, 1991. Played squash and
hockey for Gloucestershire U16
Opinions on cricket: 'Bigger seams on balls, uncovered wickets and better standard of
umpiring at 2nd XI level.'
Best batting: 1* Gloucestershire v Essex, Bristol 1991
Best bowling: 2-69 Gloucestershire v Leicestershire, Hinckley 1991

1991 Season

	M	Inns	NO	Runs	HS	Avge	100s	50s	Ct	St	O	M	Runs	Wkts	Avge	Best	5wl	10wM
Test																		
All First	2	2	1	1	1 *	1.00	-	-	-	-	25	0	138	3	46.00	2-69	-	-
1-day Int																		
NatWest																		
B&H																		
Refuge																		

Career Performances

	M	Inns	NO	Runs	HS	Avge	100s	50s	Ct	St	Balls	Runs	Wkts	Avge	Best	5wI	10wM
Test																	
All First	2	2	1	1	1 *	1.00	-	-	-	-	150	138	3	46.00	2-69	-	-
1-day Int																	
NatWest																	
B&H																	
Refuge																	

DENNIS, S. J.   Glamorgan

Name: Simon John Dennis
Role: Right-hand bat, left-arm
fast-medium bowler
Born: 18 October 1960, Scarborough
Height: 6ft 1in **Weight:** 14st
Nickname: Donkey
County debut: 1980 (Yorks),
1989 (Glamorgan)
County cap: 1983 (Yorks)
50 wickets in a season: 1
1st-Class 50s scored: 1
1st-Class 5 w. in innings: 7
1st-Class catches: 26
One-Day 50s: 1
Place in bowling averages: (1990 125th
av. 48.68)
Strike rate: (career 63.14)
Parents: Margaret and Geoff
Marital status: Single
Family links with cricket: Father captained Scarborough for many years.
Uncle, Frank Dennis, played for Yorkshire 1928-33. Uncle, Sir Leonard Hutton, played for Yorkshire and England
Education: Northstead County Primary School; Scarborough College
Qualifications: 7 O-levels, 1 A-level, City and Guilds Programming in COBOL
Career outside cricket: Joined Retail Computer Solutions
Off-season: Retired from first-class cricket, working on the Development side of Retail Computer Solutions
Overseas tours: ESCA to India 1978-79; England YC to Australia 1980
Overseas teams played for: Orange Free State 1982-83
Cricketers particularly admired: Dennis Lillee, John Lever
Relaxations: Car maintenance, wine- and beer-making. Photography and real ale. Home

147

computer, video games. 'Also terrible snooker player.'
Extras: Sunil Gavaskar was first first-class wicket. Left Yorkshire at end of 1988 season
Opinions on cricket: 'I think that to bring money into the game we should play a 60-over league on Saturdays, a 40-over league on Sundays and 17 four-day games in the week. I would also like to see more effort put into finding players winter work with a view to a future career.'
Best batting: 53* Yorkshire v Nottinghamshire, Trent Bridge 1984
Best bowling: 5-35 Yorkshire v Somerset, Sheffield 1981

1991 Season

	M	Inns	NO	Runs	HS	Avge	100s	50s	Ct	St	O	M	Runs	Wkts	Avge	Best	5wI	10wM
Test																		
All First	3	2	0	3	3	1.50	-	-	-	-	36.3	9	98	3	32.66	3-31	-	-
1-day Int																		
NatWest																			
B&H	3	2	0	55	50	27.50	-	1	-	-	33	3	119	0	-		-	-
Refuge	3	2	0	9	6	4.50	-	-	2	-	18	0	95	1	95.00	1-36	-

Career Performances

	M	Inns	NO	Runs	HS	Avge	100s	50s	Ct	St	Balls	Runs	Wkts	Avge	Best	5wI	10wM
Test																	
All First	104	100	29	669	53 *	9.42	-	1	26	-	16044	8426	254	33.17	5-35	7	-
1-day Int																	
NatWest	10	3	0	15	14	5.00	-	-	2	-	536	357	6	59.50	2-45	-
B&H	19	10	1	71	50	7.88	-	1	1	-	1086	645	11	58.63	3-41	-
Refuge	72	34	14	150	16 *	7.50	-	-	14	-	2813	2269	45	50.42	3-19	-

DERRICK, J.   Glamorgan

Name: John Derrick
Role: Right-hand bat, right-arm medium bowler
Born: 15 January 1963, Aberdare
Height: 6ft 1in **Weight:** 14st 5lbs
Nickname: JD, Bo
County debut: 1983
County cap: 1988
1st-Class 50s: 11
1st-Class 5 w. in innings: 2
1st-Class catches: 40
Strike rate: (career 73.39)
Parents: John Raymond and Megan Irene
Wife and date of marriage: Anne Irene, 20 April 1985

Children: Liam Kyle, 3 April 1987
Family links with cricket: Father and brother play for Aberdare
Education: Glynhafod and Blaengwawr Primary Schools: Blaengwawr Comprehensive
Qualifications: School Certificate
Career outside cricket: Coaching cricket
Overseas teams played for: Toombul, Brisbane 1982-85; Te Puke and Bay of Plenty Red Team, New Zealand 1985-86; Northern Districts, New Zealand 1986-87
Cricketers particularly admired: Geoff Boycott, John Snow, Dennis Lillee, Graeme Hick
Other sports followed: Rugby, football (Chelsea)
Relaxations: 'Days of when I can take my little boy for walks, TV and videos.'
Extras: Retired at end of 1991 season
Opinions on cricket: 'In favour of four-day matches for the Championship, to be played on good wickets.'
Best batting: 78* Glamorgan v Derbyshire, Abergavenny 1986
Best bowling: 6-54 Glamorgan v Leicestershire, Leicester 1988

1991 Season

	M	Inns	NO	Runs	HS	Avge	100s	50s	Ct	St	O	M	Runs	Wkts	Avge	Best	5wl	10wM
Test																		
All First	1	1	1	12	12*	-	-	-	1	-	7	3	16	0	-	-	-	-
1-day Int																		
NatWest	1	0	0	0	0	-	-	-	-	-	12	0	59	1	59.00	1-59	-	
B&H																		
Refuge	4	4	1	39	25	13.00	-	-	-	-	14.2	0	79	5	15.80	4-25	-	

Career Performances

	M	Inns	NO	Runs	HS	Avge	100s	50s	Ct	St	Balls	Runs	Wkts	Avge	Best	5wl	10wM
Test																	
All First	95	125	38	1995	78*	22.93	-	11	40	-	10055	5213	137	38.05	6-54	2	-
1-day Int																	
NatWest	8	3	1	10	4	5.00	-	-	2	-	423	237	13	18.23	4-14	-	
B&H	16	9	2	87	42	12.42	-	-	4	-	756	428	19	22.52	4-53	-	
Refuge	77	49	14	414	26	11.82	-	-	11	-	2423	2074	62	33.45	5-32	1	

DILLEY, G. R. Worcestershire

Name: Graham Roy Dilley
Role: Left-hand bat, right-arm
fast bowler
Born: 18 May 1959, Dartford
Height: 6ft 4in **Weight:** 15st
Nickname: Picca
County debut: 1977 (Kent), 1987 (Worcs)
County cap: 1980 (Kent), 1987 (Worcs)
Test debut: 1979-80
Tests: 41
One-Day Internationals: 36
50 wickets in a season: 3
1st-Class 50s scored: 4
1st-Class 5 w. in innings: 34
1st-Class 10 w. in match: 3
1st-Class catches: 75

Place in bowling averages: 9th av. 22.24
(1990 49th av. 46.25)
Strike rate: 49.51 (career 52.88)
Parents: Geoff and Jean
Wife and date of marriage: Helen, 6 November 1980
Children: Paul and Christopher
Family links with cricket: Father and grandfather both played local cricket. Wife is sister of former Kent colleague Graham Johnson
Education: Dartford West Secondary School
Qualifications: 3 O-levels
Overseas tours: England to Australia and India 1979-80; West Indies 1980-81; India and Sri Lanka 1981-82; New Zealand and Pakistan 1983-84; Australia 1986-87; Pakistan, New Zealand and Australia 1987-88; unofficial English team to South Africa 1989-90
Overseas teams played for: Natal 1985-86
Relaxations: Music; playing golf
Extras: Cricket Writers' Club Young Cricketer of the Year 1980. Missed 1984 season after suffering back injury on 1983-84 tour. Joined Worcestershire in 1987. Banned from Test cricket for joining tour to South Africa in 1989-90. Autobiography *Swings and Roundabouts*, 1988
Opinions on cricket: 'For years counties have held almost a feudal grip on their players. Unhappy employees have been forced to show a false sense of loyalty with the hope of a lucrative benefit. The system had one merit in that a player around the age of 30 to 35 was given the chance to make enough money in a year to make himself financially secure for life. But it failed to take into account others less fortunate who might have been forced out of the game at a younger age without any lump sum, or any formal training.'
Best batting: 81 Kent v Northamptonshire, Northampton 1979

Best bowling: 7-63 Natal v Transvaal, Johannesburg 1985-86

1991 Season

	M	Inns	NO	Runs	HS	Avge	100s	50s	Ct	St	O	M	Runs	Wkts	Avge	Best	5wI	10wM
Test																		
All First	11	11	5	37	15 *	6.16	-	-	3	-	305.2	62	823	37	22.24	5-91	1	-
1-day Int																		
NatWest	2	1	1	7	7 *	-	-	-	1	-	18	3	47	2	23.50	1-12	-	
B&H	5	0	0	0	0	-	-	-	-	-	49.2	4	200	11	18.18	4-35	-	
Refuge	2	0	0	0	0	-	-	-	-	-	12	0	72	2	36.00	2-48	-	

Career Performances

	M	Inns	NO	Runs	HS	Avge	100s	50s	Ct	St	Balls	Runs	Wkts	Avge	Best	5wI	10wM
Test	41	58	19	521	56	13.35	-	2	10	-	8192	4107	138	29.76	6-38	6	-
All First	232	249	92	2278	81	14.51	-	4	75	-	34268	17338	648	26.75	7-63	34	3
1-day Int	36	18	8	114	31 *	11.40	-	-	4	-	2043	1291	48	26.89	4-23	-	
NatWest	23	14	5	112	25	12.44	-	-	6	-	1396	716	37	19.35	5-29	1	
B&H	55	27	9	159	37 *	8.83	-	-	8	-	3021	1733	88	19.69	4-14	-	
Refuge	74	27	8	252	33	13.26	-	-	21	-	3038	2089	79	26.44	4-20	-	

DOBSON, M. C.   Kent

Name: Mark Christopher Dobson
Role: Right-hand opening bat, slow left-arm bowler
Born: 24 October 1967, Canterbury
Height: 5ft 10in **Weight:** 12st 11lbs
Nickname: Dobbo
County debut: 1989
1st-Class 50s scored: 2
1st-Class catches: 2
Parents: Bryan and Yvonne
Marital status: Single
Family links with cricket: Father played local club cricket, uncle played for the RAF
Education: Simon Langton Grammar School for Boys, Canterbury
Qualifications: 8 O-levels, 2 A-levels; qualified coach
Off-season: 'Trying to start a successful career outside cricket.'
Overseas tours: Kent Schools U17 to Canada 1982

Overseas teams played for: Glenwood OB, Durban 1989; Green Point, Cape Town 1990
Cricketers particularly admired: Roy Pienaar and Richard Davis. 'Learnt most from my father and Colin Page.'
Other sports followed: 'Play Kent League football for Herne Bay.'
Relaxations: Running and gym work, reading
Extras: 'Released by Kent in early August after scoring 750 runs in only 10 matches at an average of 50 in the 2nd XI Championship. When allowed to bowl I also took 17 wickets.'
Best batting: 52 Kent v Glamorgan, Canterbury 1989
Best bowling: 2-20 Kent v Glamorgan, Canterbury 1989

1991 Season

	M	Inns	NO	Runs	HS	Avge	100s	50s	Ct	St	O	M	Runs	Wkts	Avge	Best	5wI	10wM
Test																		
All First	1	2	1	63	50	63.00	-	1	1	-	8	1	17	0	-	-	-	-
1-day Int																		
NatWest																		
B&H																		
Refuge																		

Career Performances

	M	Inns	NO	Runs	HS	Avge	100s	50s	Ct	St	Balls	Runs	Wkts	Avge	Best	5wI	10wM
Test																	
All First	9	14	2	206	52	17.16	-	2	1	-	778	441	8	55.12	2-20	-	-
1-day Int																	
NatWest																	
B&H																	
Refuge	1	1	0	21	21	21.00	-	-	1	-							

DODEMAIDE, A. I. C.   Sussex

Name: Anthony Ian Christopher Dodemaide
Role: Right-hand bat, right-arm fast-medium bowler
Born: 5 October 1963, Williamstown, Victoria, Australia
Height: 6ft 2in **Weight:** 13st 7lbs
Nickname: Dodders
County debut: 1989
County cap: 1989
Test debut: 1987-88
Tests: 8
One-Day Internationals: 12
1000 runs in a season: 1
50 wickets in a season: 3

1st-Class 50s scored: 22
1st-Class 100s scored: 3
1st-Class 5 w. in innings: 11
1st-Class catches: 71
Place in batting averages: 127th av. 28.66
(1990 144th av. 33.36)
Place in bowling averages: 52nd av. 30.31
(1990 99th av. 40.27)
Strike rate: 64.33 (career 71.03)
Parents: Ian and Irene
Wife and date of marriage: Danielle,
7 April 1989
Family links with cricket: 'Brother Alan
plays district cricket in Melbourne. Brother
Warren and several uncles were keen club
cricketers around home town Footscray.'
Education: St Johns & Chisholm College,
Braybrook, Footscray; Chisholm Institute of
Technology, Melbourne
Qualifications: Higher School Certificate, Bachelor of Applied Science (Physics)
Off-season: Playing for Victoria in Sheffield Shield
Overseas tours: Australia U19 to England 1983; Australia U25 to Zimbabwe 1985;
Australia to Pakistan 1988-89
Cricketers particularly admired: Sunil Gavaskar, Imran Khan, Richard Hadlee, Terry
Alderman
Other sports followed: 'Will watch most sports.'
Relaxations: Watching movies (particularly old ones), reading, listening to music,
playing golf and 'social tennis'
Extras: Played for Sussex 2nd XI on Esso Scholarship Scheme in 1985. Completed double
of 1000 runs and 50 wickets in 1990. Released by Sussex at the end of the 1991 season
Opinions on cricket: 'Too much emphasis in the English season on the one-day game (40,
55 and 60 overs) compared to Championship cricket which could adversely affect the
development of young players.'
Best batting: 112 Sussex v Somerset, Hove 1990
Best bowling: 6-58 Australia v New Zealand, Melbourne 1987-88

1991 Season

	M	Inns	NO	Runs	HS	Avge	100s	50s	Ct	St	O	M	Runs	Wkts	Avge	Best	5wI	10wM
Test																		
All First	20	30	9	602	100 *	28.66	1	1	8	-	579	116	1637	54	30.31	5-130	1	-
1-day Int																		
NatWest	2	2	2	59	32 *	-	-	-	1	-	21	3	64	2	32.00	2-12	-	
B&H	1	0	0	0	0	-	-	-	-	-	7	3	17	1	17.00	1-17	-	
Refuge	11	8	3	96	31 *	19.20	-	-	3	-	70	5	260	7	37.14	2-22	-	

	M	Inns	NO	Runs	HS	Avge	100s	50s	Ct	St	Balls	Runs	Wkts	Avge	Best	5wl	10wM
Test	8	12	3	171	50	19.00	-	1	6	-	1861	803	28	28.67	6-58	1	-
All First	140	214	52	4711	112	29.08	3	22	71	-	27132	12978	393	33.02	6-58	11	-
1-day Int	12	8	5	84	30	28.00	-	-	4	-	655	360	20	18.00	5-21	1	
NatWest	7	5	2	68	32 *	22.66	-	-	1	-	473	245	14	17.50	6-9	1	
B&H	9	5	1	139	38	34.75	-	-	2	-	558	333	13	25.61	3-26	-	
Refuge	40	34	14	572	40 *	28.60	-	-	13	-	1702	1157	42	27.54	4-40	-	

D'OLIVEIRA, D. B. Worcestershire

Name: Damian Basil D'Oliveira
Role: Right-hand bat, off-break
bowler, slip or boundary fielder
Born: 19 October 1960, Cape Town,
South Africa
Height: 5ft 8in **Weight:** 11st 10lbs
Nickname: Dolly
County debut: 1982
County cap: 1985
1000 runs in a season: 4
1st-Class 50s scored: 39
1st-Class 100s scored: 9
1st-Class 200s scored: 1
1st-Class catches: 174
One-Day 50s: 16
One-Day 100s: 1
Place in batting averages: 145th av. 26.63
(1990 116th av. 38.27)
Parents: Basil and Naomi
Wife and date of marriage: Tracey Michele, 26 September 1983
Children: Marcus Damian, 27 April 1986; Dominic James, 29 April 1988; 3rd child
expected February 1992
Family links with cricket: Father played for Worcestershire and England
Education: St George's RC Primary School; Blessed Edward Oldcorne Secondary School
Qualifications: 3 O-levels, 5 CSEs
Overseas tours: English Counties XI to Zimbabwe 1985
Cricketers particularly admired: Greg Chappell, Viv Richards, Dennis Lillee, Malcolm
Marshall, Richard Hadlee
Other sports followed: 'Most others, but not horse racing.'
Relaxations: 'Watching films, TV, eating out, and playing with the kids.'
Best batting: 237 Worcestershire v Oxford University, The Parks 1991

Best bowling: 2-17 Worcestershire v Gloucestershire, Cheltenham 1986

1991 Season

	M	Inns	NO	Runs	HS	Avge	100s	50s	Ct	St	O	M	Runs	Wkts	Avge	Best	5wl	10wM
Test																		
All First	17	24	2	586	237	26.63	1	1	21	-	51	16	146	1	146.00	1-36	-	-
1-day Int																		
NatWest	2	2	1	23	13	23.00	-	-	1	-								
B&H	7	6	0	79	25	13.16	-	-	3	-								
Refuge	18	16	3	319	54	24.53	-	1	7	-								

Career Performances

	M	Inns	NO	Runs	HS	Avge	100s	50s	Ct	St	Balls	Runs	Wkts	Avge	Best	5wl	10wM
Test																	
All First	199	312	21	8132	237	27.94	9	39	174	-	1972	1176	27	43.55	2-17	-	-
1-day Int																	
NatWest	22	21	4	468	99	27.52	-	3	3	-	258	151	8	18.87	2-17	-	
B&H	44	40	4	776	66	21.55	-	4	17	-	228	148	5	29.60	3-12	-	
Refuge	141	126	13	2622	103	23.20	1	9	30	-	234	232	7	33.14	3-23	-	

DONALD, A. A.   Warwickshire

Name: Allan Anthony Donald
Role: Right-hand bat, right-arm
fast bowler
Born: 20 October 1966, Bloemfontein,
South Africa
Height: 6ft 3in **Weight:** 13st 7lbs
County debut: 1987
County cap: 1989
50 wickets in a season: 2
1st-Class 5 w. in innings: 24
1st-Class 10 w. in match: 3
1st-Class catches: 38
Place in bowling averages: 4th av. 19.68
(1990 76th av. 37.55)
Strike rate: 37.74 (career 46.77)
Parents: Stuart and Francina
Wife and date of marriage: Tina, 1991
Education: Grey College High School
and Technical High School, Bloemfontein
Qualifications: Matriculation

Off-season: Playing cricket in South Africa
Overseas tours: South Africa to India 1991-92; World Cup, Australia 1991-92
Overseas teams played for: Orange Free State, South Africa 1985-90
Cricketers particularly admired: Ian Botham, Imran Khan, Richard Hadlee, Malcolm Marshall, Robin Smith, Dean Jones, Dermot Reeve, Curtly Ambrose, Ian Bishop
Other sports followed: Rugby, football
Relaxations: Playing tennis, listening to music
Extras: Played for South African XI v Australian XI in 1986-87 and v English XI in 1989-90. Retained by Warwickshire for 1991 season ahead of Tom Moody. Toured with South Africa on first-ever visit to India 1991. Selected for South Africa's first tour to India on their return to international cricket
Opinions on cricket: 'All Championship matches should be four-day games.'
Best batting: 40 Warwickshire v Yorkshire, Edgbaston 1989
Best bowling: 8-37 Orange Free State v Transvaal, Johannesburg 1986-87

1991 Season

	M	Inns	NO	Runs	HS	Avge	100s	50s	Ct	St	O	M	Runs	Wkts	Avge	Best	5wI	10wM
Test																		
All First	21	21	9	96	18	8.00	-	-	10	-	522.3	91	1634	83	19.68	6-69	8	2
1-day Int																		
NatWest	4	2	1	3	2 *	3.00	-	-	-	-	42	4	132	6	22.00	4-16	-	
B&H	5	3	2	8	6 *	8.00	-	-	1	-	49	2	266	11	24.18	4-55	-	
Refuge	8	1	0	7	7	7.00	-	-	3	-	58	1	264	8	33.00	2-7	-	

Career Performances

	M	Inns	NO	Runs	HS	Avge	100s	50s	Ct	St	Balls	Runs	Wkts	Avge	Best	5wI	10wM
Test																	
All First	126	150	57	1033	46 *	11.10	-	-	38	-	21342	10393	450	23.09	8-37	24	3
1-day Int																	
NatWest	12	3	1	3	2 *	1.50	-	-	1	-	714	357	30	11.90	5-12	2	
B&H	13	7	5	38	23 *	19.00	-	-	2	-	757	557	21	26.52	4-28	-	
Refuge	28	15	6	118	18 *	13.11	-	-	8	-	1278	902	34	26.52	4-32	-	

DONELAN, B. T. P.   Sussex

Name: Bradleigh Thomas Peter Donelan
Role: Right-hand bat, off-spin bowler
Born: 3 January 1968, Park Royal, Middlesex
Height: 6ft 1in **Weight:** 12st 7lbs
Nickname: Rooster, Freddie, Claw
County debut: 1989
1st-Class 50s: 3

1st-Class 5 w. in innings: 2
1st-Class 10 w. in match: 1
1st-Class catches: 8
Place in batting averages: 81st av. 35.30
(1990 165th av. 30.14)
Place in bowling averages: 81st av. 34.17
(1990 130th av. 50.00)
Strike rate: 375.26 (career 81.54)
Parents: Terry and Patricia
Marital status: Single
Education: Our Lady of Grace Junior
School, Finchley Catholic High School
Qualifications: 8 CSEs
Off-season: Coaching at Lord's, otherwise
having a winter off
Overseas tours: Christians in Sport to
India 1990
Overseas teams played for: Northcote,

Melbourne 1987-88; Southland CA and
Otago B, 1988-90; Wellington B 1990-91
Cricketers particularly admired: Robin Smith for his guts and determination,
Martin Crowe for his dedication, Graham Gooch and Allan Border
Other sports followed: Football, golf, tennis – any sport apart from horse racing.
Injuries: Knee injury diagnosed as patella tendonitis – two steroid injections needed in
right knee, one in March and one in August.
Relaxations: 'Wining and dining and generally spending a lot of time with my girlfriend
Kim (when I get the opportunity). Music and sleeping.'
Extras: Was a product of the MCC ground staff – there for 2½ years before joining Sussex
in 1989
Opinions on cricket: 'Too much county cricket played. Players play although not fully fit
and can do more harm than good. We need time in between games so we are fresh and
not stale, and can study our opposition. Four-day Championship cricket is a must, and
played on wickets that are prepared to last 4 days.'
Best batting: 61 Sussex v Kent, Hove 1991
Best bowling: 6-62 Sussex v Gloucestershire, Hove 1991

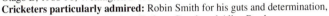

1991 Season

	M	Inns	NO	Runs	HS	Avge	100s	50s	Ct	St	O	M	Runs	Wkts	Avge	Best	5wI	10wM
Test																		
All First	13	15	5	353	61	35.30	-	2	3	-	426.3	112	1162	34	34.17	6-62	2	1
1-day Int																		
NatWest																		
B&H	1	1	1	8	8 *	-	-	-	-	-	11	0	54	0	-	-	-	-
Refuge	2	1	0	19	19	19.00	-	-	1	-	15	1	58	1	58.00	1-35	-	

Career Performances

	M	Inns	NO	Runs	HS	Avge	100s	50s	Ct	St	Balls	Runs	Wkts	Avge	Best	5wI	10wM
Test																	
All First	33	37	14	605	61	26.30	-	3	11	-	5545	2795	68	41.10	6-62	2	1
1-day Int																	
NatWest																	
B&H	1	1	1	8	8*	-	-	-	-	-	66	54	0	-	-	-	
Refuge	6	2	0	23	19	11.50	-	-	1	-	228	175	3	58.33	1-23	-	

DOWNTON, P. R. Middlesex

Name: Paul Rupert Downton
Role: Right-hand bat, wicket-keeper
Born: 4 April 1957, Farnborough, Kent
Height: 5ft 10in **Weight:** 12st 4lbs
Nickname: Nobby
County debut: 1977 (Kent),
1980 (Middlesex)
County cap: 1979 (Kent),
1981 (Middlesex)
Benefit: 1990
Test debut: 1980-81
Tests: 30
One-Day Internationals: 28
1000 runs in a season: 1
1st-Class 50s scored: 43
1st-Class 100s scored: 6
1st-Class catches: 690
1st-Class stumpings: 89
One-Day 50s: 9
Place in batting averages: (1990 189th av. 26.68)
Parents: George Charles and Jill Elizabeth
Wife and date of marriage: Alison, 19 October 1985
Children: Phoebe Alice, 16 December 1987; Jonathan George, 20 September 1989
Family links with cricket: Father kept wicket for Kent 1948-49
Education: Sevenoaks School; Exeter University
Qualifications: 9 O-levels, 3 A-levels; Law degree (LLB); NCA coaching certificate
Career outside cricket: Stockbroker
Overseas tours: England YC to West Indies 1976; England to Pakistan and New Zealand 1977-78; West Indies 1980-81; India and Australia 1984-85; West Indies 1985-86
Cricketers particularly admired: Alan Knott, Rod Marsh
Other sports followed: Golf and rugby (England U19 and Exeter U 1st XV)

Relaxations: Reading, playing golf
Extras: Forced to retire from first-class cricket in mid-season 1991 as a result of eye injury of 1990 (hit in the eye by a bail) from which he never fully recovered
Opinions on cricket: 'I can't understand why the game clings on to the past. Uncovering wickets is simply an excuse to prolong the three-day game, whereas I'm convinced four-day cricket is the way forward. It has been proven that groundsmen can produce wickets that last given reasonable weather: they certainly will be able to if you reduce the number of wickets they have to prepare. Quality not quantity must be right.'
Best batting: 126* Middlesex v Oxford University, The Parks 1986
Best bowling: 1-4 Middlesex v Surrey, The Oval 1990

1991 Season

	M	Inns	NO	Runs	HS	Avge	100s	50s	Ct	St	O	M	Runs	Wkts	Avge	Best	5wI	10wM
Test																		
All First	5	6	2	189	51 *	47.25	-	1	11	1								
1-day Int																		
NatWest																		
B&H	4	3	1	134	58	67.00	-	1	7	1								
Refuge	3	2	0	8	5	4.00	-	-	1	2								

Career Performances

	M	Inns	NO	Runs	HS	Avge	100s	50s	Ct	St	Balls		Runs	Wkts	Avge	Best	5wI	10wM
Test	30	48	8	785	74	19.62	-	4	70	5								
All First	314	405	76	8270	126 *	25.13	6	43	690	89	55		9	1	9.00	1-4	-	-
1-day Int	18	20	5	242	44 *	16.13	-	-	26	3								
NatWest	39	28	7	556	69	26.47	-	2	54	7								
B&H	57	43	15	781	80 *	27.89	-	4	62	10								
Refuge	162	113	34	1669	70	21.12	-	3	136	43								

60. Which current Sussex player played for Sussex 2nd XI at age 14?

61. Which player topped the first-class bowling averages last season for Lancashire?

EALHAM, M. A.   Kent

Name: Mark Alan Ealham
Role: Right-hand bat, right-arm
medium bowler
Born: 27 August 1969, Ashford
Height: 5ft 10in **Weight:** 13st
Nickname: Ealy, Skater, Burger
County debut: 1989
1st-Class 5 w. in innings: 2
1st-Class catches: 3
Place in batting averages: 178th av. 22.50
Place in bowling averages: 5th av. 20.82
Strike rate 41.58 (career 51.76)
Parents: Alan George Ernest and Sue
Marital status: Single
Family links with cricket: 'My father
played county cricket for Kent.'
Education: Stour Valley Secondary
School
Qualifications: 9 CSEs

Off-season: 'Working for uncle in plumbing
business and some coaching.'
Cricketers particularly admired: Ian Botham, Viv Richards, Malcolm Marshall, Robin
Smith
Other sports followed: Football, golf, snooker and many others
Relaxations: Playing golf and snooker, watching films, music
Extras: 'Enjoyed playing for Ashford CC since the age of 11.'
Opinions on cricket: 'Continue with four-day cricket with each county playing each other
once.'
Best batting: 45 Kent v Lancashire, Old Trafford 1989
Best bowling: 5-39 Kent v Sussex, Hove 1991

1991 Season

	M	Inns	NO	Runs	HS	Avge	100s	50s	Ct	St	O	M	Runs	Wkts	Avge	Best	5wI	10wM
Test																		
All First	4	7	1	135	37	22.50	-	-	3	-	118.1	24	354	17	20.82	5-39	2	-
1-day Int																		
NatWest																		
B&H	2	1	1	0	0*	-	-	-	2	-	19	1	78	1	78.00	1-46	-	
Refuge	5	5	1	46	18	11.50	-	-	-	-	38	0	178	7	25.42	3-36	-	

Career Performances

	M	Inns	NO	Runs	HS	Avge	100s	50s	Ct	St	Balls	Runs	Wkts	Avge	Best	5wI	10wM
Test																	
All First	8	12	3	204	45	22.66	-	-	3	-	1089	592	21	28.19	5-39	2	-
1-day Int																	
NatWest																	
B&H	6	4	2	22	17 *	11.00	-	-	3	-	294	219	9	24.33	4-57	-	
Refuge	23	16	5	150	29 *	13.63	-	-	11	-	846	687	21	32.71	3-26	-	

EAST, D. E. Essex

Name: David Edward East
Role: Right-hand bat, wicket-keeper
Born: 27 July 1959, Clapton
Height: 5ft 10in **Weight:** 12st 10lbs
Nickname: 'Various insults but Ethel
seems most popular, and Easty.'
County debut: 1981
County cap: 1982
Benefit: 1991
1st-Class 50s scored: 17
1st-Class 100s scored: 4
1st-Class catches: 480
1st-Class stumpings: 53
Parents: Edward William and Joan Lillian
Wife and date of marriage: Jeanette Anne,
14 September 1984
Children: Matthew David Leonard,
8 November 1986

Family links with cricket: Father played for
Hadley CC, an Essex touring side
Education: Millfields Primary; Hackney Downs School; University of East Anglia,
Norwich
Qualifications: BSc (Hons) Biological Sciences, Advanced Cricket Coach
Overseas teams played for: Avendale, Cape Town 1984-85
Cricketers particularly admired: Alan Knott, 'who is simply the best as far as I am
concerned'
Other sports followed: Interested in most but loathes horse and dog racing
Extras: World record holder for most catches in an innings (8) on his birthday in 1985.
Released by Essex at the end of the 1991 season
Best batting: 134 Essex v Gloucestershire, Ilford 1988

	M	Inns	NO	Runs	HS	Avge	100s	50s	Ct	St	O	M	Runs	Wkts	Avge	Best	5wl	10wM
Test																		
All First																		
1-day Int																		
NatWest																		
B&H																		
Refuge	1	1	0	2	2	2.00	-	-	-	-								

Career Performances

	M	Inns	NO	Runs	HS	Avge	100s	50s	Ct	St	Balls	Runs	Wkts	Avge	Best	5wl	10wM
Test																	
All First	190	254	32	4553	134	20.50	4	17	480	53	26	17	0	-		-	-	-
1-day Int																	
NatWest	21	16	5	142	28	12.90	-	-	29	3							
B&H	38	22	5	235	33	13.82	-	-	54	1							
Refuge	110	59	19	510	43	12.75	-	-	88	15							

ELLCOCK, R. M. — Middlesex

Name: Ricardo McDonald Ellcock
Role: Right-hand bat, right-arm fast bowler
Born: 17 June 1965, St Thomas, Barbados
Height: 5ft 11in **Weight:** 13st 7lbs
Nickname: Ricky
County debut: 1982 (Worcs),1989 (Middx)
1st-Class 5 w. in innings: 1
1st-Class catches: 9
Parents: Everson (deceased) and Ione
Family links with cricket: Brother played for Barbados in the Shell Shield
Education: Welches Mixed, Combermere and Malvern College
Qualifications: 8 O-levels
Off-season: Getting fit and recovering from back operation
Overseas tours: England to West Indies 1989-90
Overseas teams played for: Carlton, Barbados; Birkenhead, Auckland
Cricketers particularly admired: Alvin Kallicharran, Malcolm Marshall, Victor Sandiford ('a friend in Barbados')

Other sports followed: Motor sport and football (Spurs)
Injuries: Recurrence of back injury, requiring second operation
Best batting: 45* Worcestershire v Essex, Worcester 1984
Best bowling: 5-35 Middlesex v Yorkshire, Headingley 1989

1991 Season

	M	Inns	NO	Runs	HS	Avge	100s	50s	Ct	St	O	M	Runs	Wkts	Avge	Best	5wI	10wM
Test																		
All First	4	1	1	26	26 *	-	-	-	1	-	62	15	204	8	25.50	4-60	-	-
1-day Int																		
NatWest																		
B&H	1	1	0	0	0	0.00	-	-	-	-	10	0	55	1	55.00	1-55	-	
Refuge	2	1	1	8	8 *	-	-	-	-	-	11	0	58	1	58.00	1-33	-	

Career Performances

	M	Inns	NO	Runs	HS	Avge	100s	50s	Ct	St	Balls	Runs	Wkts	Avge	Best	5wI	10wM
Test																	
All First	46	47	13	424	45 *	12.47	-	-	9	-	5652	3395	117	29.01	5-35	1	-
1-day Int																	
NatWest	5	2	1	6	6	6.00	-	-	2	-	324	237	11	21.54	4-43	-	
B&H	4	3	1	16	12	8.00	-	-	1	-	210	153	4	38.25	2-45	-	
Refuge	18	8	3	32	13	6.40	-	-	4	-	711	477	22	21.68	4-43	-	

ELLISON, R. M. Kent

Name: Richard Mark Ellison
Role: Left-hand bat, right-arm medium
bowler
Born: 21 September 1959, Ashford, Kent
Height: 6ft 2¹/₂in **Weight:** 14st
Nickname: Elly
County debut: 1981
County cap: 1983
Benefit: 1993
Test debut: 1984
Tests: 11
One-Day Internationals: 14
50 wickets in a season: 4
1st-Class 50s scored: 19
1st-Class 100s scored: 1
1st-Class 5 w. in innings: 16
1st-Class 10 w. in match: 2

One-Day 50s: 4
1st-Class catches: 72
Place in batting averages: 181st av. 21.84 (1990 10th av. 39.41)
Place in bowling averages: 59th av. 31.48 (1990 132nd av. 50.68)
Strike rate: 61.80 (career 61.69)
Parents: Peter Richard Maxwell (deceased) and Bridget Mary
Wife and date of marriage: Fiona, 28 September 1985
Children: Charles Peter, 26 January 1991
Family links with cricket: Brother Charles Christopher gained blue at Cambridge University 1981-86. Grandfather played with Grace brothers and was secretary of Derby CCC in about 1915
Education: Friars Preparatory School, Great Chart, Ashford; Tonbridge School; St Luke's College; Exeter University
Qualifications: 8 O-levels, 2 A-levels; Degree B Ed.; Teacher
Career outside cricket: 'Seems to change each year.'
Off-season: 'Trying to find a job.'
Overseas tours: With England to India and Australia 1984-85; Sharjah 1984-85; West Indies 1985-86; unofficial English tour to South Africa 1989-90
Cricketers particularly admired: Malcolm Marshall, Richard Hadlee, Chris Tavare, Terry Alderman
Other sports followed: Anything but horse racing and greyhounds
Injuries: 'Slid into wrought-iron bench at Old Trafford and broke my nose. Usual back injuries and niggles.'
Relaxations: Social drinking, good food, music: Chris Rea, Dire Straits, New Order
Extras: Did not play at all in 1987 due to back injury. One of *Wisden's* Five Cricketers of the Year, 1985. Debut for Canterbury Amateur Operatic Society in April 1989, in 'Fiddler on the Roof'. Banned from Test cricket after touring South Africa in 1989-90
Best batting: 108 Kent v Oxford University, The Parks 1984
Best bowling: 7-33 Kent v Warwickshire, Tunbridge Wells 1991

1991 Season

	M	Inns	NO	Runs	HS	Avge	100s	50s	Ct	St	O	M	Runs	Wkts	Avge	Best	5wI	10wM
Test																		
All First	17	26	7	415	61 *	21.84	-	3	10	-	484.1	102	1480	47	31.48	7-33	2	-
1-day Int																		
NatWest															•				
B&H	5	4	1	34	15	11.33	-	-	1	-	52	7	199	5	39.80	2-19	-	
Refuge	8	7	5	102	29 *	51.00	-	-	2	-	52	1	272	7	38.85	2-29	-	

62. Which bowler holds the record for most wickets for Somerset in a career?

Career Performances

	M	Inns	NO	Runs	HS	Avge	100s	50s	Ct	St	Balls	Runs	Wkts	Avge	Best	5wI	10wM
Test	11	16	1	202	41	13.46	-	-	2	-	2264	1048	35	29.94	6-77	3	1
All First	185	258	63	4631	108	23.74	1	19	72	-	27269	12400	442	28.05	7-33	16	2
1-day Int	14	12	4	86	24	10.75	-	-	2	-	696	510	12	42.50	3-42	-	
NatWest	20	16	7	302	49 *	33.55	-	-	1	-	1203	620	29	21.37	4-19	-	
B&H	35	28	7	444	72	21.14	-	1	8	-	1999	1129	45	25.08	4-28	-	
Refuge	93	73	33	1083	84	27.07	-	3	13	-	3528	2678	95	28.18	4-25	-	

EMBUREY, J. E. Middlesex

Name: John Ernest Emburey
Role: Right-hand bat, off-spin bowler
Born: 20 August 1952, Peckham
Height: 6ft 2in **Weight:** 14st
Nickname: Embers, Ern
County debut: 1973
County cap: 1977
Benefit: 1986
Test debut: 1978
Tests: 60
One-Day Internationals: 58
50 wickets in a season: 13
1st-Class 50s scored: 42
1st-Class 100s scored: 4
1st-Class 5 w. in innings: 60
1st-Class 10 w. in match: 9
1st-Class catches: 382
One-Day 50s: 2
Place in batting averages: 183rd av. 21.72
(1990 177th av. 28.08)
Place in bowling averages: 64th av. 31.91 (1990 39th av. 32.08)
Strike rate: 79.98 (career 70.99)
Parents: John (deceased) and Rose
Wife and date of marriage: Susie, 20 September 1980
Children: Clare, 1 March 1983; Chloe, 31 October 1985
Education: Peckham Manor Secondary School
Qualifications: O-levels, advanced cricket coaching certificate
Off-season: Assisting Middlesex CCC
Overseas tours: With England to Australia 1978-79; Australia and India 1979-80; West Indies 1980-81; India and Sri Lanka 1981-82; West Indies 1985-86; Australia 1986-87; Pakistan, Australia and New Zealand 1987-88; unofficial English tours to South Africa

1981-82 and 1989-90
Overseas teams played for: Western Province 1982-84
Cricketers particularly admired: Ken Barrington, Derek Underwood
Other sports followed: Golf
Relaxations: Reading, gardening
Extras: Played for Surrey Young Cricketers 1969-70. Phil Edmonds of Middlesex and England was the best man at his wedding. Middlesex vice-captain since 1983. One of *Wisden's* Five Cricketers of the Year, 1983. Captain of England v West Indies for two Tests in 1988. Banned from Test cricket for three years for touring South Africa in 1981-82, and for five more for touring in 1989-90. Published autobiography *Emburey* in 1988
Opinions on cricket: 'We should play either three-day cricket or four-day, not both.'
Best batting: 133 Middlesex v Essex, Chelmsford 1983
Best bowling: 7-27 Middlesex v Gloucestershire, Cheltenham 1989

1991 Season

	M	Inns	NO	Runs	HS	Avge	100s	50s	Ct	St	O	M	Runs	Wkts	Avge	Best	5wI	10wM
Test																		
All First	24	33	4	630	74	21.72	-	3	25	-	906.3	246	2170	68	31.91	7-71	1	-
1-day Int																		
NatWest	2	2	0	3	2	1.50	-	-	-	-	24	7	65	2	32.50	2-52	-	--
B&H	4	3	0	38	23	12.66	-	-	3	-	44	3	167	9	18.55	5-37	1	
Refuge	15	11	4	142	33 *	20.28	-	-	2	-	114	6	528	28	18.85	5-23	1	

Career Performances

	M	Inns	NO	Runs	HS	Avge	100s	50s	Ct	St	Balls	Runs	Wkts	Avge	Best	5wI	10wM
Test	60	89	18	1540	75	21.69	-	8	33	-	14227	5105	138	36.99	7-78	6	-
All First	423	535	106	9762	133	22.75	4	42	382	-	91226	33530	1285	26.09	7-27	60	9
1-day Int	58	43	10	471	34	14.27	-	-	19	-	3281	2226	75	29.68	4-37	-	
NatWest	49	31	11	452	36 *	22.60	-	-	17	-	3291	1506	51	29.52	3-11	-	
B&H	66	48	14	574	50	16.88	-	1	35	-	3456	1780	66	26.97	5-37	1	
Refuge	210	148	49	1648	50	16.64	-	1	68	-	8892	6482	303	21.39	5-23	2	

63. What were the christian names of D.V.P. Wright of Kent and England?

EVANS, K. P.   Nottinghamshire

Name: Kevin Paul Evans
Role: Right-hand bat, right-arm medium
bowler, slip fielder
Born: 10 September 1963, Calverton,
Nottingham
Height: 6ft 2in **Weight:** 13st
Nickname: Ghost
County debut: 1984
County cap: 1990
1st-Class 50s scored: 9
1st-Class 100s scored: 1
1st-Class 5 w. in innings: 2
1st-Class catches: 57
One-Day 50s: 1
Place in batting averages: 148th av. 26.27
(1990 68th av. 46.12)
Place in bowling averages: 67th av. 31.95
(1990 65th av. 36.23)
Strike rate: 63.75 (career 65.26)
Parents: Eric and Eileen

Wife and date of marriage: Sandra, 19 March 1988
Family links with cricket: Brother Russell played for Notts. Father played local cricket
Education: William Lee Primary; Colonel Frank Seely Comprehensive, Calverton
Qualifications: 10 O-levels, 3 A-levels. Qualified coach
Off-season: Working for Pork Farms, Nottingham
Cricketers particularly admired: Richard Hadlee
Other sports followed: Football, tennis, squash
Injuries: Broken thumb, missed last six weeks of the season
Relaxations: Listening to music, reading, DIY, gardening
Extras: With brother Russell, first brothers to bat together for Nottinghamshire in first-
class cricket for fifty years
Opinions on cricket: 'We should play 17 four-day matches, but change the bonus point
system, so that the batsman can concentrate on hitting the bad ball rather than improvising
on the good ones.'
Best batting: 100* Nottinghamshire v Somerset, Weston-super-Mare 1990
Best bowling: 5-52 Nottinghamshire v Leicestershire, Trent Bridge 1991

---

64. Who captained the 1963 West Indies in England?

1991 Season

	M	Inns	NO	Runs	HS	Avge	100s	50s	Ct	St	O	M	Runs	Wkts	Avge	Best	5wl	10wM
Test																		
All First	15	18	7	289	56 *	26.27	-	1	6	-	425	89	1278	40	31.95	5-52	2	-
1-day Int																		
NatWest	2	2	0	22	20	11.00	-	-	1	-	23	3	82	0	-		-	-
B&H	3	2	2	6	5 *	-	-	-	1	-	32	2	132	6	22.00	4-43	-	
Refuge	16	6	3	47	14 *	15.66	-	-	1	-	118	2	679	18	37.72	3-41	-	

Career Performances

	M	Inns	NO	Runs	HS	Avge	100s	50s	Ct	St	Balls	Runs	Wkts	Avge	Best	5wl	10wM
Test																	
All First	70	99	26	1936	100 *	26.52	1	9	57	-	8745	4682	134	34.94	5-52	2	-
1-day Int																	
NatWest	12	8	1	49	20	7.00	-	-	4	-	708	393	11	35.72	4-30	-	
B&H	15	11	4	130	31 *	18.57	-	-	7	-	824	550	21	26.19	4-43	-	
Refuge	71	40	16	415	55 *	17.29	-	1	12	-	2816	2489	73	34.09	4-28	-	

FAIRBROTHER, N. H.   Lancashire

Name: Neil Harvey Fairbrother
Role: Left-hand bat, left-arm medium bowler, county captain
Born: 9 September 1963, Warrington, Cheshire
Height: 5ft 8in **Weight:** 11st
Nickname: Harvey
County debut: 1982
County cap: 1985
Test debut: 1987
Tests: 7
One-Day Internationals: 11
1000 runs in a season: 8
1st-Class 50s scored: 65
1st-Class 100s scored: 25
1st-Class 200s scored: 1
1st-Class 300s scored: 1
1st-Class catches: 132
One-Day 50s: 37
One-Day 100s: 6
Place in batting averages: 37th av. 46.26 (1990 11th av. 69.60)
Parents: Les and Barbara

Wife and date of marriage: Audrey, 23 September 1988
Children: Rachael Elizabeth, 4 April 1991
Family links with cricket: Father and two uncles played local league cricket
Education: St Margaret's Church of England School, Oxford; Lymn Grammar School
Qualifications: 5 O-levels
Off-season: Touring with England
Overseas tours: England to Sharjah 1986-87; World Cup, Pakistan, Australia and New Zealand 1987-88; England A to Pakistan 1990-91; England to New Zealand 1991-92
Cricketers particularly admired: Clive Lloyd, Allan Border
Other sports followed: Football, Rugby Union, Rugby League
Relaxations: Music and playing sport
Extras: 'I was named after the Australian cricketer Neil Harvey, who was my mum's favourite cricketer.' England YC v Australia 1983. His innings of 366 was the third highest score ever made in the County Championship, the second highest first-class score by a Lancashire batsman and the best at The Oval. Appointed Lancashire captain for 1992
Best batting: 366 Lancashire v Surrey, The Oval 1990
Best bowling: 2-91 Lancashire v Nottinghamshire, Old Trafford 1987

1991 Season

	M	Inns	NO	Runs	HS	Avge	100s	50s	Ct	St	O	M	Runs	Wkts	Avge	Best	5wI	10wM
Test																		
All First	19	29	6	1064	121	46.26	5	3	19	-								
1-day Int	3	3	1	122	113	61.00	1	-	2	-								
NatWest	2	2	0	92	68	46.00	-	1	-	-								
B&H	7	7	2	225	53 *	45.00	-	2	5	-								
Refuge	17	16	5	451	62	41.00	-	2	6	-								

Career Performances

	M	Inns	NO	Runs	HS	Avge	100s	50s	Ct	St	Balls	Runs	Wkts	Avge	Best	5wI	10wM
Test	7	9	1	64	33 *	8.00	-	-	4	-	12	9	0	-	-	-	-
All First	207	325	47	11465	366	41.24	25	65	132	-	656	423	5	84.60	2-91	-	-
1-day Int	14	14	3	354	113	32.18	1	2	7	-							
NatWest	23	22	4	993	93 *	55.16	-	9	9	-	18	16	0	-	-	-	-
B&H	39	38	11	1194	116 *	44.22	1	8	20	-							
Refuge	126	116	25	3395	116 *	37.30	4	18	30	-	12	15	0	-	-	-	-

65. Which England and Yorkshire cricketer retired as MCC head coach at Lord's last year after 13 years.

Name: Paul Farbrace
Role: Right-hand bat, wicket-keeper
Born: 7 July 1967, Ash, nr Canterbury
Height: 5ft 10in **Weight:** 12st
Nickname: Farby
County debut: 1987 (Kent), 1990 (Middx)
1st-Class 50s scored: 3
1st-Class catches: 81
1st-Class stumpings: 12
Place in batting averages: 221st av. 15.45
(1990 217th av. 20.66)
Parents: David and Betty
Wife and date of marriage: Elizabeth
Jane, 27 July 1985
Children: Jemma, 30 March 1985;
Eleanor, 3 September 1988
Family links with cricket: Father
played. Two brothers, Ian and Colin play
village cricket
Education: Ash CE Primary School; Geoffrey Chaucer School, Canterbury
Qualifications: O-levels, NCA Advanced Coach, NCA Staff Coach
Career outside cricket: HM Customs and Excise; BBC Radio Kent sports reporter;
postman; cricket and football coach
Off-season: Working for BBC Radio Kent, and coaching cricket and football at Hampton
School
Overseas tours: Kent Schools to Canada 1983
Cricketers particularly admired: 'Alan Knott and all of the current Middlesex staff for
their different views on the game and their different aims in cricket.'
Other sports followed: All sports except those with horses
Relaxations: 'Football, reading, my wife and children.'
Extras: Played County Schools football, had England Schools U18 trial, attracted
attention from Notts County and Coventry City. Captained Kent v Essex in a five-a-side
cricket game in Dartford Tunnel in February 1989 to raise money for Children in Need
Opinions on cricket: 'None – Dean Headley has enough for us all.'
Best batting: 79 Middlesex v Cambridge University, Fenner's 1990
Best bowling: 1-64 Middlesex v Essex, Lord's 1991

---

66. Which current England Test player is a professional artist?

1991 Season

	M	Inns	NO	Runs	HS	Avge	100s	50s	Ct	St	O	M	Runs	Wkts	Avge	Best	5wI	10wM
Test																		
All First	20	27	5	326	50	14.81	-	1	46	8	4.1	0	64	1	64.00	1-64	-	-
1-day Int																		
NatWest	2	2	1	20	13 *	20.00	-	-	1	1								
B&H																			
Refuge	12	8	3	67	26 *	13.40	-	-	9	6								

Career Performances

	M	Inns	NO	Runs	HS	Avge	100s	50s	Ct	St	Balls	Runs	Wkts	Avge	Best	5wI	10wM
Test																	
All First	36	47	10	643	79	17.37	-	3	81	12	25	64	1	64.00	1-64	-	-
1-day Int																	
NatWest	6	4	1	41	17	13.66	-	-	8	1							
B&H																		
Refuge	18	12	4	73	26 *	9.12	-	-	11	10							

FELTHAM, M. A. Surrey

Name: Mark Andrew Feltham
Role: Right-hand bat, right-arm
fast-medium bowler
Born: 26 June 1963, London
Height: 6ft 2in **Weight:** 14st
Nickname: Felts, Felpsy, Boff
or Douglas
County debut: 1983
County cap: 1990
50 wickets in a season: 1
1st-Class 50s scored: 6
1st-Class 100s scored: 1
1st-Class 5 w. in innings: 6
1st-Class catches: 45
One-Day 50s: 2
Place in batting averages: 124th av. 28.84
(1990 171st av. 29.15)
Place in bowling averages: 54th av. 30.71
(1990 24th av. 28.75)
Strike rate: 59.80 (career 59.04)
Parents: Leonard William and Patricia Louise
Wife and date of marriage: Debi, 22 September 1990

Family links with cricket: 'Mum responsible for fund-raising to build new development at Foster's Oval.'
Education: Roehampton Church School; Tiffin Boys' School
Qualifications: 7 O-levels; advanced cricket coach
Career outside cricket: Marketing and sales
Off-season: 'Getting fitter than I've ever been before.'
Cricketers particularly admired: Ian Botham, Gordon Greenidge, Waqar Younis and Sylvester Clarke
Other sports followed: Football, American football and most others
Injuries: Missed two games with abdominal strain and one with groin strain
Relaxations: Music, particularly Luther Vandross; Woody Allen films
Extras: 'I write a weekly column in *Wandsworth Borough News*. Dismissed both Clive Rice and Richard Hadlee in their last innings in county cricket.'
Opinions on cricket: '17 four-day matches and day/night cricket with coloured clothing and names on backs.'
Best batting: 101 Surrey v Middlesex, The Oval 1990
Best bowling: 6-53 Surrey v Leicestershire, The Oval 1990

1991 Season

	M	Inns	NO	Runs	HS	Avge	100s	50s	Ct	St	O	M	Runs	Wkts	Avge	Best	5wI	10wM
Test																		
All First	13	18	5	375	69 *	28.84	-	1	4	-	349	57	1075	35	30.71	4-36	-	-
1-day Int																		
NatWest	1	0	0	0	0	-	-	-	-	-	10	1	46	1	46.00	1-46	-	
B&H	2	2	0	6	4	3.00	-	-	1	-	21.2	1	103	3	34.33	2-45	-	
Refuge	9	7	3	93	23 *	23.25	-	-	3	-	65.1	2	337	9	37.44	3-44	-	

Career Performances

	M	Inns	NO	Runs	HS	Avge	100s	50s	Ct	St	Balls	Runs	Wkts	Avge	Best	5wI	10wM
Test																	
All First	101	123	32	2089	101	22.95	1	6	45	-	15767	8141	267	30.49	6-53	6	-
1-day Int																	
NatWest	13	9	3	72	19 *	12.00	-	-	1	-	784	587	13	45.15	2-27	--	
B&H	24	16	3	143	29	11.00	-	-	6	-	1342	920	33	27.87	5-28	1	
Refuge	85	59	17	777	61	18.50	-	2	18	-	3264	2807	78	35.98	4-35	-	

67. What is the name of South Africa's limited-overs competition?

68. Which player topped the first-class bowling averages last season for Middlesex?

FELTON, N. A. Northamptonshire

Name: Nigel Alfred Felton
Role: Left-hand bat
Born: 24 October 1960, Guildford
Height: 5ft 7in **Weight:** 10st 7lbs
Nickname: Gringo, Ninja
County debut: 1982 (Somerset),
1989 (Northamptonshire)
County cap: 1986 (Somerset),
1990 (Northamptonshire)
1000 runs in a season: 3
1st-Class 50s scored: 42
1st-Class 100s scored: 12
1st-Class catches: 81
One-Day 50s: 14
Place in batting averages: 193rd av. 19.88
(1990 99th av. 41.56)
Parents: Ralph and Enid
Wife and date of marriage: Jill-Marie,
October 1989

Family links with cricket: Father played non-white cricket in Cape Town and club cricket in the UK
Education: Hawes Down Secondary School, Kent; Millfield School, Somerset; Loughborough University
Qualifications: 6 O-levels, 2 A-levels, BSc (Hons), Certificate of Education PE/Sports Sciences, qualified teacher
Career outside cricket: Sales and Marketing, Kerrypak, Bristol, manufacturers of netting and suppliers throughout the world
Off-season: Returning to Cape Town to coach within the newly unified cricket board. Playing for Primrose CC in the newly unified league
Overseas tours: England ESCA to India 1976-77; England YC to Australia 1979; Somerset to Barbados 1986; to Sierra Leone 1988
Overseas teams played for: Waneroo, Perth, Western Australia 1984-86; Cape Town CC 1988; Primrose, Cape Town 1991-92
Cricketers particularly admired: Richard Hadlee, Graham Gooch
Other sports followed: Most ball games
Injuries: Calf problems and back problems since car accident in 1988
Relaxations: 'Spending time with my wife.'
Extras: Played a season for Kent in 1980 after leaving Millfield and joined Somerset at end of first year at Loughborough. Released by Somerset at end of 1988 season
Opinions on cricket: 'I'm in favour of four-day cricket. Those in authority seem to get lost in the accountability stakes. Management courses should be compulsory for people in power. Clubs should be run like businesses.'

Best batting: 173* Somerset v Kent, Taunton 1983
Best bowling: 1-48 Northamptonshire v Derbyshire, Northampton 1990

1991 Season

	M	Inns	NO	Runs	HS	Avge	100s	50s	Ct	St	O	M	Runs	Wkts	Avge	Best	5wI	10wM
Test																		
All First	16	28	3	497	55	19.88	-	1	5	-	6	0	66	0	-	-	-	-
1-day Int																		
NatWest	2	2	0	65	54	32.50	-	1	1	-								
B&H	5	5	0	119	44	23.80	-	-	2	-								
Refuge	9	8	0	203	69	25.37	-	2	4	-								

Career Performances

	M	Inns	NO	Runs	HS	Avge	100s	50s	Ct	St	Balls	Runs	Wkts	Avge	Best	5wI	10wM
Test																	
All First	160	273	15	7601	173 *	29.46	12	42	81	-	204	252	2	126.00	1-48	-	-
1-day Int																	
NatWest	18	18	2	587	87	36.68	-	5	7	-							
B&H	17	17	0	281	50	16.52	-	1	4	-							
Refuge	71	66	9	1395	96	24.47	-	8	23	-	6	7	0	-	-	-	-

FIELD-BUSS, M. G. Nottinghamshire

Name: Michael Gwyn Field-Buss
Role: Right-hand bat, off-break bowler
Born: 23 September 1964, Malta
Height: 5ft 10in **Weight:** 11st
Nickname: Mouse
County debut: 1987 (Essex), 1989 (Notts)
1st-Class catches: 2
Parents: Gwyn and Monica
Marital status: Engaged to Paula
Family links with cricket: Father
played local cricket with Ilford RAFA
Education: Wanstead High School
Qualifications: Qualified coach
Overseas teams played for: Werribee,
Melbourne 1987-88
Cricketers particularly admired: 'Bill
Morris (coach at Ilford Cricket School)
during my early years, Ray East and David
Acfield at Essex, Eddie Hemmings at Notts.'

Other sports followed: 'Watching Leyton Orient (although I support Arsenal). Keen on most other sports.'

Relaxations: 'Spending as much time as possible with my wife, Paula, and my family, listening to music and playing football.'

Opinions on cricket: 'I don't think that four-day cricket is needed. Let the home side prepare the wicket they want. That way, unless it is dangerous, you don't need to dock points. The home side will of course prepare a wicket to their benefit but the visitors will also know what to expect and can act accordingly. 2nd team grounds are still not up to 1st team standard – not enough 2nd XI games are played on county grounds.'

Best batting: 34* Essex v Middlesex, Lord's 1987

Best bowling: 4-33 Nottinghamshire v Somerset, Trent Bridge 1989

1991 Season

	M	Inns	NO	Runs	HS	Avge	100s	50s	Ct	St	O	M	Runs	Wkts	Avge	Best	5wI	10wM
Test																		
All First	3	2	0	41	25	20.50	-	-	1	-	53	11	187	1	187.00	1-73	-	-
1-day Int																		
NatWest																		
B&H																		
Refuge	3	2	2	0	0*	-	-	-	-	-	24	1	107	5	21.40	2-22	-	

Career Performances

	M	Inns	NO	Runs	HS	Avge	100s	50s	Ct	St	Balls	Runs	Wkts	Avge	Best	5wI	10wM
Test																	
All First	10	11	2	109	34 *	12.11	-	-	2	-	899	414	11	37.63	4-33	-	-
1-day Int																	
NatWest																	
B&H																	
Refuge	5	4	2	5	5	2.50	-	-	-	-	198	161	5	32.20	2-22	-	

69. What Australian Test batting record is held by Carl Rackemann?

70. Which former England player is the Surrey coach?

71. Who were known as 'the three W's'?

FITTON, J. D.   Lancashire

Name: John Dexter Fitton
Role: Left-hand bat, off-break bowler
Born: 24 August 1965, Rochdale
Height: 5ft 10in **Weight:** 12st 7lbs
Nickname: Jo, Ted, Philbert, Lord
County debut: 1987
1st-Class 50s: 1
1st-Class 5 w. in innings: 3
1st-Class catches: 10
Place in batting averages: 184th av. 21.70
(1990 242nd av. 16.62)
Place in bowling averages: 143rd av. 69.08
(1990 157th av. 103.35)
Strike rate: 118.50 (career 106.72)
Parents: Derek (deceased) and Jean
Marital status: Single
Family links with cricket: Father
dedicated cricketer for 20 years with
Littleboro in Central Lancashire

League and Robinsons in North Manchester League
Education: Redbrook High School; Oulder Hill Upper School; Rochdale College
Qualifications: 4 O-levels, Diploma in Business Studies
Career outside cricket: Export administration at Hanson Springs, Rochdale
Off-season: Playing for Sydenham CC in Christchurch, New Zealand
Overseas tours: Lancashire to Jamaica, Zimbabwe and Western Australia
Overseas teams played for: Sydenham, New Zealand 1988-91
Cricketers particularly admired: 'Everyone at Old Trafford, especially Nick Speak and Graham Lloyd for the enthusiasm and happiness they put into everyday work, David Gower, Mike Gatting and Eddie Hemmings.'
Other sports followed: 'Watch Manchester City FC and Rochdale Hornets, golf, own a couple of greyhounds.'
Relaxations: Watching 'Only Fools and Horses', 'Fawlty Towers' and Richard Pryor films. Listening to Luther Vandross, discussing Manchester football with Lloyd and Fairbrother
Extras: Was the youngest player to take 50 wickets and score 500 runs for Rochdale in the Central Lancashire League. Captained Lancashire U19, North of England, and NAYC in 1984
Opinions on cricket: 'We should play 17 four-day games. Tea should be 30 minutes. Spinners should be pushed into one-day cricket earlier.'
Best batting: 60 Lancashire v Northamptonshire, Lytham 1991
Best bowling: 6-59 Lancashire v Yorkshire, Old Trafford 1988

1991 Season

	M	Inns	NO	Runs	HS	Avge	100s	50s	Ct	St	O	M	Runs	Wkts	Avge	Best	5wI	10wM
Test																		
All First	8	11	1	217	60	21.70	-	1	-	-	237.1	39	829	12	69.08	2-42	-	-
1-day Int																		
NatWest																		
B&H	1	0	0	0	0	-	-	-	-	-	11	0	47	1	47.00	1-47	-	
Refuge	2	2	1	22	14 *	22.00	-	-	-	-	16	0	98	3	32.66	2-67	-	

Career Performances

	M	Inns	NO	Runs	HS	Avge	100s	50s	Ct	St	Balls	Runs	Wkts	Avge	Best	5wI	10wM
Test																	
All First	44	52	13	736	60	18.87	-	1	10	-	7364	3894	69	56.43	6-59	3	-
1-day Int																	
NatWest																	
B&H	1	0	0	0	0	-	-	-	-	-	66	47	1	47.00	1-47	-	
Refuge	5	3	1	22	14 *	11.00	-	-	-	-	192	176	5	35.20	2-67	-	

FLEMING, M. V. Kent

Name: Matthew Valentine Fleming
Role: Right-hand bat, right-arm
medium bowler
Born: 12 December 1964, Macclesfield
Height: 6ft **Weight:** 12st 4lbs
Nickname: Jazzer
County debut: 1988
County cap: 1990
1st-Class 50s scored: 11
1st-Class 100s scored: 3
1st-Class catches: 21
One-Day 50s: 3
Place in batting averages: 103rd av. 31.62
(1990 121st av. 37.69)
Place in bowling averages: 98th av. 35.81
(1990 126th av. 48.72)
Strike rate: 80.25 (career 102.11)
Parents: Valentine and Elizabeth
Wife and date of marriage: Caroline,
23 September 1989
Family links with cricket: 'Great-grandfather Leslie played for England and apparently
hit an all-run 7 at Lord's.'

Education: St Aubyns School, Rottingdean; Eton College
Qualifications: 8 O-levels, 3 A-levels
Career outside cricket: Corporate hospitality
Off-season: Working with Andy Needham (ex-Surrey and Middlesex)
Overseas teams played for: Avendale, Cape Town 1984
Cricketers particularly admired: 'Everyone who is still fit and enthusiastic in September.'
Other sports followed: Shooting, fishing, golf, football (Arsenal FC)
Extras: Ex-army officer in the Royal Green Jackets. First two scoring shots in Championship cricket were sixes
Opinions on cricket: 'Four-day cricket should be introduced for all Championship matches. Leg byes should be scrapped, certainly in one-day cricket if not all. B & H Cup should start later in the season.'
Best batting: 116 Kent v West Indies, Canterbury 1991
Best bowling: 3-28 Kent v Yorkshire, Harrogate 1991

1991 Season

	M	Inns	NO	Runs	HS	Avge	100s	50s	Ct	St	O	M	Runs	Wkts	Avge	Best	5wl	10wM
Test																		
All First	20	32	3	917	116	31.62	2	6	14	-	214	46	573	16	35.81	3-28	-	-
1-day Int																		
NatWest	2	2	1	56	35 *	56.00	-	-	-	-	12.2	1	44	1	44.00	1-6	-	
B&H	5	5	0	90	52	18.00	-	1	-	-	44	0	170	5	34.00	2-52	-	
Refuge	14	14	0	336	77	24.00	-	2	5	-	102.3	1	576	17	33.88	4-45	-	

Career Performances

	M	Inns	NO	Runs	HS	Avge	100s	50s	Ct	St	Balls	Runs	Wkts	Avge	Best	5wl	10wM
Test																	
All First	47	76	12	2101	116	32.82	3	11	21	-	4493	2090	44	47.50	3-28	-	-
1-day Int																	
NatWest	4	4	1	75	35 *	25.00	-	-	1	-	164	85	4	21.25	2-4	-	
B&H	12	11	0	175	52	15.90	-	1	1	-	594	354	10	35.40	2-52	-	
Refuge	41	39	7	687	77	21.46	-	2	12	-	1659	1434	46	31.17	4-45	-	

72. Which player topped the first-class bowling averages last season for Leicestershire?

FLETCHER, I.

Somerset

Name: Ian Fletcher
Role: Right-hand bat, right-arm
medium bowler
Born: 31 August 1971,
Sawbridgeworth, Herts
Height: 5ft 11in
County debut: 1991
1st-Class 50s: 1
1st-Class catches: 0
Education: Millfield School, Somerset
Extras: Played for Hertfordshire in
NatWest Trophy 1990 and for Combined
Universities in B&H Cup 1991
Best batting: 56 Somerset v Hampshire,
Southampton 1991

1991 Season

	M	Inns	NO	Runs	HS	Avge	100s	50s	Ct	St	O	M	Runs	Wkts	Avge	Best	5wI	10wM
Test																		
All First	1	2	1	58	56	58.00	-	1	-	-								
1-day Int																		
NatWest																		
B&H	1	1	0	9	9	9.00	-	-	1	-								
Refuge																		

Career Performances

	M	Inns	NO	Runs	HS	Avge	100s	50s	Ct	St	Balls	Runs	Wkts	Avge	Best	5wI	10wM
Test																	
All First	1	2	1	58	56	58.00	-	1	-	-							
1-day Int																	
NatWest	1	1	0	1	1	1.00	-	-	-	-							
B&H	1	1	0	9	9	9.00	-	-	1	-							
Refuge																	

73. What have the following England Test cricketers got in common –
Wilfred Rhodes, Frank Woolley and Percy Fender?

FLETCHER, S. D.   Lancashire

Name: Stuart David Fletcher
Role: Right-hand bat, right-arm
medium bowler
Born: 8 June 1964, Keighley
Height: 5ft 10in **Weight:** 12st
Nickname: Fletch, Godber, Norman
Stanley, Dr Death, Ghostie
County debut: 1983 (Yorkshire)
County cap: 1988 (Yorkshire)
50 wickets in a season: 1
1st-Class 5 w. in innings: 5
1st-Class catches: 25
Place in bowling averages: 105th
av. 38.25 (1990 59th av. 35.69)
Strike rate: 71.45 (career 62.23)
Parents: Brough and Norma Hilda
Wife and date of marriage: Katharine,
4 October 1986
Children: Craig, 26 July 1989
Family links with cricket: Father played league cricket
Education: Woodhouse Primary; Reins Wood Secondary
Qualifications: O-level English and Woodwork; City and Guilds in coachbuilding
Cricketers particularly admired: Ian Botham, Arnie Sidebottom
Other sports followed: Watches Leeds United FC
Relaxations: Watching TV, snooker and golf
Extras: Released by Yorkshire at end of 1991 season and signed 3-year contract with
Lancashire
Best batting: 28* Yorkshire v Kent, Tunbridge Wells 1984
Best bowling: 8-58 Yorkshire v Essex, Sheffield 1988

1991 Season

	M	Inns	NO	Runs	HS	Avge	100s	50s	Ct	St	O	M	Runs	Wkts	Avge	Best	5wI	10wM
Test																		
All First	13	11	2	48	9 *	5.33	-	-	5	-	238.1	45	765	20	38.25	6-70	1	-
1-day Int																		
NatWest	1	1	0	9	9	9.00	-	-	-	-	5	0	15	0	-	-	-	-
B&H	6	2	1	3	2 *	3.00	-	-	4	-	49.2	6	208	8	26.00	4-51	-	
Refuge	12	3	2	15	11 *	15.00	-	-	6	-	80	2	426	18	23.66	3-26	-	

Career Performances

	M	Inns	NO	Runs	HS	Avge	100s	50s	Ct	St	Balls	Runs	Wkts	Avge	Best	5wI	10wM
Test																	
All First	107	91	31	414	28 *	6.90	-	-	25	-	14562	7966	234	34.04	8-58	5	-
1-day Int																	
NatWest	15	7	4	36	16 *	12.00	-	-	2	-	913	576	15	38.40	3-34	-	
B&H	27	6	3	20	15 *	6.66	-	-	6	-	1405	974	35	27.82	4-34	-	
Refuge	86	18	11	49	11 *	7.00	-	-	26	-	3632	3135	114	27.50	4-11	-	

FOLLEY, I. Derbyshire

Name: Ian Folley
Role: Right-hand bat, slow left-arm bowler
Born: 9 January 1963
Height: 5ft 9½in **Weight:** 11st
Nickname: Thatch, Vicar, Reverend, Foll, Neil
County debut: 1982 (Lancashire)
County cap: 1987 (Lancashire)
1st-Class 50s scored: 1
1st-Class 5 w. in innings: 10
1st-Class 10 w. in match: 1
1st-Class catches: 60
Strike rate: (career 70.47)
Parents: James and Constance
Wife and date of marriage: Julie, 27 September 1986
Education: Mansfield High School, Nelson; Colne College
Qualifications: 5 O-levels, Business Studies diploma
Overseas tours: NCA to Denmark 1981; Lancashire to Barbados 1982; New York 1985; Jamaica 1987 and 1988
Overseas teams played for: Glenorchy, Tasmania 1985-86; Brighton, Tasmania 1987-88
Other sports followed: 'I am a bad watcher.'
Cricketers particularly admired: Clive Lloyd, Viv Richards, Graeme Hick, Malcolm Marshall
Relaxations: Interested in rallying and saloon-car racing, listening to music (detests disco music)
Extras: Represented Lancashire Schools U15 and U19 as captain. Represented Lancashire Federation 1979-81. Played for England U19 v India U19 in 198, also played for Young England v West Indies. In 1984 changed from left-arm medium to slow left-arm bowler.

Best batting: 69 Lancashire v Yorkshire, Old Trafford 1985
Best bowling: 7-15 Lancashire v Warwickshire, Southport 1987

1991 Season

	M	Inns	NO	Runs	HS	Avge	100s	50s	Ct	St	O	M	Runs	Wkts	Avge	Best	5wI	10wM
Test																		
All First	4	5	1	20	17 *	5.00	-	-	2	-	127	14	469	3	156.33	1-60	-	-
1-day Int																		
NatWest																			
B&H																			
Refuge	2	1	1	6	6 *	-	-	-	-	-	8	0	54	0	-	-	-	-

Career Performances

	M	Inns	NO	Runs	HS	Avge	100s	50s	Ct	St	Balls	Runs	Wkts	Avge	Best	5wI	10wM
Test																	
All First	140	163	50	1485	69	13.14	-	1	60	-	20225	9359	287	32.61	7-15	10	1
1-day Int																	
NatWest	4	2	1	4	3 *	4.00	-	-	1	-	237	114	7	16.28	2-10	-	
B&H	11	5	5	21	11 *	-	-	-	2	-	504	215	14	15.35	4-18	-	
Refuge	27	11	7	62	19	15.50	-	-	3	-	912	757	14	54.07	3-23	-	

FORDHAM, A.   Northamptonshire

Name: Alan Fordham
Role: Right-hand bat, occasional
right-arm medium bowler
Born: 9 November 1964, Bedford
Height: 6ft 1in **Weight:** 13st
Nickname: Fordy
County debut: 1986
County cap: 1990
1000 runs in a season: 2
1st-Class 50s scored: 25
1st-Class 100s scored: 10
1st-Class 200s scored: 1
1st-Class catches: 51
One-Day 50s: 15
One-Day 100s: 2
Place in batting averages: 32nd av. 47.17
(1990 85th av. 44.17)
Parents: Clifford and Ruth
Marital status: Single

Family links with cricket: Brother John played school and college cricket
Education: Bedford Modern School; Durham University
Qualifications: 9 O-levels, 3 A-levels, BSc (Hons) Chemistry, NCA senior coaching award
Career outside cricket: 'No definite plans as yet.'
Off-season: Teaching
Overseas tours: Bedford Modern to Barbados 1983; Gentlemen of Leicestershire to Jersey and Guernsey 1987; International Ambassadors XI/Christians in Sport to India 1990
Overseas teams played for: Richmond, Melbourne 1983-84; Camberwell, Melbourne 1987-88; Curtin University, Perth, Western Australia 1988; Nirman Schools XI, Dhaka, Bangladesh 1989-90
Cricketers particularly admired: Allan Lamb, Bob Willis, Mike Brearley
Other sports followed: Rugby union
Relaxations: Music, squash, travel
Extras: Has appeared for Bedfordshire in Minor Counties Championship. Played for Combined Universities in B & H Cup 1987. Shared county record stand of 393 with Allan Lamb v Yorkshire at Headingley in 1990. Only white man to have played league cricket in Bangladesh
Opinions on cricket: 'My doubts about four-day Championship cricket have been cast aside. We have had some great games in 1991; it is definitely the way forward.'
Best batting: 206* Northamptonshire v Yorkshire, Headingley 1990
Best bowling: 1-25 Northamptonshire v Yorkshire, Northampton 1990

1991 Season

	M	Inns	NO	Runs	HS	Avge	100s	50s	Ct	St	O	M	Runs	Wkts	Avge	Best	5wI	10wM
Test																		
All First	24	42	3	1840	165	47.17	4	9	8	-	13	0	78	1	78.00	1-42	-	-
1-day Int																		
NatWest	4	4	1	288	132 *	96.00	1	2	-	-	1.3	0	3	1	3.00	1-3	-	
B&H	5	5	1	183	93 *	45.75	-	2	1	-								
Refuge	16	15	0	509	76	33.93	-	4	3	-								

Career Performances

	M	Inns	NO	Runs	HS	Avge	100s	50s	Ct	St	Balls	Runs	Wkts	Avge	Best	5wI	10wM
Test																	
All First	79	139	14	4917	206 *	39.33	10	25	51	-	144	127	2	63.50	1-25	-	-
1-day Int																	
NatWest	9	9	1	543	132 *	67.87	2	3	2	-	21	6	1	6.00	1-3	-	
B&H	11	10	1	292	93 *	32.44	-	3	2	-							
Refuge	43	40	1	1149	76	29.46	-	9	9	-							

Name: Daren Joseph Foster
Role: Right-hand bat, right-arm
fast-medium bowler
Born: 14 March 1966, London
Height: 5ft 9in **Weight:** 10st 7lbs
Nickname: DJ, Fossie
County debut: 1986 (Som), 1991 (Glam)
1st-Class 5 w. in innings: 1
1st-Class catches: 7
Place in bowling averages: 68th av. 32.56
Strike rate: 53.72 (career 66.41)
Parents: Vivian and Sadie
Marital status: Single
Children: Marcella and Daren Danny
Family links with cricket: Cousin
Morris Foster played for Jamaica
Education: Somerset School; Haringey
College; Southgate Technical College
Qualifications: 2 O-levels, 1 CSE,
Pre-vocational Studies pass, Commercial Studies pass and credit
Overseas teams played for: West Geelong, Victoria 1988-89
Cricketers particularly admired: Clive Lloyd, Vivian Richards, Malcolm Marshall, Ian
Botham and Michael Holding
Other sports followed: All sports
Injuries: Back and knee
Relaxations: Music
Extras: Took career best 6-84 on his first Championship appearance for Glamorgan,
against his old county Somerset. Appeared for both Surrey and Middlesex 2nd XIs in 1985
Opinions on cricket: 'I would like to play more four-day cricket, there would be more
good results. Coloured clothing should come into one-day cricket.'
Best batting: 20 Somerset v Hampshire, Southampton 1988
Best bowling: 6-84 Glamorgan v Somerset, Taunton 1991

1991 Season

	M	Inns	NO	Runs	HS	Avge	100s	50s	Ct	St	O	M	Runs	Wkts	Avge	Best	5wI	10wM
Test																		
All First	9	9	3	35	13 *	5.83	-	-	3	-	223.5	35	814	25	32.56	6-84	1	-
1-day Int																		
NatWest																		
B&H																		
Refuge	4	3	2	2	2 *	2.00	-	-	1	-	26	0	112	6	18.66	3-30	-	

Career Performances

	M	Inns	NO	Runs	HS	Avge	100s	50s	Ct	St	Balls	Runs	Wkts	Avge	Best	5wI	10wM
Test																	
All First	37	35	14	161	20	7.66	-	-	7	-	4915	3024	74	40.86	6-84	1	-
1-day Int																	
NatWest	2	1	0	0	0	0.00	-	-	1	-	90	32	1	32.00	1-15	-	
B&H	7	1	0	0	0	0.00	-	-	-	-	420	263	6	43.83	2-26	-	
Refuge	22	9	7	15	8 *	7.50	-	-	3	-	815	635	18	35.27	4-26	-	

FOSTER, N. A. Essex

Name: Neil Alan Foster
Role: Right-hand bat, right-arm
fast-medium bowler, outfielder
Born: 6 May 1962, Colchester
Height: 6ft 3in **Weight:** 13st
Nickname: Fozzy, Nibbler, Norbie
County debut: 1980
County cap: 1983
Test debut: 1983
Tests: 28
One-Day Internationals: 48
50 wickets in a season: 9
1st-Class 50s scored: 8
1st-Class 100s scored: 1
1st-Class 5 w. in innings: 42
1st-Class 10 w. in match: 7
1st-Class catches: 92
Place in batting averages: 131st av. 28.50
(1990 190th av. 26.50)
Place in bowling averages: 6th av. 20.96 (1990 11th av. 26.61)
Strike rate: 44.54 (career 49.01)
Parents: Jean and Alan
Wife and date of marriage: Romany, 21 September 1985
Family links with cricket: Father and brother both play local cricket
Education: Broomgrove Infant & Junior Schools; Philip Morant Comprehensive, Colchester
Qualifications: 8 O-levels, 1 A-level, NCA coaching award. Has consumer credit licence
for Financial Consultancy
Career outside cricket: PE teacher at Holmwood House Prep School, Colchester
Overseas tours: England YC to West Indies 1980; England to New Zealand and Pakistan
1983-84; India and Australia 1984-85; West Indies 1985-86; Australia 1986-87; Pakistan,
Australia and New Zealand 1987-88; unofficial English team to South Africa 1989-90

Other sports followed: Golf, football

Injuries: Knee injured

Relaxations: Music, golf

Extras: Was summoned from school at short notice to play for Essex v Kent at Ilford. First ball went for 4 wides, but he finished with figures of 3 for 51. Played for England YC v India 1981. Banned from Test cricket for touring South Africa in 1989-90. Leading first-class wicket-taker in 1990 season. Britannic Assurance/*Sunday Express* Cricketer of the Year 1991

Opinions on cricket: 'We need to have the balance right between bat and ball. Last season the balance was perfect in four-day matches for most counties but favoured batsmen too much in three-day games, hence contrived finishes which always tend to favour the weaker teams.'

Best batting: 107* Essex v Sussex, Horsham 1991

Best bowling: 8-99 Essex v Lancashire, Old Trafford 1991

1991 Season

	M	Inns	NO	Runs	HS	Avge	100s	50s	Ct	St	O	M	Runs	Wkts	Avge	Best	5wI	10wM
Test																		
All First	22	22	4	513	107 *	28.50	1	1	11	-	757.2	185	2138	102	20.96	8-99	7	1
1-day Int																		
NatWest	3	2	1	19	10 *	19.00	-	-	1	-	31.5	6	127	4	31.75	2-57	-	-
B&H	6	3	1	60	39 *	30.00	-	-	-	-	61	8	185	7	26.42	2-28	-	
Refuge	7	6	4	148	57	74.00	-	1	1	-	41	1	161	6	26.83	3-28	-	

Career Performances

	M	Inns	NO	Runs	HS	Avge	100s	50s	Ct	St	Balls	Runs	Wkts	Avge	Best	5wI	10wM
Test	28	43	7	410	39	11.38	-	-	7	-	6081	2797	88	31.78	8-107	5	1
All First	210	243	56	3782	107 *	20.22	2	9	103	-	42596	20667	869	23.78	8-99	49	8
1-day Int	48	25	12	150	24	11.53	-	-	12	-	2627	1836	59	31.11	3-20	-	
NatWest	20	12	2	138	26	13.80	-	-	3	-	1321	679	38	17.86	4-9	-	
B&H	45	17	8	205	39 *	22.77	-	-	7	-	2716	1601	75	21.34	5-32	1	
Refuge	76	42	16	552	57	21.23	-	1	19	-	3158	2284	99	23.07	5-17	1	

74. Which former Lancashire and England player was awarded an honorary degree last summer by Lancaster University?

FOTHERGILL, A. R. Durham

Name: Andrew Robert Fothergill
Role: Right-hand bat, wicket-keeper
Born: 10 February 1962,
Newcastle-upon-Tyne
Height: 6ft **Weight:** 12st 10lbs
One-Day 50s:
Marital status: Divorced
Education: Eastbourne Comprehensive
Career outside cricket: Sales –
supermarket fixtures and fittings
Off-season: as above
Cricketers particularly admired: Alan
Knott and Jack Russell
Relaxations: Playing football for Bishop
Auckland in HFS Loans League, going to
restaurants
Extras: Played for Minor Counties in the
B&H Cup 1989, 1990, 1991

1991 Season

	M	Inns	NO	Runs	HS	Avge	100s	50s	Ct	St	O	M	Runs	Wkts	Avge	Best	5wI	10wM
Test																		
All First																		
1-day Int																		
NatWest	1	1	0	24	24	24.00	-	-	2	-								
B&H	4	4	1	24	15 *	8.00	-	-	2	-								
Refuge																		

Career Performances

	M	Inns	NO	Runs	HS	Avge	100s	50s	Ct	St	Balls	Runs	Wkts	Avge	Best	5wI	10wM
Test																	
All First	1	1	0	3	3	3.00	-	-	-	-							
1-day Int																	
NatWest	7	6	2	66	24	16.25	-	-	6	3							
B&H	9	8	2	89	45 *	14.83	-	-	9	-							
Refuge																	

75. Who has scored the most runs ever for South Australia?

FOWLER, G.   Lancashire

Name: Graeme Fowler
Role: Left-hand opening bat, occasional
wicket-keeper, 1st slip, 'slow right-hand
declaration bowler'
Born: 20 April 1957, Accrington
Height: 5ft 9in **Weight:** 'Near 11st'
Nickname: Fow, Foxy
County debut: 1979
County cap: 1981
Benefit: 1991 (£152,000)
Test debut: 1982
Tests: 21
One-Day Internationals: 26
1000 runs in a season: 8
1st-Class 50s scored: 75
1st-Class 100s scored: 34
1st-Class 200s scored: 2
1st-Class catches: 136
1st-Class stumpings: 5
One-Day 50s: 47
One-Day 100s: 7

Place in batting averages: 112th av. 30.74 (1990 154th av. 32.34)
Marital status: Single
Education: Accrington Grammar School; Bede College, Durham University
Qualifications: Certificate of Education, advanced cricket coach
Career outside cricket: 'Some radio and TV work.'
Off-season: Closing off benefit year.
Overseas tours: England to Australia and New Zealand 1982-83; New Zealand and
Pakistan 1983-84; India and Australia 1984-85
Overseas teams played for: Tasmania 1981-82
Cricketers particularly admired: David Lloyd and Paul Allott
Other sports followed: 'Bits of everything.'
Injuries: 'Plastic surgery on my top lip. Ball came off wicket-keeper's elbow into my face
at first slip. Couldn't laugh without pain for two weeks.'
Relaxations: Music, gardening, playing drums
Extras: Played for Accrington and Rawtenshall in Lancashire League: at 15 he was the
youngest opener in the League. Played for England YC in 1976. Published *Fox on the Run*,
a cricketing diary from 1984 to 1986, which won Channel 4's Sports Book of the Year
Award. First Englishman to score a double century in India
Opinions on cricket: 'Good game isn't it!'
Best batting: 226 Lancashire v Kent, Maidstone 1984
Best bowling: 2-34 Lancashire v Warwickshire, Old Trafford 1986

1991 Season

	M	Inns	NO	Runs	HS	Avge	100s	50s	Ct	St	O	M	Runs	Wkts	Avge	Best	5wI	10wM
Test																		
All First	19	33	2	953	113	30.74	2	3	2	-	7	0	41	1	41.00	1-41	-	-
1-day Int																		
NatWest	2	2	0	80	71	40.00	-	1	-	-								
B&H	7	7	0	320	136	45.71	1	2	2	-								
Refuge	17	17	1	572	59	35.75	-	3	2	-								

Career Performances

	M	Inns	NO	Runs	HS	Avge	100s	50s	Ct	St	Balls	Runs	Wkts	Avge	Best	5wI	10wM
Test	21	37	0	1307	201	35.32	3	8	10	-	18	11	0	-	-	-	-
All First	263	444	25	15180	226	36.22	34	75	136	5	377	306	9	34.00	2-34	-	-
1-day Int	26	26	2	744	81 *	31.00	-	4	4	2							
NatWest	28	28	0	811	122	28.96	2	3	9	2							
B&H	58	57	1	1631	136	29.12	1	12	17	1							
Refuge	162	157	10	4709	112	32.03	5	28	60	-	6	1	0	-	-	-

FRASER, A. G. J. Essex

Name: Alastair Gregory James Fraser
Role: Right-hand bat, right-arm
fast-medium bowler
Born: 17 October 1967, Edgware
Height: 6ft 1in **Weight:** 12st 7lbs
Nickname: Junior
County debut: 1986 (Middx), 1991 (Essex)
1st-Class 50s scored: 1
1st-Class catches: 0
Strike rate: (career 69.11)
Parents: Don and Irene
Marital status: Single
Family links with cricket: Father played
club cricket, brother Angus plays for
Middlesex
Education: Gayton High School, Harrow;
John Lyon School, Harrow Weald
Sixth Form College
Qualifications: 4 O-levels, qualified cricket coach
Overseas tours: England YC to Sri Lanka 1987; NCA U19 to Bermuda
Overseas teams played for: Plimmerton, Wellington 1986-88; Green Point, Cape Town
1988-89

Cricketers particularly admired: Malcolm Marshall, Ian Botham
Other sports followed: Rugby, football
Relaxations: Watching Liverpool FC when possible, snooker
Extras: Joined Essex from Middlesex in 1990.
Best batting: 52* Essex v Sussex, Horsham 1991
Best bowling: 3-46 Middlesex v New Zealand, Lord's 1986

1991 Season

	M	Inns	NO	Runs	HS	Avge	100s	50s	Ct	St	O	M	Runs	Wkts	Avge	Best	5wl	10wM
Test																		
All First	3	2	1	75	52 *	75.00	-	1	-	-	19	5	44	0	-		-	-	-
1-day Int																		
NatWest																		
B&H																		
Refuge	2	0	0	0	0	-	-	-	1	-	14	0	54	1	54.00	1-21	-	

Career Performances

	M	Inns	NO	Runs	HS	Avge	100s	50s	Ct	St	Balls	Runs	Wkts	Avge	Best	5wl	10wM
Test																	
All First	8	7	4	126	52 *	42.00	-	1	-	-	622	291	9	32.33	3-46	-	-
1-day Int																	
NatWest																	
B&H																	
Refuge	7	1	1	2	2 *	-	-	-	1	-	288	191	6	31.83	2-35	-	

FRASER, A. R. C.   Middlesex

Name: Angus Robert Charles Fraser
Role: Right-hand bat ('late-order stroke-player'), right-arm fast-medium bowler, gully fielder ('from now on')
Born: 8 August 1965, Billinge, Lancashire
Height: 6ft 5½in **Weight:** 15st 7lbs ('when fit')
Nickname: Gus, Lard
County debut: 1984
County cap: 1988
Test debut: 1989
Tests: 11
One-Day Internationals: 24
50 wickets in a season: 3
1st-Class 50s scored: 1
1st-Class 5 w. in innings: 16
1st-Class 10 w. in match: 2

1st-Class catches: 16
Place in batting averages: (1990 226th av. 19.45)
Place in bowling averages: (1990 13th av. 26.89)
Strike rate: (career 59.48)
Parents: Don and Irene
Marital status: Single
Family links with cricket: Brother Alastair plays for Essex. Parents are keen followers
Education: Gayton High School, Harrow; Orange Senior High School, Edgware
Qualifications: 7 O-levels, qualified cricket coach
Career outside cricket: 'Haven't thought about it too hard, who knows? All that most cricketers do until they retire is play cricket. Working for Whittingdale whilst injured this summer has given me the chance to see what a job in the city is like.'

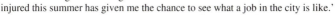

Off-season: 'I don't know - working for Whittingdale? Hopefully recovering from injury and getting fit.'
Overseas tours: Thames Valley Gentlemen to Barbados 1985; Middlesex to La Manga 1985 and 1986; Portugal 1991; England to India (Nehru Cup) and West Indies 1989-90; Australia 1990-91
Overseas teams played for: Plimmerton, Wellington 1985-86 and 1987-88; Western Suburbs, Sydney 1988-89
Cricketers particularly admired: Richard Hadlee, Allan Border, Graham Gooch and Robert Sims 'for his thoughts on cricket and his valuable comments'
Other sports followed: 'Rugby, football, golf, most except horse racing.'
Injuries: 'Hip knackered'
Relaxations: 'Sorting out the problems of the world and cricket over a pint with friends. Having a good moan. Driving.'
Extras: Sponsored by local Benskins pub, 'The Seven Balls' – one pint for first-class wickets, two pints for Test wickets ('I've been thirsty this year!'). Middlesex Player of the Year 1988 and 1989. Selected for England tour to New Zealand 1991-92 but ruled out by injury.
Opinions on cricket: 'You'd never guess that the people who make most of the decisions in cricket are batsmen, would you? Most opinions given by cricketers aren't really listened to anyway! Players should be talked to more about changes that are made to the game, having the views of the odd bowler wouldn't be a bad thing. Rebels should serve out their ban.'
Best batting: 92 Middlesex v Surrey, The Oval 1990
Best bowling: 7-77 Middlesex v Kent, Canterbury 1989

1991 Season

	M	Inns	NO	Runs	HS	Avge	100s	50s	Ct	St	O	M	Runs	Wkts	Avge	Best	5wI	10wM
Test																		
All First	2	2	0	12	12	6.00	-	-	2	-	39.5	12	91	6	15.16	4-24	-	-
1-day Int																		
NatWest																		
B&H																		
Refuge	2	1	1	8	8 *	-	-	-	1	-	16	0	78	2	39.00	1-34	-	

Career Performances

	M	Inns	NO	Runs	HS	Avge	100s	50s	Ct	St	Balls	Runs	Wkts	Avge	Best	5wI	10wM
Test	11	14	1	88	29	6.76	-	-	1	-	3106	1255	47	26.70	6-82	4	-
All First	101	114	27	1022	92	11.74	-	1	16	-	19749	8103	332	24.40	7-77	16	2
1-day Int	24	10	4	69	38 *	11.50	-	-	-	-	1336	797	23	34.65	3-22	-	
NatWest	15	3	2	27	19	27.00	-	-	-	-	1065	529	28	18.89	4-34	-	
B&H	15	8	3	36	13 *	7.20	-	-	3	-	913	517	15	34.46	3-39	-	
Refuge	64	28	13	164	30 *	10.93	-	-	9	-	2773	1812	64	28.31	4-28	-	

FRENCH, B. N.   Nottinghamshire

Name: Bruce Nicholas French
Role: Right-hand bat, wicket-keeper
Born: 13 August 1959, Warsop, Notts
Height: 5ft 8in **Weight:** 10st
Nickname: Frog
County debut: 1976
County cap: 1980
Benefit: 1991
Test debut: 1986
Tests: 16
One-Day Internationals: 13
1st-Class 50s scored: 23
1st-Class 100s scored: 1
1st-Class catches: 731
1st-Class stumpings: 81
Place in batting averages: 217th av. 15.75
(1990 220th av. 20.24)
Parents: Maurice and Betty
Wife and date of marriage: Ellen Rose, 9 March 1978
Children: Charles Daniel, 31 August 1978; Catherine Ellen, 28 December 1980
Family links with cricket: Brothers, Neil, David, Charlie, Joe, play for Welbeck CC and father is Treasurer. Neil also plays for Lincolnshire

Education: Meden School, Warsop
Qualifications: O-level and CSE
Overseas tours: England to India and Sri Lanka 1984-85; West Indies 1985-86; Australia 1986-87; World Cup, Pakistan, Australia and New Zealand 1987-88; unofficial English team to South Africa 1989-90
Cricketers particularly admired: Bob Taylor
Other sports followed: Rock climbing, fell walking and all aspects of mountaineering
Injuries: Missed most of 1988 season following operations in May on index finger of left hand, and in 1989 broke the same finger again, missing end of season. Previously, French was bitten by a dog whilst jogging in the Caribbean in 1985-86; had to be carried off the field with a cut head and concussion after being struck by a short-pitched delivery from Richard Hadlee; contracted a chest infection after being hit in the chest by a ball in Australia in 186-87; in Pakistan in 1987-88, he needed stitches in a cut eye and on the way to hospital a car struck his legs
Relaxations: Reading, pipe smoking and drinking Theakston's Ale
Extras: Youngest player to play for Nottinghamshire, aged 16 years 10 months. Equalled Nottinghamshire record for dismissals in match with 10 (7ct, 3st), and in innings with 6 catches; also set new county record for dismissals in a season with 87 (75ct, 12st). Banned from Test cricket for touring South Africa in 1989-90. Made his maiden first-class 100 in 1990 in 15th season of county cricket
Best batting: 105* Nottinghamshire v Derbyshire, Derby 1990
Best bowling: 1-37 Nottinghamshire v Derbyshire, Derby 1991

1991 Season

	M	Inns	NO	Runs	HS	Avge	100s	50s	Ct	St	O	M	Runs	Wkts	Avge	Best	5wI	10wM
Test																		
All First	21	24	4	315	65	15.75	-	2	54	8	14	4	48	1	48.00	1-37	-	-
1-day Int																		
NatWest	3	2	0	8	7	4.00	-	-	7	-								
B&H	4	1	1	37	37 *	-	-	-	3	-								
Refuge	17	11	6	137	31	27.40	-	-	17	1								

Career Performances

	M	Inns	NO	Runs	HS	Avge	100s	50s	Ct	St	Balls	Runs	Wkts	Avge	Best	5wI	10wM
Test	16	21	4	308	59	18.11	-	1	38	1							
All First	323	424	84	6461	105 *	19.00	1	23	731	91	90	70	1	70.00	1-37	-	-
1-day Int	13	8	3	34	9 *	6.80	-	-	13	3							
NatWest	28	23	5	346	49	19.22	-	-	45	4							
B&H	56	40	12	401	48 *	14.32	-	-	58	11							
Refuge	154	94	31	933	37	14.81	-	-	121	17							

FROST, M.   Glamorgan

Name: Mark Frost
Role: Right-hand bat, right-arm
medium-fast bowler
Born: 21 October 1962, Barking
Height: 6ft 2in **Weight:** 14st
Nickname: Harold, Frosty, Jack
County debut: 1988 (Surrey),
1990 (Glamorgan)
County cap: 1991
50 wickets in a season: 2
1st-Class 5 w. in innings: 4
1st-Class 10 w. in match: 2
1st-Class catches: 5
Place in bowling averages: 41st av. 28.73
(1990 54th av. 34.69)
Strike rate: 49.23 (career 56.24)
Parents: George and Joyce
Wife and date of marriage: Janet,
28 September 1991
Family links with cricket: All three brothers play
Education: Alexandra High School, Tipton; St Peter's, Wolverhampton; University of
Durham
Qualifications: 10 O-levels, 4 A-levels, BA (Hons) Geography
Off-season: Working for South Glamorgan County Council
Overseas tours: Christians in Sport to India 1985; Surrey to Sharjah 1988; Glamorgan to
Zimbabwe 1991
Cricketers particularly admired: Jack Breakwell, Andy Webster, Ron Headley, Chris
Derham, Nick Peters, Geoff Arnold, Pete Frost
Other sports followed: Soccer, rugby, tennis, athletics
Injuries: Back strain, knuckle bruising
Relaxations: Hill walking, climbing, listening to compact discs, theatre going. 'Climbing
snowy mountains in Scotland with Janet. Converting Tony Cottey.'
Extras: Member of Christians in Sport. Played for Old Hill CC, winners of Cockspur Cup
in 1987 and for Staffordshire before joining Surrey. Released by Surrey at end of 1989
season and joined Glamorgan
Opinions on cricket: 'The cricket ball should be standardised so that they all deteriorate,
shine, or go soft in the same way. There should be no declarations so that batsmen have to
give up their wickets to tired seamers!'
Best batting: 12 Glamorgan v Warwickshire, Edgbaston 1990
Best bowling: 7-99 Glamorgan v Gloucestershire, Cheltenham 1991

1991 Season

	M	Inns	NO	Runs	HS	Avge	100s	50s	Ct	St	O	M	Runs	Wkts	Avge	Best	5wI	10wM
Test																		
All First	20	12	5	19	8 *	2.71	-	-	1	-	533.2	90	1868	65	28.73	7-99	1	1
1-day Int																		
NatWest	3	1	0	3	3	3.00	-	-	3	-	31	2	137	2	68.50	1-45	-	
B&H	4	2	1	0	0 *	0.00	-	-	-	-	40	6	177	5	35.40	3-38	-	
Refuge	10	3	2	2	2	2.00	-	-	3	-	70	2	357	14	25.50	3-35	-	

Career Performances

	M	Inns	NO	Runs	HS	Avge	100s	50s	Ct	St	Balls	Runs	Wkts	Avge	Best	5wI	10wM
Test																	
All First	54	43	14	83	12	2.86	-	-	5	-	8380	4992	149	33.50	7-99	4	2
1-day Int																	
NatWest	6	1	0	3	3	3.00	-	-	3	-	372	260	5	52.00	3-50	-	
B&H	8	4	2	4	3	2.00	-	-	-	-	476	323	14	23.07	4-25	-	
Refuge	24	6	4	11	6	5.50	-	-	4	-	976	862	30	28.73	4-30	-	

GARNHAM, M. A.　　　　　　Essex

Name: Michael Anthony Garnham
Role: Right-hand bat, wicket-keeper
Born: 20 August 1960, Johannesburg
Height: 5ft 10³/₄in **Weight:** 12st
Nickname: Bones, Fred
County debut: 1979 (Gloucs),
1980 (Leics), 1989 (Essex)
County cap: 1989 (Essex)
1st-Class 50s scored: 22
1st-Class 100s scored: 4
1st-Class catches: 320
1st-Class stumpings: 28
One-Day 50s: 2
One-Day 100s: 1
Place in batting averages: 34th av. 46.95
(1990 170th av. 29.28)
Parents: Pauline Anne and Robert Arthur
Wife and date of marriage: Lorraine,
15 September 1984
Children: Laura Clare, 3 November 1988; Eleanor Louise, 22 October 1990
Family links with cricket: Father was a club cricketer in Essex. He lost the sight of an eye keeping wicket

Education: Camberwell Grammar, Melbourne, Australia; Scotch College, Perth, Australia; Park School, Barnstaple, North Devon; North Devon College; University of East Anglia (for one year)

Qualifications: 10 O-levels, 2 A-levels

Overseas tours: England Schools to India 1977-78; England YC to Australia 1979

Cricketers particularly admired: Bob Taylor

Other sports followed: Squash

Relaxations: Carpentry – furniture making, building and DIY

Extras: Moved to England in 1975 after living in Australia for ten years and in South Africa for four years. Played for Devon in 1976 and 1977 before joining Gloucestershire. Signed for Leicestershire in 1980 and was banned by the registration committee from competitive first-team cricket for a month for breach of registration regulations. Retired at end of 1985, but returned for one one-day and one three-day game in 1988 following injury to Phil Whitticase. Signed for Essex in 1989, having been playing for Cambridgeshire. 'Having run a business making keeping gloves, I wear gloves I have made myself.'

Opinions on cricket: 'I hope that we soon can organise a sensible system of county cricket built around 17 four-day games, with a comprehensive review of the distribution of the game's income. It cannot be beyond our wit to produce the cricket that everyone seems to want without the financial hardships that some administrators predict.'

Best batting: 123 Essex v Leicestershire, Leicester 1991

1991 Season

	M	Inns	NO	Runs	HS	Avge	100s	50s	Ct	St	O	M	Runs	Wkts	Avge	Best	5wI	10wM
Test																		
All First	25	29	8	986	123	46.95	3	5	62	-	4	0	39	0	-	-	-	-
1-day Int																		
NatWest	3	2	1	21	12 *	21.00	-	-	3	-								
B&H	6	4	1	27	11	9.00	-	-	7	1								
Refuge	13	9	3	67	18 *	11.16	-	-	10	3								

Career Performances

	M	Inns	NO	Runs	HS	Avge	100s	50s	Ct	St	Balls	Runs	Wkts	Avge	Best	5wI	10wM
Test																	
All First	147	193	42	4387	123	29.05	4	22	320	28	24	39	0	-	-	-	-
1-day Int																	
NatWest	19	16	5	318	110	28.90	1	-	13	2							
B&H	49	34	12	467	55	21.22	-	1	45	5							
Refuge	126	92	21	1174	79 *	16.53	-	1	110	17							

GATTING, M. W. Middlesex

Name: Michael William Gatting
Role: Right-hand bat, right-arm
medium bowler, slip fielder
Born: 6 June 1957, Kingsbury, Middlesex
Height: 5ft 10in **Weight:** 15st
Nickname: Gatt, Jabba
County debut: 1975
County cap: 1977
Benefit: 1988 (£205,000)
Test debut: 1977-78
Tests: 68
One-Day Internationals: 85
1000 runs in a season: 13
1st-Class 50s scored: 134
1st-Class 100s scored: 66
1st-Class 200s scored: 5
1st-Class 5 w. in innings: 2
1st-Class catches: 360
One-Day 50s: 67
One-Day 100s: 11
Place in batting averages: 3rd av. 73.46 (1990 31st av. 56.80)
Parents: Bill and Vera
Wife and date of marriage: Elaine, September 1980
Children: Andrew, 21 January 1983; James, 11 July 1986
Family links with cricket: Father used to play club cricket. Brother Steve played for Middlesex 2nd XI
Education: Wykeham Primary School; John Kelly Boys' High School
Qualifications: 4 O-levels
Overseas tours: England to New Zealand and Pakistan 1977-78; West Indies 1980-81; India and Sri Lanka 1981-82; New Zealand and Pakistan 1983-84; India 1984-85; West Indies 1985-86; Australia 1986-87; World Cup, Pakistan, Australia and New Zealand 1987-88; unofficial English team to South Africa 1989-90
Cricketers particularly admired: Sir Gary Sobers, Sir Leonard Hutton
Other sports followed: Football, tennis, swimming, golf, squash
Injuries: Scalded chest, hamstring, disclocated finger
Relaxations: Reading science fiction thrillers, 'hooked on Tolkien' and a great fan of 'Dr Who'; music, 'the only music I dislike is punk rock and heavy metal.'
Extras: Awarded OBE in Queen's Birthday Honours for services to cricket. Captain of Middlesex since 1983. Captain of England from 1986 to 1988. Published autobiography *Leading From the Front* in 1988. Won a bronze medal for ballroom dancing at the Neasden Ritz. Played football for Edgware Town as a teenager. Started as a goalkeeper, but also played centre-half for Middlesex Schools. Was recommended to West Ham, had a trial

with QPR and offered an apprenticeship by Watford. His brother Steve has had a successful football career with Arsenal and Brighton. Mike started his cricket career as wicket-keeper for his school team. He toured West Indies with England Young Cricketers in 1976 and 'to my immense pleasure (and to most other people's total disbelief) I was given the job of opening the bowling in the 'Test' matches.' One of *Wisden's* Five Cricketers of the Year, 1983. His finest achievement was as captain of England on victorious tour of Australia, 1986-87, when they won the Ashes, the Perth Challenge Cup and World Series Cup. Was relieved of England captaincy after the First Test against West Indies in 1988. Captain of unofficial English team in South Africa in 1989-90 and has been banned from Test cricket for five years. Captained Middlesex to Championship title in 1990

Opinions on cricket: 'There seems to be far too much cricket compressed into our domestic season and with all the travelling involved, it leaves most of us rather jaded by the time September comes.'

Best batting: 258 Middlesex v Somerset, Bath 1984
Best bowling: 5-34 Middlesex v Glamorgan, Swansea 1982

1991 Season

	M	Inns	NO	Runs	HS	Avge	100s	50s	Ct	St	O	M	Runs	Wkts	Avge	Best	5wI	10wM
Test																		
All First	22	39	11	2057	215 *	73.46	8	6	14	-	30.2	5	99	0	-		-	-	-
1-day Int																			
NatWest	2	2	0	150	85	75.00	-	2	2	-	1	0	8	1	8.00	1-8	-	
B&H	4	4	0	169	112	42.25	1	-	1	-								
Refuge	15	15	2	525	111	40.38	1	4	5	-	24.5	0	119	2	59.50	2-34	-	

Career Performances

	M	Inns	NO	Runs	HS	Avge	100s	50s	Ct	St	Balls	Runs	Wkts	Avge	Best	5wI	10wM
Test	68	117	14	3870	207	37.57	9	18	51	-	752	317	4	79.25	1-14	-	-
All First	408	640	101	26512	258	49.18	66	134	360	-	9677	4428	154	28.75	5-34	2	-
1-day Int	85	82	17	2049	115 *	31.52	1	9	22	-	386	334	10	33.40	3-32	-	
NatWest	53	52	13	1894	132 *	48.56	2	13	21	-	1004	643	19	33.84	2-14	-	
B&H	73	68	17	2444	143 *	47.92	3	17	22	-	1382	940	41	22.92	4-49	-	
Refuge	192	177	23	4931	124 *	32.01	5	28	61	-	3082	2587	85	30.43	4-30	-	

GERRARD, M. J.   Gloucestershire

Name: Martin James Gerrard
Role: Right-hand bat, left-arm medium-fast bowler
Born: 19 May 1967, Bristol
Height: 6ft 2in **Weight:** 13st
Nickname: Noddy, Clunk
County debut: 1991

1st-Class 5 w. in innings: 1
1st-Class 10 w. in match: 1
1st-Class catches: 2
Place in bowling averages: 36th av. 27.66
Strike rate: 52.73 (career 52.73)
Parents: Donald and Jean
Marital status: Single
Education: Grittleton House School;
St Brendan's Sixth Form College;
Polytechnic of Wales
Qualifications: A-level Geography,
HND in Mineral Surveying
Career outside cricket: Construction
engineer
Off-season: Playing in South Africa
Overseas teams played for: Vaal Reefs
and Western Transvaal 1991-92
Cricketers particularly admired: Ian
Botham, Sir Richard Hadlee, Jack Russell
Other sports followed: All sport, especially rugby and golf
Relaxations: Playing golf, reading sports autobiographies
Extras: Recorded his first 10 wickets in a match on only his fifth first-class appearance
Best batting: 42 Gloucestershire v Somerset, Bristol 1991
Best bowling: 6-40 Gloucestershire v Sri Lanka, Bristol 1991

1991 Season

	M	Inns	NO	Runs	HS	Avge	100s	50s	Ct	St	O	M	Runs	Wkts	Avge	Best	5wI	10wM
Test																		
All First	8	9	5	49	42	12.25	-	-	2	-	131.5	20	415	15	27.66	6-40	1	1
1-day Int																		
NatWest	1	0	0	0	0	-	-	-	-	-	2	0	10	0	-	-	-	-
B&H																		
Refuge	4	4	1	17	7	5.66	-	-	-	-	29	3	164	3	54.66	1-35	-	

Career Performances

	M	Inns	NO	Runs	HS	Avge	100s	50s	Ct	St	Balls	Runs	Wkts	Avge	Best	5wI	10wM
Test																	
All First	8	9	5	49	42	12.25	-	-	2	-	791	415	15	27.66	6-40	1	1
1-day Int																	
NatWest	1	0	0	0	0	-	-	-	-	-	12	10	0	-	-	-	-
B&H																	
Refuge	4	4	1	17	7	5.66	-	-	-	-	174	164	3	54.66	1-35	-	

GIDDINS, E. S. H.   Sussex

Name: Edward Simon Hunter Giddins
Role: Right-hand bat, right-arm
medium-fast bowler
Born: 20 July 1971, Eastbourne
Height: 6ft 4in **Weight:** 14st 7lbs
Nickname: Guv'nor
County debut: 1991
1st-Class catches: 0
Parents: Simon and Pauline
Marital status: Single
Family links with cricket: 'Father played
lacrosse.'
Education: St Bede's Prep School,
Eastbourne College
Qualifications: 'I've got a few O-levels
and GCSEs but not all that many A-levels
or degrees.'
Off-season: Ski-guide in Meribel
Overseas teams played for: Discovery Bay
Hotel, Barbados 1991
Cricketers particularly admired: Simon Aldis, Ted James, Graham Dilley
Other sports followed: 'Most sports but not football.'
Injuries: 'I have had an uncharacteristic nightmare: May-August – shin stress fracture,
August-September – viruses.'
Relaxations: Golf and conchology. 'Never go to nightclubs because I believe it could
affect my cricket.'
Opinions on cricket: 'A great game to be involved with – at temperatures above 20°
centigrade.'
Best batting: 14* Sussex v Middlesex, Lord's 1991
Best bowling: 1-29 Sussex v Hampshire, Hove 1991

1991 Season

	M	Inns	NO	Runs	HS	Avge	100s	50s	Ct	St	O	M	Runs	Wkts	Avge	Best	5wI	10wM
Test																		
All First	2	1	1	14	14 *	-	-	-	-	-	56.2	6	186	2	93.00	1-29	-	-
1-day Int																		
NatWest																			
B&H	1	1	0	0	0	0.00	-	-	-	-	8	2	46	1	46.00	1-46	-	
Refuge	2	0	0	0	0	-	-	-	-	-	7	0	38	0	-	-	-	

200

Career Performances

	M	Inns	NO	Runs	HS	Avge	100s	50s	Ct	St	Balls	Runs	Wkts	Avge	Best	5wI	10wM
Test																	
All First	2	1	1	14	14 *	-	-	-	-	-	338	186	2	93.00	1-29	-	-
1-day Int																	
NatWest																	
B&H	1	1	0	0	0	0.00	-	-	-	-	48	46	1	46.00	1-46	-	
Refuge	2	0	0	0	0	-	-	-	-	-	42	38	0	-	-	-	

GIDLEY, M. I. Leicestershire

Name: Martyn Ian Gidley
Role: Left-hand bat, off-spin bowler
Born: 30 September 1968, Leicester
Height: 6ft 1in **Weight:** 12st
Nickname: Gidders
County debut: 1989
1st-Class 50s scored: 3
1st-Class catches: 9
Place in batting averages: 222nd av. 15.28
Parents: Barry and Susan
Marital status: Single
Family links with cricket: Father plays
club cricket, brother plays for
Leicestershire Schools
Education: Loughborough Grammar School
Qualifications: 7 O-levels, 3 A-levels
Off-season: Playing and coaching in
Orange Free State

Overseas teams played for: Harmony,
OFS 1989-91; Orange Free State B 1990-91
Cricketers particularly admired: David Gower, John Emburey. 'Have learnt a lot from
Bobby Simpson, Leicestershire's cricket manager.'
Other sports followed: Football (Manchester United), golf, pool
Injuries: Pulled muscle in side, out for a week
Relaxations: Listen to most types of chart music
Extras: Leicestershire U19 Player of the Year 1987, England Schools U19 1987
Opinions on cricket: 'There is too much cricket played. There should be tighter
restrictions on who can play for England.'
Best batting: 80 Leicestershire v Derbyshire, Leicester 1991
Best bowling: 3-51 Orange Free State B v Western Province B, Bloemfontein 1990-91

1991 Season

	M	Inns	NO	Runs	HS	Avge	100s	50s	Ct	St	O	M	Runs	Wkts	Avge	Best	5wI	10wM
Test																		
All First	6	9	2	107	80	15.28	-	1	4	-	107.4	29	323	4	80.75	2-58	-	-
1-day Int																		
NatWest																		
B&H																		
Refuge	2	2	1	14	12 *	14.00	-	-	-	-	4	0	33	0	-		-	-

Career Performances

	M	Inns	NO	Runs	HS	Avge	100s	50s	Ct	St	Balls	Runs	Wkts	Avge	Best	5wI	10wM
Test																	
All First	16	22	5	416	80	24.47	-	3	9	-	1823	868	14	62.00	3-51	-	
1-day Int																	
NatWest																	
B&H	3	2	2	21	20 *	-	-	-	-	-	72	39	0	-		-	
Refuge	8	7	5	51	14 *	25.50	-	-	-	-	211	221	5	44.20	3-45	-	

GILBERT, D. R.   Gloucestershire

Name: David Robert Gilbert
Role: Right-hand bat, right-arm
fast-medium bowler, specialist fine-leg
Born: 29 December 1960,
Sydney, Australia
Height: 6ft 1in **Weight:** 13st
Nickname: Lizard
County debut: 1991
Test debut: 1985
Tests: 9
One-Day Internationals: 14
50 wickets in a season: 1
1st-Class 50s scored: 1
1st-Class 100s scored: 1
1st-Class 5 w. in innings: 11
1st-Class 10 w. in match: 1
1st-Class catches: 28
Place in batting averages: 231st av. 14.42
Place in bowling averages: 43rd av. 29.14
Strike rate: 60.82 (career 64.03)
Parents: Robert and Yvonne (deceased)
Wife and date of marriage: Hilary Louise, 3 September 1988

Children: Adele Yvonne, 4 January 1991
Family links with cricket: Uncles played Sydney club cricket
Education: Marist Bros, Eastwood, Sydney; Sydney Technical College
Qualifications: Australian Higher School Certificate. Estate Agent Valuer (Surveyor)
Career outside cricket: 'Work for Tasmanian Cricket Association – coaching, promotions etc. Probably go back to estate agency work one day.'
Off-season: Playing for Tasmania in Sheffield Shield
Overseas tours: New South Wales to New Zealand 1985; Zimbabwe 1987; Australian Youth XI to Zimbabwe 1985; Australia to England 1985; New Zealand 1986; Sharjah 1986; India 1986
Overseas teams played for: New South Wales 1983-88; Tasmania 1988-92
Cricketers particularly admired: For sheer cricket ability – Richard Hadlee; for good times – John Dyson, Dirk Welham, Simon Davis, Steve Waugh
Other sports followed: Most sports – 'big golf fan'
Injuries: Hamstring strain and rib injury – missed two games
Relaxations: 'Renovating an old house (mine), gardening, browsing through antique shops, going to the cinema.'
Extras: Hat-trick for NSW v Victoria 1985 and another for Lincolnshire in 1984. Has played in English league cricket in five counties (Essex, Yorkshire, Lancashire, Surrey and Kent). MCC member. Contracted to Gloucestershire for 1991 season only
Opinions on cricket: 'New ball after 85 overs (as per Test cricket), 17 four-day games – 100 overs per day 11am-6pm. Install bowling machine for Sunday league!'
Best batting: 117 Australians v Delhi, Baroda 1986-87
Best bowling: 8-55 Gloucestershire v Kent, Canterbury 1991

1991 Season

	M	Inns	NO	Runs	HS	Avge	100s	50s	Ct	St	O	M	Runs	Wkts	Avge	Best	5wI	10wM
Test																		
All First	22	28	7	303	28 *	14.42	-	-	5	-	648.5	137	1865	64	29.14	8-55	1	-
1-day Int																		
NatWest	1	0	0	0	0	-	-	-	1	-	12	0	41	2	20.50	2-41	-	
B&H	4	3	0	25	16	8.33	-	-	-	-	44	5	138	3	46.00	1-31	-	
Refuge	11	5	2	17	10 *	5.66	-	-	1	-	77.4	1	391	6	65.16	2-27	-	

Career Performances

	M	Inns	NO	Runs	HS	Avge	100s	50s	Ct	St	Balls	Runs	Wkts	Avge	Best	5wI	10wM
Test	9	12	4	57	15	7.12	-	-	-	-	1647	843	16	52.68	3-48	-	
All First	117	137	50	1298	117	14.92	1	1	28	-	21708	10765	339	31.75	8-55	11	1
1-day Int	14	8	3	39	8	7.80	-	-	3	-	684	552	18	30.66	5-56	1	
NatWest	1	0	0	0	0	-	-	-	1	-	72	41	2	20.50	2-41	-	
B&H	4	3	0	25	16	8.33	-	-	-	-	264	138	3	46.00	1-31	-	
Refuge	11	5	2	17	10 *	5.66	-	-	1	-	466	391	6	65.16	2-27	-	

GLENDENEN, J. D. Durham

Name: John David Glendenen
Role: Right-hand opening bat, right-arm
medium bowler
Born: 20 June 1965, Middlesbrough
Height: 6ft **Weight:** 12st 10lbs
Nickname: Glendo
One-Day 100s: 1
Parents: David and Jackie
Marital status: Single
Family links with cricket: Father played
cricket for Middlesbrough for 25 years in
the NYSD League
Education: Ormesby Secondary School
Off-season: Playing for Manly, Sydney
Overseas teams played for: Manly,
Sydney 1989-92
Other sports followed: All sports
Injuries: Broken big toe (twice)
Relaxations: Music

Extras: Has cored six centuries for Durham including 109 against Glamorgan in the
NatWest Trophy 1991. Has played 2nd XI cricket for Yorkshire (1983-86), Gloucestershire
(1988) and Somerset (1989)

1991 Season

	M	Inns	NO	Runs	HS	Avge	100s	50s	Ct	St	O	M	Runs	Wkts	Avge	Best	5wI	10wM
Test																		
All First																		
1-day Int																		
NatWest	1	1	0	109	109	109.00	1	-	-	-								
B&H																		
Refuge																		

Career Performances

	M	Inns	NO	Runs	HS	Avge	100s	50s	Ct	St	Balls	Runs	Wkts	Avge	Best	5wI	10wM
Test																	
All First																	
1-day Int																	
NatWest	3	3	0	129	109	43.00	1	-	-	-							
B&H																	
Refuge																	

GOLDSMITH, S. C. Derbyshire

Name: Steven Clive Goldsmith
Role: Right-hand bat, right-arm
medium-slow 'nagger'
Born: 19 December 1964, Ashford, Kent
Height: 5ft 10½in **Weight:** 12st 10lbs
Nickname: Goldy, Nagger, Ox
County debut: 1987 (Kent),
1988 (Derbyshire)
1000 runs in a season: 1
1st-Class 50s: 11
1st-Class 100s: 1
1st-Class catches: 34
One-Day 50s: 3
Place in batting averages: 146th av. 26.52
(1990 241st av. 16.68)
Place in bowling averages: 76th av. 33.72)
Strike rate: 62.33 (career 84.00)
Parents: Tony and Daphne
Wife and date of marriage: Joanne,
10 March 1990
Family links with cricket: Father played club cricket in Kent and Surrey leagues
Education: Simon Langton Grammar School, Canterbury
Qualifications: 8 O-levels, NCA coaching qualification
Career outside cricket: 'No career but always looking for anything that sells.'
Off-season: Clovelly Hotel – 'all sorts of work'
Overseas teams played for: Essendon, Melbourne 1984-85; Pirates, Durban 1989-91
Cricketers particularly admired: David Gower, Peter Bowler, Mohammad Azharuddin, Ian Bishop, Dominic Cork and Mark Spencer
Other sports followed: Motor sport, golf, hockey 'and most others'
Injuries: Cartilage in right knee at the start of the season, tendonitis in right shoulder
Relaxations: Classic cars, golf and watching Nick Owen on TV, Tony Hancock and comedy
Extras: Spent four years on Kent staff until released at end of the 1987 season.
Opinions on cricket: 'Four-day cricket should come in across the board by 1993 season. Coloured clothing should be used in the B & H and Sunday league. Should look at six major grounds with a view to erecting floodlights and introducing a day/night inter-county series.'
Best batting: 127 Derbyshire v Sri Lankans, Derby 1991
Best bowling: 3-42 Derbyshire v Yorkshire, Scarborough 1991

1991 Season

	M	Inns	NO	Runs	HS	Avge	100s	50s	Ct	St	O	M	Runs	Wkts	Avge	Best	5wI	10wM
Test																		
All First	16	26	3	610	127	26.52	1	2	2	-	187	32	607	18	33.72	3-42	-	-
1-day Int																		
NatWest																		
B&H																		
Refuge	10	8	1	165	67 *	23.57	-	1	4	-	60	3	345	7	49.28	3-48	-	

Career Performances

	M	Inns	NO	Runs	HS	Avge	100s	50s	Ct	St	Balls	Runs	Wkts	Avge	Best	5wI	10wM
Test																	
All First	65	107	9	2373	127	24.21	1	11	34	-	2184	1152	26	44.30	3-42	-	-
1-day Int																	
NatWest	5	4	0	42	21	10.50	-	-	-	-	62	43	1	43.00	1-20	-	
B&H	14	10	3	159	45 *	22.71	-	-	9	-	60	38	3	12.66	3-38	-	
Refuge	45	38	9	732	67 *	25.24	-	3	13	-	462	465	7	66.42	3-48	-	

GOOCH, G. A. Essex

Name: Graham Alan Gooch
Role: Right-hand bat,
right-arm medium bowler
Born: 23 July 1953, Leytonstone
Height: 6ft **Weight:** 13st
Nickname: Zap, Goochie
County debut: 1973
County cap: 1975
Benefit: 1985 (£153,906)
Test debut: 1975
Tests: 91
One-Day Internationals: 96
1000 runs in a season: 15
1st-Class 50s scored: 170
1st-Class 100s scored: 89
1st-Class 200s scored: 9
1st-Class 5 w. in innings: 3
1st-Class catches: 456
One-Day 50s: 105
One-Day 100s: 33
Place in batting averages: 5th av. 70.77 (1990 1st av. 101.70)
Parents: Alfred and Rose

Wife and date of marriage: Brenda, 23 October 1976

Children: Hannah; Megan and Sally (twins)

Family links with cricket: Father played local cricket for East Ham Corinthians. Second cousin, Graham Saville, played for Essex CCC and is now England YC team manager

Education: Cannhall School and Norlington Junior High School, Leytonstone; Redbridge Technical College

Qualifications: 6 CSEs; four-year apprenticeship in tool-making

Off-season: Captaining England in New Zealand and Australia

Overseas tours: England YC to West Indies 1972; England to Australia 1978-79; Australia and India 1979-80; West Indies 1980-81; India and Sri Lanka 1981-82; World Cup and Pakistan 1987-88; India and West Indies 1989-90; Australia 1990-91; New Zealand 1991-92; Australia (World Cup) 1991-92; unofficial English team to South Africa 1981-82

Overseas teams played for: Western Province, South Africa 1982-84

Cricketers particularly admired: Bob Taylor, a model sportsman; Mike Procter for his enthusiasm; Barry Richards for his ability

Other sports followed: Squash, soccer, golf. Has trained with West Ham United FC

Relaxations: 'Relaxing at home.'

Extras: One of *Wisden's* Five Cricketers of the Year, 1979. Captained English rebel team in South Africa in 1982 and was banned from Test cricket for three years. Hit a hole in one at Tollygunge Golf Club during England's tour in India, 1981-82. Appointed Essex captain 1986, but resigned captaincy at end of 1987; reappointed in 1989 following retirement of Keith Fletcher. Captain of England for last two Tests of 1988 season against West Indies and Sri Lanka in 1988 and chosen to captain England on the cancelled tour of India in 1988-89. Reappointed captain for the tour to India and West Indies in 1989-90, and led England to their first Test victory over West Indies for sixteen years. His 333 in the Lord's Test against India was the third highest score ever by an English batsman in a Test match, and by also hitting 123 in the second innings he created a record Test aggregate of 456 runs and became the first man to hit a triple century and a century in the same first-class match. His aggregate for the season (2746 runs at 101.70) was the best since 1961 and he was only the fourth batsman to finish an English season with an average better than 100. When he first joined Essex, he was a wicket-keeper and batted at number 11 in his first match. He went on a Young England tour to the West Indies as second wicket-keeper to Andy Stovold of Gloucestershire. Autobiography *Out of the Wilderness* published in 1988; *Test of Fire*, an account of the West Indies tour, published in 1990

Opinions on cricket: Regarding four-day cricket: 'We have had some excellent four-day games, and purely in cricketing terms I believe it is worth trying, as long as it is scheduled so that Test cricketers are available for almost all the games.'

Best batting: 333 England v India, Lord's 1990

Best bowling: 7-14 Essex v Worcestershire, Ilford 1982

---

76. Who captained the 1965 South Africans in England?

1991 Season

	M	Inns	NO	Runs	HS	Avge	100s	50s	Ct	St	O	M	Runs	Wkts	Avge	Best	5wI	10wM
Test	6	11	1	692	174	69.20	2	2	6	-	8	1	14	0	-	-	-	-
All First	20	31	4	1911	259	70.77	6	6	22	-	63.1	22	215	4	53.75	2-16	-	-
1-day Int	3	3	0	65	54	21.66	-	1	2	-	18	1	77	3	25.66	1-9	-
NatWest	3	3	0	202	95	67.33	-	3	-	-	18	3	67	3	22.33	2-30	-
B&H	6	6	0	202	72	33.66	-	1	3	-	56	2	235	7	33.57	2-19	-
Refuge	8	7	1	358	107	59.66	1	3	3	-	43	2	175	6	29.16	3-25	-

Career Performances

	M	Inns	NO	Runs	HS	Avge	100s	50s	Ct	St	Balls	Runs	Wkts	Avge	Best	5wI	10wM
Test	91	166	6	7028	333	43.92	15	39	94	-	1989	800	17	47.05	2-12	-	-
All First	459	777	62	33897	333	47.40	89	170	456	-	16906	7644	219	34.90	7-14	3	-
1-day Int	96	94	5	3641	142	40.91	8	20	34	-	1946	1423	36	39.52	3-19	-
NatWest	42	41	2	2022	144	51.84	5	13	20	-	1585	808	28	28.85	3-31	-
B&H	93	92	10	4156	198 *	50.68	9	29	61	-	3563	2079	67	31.03	3-24	-
Refuge	219	215	20	6724	176	34.48	11	43	78	-	5456	4120	141	29.22	4-33	-

GOUGH, D. Yorkshire

Name: Darren Gough
Role: Right-hand bat, right-arm
fast-medium bowler
Born: 18 September 1970, Barnsley
Height: 5ft 11in **Weight:** 12st 11lbs
Nickname: Dazzler, Guzzler, Son of
County debut: 1989
1st-Class 50s: 2
1st-Class 5 w. in innings: 1
1st-Class catches: 4
Place in batting averages: 137th av. 27.90
(1990 270th av. 11.18)
Place in bowling averages: 137th av. 52.50
(1990 71st av. 37.03)
Strike rate: 90.00 (career 70.92)
Parents: Trevor and Christine
Marital status: Single
Family links with cricket: 'Brother
Adrian plays in local league for Monk
Bretton where I started.'
Education: St Helens Primary; Priory Comprehensive; Horsforth College (part-time)
Qualifications: 2 O-levels, 5 CSEs, BTec Leisure, Distinction Coaching Award 1

Career outside cricket: Straight from school into cricket
Off-season: 'Trying to improve my fitness!'
Overseas tours: England YC to Australia 1989-90; Yorkshire to Barbados 1990
Overseas teams played for: East Christchurch Shirley, New Zealand 1990-91
Cricketers particularly admired: Ian Botham, Richard Hadlee 'and in our team Peter Hartley for his approach to the game.'
Other sports followed: Football, golf
Injuries: Sore shins all season
Relaxations: 'Watching videos, having the odd drink in discos.'
Extras: 'Had trials with Rotherham United FC but wasn't good enough.'
Opinions on cricket: 'It's a batter's game.'
Best batting: 72 Yorkshire v Northamptonshire, Northampton 1991
Best bowling: 5-41 Yorkshire v Lancashire, Scarborough 1991

1991 Season

	M	Inns	NO	Runs	HS	Avge	100s	50s	Ct	St	O	M	Runs	Wkts	Avge	Best	5wI	10wM
Test																		
All First	13	14	3	307	72	27.90	-	2	3	-	270	55	945	18	52.50	5-41	1	-
1-day Int																		
NatWest	1	1	0	2	2	2.00	-	-	-	-	8	2	18	0	-	-	-	-
B&H	1	1	0	1	1	1.00	-	-	-	-	8	0	41	2	20.50	2-41	-	
Refuge	10	7	1	105	72 *	17.50	-	1	4	-	60.2	1	316	7	45.14	2-32	-	

Career Performances

	M	Inns	NO	Runs	HS	Avge	100s	50s	Ct	St	Balls	Runs	Wkts	Avge	Best	5wI	10wM
Test																	
All First	29	33	10	441	72	19.17	-	2	4	-	3688	2155	52	41.44	5-41	1	-
1-day Int																	
NatWest	3	1	0	2	2	2.00	-	-	1	-	162	85	4	21.25	2-22	-	
B&H	2	1	0	1	1	1.00	-	-	-	-	84	68	2	34.00	2-41	-	
Refuge	15	9	2	126	72 *	18.00	-	1	6	-	518	462	9	51.33	2-32	-	

77. Which England qualified player came highest in the first-class averages last season?

78. Which county has won the County Championship the most times, and how many?

Name: Ian James Gould
Role: Left-hand bat, wicket-keeper
Born: 19 August 1957, Taplow, Bucks
Height: 5ft 7in **Weight:** 12st 4lbs
Nickname: Gunner
County debut: 1975 (Middlesex),
1981 (Sussex)
County cap: 1977 (Middlesex),
1981 (Sussex)
Benefit: 1990 (£87,097)
One-Day Internationals: 18
1st-Class 50s scored: 47
1st-Class 100s scored: 4
1st-Class catches: 536
1st-Class stumpings: 67
One-Day 50s: 20
Place in batting averages: (1990 205th
av. 23.50)
Parents: Doreen and George
Wife and date of marriage: Joanne, 25 September 1986
Children: Gemma Louise, Michael James Thomas
Education: Westgate Secondary Modern, Slough
Career outside cricket: Cricket coach and soccer coach
Off-season: Coaching
Overseas tours: England YC to West Indies 1976; Derrick Robins' XI to Canada 1978-79; International XI to Pakistan 1980-81; England to Australia and New Zealand 1982-83; MCC to Namibia
Overseas teams played for: Auckland 1979-80
Cricketers particularly admired: David Gower, John Lever, Josh Gifford
Other sports followed: Soccer – 'watch the "Gunners" when possible.'
Relaxations: 'Horse racing – listening to Josh Gifford explain to an owner why his horse hasn't run so well.'
Extras: Captain of Sussex in 1986 and 1987
Opinions on cricket: 'I am a fan of four-day cricket as long as it is played on good pitches. Perhaps more people should allow the groundsman to get on with his job and the players should get on with their's.'
Best batting: 128 Middlesex v Worcestershire, Worcester 1978
Best bowling: 3-10 Sussex v Surrey, The Oval 1989

---

79. Who won the first County Championship in 1890?

1991 Season

	M	Inns	NO	Runs	HS	Avge	100s	50s	Ct	St	O	M	Runs	Wkts	Avge	Best	5wI	10wM
Test																		
All First																		
1-day Int																		
NatWest																		
B&H																		
Refuge	1	1	0	21	21	21.00	-	-	-	-								

Career Performances

	M	Inns	NO	Runs	HS	Avge	100s	50s	Ct	St	Balls	Runs	Wkts	Avge	Best	5wI	10wM
Test																	
All First	297	399	63	8756	128	26.06	4	47	536	67	478	365	7	52.14	3-10	-	-
1-day Int	18	14	2	155	42	12.91	-	-	15	3							
NatWest	33	24	2	443	88	20.13	-	2	26	7							
B&H	62	54	9	761	72	16.91	-	4	55	5	20	16	1	16.00	1-0	-	
Refuge	191	170	27	2907	84 *	20.32	-	14	139	22							

GOWER, D. I.   Hampshire

Name: David Ivon Gower
Role: Left-hand bat, off-break bowler
Born: 1 April 1957, Tunbridge Wells
Height: 5ft 11¾in **Weight:** 11st 11lbs
Nickname: Lubo
County debut: 1975 (Leicestershire),
1990 (Hampshire)
County cap: 1977 (Leicestershire),
1990 (Hampshire)
Benefit: 1987 (£121,546)
Test debut: 1978
Tests: 114
One-Day Internationals: 114
1000 runs in a season: 11
1st-Class 50s scored: 123
1st-Class 100s scored: 48
1st-Class 200s scored: 2
1st-Class catches: 255
1st-Class stumpings: 1
One-Day 50s: 52
One-Day 100s: 18
Place in batting averages: 84th av. 34.60 (1990 66th av.46.77)

Parents: Richard Hallam and Sylvia Mary
Marital status: Single
Family links with cricket: Father was club cricketer
Education: Marlborough House School; King's School, Canterbury; University College, London (did not complete law course)
Qualifications: 8 O-levels, 3 A-levels
Career outside cricket: Head PR Ltd
Off-season: see above
Overseas tours: English Schools XI to South Africa 1974-75; England YC to West Indies 1976; England to Australia 1978-79; Australia and India 1979-80; West Indies 1980-81; India and Sri Lanka 1981-82; Australia and New Zealand 1982-83; New Zealand and Pakistan 1983-84; India and Australia 1984-85; West Indies 1985-86; Australia 1986-87; Australia 1990-91
Cricketers particularly admired: Graeme Pollock, Gary Sobers, Allan Border
Other sports followed: Rugby, tennis, golf, soccer
Injuries: 'No excuses!'
Relaxations: Wildlife photography, wine, winter sports, flying, lawn mowing
Extras: Played for King's Canterbury 1st XI for three years. One of *Wisden's* Five Cricketers of the Year, 1978. Books include *Anyone for Cricket* (1979), *With Time to Spare* (1980), *Heroes and Contemporaries* (1983), *A Right Ambition* (1986), and he writes regular column for *Wisden Cricket Monthly*. England and Leicestershire captain 1984-86. Declared himself not available for England tour 1987-88. Reappointed Leicestershire captain for 1988 and reappointed captain of England v Australia in 1989. Sacked as captain and player after losing the Ashes to Allan Border's team. Resigned the Leicestershire captaincy at the end of the season and decided to join Hampshire. Surprisingly not selected for England's winter tours to either India or West Indies, but when in the Caribbean writing for *The Times*, he was called into the England side for their match v Barbados. Made sure of a fifth tour to Australia with 157* v India at The Oval when he became England's second highest Test run-maker. In the absence of Mark Nicholas through injury, captained Hampshire to victory in the NatWest Trophy final 1991
Best batting: 228 Leicestershire v Glamorgan, Leicester 1989
Best bowling: 3-47 Leicestershire v Essex, Leicester 1977

1991 Season

	M	Inns	NO	Runs	HS	Avge	100s	50s	Ct	St	O	M	Runs	Wkts	Avge	Best	5wI	10wM
Test																		
All First	23	38	5	1142	80 *	34.60	-	8	13	-	0.1	0	4	0	-	-	-	-
1-day Int																		
NatWest	5	3	1	82	54 *	41.00	-	1	-	-								
B&H	5	5	0	97	63	19.40	-	1	1	-								
Refuge	8	7	0	111	45	15.85	-	-	4	-								

Career Performances

	M	Inns	NO	Runs	HS	Avge	100s	50s	Ct	St	Balls	Runs	Wkts	Avge	Best	5wI	10wM
Test	114	199	16	8081	215	44.15	18	38	73	-	36	20	1	20.00	1-1	-	-
All First	412	666	62	23978	228	39.69	48	123	255	1	260	227	4	56.75	3-47	-	-
1-day Int	114	111	8	3170	158	30.77	7	12	44	-	5	14	0	-	-	-	-
NatWest	43	40	6	1757	156	51.67	5	8	15	-	15	16	0	-	-	-	-
B&H	61	60	7	1367	114 *	25.79	1	3	24	-							
Refuge	160	157	23	4700	135 *	35.07	5	29	64	-							

GRAVENEY, D. A.   Durham

Name: David Anthony Graveney
Role: Right-hand bat, slow
left-arm bowler
Born: 2 January 1953, Bristol
Height: 6ft 4in **Weight:** 14st
Nickname: Gravity, Grav
County debut: 1972 Gloucestershire),
1991 (Somerset)
County cap: 1976 (Gloucestershire)
Benefit: 1986
50 wickets in a season: 7
1st-Class 50s scored: 15
1st-Class 100s scored: 2
1st-Class 5 w. in innings: 38
1st-Class 10 w. in match: 7
1st-Class catches: 211
One-Day 50s: 1
Place in batting averages: (1990 265th
av. 11.88)

Place in bowling averages: 110th av. 39.27 (1990 82nd av. 38.35)
Strike rate: 77.32 (career 69.00)
Parents: Ken and Jeanne (deceased)
Wife and date of marriage: Julie, 23 September 1978
Children: Adam, 13 October 1982
Family links with cricket: Son of J. K. Graveney, captain of Gloucestershire, who took
10 wickets for 66 runs v Derbyshire at Chesterfield in 1949, and nephew of Tom Graveney
of Gloucestershire, Worcestershire and England. Brother, John, selected for English
Public Schools v English Schools at Lord's
Education: Millfield School, Somerset
Career outside cricket: Company director. Accountant
Overseas tours: Unofficial England tour to South Africa 1989-90

Other sports followed: Golf, soccer, squash
Relaxations: 'Playing sport, TV and cinema. Relaxing at a good pub.'
Extras: Treasurer of Cricketers' Association. Captain of Gloucestershire, 1981 to 1988. Third member of the Graveney family to be dismissed by Gloucester CCC – Uncle Tom as captain in 1960 and father Ken as chairman in 1982 – when he was sacked as captain. Player-manager of unofficial tour to South Africa 1989-90. Left Gloucestershire at end of 1990 season and joined Somerset. Left Somerset at the end of the 1991 season to captain Durham in their first season as a first-class county
Best batting: 119 Gloucestershire v Oxford University, The Parks 1980
Best bowling: 8-85 Gloucestershire v Nottinghamshire, Cheltenham 1974

1991 Season

	M	Inns	NO	Runs	HS	Avge	100s	50s	Ct	St	O	M	Runs	Wkts	Avge	Best	5wI	10wM
Test																		
All First	21	14	7	59	17	8.42	-	-	10	-	708.2	152	2160	55	39.27	7-105	2	-
1-day Int																		
NatWest	3	0	0	0	0	-	-	-	1	-	31	5	92	3	30.66	1-24	-	
B&H	1	1	1	3	3 *	-	-	-	-	-	7	0	33	0	-		-	-
Refuge	10	3	3	20	14 *	-	-	-	1	-	60	2	253	11	23.00	3-21	-	

Career Performances

	M	Inns	NO	Runs	HS	Avge	100s	50s	Ct	St	Balls	Runs	Wkts	Avge	Best	5wI	10wM
Test																	
All First	404	501	149	6168	119	17.52	2	15	211	-	61001	26113	884	29.54	8-85	38	7
1-day Int																	
NatWest	41	25	9	292	44	18.25	-	-	18	-	2296	1225	51	24.02	5-11	1	
B&H	68	43	16	425	49 *	15.74	-	-	16	-	2792	1705	51	33.43	3-13	-	
Refuge	221	134	52	1292	56 *	15.75	-	1	53	-	6091	4684	142	32.98	4-22	-	

GRAYSON, P. A. Yorkshire

Name: Paul Adrian Grayson
Role: Right-hand bat, slow left-arm bowler
Born: 31 March 1971, Ripon
Height: 6ft 1in **Weight:** 12st 2lbs
Nickname: PG, Larry, Ravi
County debut: 1990
1st-Class catches: 3
Parents: Adrian and Carol
Marital status: Single
Family links with cricket: 'Dad played good league cricket and is also an NCA staff coach; brother also plays.'

Education: Bedale Comprehensive School
Qualifications: 8 CSEs, BTec in Leisure, NCA senior coaching award
Off-season: Playing and coaching in Wellington, New Zealand
Overseas tours: England YC to Australia 1989-90; Yorkshire to Barbados 1990
Overseas teams played for: Petone, Wellington 1991-92
Cricketers particularly admired: Graham Gooch, Martyn Moxon, Phil Carrick
Other sports followed: Keen supporter of Leeds United
Injuries: Missed two weeks with a thigh strain
Relaxations: Playing golf, watching most sports programmes on TV, reading newspapers

Extras: Brother Simon is a professional footballer with Leeds United. Played for England YC v New Zealand 1989 and Pakistan 1990. Turned down an offer by Middlesex
Best batting: 44* Yorkshire v Somerset, Scarborough 1990
Best bowling: 1-3 Yorkshire v Oxford University, The Parks 1991

1991 Season

	M	Inns	NO	Runs	HS	Avge	100s	50s	Ct	St	O	M	Runs	Wkts	Avge	Best	5wI	10wM
Test																		
All First	2	2	1	18	18 *	18.00	-	-	1	-	27	10	56	1	56.00	1-3	-	-
1-day Int																		
NatWest																		
B&H																		
Refuge	1	0	0	0	0	-	-	-	-	-	5	0	32	1	32.00	1-32	-	

Career Performances

	M	Inns	NO	Runs	HS	Avge	100s	50s	Ct	St	Balls	Runs	Wkts	Avge	Best	5wI	10wM
Test																	
All First	7	10	5	163	44 *	32.60	-	-	3	-	642	326	2	163.00	1-3	-	-
1-day Int																	
NatWest																	
B&H																	
Refuge	1	0	0	0	0	-	-	-	-	-	30	32	1	32.00	1-32	-	

GREEN, S. J.   Warwickshire

Name: Simon James Green
Role: Right-hand bat, left-arm medium bowler
Born: 19 March 1970, Bloxwich
Height: 6ft 2½in **Weight:** 13st
Nickname: Charlie, Digger
County debut: 1988
1st-Class 50s scored: 1
1st-Class catches: 2
Parents: Albert and Jennifer
Education: West House Prep School; Old Swinford Hospital
Qualifications: 3 O-levels, coaching qualification
Overseas teams played for: Albany, Western Australia 1988-89; Phoenix, Western Australia 1989-90
Cricketers particularly admired: Dennis Lillee, Allan Donald, Paul Smith, Robin Smith, Ian Botham

Other sports followed: Football (Derby County) and Formula 1 Grand Prix
Injuries: Double fracture of the thumb
Relaxations: Playing hockey and football, listening to music
Extras: 'Was out first ball in my 2nd and 1st team debuts.'
Opinions on cricket: 'Four-day cricket should be played instead of three-day, so that you can get proper results in games, not teams setting easy targets on the last day of a three-day game.'
Best batting: 77* Warwickshire v Somerset, Edgbaston 1991

1991 Season

	M	Inns	NO	Runs	HS	Avge	100s	50s	Ct	St	O	M	Runs	Wkts	Avge	Best	5wl	10wM
Test																		
All First	1	1	1	77	77*	-		-	1	-	-							
1-day Int																		
NatWest																		
B&H																		
Refuge	2	2	0	7	5	3.50	-	-	-	-	-							

Career Performances

	M	Inns	NO	Runs	HS	Avge	100s	50s	Ct	St	Balls	Runs	Wkts	Avge	Best	5wI	10wM
Test																	
All First	5	8	1	168	77 *	24.00	-	1	2	-							
1-day Int																	
NatWest	1	1	0	1	1	1.00	-	-	-	-							
B&H	1	1	0	0	0	0.00	-	-	-	-							
Refuge	7	6	1	43	25	8.60	-	-	-	-							

GREENFIELD, K. Sussex

Name: Keith Greenfield
Role: Right-hand bat, right-arm
off-break bowler
Born: 6 December 1968, Brighton
Height: 6ft **Weight:** 12st 4lbs
Nickname: Grubby
County debut: 1987
1st-Class 50s scored: 2
1st-Class 100s scored: 3
1st-Class catches: 22
Place in batting averages: 114th av. 30.30
Parents: Leslie Ernest and Sheila
Marital status: Single
Education: Coldgan First and
Middle Schools, Falmer High School
Qualifications: 3 O-level, BTec Leisure
Centre Management certificate, junior,
senior and advanced coaching certificates
Off-season: Coaching at schools around
Sussex and at the county ground, Hove
Overseas teams played for: Cornwall, Auckland 1988-90
Cricketers particularly admired: Derek Randall, Ian Botham
Other sports followed: 'All sports interest me.'
Injuries: Bruising on right forearm when hit fielding at short-leg – missed two games
Relaxations: 'Eating at good restaurants, music, films.'
Extras: First person taken on Youth Training Scheme to become a professional cricketer
at Sussex. Only uncapped player to have captained Sussex at Hove (v Cambridge Univ),
scored century in this game. Captained 2nd XI to Championship title in 1990
Opinions on cricket: 'Should play four-day cricket in all Championship matches.'
Best batting: 127* Sussex v Cambridge University, Hove 1991

1991 Season

	M	Inns	NO	Runs	HS	Avge	100s	50s	Ct	St	O	M	Runs	Wkts	Avge	Best	5wI	10wM
Test																		
All First	9	14	1	394	127 *	30.30	2	1	15	-	6	0	30	0	-	-	-	-
1-day Int																		
NatWest																		
B&H	2	2	1	33	33	33.00	-	-	3	-	18	0	89	1	89.00	1-35	-	
Refuge	15	14	3	341	78 *	31.00	-	3	1	-	25.3	0	154	0	-	-	-	

Career Performances

	M	Inns	NO	Runs	HS	Avge	100s	50s	Ct	St	Balls	Runs	Wkts	Avge	Best	5wI	10wM
Test																	
All First	19	32	3	790	127 *	27.24	3	2	22	-	57	49	0	-	-	-	-
1-day Int																	
NatWest																	
B&H	3	3	1	33	33	16.50	-	-	3	-	108	89	1	89.00	1-35	-	
Refuge	21	19	4	389	78 *	25.93	-	3	2	-	153	154	0	-	-	-	

GREIG, I. A.   Surrey

Name: Ian Alexander Greig
Role: Right-hand bat, right-arm
medium bowler, slip fielder
Born: 8 December 1955, Queenstown,
South Africa
Height: 5ft 11½in **Weight:** 12st
Nickname: Wash, Greigy
County debut: 1980 (Sussex),
1987 (Surrey)
County cap: 1981 (Sussex),
1987 (Surrey)
Test debut: 1982
Tests: 2
1000 runs in a season: 2
50 wickets in a season: 3
1st-Class 50s scored: 40
1st-Class 100s scored: 8
1st-Class 200s scored: 1
1st-Class 5 w. in innings: 10
1st-Class 10 w. in match: 2
1st-Class catches: 152
One-Day 50s: 6

Place in batting averages: 177th av. 22.59 (1990 35th av. 54.73)
Place in bowling averages: 121st av. 42.60 (1990 151st av. 66.00)
Strike rate: 99.30 (career 59.82)
Parents: Sandy (deceased) and Joyce
Wife and date of marriage: Cheryl, 8 January 1983
Children: Michelle, 17 December 1984; Andrew, 20 January 1987
Family links with cricket: Brother of Tony, former captain of Sussex and England; brother-in-law Phillip Hodson played for Cambridge University and Yorkshire
Education: Queens College, Queenstown; Downing College, Cambridge
Qualifications: MA Law (Cantab)
Off-season: Marketing/cricket activities at Surrey CCC
Overseas teams played for: Border, South Africa 1974-75, 1979-80; Griqualand West, South Africa 1975-76
Cricketers particularly admired: Garth le Roux, Richard Hadlee
Other sports followed: Rugby
Relaxations: Relaxing with family, barbecues, fly-fishing
Extras: Wombwell Cricket Lovers' Society County Captain of the Year 1991. Retired as captain of Surrey at the end of the 1991 season
Opinions on cricket: 'I still firmly believe that four-day cricket is the answer to English cricket and producing a better equipped England XI. If four-day cricket (x17) is going to happen, then the current three-day playing conditions will have to be altered to get away from the current three-day declarations etc. Perhaps uncovering the wickets is the answer.'
Best batting: 291 Surrey v Lancashire, The Oval 1990
Best bowling: 7-43 Sussex v Cambridge University, Fenner's 1981

1991 Season

	M	Inns	NO	Runs	HS	Avge	100s	50s	Ct	St	O	M	Runs	Wkts	Avge	Best	5wI	10wM
Test																		
All First	20	31	4	610	72	22.59	-	3	7	-	165.3	34	426	10	42.60	3-30	-	-
1-day Int																		
NatWest	3	3	1	35	20	17.50	-	-	-	-								
B&H	4	4	0	93	47	23.25	-	-	2	-	9.2	0	26	2	13.00	2-26	-	
Refuge	13	10	2	162	68 *	20.25	-	1	4	-	29.5	0	146	6	24.33	3-10	-	

Career Performances

	M	Inns	NO	Runs	HS	Avge	100s	50s	Ct	St	Balls	Runs	Wkts	Avge	Best	5wI	10wM
Test	2	4	0	26	14	6.50	-	-	-	-	188	114	4	28.50	4-53	-	-
All First	253	339	50	8301	291	28.72	8	40	152	-	25065	13023	419	31.08	7-43	10	2
1-day Int																	
NatWest	24	20	3	390	82	22.94	-	2	6	-	970	579	22	26.31	4-31	-	
B&H	57	52	4	685	51	14.27	-	1	12	-	2602	1630	59	27.62	5-35	1	
Refuge	144	121	35	1996	68 *	23.20	-	3	34	-	4301	3642	126	28.90	5-30	2	

GRIFFITH, F. A. Derbyshire

Name: Frank Alexander Griffith
Role: Right-hand bat, right-arm medium bowler
Born: 15 August 1968, Leyton
Height: 6ft **Weight:** 12st
Nickname: Sir Learie
County debut: 1988
1st-Class catches: 6
Parents: Alex and Daisy
Marital status: Single
Education: William Morris High School, Walthamstow
Qualifications: Food and nutrition and art O-levels; NCA coaching certificate
Cricketers particularly admired: Collis King, Franklyn Stephenson
Other sports followed: Table tennis, basketball, football
Relaxations: Listening to music
Extras: Attended Haringey Cricket College
Opinions on cricket: 'We must play more four-day games in order to get more results.'
Best batting: 37* Derbyshire v Northamptonshire, Northampton 1988
Best bowling: 4-47 Derbyshire v Lancashire, Old Trafford 1988

1991 Season

	M	Inns	NO	Runs	HS	Avge	100s	50s	Ct	St	O	M	Runs	Wkts	Avge	Best	5wI	10wM
Test																		
All First	2	3	0	11	6	3.66	-	-	-	-	31	6	125	2	62.50	1-16	-	-
1-day Int																		
NatWest																		
B&H																		
Refuge	5	4	1	47	20	15.66	-	-	-	-	23	0	132	3	44.00	3-37	-	

Career Performances

	M	Inns	NO	Runs	HS	Avge	100s	50s	Ct	St	Balls	Runs	Wkts	Avge	Best	5wI	10wM
Test																	
All First	13	21	1	219	37 *	10.95	-	-	6	-	1095	644	18	35.77	4-47	-	-
1-day Int																	
NatWest																	
B&H	1	1	0	10	10	10.00	-	-	-	-							
Refuge	15	13	2	83	20	7.54	-	-	-	-	468	414	12	34.50	3-37	-	

HALL, J. W.   Sussex

Name: James William Hall
Role: Right-hand opening batsman
Born: 30 March 1968, Chichester
Height: 6ft 3in **Weight:** 13st 7lbs
Nickname: Gus
County debut: 1990
1000 runs in a season: 1
1st-Class 50s scored: 9
1st-Class 100s scored: 3
1st-Class catches: 14
Place in batting averages: 128th av. 28.58
(1990 152nd av. 32.57)
Parents: Maurice and Marlene (deceased)
Marital status: Single
Family links with cricket: Father
played club cricket for Chichester
Education: Chichester Boys' High School
Qualifications: 9 O-levels
Off-season: Playing club cricket in Auckland
Overseas teams played for: Southern Districts, Perth, Western Australia 1986-87;
Swanbourne, Perth 1988-89; University St Helliers, Auckland 1991-92
Cricketers particularly admired: Alan Wells, Allan Green, David Smith
Other sports followed: Football (Brighton & Hove Albion and Carlisle United)
Injuries: Blood poisoning, torn shoulder muscles, split webbing on right hand
Relaxations: 'Eating out, drinking bottled beer, spending money at Sammy Gordon's
clothes shop in Brighton.'
Extras: Scored 53 on first XI debut v Zimbabwe and scored maiden first-class 100 in same
week (120* v New Zealand). Over 1000 runs in debut season of first-class cricket. Run out
without facing a ball on NatWest debut v Glamorgan ('thanks Neil'). Whittingdale Young
Cricketer of the Month for May 1991
Opinions on cricket: 'Over rate fines should be scrapped.'
Best batting: 125 Sussex v Nottinghamshire, Trent Bridge 1990

1991 Season

	M	Inns	NO	Runs	HS	Avge	100s	50s	Ct	St	O	M	Runs	Wkts	Avge	Best	5wI	10wM
Test																		
All First	15	26	2	686	117 *	28.58	1	4	8	-								
1-day Int																		
NatWest																			
B&H	4	4	0	150	71	37.50	-	1	-	-								
Refuge	3	3	0	96	50	32.00	-	1	-	-								

Career Performances

	M	Inns	NO	Runs	HS	Avge	100s	50s	Ct	St	Balls	Runs	Wkts	Avge	Best	5wl	10wM
Test																	
All First	35	63	4	1826	125	30.94	3	9	14	-							
1-day Int																	
NatWest	1	1	0	0	0	0.00	-	-	-	-							
B&H	4	4	0	150	71	37.50	-	1	-	-							
Refuge	3	3	0	96	50	32.00	-	1	-	-							

HALLETT, J. C. Somerset

Name: Jeremy Charles Hallett
Role: Right-hand bat, right-arm
medium-fast bowler
Born: 18 October 1970, Yeovil
Height: 6ft 2in **Weight:** 12st
Nickname: Chicks, Pikey
County debut: 1990
1st-Class catches: 4
Place in bowling averages: 138th av. 53.08
Strike rate: 89.25 (career 81.44)
Parents: Glyn and Rosemarie
Marital status: Single
Family links with cricket: 'Father has
played Somerset League cricket for years.'
Education: Wells Cathedral Junior
School; Millfield School;
Durham University
Qualifications: 10 O-levels, 3 A-levels
Off-season: At Durham University
Overseas tours: England YC to Australia 1989-90
Cricketers particularly admired: Malcolm Marshall, Viv Richards, Terry Alderman,
Richard Hadlee, Martin Crowe, Jimmy Cook
Other sports followed: Soccer (Yeovil Town), golf, 'all sports really'
Relaxations: 'Films, music, playing golf, a good pub, food!'
Extras: Cricketer of the Series, England YC v Australia 1989-90. Also played v New
Zealand 1989 and Pakistan 1990. Somerset Young Player of the Year 1990. Played for
Combined Universities in B&H Cup 1991
Opinions on cricket: 'Four-day cricket has to be beneficial to the English game. Quality
not quantity of cricket should be the aim.'
Best batting: 15 Somerset v Gloucestershire, Bristol 1991
Best bowling: 3-154 Somerset v Worcestershire, Worcester 1991

1991 Season

	M	Inns	NO	Runs	HS	Avge	100s	50s	Ct	St	O	M	Runs	Wkts	Avge	Best	5wI	10wM
Test																		
All First	8	5	1	35	15	8.75	-	-	4	-	178.3	31	637	12	53.08	3-154	-	-
1-day Int																		
NatWest	1	0	0	0	0	-	-	-	-	-	12	1	31	0	-		-	
B&H	4	2	0	5	5	2.50	-	-	1	-	43.1	0	149	6	24.83	3-36	-	
Refuge	6	1	0	1	1	1.00	-	-	1	-	40	0	198	5	39.60	2-32	-	

Career Performances

	M	Inns	NO	Runs	HS	Avge	100s	50s	Ct	St	Balls	Runs	Wkts	Avge	Best	5wI	10wM
Test																	
All First	11	6	1	35	15	7.00	-	-	4	-	1466	875	18	48.61	3-154	-	-
1-day Int																	
NatWest	1	0	0	0	0	-	-	-	-	-	72	31	0	-		-	
B&H	6	2	0	5	5	2.50	-	-	1	-	325	219	7	31.28	3-36	-	
Refuge	15	4	3	8	4 *	8.00	-	-	1	-	513	444	12	37.00	3-41	-	

HANCOCK, T. H. C.　　　　Gloucestershire

Name: Timothy Harold Coulter Hancock
Role: Right-hand bat, occasional right-arm medium bowler, short-leg or cover fielder
Born: 20 April 1972
Height: 5ft 10¹/₂in **Weight:** 13st
Nickname: Herbie, Dumper
County debut: 1991
1st-Class 50s: 1
1st-Class catches: 7
Place in batting averages: 241st av. 13.28
Parents: John and Jenifer
Marital status: Single
Family links with cricket: 'Dad plays and so does my brother.'
Education: St Edwards, Oxford; Henley College
Qualifications: 8 GCSEs
Off-season: In South Africa
Cricketers particularly admired: Ian Botham, Robin Smith, Richie Richardson, Desmond Haynes
Other sports followed: Rugby union
Relaxations: 'Going down the pub with a few mates, sleeping.'

Opinions on cricket: 'There is too much poor umpiring in second team cricket and not enough result wickets.'
Best batting: 51 Gloucestershire v Sussex, Hove 1991

1991 Season

	M	Inns	NO	Runs	HS	Avge	100s	50s	Ct	St	O	M	Runs	Wkts	Avge	Best	5wI	10wM
Test																		
All First	5	9	2	93	51	13.28	-	1	7	-								
1-day Int																		
NatWest																		
B&H																		
Refuge	5	3	0	20	20	6.66	-	-	1	-								

Career Performances

	M	Inns	NO	Runs	HS	Avge	100s	50s	Ct	St	Balls	Runs	Wkts	Avge	Best	5wI	10wM
Test																	
All First	5	9	2	93	51	13.28	-	1	7	-							
1-day Int																	
NatWest																	
B&H																	
Refuge	5	3	0	20	20	6.66	-	-	1	-							

HANLEY, R.   Sussex

Name: Robin Hanley
Role: Right-hand bat
Born: 5 January 1968, Tonbridge, Kent
Height: 6ft 2in **Weight:** 14st
Nickname: Ninj, Ninja, Spook
County debut: 1990
Parents: Peter and Janet
Marital status: Single
Family links with cricket: Brother good local player, grandfather founded Woodside Green CC in Surrey
Education: Willingdon School; Eastbourne Sixth Form College
Qualifications: 6 O-levels
Off-season: Coaching cricket
Overseas teams played for: Bayswater Morley, Perth, Western Australia, 1987-88;

Lake View, Kalgoorlie 1989-90; Brighton, Tasmania 1990-91
Cricketers particularly admired: John Tompsett and Mike Turner (Eastbourne CC)
Other sports followed: Boxing
Injuries: Tore muscles in lower back pre-season
Relaxations: Fitness training, martial arts, archery
Extras: Played a season of Central Lancashire League cricket for Rochdale in 1989. Has also played for NCA YC, NAYC, English Schools U19
Opinions on cricket: 'In favour of coloured clothing etc, put forward for Sunday league.'
Best batting: 28 Sussex v Warwickshire, Eastbourne 1990

1991 Season

	M	Inns	NO	Runs	HS	Avge	100s	50s	Ct	St	O	M	Runs	Wkts	Avge	Best	5wl	10wM
Test																		
All First	2	2	0	19	19	9.50	-	-	-	-								
1-day Int																		
NatWest																		
B&H																		
Refuge	1	1	0	2	2	2.00	-	-	1	-								

Career Performances

	M	Inns	NO	Runs	HS	Avge	100s	50s	Ct	St	Balls	Runs	Wkts	Avge	Best	5wl	10wM
Test																	
All First	4	6	0	51	28	8.50	-	-	-	-							
1-day Int																	
NatWest																	
B&H																	
Refuge	3	2	0	13	11	6.50	-	-	2	-							

80. Who is the only current county player to have scored four centuries for England v Australia?

81. What do Doug Walters, Greg Chappell and Kepler Wessels have in common?

82. Who did Salim Malik replace as Essex's overseas player in 1991?

HANSFORD, A. R. Sussex

Name: Alan Roderick Hansford
Role: Right-hand bat, right-arm
medium-fast bowler
Born: 1 October 1968, Burgess Hill,
West Sussex
Height: 6ft **Weight:** 13st 7lbs
Nickname: Skater
County debut: 1989
1st-Class 5 w. in innings: 1
1st-Class catches: 3
Parents: John and Muriel
Marital status: Single
Family links with cricket: Father
played club cricket primarily in Dorset.
Four brothers all play or played county
youth and club cricket
Education: Oakmeeds Community
School, Burgess Hill; Haywards Heath
Sixth Form College; University of Surrey
Qualifications: 10 O-levels, 3 A-levels, presently studying for BSc (Hons) Maths and
Statistics
Cricketers particularly admired: Ian Botham, Viv Richards, Malcolm Marshall, Sylvester
Clarke, Phil Edmonds
Relaxations: Eating out, statistics, crosswords
Extras: Took wicket with 4th ball in first-class cricket. Was member of 1989 Combined
Universities side. Released by Sussex at the end of the 1991 season
Opinions on cricket: 'The lunch and tea intervals should be lengthened to one hour and
half-an-hour respectively. Coaches should generally become less rigid re unorthodox and
individual bowling and batting techniques. All Championship cricket should be four-day,
but bring back the bigger seam.'
Best batting: 29 Sussex v Hampshire, Southampton 1990
Best bowling: 5-79 Sussex v Hampshire, Hove 1989

1991 Season

	M	Inns	NO	Runs	HS	Avge	100s	50s	Ct	St	O	M	Runs	Wkts	Avge	Best	5wI	10wM
Test																		
All First																		
1-day Int																		
NatWest																		
B&H	4	2	1	13	*	13.00	-	-	-	-	32.5	3	125	1	125.00	1-55	-	
Refuge																		

Career Performances

	M	Inns	NO	Runs	HS	Avge	100s	50s	Ct	St	Balls	Runs	Wkts	Avge	Best	5wl	10wM
Test																	
All First	9	10	3	108	29	15.42	-	-	3	-	1747	910	27	33.70	5-79	1	-
1-day Int																	
NatWest	1	1	1	5	5 *	-	-	-	-	-	72	48	2	24.00	2-48	-	
B&H	13	6	4	25	13 *	12.50	-	-	1	-	773	557	8	69.62	2-11	-	
Refuge	12	4	2	10	5 *	5.00	-	-	1	-	528	460	17	27.05	5-32	1	

HARDEN, R. J.   Somerset

Name: Richard John Harden
Role: Right-hand bat, left-arm
medium bowler
Born: 16 August 1965, Bridgwater
Height: 5ft 11in **Weight:** 13st 7lbs
Nickname: Sumo, Curtis
County debut: 1985
County cap: 1989
1000 runs in a season: 2
1st-Class 50s scored: 36
1st-Class 100s scored: 12
One-Day 50s: 9
1st-Class catches: 86
Place in batting averages: 44th av. 43.71
(1990 23rd av. 60.83)
Parents: Chris and Ann
Marital status: Single
Family links with cricket: Grandfather
played club cricket for Bridgwater
Education: Kings College, Taunton

Qualifications: 8 O-levels, 2 A-levels. Coaching award
Overseas teams: Central Districts, New Zealand
Cricketers particularly admired: Viv Richards, Jimmy Cook
Other sports followed: Squash, golf, rugby
Relaxations: 'Love my domestic duties (dusting, hoovering, etc) rather than golf. Good food and the odd drink.'
Opinions on cricket: 'We should play 17 four-day games, but must be played on decent pitches.'
Best batting: 134 Somerset v Derbyshire, Derby 1991
Best bowling: 2-7 Central Districts v Canterbury, Blenheim 1987-88

227

1991 Season

	M	Inns	NO	Runs	HS	Avge	100s	50s	Ct	St	O	M	Runs	Wkts	Avge	Best	5wI	10wM
Test																		
All First	24	39	8	1355	134	43.71	3	9	21	-	23.5	0	122	3	40.66	2-70	-	-
1-day Int																		
NatWest	3	3	0	69	39	23.00	-	-	1	-								
B&H	4	4	0	26	21	6.50	-	-	-	-								
Refuge	15	15	1	342	79 *	24.42	-	1	1	-								

Career Performances

	M	Inns	NO	Runs	HS	Avge	100s	50s	Ct	St	Balls	Runs	Wkts	Avge	Best	5wI	10wM
Test																	
All First	135	212	36	6515	134	37.01	12	36	86	-	1379	921	19	48.47	2-7	-	-
1-day Int																	
NatWest	9	7	0	112	39	16.00	-	-	5	-							
B&H	28	27	3	420	53 *	17.50	-	1	7	-							
Refuge	85	82	15	1856	79 *	27.70	-	8	19	-	1	0	0	-		-	-

HARDY, J. J. E. Gloucestershire

Name: Jonathan James Ean Hardy
Role: Left-hand bat
Born: 2 October 1960, Nakuru, Kenya
Height: 6ft 3in **Weight:** 13st 7lbs
Nickname: JJ
County debut: 1984 (Hampshire),
1986 (Somerset), 1991 (Gloucestershire)
County cap: 1987 (Somerset)
1000 runs in a season: 1
1st-Class 50s scored: 36
1st-Class 100s scored: 4
One-Day 50s: 9
One-Day 100s: 2
1st-Class catches: 80
Place in batting averages: 200th av. 18.61
(1990 148th av. 32.81)
Parents: Ray and Petasue
Wife and date of marriage: Janet,
25 September 1987
Family links with cricket: Father played for Yorkshire Schools
Education: Pembroke House, Gilgil, Kenya; Canford School, Dorset
Qualifications: 10 O-levels, 3 A-levels (English, Economics, Geography)

Off-season: Playing for Cape Town CC – 'wine-tasting for T.J. wines'
Overseas teams played for: Western Province 1987-91
Cricketers particularly admired: Graeme Pollock, Greg Chappell, Malcolm Marshall, Jimmy Cook
Other sports followed: Hockey (captain Dorset U19), rugby, squash
Injuries: 'Numerous – wrist, knee, Achilles tendon.'
Relaxations: Photography, walking
Extras: Suffered from bilharzia, a tropical parasitic disease, from 1980 to February 1986. Released by Somerset at end of 1990 season and joined Gloucestershire
Opinions on cricket: 'Every effort should be made to prevent the county season becoming just a mental and physical endurance test.'
Best batting: 119 Somerset v Gloucestershire, Taunton 1987

1991 Season

	M	Inns	NO	Runs	HS	Avge	100s	50s	Ct	St	O	M	Runs	Wkts	Avge	Best	5wl	10wM
Test																		
All First	10	15	2	242	52	18.61	-	1	-	-								
1-day Int																		
NatWest	2	2	0	93	70	46.50	-	1	-	-								
B&H	1	1	0	6	6	6.00	-	-	-	-								
Refuge	9	8	1	171	54	24.42	-	1	2	-								

Career Performances

	M	Inns	NO	Runs	HS	Avge	100s	50s	Ct	St	Balls	Runs	Wkts	Avge	Best	5wl	10wM
Test																	
All First	142	236	31	6120	119	29.85	4	36	80	-	25	26	0	-	-	-	-
1-day Int																	
NatWest	10	10	1	284	100	31.55	1	2	4	-							
B&H	20	20	1	500	109	26.31	1	2	9	-							
Refuge	64	56	8	1061	94 *	22.10	-	5	19	-							

83. Which player topped the first-class bowling averages last season for Northamptonshire?

84. How many centuries did Geoff Boycott score against the West Indies: 0, 5, or 7?

HARTLEY, P. J. Yorkshire

Name: Peter John Hartley
Role: Right-hand bat, right-arm
medium-fast bowler
Born: 18 April 1960, Keighley
Height: 6ft **Weight:** 13st 2lbs
Nickname: Daisy, Jack
County debut: 1982 (Warwicks),
1985 (Yorks)
County cap: 1987 (Yorks)
50 wickets in a season: 2
1st-Class 50s scored: 6
1st-Class 100s scored: 1
1st-Class 5 w. in innings: 9
1st-Class catches: 35
Place in batting averages: 174th av. 23.00
(1990 249th av. 15.57)
Place in bowling averages: 87th av. 35.02
(1990 53rd av. 34.25)

Strike rate: 62.70 (career 59.20)
Parents: Thomas and Molly
Wife and date of marriage: Sharon, 12 March 1988
Family links with cricket: Father played local league cricket
Education: Greenhead Grammar School; Bradford College
Qualifications: City & Guilds in textile design and management
Off-season: 'Trying to find employment and working on my golf swing.'
Overseas teams played for: Melville, New Zealand; Adelaide, Australia; Harmony and
Orange Free State, South Africa
Cricketers particularly admired: Dennis Lillee, Malcolm Marshall, Richard Hadlee
Other sports followed: Golf, football (Chelsea)
Injuries: Two broken thumbs
Relaxations: Golf, walking the dog
Opinions on cricket: 'Wickets are now too much in favour of the batters.'
Best batting: 127* Yorkshire v Lancashire, Old Trafford 1988
Best bowling: 6-57 Yorkshire v Warwickshire, Sheffield 1990

---

85. Which two England players 'buzzed' the England v Queensland
match on an aerial joy-ride in 1991?

86. Who captained the 1967 Indians in England?

1991 Season

	M	Inns	NO	Runs	HS	Avge	100s	50s	Ct	St	O	M	Runs	Wkts	Avge	Best	5wI	10wM
Test																		
All First	20	24	10	322	50 *	23.00	-	1	3	-	522.3	100	1751	50	35.02	6-151	3	-
1-day Int																		
NatWest	1	1	1	6	6 *	-	-	-	-	-	8	1	19	0	-		-	-
B&H	5	4	1	15	13	5.00	-	-	1	-	46	5	185	5	37.00	2-7	-	
Refuge	13	8	2	32	11	5.33	-	-	2	-	92.2	3	416	13	32.00	3-6	-	

Career Performances

	M	Inns	NO	Runs	HS	Avge	100s	50s	Ct	St	Balls	Runs	Wkts	Avge	Best	5wI	10wM
Test																	
All First	104	115	32	1894	127 *	22.81	1	6	35	-	15276	9083	258	35.20	6-57	9	-
1-day Int																	
NatWest	10	6	3	104	52	34.66	-	1	-	-	599	361	24	15.04	5-46	1	
B&H	22	12	4	66	29 *	8.25	-	-	6	-	1236	834	34	24.52	5-43	1	
Refuge	61	41	14	323	51	11.96	-	1	8	-	2519	1998	72	27.75	5-38	1	

HAYHURST, A. N.   Somerset

Name: Andrew Neil Hayhurst
Role: Right-hand bat, right-arm medium bowler
Born: 23 November 1962, Davyhulme, Manchester
Height: 6ft **Weight:** 13st
Nickname: Bull
County debut: 1985 (Lancs), 1990 (Somerset)
1000 runs in a season: 1
1st-Class 50s scored: 13
1st-Class 100s scored: 8
1st-Class catches: 25
One-Day 50s: 9
Place in batting averages: 88th av. 33.70 (1990 27th av. 57.74)
Place in bowling averages: 144th av. 70.90 (1990 147th av. 63.94)
Strike rate: 112.09 (career 80.45)
Parents: William and Margaret
Wife and date of marriage: April, 17 February 1990
Family links with cricket: Father played club cricket for Worsley in the Manchester and

231

District Cricket Association
Education: St Mark's Primary School; Worsley Wardley High; Eccles Sixth Form College; Leeds Polytechnic (Carnegie College of PE)
Qualifications: 8 O-levels, 3 A-levels, BA (Hons) Human Movement
Career outside cricket: Teacher/coach
Off-season: Coaching in West Country
Overseas tours: Lancashire to Jamaica 1987 and 1988; Zimbabwe 1989; Bahamas 1990
Overseas teams played for: South Launceston, Tasmania 1987-89
Cricketers particularly admired: Viv Richards, Richard Hadlee, Jimmy Cook
Other sports followed: All sports, especially football (Manchester United)
Injuries: Rib cartilage – three weeks, on-going tendonitis in left knee
Relaxations: Animals – bull terriers, decorating, gardening, good food
Extras: Played for Greater Manchester U19 at football. Scored a record 197 runs whilst playing for North of England v South, Southampton 1982. Holds record for number of runs in Manchester & District Cricket Association League, whilst playing for Worsley CC in 1984: 1193 runs (av. 70.17). Represented Greater Manchester U19s at football. Released by Lancashire at the end of 1989 season and joined Somerset on a three-year contract, 1990. Made 110* on his first-class debut for Somerset
Opinions on cricket: 'Would still like to see four-day cricket. If not we need a swing back to better "cricket wickets" to avoid contrived finishes.'
Best batting: 172* Somerset v Gloucestershire, Bath 1991
Best bowling: 4-27 Lancashire v Middlesex, Old Trafford 1987

1991 Season

	M	Inns	NO	Runs	HS	Avge	100s	50s	Ct	St	O	M	Runs	Wkts	Avge	Best	5wI	10wM
Test																		
All First	19	32	5	910	172 *	33.70	3	1	5	-	205.3	32	780	11	70.90	2-42	-	-
1-day Int																		
NatWest	3	3	1	154	91 *	77.00	-	2	1	-	35.3	4	137	8	17.12	5-60	1	
B&H	2	2	0	102	70	51.00	-	1	1	-	5.1	0	18	0	-	-	-	
Refuge	13	11	5	163	35	27.16	-	-	2	-	61.3	0	308	9	34.22	3-38	-	

Career Performances

	M	Inns	NO	Runs	HS	Avge	100s	50s	Ct	St	Balls	Runs	Wkts	Avge	Best	5wI	10wM
Test																	
All First	83	130	19	3654	172 *	32.91	8	13	25	-	6195	3511	77	45.59	4-27	-	-
1-day Int																	
NatWest	12	11	2	399	91 *	44.33	-	3	3	-	656	416	17	24.47	5-60	1	
B&H	16	14	1	257	76	19.76	-	2	1	-	564	371	13	28.53	4-50	-	
Refuge	69	54	11	1077	84	25.04	-	4	10	-	2124	1820	47	38.72	4-37	-	

HAYNES, D. L.   Middlesex

Name: Desmond Leo Haynes
Role: Right-hand bat, right-arm bowler
Born: 15 February 1956, St James,
Barbados, West Indies
County debut: 1989
County cap: 1989
Test debut: 1977-78
Tests: 102
One-Day Internationals: 182
1000 runs in a season: 2
1st-Class 50s scored: 101
1st-Class 100s scored: 45
1st-Class 200s scored: 3
1st-Class catches: 152
1st-Class stumpings: 1
One-Day 50s: 56
One-Day 100s: 19
Place in batting averages: 48th av. 42.41

(1990 14th av. 69.00)
Wife and date of marriage: Dawn, 14 September 1991
Education: Federal HS, Barbados
Off-season: Touring with West Indies in Pakistan and Australia
Overseas teams played for: Barbados 1976-92
Overseas tours: World Series Cricket (Kerry Packer) 1978-79; West Indies to Australia 1979-80, 1981-82, 1984-85, 1988-89, 1991-92; New Zealand 1979-80, 1986-87; England 1980, 1984, 1988, 1991; Pakistan 1980-81, 1986-87, 1990-91, 1991-92; India 1983-84, 1987-88, 1989-90; West Indies B to Zimbabwe 1981
Extras: Played for Scotland in the B&H Cup. Captained West Indies v England, Port of Spain in 1989-90 and on tour of Pakistan 1990-91. Vice-captain (to Viv Richards) on England tour 1991 and promoted to vice-captain (to Richie Richardson) of tours to Pakistan and Australia 1991-92 when Gus Logie was ruled out after being injured in a car accident. Britannic Assurance Player of the Year 1990
Best batting: 255* Middlesex v Sussex, Lord's 1990
Best bowling: 1-2 West Indies v Pakistan, Lahore 1980-81

---

87. Which player topped the first-class bowling averages
last season for Nottinghamshire?

88. Who is the MCC Head Coach?

1991 Season

	M	Inns	NO	Runs	HS	Avge	100s	50s	Ct	St	O	M	Runs	Wkts	Avge	Best	5wl	10wM
Test	5	10	3	323	75 *	46.14	-	3	2	-								
All First	13	22	5	721	151	42.41	1	4	4	-								
1-day Int																		
NatWest																		
B&H																		
Refuge																		

Career Performances

	M	Inns	NO	Runs	HS	Avge	100s	50s	Ct	St	Balls	Runs	Wkts	Avge	Best	5wl	10wM
Test	102	178	21	6644	184	42.31	16	36	59	-	18	8	1	8.00	1-2	-	-
All First	274	468	56	19147	255 *	46.47	45	101	152	1	400	196	6	32.66	1-2	-	-
1-day Int	182	181	23	6780	152 *	42.91	16	39	42	-	30	24	0	-	-	-	
NatWest	9	9	2	575	149 *	82.14	1	6	2	-	120	59	1	59.00	1-41	-	
B&H	9	9	0	457	131	50.77	1	3	6	-	180	89	2	44.50	1-9	-	
Refuge	28	27	2	951	107 *	38.04	1	8	12	-	320	300	4	75.00	1-16	-	

HAYNES, G. R.   Worcestershire

Name: Gavin Richard Haynes
Role: Right-hand bat, right-arm
medium bowler
Born: 29 September 1969
Height: 5ft 10in **Weight:** 12st 6lbs
Nickname: Splash
County debut: 1991
1st-Class catches: 2
Parents: Nicholas and Dorothy
Marital status: Single
Family links with cricket: Father played
club cricket and manages Worcester U14 side
Education: Gigmill Junior School;
High Park Comprehensive; King Edward V
College, Stourbridge
Qualifications: 5 O-levels, 1 A-level, senior
cricket coaching award
Career outside cricket: 'Anything going'
Off-season: 'Finding a job'
Overseas teams played for: Sunrise Sports Club, Zimbabwe 1989-90
Cricketers particularly admired: Ian Botham, Graeme Hick, Graham Gooch, Malcolm
Marshall

Other sports followed: Football (Aston Villa)

Injuries: Thigh strain - missed one week, partially dislocated shoulder – missed one week, torn calf muscle

Relaxations: Playing golf or squash, watching videos

Extras: Represented England Schools U15

Opinions on cricket: 'The standard of 2nd XI wickets should be improved, especially at out grounds. More should be done to find employment for cricketers in the winter.'

Best batting: 16 Worcestershire v Nottinghamshire, Worcester 1991

16 Worcestershire v Sri Lanka, Worcester 1991

1991 Season

	M	Inns	NO	Runs	HS	Avge	100s	50s	Ct	St	O	M	Runs	Wkts	Avge	Best	5wI	10wM
Test																		
All First	4	4	1	51	16	17.00	-	-	2	-	19.2	2	82	0	-	-	-	-
1-day Int																		
NatWest																		
B&H																		
Refuge																		

Career Performances

	M	Inns	NO	Runs	HS	Avge	100s	50s	Ct	St	Balls	Runs	Wkts	Avge	Best	5wI	10wM
Test																	
All First	4	4	1	51	16	17.00	-	-	2	-	116	82	0	-	-	-	-
1-day Int																	
NatWest																	
B&H																	
Refuge																	

89. True or false: Mark and Steve Waugh are the only twins to have played Test cricket for Australia?

90. Who scored the most centuries for the West Indies v England, Viv Richards or Gary Sobers?

HEADLEY, D. W.   Middlesex

Name: Dean Warren Headley
Role: Right-hand bat, right-arm fast-medium bowler
Born: 27 January 1970, Stourbridge
Height: 6ft 4in **Weight:** 13st 7lbs
Nickname: Elma, Murphy
County debut: 1991
1st-Class 50s scored: 1
1st-Class 5 w. in innings: 1
1st-Class catches: 5
Place in batting averages: 238th av. 13.42
Place in bowling averages: 124th av. 43.37
Strike rate: 68.17 (career 68.17)
Parents: Ronald George Alphonso and Gail
Marital status: Single
Family links with cricket: Father Ron played for Worcestershire and West Indies and grandfather George played for Jamaica and West Indies

Education: Gigmill Junior School; Oldswinford Hospital School; Royal Grammar School, Worcester
Qualifications: 7 O-levels
Career outside cricket: 'Not yet established, but director of father's company.'
Off-season: Playing club cricket in Jamaica
Overseas tours: RGS Worcester to Zimbabwe 1988; Christians in Sport to India 1990
Cricketers particularly admired: Clive Lloyd, Michael Holding, Robin Smith, Malcolm Marshall – 'learned most from my father Ron'
Other sports followed: Rugby, football
Injuries: Severe bruising on left hip – out for seven weeks
Relaxations: Music, socialising, with friends and colleagues
Extras: Took 5 wickets on debut including a wicket with his first ball in Championship cricket. Played for Worcestershire 2nd XI 1988-89
Opinions on cricket: 'There should be no limitation on bouncers. Umpires must use their own discretion on intimidatory bowling. A bouncer is a legitimate ball, just as a yorker is. Cricket should become more commercial and better marketed. Wickets should be more conducive to results. Thus wickets should be prepared for scores of no more than 300 in three-day cricket to avoid contrived results.'
Best batting: 76 Middlesex v Hampshire, Lord's 1991
Best bowling: 5-46 Middlesex v Yorkshire, Lord's 1991

1991 Season

	M	Inns	NO	Runs	HS	Avge	100s	50s	Ct	St	O	M	Runs	Wkts	Avge	Best	5wI	10wM
Test																		
All First	12	15	1	202	76	14.42	-	1	5	-	329.3	51	1258	29	43.37	5-46	2	-
1-day Int																		
NatWest	1	1	1	11	11 *	-	-	-	-	-	12	0	51	0	-	-	-	-
B&H	4	3	0	30	26	10.00	-	-	1	-	42.1	4	180	3	60.00	1-34	-	
Refuge	8	2	1	10	6 *	10.00	-	-	-	-	56	0	296	1	296.00	1-70	-	

Career Performances

	M	Inns	NO	Runs	HS	Avge	100s	50s	Ct	St	Balls	Runs	Wkts	Avge	Best	5wI	10wM
Test																	
All First	12	15	1	202	76	14.42	-	1	5	-	1977	1258	29	43.37	5-46	2	-
1-day Int																	
NatWest	1	1	1	11	11 *	-	-	-	-	-	72	51	0	-	-	-	-
B&H	4	3	0	30	26	10.00	-	-	1	-	253	180	3	60.00	1-34	-	
Refuge	8	2	1	10	6 *	10.00	-	-	-	-	336	296	1	296.00	1-70	-	

HEGG, W. K. Lancashire

Name: Warren Kevin Hegg
Role: Right-hand bat, wicket-keeper
Born: 23 February 1968, Radcliffe, Lancashire
Height: 5ft 10in **Weight:** 12st 7lbs
Nickname: Chucky
County debut: 1986
1st-Class 50s scored: 12
1st-Class 100s scored: 2
1st-Class catches: 251
1st-Class stumpings: 29
Place in batting averages: 97th av. 32.66 (1990 95th av. 42.12)
Parents: Kevin and Glenda
Marital status: Single
Family links with cricket: Father and brother Martin play in local leagues
Education: Unsworth High School; Stand College, Whitefield
Qualifications: 5 O-levels, 7 CSEs; qualified coach
Career outside cricket: Groundsman – worked in textile warehouse
Off-season: England A tour to Bermuda and West Indies

Overseas tours: NCA North U19 to Bermuda 1985; England U19 to Sri Lanka 1986-87; Youth World Cup in Australia 1988; England A to Pakistan and Sri Lanka 1990-91; Bermuda and West Indies 1991-92

Overseas teams played for: Sheffield, Tasmania 1988-90

Cricketers particularly admired: Ian Botham, Alan Knott, Bob Taylor, Gehan Mendis (for perseverance)

Other sports followed: Football, golf, fishing, Aussie rules

Injuries: Sore heel – missed one game

Relaxations: Listening to music, walking on my own

Extras: First player to make county debut from Lytham CC. Youngest player to score a 100 for Lancashire for thirty years, 130 v Northamptonshire in fourth first-class game. Eleven victims in match v Derbyshire – to equal world record

Opinions on cricket: 'Players should be given more time to prepare for games. There should always be a travelling day for long journeys.'

Best batting: 130 Lancashire v Northamptonshire, Northampton 1987

1991 Season

	M	Inns	NO	Runs	HS	Avge	100s	50s	Ct	St	O	M	Runs	Wkts	Avge	Best	5wI	10wM
Test																		
All First	22	32	8	784	97	32.66	-	3	43	3								
1-day Int																		
NatWest	2	1	0	7	7	7.00	-	-	4	-								
B&H	7	2	1	13	13 *	13.00	-	-	6	-								
Refuge	18	8	5	152	47 *	50.66	-	-	22	1								

Career Performances

	M	Inns	NO	Runs	HS	Avge	100s	50s	Ct	St	Balls	Runs	Wkts	Avge	Best	5wI	10wM
Test																		
All First	109	155	27	3080	130	24.06	2	12	251	29	6	7	0	-	-	-	-
1-day Int																		
NatWest	12	7	1	111	29	18.50	-	-	14	-								
B&H	23	9	4	94	31 *	18.80	-	-	33	1								
Refuge	71	32	16	279	47 *	17.43	-	-	77	9								

91. Which England-qualified player came highest in the first-class bowling averages last season where 10 wickets is a qualification?

HEMMINGS, E. E.　　　Nottinghamshire

Name: Edward Ernest Hemmings
Role: Right-hand bat, off-break bowler
Born: 20 February 1949, LeamingtonSpa, Warwickshire
Height: 5ft 10in **Weight:** 13st
Nickname: Eddie, Whale, Fossil 'with many thanks to Angus Fraser for the last of my nicknames'
County debut: 1966 (Warwicks), 1979 (Notts)
County cap: 1974 (Warwicks), 1980 (Notts)
Benefit: 1987
Test debut: 1982
Tests: 16
One-Day Internationals: 33
50 wickets in a season: 14
1st-Class 50s scored: 26
1st-Class 100s scored: 1
1st-Class 5 w. in innings: 666
1st-Class 10 w. in match: 14
1st-Class catches: 194
One-Day 50s: 1
Place in batting averages: 248th av. 11.91 (1990 210th av. 22.20)
Place in bowling averages: 103rd av. 37.41 (1990 64th av. 36.15)
Strike rate: 83.28 (career 66.68)
Parents: Edward and Dorothy Phyliss
Wife and date of marriage: Christine Mary, 23 October 1971
Children: Thomas Edward, 26 July 1977; James Oliver, 9 September 1979
Family links with cricket: Father and father's father played Minor Counties and League cricket
Education: Campion School, Leamington Spa
Off-season: Touring Australia with England
Overseas tours: England to Australia and New Zealand 1982-83; World Cup, Pakistan, Australia and New Zealand 1987-88; India and West Indies 1989-90; Australia 1990-91
Cricketers particularly admired: Tim Robinson, Clive Rice, John Jameson
Other sports followed: Golf, football
Relaxations: 'Watching football at any level – especially junior. Dining out with my wife. Golf, real ale – and sleeping it off!'
Extras: Took a hat-trick for Warwickshire in 1977; hit first century – 127* for Nottinghamshire v Yorkshire at Worksop, July 1982 – after sixteen years in first-class game
Opinions on cricket: 'I think this year has gone to prove the old motto, "never give up trying".'

Best batting: 127* Nottinghamshire v Yorkshire, Worksop 1982
Best bowling: 10-175 International XI v West Indies XI, Kingston 1982-83

1991 Season

	M	Inns	NO	Runs	HS	Avge	100s	50s	Ct	St	O	M	Runs	Wkts	Avge	Best	5wI	10wM
Test																		
All First	16	16	4	143	29 *	11.91	-	-	4	-	638.3	171	1721	46	37.41	6-46	2	-
1-day Int																		
NatWest	3	2	2	22	17 *	-	-	-	-	-	33	3	135	2	67.50	1-27	-	
B&H	4	1	0	9	9	9.00	-	-	-	-	44	4	201	4	50.25	2-49	-	
Refuge	15	4	1	28	17	9.33	-	-	7	-	112.1	4	488	14	34.85	4-26	-	

Career Performances

	M	Inns	NO	Runs	HS	Avge	100s	50s	Ct	St	Balls	Runs	Wkts	Avge	Best	5wI	10wM
Test	16	21	4	383	95	22.52	-	2	5	-	4437	1825	43	42.44	6-58	1	-
All First	475	616	141	9165	127 *	19.29	1	26	194	-	92430	40859	1386	29.48	10-175	66	14
1-day Int	33	12	6	30	8 *	5.00	-	-	5	-	1752	1293	37	34.94	4-52	-	
NatWest	42	30	11	255	31 *	13.42	-	-	8	-	2794	1591	46	34.58	3-27	-	
B&H	85	51	16	496	61 *	14.17	-	1	19	-	5083	2716	76	35.73	4-47	-	
Refuge	268	169	52	1634	44 *	13.96	-	-	82	-	10429	7986	273	29.25	5-22	4	

HEMP, D. L.   Glamorgan

Name: David Lloyd Hemp
Role: Left-hand bat, right-arm medium bowler
Born: 15 November 1970, Bermuda
Height: 6ft **Weight:** 12st
Nickname: Hempy
County debut: 1991
Parents: Clive and Elisabeth
Marital status: Single
Family links with cricket: Father plays for Ffynone and brother plays for Swansea
Education: Olchfa Comprehensive School; Millfield School
Qualifications: 5 O-levels, 2 A-levels
Off-season: Touring with South Wales Cricket Association to New Zealand and Australia
Overseas tours: Welsh Schools U19 to Australia 1986-87; Welsh Cricket Association U18 to Barbados 1987; South Wales Cricket Association to New Zealand and

Australia 1991-92

Cricketers particularly admired: David Gower, Viv Richards, Graeme Hick
Other sports followed: Football
Relaxations: Watching football and TV, listening to music
Extras: Scored 258* for Wales V MCC 1991. In 1990 scored 104* & 101* for Welsh Schools U19 v Scottish Schools U19 and 120 & 102* v Irish Schools U19
Opinions on cricket: 'More four-day cricket should be played. 2nd team games should all be played on county grounds rather than club grounds as the quality of wickets is usually poorer at clubs, also they do not have such good facilities for covering wickets.'
Best batting: 8 Glamorgan v Hampshire, Southampton 1991

1991 Season

	M	Inns	NO	Runs	HS	Avge	100s	50s	Ct	St	O	M	Runs	Wkts	Avge	Best	5wl	10wM
Test																		
All First	1	2	1	12	8	12.00	-	-	-	-								
1-day Int																		
NatWest																		
B&H																		
Refuge	1	1	0	7	7	7.00	-	-	-	-								

Career Performances

	M	Inns	NO	Runs	HS	Avge	100s	50s	Ct	St	Balls	Runs	Wkts	Avge	Best	5wl	10wM
Test																	
All First	1	2	1	12	8	12.00	-	-	-	-							
1-day Int																	
NatWest																	
B&H																	
Refuge	1	1	0	7	7	7.00	-	-	-	-							

92. Which player topped the first-class bowling averages last season for Somerset?

HENDERSON, P. W. — Durham

Name: Paul William Henderson
Role: Right-hand bat, right-arm fast-medium bowler
Born: 22 October 1974, Stockton-on-Tees
Marital status: Single
Education: Billingham Campus School
Off-season: Touring with Durham
Overseas tours: Durham to Zimbabwe 1991-92
Extras: Made his debut for Durham in 1991 aged 16 against Durham University. Scored 61* against Cumberland. Played in 1991 friendly one-day games against Leicestershire and Essex

Career Perfomances – no appearance in first-class cricket or any one-day competition

HEPWORTH, P. N. — Leicestershire

Name: Peter Nash Hepworth
Role: Right-hand bat, off-spinbowler
Born: 4 May 1967, Ackworth, West Yorkshire
Height: 6ft 1in **Weight:** 12st 7lbs
Nickname: Nash, Hepps, Heppers
County debut: 1988
1st-Class 50s scored: 6
1st-Class 50s scored: 2
1st-Class catches: 23
Place in batting averages: 95th av. 32.91 (1990 159th av. 30.83)
Place in bowling averages: 74th av. 33.07
Strike rate: 51.14 (career 51.14)
Parents: George and Zena
Marital status: Single
Family links with cricket: Father and uncle played cricket for Ackworth

Education: Bell Lane School, Ackworth; Ackworth Middle School; Hemsworth High School
Qualifications: 8 CSEs, NCA senior coaching certificate
Career outside cricket: Builder (with family firm), cricket coach
Off-season: Coaching and playing in Bloemfontein, South Africa
Overseas tours: Hull CC to Barbados
Cricketers particularly admired: Geoff Boycott – for his expert advice, Don Wilson – for his attitude with young players, David Gower – for his effortless strokeplay
Other sports followed: Rugby league (Featherstone Rovers), football (Leeds United)
Relaxations: Playing football for Ackworth. Listening to music, going to cinema. Reading war stories. TV addict
Extras: Started playing for Ackworth Cricket Club following the likes of Neil Lloyd (the best young cricketer I've ever seen), Graham Stevenson, Tim Boon, Geoff Boycott
Opinions on cricket: 'Both pitches and run-ups should be uncovered – bowling and batting skills would then be put to the test. The pitches seem to be better every year and the spin bowlers are now being given a chance by the majority of counties.'
Best batting: 115 Leicestershire v Essex, Leicester 1991
115 Leicestershire v Cambridge University, Fenner's 1991
Best bowling: 3-51 Leicestershire v Kent, Canterbury 1991

1991 Season

	M	Inns	NO	Runs	HS	Avge	100s	50s	Ct	St	O	M	Runs	Wkts	Avge	Best	5wI	10wM
Test																		
All First	23	38	4	1119	115	32.91	2	4	19	-	119.2	20	463	14	33.07	3-51	-	-
1-day Int																		
NatWest																		
B&H	3	2	0	42	33	21.00	-	-	1	-	20	2	83	5	16.60	4-39	-	
Refuge	8	6	1	56	31	11.20	-	-	1	-	27	1	140	6	23.33	2-33	-	

Career Performances

	M	Inns	NO	Runs	HS	Avge	100s	50s	Ct	St	Balls	Runs	Wkts	Avge	Best	5wI	10wM
Test																	
All First	36	60	6	1499	115	27.75	2	6	23	-	716	463	14	33.07	3-51	-	-
1-day Int																	
NatWest																	
B&H	3	2	0	42	33	21.00	-	-	1	-	120	83	5	16.60	4-39	-	
Refuge	14	10	2	145	38	18.12	-	-	1	-	162	140	6	23.33	2-33	-	

93. Who is the only batsman to have an average of over 200 in a Test series?

HICK, G. A. Worcestershire

Name: Graeme Ashley Hick
Role: Right-hand bat, off-break bowler
Born: 23 May 1966, Salisbury, Rhodesia
Height: 6ft 3in **Weight:** 14st 7lbs
Nickname: Hicky, Ash
County debut: 1984
County cap: 1986
Test debut: 1991
Tests: 4
One-Day Internationals: 3
1000 runs in a season: 7
1st-Class 50s scored: 66
1st-Class 100s scored: 60
1st-Class 200s scored: 7
1st-Class 5 w. in innings: 4
1st-Class 10 w. in match: 1
1st-Class catches: 229
One-Day 50s: 43
One-Day 100s: 9

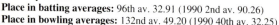

Place in batting averages: 96th av. 32.91 (1990 2nd av. 90.26)
Place in bowling averages: 132nd av. 49.20 (1990 40th av. 32.25)
Strike rate: 91.00 (career 72.67)
Parents: John and Eve
Wife and date of marriage: Jackie, 5 October 1991
Family links with cricket: Father served on Zimbabwe Cricket Union Board of Control since 1984; also played representative cricket in Zimbabwe
Education: Banket Primary; Prince Edward Boys' High School, Zimbabwe
Qualifications: 4 O-levels, NCA coaching award
Off-season: Touring with England
Overseas tours: Zimbabwe to England for 1983 World Cup; Sri Lanka 1983-84; England 1985; England to New Zealand
Overseas teams played for: Old Hararians in Zimbabwe 1982-90; Northern Districts 1987-89; Queensland 1990-91
Cricketers particularly admired: Duncan Fletcher (Zimbabwe captain) for approach and understanding of the game, David Houghton, Basil D'Oliveira
Other sports followed: Follows Liverpool FC, golf, tennis, squash, hockey
Relaxations: 'Leaning against Steve Rhodes at first-slip.'
Extras: Made first 100 aged 6 for school team; youngest player participating in 1983 Prudential World Cup (aged 17); youngest player to represent Zimbabwe. Scored 1234 runs in Birmingham League and played for Worcestershire 2nd XI in 1984 – hitting six successive 100s. In 1986, at age 20, he became the youngest player to score 2000 runs in an English season. One of *Wisden's* Five Cricketers of the Year, 1986. In 1988 he made

405* v Somerset, the highest individual score in England since 1895, and scored 1000 first-class runs by end of May 1988, hitting a record 410 runs in April. In 1990 became youngest batsman ever to make 50 first-class 100s and scored 645 runs without being dismissed – a record for English cricket. Qualified as an English player in 1991. Published *Hick 'n' Dilley Circus* and *A Champion's Diary*. Also played hockey for Zimbabwe

Opinions on cricket: 'What a great game.'

Best batting: 405* Worcestershire v Somerset, Taunton 1988

Best bowling: 5-37 Worcestershire v Gloucestershire, Worcester 1990

1991 Season

	M	Inns	NO	Runs	HS	Avge	100s	50s	Ct	St	O	M	Runs	Wkts	Avge	Best	5wI	10wM
Test	4	7	0	75	43	10.71	-	-	8	-	24	5	95	2	47.50	2-77	-	-
All First	22	36	2	1119	186	32.91	3	5	26	-	151.4	34	492	10	49.20	5-42	1	-
1-day Int	3	3	1	129	86 *	64.50	-	1	-	-								
NatWest	2	2	0	10	10	5.00	-	-	1	-	5	2	11	0	-	-	-	-
B&H	7	7	2	297	88	59.40	-	4	8	-								
Refuge	12	10	1	433	109	48.11	1	2	3	-	27.2	1	138	9	15.33	5-35	1	

Career Performances

	M	Inns	NO	Runs	HS	Avge	100s	50s	Ct	St	Balls	Runs	Wkts	Avge	Best	5wI	10wM
Test	4	7	0	75	43	10.71	-	-	8	-	144	95	2	47.50	2-77	-	-
All First	202	327	38	17184	405 *	59.46	60	66	229	-	9517	4848	129	37.58	5-37	4	-
1-day Int	3	3	1	129	86 *	64.50	-	1	-	-							
NatWest	20	20	5	927	172 *	61.80	3	4	9	-	621	354	9	39.33	4-54	-	
B&H	32	32	6	1329	109	51.11	3	11	23	-	378	260	7	37.14	3-36	-	
Refuge	98	95	16	3518	114 *	44.53	3	27	20	-	1262	1159	42	27.59	5-35	1	

94. Who has taken the most wickets in one Ashes series, and how many?

95. Which Australian Test captain was nicknamed 'The Big Ship'?

HINKS, S. G.   Gloucestershire

Name: Simon Graham Hinks
Role: Left-hand opening bat
Born: 12 October 1960, Northfleet, Kent
Height: 6ft 2in **Weight:** 12st 10lbs
Nickname: Hinksy
County debut: 1982
County cap: 1985
1000 runs in a season: 3
1st-Class 50s scored: 35
1st-Class 100s scored: 11
1st-Class 200s scored: 1
One-Day 50s: 21
Place in batting averages: 175th av. 22.91
(1990 124th av. 36.93)
Parents: Mary and Graham
Wife and date of marriage: Vicki,
September 1990
Children: Megan Rose, 15 June 1991
Family links with cricket: Father captained
Gravesend CC and is now chairman. Brother Jonathan captains Gravesend and has played
for Kent U19
Education: Dover Road Infant and Junior Schools, Northfleet; St George's C of E School,
Gravesend; Sheffield University
Qualifications: 5 O-levels, 1 A-level; senior cricket coach; Diploma in Leisure Management
Career outside cricket: Sales rep for Reed Corrugated Cases
Off-season: 'Negotiating a new contract'
Cricketers particularly admired: 'Admired Clive Lloyd's style and power and anyone
who has proved themselves over a long period.'
Other sports followed: All sports
Injuries: Groin injury – out for three weeks
Relaxations: Sport, TV, DIY, gardening
Extras: Left Kent at the end of 1991 season and signed three-year contract with
Gloucestershire
Opinions on cricket: 'Learn from your mistakes before it is too late. Wear the right tie.'
Best batting: 234 Kent v Middlesex, Canterbury 1990
Best bowling: 2-18 Kent v Nottinghamshire, Trent Bridge 1989

---

96. Who has scored the most runs in all Test cricket?

1991 Season

	M	Inns	NO	Runs	HS	Avge	100s	50s	Ct	St	O	M	Runs	Wkts	Avge	Best	5wI	10wM
Test																		
All First	9	14	2	275	61 *	22.91	-	2	6	-								
1-day Int																		
NatWest	1	1	0	34	34	34.00	-	-	-	-								
B&H																		
Refuge	5	5	0	99	35	19.80	-	-	1	-								

Career Performances

	M	Inns	NO	Runs	HS	Avge	100s	50s	Ct	St	Balls	Runs	Wkts	Avge	Best	5wI	10wM
Test																	
All First	154	267	15	7569	234	30.03	11	35	96	-	580	367	8	45.87	2-18	-	-
1-day Int																	
NatWest	11	11	2	414	95	46.00	-	3	3	-	18	23	0	-	-	-	
B&H	32	31	1	708	85	23.60	-	4	7	-	246	198	5	39.60	1-15	-	
Refuge	91	91	6	2084	99	24.51	-	14	26	-	150	139	4	34.75	1-3	-	

HODGSON, G. D. Gloucestershire

Name: Geoffrey Dean Hodgson
Role: Right-hand opening bat
Born: 22 October 1966, Carlisle
Height: 6ft 1in **Weight:** 13st
Nickname: Deano
County debut: 1987 (Warwicks), 1989 (Gloucs)
1000 runs in a season: 2
1st-Class 50s scored: 17
1st-Class 100s scored: 3
1st-Class catches: 20
One-Day 50s: 1
Place in batting averages: 118th av. 29.75 (1990 125th av. 36.66)
Parents: John Geoffrey and Dorothy Elizabeth
Marital status: Single
Education: Nelson Thomlinson Comp., Wigton; Loughborough University
Qualifications: 11 O-levels, 4 A-levels, BSc (Hons) Human Biological Sciences, NCA qualified cricket coach, PFA qualified football coach, LTA qualified tennis coach

Off-season: Playing and coaching in Argentina

Overseas tours: NCA North U19 to Bermuda 1985

Overseas teams played for: Southern Districts, Queensland 1988-89; Wests, Brisbane 1990-91

Cricketers particularly admired: Dennis Amiss, Barry Richards, Sunil Gavaskar. 'I learnt a lot from Graham Wiltshire, Eddie Barlow, Neal Abberley and Alan Ormrod, and all the Gloucestershire players have been very helpful.'

Other sports followed: Football, international rugby, golf, tennis, skiing

Injuries: 'Rotator cuff injury to shoulder stopped me from throwing for the last four months of the season.'

Relaxations: Listening to music ('all types depending on mood'), reading thrillers and autobiographies, watching comedies and thrillers, going to wine bars

Extras: Played Minor County Cricket for Cumberland 1982-88; also played for Lancashire and Worcestershire 2nd XIs; first-class debut for Gloucestershire in 1989

Opinions on cricket: '1. Championship to consist of 17 four-day games on good covered wickets. Each day to consist of three 2-hour sessions with an over rate of 17 per hour. A higher required rate hinders the development of fast bowlers and doesn't always mean that spinners bowl more. **2.** Both B&H and NatWest should be knock-outs, not starting before June, Games to be played Sat, Sun, Mon. **3.** Sunday league to be in two divisions (North and South) with play-offs for top two in each division. Competition to be played in April, May and September. **4.** Better fixture arrangement to reduce travelling. **5.** Increased awareness of players' needs in the winter *or* all-year contracts with players promoting cricket at schools in the area from January to April.

Best batting: 126 Gloucestershire v Zimbabwe, Bristol 1990

1991 Season

	M	Inns	NO	Runs	HS	Avge	100s	50s	Ct	St	O	M	Runs	Wkts	Avge	Best	5wI	10wM
Test																		
All First	23	39	2	1101	105	29.75	1	7	8	-								
1-day Int																		
NatWest	1	1	0	7	7	7.00	-	-	1	-								
B&H	3	3	0	19	9	6.33	-	-	1	-								
Refuge																			

Career Performances

	M	Inns	NO	Runs	HS	Avge	100s	50s	Ct	St	Balls	Runs	Wkts	Avge	Best	5wI	10wM
Test																	
All First	50	83	6	2481	126	32.22	3	17	20	-							
1-day Int																	
NatWest	5	5	0	175	52	35.00	-	1	1	-							
B&H	4	4	0	20	9	5.00	-	-	1	-							
Refuge	13	12	2	188	39	18.80	-	-	7	-							

HOLLOWAY, P. C. L. Warwickshire

Name: Piran Christopher Laity Holloway
Role: Left-hand bat, wicket-keeper
Born: 1 October 1970, Helston, Cornwall
Height: 5ft 8in **Weight:** 10st 7lbs
County debut: 1988
1st-Class 50s scored: 2
1st-Class catches: 17
1st-Class stumpings: 1
Parents: Chris and Mary
Marital status: Single
Education: Nansloe CP School, Helston;
Taunton School
Qualifications: 6 O-levels
Overseas tours: Millfield School to
Barbados 1986
Cricketers particularly admired:
Ian Botham, David Gower, Alan Knott
Other sports followed: Rugby, soccer
Relaxations: Rock music, watching films,
keeping fit

Extras: Played England Schools U15 (awarded Jack Hobbs Award by Cricket Society),
England Schools U17 (Wicket-keeping Award).
Best batting: 89* Warwickshire v Leicestershire, Leicester 1991

1991 Season

	M	Inns	NO	Runs	HS	Avge	100s	50s	Ct	St	O	M	Runs	Wkts	Avge	Best	5wI	10wM
Test																		
All First	6	9	5	263	89 *	65.75	-	2	9	-								
1-day Int																		
NatWest	1	1	0	2	2	2.00	-	-	2	1								
B&H	4	4	0	59	27	14.75	-	-	4	-								
Refuge	5	3	2	67	34 *	67.00	-	-	2	-								

Career Performances

	M	Inns	NO	Runs	HS	Avge	100s	50s	Ct	St	Balls	Runs	Wkts	Avge	Best	5wI	10wM
Test																	
All First	9	14	5	303	89 *	33.66	-	2	17	1							
1-day Int																	
NatWest	1	1	0	2	2	2.00	-	-	2	1							
B&H	4	4	0	59	27	14.75	-	-	4	-							
Refuge	7	5	3	87	34 *	43.50	-	-	3	-							

HOLMES, G. C. Glamorgan

Name: Geoffrey Clark Holmes
Role: Right-hand bat, right-arm medium bowler
Born: 16 September 1958, Newcastle-on-Tyne
Height: 5ft 10in **Weight:** 11st 2lbs
County debut: 1978
County cap: 1985
Benefit: 1991
1000 runs in a season: 3
1st-Class 50s scored: 37
1st-Class 100s scored: 11
1st-Class 5 w. in innings: 2
1st-Class catches: 85
One-Day 50s: 18
Place in batting averages: 195th av. 19.42 (1990 94th av. 42.27)
Parents: George and Rita
Wife: Christine
Children: Victoria
Family links with cricket: Father played in the Northumberland League
Education: West Denton High School
Qualifications: 6 O-levels, 2 A-levels; advanced cricket coach
Overseas teams played for: Border, South Africa 1989-90
Cricketers particularly admired: Geoff Boycott, John Snow
Other sports followed: Soccer, and most others
Relaxations: Reading (especially cricket books), TV, sport, 3-card brag
Extras: Persistent back injury forced him to retire at the end of the 1991 season
Opinions on cricket: 'I think we play too much county cricket and would like to see 17 Championship matches per season. I would like to see one of the one-day competitions played as day/night matches, under floodlights.'
Best batting: 182 Border v Western Province B, East London 1989-90
Best bowling: 5-38 Glamorgan v Essex, Colchester 1988

---

97. Who has taken the most Test wickets?

98. Which player topped the first-class bowling averages last season for Surrey?

1991 Season

	M	Inns	NO	Runs	HS	Avge	100s	50s	Ct	St	O	M	Runs	Wkts	Avge	Best	5wI	10wM
Test																		
All First	7	8	1	136	54	19.42	-	1	1	-								
1-day Int																		
NatWest																		
B&H	4	4	1	92	35 *	30.66	-	-	-	-								
Refuge	9	8	2	240	72	40.00	-	2	3	-	1.5	0	24	0	-		-	-

Career Performances

	M	Inns	NO	Runs	HS	Avge	100s	50s	Ct	St	Balls	Runs	Wkts	Avge	Best	5wl	10wM
Test																	
All First	209	335	51	8092	182	28.49	11	37	85	-	6932	3963	88	45.03	5-38	2	-
1-day Int																	
NatWest	15	14	0	280	57	20.00	-	1	5	-	492	220	11	20.00	5-24	1	
B&H	34	32	7	744	70	29.76	-	5	11	-	938	650	25	26.00	3-26	-	
Refuge	131	118	22	2438	73	25.39	-	12	37	-	2772	2519	97	25.96	5-2	3	

HOOPER, C. L.　　　　　　　　　　Kent

Name: Carl Llewellyn Hooper
Role: Right-hand bat, off-break bowler
Born: 15 December 1966, Guyana
Height: 6ft **Weight:** 13st
Test debut: 1987-88
Tests: 32
One-Day Internationals: 58
1st-Class 50s scored: 28
1st-Class 100s scored: 10
1st-Class 5 w. in innings: 5
1st-Class catches: 92
One-Day 50s: 3
One-Day 100s: 1
Place in batting averages: 1st av. 93.81
Place in bowling averages: 32nd av. 27.00
Strike rate: 65.09 (career 70.57)
Off-season: Touring with West Indies
Overseas tours: West Indies to India and
Pakistan 1987-88; Australia 1988-89;
Pakistan 1990-91; England 1991; Pakistan and Australia 1991-92
Extras: Signed a two-year contract to play for Kent from 1992
Best batting: 196 West Indies v Hampshire, Southampton 1991

Best bowling: 5-33 West Indies v Queensland, Brisbane 1988-89

1991 Season

	M	Inns	NO	Runs	HS	Avge	100s	50s	Ct	St	O	M	Runs	Wkts	Avge	Best	5wl	10wM
Test	5	9	2	271	111	38.71	1	2	9	-	64	13	137	2	68.50	1-10	-	-
All First	16	25	9	1501	196	93.81	5	8	20	-	336.2	71	837	31	27.00	5-94	1	-
1-day Int	3	3	0	84	48	28.00	-	-	-	-	15.5	0	98	3	32.66	2-18	-	
NatWest																		
B&H																		
Refuge																		

Career Performances

	M	Inns	NO	Runs	HS	Avge	100s	50s	Ct	St	Balls	Runs	Wkts	Avge	Best	5wl	10wM
Test	32	54	4	1409	134	28.18	3	7	29	-	2920	1247	15	83.13	2-28	-	-
All First	95	142	17	5136	196	41.08	10	28	92	-	10304	4611	146	31.58	5-33	5	-
1-day Int	56	47	14	1037	113 *	31.42	1	3	23	-	1788	1407	43	32.72	3-22	-	
NatWest																		
B&H																		
Refuge																		

HOUSEMAN, I. J.   Yorkshire

Name: Ian James Houseman
Role: Right-hand bat, right-arm fast-medium bowler
Born: 12 October 1969, Harrogate, North Yorkshire
Height: 5ft 10in **Weight:** 11st 10lbs
Nickname: Turk, Tessa, Toff 'and many others'
County debut: 1989
Parents: Eric and Jennifer
Marital status: Single
Family links with cricket: Father is a Yorkshire committee man; sister Fiona played for Yorkshire U19
Education: Harrogate Grammar School, Loughborough University
Qualifications: 10 O-levels, 5 A-levels
Off-season:' Touring Australia for a month and working at home.'
Cricketers particularly admired: Michael

Holding, Fred Trueman, Richard Hadlee, Dennis Lillee
Other sports followed: Rugby league (Leeds), golf
Relaxations: Golf
Extras: Played for England YC v New Zealand 1989
Opinions on cricket: 'Tighten the qualification rules for England. Too much cricket is played at all levels but especially first-class. I'd also like to see some more genuine attempts to bring back some pace and bounce into many English county pitches.'
Best batting: 18 Yorkshire v Sussex, Middlesbrough 1989
Best bowling: 2-26 Yorkshire v Indians, Headingley 1990

1991 Season

	M	Inns	NO	Runs	HS	Avge	100s	50s	Ct	St	O	M	Runs	Wkts	Avge	Best	5wI	10wM
Test																		
All First	1	0	0	0	0	-	-	-	-	-	21	4	52	1	52.00	1-52	-	-
1-day Int																		
NatWest																		
B&H																		
Refuge																		

Career Performances

	M	Inns	NO	Runs	HS	Avge	100s	50s	Ct	St	Balls	Runs	Wkts	Avge	Best	5wI	10wM
Test																	
All First	5	2	1	18	18	18.00	-	-	-	-	480	311	3	103.66	2-26	-	-
1-day Int																	
NatWest																	
B&H																	
Refuge																	

99. Which Englishman has taken the most Test wickets?

100. Who captained the 1969 New Zealanders in England?

101. Which wicket-keeper has the most dismissals in Test cricket?

HUGHES, D. P. Lancashire

Name: David Paul Hughes
Role: Right-hand bat, slow left-arm bowler
Born: 13 May 1947, Newton-le-Willows
Height: 5ft 11in **Weight:** 12st
Nickname: Yozzer
County debut: 1967
County cap: 1970
Benefit: 1981
1000 runs in a season: 2
50 wickets in a season: 4
1st-Class 50s scored: 45
1st-Class 100s scored: 8
1st-Class 5 w. in innings: 20
1st-Class 10 w. in match: 2
1st-Class catches: 325
One-Day 50s: 10
Place in batting averages: 201st av. 18.50
(1990 204th av. 23.70)

Place in bowling averages: 81st av. 38.25
(1989 41st av. 25.25)
Strike rate: (career 66.34)
Parents: Both deceased
Wife and date of marriage: Christine, March 1973
Children: James, July 1975
Family links with cricket: Father, Lloyd, a professional with Bolton League club Walkden, before and after Second World War
Education: Newton-le-Willows Grammar School
Qualifications: NCA coaching certificate
Overseas tours: England Counties side to West Indies 1974-75
Overseas teams played for: Tasmania, while coaching there 1975-77
Cricketers particularly admired: 'At the start of my career I spoke to all the leading left-arm spin bowlers in the game for help.'
Relaxations: Golf
Extras: Hit 24 runs off John Mortimer v Gloucestershire in penultimate over in Gillette Cup semi-final in 1972. Hit 26 runs off last over of innings v Northamptonshire in Gillette Final at Lord's, 1976. Bowled 13 consecutive maiden overs v Gloucestershire at Bristol, 1980. Appointed Lancashire captain 1987. One of *Wisden's* Five Cricketers of the Year, 1987. Led Lancashire to B&H and NatWest double in 1990 – the first time any county has won both knockout competitions in the same year. He has played in nine Lord's finals but stood down to make way for another batsman in the 1991 NatWest final which Lancashire lost to Hampshire. Appointed Lancashire's assistant cricket manager at the end of the 1991 season

Best batting: 153 Lancashire v Glamorgan, Old Trafford 1983
Best bowling: 7-24 Lancashire v Oxford University, The Parks 1970

1991 Season

	M	Inns	NO	Runs	HS	Avge	100s	50s	Ct	St	O	M	Runs	Wkts	Avge	Best	5wI	10wM
Test																		
All First	8	9	3	111	51	18.50	-	1	4	-	85.2	21	245	5	49.00	2-7	-	-
1-day Int																		
NatWest	2	1	1	5	5*	-	-	-	-	3	-	0.5	0	5	0	-		-	-
B&H	2	1	1	1	1*	-	-	-	-	1	-							
Refuge	6	1	1	4	4*	-	-	-	-	3	-	6	0	33	0	-		-	-

Career Performances

	M	Inns	NO	Runs	HS	Avge	100s	50s	Ct	St	Balls	Runs	Wkts	Avge	Best	5wI	10wM
Test																	
All First	447	587	109	10419	153	21.79	8	45	325	-	43458	19858	655	30.31	7-24	20	2
1-day Int																	
NatWest	61	41	17	815	71	33.95	-	1	22	-	1825	1190	44	27.04	4-61	-	
B&H	79	59	16	979	52	22.76	-	1	20	-	1424	754	29	26.00	5-23	1	
Refuge	307	221	52	3049	92	18.04	-	8	98	-	4999	3714	172	21.59	6-29	5	

102. Who topped the first-class bowling averages last season for Sussex?

103. Which England wicket-keeper had the most Test dismissals, Evans, Knott or Taylor?

104. Which non-wicket-keeper has caught most Test catches?

HUGHES, J. G. — Northamptonshire

Name: John Gareth Hughes
Role: Right-hand bat, right-arm medium bowler
Born: 3 May 1971, Wellingborough
Height: 6ft 1in **Weight:** 14st
Nickname: Yozzer
County debut: 1990
Parents: John and Jennifer
Marital status: Single
Family links with cricket: Grandfather, father and brother have played/play for Little Harrowden, whilst uncle umpires for the same team
Education: Sir Christopher Hatton School, Wellingborough; Sheffield City Polytechnic
Off-season: Studying at Polytechnic for BEd (Hons) in Physical Education
Overseas tours: Northampton Cricket Association U15 to Netherlands 1985
Cricketers particularly admired: David Capel, Greg Thomas, Angus Fraser, Neil Foster
Other sports followed: Football
Extras: Played for ESCA and made his 2nd XI debut in 1987. Played football for Northamptonshire U15 and U19. Grandfather was Welsh international footballer and father played football for Scotland youth team
Best batting: 2 Northamptonshire v Hampshire, Bournemouth 1990
Best bowling: 2-57 Northamptonshire v Derbyshire, Chesterfield 1990

1991 Season

	M	Inns	NO	Runs	HS	Avge	100s	50s	Ct	St	O	M	Runs	Wkts	Avge	Best	5wI	10wM
Test																		
All First	1	0	0	0	0	-	-	-	-	-	12	1	43	1	43.00	1-43	-	-
1-day Int																		
NatWest																		
B&H																		
Refuge																		

105. Who has scored the most centuries for England v Australia?

Career Performances

	M	Inns	NO	Runs	HS	Avge	100s	50s	Ct	St	Balls	Runs	Wkts	Avge	Best	5wI	10wM
Test																	
All First	5	7	0	4	2	0.57	-	-	-	-	468	336	4	84.00	2-57	-	-
1-day Int																	
NatWest																	
B&H																	
Refuge	1	1	1	1	1 *	-	-	-	-	-	24	16	0	-	-	-	-

HUGHES, S. P. Durham

Name: Simon Peter Hughes
Role: Right-hand bat, right-arm fast-medium bowler
Born: 20 December 1959, Kingston, Surrey
Height: 5ft 10in **Weight:** 11st 7lbs
Nickname: Yozzer, Spam, Yule
County debut: 1980 (Middlesex)
County cap: 1981 (Middlesex)
Benefit: 1991 (£110,000)
50 wickets in a season: 2
1st-Class 50s scored: 1
1st-Class 5 w. in innings: 9
1st-Class catches: 43
Place in bowling averages: (1990 89th av. 39.00)
Strike rate: (career 57.60)
Parents: Peter and Erica
Wife and date of marriage: Jan, 31 March 1990
Family links with cricket: Father very keen coach and player who owned indoor cricket school. 'Uncle once hit a ball over the school pavilion!'
Education: Latymer Upper School, Hammersmith; Durham University
Qualifications: 10 O-levels, 4 A-levels, BA General Studies
Career outside cricket: 'Write column for *The Independent* newspaper and broadcast on radio and TV.'
Off-season: Visiting friends abroad
Overseas tours: Middlesex to Zimbabwe 1980; International XI to India 1980; Bristol University to Sri Lanka 1987; International Ambassadors to India 1985-90
Overseas teams played for: Colts CC, Colombo 1979; Northern Transvaal 1982-83; Grosvenor Fynnland, Natal 1983-84; Auckland University 1984-85; Freemantle, Western Australia 1985-86; Sydney University 1986-87; Grafton, New Zealand 1988-89

Cricketers particularly admired: John Emburey, Clive Radley, Malcolm Marshall, Richard Hadlee
Other sports followed: Soccer, rugby, tennis, golf
Injuries: Broke collar bone on the Cresta Run
Relaxations: Travelling, people, Asian food, comedy
Extras: Took 4-82 v Kent on Championship debut, and played in County Championship and Gillette Cup winning sides in first season in 1980. Awarded cap after only 20 matches. Middlesex/Austin Reed Player of the Year 1986
Opinions on cricket: 'Having an 18th county is actually a bit of a mistake!'
Best batting: 53 Middlesex v Cambridge University, Fenner's 1988
Best bowling: 7-35 Middlesex v Surrey, The Oval 1986

1991 Season

	M	Inns	NO	Runs	HS	Avge	100s	50s	Ct	St	O	M	Runs	Wkts	Avge	Best	5wI	10wM
Test																		
All First	5	5	2	11	5	3.66	-	-	2	-	107.5	25	388	6	64.66	2-44	-	-
1-day Int																		
NatWest	1	1	1	0	0 *	-	-	-	-	-	11	2	24	2	12.00	2-24	-	
B&H																		
Refuge	6	2	0	8	4	4.00	-	-	-	-	47	3	214	8	26.75	2-29	-	

Career Performances

	M	Inns	NO	Runs	HS	Avge	100s	50s	Ct	St	Balls	Runs	Wkts	Avge	Best	5wI	10wM
Test																	
All First	179	193	63	1509	53	11.60	-	1	43	-	24424	12915	424	30.46	7-35	9	-
1-day Int																	
NatWest	24	13	8	45	11	9.00	-	-	1	-	1472	904	41	22.04	4-20	-	
B&H	24	15	7	71	22	8.87	-	-	3	-	1194	807	35	23.05	4-34	-	
Refuge	99	38	18	263	22 *	13.15	-	-	13	-	4100	3394	123	27.59	5-23	1	

HUNT, A. J.   Gloucestershire

Name: Alan Jeffrey Hunt
Role: Right-hand opening bat, 'non-bowler'
Born: 28 December 1968, Birmingham
Height: 5ft 10in **Weight:** 11st 8lbs
Nickname: Fox
County debut: 1991
1st-Class catches: 1
Parents: George and Marlene
Marital status: Single
Family links with cricket: Father played a bit (Works league), grandfather played in the

Birmingham League
Education: Dartmouth High School;
Dartmouth Sixth Form College
Qualifications: 5 O-levels, 2 A-levels
Career outside cricket: Salesman,
Insurance
Off-season: 'Playing football (semi-pro),
any job going.'
Overseas tours: Gloucestershire to Kenya
1991
Cricketers particularly admired:
Geoffrey Boycott, Dennis Amiss,
Eddie Barlow, Paul Romaines, Graham
Warner (capt of M&B, Birmingham
League club)
Other sports followed: Football (West
Bromwich Albion), any other ball sport
Injuries: 'The odd strain here and there.'
Relaxations: 'A quiet pint after the game, a
nice Cantonese meal with my girlfriend.'

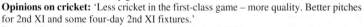

Opinions on cricket: 'Less cricket in the first-class game – more quality. Better pitches for 2nd XI and some four-day 2nd XI fixtures.'
Best batting: 12 Gloucestershire v Sri Lanka, Bristol 1991

1991 Season

	M	Inns	NO	Runs	HS	Avge	100s	50s	Ct	St	O	M	Runs	Wkts	Avge	Best	5wI	10wM
Test																		
All First	1	2	0	15	12	7.50	-	-	1	-								
1-day Int																		
NatWest																		
B&H																		
Refuge																		

Career Performances

	M	Inns	NO	Runs	HS	Avge	100s	50s	Ct	St	Balls	Runs	Wkts	Avge	Best	5wI	10wM
Test																	
All First	1	2	0	15	12	7.50	-	-	1	-							
1-day Int																	
NatWest																	
B&H																	
Refuge																	

HUSSAIN, N.   Essex

Name: Nasser Hussain
Role: Right-hand bat
Born: 28 March 1968, Madras, India
Height: 6ft 1in
Nickname: Bunny
County debut: 1987
Test debut: 1989-90
Tests: 3
One-Day Internationals: 2
1000 runs in a season: 1
1st-Class 50s scored: 19
1st-Class 100s scored: 9
1st-Class catches: 95
One-Day 50s: 6
One-Day 100s: 1
Place in batting averages: 18th av. 54.16
(1990 122nd av. 37.60)

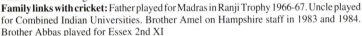

Parents: Jawad and Shireen
Marital status: Single
Family links with cricket: Father played for Madras in Ranji Trophy 1966-67. Uncle played for Combined Indian Universities. Brother Amel on Hampshire staff in 1983 and 1984. Brother Abbas played for Essex 2nd XI
Education: Forest School; Durham University
Qualifications: 9 O-levels, 3 A-levels; BSc (Hons) in Geology; NCA cricket coaching award
Off-season: Touring with England A to Bermuda and West Indies
Overseas tours: England YC to Sri Lanka
1987 and Australia for Youth World Cup 1988; England to India and West Indies 1990; England A to Pakistan and Sri Lanka 1990-91; England A to Bermuda and West Indies 1991-92
Overseas teams played for: Madras 1986-87
Cricketers particularly admired: 'They are all in the Essex dressing room, plus David Gower.'
Other sports followed: Golf, football, American football
Relaxations: Music, TV
Extras: Played for England Schools U15 for two years (one as captain). Youngest player to play for Essex Schools U11 at the age of 8 and U15 at the age of 12. At 15, was considered the best young leg-spin bowler in the country. Cricket Writers' Club Young Cricketer of the Year, 1989. One of four players asked to stand by as reserves for England's World Cup squad 1992
Best batting: 197 Essex v Surrey, The Oval 1990

1991 Season

	M	Inns	NO	Runs	HS	Avge	100s	50s	Ct	St	O	M	Runs	Wkts	Avge	Best	5wI	10wM
Test																		
All First	25	33	8	1354	196	54.16	3	8	38	-	8.3	0	50	0	-	-	-	-
1-day Int																		
NatWest	3	2	0	114	97	57.00	-	1	4	-								
B&H	6	5	1	46	26	11.50	-	-	2	-								
Refuge	14	12	3	256	48	28.44	-	-	4	-								

Career Performances

	M	Inns	NO	Runs	HS	Avge	100s	50s	Ct	St	Balls	Runs	Wkts	Avge	Best	5wI	10wM
Test	3	5	0	100	35	20.00	-	-	1	-							
All First	78	114	19	4265	197	44.89	9	19	95	-	183	160	0	-	-	-	-
1-day Int	2	2	1	17	15 *	17.00	-	-	1	-							
NatWest	5	4	1	140	97	46.66	-	1	4	-							
B&H	19	17	3	496	118	35.42	1	3	7	-							
Refuge	45	38	9	813	66 *	28.03	-	2	23	-							

HUTCHINSON, I. J. F.   Middlesex

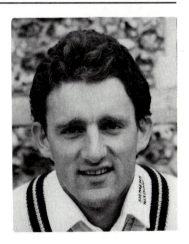

Name: Ian James Frederick Hutchinson
Role: Right-hand opening bat, right-arm
medium bowler
Born: 31 October 1964, Welshpool
Height: 6ft 1in **Weight:** 13st 5lbs
Nickname: Hutch
County debut: 1987
1st-Class 50s scored: 2
1st-Class 100s scored: 5
1st-Class 200s scored: 1
1st-Class catches: 29
Place in batting averages: 130th av. 28.52
Parents: Alan Trevor and Gillian Catharine
Wife and date of marriage: Louise,
19 September 1987
Family links with cricket: Father played
league cricket, grandfather played for
Leicestershire 2nd XI
Education: Kingsland Grange Prep School;
Shrewsbury School
Qualifications: 10 O-levels, 2 A-levels, cricket coach, full licence (insurance)
Career outside cricket: Insurance broker and fives coach

Off-season: Working as insurance broker and fives coach
Overseas tours: Middlesex pre-season tours to Spain and Portugal
Cricketers particularly admired: Geoff Boycott
Other sports followed: 'Almost everything other than horse-racing.'
Injuries: Sprained ankle and strained side
Relaxations: 'Holidays.'
Extras: 'Took the wicket of Carl Hooper with my 2nd ball in first-class cricket!'
Opinions on cricket: 'I think it's magic!'
Best batting: 201* Middlesex v Oxford University, The Parks 1989
Best bowling: 1-18 Middlesex v West Indies, Lord's 1991

1991 Season

	M	Inns	NO	Runs	HS	Avge	100s	50s	Ct	St	O	M	Runs	Wkts	Avge	Best	5wI	10wM
Test																		
All First	14	24	1	656	125	28.52	2	2	15	-	12	0	29	1	29.00	1-18	-	-
1-day Int																		
NatWest	2	2	0	40	23	20.00	-	-	2	-	2	0	17	0	-		-	-
B&H	1	1	0	8	8	8.00	-	-	-	-								
Refuge	5	5	0	104	42	20.80	-	-	2	-	2	0	10	1	10.00	1-10	-	

Career Performances

	M	Inns	NO	Runs	HS	Avge	100s	50s	Ct	St	Balls	Runs	Wkts	Avge	Best	5wI	10wM
Test																	
All First	27	46	4	1435	201*	34.16	5	2	29	-	72	29	1	29.00	1-18	-	-
1-day Int																	
NatWest	4	3	0	41	23	13.66	-	-	5	-	12	17	0	-		-	-
B&H	1	1	0	8	8	8.00	-	-	-	-							
Refuge	13	12	1	164	42	14.90	-	-	6	-	12	10	1	10.00	1-10	-	

HUTTON, S.   Durham

Name: Stewart Hutton
Role: Left-hand bat, cover fielder
Born: 30 November 1969, Stockton-on-Tees
Height: 6ft **Weight:** 12st

106. Who captained England A to Bermuda and West Indies during the 1991-92 off-season?

Nickname: Len
Parents: Leonard and Mavis
Marital status: Single
Education: De Brus Comprehensive;
Cleveland Technical College
Qualifications: 6 O-levels (equivalent),
A-level Economics
Overseas tours: Durham to Zimbabwe
1991-92
Cricketers particularly admired:
Mike Gatting
Other sports followed: Golf, football
Injuries: Broken left thumb
Relaxations: Playing golf
Extras: Played for Durham in two friendly
one-day games in 1991, against Victoria
and Essex

No appearances in first-class cricket or any one-day competition

IGGLESDEN, A. P. Kent

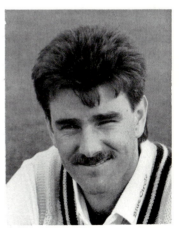

Name: Alan Paul Igglesden
Role: Right-hand bat, right-arm fast-medium
bowler, outfielder
Born: 8 October 1964, Farnborough, Kent
Height: 6ft 6in **Weight:** 14st 12lbs
Nickname: Iggy, Norman
County debut: 1986
Test debut: 1989
Tests: 1
50 wickets in a season: 3
1st-Class 5 w. in innings: 11
1st-Class 10 w. in match: 2
1st-Class catches: 24
Place in batting averages: (1990 259th
av. 13.12)
Place in bowling averages: 33rd av. 27.02
(1990 61st av. 35.93)
Strike rate: 56.52 (career 52.18)
Parents: Alan Trevor and Gillian Catharine

Wife and date of marriage: Hilary Moira,
20 January 1990
Family links with cricket: Brother Kevin plays for Holmesdale in the Kent League
Education: St Mary's Primary School; Hosey School; Churchill Secondary School, Westerham
Qualifications: 9 CSEs, coaching certificate
Off-season: Playing and coaching at Green Point, Cape Town
Overseas tours: With England A to Zimbabwe and Kenya 1989-90; Fred Rumsey's XI to Barbados 1990
Overseas teams played for: Avendale, Cape Town 1985-89; Western Province 1987-91; Green Point, Cape Town 1991-92
Cricketers particularly admired: Terry Alderman, Dennis Lillee, Chris Penn, Mark Benson, Roy Pienaar, Peter Kirsten, Gavin Daitsch
Other sports followed: 'Very keen Crystal Palace supporter'
Injuries: Torn side muscle – missed last two games of the season
Relaxations: 'Music, golf, keeping fit, a meal and a few beers with my wife and a few friends, the Granville pub.'
Opinions on cricket: 'We play too much cricket in England but we can't complain , it's a privilege to have such an enjoyable profession.'
Best batting: 41 Kent v Surrey, Canterbury 1988
Best bowling: 6-34 Kent v Surrey, Canterbury 1988

1991 Season

	M	Inns	NO	Runs	HS	Avge	100s	50s	Ct	St	O	M	Runs	Wkts	Avge	Best	5wI	10wM
Test																		
All First	19	17	4	101	16 *	7.76	-	-	4	-	471	94	1351	50	27.02	5-36	1	-
1-day Int																		
NatWest	1	0	0	0	0	-	-	-	1	-	9.2	1	29	4	7.25	4-29	-	
B&H	5	2	1	29	26 *	29.00	-	-	1	-	50.5	7	224	10	22.40	3-24	-	
Refuge	14	5	3	18	13 *	9.00	-	-	3	-	109	6	461	23	20.04	4-59	-	

Career Performances

	M	Inns	NO	Runs	HS	Avge	100s	50s	Ct	St	Balls	Runs	Wkts	Avge	Best	5wI	10wM
Test	1	1	1	2	2 *	-	-	-	1	-	222	146	3	48.66	2-91	-	-
All First	87	93	32	603	41	9.88	-	-	24	-	14717	7862	282	27.87	6-34	11	2
1-day Int																	
NatWest	7	3	2	16	12 *	16.00	-	-	3	-	356	203	12	16.91	4-29	-	
B&H	15	6	4	37	26 *	18.50	-	-	4	-	845	590	21	28.09	3-24	-	
Refuge	42	17	9	49	13 *	6.12	-	-	10	-	1876	1261	61	20.67	5-13	1	

ILLINGWORTH, R. K.   Worcestershire

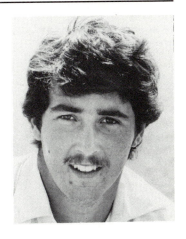

Name: Richard Keith Illingworth
Role: Right-hand bat, slow left-arm bowler
Born: 23 August 1963, Bradford
Height: 6ft **Weight:** 13st 4lbs
Nickname: Lucy, Harry
County debut: 1982
County cap: 1986
Test debut: 1991
Tests: 2
One-Day Internationals: 3
50 wickets in a season: 3
1st-Class 50s scored: 10
1st-Class 100s scored: 3
1st-Class 5 w. in innings: 19
1st-Class 10 w. in match: 4
1st-Class catches: 97
Place in batting averages: 166th av. 23.81
(1990 146th av. 33.25)
Place in bowling averages: 90th av. 35.31
(1990 20th av. 28.29)
Strike rate: 87.00 (career 77.86)
Parents: Keith and Margaret
Wife and date of marriage: Anne, 20 September 1985
Children: Miles, 28 August 1987; Thomas, 20 April 1989
Family links with cricket: Father played Bradford League cricket
Education: Wrose Brow Middle; Salts Grammar School ('same school as the late Jim Laker')
Qualifications: 6 O-levels, senior coaching award holder
Career outside cricket: Buyer for Golding Pipeworks
Off-season: Touring with England
Overseas tours: England A to Zimbabwe and Kenya 1989-90; Pakistan and Sri Lanka 1990-91; England to New Zealand 1991-92
Overseas teams played for: Natal 1988-89
Other sports followed: Football (follows Leeds United, Bradford City)
Injuries: Broken right thumb – missed three weeks
Relaxations: 'Listening to music. Playing with Miles and Thomas.'
Extras: Took 11 for 108 on South African first-class debut for Natal B v Boland 1988. Scored 120 not out as a nightwatchman for Worcestershire v Warwickshire 1988 and 106 for England A v Zimbabwe 1989-90. 11th person in history to take a wicket with their first ball in Test cricket
Best batting: 120* Worcestershire v Warwickshire, Worcester 1987
Best bowling: 7-50 Worcestershire v Oxford University, The Parks 1985

1991 Season

	M	Inns	NO	Runs	HS	Avge	100s	50s	Ct	St	O	M	Runs	Wkts	Avge	Best	5wl	10wM
Test	2	4	2	31	13	15.50	-	-	1	-	56.4	10	213	4	53.25	3-110	-	-
All First	22	29	7	524	56 *	23.81	-	1	8	-	551.1	155	1342	38	35.31	5-43	3	-
1-day Int	3	1	1	9	9 *	-	-	-	4	-	32	3	115	3	38.33	2-53	-	
NatWest	2	1	0	10	10	10.00	-	-	2	-	16	2	59	2	29.50	1-12	-	
B&H	6	2	2	18	17 *	-	-	-	2	-	49	2	189	2	94.50	2-50	-	
Refuge	15	4	3	90	25 *	90.00	-	-	6	-	100	4	473	16	29.56	5-49	1	

Career Performances

	M	Inns	NO	Runs	HS	Avge	100s	50s	Ct	St	Balls	Runs	Wkts	Avge	Best	5wl	10wM
Test	2	4	2	31	13	15.50	-	-	1	-	340	213	4	53.25	3-110	-	-
All First	222	244	64	3800	120 *	21.11	3	10	97	-	37202	15116	482	31.36	7-50	19	4
1-day Int	3	1	1	9	9 *	-	-	-	4	-	192	115	3	38.33	2-53	-	
NatWest	21	9	2	65	22	9.28	-	-	6	-	1213	611	19	32.15	4-20	-	
B&H	33	17	10	159	36 *	22.71	-	-	7	-	1560	969	24	40.37	4-36	-	
Refuge	114	50	24	311	25 *	11.96	-	-	29	-	4036	3041	133	22.86	5-24	2	

ILOTT, M. C. Essex

Name: Mark Christopher Ilott
Role: Left-hand bat (nightwatchman),
left-arm fast bowler
Born: 27 August 1970, Watford
Height: 6ft 1½in **Weight:** 13st
Nickname: Ramble, Touché, Headless
County debut: 1988
1st-Class 5 w. in innings: 2
1st-Class catches: 2
Place in batting averages: (1990 251st
av. 15.37)
Place in bowling averages: (1990 47th
av. 33.41)
Strike rate: (career 64.05)
Parents: John and Glenys
Marital status: Single
Family links with cricket: 'Brother plays
Minor Counties for Hertfordshire, Dad is
president of Watford Town CC and Grandad

played for Ruislip Manor for many years – Mum is tea-maker *extraordinaire*.'
Education: Francis Combe School
Qualifications: 6 O-levels, 2 AO-levels, 2 A-levels, coaching qualification

Career outside cricket: Odd job man
Off-season: 'Recovering from operation, getting fit.'
Overseas tours: England A to Sri Lanka 1990-91
Overseas teams played for: East Torrens District, Adelaide 1989-91
Cricketers particularly admired: John Lever, Malcolm Marshall, Steve Andrew, Nasser Hussain
Other sports followed: Tennis, football, golf
Injuries: Stress fracture of spine. Had surgery in August – missed almost all of last season
Relaxations: Swimming, golf, tennis, reading, eating
Extras: Youngest player ever to play for Hertfordshire
Best batting: 42* Essex v Kent, Chelmsford 1990
Best bowling: 5-34 Essex v Derbyshire, Derby 1990

1991 Season

	M	Inns	NO	Runs	HS	Avge	100s	50s	Ct	St	O	M	Runs	Wkts	Avge	Best	5wI	10wM
Test																		
All First	1	0	0	0	0	-	-	-	-	-	21.4	7	62	3	20.66	2-30	-	-
1-day Int																		
NatWest																		
B&H	3	0	0	0	0	-	-	-	-	-	31	6	101	5	20.20	3-34	-	
Refuge	2	1	0	0	0	0.00	-	-	1	-	14	1	54	3	18.00	2-26	-	

Career Performances

	M	Inns	NO	Runs	HS	Avge	100s	50s	Ct	St	Balls	Runs	Wkts	Avge	Best	5wI	10wM
Test																	
All First	19	17	7	167	42 *	16.70	-	-	3	-	3395	1716	53	32.37	5-34	2	-
1-day Int																	
NatWest	1	0	0	0	0	-	-	-	-	-	54	45	1	45.00	1-45	-	
B&H	5	0	0	0	0	-	-	-	-	-	282	162	5	32.40	3-34	-	
Refuge	12	5	1	14	6	3.50	-	-	2	-	552	385	12	32.08	2-24	-	

---

107. Who scored the fastest first-class century last season?

IRANI, R.   Lancashire

Name: Ronnie Irani
Role: Right-hand bat, right-arm medium
bowler
Born: 26 October 1971, Leigh
Height: 6ft 4in **Weight:** 13st
Nickname: Imre, Moon, Ronski
County debut: 1990
1st-Class catches: 0
Parents: John and Glenys
Marital status: Single
Family links with cricket: 'Father played
local league cricket in Bolton for 30 years,
mother did teas for 20 years! '
Education: Church Road Primary School;
Smithills Comprehensive School
Qualifications: 9 GCSEs
Career outside cricket: 'Opened two
greengrocery outlets (health shops) with
partner, Fil Adams-Mercer, and planning to
open a few more.'

Off-season: 'Being a director of FAM Foods Ltd I am up at 3am buying our fresh produce,
and during the day I make sure all is in good order. My day finishes at 6.30pm.'
Overseas tours: England U19 to Australia 1990-91
Cricketers particularly admired: Ian Botham, Imran Khan, Richie Richardson
Other sports followed: Football, boxing, Thai boxing, golf, American football and motor
racing
Injuries: Sore knee
Relaxations: Films, Thai boxing, watching football
Extras: Played for England U19 in home series against Australia 1991, scoring a century
and three 50s in six innings
Best batting: 31* Lancashire v Oxford University, The Parks 1991
Best bowling: 1-12 Lancashire v Zimbabwe, Old Trafford 1990

1991 Season

	M	Inns	NO	Runs	HS	Avge	100s	50s	Ct	St	O	M	Runs	Wkts	Avge	Best	5wI	10wM
Test																		
All First	1	1	1	31	31 *	-	-	-	-	-	32.2	5	82	0	-	-	-	-
1-day Int																		
NatWest																			
B&H																			
Refuge																			

Career Performances

	M	Inns	NO	Runs	HS	Avge	100s	50s	Ct	St	Balls	Runs	Wkts	Avge	Best	5wI	10wM
Test																	
All First	2	1	1	31	31 *	-	-	-	-	-	326	155	2	77.50	1-12	-	-
1-day Int																	
NatWest																	
B&H																	
Refuge																	

JACK, S. D. Lancashire

Name: Steven Douglas Jack
Role: Right-hand bat, right-arm fast bowler
Born: 4 August 1970, Durban
Height: 6ft 3in **Weight:** 13st 9lbs
Nickname: Charger
1st-Class 5 w. in innings: 3
1st-Class 10 w. in match: 1
1st-Class catches: 4
Strike rate: (career 38.45)
Parents: Andy and Shirley
Marital status: Single
Family links with cricket: Father played
league cricket in Durban
Education: Greenwood High School,
Durban; Witwatersrand University
Career outside cricket:
Studying Commerce
Off-season: Playing for Transvaal and
'hoping to play for South Africa'

Overseas teams played for:
Transvaal 1990-92
Cricketers particularly admired: Clive Rice, Jimmy Cook, Dennis Lillee
Other sports followed: All sports, particularly golf
Injuries: 'Ankle injury has forced me to miss most of the 1991-92 season.'
Relaxations: Golf, watching sport, 'doing nothing'
Extras: South African Cricketer of the Year 1991. Leading wicket-taker in the Currie Cup
1990-91
Opinions on cricket: 'Wickets must be prepared to provide a fair contest between bat and
ball. Good wickets produce good players.'
Best batting: 26 Transvaal v Eastern Province, Port Elizabeth 1990-91
Best bowling: 8-51 Transvaal v Eastern Province, Port Elizabeth 1990-91

Career Performances

	M	Inns	NO	Runs	HS	Avge	100s	50s	Ct	St	Balls	Runs	Wkts	Avge	Best	5wI	10wM
Test																	
All First	12	14	5	143	26	15.88	-	-	4	-	2307	1072	60	17.86	8-51	3	1
1-day Int																	
NatWest																	
B&H																	
Refuge																	

JAMES, K. D. Hampshire

Name: Kevan David James
Role: Left-hand bat, left-arm medium bowler
Born: 18 March 1961, Lambeth, South London
Height: 6ft ^{1}/2in **Weight:** 12st 6lbs
Nickname: Jambo, Jaimo
County debut: 1980 (Middlesex), 1985 (Hampshire)
County cap: 1989
1000 runs in a season: 1
1st-Class 50s scored: 16
1st-Class 100s scored: 7
1st-Class 5 w. in innings: 7
1st-Class catches: 37
One-Day 50s: 3
Place in batting averages: 31st av. 47.18
Place in bowling averages: 73rd av. 33.02
Strike rate: 64.80 (career 63.03)
Parents: David (deceased) and Helen
Wife and date of marriage: Debbie, October 1987
Family links with cricket: Late father played club cricket in North London, brother Martin plays for Hertfordshire
Education: Edmonton County High School
Qualifications: 5 O-levels; qualified coach
Off-season: 'Developing my South African wine business.'
Overseas tours: England YC tour of Australia 1978-79; West Indies 1979-80
Overseas teams played for: Wellington, New Zealand 1982-83
Cricketers particularly admired: Chris Smith
Other sports followed: Football (Spurs)

Extras: Released by Middlesex at end of 1984 season and joined Hampshire
Best batting: 162 Hampshire v Glamorgan, Cardiff 1989
Best bowling: 6-22 Hampshire v Australia, Southampton 1985

1991 Season

	M	Inns	NO	Runs	HS	Avge	100s	50s	Ct	St	O	M	Runs	Wkts	Avge	Best	5wl	10wM
Test																		
All First	24	37	10	1274	134 *	47.18	2	6	9	-	442.5	99	1354	41	33.02	4-32	-	-
1-day Int																		
NatWest	3	1	0	0	0	0.00	-	-	1	-	22	3	97	1	97.00	1-50	-	
B&H	2	1	0	2	2	2.00	-	-	-	-	22	0	100	1	100.00	1-45	-	
Refuge	13	12	2	176	58 *	17.60	-	1	3	-	66	3	304	11	27.63	3-24	-	

Career Performances

	M	Inns	NO	Runs	HS	Avge	100s	50s	Ct	St	Balls	Runs	Wkts	Avge	Best	5wl	10wM
Test																	
All First	117	160	34	4230	162	33.57	7	16	37	-	12922	6447	205	31.44	6-22	7	-
1-day Int																	
NatWest	14	9	2	132	42	18.85	-	-	1	-	814	569	17	33.47	3-22	-	
B&H	26	18	2	258	45	16.12	-	-	2	-	1423	922	25	36.88	3-31	-	
Refuge	86	57	20	888	66	24.00	-	3	29	-	3463	2446	75	32.61	4-23	-	

JAMES, S. P.   Glamorgan

Name: Stephen Peter James
Role: Right-hand opening bat, cover fielder
Born: 7 September 1967, Lydney
Height: 6ft **Weight:** 12st 8lbs
Nickname: Jamer, Dougie, Pedro, Sid
County debut: 1985
1000 runs in a season: 1
1st-Class 50s scored: 11
1st-Class 100s scored: 7
1st-Class catches: 33
One-Day 50s: 3
Place in batting averages: 125th av. 28.81
(1990 134th av. 34.48)
Parents: Peter and Margaret
Marital status: Single
Family links with cricket: Father played
for Gloucestershire 2nd XI
Education: Monmouth School;

University College, Swansea; Cambridge University
Qualifications: BA (Hons) Classics; BA (Hons) Land Economy
Off-season: Playing and coaching in Zimbabwe
Overseas tours: Welsh Schools to Barbados 1984; Monmouth Schools to Sri Lanka 1985; Combined Universities to Barbados 1989; Glamorgan to Trinidad 1990; Zimbabwe 1991
Overseas teams played for: Bionics, Zimbabwe 1990-91
Cricketers particularly admired: Geoff Boycott, Michael Atherton, Graham Gooch, Graham Burgess
Other sports followed: All sports, especially Rugby Union
Injuries: 'Nothing serious but I still spent a lot of time with our physio!'
Relaxations: 'Music, videos and socialising – former fitness fanatic!'
Extras: Scored maiden century in only second first-class game. Played rugby for Lydney and Gloucestershire and Cambridge University and was on the substitutes bench for 1988 and 1989 Varsity matches
Opinions on cricket: '2nd XI pitches are too often sub-standard, making it very difficult to get the necessary scores to challenge for a 1st team place.'
Best batting: 151* Cambridge University v Warwickshire, Fenner's 1989

1991 Season

	M	Inns	NO	Runs	HS	Avge	100s	50s	Ct	St	O	M	Runs	Wkts	Avge	Best	5wl	10wM
Test																		
All First	11	19	3	461	70	28.81	-	2	8	-								
1-day Int																		
NatWest																		
B&H																		
Refuge	2	2	0	34	23	17.00	-	-	1	-								

Career Performances

	M	Inns	NO	Runs	HS	Avge	100s	50s	Ct	St	Balls	Runs	Wkts	Avge	Best	5wl	10wM
Test																	
All First	53	92	7	2691	151 *	31.65	7	11	33	-							
1-day Int																	
NatWest	2	2	0	32	26	16.00	-	-	-	-							
B&H	8	8	0	273	65	34.12	-	3	3	-							
Refuge	5	5	0	64	23	12.80	-	-	2	-							

108. Who topped the first-class bowling averages last season for Warwickshire?

JARVIS, P. W.   Yorkshire

Name: Paul William Jarvis
Role: Right-hand bat, right-arm
fast-medium bowler
Born: 29 June 1965, Redcar, North
Yorkshire
Height: 5ft 11in **Weight:** 12st 4lbs
Nickname: Jarv, Beaver, Gnasher
County debut: 1981
County cap: 1986
Test debut: 1987-88
Tests: 6
One-Day Internationals: 5
50 wickets in a season: 3
1st-Class 50s scored: 1
1st-Class 5 w. in innings: 18
1st-Class 10 w. in match: 3
1st-Class catches: 34
Place in batting averages: (1990 234th
av. 17.66)
Place in bowling averages: 3rd av. 19.58
(1990 78th av. 37.64)
Strike rate: 47.50 (career 51.40)
Parents: Malcolm and Marjorie
Wife and date of marriage: Wendy Jayne, 3 December 1988
Children: Alexander Michael, 13 July 1989
Family links with cricket: Father still plays league cricket, now for Gwent CC; brother
Andrew now plays for Methley CC in the Yorkshire Council League
Education: Bydales Comprehensive School, Marske, Cleveland
Qualifications: 4 O-levels
Off-season: Looking for employment
Overseas tours: England to World Cup and Pakistan 1986-87; Australia and New Zealand
1987-88; unofficial English team to South Africa 1989-90
Overseas teams played for: Mossman Middle Harbour, Sydney 1984-85; Avendale,
Cape Town 1985-86; Manly Warringah, Sydney 1987
Cricketers particularly admired: Dennis Lillee, Richard Hadlee, Malcolm Marshall
Other sports followed: Most sports
Injuries: Torn hamstring in left knee
Relaxations: Fishing, golf, DIY, cooking, eating out, going to pubs
Extras: Youngest player ever to play for Yorkshire in County Championship (16 years,
2 months, 13 days) and youngest player to take hat-trick in JPL and Championship. Played
for England YC v West Indies 1982 and Australia 1983. Banned from Test cricket for
joining tour of South Africa

Opinions on cricket: 'Four-day cricket should now be introduced for all Championship matches. It produces positive and not contrived results.'
Best batting: 59* Yorkshire v Nottinghamshire, Trent Bridge 1989
Best bowling: 7-55 Yorkshire v Surrey, Headingley 1986

1991 Season

	M	Inns	NO	Runs	HS	Avge	100s	50s	Ct	St	O	M	Runs	Wkts	Avge	Best	5wI	10wM
Test																		
All First	4	5	2	114	37 *	38.00	-	-	-	-	95	26	235	12	19.58	4-28	-	-
1-day Int																		
NatWest																		
B&H	5	3	2	15	12 *	15.00	-	-	-	-	44.2	9	142	6	23.66	2-13	-	
Refuge	3	3	0	18	9	6.00	-	-	-	-	23	3	103	2	51.50	2-37	-	

Career Performances

	M	Inns	NO	Runs	HS	Avge	100s	50s	Ct	St	Balls	Runs	Wkts	Avge	Best	5wI	10wM
Test	6	9	2	109	29 *	15.57	-	-	-	-	1347	708	14	50.57	4-107	-	-
All First	128	148	47	1522	59 *	15.06	-	1	34	-	21436	11407	417	27.35	7-55	18	3
1-day Int	5	2	1	5	5 *	5.00	-	-	-	-	287	187	6	31.16	4-33	-	
NatWest	13	7	2	62	16	12.40	-	-	3	-	847	520	16	32.50	4-41	-	
B&H	29	12	4	103	42	12.87	-	-	4	-	1640	918	45	20.40	4-43	-	
Refuge	81	39	17	217	29 *	9.86	-	-	20	-	3474	2499	119	21.00	6-27	2	

109. What legendary Test fast bowler now runs a florist business?

JEAN-JACQUES, M.   Derbyshire

Name: Martin Jean-Jacques
Role: Right-hand bat, right-arm fast-medium
pace bowler
Born: 2 August 1960, Soufriere, Dominica
Height: 5ft 11in **Weight:** 12st 7lbs
Nickname: JJ
County debut: 1986
1st-Class 50s scored: 1
1st-Class 5 w. in innings: 2
1st-Class 10 w. in match: 1
1st-Class catches: 11
Place in batting averages: (1990 257th
av. 13.37)
Place in bowling averages: 165th av. 41.33
(1990 112th av. 44.24)
Strike rate: 70.75 (career 60.92)
Education: Scotts Head Primary, Dominica;
Aylestone High, London
Career outside cricket: Electrician
Cricketers particularly admired: Michael Holding
Other sports followed: Football
Relaxations: Listening to music – reggae and soul
Extras: Played Minor Counties cricket for Buckinghamshire. On debut for Derbyshire (v
Yorkshire) put on a record 132 with Alan Hill for the 10th wicket
Best batting: 73 Derbyshire v Yorkshire, Sheffield 1986
Best bowling: 8-77 Derbyshire v Kent, Derby 1986

1991 Season

	M	Inns	NO	Runs	HS	Avge	100s	50s	Ct	St	O	M	Runs	Wkts	Avge	Best	5wI	10wM
Test																		
All First	5	7	1	35	28	5.83	-	-	-	-	141.3	26	496	12	41.33	4-54	-	-
1-day Int																		
NatWest																		
B&H																		
Refuge	3	2	0	23	23	11.50	-	-	1	-	18	1	124	2	62.00	2-56	-	

110. Who does Allan Donald play for in South Africa?

Career Performances

	M	Inns	NO	Runs	HS	Avge	100s	50s	Ct	St	Balls	Runs	Wkts	Avge	Best	5wI	10wM
Test																	
All First	51	64	14	581	73	11.62	-	1	11	-	6702	3956	110	35.96	8-77	2	1
1-day Int																	
NatWest	8	5	3	28	16	14.00	-	-	1	-	444	310	12	25.83	3-23	-	
B&H	4	2	1	4	2*	4.00	-	-	2	-	180	164	5	32.80	3-22	-	
Refuge	29	14	1	92	23	7.07	-	-	5	-	1074	1020	27	37.77	3-36	-	

JESTY, T. E. Lancashire

Name: Trevor Edward Jesty
Role: Right-hand bat, right-arm medium bowler
Born: 2 June 1948, Gosport, Hampshire
Height: 5ft 9in **Weight:** 11st 10lbs
Nickname: Jets
County debut: 1966 (Hampshire), 1985 (Surrey), 1988 (Lancs)
County cap: 1971 (Hampshire), 1985 (Surrey)
Benefit: 1982
One-Day Internationals: 10
1000 runs in a season: 10
50 wickets in a season: 2
1st-Class 50s scored: 110
1st-Class 100s scored: 35
1st-Class 200s scored: 2
1st-Class 5 w. in innings: 19
1st-Class catches: 265
1st-Class stumpings: 1
One-Day 50s: 44
One-Day 100s: 7
Place in batting averages: (1990 90th av. 43.61)
Parents: Aubrey Edward and Sophia
Wife and date of marriage: Jacqueline, 12 September 1970
Children: Graeme Barry, 27 September 1972; Lorna Samantha, 7 November 1976
Family links with cricket: Brother Aubrey, a wicket-keeper and left-hand bat, could have joined Hampshire staff, but decided to continue with his apprenticeship
Education: Privet County Secondary Modern, Gosport
Overseas tours: England to Australia and New Zealand 1982-83
Overseas teams played for: Border, South Africa 1973-74; Griqualand West, South

Africa 1974-75 and 1975-76; Canterbury, New Zealand 1979-80
Cricketers particularly admired: Barry Richards
Relaxations: Watching soccer, gardening, golf
Extras: Took him ten years to score maiden first-class century. Missed most of 1980 season through injury. Considered to be most unlucky not to be chosen for England tour of Australia 1982-83, then was called in as a replacement. One of *Wisden's* Five Cricketers of the Year, 1982. Left Hampshire at end of 1984 when not appointed captain. Captaincy of Surrey 1985. Released by Surrey at end of 1987 season and joined Lancashire 1988
Best batting: 248 Hampshire v Cambridge University, Fenner's 1984
Best bowling: 7-75 Hampshire v Worcestershire, Southampton 1976

1991 Season

	M	Inns	NO	Runs	HS	Avge	100s	50s	Ct	St	O	M	Runs	Wkts	Avge	Best	5wI	10wM
Test																		
All First	1	2	2	126	122 *	-		1	-	-	-							
1-day Int																		
NatWest																		
B&H																		
Refuge																		

Career Performances

	M	Inns	NO	Runs	HS	Avge	100s	50s	Ct	St	Balls	Runs	Wkts	Avge	Best	5wI	10wM
Test																	
All First	490	777	107	21916	248	32.71	35	110	265	1	36858	16075	585	27.47	7-75	19	-
1-day Int	10	10	4	127	52 *	21.16	-	1	5	-	108	93	1	93.00	1-23	-	
NatWest	41	35	2	976	118	29.57	2	5	15	-	1884	1038	39	26.61	6-46	1	
B&H	75	71	11	2150	105	35.83	1	15	16	-	3118	1797	74	24.28	5-39	1	
Refuge	292	268	37	5737	166 *	24.83	4	23	63	-	7827	6151	249	24.70	6-20	3	

111. Which former county player is now team manager of Nottinghamshire?

JOHNSON, P.   Nottinghamshire

Name: Paul Johnson
Role: Right-hand bat, right-arm occasional bowler
Born: 24 April 1965, Newark
Height: 5ft 7in **Weight:** 11st 7lbs
Nickname: Gus, Johno, Midge
County debut: 1982
County cap: 1986
1000 runs in a season: 4
1st-Class 50s scored: 55
1st-Class 100s scored: 20
1st-Class catches: 131
1st-Class stumpings: 1
One-Day 50s: 17
One-Day 100s: 6
Place in batting averages: 26th av. 48.46
(1990 118th av. 37.95)
Parents: Donald Edward and Joyce
Marital status: Divorced
Family links with cricket: Father played local cricket and is a qualified coach
Education: Grove Comprehensive School, Newark
Qualifications: 9 CSEs, advanced coach
Off-season: Working at Nottinghamshire CCC and touring with England A
Overseas tours: England A to Bermuda and West Indies 1991-92
Cricketers particularly admired: 'Clive Rice and Jimmy Cook – both great players who always have time to talk to players and the public.'
Other sports followed: Watches ice-hockey (Nottingham Panthers), football (Forest and County), golf
Injuries: Broken right thumb – missed end of season, strained hamstring
Relaxations: 'Listening to music, crosswords and reading autobiographies.'
Extras: Played for English Schools in 1980-81 and England YC 1982 and 1983. Youngest player ever to join the Nottinghamshire CCC staff. Made 235 for Nottinghamshire 2nd XI, July 1982, aged 17. Won Man of Match award in first NatWest game (101* v Staffordshire); missed 1985 final due to appendicitis
Opinions on cricket: 'Who would take any notice?'
Best batting: 165* Nottinghamshire v Northamptonshire, Trent Bridge 1990
Best bowling: 1-9 Nottinghamshire v Oxford University, Trent Bridge 1984

---

112. Who captained the 1971 Pakistanis in England?

1991 Season

	M	Inns	NO	Runs	HS	Avge	100s	50s	Ct	St	O	M	Runs	Wkts	Avge	Best	5wI	10wM
Test																		
All First	23	37	7	1454	124	48.46	3	11	12	-	12.2	1	62	2	31.00	1-26	-	-
1-day Int																		
NatWest	3	3	0	66	48	22.00	-	-	-	-								
B&H	4	4	1	144	102 *	48.00	1	-	1	-								
Refuge	17	15	1	370	80	26.42	-	3	6	-								

Career Performances

	M	Inns	NO	Runs	HS	Avge	100s	50s	Ct	St	Balls	Runs	Wkts	Avge	Best	5wI	10wM
Test																	
All First	192	317	33	10099	165 *	35.56	20	55	131	1	448	480	5	96.00	1-9	-	-
1-day Int																	
NatWest	20	20	2	461	101 *	25.61	1	-	5	-	12	16	0	-	-	-	
B&H	33	31	4	712	104 *	26.37	2	3	12	-							
Refuge	120	111	12	2542	114	25.67	3	14	44	-							

JONES, A. N.   Sussex

Name: Adrian Nicholas Jones
Role: Left-hand bat, right-arm fast bowler, outfielder
Born: 22 July 1961, Woking
Height: 6ft 2in **Weight:** 14st
Nickname: Quincy, Jonah, Billy
County debut: 1981 (Sussex), 1987 (Somerset)
County cap: 1986 (Sussex), 1987 (Somerset)
50 wickets in a season: 5
1st-Class 5 w. in innings: 12
1st-Class 10 w. in match: 1
1st-Class catches: 41
Place in batting averages: 253rd av. 10.66
Place in bowling averages: 83rd av. 33.64
(1990 68th av. 36.69)
Strike rate: 55.50 (career 53.99)
Parents: William Albert and Emily Doris
Wife and date of marriage:
Elizabeth Antoinette, 1 October 1988
Children: Amy Elizabeth, 2 May 1990
Family links with cricket: Father and brother, Glynne, both fine club cricketers

Education: Forest Grange Preparatory School; Seaford College
Qualifications: 8 O-levels, 2 A-levels, NCA coaching qualification, financial planning and advising qualifications
Career outside cricket: Sales Director, Hughes and Hughes Ltd
Off-season: as above
Overseas teams played for: Border 1981-82; Orange Free State 1986
Cricketers particularly admired: Imran Khan, Geoff Arnold, Garth le Roux, Jimmy Cook, Tony Pigott, Waqar Younis, Sylvester Clarke
Other sports followed: 'Play golf badly; hockey slightly better; rugby like an animal.'
Injuries: Ankle injury, operated on at the end of 1991 season
Relaxations: 'UB40, watching Laurel and Hardy films, walking, eating, good wine and port.'
Extras: Played for England YC in 1981. Left Sussex to join Somerset at end of 1986 season, but returned for start of 1991 season
Opinions on cricket: 'There should be an alternative system for the awarding of a benefit rather than the present haphazard method. Perhaps an endowment scheme taken out when the player is capped. Too much notice is taken of averages.'
Best batting: 43* Somerset v Leicestershire, Taunton 1989
Best bowling: 7-30 Somerset v Hampshire, Southampton 1988

1991 Season

	M	Inns	NO	Runs	HS	Avge	100s	50s	Ct	St	O	M	Runs	Wkts	Avge	Best	5wI	10wM
Test																		
All First	23	18	6	128	28	10.66	-	-	1	-	527.2	74	1918	57	33.64	5-46	2	-
1-day Int																		
NatWest	2	1	1	0	0 *	-	-	-	-	-	12	0	76	2	38.00	2-46	-	
B&H	3	1	1	0	0 *	-	-	-	-	-	30.4	4	117	7	16.71	3-33	-	
Refuge	15	7	6	18	7 *	18.00	-	-	5	-	81.2	5	448	22	20.36	5-32	1	

Career Performances

	M	Inns	NO	Runs	HS	Avge	100s	50s	Ct	St	Balls	Runs	Wkts	Avge	Best	5wI	10wM
Test																	
All First	160	138	57	942	43 *	11.63	-	-	41	-	21437	12398	397	31.22	7-30	12	1
1-day Int																	
NatWest	14	5	3	13	7	6.50	-	-	2	-	707	518	16	32.37	4-26	-	
B&H	29	14	6	78	25	9.75	-	-	2	-	1528	1083	57	19.00	5-53	1	
Refuge	94	32	22	168	37	16.80	-	-	17	-	3477	2946	139	21.19	7-41	4	

113. Which player completed a set of centuries against all first-class counties last season? And which was the final county?

JONES, D. M.   Durham

Name: Dean Mervyn Jones
Role: Right-hand bat
Born: 24 March 1963, Melbourne, Australia
Height: 6ft 1½in **Weight:** 13st 2lbs
Nickname: Deano
Test debut: 1983-84
Tests: 44
One-Day Internationals: 115
1st-Class 50s scored: 44
1st-Class 100s scored: 25
1st-Class 200s scored: 2
1st-Class catches: 96
One-Day 50s: 33
One-Day 100s: 7
Wife and date of marriage: Jane,
24 April 1986
Children: Phoebe, 26 June 1991
Family links with cricket: Father was
captain/coach of Carlton, Victoria for
18 years

Education: Mt Waverley High School, Victoria
Qualifications: Higher School Certificate
Career outside cricket: Public Servant - Correctional Services
Off-season: Playing in Australia
Overseas tours: Young Australians to Zimbabwe 1983 and 1985; Australia to West Indies 1984 and 1991; England 1985 and 1989; India 1986 and 1987 (World Cup); Sharjah 1986 and 1990; Pakistan 1988; New Zealand 1989; USA 1990
Overseas teams played for: Victoria, Australia
Cricketers particularly admired: Allan Border, Geoff Boycott, Sunil Gavaskar; Viv Richards, Javed Miandad
Other sports followed: Golf, baseball
Relaxations: Golf and looking after my two Rottweilers, Jessica and Stanley
Extras: Played for Victoria on their tour to England in 1991, culminating in the Britannic Assurance Challenge against Essex
Opinions on cricket: 'One-day cricket at international level should have a uniform number of overs and rules and regulations. My favourite is the Australian form.'
Best batting: 248 Australian XI v Warwickshire, Edgbaston 1988

---

114. Which England Test captain was born in Peru?

1991 Season

	M	Inns	NO	Runs	HS	Avge	100s	50s	Ct	St	O	M	Runs	Wkts	Avge	Best	5wI	10wM
Test																		
All First	1	2	0	34	25	17.00	-	-	-	-								
1-day Int																		
NatWest																		
B&H																		
Refuge																		

Career Performances

	M	Inns	NO	Runs	HS	Avge	100s	50s	Ct	St	Balls	Runs	Wkts	Avge	Best	5wI	10wM
Test	44	75	9	3045	216	46.13	9	11	27	-	198	64	1	64.00	1-5	-	-
All First	133	217	19	9353	248	47.23	25	44	96	-	1675	848	12	70.66	1-0	-	-
1-day Int	115	113	21	4576	145	49.73	7	33	40	-	106	81	3	27.00	2-34	-	
NatWest																	
B&H																	
Refuge																	

KEECH, M.　　　　　　　　　　　Middlesex

Name: Matthew Keech
Role: Right-hand bat, right-arm medium bowler
Born: 21 October 1970
Height: 6ft **Weight:** 13st 6lbs
County debut: 1991
1st-Class 50s scored: 2
1st-Class catches: 4
Place in batting averages: 192nd av. 20.00
Parents: Ron and Brenda
Marital status: Single
Education: Northumberland Park School, Tottenham
Qualifications: 5 O-levels, NCA coaching certificate
Off-season: At home coaching cricket
Overseas tours: England U19 to Australia 1989-90
Overseas teams played for: Mossman, Sydney 1988-89; Lancaster Park, Christchurch NZ 1990-91
Cricketers particularly admired: Mike Gatting, Richard Hadlee, Paul Downton
Other sports followed: Most other sports except horse racing

Relaxations: Listening to music, watching videos
Opinions on cricket: 'All Championship games should be four-day.'
Best batting: 58* Middlesex v Nottinghamshire, Lord's 1991

1991 Season

	M	Inns	NO	Runs	HS	Avge	100s	50s	Ct	St	O	M	Runs	Wkts	Avge	Best	5wI	10wM
Test																		
All First	15	24	3	420	58 *	20.00	-	2	4	-	14	6	36	0	-		-	-
1-day Int																		
NatWest																		
B&H	2	2	0	84	47	42.00	-	-	1	-								
Refuge	12	12	3	195	49 *	21.66	-	-	2	-								

Career Performances

	M	Inns	NO	Runs	HS	Avge	100s	50s	Ct	St	Balls	Runs	Wkts	Avge	Best	5wI	10wM
Test																	
All First	15	24	3	420	58 *	20.00	-	2	4	-	84	36	0	-		-	-
1-day Int																	
NatWest																	
B&H	2	2	0	84	47	42.00	-	-	1	-							
Refuge	12	12	3	195	49 *	21.66	-	-	2	-							

KELLEHER, D. J. M. Kent

Name: Daniel John Michael Kelleher
Role: Right-hand bat, right-arm medium
bowler, outfielder
Born: 5 May 1966, London
Height: 6ft **Weight:** 12st 13lbs
Nickname: Donk, Shots
County debut: 1987
1st-Class 50s scored: 2
1st-Class 5 w. in innings: 2
1st-Class catches: 8
Place in batting averages: (1990 262nd
av. 12.62)
Parents: John and Joan
Marital status: Single
Family links with cricket: Uncle played
county cricket for Surrey and
Northamptonshire. Father played club
cricket

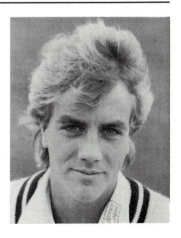

Education: St Mary's Grammar School, Sidcup; Erith College of Technology
Qualifications: O-levels
Cricketers particularly admired: Ian Botham, David Gower, Richard Davis
Other sports followed: Rugby, American football, tennis, golf, skiing
Relaxations: Watching TV, music, 'watching Richard Davis bat.'
Extras: Played rugby and cricket for Kent schools. Released by Kent at the end of the 1991 season
Opinions on cricket: 'Too much cricket is played.'
Best batting: 53* Kent v Derbyshire, Dartford 1989
Best bowling: 6-109 Kent v Somerset, Bath 1987

1991 Season

	M	Inns	NO	Runs	HS	Avge	100s	50s	Ct	St	O	M	Runs	Wkts	Avge	Best	5wl	10wM
Test																		
All First	1	2	1	39	29 *	39.00	-	-	-	-	26	5	47	3	15.66	3-25	-	-
1-day Int																		
NatWest																			
B&H																			
Refuge																			

Career Performances

	M	Inns	NO	Runs	HS	Avge	100s	50s	Ct	St	Balls	Runs	Wkts	Avge	Best	5wl	10wM
Test																	
All First	34	43	6	565	53 *	15.27	-	2	8	-	4906	2533	77	32.89	6-109	2	-
1-day Int																	
NatWest	3	2	1	21	21	21.00	-	-	1	-	158	95	5	19.00	3-16	-
B&H	7	3	3	15	11 *	-	-	-	2	-	456	269	6	44.83	1-23	-
Refuge	21	11	2	55	19	6.11	-	-	4	-	875	556	11	50.54	2-25	-

KELLETT, S. A.   Yorkshire

Name: Simon Andrew Kellett
Role: Opening bat, occasional right-arm medium bowler
Born: 16 October 1967, Mirfield
Height: 6ft 2in **Weight:** 13st
Nickname: Kel, Skerrett
County debut: 1989
1000 runs in a season: 1
1st-Class 50s scored: 14
1st-Class 100s scored: 2
1st-Class catches: 28
Place in batting averages: 77th av. 36.17 (1990 158th av. 27.82)

Parents: Brian and Valerie
Marital status: Single
Family links with cricket: Father played local league cricket
Education: Whitcliffe Mount High School; Huddersfield Technical College
Qualifications: 3 O-levels; Sports Management course
Off-season: Playing cricket in New Zealand
Overseas teams played for: North Shore, New Zealand
Cricketers particularly admired: Martyn Moxon, Graeme Hick, Robin Smith, Tony Greig
Other sports followed: Rugby league (Bradford Northern), horse racing, football
Injuries: Fractured thumb
Relaxations: Watching sport, eating out, playing golf
Extras: Captained NAYC against MCC; captained Yorkshire U19s to Cambridge Festival win; was out to first ball in first-class cricket
Opinions on cricket: 'Four-day cricket is good for the development of Test cricketers.'
Best batting: 125* Yorkshire v Derbyshire, Chesterfield 1991

1991 Season

	M	Inns	NO	Runs	HS	Avge	100s	50s	Ct	St	O	M	Runs	Wkts	Avge	Best	5wI	10wM
Test																		
All First	24	40	5	1266	125 *	36.17	2	8	19	-	4	0	7	0	-	-	-	-
1-day Int																		
NatWest																			
B&H	5	3	1	46	44	23.00	-	-	-	-								
Refuge	6	6	1	66	26	13.20	-	-	2	-	3	0	16	0	-	-	-	

Career Performances

	M	Inns	NO	Runs	HS	Avge	100s	50s	Ct	St	Balls	Runs	Wkts	Avge	Best	5wI	10wM
Test																	
All First	42	71	8	2045	125 *	32.46	2	14	28	-	24	7	0	-	-	-	-
1-day Int																	
NatWest	3	1	0	0	0	0.00	-	-	-	-							
B&H	8	6	1	142	45	28.40	-	-	-	-							
Refuge	10	10	1	136	32	15.11	-	-	3	-	18	16	0	-	-	-	

KENDRICK, N. M. Surrey

Name: Neil Michael Kendrick
Role: Right-hand bat, slow left-arm bowler, gully fielder
Born: 11 November 1967, Bromley
Height: 5ft 11in **Weight:** 11st 7lbs
Nickname: Kendo, Rat, Merson
County debut: 1988
1st-Class 50s scored: 1
1st-Class 5 w. in innings: 2
1st-Class 10 w. in match: 1
1st-Class catches: 19
Place in batting averages: (1990 250th av. 15.50)
Place in bowling averages: 8th av. 21.83 (1990 122nd av. 47.76)
Strike rate: 52.50 (career 74.15)
Parents: Michael Hall and Anne Patricia
Marital status: Single
Family links with cricket: Father plays club cricket for Old Wilsonians, and sister has represented Kent Ladies
Education: Hayes Primary; Wilsons Grammar School
Qualifications: 7 O-levels, 1 A-level; coaching certificate
Career outside cricket: Working for office equipment company
Cricketers particularly admired: Phil Edmonds, Bishen Bedi, 'for the way they made it look so easy'
Other sports followed: 'Support Arsenal but saw a lot of Charlton last year.'
Relaxations: 'Listening to music – mainly soul plus Stone Roses and Happy Mondays.'
Opinions on cricket: 'Please can we have four-day cricket. The pitches must remain good, but the balls have too small a seam. As a spinner they are very difficult to grip.'
Best batting: 52* Surrey v Middlesex, Lord's 1990
Best bowling: 5-54 Surrey v Lancashire, Old Trafford 1991

1991 Season

	M	Inns	NO	Runs	HS	Avge	100s	50s	Ct	St	O	M	Runs	Wkts	Avge	Best	5wI	10wM
Test																		
All First	2	4	1	58	24	19.33	-	-	1	-	105	26	262	12	21.83	5-54	2	1
1-day Int																		
NatWest																		
B&H																		
Refuge																		

Career Performances

	M	Inns	NO	Runs	HS	Avge	100s	50s	Ct	St	Balls	Runs	Wkts	Avge	Best	5wI	10wM
Test																	
All First	19	20	7	207	52 *	15.92	-	1	19	-	3263	1692	44	38.45	5-54	2	1
1-day Int																	
NatWest																	
B&H																	
Refuge	1	1	1	2	2 *	-	-	-	-	-	18	20	0	-		-	-

KERSEY, G. J. Kent

Name: Graham James Kersey
Role: Right-hand bat, wicket-keeper
Born: 19 May 1971, Greenwich
Height: 5ft 7in **Weight:** 10st 4lbs
Nickname: Scuz
County debut: 1991
1st-Class catches: 7
Parents: Don and Beryl
Marital status: Single
Family links with cricket: Brother plays for local club side, Bexley
Education: Bexley-Erith Technical High School
Qualifications: 6 O-levels, 1 A-level
Career outside cricket: Groundsman, installing air-conditioning
Off-season: Playing in Cape Town
Overseas tours: Kent Schools U17 to Singapore and New Zealand 1987-88
Overseas teams played for: Eastern Suburbs District, Brisbane 1989-91
Cricketers particularly admired: Alan Knott, Jack Russell, David Gower
Other sports followed: Football
Relaxations: Keeping fit, watching films, listening to music
Opinions on cricket: 'Rules about qualifying for England are not nearly strict enough.'
Best batting: 27* Kent v Surrey, The Oval 1991

---

115. Which England Test captain was born in Italy?

1991 Season

	M	Inns	NO	Runs	HS	Avge	100s	50s	Ct	St	O	M	Runs	Wkts	Avge	Best	5wI	10wM
Test																		
All First	2	1	1	27	27 *	-	-	-	7	-								
1-day Int																			
NatWest																			
B&H																			
Refuge																			

Career Performances

	M	Inns	NO	Runs	HS	Avge	100s	50s	Ct	St	Balls	Runs	Wkts	Avge	Best	5wI	10wM
Test																	
All First	2	1	1	27	27 *	-	-	-	7	-							
1-day Int																		
NatWest																		
B&H																		
Refuge																		

KIRNON, S.   Glamorgan

Name: Samuel Kirnon
Role: Right-hand bat, right-arm fast-medium bowler
Born: 25 December 1963
Height: 5ft 9$\frac{1}{2}$in **Weight:** 12st 7lbs
Nickname: Sammy
County debut: 1991 (one-day)
Parents: William and Ethel
Wife and date of marriage: Shirley Anne, 20 April 1990
Family links with cricket: Father played for Montserrat, West Indies. Cousin L. O'Brien still plays for Montserrat
Education: Montserrat Secondary School, West Indies
Career outside cricket: PT Instructor with the British Army
Off-season: Playing cricket in Montserrat
Overseas tours: BAOR to Barbados 1986 and 1988; Royal Artillery to Barbados 1990
Overseas teams played for: Nijmegen, Holland 1984-90
Cricketers particularly admired: Richie Richardson, David Hemp, Steve Bastien

Other sports followed: Boxing, athletics
Relaxations: Playing squash, listening to music
Opinions on cricket: 'More one-day cricket. Four-day games in the week.'

1991 Season

	M	Inns	NO	Runs	HS	Avge	100s	50s	Ct	St	O	M	Runs	Wkts	Avge	Best	5wI	10wM
Test																		
All First																		
1-day Int																		
NatWest																		
B&H																		
Refuge	1	1	0	0	0	0.00	-	-	-	-	8	0	48	2	24.00	2-48	-	

Career Performances

	M	Inns	NO	Runs	HS	Avge	100s	50s	Ct	St	Balls	Runs	Wkts	Avge	Best	5wI	10wM
Test																	
All First																	
1-day Int																	
NatWest																	
B&H																	
Refuge	1	1	0	0	0	0.00	-	-	-	-	48	48	2	24.00	2-48	-	

KNIGHT, N. V. Essex

Name: Nicholas Verity Knight
Role: Left-hand bat, right-arm medium
bowler, close fielder
Born: 28 November 1969, Watford
Height: 6ft **Weight:** 12st 8lbs
Nickname: Knighty, Stitch
County debut: 1991
1st-Class 50s scored: 3
1st-Class 100s scored: 1
1st-Class catches: 5
Place in batting averages: 25th av. 49.00
Parents: John and Rosemary
Marital status: Single
Family links with cricket: Father played
for Cambridgeshire
Education: Felsted Prep; Felsted School;
Loughborough University
Qualifications: 9 O-levels, 3 A-level;

BSc (Hons) Sociology
Off-season: Playing cricket in Australia
Overseas tours: Felsted School to Australia 1986-87
Cricketers particularly admired: Graham Gooch, Keith Fletcher, David Gower and Gordon Barker – 'my coach at Felsted'
Other sports followed: Rugby, hockey
Relaxations: 'Eating lots of food.'
Extras: Captain of England Schools 1987 and 1988, captain of Young England v New Zealand 1989, captain of Combined Universities 1991. Played hockey for Essex and Young England. Played rugby for Eastern Counties.
Opinions on cricket: 'I would like more four-day cricket.'
Best batting: 101* Essex v Lancashire, Old Trafford 1991

1991 Season

	M	Inns	NO	Runs	HS	Avge	100s	50s	Ct	St	O	M	Runs	Wkts	Avge	Best	5wI	10wM
Test																		
All First	7	10	1	441	101 *	49.00	1	3	5	-	5	0	32	0	-	-	-	-
1-day Int																		
NatWest																			
B&H	4	4	0	62	36	15.50	-	-	5	-	1	0	4	0	-		-	-
Refuge	2	2	1	31	31 *	31.00	-	-	2	-								

Career Performances

	M	Inns	NO	Runs	HS	Avge	100s	50s	Ct	St	Balls	Runs	Wkts	Avge	Best	5wI	10wM
Test																	
All First	7	10	1	441	101 *	49.00	1	3	5	-	30	32	0	-	-	-	-
1-day Int																	
NatWest																		
B&H	6	6	0	87	36	14.50	-	-	5	-	6	4	0	-	-	-	
Refuge	2	2	1	31	31 *	31.00	-	-	2	-							

116. Who topped the first-class bowling averages last season for Worcestershire?

KRIKKEN, K. M. G.   Derbyshire

Name: Karl Matthew Giles Krikken
Role: Right-hand bat, wicket-keeper
Born: 9 April 1969, Bolton
Height: 5ft 10in **Weight:** 12st
Nickname: Filthy, Farmer, Krikk,
County debut: 1987 (one-day),
1989 (first-class)
1st-Class 50s scored: 4
1st-Class catches: 123
1st-Class stumpings: 7
Place in batting averages: 171st av. 23.23
(1990 231st av. 18.07)
Parents: Brian and Irene
Marital status: Engaged to Liz
Family links with cricket: Father kept
wicket for Lancashire and Worcestershire
Education: Bolton High Street; Blackrod
High School
Off-season: 'Doing what Liz tells me and
working on my game.'
Overseas teams played for: Bushmans XI, Griqualand West, South Africa 1988-89
Cricketers particularly admired: Bernie Maher ('keeping ability), John Morris (mental strength), Steve Goldsmith (ability to hit stationary ball)
Other sports followed: Bowls, body-building, fell walking
Relaxations: 'Doing jobs around the house for Liz'
Extras: 'Caught more than I dropped last season – I'm really chuffed.' Played first first-class game in South Africa as an overseas professional. Wicket-keeper with most dismissals in 1990
Opinions on cricket: 'No one-day cricket. 34 Championship games.'
Best batting: 77* Derbyshire v Somerset, Taunton 1990

1991 Season

	M	Inns	NO	Runs	HS	Avge	100s	50s	Ct	St	O	M	Runs	Wkts	Avge	Best	5wI	10wM
Test																		
All First	24	38	8	697	65	23.23	-	2	58	3								
1-day Int																		
NatWest																		
B&H																		
Refuge	7	4	1	67	44 *	22.33	-	-	9	3								

Career Performances

	M	Inns	NO	Runs	HS	Avge	100s	50s	Ct	St	Balls	Runs	Wkts	Avge	Best	5wI	10wM
Test																	
All First	51	77	13	1293	77 *	20.20	-	4	123	7	36	40	0	-	-	-	-
1-day Int																	
NatWest																		
B&H																		
Refuge	12	7	1	97	44 *	16.16	-	-	12	3							

LAMB, A. J.   Northamptonshire

Name: Allan Joseph Lamb
Role: Right-hand bat, right-arm medium
bowler, county captain
Born: 20 June 1954, Langebaanweg,
Cape Province, South Africa
Height: 5ft 8in **Weight:** 12st
Nickname: Lambie, Legger, Joe
County debut: 1978
County cap: 1978
Benefit: 1988 (£134,000)
Test debut: 1982
Tests: 74
One-Day Internationals: 110
1000 runs in a season: 11
1st-Class 50s scored: 136
1st-Class 100s scored: 72
1st-Class 200s scored: 2
1st-Class catches: 305
One-Day 50s: 73
One-Day 100s: 14
Place in batting averages: 63rd av. 38.60 (1990 18th av. 63.84)
Parents: Michael and Joan
Wife and date of marriage: Lindsay, 8 December 1979
Children: Katie-Ann and Richard Edward Thomas
Family links with cricket: Father and brother played in the B section of the Currie Cup
Education: Wynberg Boys' High School; Abbotts College
Qualifications: Matriculation
Career outside cricket: Promotions company
Off-season: Touring with England
Overseas tours: With England to Australia and New Zealand 1982-83; New Zealand and
Pakistan 1983-84; India and Australia 1984-85; West Indies 1985-86; Australia 1986-87;

World Cup in India and Pakistan 1987-88; India and West Indies 1989-90; Australia 1990-91; New Zealand 1991-92
Overseas teams played for: Western Province 1972-81; Orange Free State 1987-88
Cricketers particularly admired: Dennis Lillee, Viv Richards
Other sports followed: Tennis, golf, rugby and horse racing
Relaxations: Fly fishing (trout and salmon)
Extras: Was primarily a bowler when he first played school cricket in South Africa. Made first-class debut for Western Province in 1972-73. Top of first-class batting averages in 1980. One of *Wisden's* Five Cricketers of the Year, 1980. Qualified to play for England in 1982. Appointed Northamptonshire captain 1989. Captained England in Tests v West Indies in 1989-90 and v Australia in 1990-91 after injuries to Graham Gooch. Made a century in his first Test as captain v West Indies at Bridgetown. Hit three 100s in consecutive Tests v West Indies 1984
Opinions on cricket: 'Get our one-day domestic game in line with overseas, ie we should play 50 overs as they do abroad, our longer competition could be 55 not 60.'
Best batting: 294 Orange Free State v Eastern Province, Bloemfontein 1987-88
Best bowling: 2-29 Northamptonshire v Lancashire, Lytham 1991

1991 Season

	M	Inns	NO	Runs	HS	Avge	100s	50s	Ct	St	O	M	Runs	Wkts	Avge	Best	5wI	10wM
Test	4	7	0	88	29	12.57	-	-	7	-								
All First	19	30	2	1081	194	38.60	3	5	21	-	3.4	0	29	2	14.50	2-29	-	-
1-day Int	2	2	0	80	62	40.00	-	1	-	-								
NatWest	4	3	0	84	31	28.00	-	-	1	-								
B&H	5	5	0	150	48	30.00	-	-	2	-								
Refuge	12	12	0	212	61	17.66	-	1	5	-								

Career Performances

	M	Inns	NO	Runs	HS	Avge	100s	50s	Ct	St	Balls	Runs	Wkts	Avge	Best	5wI	10wM
Test	74	131	10	4264	139	35.24	13	16	73	-	30	23	1	23.00	1-6	-	-
All First	389	648	95	26472	294	47.87	72	136	305	-	299	193	8	24.12	2-29	-	-
1-day Int	110	106	16	3710	118	41.22	4	24	30	-	6	3	0	-	-	-	-
NatWest	39	38	2	1401	103	38.91	2	10	10	-	8	12	1	12.00	1-4	-	
B&H	62	56	9	2173	126 *	46.23	4	14	23	-	6	11	1	11.00	1-11	-	
Refuge	146	141	18	4406	132 *	35.82	4	25	35	-							

117. Which England Test captain was born in Australia?

LAMPITT, S. R. Worcestershire

Name: Stuart Richard Lampitt
Role: Right-hand bat, right-arm fast-medium bowler
Born: 29 July 1966, Wolverhampton
Height: 5ft 11in **Weight:** 14st
Nickname: Jed
County debut: 1985
County cap: 1989
50 wickets in a season: 2
1st-Class 50s scored: 4
1st-Class 5 w. in innings: 8
1st-Class catches: 29
Place in batting averages: 111th av. 30.76 (1990 229th av. 18.73)
Place in bowling averages: 46th av. 29.33 (1990 44th av. 32.56)
Strike rate: 53.96 (career 55.79)
Parents: Joseph Charles and Muriel Ann
Marital status: Single

Family links with cricket: 'Dad talks a good game.'
Education: Kingswinford Secondary School; Dudley Technical College
Qualifications: 7 O-levels; Diploma in Business Studies
Career outside cricket: 'None as yet – still looking.'
Off-season: 'Coaching somewhere in the world.'
Overseas tours: NCA U19 to Bermuda; Worcestershire to Bahamas 1990; Zimbabwe 1991
Overseas teams played for: Mangere, Auckland 1987-89
Cricketers particularly admired: Ian Botham
Other sports followed: Any ball sport, particularly football (Wolves) and golf
Injuries: Shoulder – out for a week
Relaxations: Golf, listening to music, ornithology, especially around the Worcestershire area
Extras: Took five wickets and made 42 for Stourbridge in Final of the Cockspur Cup at Lord's in 1987. One of the Whittingdale Young Players of the Year 1990
Opinions on cricket: 'If the new ball and four-day cricket was meant to produce better Test players of the future please explain to me why the four-day matches are still finishing in just over two days. Are we being strong enough on under-prepared and "fixed" wickets? Surely some standard can be obtained by the people who decide everything else for us! The game could be managed better, ie marketed better.'
Best batting: 93 Worcestershire v Derbyshire, Kidderminster 1991
Best bowling: 5-32 Worcestershire v Kent, Worcester 1989

1991 Season

	M	Inns	NO	Runs	HS	Avge	100s	50s	Ct	St	O	M	Runs	Wkts	Avge	Best	5wI	10wM
Test																		
All First	22	23	6	523	93	30.76	-	4	6	-	503.4	84	1643	56	29.33	5-70	4	-
1-day Int																		
NatWest	2	1	0	7	7	7.00	-	-	-	-	12.4	1	65	2	32.50	1-4	-	
B&H	5	0	0	0	0	-	-	-	1	-	48.1	4	211	11	19.18	4-46	-	
Refuge	14	3	1	5	4	2.50	-	-	2	-	84	1	477	10	47.70	3-23	-	

Career Performances

	M	Inns	NO	Runs	HS	Avge	100s	50s	Ct	St	Balls	Runs	Wkts	Avge	Best	5wI	10wM
Test																	
All First	70	70	17	1100	93	20.75	-	4	29	-	8378	4416	151	29.24	5-32	8	-
1-day Int																	
NatWest	9	4	2	19	9 *	9.50	-	-	2	-	458	307	14	21.92	5-22	1	
B&H	11	4	1	52	41	17.33	-	-	5	-	619	461	17	27.11	4-46	-	
Refuge	48	18	7	143	25 *	13.00	-	-	14	-	1470	1361	44	30.93	5-67	1	

LARKINS, W. Durham

Name: Wayne Larkins
Role: Right-hand bat, right-arm medium bowler
Born: 22 November 1953
Height: 5ft 11in **Weight:** 12st
Nickname: Ned
County debut: 1972
County cap: 1976
Benefit: 1986
Test debut: 1979-80
Tests: 13
One-Day Internationals: 25
1000 runs in a season: 11
1st-Class 50s scored: 96
1st-Class 100s scored: 49
1st-Class 200s scored: 3
1st-Class 5 w. in innings: 1
1st-Class catches: 244
One-Day 50s: 50
One-Day 100s: 17
Place in batting averages: 74th av. 36.50 (1990 178th av. 28.04)
Parents: Mavis (father deceased)

Wife and date of marriage: Jane Elaine, 22 March 1975

Children: Philippa Jane, 30 May 1981

Family links with cricket: Father was umpire. Brother, Melvin, played for Bedford Town for many years

Education: Bushmead, Eaton Socon, Huntingdon

Overseas tours: England to Australia and India 1979-80; India and Sri Lanka 1981-82; India and West Indies 1989-90; Australia 1990-91; unofficial English team to South Africa 1981-82

Other sports followed: Golf, football (was on Notts County's books), squash

Relaxations: Gardening

Extras: Banned from Test cricket for three years for joining rebel tour of South Africa in 1982. Recalled to Test team in 1986 but withdrew due to thumb injury and missed another Test recall in 1987 because of a football injury. Eventually returned to Test cricket in the West Indies in 1989-90, nine years after his last appearance

Best batting : 252 Northamptonshire v Glamorgan, Cardiff 1983

Best bowling : 5-59 Northamptonshire v Worcestershire, Worcester 1984

1991 Season

	M	Inns	NO	Runs	HS	Avge	100s	50s	Ct	St	O	M	Runs	Wkts	Avge	Best	5wI	10wM
Test																		
All First	9	16	6	365	75	36.50	-	2	6	-	6	4	2	0	-		-	-	-
1-day Int																		
NatWest	2	2	0	39	31	19.50	-	-	2	-								
B&H																		
Refuge	8	8	0	363	108	45.37	1	3	2	-								

Career Performances

	M	Inns	NO	Runs	HS	Avge	100s	50s	Ct	St	Balls	Runs	Wkts	Avge	Best	5wI	10wM
Test	13	25	1	493	64	20.54	-	3	8	-							
All First	414	721	48	22848	252	33.94	49	96	244	-	3451	1854	42	44.14	5-59	1	-
1-day Int	25	24	0	591	124	24.62	1	-	9	-	15	22	0	-	-	-	
NatWest	44	43	3	1436	121 *	35.90	1	11	19	-	455	274	4	68.50	2-38	-	
B&H	70	66	3	2088	132	33.14	5	8	14	-	675	444	16	27.75	4-37	-	
Refuge	239	230	13	6088	172 *	28.05	10	31	71	-	2033	1679	57	29.45	5-32	1	

118. Who has made the most Test appearances for West Indies?

LATHWELL, M. N.

Somerset

Name: Mark Nicholas Lathwell
Role: Right-hand bat, right-arm medium bowler
Born: 26 December 1971, Bletchley, Bucks
Height: 5ft 7in **Weight:** 11st
Nickname: Lathers, Rowdy
County debut: 1991
1st-Class catches: 0
Parents: Derek Peter and Valerie
Marital status: Single
Family links with cricket: Father and brother play local league cricket
Education: Overstone Primary, Wing, Bucks; Southmead Primary, Braunton, N Devon; Braunton Comprehensive
Qualifications: 5 GCSEs
Career outside cricket: 'Worked in a bank.'
Off-season: 'Working locally.'
Cricketers particularly admired:
Ian Botham, Graham Gooch
Other sports followed: Darts, snooker/pool, squash 'and lots more'
Relaxations: Drinking, eating, sleeping
Extras: Spent one season on Lord's groundstaff. Played for England U19 v Australia 1991
Best batting: 43 Somerset v Worcestershire, Worcester 1991
Best bowling: 1-29 Somerset v Sri Lanka, Taunton 1991

1991 Season

	M	Inns	NO	Runs	HS	Avge	100s	50s	Ct	St	O	M	Runs	Wkts	Avge	Best	5wI	10wM
Test																		
All First	2	3	0	63	43	21.00	-	-	-	-	28	9	99	1	99.00	1-29	-	-
1-day Int																		
NatWest	1	1	0	16	16	16.00	-	-	-	-								
B&H																			
Refuge	2	2	0	35	20	17.50	-	-	1	-	4	0	19	0	-		-	-

119. Who topped the first-class batting averages last season for Gloucestershire?

Career Performances

	M	Inns	NO	Runs	HS	Avge	100s	50s	Ct	St	Balls	Runs	Wkts	Avge	Best	5wI	10wM
Test																	
All First	2	3	0	63	43	21.00	-	-	-	-	168	99	1	99.00	1-29	-	-
1-day Int																	
NatWest	1	1	0	16	16	16.00	-	-	-	-							
B&H																	
Refuge	2	2	0	35	20	17.50	-	-	1	-	24	19	0	-		-	-

LAWRENCE, D. V. Gloucestershire

Name: David Valentine Lawrence
Role: Right-hand bat, right-arm fast bowler
Born: 28 January 1964, Gloucester
Height: 6ft 2in **Weight:** 16st 5lbs
Nickname: Syd
County debut: 1981
County cap: 1985
Test debut: 1988
Tests: 4
One-Day Internationals: 1
50 wickets in a season: 5
1st-Class 50s scored: 2
1st-Class 5 w. in innings: 20
1st-Class 10 w. in match: 1
1st-Class catches: 40
Place in batting averages: 208th av. 17.32
Place in bowling averages: 17th av. 24.18
(1990 51st av. 34.12)
Strike rate: 41.77 (career 52.04)
Parents: Joseph and Hilda Joyce
Children: Buster, November 1991
Family links with cricket: Father played club cricket in Jamaica
Education: Linden School, Gloucester
Qualifications: 3 CSEs
Career outside cricket: 'Ducking and diving, wheeling and dealing.'
Off-season: Touring with England
Overseas tours: England B to Sri Lanka 1986; England A to Zimbabwe 1989-90; England to New Zealand 1991-92
Overseas teams played for: Tasmania 1984; Scarborough, Perth, Western Australia 1984-85; Manly, Sydney 1987; Freemantle, Western Australia 1989
Cricketers particularly admired: Dennis Lillee, Richard Hadlee, Michael Holding

Other sports followed: Rugby union and league, American football, golf

Relaxations: Clothes, music, aerobics, eating out ('preferably Mexican'), looking after doberman dog called Arnold

Extras: Called up to join the England A tour in 1989-90 when Chris Lewis joined the senior squad in the West Indies. Took a hat-trick v Nottinghamshire in 1990

Opinions on cricket: 'We play too much cricket. Sunday league should be abolished. If more Minor Counties were brought in there could be a two-division Championship with promotion and relegation prospects.'

Best batting: 66 Gloucestershire v Glamorgan, Abergavenny 1991

Best bowling: 7-47 Gloucestershire v Surrey, Cheltenham 1988

1991 Season

	M	Inns	NO	Runs	HS	Avge	100s	50s	Ct	St	O	M	Runs	Wkts	Avge	Best	5wI	10wM
Test	3	4	0	50	34	12.50	-	-	-	-	116.2	17	494	14	35.28	5-106	1	-
All First	18	26	1	433	66	17.32	-	1	4	-	515.1	79	1790	74	24.18	6-67	4	1
1-day Int	1	0	0	0	0	-	-	-	-	-	11	1	67	4	16.75	4-67	-	
NatWest	2	2	2	7	5 *	-	-	-	-	-	21	3	65	7	9.28	5-17	1	
B&H	4	3	1	51	23	25.50	-	-	-	-	44	7	137	13	10.53	6-20	1	
Refuge	8	7	2	82	38 *	16.40	-	1	-	-	55	1	285	11	25.90	4-27	-	

Career Performances

	M	Inns	NO	Runs	HS	Avge	100s	50s	Ct	St	Balls	Runs	Wkts	Avge	Best	5wI	10wM
Test	4	5	0	54	34	10.80	-	-	-	-	914	605	17	35.58	5-106	1	-
All First	178	203	35	1809	66	10.76	-	2	44	-	25867	15962	497	32.11	7-47	20	1
1-day Int	1	0	0	0	0	-	-	-	-	-	66	67	4	16.75	4-67	-	
NatWest	20	10	5	11	5 *	2.20	-	-	2	-	1108	763	28	27.25	5-17	1	
B&H	29	12	6	94	23	15.66	-	-	6	-	1614	1050	44	23.86	6-20	2	
Refuge	59	23	8	179	38 *	11.93	-	-	15	-	2430	2115	75	28.20	5-18	1	

120. Who has made the most Test appearances for New Zealand?

121. Who has made the most Test appearances for India?

LEATHERDALE, D. A.   Worcestershire

Name: David Anthony Leatherdale
Role: Right-hand bat, right-arm medium bowler, cover fielder
Born: 26 November 1967, Bradford
Height: 5ft 10in **Weight:** 11st 2lbs
Nickname: Lugs, Spock
County debut: 1988
1st-Class 50s scored: 4
1st-Class 100s scored: 1
1st-Class catches: 22
One-Day 50s: 2
Place in batting averages: 8th av. 63.16
(1990 194th av. 18.59)
Parents: Paul and Rosalyn
Wife's name: Vanessa
Children: Callum Edward, 6 July 1990
Family links with cricket: Brother
plays for East Bierley in Bradford League.
Brother-in-law played for Young England
in 1979. Father played local cricket
Education: Bolton Royd Primary School; Pudsey Grangefield Secondary School
Qualifications: 8 O-levels, 2 A-levels; NCA coaching award (stage 1)
Off-season: Working for Golding Pipework Services (Birmingham)
Overseas teams played for: Pretoria Police, South Africa 1987-88
Cricketers particularly admired: Mark Scott, George Batty, Peter Kippax
Other sports followed: Football, American football
Relaxations: Golf
Opinions on cricket: 'A full circuit of 2nd XI cricket will make it easier for 2nd XI players to move up into first-class cricket.'
Best batting: 157 Worcestershire v Somerset, Worcester 1991
Best bowling: 1-12 Worcestershire v Northamptonshire, Worcester 1988

1991 Season

	M	Inns	NO	Runs	HS	Avge	100s	50s	Ct	St	O	M	Runs	Wkts	Avge	Best	5wI	10wM
Test																		
All First	5	6	0	379	157	63.16	1	2	4	-	2	0	6	0	-	-	-	-
1-day Int																		
NatWest																		
B&H																		
Refuge	4	4	1	27	15	9.00	-	-	1	-								

Career Performances

	M	Inns	NO	Runs	HS	Avge	100s	50s	Ct	St	Balls	Runs	Wkts	Avge	Best	5wI	10wM
Test																	
All First	26	35	2	881	157	26.69	1	4	22	-	54	26	1	26.00	1-12	-	-
1-day Int																	
NatWest	7	6	1	94	43	18.80	-	-	-	-							
B&H	2	0	0	0	0	-	-	-	-	-							
Refuge	27	23	5	314	62*	17.44	-	2	9	-	54	58	0	-		-	-

LEFEBVRE, R. P. Somerset

Name: Roland Phillippe Lefebvre
Role: Right-hand bat, right-arm medium bowler
Born: 7 February 1963, Rotterdam
Height: 6ft 1in **Weight:** 12st
Nickname: Tulip, Clogsy, Dopie
County debut: 1990
County cap: 1991
1st-Class 50s scored: 2
1st-Class 100s scored: 1
1st-Class 5 w. in innings: 2
1st-Class catches: 17
Place in batting averages: 150 av. 26.14 (1990 243rd av. 16.46)
Place in bowling averages: 140th av. 59.72 (1990 107th av. 41.32)
Strike rate: 121.66 (career 106.67)
Parents: Pierre Joseph Ernest
Marital status: Single
Family links with cricket: Father and two brothers play club cricket in Holland
Education: Montessori Lyceum, Rotterdam; Hague Academy of Physiotherapy
Qualifications: Qualified physiotherapist
Career outside cricket: Physiotherapy
Off-season: Has set up a private practice at the County Ground, Taunton with Somerset CCC physiotherapist Ray Heard
Overseas tours: Holland tours to England, Canada, Denmark, New Zealand, Barbados, Zimbabwe and Dubai
Overseas teams played for: VOC Rotterdam, Flamingos
Cricketers particularly admired: Nolan Clarke, Anton Bakker, Rob van Weelde, Renee Schoonheim, Dick Abed, Rob Hennink
Other sports followed: Cycling, speed skating and most other sports

Injuries: Pulled hamstring
Relaxations: Playing the piano, music of various kinds, golf, travelling
Extras: More than 70 caps for Holland. Played in 1986 and 1990 ICC Trophy competitions – voted player of tournament 1990; was a member of the Dutch team that beat England (captained by Peter Roebuck) in 1989 and West Indies in 1991. First Dutch player to score a first-class hundred
Opinions on cricket: 'Too much cricket is being played.'
Best batting: 100 Somerset v Worcestershire, Weston-super-Mare 1991
Best bowling: 6-53 Canterbury v Auckland, Auckland 1990-91

1991 Season

	M	Inns	NO	Runs	HS	Avge	100s	50s	Ct	St	O	M	Runs	Wkts	Avge	Best	5wI	10wM
Test																		
All First	16	18	4	366	100	26.14	1	1	6	-	365	74	1075	18	59.72	3-51	-	-
1-day Int																		
NatWest	3	2	1	34	21 *	34.00	-	-	1	-	36	7	89	6	14.83	3-27	-	
B&H	4	4	2	51	23 *	25.50	-	-	1	-	38	6	150	4	37.50	3-44	-	
Refuge	13	11	1	107	27	10.70	-	-	4	-	87	5	367	15	24.46	3-29	-	

Career Performances

	M	Inns	NO	Runs	HS	Avge	100s	50s	Ct	St	Balls	Runs	Wkts	Avge	Best	5wI	10wM
Test																	
All First	40	40	10	645	100	21.50	1	2	17	-	6819	2849	69	41.29	6-53	2	-
1-day Int																	
NatWest	5	2	1	34	21 *	34.00	-	-	1	-	345	150	15	10.00	7-15	1	
B&H	10	7	3	121	37	30.25	-	-	1	-	578	380	9	42.22	3-44	-	
Refuge	25	18	3	193	28	12.86	-	-	8	-	1019	835	26	32.11	4-35	-	

122. Who has made the most Test appearances for Pakistan?

LENHAM, N. J. Sussex

Name: Neil John Lenham
Role: Right-hand bat, right-arm medium bowler
Born: 17 December 1965, Worthing
Height: 5ft 11in **Weight:** 11st
Nickname: Pin
County debut: 1984
County cap: 1990
1000 runs in a season: 2
1st-Class 50s scored: 25
1st-Class 100s scored: 9
1st-Class catches: 44
One-Day 50s: 10
Place in batting averages: 75th av. 36.36 (1990 98th av. 41.57)
Parents: Leslie John and Valerie Anne
Marital status: Single
Family links with cricket: Father played for Sussex

Education: Broadwater Manor Prep School; Brighton College
Qualifications: 5 O-levels, 2 A-levels, advanced cricket coach
Career outside cricket: Working for Notts Sport
Off-season: Selling artificial cricket pitches for Notts Sport
Overseas tours: England U19 to West Indies (as captain) in 1985
Overseas teams played for: Port Elizabeth, South Africa 1987-88; Brighton, Tasmania 1989-90
Cricketers particularly admired: Ken McEwan, Ralph Dellor
Other sports followed: Golf, horse racing, fishing
Injuries: Shoulder injury and damaged finger
Relaxations: 'Listening to Van Morrison, gambling extremely badly, keeping tropical fish, fishing.'
Extras: Made debut for England YC in 1983. Broke record for number of runs scored in season at a public school in 1984 (1534 av. 80.74). Youngest player to appear for County 2nd XI at 14 years old. Appointed as Eastbourne's first Cricket Development Officer for 1992
Opinions on cricket: 'Four-day cricket should now be seriously considered, and the fining of poor over rates should be looked into.'
Best batting: 193 Sussex v Leicestershire, Hove 1991
Best bowling: 4-85 Sussex v Leicestershire, Leicester 1986

1991 Season

	M	Inns	NO	Runs	HS	Avge	100s	50s	Ct	St	O	M	Runs	Wkts	Avge	Best	5wI	10wM
Test																		
All First	19	33	3	1091	193	36.36	3	4	11	-	29	5	79	2	39.50	2-5	-	-
1-day Int																		
NatWest	2	2	0	85	66	42.50	-	1	-	-	18	1	60	3	20.00	2-25	-	
B&H																		
Refuge	12	12	1	272	86	24.72	-	2	2	-	8	0	63	3	21.00	1-8	-	

Career Performances

	M	Inns	NO	Runs	HS	Avge	100s	50s	Ct	St	Balls	Runs	Wkts	Avge	Best	5wI	10wM
Test																	
All First	108	184	19	5294	193	32.08	9	25	44	-	1931	1033	23	44.91	4-85	-	-
1-day Int																	
NatWest	6	6	1	196	66	39.20	-	1	-	-	216	133	7	19.00	2-12	-	
B&H	12	12	2	287	82	28.70	-	2	1	-	108	97	3	32.33	1-3	-	
Refuge	48	40	9	932	86	30.06	-	7	9	-	414	428	16	26.75	2-19	-	

LEWIS, C. C.   Nottinghamshire

Name: Christopher Clairmonte Lewis
Role: Right-hand bat, right-arm
fast-medium bowler
Born: 14 February 1968, Georgetown,
Guyana
Height: 6ft 2¹/₂in **Weight:** 13st
Nickname: Carl
County debut: 1987 (Leicestershire)
County cap: 1990 (Leicestershire)
Test debut: 1990
Tests: 7
One-Day Internationals: 14
50 wickets in a season: 1
1st-Class 50s scored: 9
1st-Class 100s scored: 1
1st-Class 5 w. in innings: 10
1st-Class 10 w. in match: 2
1st-Class catches: 51
One-Day 50s scored: 4
Place in batting averages: 86th av. 34.50 (1990 147th av. 33.19)
Place in bowling averages: 24th av. 25.27 (1990 30th av. 30.30)
Strike rate: 58.95 (career 55.62)
Parents: Philip and Patricia

Marital status: Single
Education: Willesden High School
Qualifications: 2 O-levels
Off-season: Touring with England
Overseas tours: England YC to Australia for Youth World Cup 1987; England A to Kenya and Zimbabwe 1989-90; England to West Indies 1989-90; Australia and New Zealand 1990-91; New Zealand 1991-92
Cricketers particularly admired: Richard Hadlee
Other sports followed: Snooker, football, darts, American football
Injuries: Various minor ailments – missed Oval Test with a migraine
Relaxations: Music, sleeping
Extras: Joined England's tour of West Indies in 1989-90 as a replacement for Ricky Ellcock. Suffers from Raynaud's Disease which affects his blood circulation. Left Leicestershire at the end of 1991 season and signed for Nottinghamshire
Best batting: 189* Leicestershire v Essex, Chelmsford 1990
Best bowling: 6-22 Leicestershire v Oxford University, The Parks 1988

1991 Season

	M	Inns	NO	Runs	HS	Avge	100s	50s	Ct	St	O	M	Runs	Wkts	Avge	Best	5wI	10wM
Test	3	4	1	136	65	45.33	-	1	4	-	107	39	261	8	32.62	6-111	1	-
All First	16	20	2	621	73	34.50	-	4	9	-	471.4	127	1213	48	25.27	6-111	3	-
1-day Int	2	1	0	0	0	0.00	-	-	2	-	22	3	103	4	25.75	3-62	-	
NatWest	2	1	0	6	6	6.00	-	-	2	-	21	2	60	3	20.00	3-28	-	
B&H	2	2	0	13	8	6.50	-	-	-	-	22	0	115	3	38.33	3-62	-	
Refuge	12	12	1	174	36	15.81	-	-	4	-	91.2	10	341	15	22.73	3-25	-	

Career Performances

	M	Inns	NO	Runs	HS	Avge	100s	50s	Ct	St	Balls	Runs	Wkts	Avge	Best	5wI	10wM
Test	7	9	1	206	65	25.75	-	1	9	-	1368	727	20	36.35	6-111	1	-
All First	70	101	12	2262	189*	25.41	1	9	51	-	11347	5743	204	28.15	6-22	10	2
1-day Int	14	8	0	28	7	3.50	-	-	6	-	720	552	19	29.05	4-35	-	
NatWest	9	7	0	139	53	19.85	-	1	4	-	504	284	10	28.40	3-28	-	
B&H	13	12	5	160	28	22.85	-	-	6	-	729	505	15	33.66	3-41	-	
Refuge	52	45	12	870	93*	26.36	-	3	15	-	1869	1342	52	25.80	4-13	-	

123. Who topped the first-class batting averages last season for Hampshire?

LEWIS, J. J. B.   Essex

Name: Jonathan James Benjamin Lewis
Role: Right-hand bat
Born: 21 May 1970, Middlesex
Height: 5ft 9in **Weight:** 11st
Nickname: Scrubby, JJ
County debut: 1990
1st-Class 100s scored: 1
1st-Class catches: 2
Parents: Edward and Regina
Marital status: Single
Education: King Edward VI School,
Chelmsford; Roehampton Institute of
Higher Education
Qualifications: 5 O-levels, 3 A-levels,
BSc (Hons) Sport Studies, coaching award
Career outside cricket: Penguin Pools,
Post Office, bar work
Off-season: Playing and coaching abroad
Cricketers particularly admired:
Graham Gooch, Greg Matthews, Keith Fletcher, Craig Miller
Other sports followed: Football, basketball and women's tennis
Relaxations: 'Music, pubs with real ale, listening to John Boden's theories on diet.'
Extras: Hit century on first-class debut in Essex's final Championship match of the 1990
season
Opinions on cricket: 'I do not believe close fielders should be prevented from wearing
shin pads or helmet for protection, as has been suggested.'
Best batting: 116* Essex v Surrey, The Oval 1990

1991 Season

	M	Inns	NO	Runs	HS	Avge	100s	50s	Ct	St	O	M	Runs	Wkts	Avge	Best	5wI	10wM
Test																		
All First	2	2	0	73	48	36.50	-	-	1	-								
1-day Int																		
NatWest																		
B&H																		
Refuge	1	1	0	19	19	19.00	-	-	-	-								

124. Who has made the most Test appearances for Sri Lanka?

Career Performances

	M	Inns	NO	Runs	HS	Avge	100s	50s	Ct	St	Balls	Runs	Wkts	Avge	Best	5wI	10wM
Test																	
All First	3	3	1	189	116 *	94.50	1	-	2	-							
1-day Int																	
NatWest																	
B&H																	
Refuge	1	1	0	19	19	19.00	-	-	-	-							

LLONG, N. J. Kent

Name: Nigel James Llong
Role: Right-hand bat, right-arm
off-spin bowler
Born: 11 February 1969, Ashford, Kent
Height: 6ft **Weight:** 11st 13lbs
Nickname: Nidge, Lloydie,
Stormin' Norman
County debut: 1991
1st-Class catches: 4
Parents: Richard and Peggy (deceased)
Marital status: Single
Family links with cricket: Father
and brother play local league cricket
Education: Ashford North Secondary School
Qualifications: 6 CSEs
Career outside cricket: Assistant
groundsman, barman
Off-season: 'Spending a winter at home.'

Overseas teams played for: Ashburton,
Melbourne 1988-90; Green Point, Cape Town 1990-91
Cricketers particularly admired: Eddie Hemmings, Phil Edmonds, David Gower, Dean
Jones
Other sports followed: Most ball sports
Injuries: Dislocated finger
Relaxations: 'Socialising with Dave Fulton, fellow 2nd team player.'
Opinions on cricket: 'All 2nd team venues should have proper practice facilities.'
Best batting: 42* Kent v Nottinghamshire, Trent Bridge 1991

---

125. Who captained the 1973 West Indies in England?

1991 Season

	M	Inns	NO	Runs	HS	Avge	100s	50s	Ct	St	O	M	Runs	Wkts	Avge	Best	5wl	10wM
Test																		
All First	4	7	2	63	42 *	12.60	-	-	4	-	5	1	28	0	-	-	-	-
1-day Int																		
NatWest																		
B&H																		
Refuge	3	3	0	36	23	12.00	-	-	-	-	3	0	17	0	-		-	-

Career Performances

	M	Inns	NO	Runs	HS	Avge	100s	50s	Ct	St	Balls	Runs	Wkts	Avge	Best	5wl	10wM
Test																	
All First	5	7	2	63	42 *	12.60	-	-	5	-	72	52	0	-	-	-	-
1-day Int																	
NatWest																	
B&H																	
Refuge	4	4	1	36	23	12.00	-	-	-	-	36	37	1	37.00	1-20	-	

LLOYD, G. D.   Lancashire

Name: Graham David Lloyd
Role: Right-hand bat, right-arm medium bowler
Born: 1 July 1969, Accrington
Height: 5ft 9in **Weight:** 11st 7lbs
Nickname: Bumble, Geoff
County debut: 1988
1st-Class 50s scored: 14
1st-Class 100s scored: 3
1st-Class catches: 23
One-Day 50s: 9
One-Day 100s: 1
Place in batting averages: 143rd av. 27.63
(1990 84th av. 44.22)
Parents: David and Susan
Marital status: Single
Family links with cricket: Father played for Lancashire and England
Education: Hollins County High School, Accrington
Qualifications: 3 O-levels; cricket coach
Cricketers particularly admired: Graeme Hick, Allan Lamb, David Makinson, Gary

Yates, Gordon Parsons
Other sports followed: Football, horse racing
Relaxations: Watching Manchester United and playing cards
Extras: His school did not play cricket, so he learnt at Accrington CC, playing in the same team as his father
Opinions on cricket: 'I would like to see some sort of day/ night competition with coloured clothing.'
Best batting: 117 Lancashire v Nottinghamshire, Worksop 1989
Best bowling: 1-57 Lancashire v Yorkshire, Old Trafford 1991

1991 Season

	M	Inns	NO	Runs	HS	Avge	100s	50s	Ct	St	O	M	Runs	Wkts	Avge	Best	5wI	10wM
Test																		
All First	18	30	0	829	96	27.63	-	6	11	-	10	0	57	1	57.00	1-57	-	-
1-day Int																		
NatWest	1	1	0	39	39	39.00	-	-	-	-								
B&H	3	3	2	17	10	17.00	-	-	-	-								
Refuge	18	18	4	519	79 *	37.07	-	4	4	-								

Career Performances

	M	Inns	NO	Runs	HS	Avge	100s	50s	Ct	St	Balls	Runs	Wkts	Avge	Best	5wI	10wM
Test																	
All First	40	64	3	2089	117	34.24	3	14	23	-	109	141	1	141.00	1-57	-	-
1-day Int																	
NatWest	2	2	0	75	39	37.50	-	-	-	-							
B&H	3	3	2	17	10	17.00	-	-	-	-							
Refuge	34	32	6	1096	100 *	42.15	1	9	10	-							

126. Who scored more first-class centuries after he was 40 years old than before?

LLOYD, T. A. Warwickshire

Name: Timothy Andrew Lloyd
Role: Left-hand bat, off-break bowler,
county captain
Born: 5 November 1956, Oswestry
Height: 5ft 11in **Weight:** 12st
Nickname: Towser
County debut: 1977
County cap: 1980
Benefit: 1990 (£120,000)
Test debut: 1984
Tests: 1
One-Day Internationals: 3
1000 runs in a season: 9
1st-Class 50s scored: 82
1st-Class 100s scored: 29
1st-Class 200s scored: 1
1st-Class catches: 142
One-Day 50s: 50
One-Day 100s: 2

Place in batting averages: 98th av. 32.60 (1990 198th av. 24.84)
Parents: John Romer and Gwen
Wife: Gilly
Children: Georgia, Sophie
Education: Oswestry Boys' High School; Dorset College of Higher Education
Qualifications: O-levels, 2 A-levels, HND Tourism, NCA advanced coach
Career outside cricket: Business entertainment/corporate hospitality executive
Overseas tours: English Counties XI to Zimbabwe 1984-85
Overseas teams played for: Orange Free State 1978-80
Cricketers particularly admired: Allan Border, Dennis Amiss
Other sports followed: 'Most sports, but particularly racing.'
Relaxations: 'Enjoying my home, drinking good wine and beer, eating various cuisines.
Also greyhounds, playing golf and walking.'
Extras: Played for Shropshire and Warwickshire 2nd XI in 1975. Has been captain of
Warwickshire since 1988. Was Gladstone Small's best man
Opinions on cricket: 'After-match arrangements at some grounds must be looked into

---

127. Who has made the most Test appearances for England?

---

more closely. Hygiene and refreshment seem low on some counties' list of priorities.'
Best batting: 208* Warwickshire v Gloucestershire, Edgbaston 1983
Best bowling: 3-62 Warwickshire v Surrey, Edgbaston 1985

1991 Season

	M	Inns	NO	Runs	HS	Avge	100s	50s	Ct	St	O	M	Runs	Wkts	Avge	Best	5wI	10wM
Test																		
All First	21	35	2	1076	97	32.60	-	10	10	-	16	13	26	0	-		-	-	-
1-day Int																		
NatWest	4	2	0	96	78	48.00	-	1	-	-								
B&H	5	5	0	154	58	30.80	-	1	3	-								
Refuge	13	12	3	373	56 *	41.44	-	1	4	-								

Career Performances

	M	Inns	NO	Runs	HS	Avge	100s	50s	Ct	St	Balls	Runs	Wkts	Avge	Best	5wI	10wM
Test	1	1	1	10	10 *	-	-	-	-	-							
All First	288	506	43	16256	208 *	35.11	29	82	142	-	1908	1384	17	81.41	3-62	-	-
1-day Int	3	3	0	101	49	33.66	-	-	-	-							
NatWest	33	31	3	1177	121	42.03	1	11	9	-	54	47	2	23.50	1-4	-	
B&H	52	49	3	1458	137 *	31.69	1	8	14	-	90	76	0	-	-	-	
Refuge	168	159	18	4121	90	29.22	-	31	34	-	139	149	1	149.00	1-42	-	

LLOYDS, J. W.   Gloucestershire

Name: Jeremy William Lloyds
Role: Left-hand bat, off-break bowler,
close fielder
Born: 17 November 1954, Penang,
Malaysia
Height: 5ft 11in **Weight:** 12st
Nickname: Jo'burg, JJ or Jerry
County debut: 1979 (Somerset),
1985 (Gloucs)
County cap: 1982 (Somerset),
1985 (Gloucs)
1000 runs in a season: 3
1st-Class 50s scored: 62
1st-Class 100s scored: 10
1st-Class 5 w. in innings: 13
1st-Class 10 w. in match: 1
1st-Class catches: 229
One-Day 50s: 5

Place in batting averages: 141st av. 27.69 (1990 117th av. 38.13)
Place in bowling averages: 131st av. 48.52 (1990 136th av. 57.16)
Strike rate: 95.52 (career 72.57)
Parents: Edwin William and Grace Cicely
Wife and date of marriage: Corne, March 1989
Family links with cricket: Father played for Blundell's 1st XI 1932-35, was selected for Public Schools and also played in Malaya and Singapore 1950-55. Brother, Christopher Edwin Lloyds played for Blundell's 1st XI 1964-66 and Somerset 2nd XI in 1966
Education: St Dunstan's Prep School; Blundell's School
Qualifications: 10 O-levels, NCA advanced coach
Overseas teams played for: Orange Free State 1983-88
Cricketers particularly admired: John Hampshire, Graeme Pollock, Viv Richards, Ian Botham, Derek Underwood, Brian Davison
Other sports followed: Motor racing, tennis, American football
Relaxations: Music, cinema, driving, reading
Extras: Retired at the end of the 1991 season
Opinions on cricket: 'Coloured clothing and white ball for all one-day cricket; 17 four-day games played Wednesday to Saturday. Play the B&H in May. Season to finish early in September – it drags on too long.'
Best batting: 132* Somerset v Northamptonshire, Northampton 1982
Best bowling: 7-88 Somerset v Essex, Chelmsford 1982

1991 Season

	M	Inns	NO	Runs	HS	Avge	100s	50s	Ct	St	O	M	Runs	Wkts	Avge	Best	5wI	10wM
Test																		
All First	24	35	6	803	71 *	27.69	-	8	21	-	541.2	122	1650	34	48.52	6-94	1	-
1-day Int																		
NatWest	2	2	1	17	13 *	17.00	-	-	2	-	14	1	39	0	-	-	-	-
B&H	3	2	0	43	24	21.50	-	-	2	-	9	2	14	3	4.66	3-14	-	
Refuge	12	9	1	116	42 *	14.50	-	-	4	-	12	0	75	2	37.50	2-47	-	

Career Performances

	M	Inns	NO	Runs	HS	Avge	100s	50s	Ct	St	Balls	Runs	Wkts	Avge	Best	5wI	10wM
Test																	
All First	267	408	64	10679	132 *	31.04	10	62	229	-	24169	12943	333	38.86	7-88	13	1
1-day Int																	
NatWest	21	20	6	310	73 *	22.14	-	1	12	-	401	248	4	62.00	2-35	-	
B&H	31	24	4	372	53 *	18.60	-	2	15	-	236	114	7	16.28	3-14	-	
Refuge	119	101	15	1245	65	14.47	-	2	29	-	755	678	15	45.20	2-1	-	

LONGLEY, J. I.   Kent

Name: Jonathan Ian Longley
Role: Right-hand bat
Born: 12 April 1969, New Brunswick, USA
Height: 5ft 8in **Weight:** 11st 7lbs
Nickname: Tufty
County debut: 1989
1st-Class catches: 0
One-Day 50s: 1
Parents: Dick and Helen
Marital status: Single
Education: Tonbridge School; Durham
University
Qualifications: 9 O-levels, 3 A-levels
Cricketers particularly admired: Javed
Miandad, Gordon Greenidge, Allan Border
Other sports followed: Rugby, golf
Relaxations: Music, walking the dogs
Extras: Member of the Combined
Universities team which reached the
quarter-finals of the B&H Cup in 1989

Opinions on cricket: 'The cricketers themselves should have more say in the way cricket is run in this country. Most cricketers agree that too much first-class cricket is played, which dilutes the quality of the game and is reflected in the low interest shown by the public in county cricket. More time should be given to practising specific skills. I also believe that there are too many professionals. Cricket in this country can't support them properly.'
Best batting: 17 Kent v Essex, Southend 1989

1991 Season

	M	Inns	NO	Runs	HS	Avge	100s	50s	Ct	St	O	M	Runs	Wkts	Avge	Best	5wI	10wM
Test																		
All First																		
1-day Int																		
NatWest																		
B&H	4	4	0	63	47	15.75	-	-	1	-								
Refuge	1	1	0	1	1	1.00	-	-	1	-								

128. Who topped the first-class batting averages last season for Kent?

Career Performances

	M	Inns	NO	Runs	HS	Avge	100s	50s	Ct	St	Balls	Runs	Wkts	Avge	Best	5wI	10wM
Test																	
All First	4	8	0	42	17	5.25	-	-	-	-							
1-day Int																	
NatWest																	
B&H	13	13	1	210	49	17.50	-	-	1	-							
Refuge	5	5	0	97	57	19.40	-	1	2	-							

LORD, G. J. Worcestershire

Name: Gordon John Lord
Role: Left-hand bat, slow left-arm
bowler, specialist third-man
Born: 25 April 1961, Birmingham
Height: 5ft 10in **Weight:** 'Variable
and confidential!'
Nickname: Plum
County debut: 1983 (Warwicks),
1987 (Worcs)
County cap: 1990 (Worcs)
1000 runs in a season: 1
1st-Class 50s scored: 18
1st-Class 100s scored: 5
1st-Class catches: 22
One-Day 50s: 2
One-Day 100s: 1
Place in batting averages: 189th av. 21.00
(1990 73rd av. 45.59)
Parents: Michael David and Christine
Frances
Marital status: Single
Family links with cricket: Uncle Charles Watts played for Leicestershire
Education: Warwick School; Durham University
Qualifications: 7 O-levels, 4 A-levels, BA General Studies, NCA coaching award
Overseas tours: England YC to Australia 1978-79 and West Indies 1979-80
Cricketers particularly admired: Dennis Amiss, Graeme Hick
Other sports followed: Watches rugby, squash, snooker
Extras: Released by Worcestershire at the end of 1991 season
Relaxations: All forms of music, particularly church organ music; astronomy, reading,
people, Indian cooking and eating
Best batting: 199 Warwickshire v Yorkshire, Edgbaston 1985

1991 Season

	M	Inns	NO	Runs	HS	Avge	100s	50s	Ct	St	O	M	Runs	Wkts	Avge	Best	5wI	10wM
Test																		
All First	11	18	0	378	85	21.00	-	3	2	-								
1-day Int																		
NatWest																		
B&H																		
Refuge																		

Career Performances

	M	Inns	NO	Runs	HS	Avge	100s	50s	Ct	St	Balls		Runs	Wkts	Avge	Best	5wI	10wM
Test																		
All First	85	137	10	3406	199	26.81	5	18	22	-	96		61	0	-	-	-	-
1-day Int																		
NatWest	1	1	0	0	0	0.00	-	-	1	-								
B&H	8	8	0	67	26	8.37	-	-	-	-								
Refuge	16	16	1	351	103	23.40	1	2	4	-								

LOVELL, W. G.   Essex

Name: William Guy Lovell
Role: Right-hand bat, slow left-arm bowler
Born: 16 February 1969, Whitehaven, Cumbria
Height: 6ft **Weight:** 11st 7lbs
Nickname: Shovell, Shove
County debut: 1991 (one-day)
Parents: William and Christine
Wife and date of marriage: Frances, 17 February 1990
Children: Laura, 11 September 1990
Education: Millom School, Cumbria; Barrow College of FE
Qualifications: 4 O-levels, senior cricket coach, 'served two-year apprenticeship as engineer'
Off-season: 'Spending time with the family. Preparing myself for the season, aerobics and coaching.'
Overseas tours: Cricketer Club of London to Germany and Holland 1989
Overseas teams played for: Roskell, New Zealand 1988-89

315

Cricketers particularly admired: John Childs, Robin Smith, Derek Randall
Other sports followed: Golf, football, rugby league
Injuries: Quad muscle – out for two weeks in mid-June
Relaxations: Watching TV videos, aerobics, DIY
Extras: Started playing as right-arm bowler and changed to left-arm spin with help of David Bell, the Cumbria schools coach. Was on the Leicestershire staff 1988-89 and took a hat-trick for Essex 2nd against Leicestershire 2nd XI in 1990.

1991 Season

	M	Inns	NO	Runs	HS	Avge	100s	50s	Ct	St	O	M	Runs	Wkts	Avge	Best	5wI	10wM
Test																		
All First																		
1-day Int																		
NatWest																		
B&H																		
Refuge	1	-	-	-	-	-	-	-	-	-	6	0	34	0	-	-	-	-

Career Performances

	M	Inns	NO	Runs	HS	Avge	100s	50s	Ct	St	Balls	Runs	Wkts	Avge	Best	5wI	10wM
Test																	
All First																	
1-day Int																	
NatWest																	
B&H																	
Refuge	1	-	-	-	-	-	-	-	-	-	36	34	0	-	-	-	-

129. Who has made the most Test appearances for Australia?

LOYE, M. B.   Northamptonshire

Name: Malachy Bernard Loye
Role: Right-hand bat, right-arm off-spin
bowler
Born: 27 September 1972, Northampton
Height: 6ft 2in **Weight:** 11st 6lbs
Nickname: Mal, Moon Man
County debut: 1991
1st-Class catches: 1
Parents: Patrick and Anne
Marital status: Single
Family links with cricket: Father and
brother both play for Cogenhoe
Education: Moulton Comprehensive School
Qualifications: GCSEs and coaching
certificate
Overseas tours: England U18 to
international tournament in Canada 1991
Cricketers particularly admired: Gordon
Greenidge
Other sports followed: Football, golf and basketball
Relaxations: Listening to music and playing golf
Extras: Played for England U19 in the home series against Australia 1991
Opinions on cricket: 'Too much cricket is played over a six month period. Lunch and tea
should be extended by 10 minutes.'
Best batting: 3* Northamptonshire v Worcestershire, Northampton 1991

1991 Season

	M	Inns	NO	Runs	HS	Avge	100s	50s	Ct	St	O	M	Runs	Wkts	Avge	Best	5wI	10wM
Test																		
All First	1	1	1	3	3*	-	-	-	1	-								
1-day Int																		
NatWest																		
B&H																		
Refuge																		

130. Who has made the most Test appearances for South Africa?

	M	Inns	NO	Runs	HS	Avge	100s	50s	Ct	St	Balls	Runs	Wkts	Avge	Best	5wl	10wM
Test																	
All First	1	1	1	3	3*	-	-	-	1	-							
1-day Int																	
NatWest																	
B&H																	
Refuge																	

LYNCH, M. A. Surrey

Name: Monte Allan Lynch
Role: Right-hand bat, right-arm medium and off-break bowler
Born: 21 May 1958, Georgetown, Guyana
Height: 5ft 8in **Weight:** 12st
Nickname: Mont
County debut: 1977
County cap: 1982
Benefit: 1991
One-Day Internationals: 3
1000 runs in a season: 8
1st-Class 50s scored: 66
1st-Class 100s scored: 31
1st-Class catches: 265
One-Day 50s: 34
One-Day 100s: 4
Place in batting averages: 185th av. 21.37
(1990 75th av. 45.44)
Parents: Lawrence and Doreen Austin
Marital status: Single
Family links with cricket: 'Father and most of family played at some time or another.'
Education: Ryden's School, Walton-on-Thames
Overseas tours: West Indies XI to South Africa 1983-84
Overseas teams played for: Guyana 1982-83
Other sports followed: Football, table tennis
Extras: Hitting 141* for Surrey v Glamorgan at Guildford in August 1982, off 78 balls in 88 minutes, one six hit his captain Roger Knight's car. Joined West Indies Rebels in South Africa 1983-84, although qualified for England. Appeared in all three One-Day Internationals v West Indies 1988
Best batting: 172* Surrey v Kent, The Oval 1989
Best bowling: 3-6 Surrey v Glamorgan, Swansea 1981

1991 Season

	M	Inns	NO	Runs	HS	Avge	100s	50s	Ct	St	O	M	Runs	Wkts	Avge	Best	5wI	10wM
Test																		
All First	10	17	1	342	141 *	21.37	1	1	13	-	9	1	29	0	-		-	-
1-day Int																		
NatWest	4	4	0	66	48	16.50	-	-	3	-	10	1	28	0	-		-	-
B&H	2	2	0	20	20	10.00	-	-	-	-								
Refuge	14	14	2	433	97	36.08	-	3	6	-	0.4	0	6	0	-		-	-

Career Performances

	M	Inns	NO	Runs	HS	Avge	100s	50s	Ct	St	Balls	Runs	Wkts	Avge	Best	5wI	10wM
Test																	
All First	277	443	52	13912	172 *	35.58	31	66	265	-	1991	1275	25	51.00	3-6	-	-
1-day Int	3	3	0	8	6	2.66	-	-	1	-							
NatWest	33	29	4	722	129	28.88	1	3	14	-	198	108	2	54.00	1-11	-	
B&H	49	44	3	1028	112 *	25.07	1	5	20	-	108	108	0	-		-	-
Refuge	176	163	24	4171	136	30.00	2	26	57	-	117	152	7	21.71	2-2	-	

MACLEAY, K. H. Somerset

Name: Kenneth Hervey Macleay
Role: Right-hand bat, right-arm medium bowler
Born: 2 April 1959, Bradford-on-Avon, Wiltshire
Height: 6ft 4in **Weight:** 14st
Nickname: Rip, Freddie
County debut: 1991
One-Day Internationals: 16
1st-Class 50s scored: 16
1st-Class 100s scored: 3
1st-Class 5 w. in innings: 6
1st-Class catches: 72
Place in batting averages: 139th av. 27.80
Place in bowling averages: 83rd av. 34.88
Parents: Donald and Felicity
Wife and date of marriage: Elizabeth, 1987
Family links with cricket: Father played for Devon and Combined Services
Education: Scotch College; University of Western Australia, Perth
Career outside cricket: Accountant
Off-season: as above

Overseas tours: Australia to England (World Cup) 1984
Overseas teams played for: Western Australia 1981-91
Cricketers particularly admired: Allan Border, Dennis Lillee, David Gower, Ian Botham
Other sports followed: Keen follower of most major sporting events, 'especially those involving England and Australia'
Injuries: Broken finger, inter-costal muscle strain
Relaxations: Water sports – particularly windsurfing, fishing, swimming, travelling
Opinions on cricket: 'County cricket should not be drastically altered solely on the basis of the national team's performance.'
Best batting: 114* Western Australia v New South Wales, Perth 1986-87
Best bowling: 6-93 Western Australia v New South Wales, Perth 1985-86

1991 Season

	M	Inns	NO	Runs	HS	Avge	100s	50s	Ct	St	O	M	Runs	Wkts	Avge	Best	5wI	10wM
Test																		
All First	15	21	6	417	63	27.80	-	2	5	-	284.3	54	872	25	34.88	3-40	-	-
1-day Int																		
NatWest	2	1	1	25	25 *	-	-	-	1	-	24	1	67	3	22.33	2-35	-	
B&H																		
Refuge	9	8	3	56	19	11.20	-	-	3	-	63	1	252	9	28.00	3-31	-	

Career Performances

	M	Inns	NO	Runs	HS	Avge	100s	50s	Ct	St	Balls	Runs	Wkts	Avge	Best	5wI	10wM
Test																	
All First	116	152	31	3298	114 *	27.25	3	16	72	-	21306	8708	291	29.92	6-93	6	-
1-day Int	16	13	2	139	41	12.63	-	-	2	-	857	626	15	41.73	6-39	1	
NatWest	2	1	1	25	25 *	-	-	-	1	-	144	67	3	22.33	2-35	-	
B&H																	
Refuge	9	8	3	56	19	11.20	-	-	3	-	378	252	9	28.00	3-31	-	

131. Who topped the first-class batting averages last season for Lancashire?

MAGUIRE, J. N. Leicestershire

Name: John Norman Maguire
Role: Right-hand bat, right-arm medium
bowler
Born: 15 September 1956, Murwillumbah,
NSW, Australia
County debut: 1991
Test debut: 1983-84
Tests: 3
One-Day Internationals: 23
50 wickets in a season: 1
1st-Class 50s scored: 2
1st-Class 5 w. in innings: 26
1st-Class 10 w. in match: 3
1st-Class catches: 42
Place in batting averages: 253rd av. 13.94
Place in bowling averages: 62nd av. 31.64
Strike rate: 61.24 (career 60.92)
Education: Cavendish Road State High
School; Queensland Institute of Technology

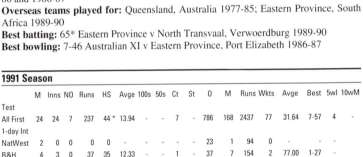

Overseas tours: Australia to West Indies 1983-84; Australian XI to South Africa 1985-86 and 1986-87
Overseas teams played for: Queensland, Australia 1977-85; Eastern Province, South Africa 1989-90
Best batting: 65* Eastern Province v North Transvaal, Verwoerdburg 1989-90
Best bowling: 7-46 Australian XI v Eastern Province, Port Elizabeth 1986-87

1991 Season

	M	Inns	NO	Runs	HS	Avge	100s	50s	Ct	St	O	M	Runs	Wkts	Avge	Best	5wl	10wM
Test																		
All First	24	24	7	237	44 *	13.94	-	-	7	-	786	168	2437	77	31.64	7-57	4	-
1-day Int																		
NatWest	2	0	0	0	0	-	-	-	-	-	23	1	94	0	-	-	-	
B&H	4	3	0	37	35	12.33	-	-	1	-	37	7	154	2	77.00	1-27	-	
Refuge	15	6	5	2	2 *	2.00	-	-	3	-	113.3	7	505	21	24.04	3-31	-	

132. Who was the oldest Test player for any country, and how old?

Career Performances

	M	Inns	NO	Runs	HS	Avge	100s	50s	Ct	St	Balls	Runs	Wkts	Avge	Best	5wl	10wM
Test	3	5	1	28	15 *	7.00	-	-	2	-	616	323	10	32.30	4-57	-	-
All First	134	152	46	1162	65 *	10.96	-	2	42	-	28208	12851	463	27.75	7-46	26	3
1-day Int	23	11	5	42	14 *	7.00	-	-	2	-	1009	769	19	40.47	3-61	-	
NatWest	2	0	0	0	0	-	-	-	-	-	138	94	0	-	-	-	
B&H	4	3	0	37	35	12.33	-	-	1	-	222	154	2	77.00	1-27	-	
Refuge	15	6	5	2	2 *	2.00	-	-	3	-	681	505	21	24.04	3-31	-	

MAHER, B. J. M. Derbyshire

Name: Bernard Joseph Michael Maher
Role: Right-hand bat, wicket-keeper
Born: 11 February 1958, Hillingdon
Height: 5ft 9¹/₂in **Weight:** 12st 3lbs
Nickname: BJ
County debut: 1981
County cap: 1987
1st-Class 50s scored: 17
1st-Class 100s scored: 4
1st-Class catches: 280
1st-Class stumpings: 14
Parents: Francis Joseph (deceased) and
Mary Anne
Marital status: Single
Family links with cricket: Brother kept
wicket for school, father was keen follower
of Derbyshire
Education: St Bernadette's Primary,
Abbotsfield; Bishopshalt Grammar
Qualifications: 10 O-levels, 3 A-levels, BSc (Hons) Economics and Accountancy,
Advanced NCA Coaching Award, qualified to Professional 2 level of Certified Accountancy
exams
Career outside cricket: Professional cricket coach in winter, also works with BBC Radio
Derby
Off-season: Coaching and playing for Taieri CC and Otago Cricket Association in New
Zealand
Overseas tours: Middlesex Cricket League to Trinidad and Tobago 1978; Loughborough
University to Amsterdam 1981
Overseas teams played for: Zingari, Pietermaritzburg, South Africa 1982-84; Ellerslie,
Auckland 1984-85; Kamo and Northland CA, New Zealand 1985-86; Northern Districts
B side 1986-87; Taieri, Otago, New Zealand 1988-90, 1991-92

Cricketers particularly admired: Malcolm Marshall, Richard Hadlee, Gordon Greenidge, Allan Border

Other sports followed: Athletics, rugby union, tennis, boxing

Relaxations: Fanatical fly-fisherman spend virtually all my spare time fishing on rivers and lakes around the country. Also enjoy walking in Snowdonia, the Lake District and the Yorkshire moors

Extras: Caught five catches on debut v Gloucestershire, 1981. Topped wicket-keepers' dismissals list with 76 victims in 1987

Opinions on cricket: '**1.** A transfer system should operate allowing players and clubs to make money. A direct result would be the improvement of youth cricket, with clubs and junior associations seeking out and coaching young talent for their future earnings potential. **2.** I believe that a paid England selector should watch every county game to ensure more (and fairer) consistency in England's team selection. **3.** I would like to see a specialised coaching clinic for the top 25 young batsmen and the top 25 young bowlers one month before players report back for training in April. The course tutors should be current seasoned professionals and recently retired players. **4.** I do not feel that there should be any restriction on the number of short-pitched balls a bowler bowls. We have tried various ways of restricting them – all of which have failed. What might be an idea would be to make the glove no longer part of the bat i.e. if a ball flies at your throat you are allowed to defend yourself with your glove without fear of being caught off it. **5.** It has long been said that Oxford and Cambridge Universities are well below standard and should not be first-class fixtures. We have maintained this status for reasons of tradition, early season practice for the counties and a breeding ground for young talent. It therefore alarms me to see Oxford with five foreigners in their side, i.e. not eligible to play for England. If we are going to have the Oxbridge fixtures as first-class let's at least have Englishmen in them. Might I suggest that the same overseas player rules as those which apply to the counties! '

Best batting: 126 Derbyshire v New Zealand, Derby 1986

Best bowling: 2-69 Derbyshire v Glamorgan, Abergavenny 1986

1991 Season

	M	Inns	NO	Runs	HS	Avge	100s	50s	Ct	St	O	M	Runs	Wkts	Avge	Best	5wI	10wM
Test																		
All First	1	1	0	5	5	5.00	-	-	-	-								
1-day Int																		
NatWest																		
B&H																		
Refuge	2	2	1	4	4	4.00	-	-	1	1								

---

133. Who was the youngest Test player ever?

Career Performances

	M	Inns	NO	Runs	HS	Avge	100s	50s	Ct	St	Balls	Runs	Wkts	Avge	Best	5wI	10wM
Test																	
All First	128	200	35	3667	126	22.22	4	17	280	14	270	234	4	58.50	2-69	-	-
1-day Int																	
NatWest	9	9	1	99	44	12.37	-	-	17	-							
B&H	20	13	2	256	50	23.27	-	1	25	1							
Refuge	74	63	13	776	78	15.52	-	1	58	10							

MALCOLM, D. E. Derbyshire

Name: Devon Eugene Malcolm
Role: Right-hand bat, right-arm
fast bowler
Born: 22 February 1963, Kingston, Jamaica
Height: 6ft 2in **Weight:** 14st 8lbs
Nickname: Dude
County debut: 1984
County cap: 1989
Test debut: 1989
Tests: 18
One-Day Internationals: 4
50 wickets in a season: 2
1st-Class 50s scored: 1
1st-Class 5 w. in innings: 8
1st-Class 10 w. in innings: 1
1st-Class catches: 20
Place in bowling averages: 84th av. 34.54
(1990 42nd av. 32.46)
Strike rate: 55.54 (career 54.53)
Parents: Albert and Brendalee (deceased)
Wife and date of marriage: Jennifer, October 1989
Education: St Elizabeth Technical High School; Richmond College; Derby College
Qualifications: College certificates, O-levels, coaching certificate
Off-season: Touring with England A
Overseas tours: England to West Indies 1989-90, Australia 1990-91; England A to Bermuda and West Indies 1991-92
Cricketers particularly admired: Michael Holding, Richard Hadlee
Relaxations: Music and swimming. Collection of 500 records and tapes – reggae, soca, jazz funk 'and especially singers like Anita Baker and Gregory Isaacs.'
Extras: Became eligible to play for England in 1987. Played league cricket for Sheffield Works and Sheffield United. Took 10 for 137 v West Indies in Port of Spain Test, 1989-90

Best batting: 51 Derbyshire v Surrey, Derby 1989
Best bowling: 7-74 England XI v Australian XI, Hobart 1990-91

1991 Season

	M	Inns	NO	Runs	HS	Avge	100s	50s	Ct	St	O	M	Runs	Wkts	Avge	Best	5wI	10wM
Test	2	3	1	9	5*	4.50	-	-	1	-	42.3	3	180	3	60.00	1-9	-	-
All First	13	17	3	93	18	6.64	-	-	1	-	388.5	53	1451	42	34.54	5-45	1	-
1-day Int																		
NatWest																			
B&H	4	3	0	37	15	12.33	-	-	-	-	39	3	151	5	30.20	2-14	-	
Refuge	9	6	3	38	18	12.66	-	-	2	-	66	2	384	15	25.60	3-43	-	

Career Performances

	M	Inns	NO	Runs	HS	Avge	100s	50s	Ct	St	Balls	Runs	Wkts	Avge	Best	5wI	10wM
Test	18	24	8	99	15*	6.18	-	-	2	-	4204	2293	61	37.59	6-77	3	1
All First	108	122	34	675	51	7.67	-	1	20	-	18595	10573	341	31.00	7-74	8	1
1-day Int	4	2	1	7	4	7.00	-	-	-	-	234	171	6	28.50	2-19	-	
NatWest	7	6	0	11	6	1.83	-	-	-	-	450	290	9	32.22	3-54	-	
B&H	12	7	2	42	15	8.40	-	-	-	-	696	431	17	25.35	5-27	1	
Refuge	27	12	4	63	18	7.87	-	-	4	-	1188	1028	39	26.35	4-21	-	

MALLENDER, N. A. Somerset

Name: Neil Alan Mallender
Role: Right-hand bat, right-arm
fast-medium bowler
Born: 13 August 1961, Kirk Sandall,
nr Doncaster
Height: 6ft **Weight:** 13st
Nickname: Ghostie
County debut: 1980 (Northants),
1987 (Somerset)
County cap: 1984 (Northants),
1987 (Somerset)
50 wickets in a season: 5
1st-Class 50s scored: 9
1st-Class 5 w. in innings: 24
1st-Class 10 w. in match: 3
1st-Class catches: 100
Place in batting averages: 236th av. 13.50
(1990 196th av. 25.28)
Place in bowling averages: 12th av. 23.07

(1990 35th av. 31.07)
Strike rate: 49.97 (career 58.66)
Parents: Ron and Jean
Wife and date of marriage: Caroline, 1 October 1984
Children: Kirstie Jane, 18 May 1988; Dominic James 21 September 1991
Family links with cricket: Brother Graham used to play good representative cricket before joining the RAF
Education: Beverley Grammar School, East Yorkshire
Qualifications: 7 O-levels
Off-season: Playing for Otago in New Zealand
Overseas tours: England YC to West Indies 1980
Overseas teams played for: Otago 1983-90
Cricketers particularly admired: Richard Hadlee, Dennis Lillee, Peter Willey
Other sports followed: Golf, rugby league, 'most sports'
Injuries: Groin, abductor strain – out for July and August
Relaxations: Golf and watching other sports
Extras: Signed a 3-year contract to play for Somerset in 1987. Equalled Somerset record for 9th wicket v Sussex at Hove in 1990 – batting with Chris Tavare. Called up to join England tour squad in New Zealand 1991-92 as cover for injured fast bowlers
Opinions on cricket: 'Four-day cricket seems to be working well, as the more dominant team seems to have the time to force a result, and there is not so much contrived cricket. I think a new ball should be available after 85 overs in county cricket – as it used to be.'
Best batting: 88 Otago v Central Districts, Oamaru 1984-85
Best bowling: 7-27 Otago v Auckland, Auckland 1984-85

1991 Season

	M	Inns	NO	Runs	HS	Avge	100s	50s	Ct	St	O	M	Runs	Wkts	Avge	Best	5wI	10wM
Test																		
All First	13	11	3	108	19	13.50	-	-	1	-	349.5	76	969	42	23.07	6-43	3	-
1-day Int																		
NatWest	1	0	0	0	0	-	-	-	-	-	12	4	23	3	7.66	3-23	-	
B&H	4	3	1	4	2 *	2.00	-	-	1	-	41	3	181	3	60.33	1-35	-	
Refuge	9	5	3	24	13 *	12.00	-	-	-	-	59	1	246	3	82.00	2-21	-	

Career Performances

	M	Inns	NO	Runs	HS	Avge	100s	50s	Ct	St	Balls	Runs	Wkts	Avge	Best	5wI	10wM
Test																	
All First	281	307	97	3408	88	16.22	-	9	100	-	43602	20483	738	27.75	7-27	24	3
1-day Int																	
NatWest	22	9	3	43	11 *	7.16	-	-	5	-	1366	631	35	18.02	7-37	1	
B&H	47	20	8	58	16 *	4.83	-	-	13	-	2589	1586	54	29.37	5-53	1	
Refuge	140	62	33	362	24	12.48	-	-	25	-	5641	4180	154	27.14	5-34	1	

MARSH, S. A. Kent

Name: Steven Andrew Marsh
Role: Right-hand bat, wicket-keeper, county vice-captain
Born: 27 January 1961, Westminster
Height: 5ft 11in **Weight:** 12st
County debut: 1982
County cap: 1986
Nickname: Marshy
1st-Class 50s scored: 24
1st-Class 100s scored: 5
One-Day 50s scored: 5
Place in batting averages: 89th av. 33.70
(1990 141st av. 33.74)
Parents: Melvyn Graham and Valerie Ann
Wife and date of marriage: Julie,
27 September 1986
Children: Hayley Ann, 15 May 1987;
Christian 20 November 1990

Family links with cricket: Father played
local cricket for Lordswood. Father-in-law, Bob Wilson, played for Kent 1954-66
Education: Walderslade Secondary School for Boys; Mid-Kent College of Higher and
Further Education
Qualifications: 6 O-levels, 2 A-levels, OND in Business Studies
Off-season: 'Working computer operator/accounts clerk for my car sponsor, Swale Motor
Co., Sittingbourne.'
Cricketers particularly admired: Robin Smith, Graham Cowdrey, Matthew Fleming
Other sports followed: 'All sport except synchronised swimming.'
Injuries: Infection in right foot – out for two weeks
Extras: Appointed Kent vice-captain for 1991. Equalled world record eight catches in an
innings v Middlesex 1991 and scored 113* in the same match
Best batting: 120 Kent v Essex, Chelmsford 1988
Best bowling: 2-20 Kent v Warwickshire, Edgbaston 1990

---

134. Who is the oldest player to have made a Test debut?

135. Who topped the first-class batting averages last season
for Northamptonshire?

1991 Season

	M	Inns	NO	Runs	HS	Avge	100s	50s	Ct	St	O	M	Runs	Wkts	Avge	Best	5wl	10wM
Test																		
All First	23	32	5	910	113 *	33.70	2	5	66	4	5	0	28	0	-		-	-	-
1-day Int																		
NatWest	2	1	0	15	15	15.00	-	-	3	-								
B&H	3	3	1	118	71	59.00	-	1	5	-								
Refuge	14	13	3	269	59	26.90	-	3	9	1								

Career Performances

	M	Inns	NO	Runs	HS	Avge	100s	50s	Ct	St	Balls	Runs	Wkts	Avge	Best	5wl	10wM
Test																	
All First	150	210	41	4596	120	27.19	5	24	324	23	106	101	2	50.50	2-20	-	-
1-day Int																	
NatWest	10	5	1	46	24 *	11.50	-	-	17	1							
B&H	30	21	5	297	71	18.56	-	1	36	2							
Refuge	89	65	14	947	59	18.56	-	4	85	10							

MARSHALL, M. D.   Hampshire

Name: Malcolm Denzil Marshall
Role: Right-hand bat, right-arm fast bowler
Born: 18 April 1958, Barbados
Height: 5ft 10½in **Weight:** 12st 8lbs
Nickname: Macko
County debut: 1979
County cap: 1981
Benefit: 1987 (£61,006)
Test debut: 1978-79
Tests: 81
One-Day Internationals: 121
50 wickets in a season: 9
1st-Class 50s scored: 47
1st-Class 100s scored: 6
1st-Class 5 w. in innings: 82
1st-Class 10 w. in match: 13
1st-Class catches: 120
One-Day 50s: 4
Place in batting averages: 182nd av. 21.77
(1990 70th av. 45.81)
Place in bowling averages: 29th av. 26.06 (1990 2nd av. 19.18)
Strike rate: 56.43 (career 43.02)

Parents: Mrs Eleanor Inniss
Children: Shelly, 24 November 1984
Family links with cricket: Cousin Errol Yearwood plays for Texaco in Barbados as a fast bowler
Education: St Giles Boys' School; Parkinson Comprehensive School, Barbados
Qualifications: School passes in Maths and English
Career outside cricket: Working for Banks Brewery
Off-season: Playing for West Indies
Overseas tours: Young West Indies to Zimbabwe 1981-82; West Indies to India and Sri Lanka 1978-79; Australia and New Zealand 1979-80; England 1980; Pakistan 1980-81; Australia 1981-82; India 1983-84; England 1984; Australia 1984-85; Pakistan and New Zealand 1986-87; England 1988; Australia 1988-89; Pakistan 1990-91; England 1991; Pakistan and Australia 1991-92
Overseas teams played for: Barbados 1977-90
Cricketers particularly admired: Wes Hall and Gary Sobers
Other sports followed: Tennis, golf
Relaxations: Soul music, reggae
Extras: Took nine wickets in debut match v Glamorgan in May 1979. Scored his first first-class century (109) in Zimbabwe, October 1981. Became the leading West Indies Test wicket-taker when he overtook Lance Gibbs's total of 309. Broke record for number of wickets taken in a 22-match English season (i.e. since 1969) with 133. Published autobiography *Marshall Arts* (1987). Nearly chose to become a wicket-keeper. 'Even now I wish sometimes I was in Jeff Dujon's place behind the stumps.' One of *Wisden's* Five Cricketers of the Year, 1982. After considering retirement, he signed a new three-year contract with Hampshire in 1990
Opinions on cricket: 'Cricket has been my life since I could stand upright and hold a cricket bat or at least our home-made apology, built from anything that looked like one. I played morning, noon and night every day of my life. Not even school could get in the way of my obsession with the game. There was no question of playing football, or anything else, for very long. It was cricket, cricket and more cricket.'
Best batting: 117 Hampshire v Yorkshire, Headingley 1990
Best bowling: 8-71 Hampshire v Worcestershire, Southampton 1982

1991 Season

	M	Inns	NO	Runs	HS	Avge	100s	50s	Ct	St	O	M	Runs	Wkts	Avge	Best	5wI	10wM
Test	5	7	1	116	67	19.33	-	1	-	-	172.1	36	442	20	22.10	4-33	-	-
All First	11	11	2	196	67	21.77	-	1	-	-	282.1	57	782	30	26.06	4-33	-	-
1-day Int	3	3	0	52	22	17.33	-	-	-	-	32	2	126	3	42.00	2-32	-	
NatWest																		
B&H																		
Refuge																		

Career Performances

	M	Inns	NO	Runs	HS	Avge	100s	50s	Ct	St	Balls	Runs	Wkts	Avge	Best	5wI	10wM
Test	81	107	11	1810	92	18.85	-	10	25	-	17585	7876	376	20.94	7-22	22	4
All First	347	439	57	9350	117	24.47	6	47	120	-	63460	27163	1475	18.41	8-71	82	13
1-day Int	121	70	17	888	66	16.75	-	2	12	-	6413	3735	142	26.30	4-23	-	
NatWest	27	19	8	310	77	28.18	-	2	2	-	1685	762	34	22.41	4-15	-	
B&H	31	25	1	340	34	14.16	-	-	6	-	1741	862	37	23.29	4-26	-	
Refuge	118	78	19	1120	46	18.98	-	-	21	-	5217	3086	128	24.10	5-13	2	

MARTIN, P. J. Lancashire

Name: Peter James Martin
Role: Right-hand bat, right-arm
fast-medium bowler
Born: 15 November 1968, Accrington
Height: 6ft 4½in **Weight:** 15st 7lbs
Nickname: Digger, Maurice, Astin
County debut: 1989
1st-Class catches: 11
Place in bowling averages: 99th av. 36.75
(1990 94th av. 39.45)
Strike rate: 75.38 (career 78.42)
Parents: Keith and Catherine Lina
Marital status: Single
Education: Danum School, Doncaster
Qualifications: 6 O-levels, 2 A-levels
Career outside cricket: None as yet -
'I was a chicken farmer in Queensland for
six months.'
Off-season: Playing cricket in Canberra,
Australia
Overseas tours: England YC to Australia for Youth World Cup, 1988 and various other
tours with Schools and NAYC
Overseas teams played for: Southern Districts, Queensland 1988-89; South Launceston,
Tasmania 1989-90; South Canberra, ACT 1990-91
Cricketers particularly admired: Paul Allott, Richard Hadlee, Wasim Akram, Ian
Botham, Dennis Lillee, 'most of the fellas on the Lancs staff.'
Other sports followed: Soccer (Man United), golf, water sports
Injuries: Left ankle injury - missed six weeks at the beginning of the season
Relaxations: Music, walking the dog
Extras: Played district football and basketball for Doncaster. Played for England A v Sri
Lanka 1991

Opinions on cricket: 'Although 17 four-day games may cause financial problems for some counties it seriously needs to be considered in the interests of future Test cricket. It also helps to avoid contrived finishes – it makes a joke of the game when someone can score a first-class hundred with declaration bowlers operating. Get rid of water hogs!'

Best batting: 29 Lancashire v Yorkshire, Scarborough 1991
Best bowling: 4-30 Lancashire v Worcestershire, Blackpool 1991

1991 Season

	M	Inns	NO	Runs	HS	Avge	100s	50s	Ct	St	O	M	Runs	Wkts	Avge	Best	5wI	10wM
Test																		
All First	16	13	8	85	29	17.00	-	-	5	-	454.4	107	1323	36	36.75	4-30	-	-
1-day Int																		
NatWest	1	0	0	0	0	-	-	-	-	-	12	2	19	2	9.50	2-19	-	
B&H																		
Refuge	6	0	0	0	0	-	-	-	-	-	39	1	174	3	58.00	2-38	-	

Career Performances

	M	Inns	NO	Runs	HS	Avge	100s	50s	Ct	St	Balls	Runs	Wkts	Avge	Best	5wI	10wM
Test																	
All First	28	22	11	149	29	13.54	-	-	11	-	4639	2324	59	39.39	4-30	-	-
1-day Int																	
NatWest	3	0	0	0	0	-	-	-	-	-	120	72	2	36.00	2-19	-	
B&H																	
Refuge	8	0	0	0	0	-	-	-	2	-	318	253	3	84.33	2-38	-	

136. Which former England Test player is Warwickshire's Director of Coaching?

MARTINDALE, D. J. R.   Nottinghamshire

Name: Duncan John Richardson Martindale
Role: Right-hand bat, cover fielder
Born: 13 December 1963, Harrogate
Height: 5ft 11½in **Weight:** 11st 11lbs
Nickname: Blowers
County debut: 1985
1st-Class 50s scored: 7
1st-Class 100s scored: 4
1st-Class catches: 23
One-Day 50s scored: 1
Place in batting averages: (1990 166th
av. 30.04)
Parents: Don and Isabel
Marital status: Single
Family links with cricket: Father and
grandfather played club cricket; great uncle
played for Nottinghamshire2nd XI
Education: Lymm Grammar School;
Trent Polytechnic
Qualifications: 9 O-levels, 2 A-levels, HND Business Studies, NCA senior coaching
award
Overseas tours: Christians in Sport to India 1990
Cricketers particularly admired: Geoff Boycott, Viv Richards, Richard Hadlee, Clive
Rice
Other sports followed: Most sports
Relaxations: Reading, travelling, meeting people, active in other sports
Extras: Scored a century (104*) in fifth first-class innings. First one-day match was 1985
NatWest Final. Member of Christians in Sport. Released by Nottingham at the end of 1991
season
Opinions on cricket: 'There is too much cricket. There should be 12-month contracts for
all players, with the county club helping players to develop careers in and out of the game.'
Best batting: 138 Nottinghamshire v Cambridge University, Fenner's 1990

1991 Season

	M	Inns	NO	Runs	HS	Avge	100s	50s	Ct	St	O	M	Runs	Wkts	Avge	Best	5wI	10wM
Test																		
All First	1	1	1	4	4 *	-	-	-	-	-	-							
1-day Int																		
NatWest																		
B&H																		
Refuge																		

	M	Inns	NO	Runs	HS	Avge	100s	50s	Ct	St	Balls	Runs	Wkts	Avge	Best	5wl	10wM
Test																	
All First	55	85	10	1861	138	24.81	4	7	23	-	12	8	0	-	-	-	-
1-day Int																	
NatWest	2	2	1	67	47	67.00	-	-	-	-							
B&H	1	1	0	0	0	0.00	-	-	-	-							
Refuge	16	12	1	276	53	25.09	-	1	5	-							

MARTYN, D. R. Leicestershire

Name: Damien Richard Martyn
Role: Right-hand bat, right-arm medium bowler
Born: 21 October 1971, Darwin, Australia
Height: 5ft 10in
County debut: 1991
1st-Class 50s scored: 3
1st-Class catches: 3
Marital status: Single
Off-season: Playing in Australia
Overseas tours: Australia U19 to England 1991
Overseas teams played for: Western Australia 1990-91
Extras: Captained Australia U19 against England 1991
Best batting: 68* Western Australia v Victoria, St Kilda 1990-91
Best bowling: 1-22 Western Australia v Victoria, St Kilda 1990-91

1991 Season

	M	Inns	NO	Runs	HS	Avge	100s	50s	Ct	St	O	M	Runs	Wkts	Avge	Best	5wl	10wM
Test																		
All First	1	2	1	95	60 *	95.00	-	1	-	-								
1-day Int																		
NatWest																		
B&H																		
Refuge																		

Career Performances

	M	Inns	NO	Runs	HS	Avge	100s	50s	Ct	St	Balls	Runs	Wkts	Avge	Best	5wI	10wM
Test																	
All First	7	13	3	353	68 *	35.30	-	3	3	-	90	44	1	44.00	1-22	-	-
1-day Int																	
NatWest																	
B&H																	
Refuge																	

MARU, R. J.   Hampshire

Name: Rajesh Jamnadass Maru
Role: Right-hand bat, slow left-arm bowler, close fielder
Born: 28 October 1962, Nairobi
Height: 5ft 6in **Weight:** 11st
Nickname: Raj
County debut: 1980 (Middlesex), 1984 (Hampshire)
County cap: 1986 (Hampshire)
50 wickets in a season: 4
1st-Class 50s scored: 6
1st-Class 5 w. in innings: 15
1st-Class 10 w. in match: 1
1st-Class catches: 201
Place in batting averages: 210th av. 17.04 (1990 172nd av. 28.88)
Place in bowling averages: 114th av. 41.02 (1990 67th av. 36.66)
Strike rate: 93.77 (career 72.69)
Parents: Jamnadass and Prabhavati
Family links with cricket: Father played in Kenya and in England for North London Polytechnic. Brother Pradip plays for Wembley in the Middlesex League and has played a couple of games for Middlesex 2nd XI
Education: Rooks Heath High; Pinner Sixth Form College
Qualifications: NCA senior cricket coach
Career outside cricket: Cricket coach
Off-season: Coaching for Hampshire CCC
Overseas tours: England YC South to Canada 1979; England YC to West Indies 1979-80; Middlesex to Zimbabwe 1980; Hampshire to Barbados 1987,1988,1990; Hampshire to Dubai 1989
Overseas teams played for: Marlborough CA, Blenheim, New Zealand 1985-87

334

Cricketers particularly admired: Malcolm Marshall, Bishen Bedi, Jimmy Cook, Richard Hadlee, Phil Edmonds, Mike Gatting, John Emburey
Other sports followed: Badminton, table tennis, squash, football, rugby – 'would watch any sport'
Relaxations: Music, watching videos, reading, DIY at home
Extras: Played for Middlesex 1980-83
Best batting: 74 Hampshire v Gloucestershire, Gloucester 1988
Best bowling: 8-41 Hampshire v Kent, Southampton 1989

1991 Season

	M	Inns	NO	Runs	HS	Avge	100s	50s	Ct	St	O	M	Runs	Wkts	Avge	Best	5wI	10wM
Test																		
All First	22	26	3	392	61	17.04	-	1	31	-	625.1	178	1641	40	41.02	5-128	1	-
1-day Int																		
NatWest	4	1	1	1	1 *	-	-	-	3	-	42	7	122	3	40.66	2-20	-	
B&H																		
Refuge	7	4	2	63	33 *	31.50	-	-	4	-	36	1	170	3	56.66	1-27	-	

Career Performances

	M	Inns	NO	Runs	HS	Avge	100s	50s	Ct	St	Balls	Runs	Wkts	Avge	Best	5wI	10wM
Test																	
All First	192	179	43	2234	74	16.42	-	6	201	-	33584	15094	462	32.67	8-41	15	1
1-day Int																	
NatWest	11	4	2	39	22	19.50	-	-	9	-	678	392	12	32.66	3-46	-	
B&H	4	1	0	9	9	9.00	-	-	1	-	162	149	4	37.25	3-46	-	
Refuge	38	15	8	110	33 *	15.71	-	-	13	-	1134	965	26	37.11	3-30	-	

137. On which ground will the final of the 1992 World Cup be played?

MAYNARD, M. P. Glamorgan

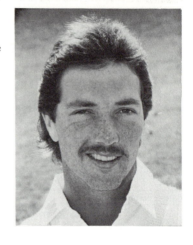

Name: Matthew Peter Maynard
Role: Right-hand bat, right-arm medium 'declaration' bowler, cover fielder
Born: 21 March 1966, Oldham, Lancashire
Height: 5ft 10$^{1}/_{2}$in **Weight:** 12st 8lbs
Nickname: Action, The Kid, Susie
County debut: 1985
County cap: 1987
Test debut: 1988
Tests: 1
1000 runs in a season: 6
1st-Class 50s scored: 53
1st-Class 100s scored: 19
1st-Class 200s scored: 2
1st-Class catches: 130
One-Day 50s: 19
One-Day 100s: 5
Place in batting averages: 11th av. 60.10
(1990 86th av. 44.14)
Parents: Ken (deceased) and Pat
Wife and date of marriage: Susan, 27 September 1986
Children: Tom, 25 March 1989
Family links with cricket: Father played for many years for Duckinfield. Brother Charlie plays for St Fagans
Education: Ysgol David Hughes, Anglesey
Qualifications: Cricket coach
Career outside cricket: 'Cricket *is* my career.'
Off-season: Playing in New Zealand
Overseas tours: North Wales XI to Barbados 1982; Glamorgan to Barbados; Unofficial England XI to South Africa 1989-90
Overseas teams played for: St Joseph's, Whakatane, New Zealand 1986-88; Gosnells, Perth, Western Australia 1988-89; Northern Districts, New Zealand 1990-92
Cricketers particularly admired: Ian Botham, Viv Richards, Bill Clutterbuck, Ken Maynard
Other sports followed: Rugby, golf, snooker, athletics
Injuries: Broken knuckle
Relaxations: 'Spending time with the family, playing golf, sleeping.'
Extras: Scored century on debut v Yorkshire at Swansea. Youngest centurion for Glamorgan and scored 1000 runs in first full season. Fastest ever 50 for Glamorgan (14 mins) v Yorkshire and youngest player to be awarded Glamorgan cap. Voted Young Cricketer of the Year 1988 by the Cricket Writers Club. Banned from Test cricket for joining tour of South Africa, 1989-90. Scored 987 runs in July 1991 including a century

in each innings against Gloucestershire at Cheltenham.

Opinions on cricket: 'The new law concerning the number of bouncers per over is ludicrous. Four-day cricket is a must.'

Best batting: 243 Glamorgan v Hampshire, Southampton 1991

Best bowling: 3-21 Glamorgan v Oxford University, The Parks 1987

1991 Season

	M	Inns	NO	Runs	HS	Avge	100s	50s	Ct	St	O	M	Runs	Wkts	Avge	Best	5wI	10wM
Test																		
All First	23	36	6	1803	243	60.10	7	5	18	-	4.5	0	34	0	-	-	-	-
1-day Int																		
NatWest	3	3	2	256	151 *	256.00	1	1	-	-								
B&H	4	4	0	94	62	23.50	-	1	2	-								
Refuge	15	15	1	458	101	32.71	1	3	9	-	1	0	2	0	-	-	-	-

Career Performances

	M	Inns	NO	Runs	HS	Avge	100s	50s	Ct	St	Balls	Runs	Wkts	Avge	Best	5wI	10wM
Test	1	2	0	13	10	6.50	-	-	-	-							
All First	155	257	32	9250	243	41.11	19	53	130	-	726	491	4	122.75	3-21	-	-
1-day Int																	
NatWest	15	15	2	510	151 *	39.23	1	3	2	-							
B&H	24	24	3	840	115	40.00	2	4	4	-	24	32	0	-	-	-	-
Refuge	89	86	5	2099	101	25.91	2	12	23	-	12	25	0	-	-	-	-

138. Who captained the 1977 Australians in England?

McCAGUE, M. J.   Kent

Name: Martin John McCague
Role: Right-hand bat, right-arm fast-medium
bowler, slip/gully fielder
Born: 24 May 1969, Larne, Northern Ireland
Height: 6ft 4in **Weight:** 15st 6lbs
Nickname: Stinger, Oz
County debut: 1991
1st-Class 5 w. in innings : 2
1st-Class catches: 4
Place in batting averages: 204th av. 17.75
Place in bowling averages: 51st av. 30.06
Strike rate: 57.56 (career 54.67)
Parents: Mal and Mary
Marital status: Single
Education: Hedland Senior High School;
Carine Tafe College, Australia
Qualifications: Apprentice electrician
Career outside cricket: Electrician
Off-season: Playing in Australia
Overseas teams played for: Western Australia 1990-91
Cricketers particularly admired: Dennis Lillee, Rob Langer, Peter Carlstein
Other sports followed: Australian Rules football, basketball
Injuries: Stress fractures, shin and foot
Relaxations: Music, golf, jigsaw puzzles
Extras: Took 5-105 in his first-class debut for Western Australia v Victoria 1990-91. 'As
a British citizen and Australian resident Kent can have other overseas players as well as
myself.'
Opinions on cricket: 'More four-day cricket. Three-day games are probably more
interesting for the public, but I am sure they don't enjoy it when runs are tossed up in order
to make declarations. Better teams will win over four days.'
Best batting: 29 Kent v Leicestershire, Leicester 1991
Best bowling: 6-88 Kent v Leicestershire, Leicester 1991

1991 Season

	M	Inns	NO	Runs	HS	Avge	100s	50s	Ct	St	O	M	Runs	Wkts	Avge	Best	5wI	10wM
Test																		
All First	8	10	2	142	29	17.75	-	-	1	-	153.3	23	481	16	30.06	6-88	1	-
1-day Int																		
NatWest	1	1	0	9	9	9.00	-	-	-	-	7	0	47	0	-	-	-	-
B&H	2	1	0	12	12	12.00	-	-	-	-	18	2	85	4	21.25	2-32	-	
Refuge	8	5	2	39	17 *	13.00	-	-	1	-	59	0	349	11	31.72	4-51	-	

Career Performances

	M	Inns	NO	Runs	HS	Avge	100s	50s	Ct	St	Balls	Runs	Wkts	Avge	Best	5wI	10wM
Test																	
All First	12	15	4	170	29	15.45	-	-	4	-	1695	933	31	30.09	6-88	2	-
1-day Int																	
NatWest	1	1	0	9	9	9.00	-	-	-	-	42	47	0	-	-	-	
B&H	2	1	0	12	12	12.00	-	-	-	-	108	85	4	21.25	2-32	-	
Refuge	8	5	2	39	17 *	13.00	-	-	1	-	354	349	11	31.72	4-51	-	

McCRAY, E. Derbyshire

Name: Ewan McCray
Role: Right-hand bat, right-arm
off-spin bowler
Born: 29 October 1964, Altrincham, Cheshire
Height: 6ft 1in **Weight:** 14st 12lbs
Nickname: Mac
County debut: 1991
1st-Class catches: 1
Parents: Malcolm and Beryl
Marital status: Single
Education: Poundswick High School,
Manchester
Qualifications: 3 O-levels
Career outside cricket: Sales
Off-season: Playing cricket in New Zealand
Overseas teams played for:
Old Johannions, Johannesburg; Taita,
Wellington, New Zealand 1991-92

Cricketers particularly admired:
'Mohammad Azharuddin for being in his own words"just an average human being who happens to play cricket".'
Other sports followed: Rugby union, golf, lacrosse, squash 'and most other sports'
Injuries: Bruised heel 'due to excessive jogging during the winter!'
Relaxations: 'Playing golf and listening to jazz and soul music supplied by Frank Griffith.'
Opinions on cricket: 'In favour of coloured clothing in one-day cricket to make the game more appealing to spectators. This way we can get more people in the grounds and professional cricketers will hopefully get paid as much as other professional sports people!'
Best batting: 37 Derbyshire v Gloucestershire, Gloucester 1991

1991 Season

	M	Inns	NO	Runs	HS	Avge	100s	50s	Ct	St	O	M	Runs	Wkts	Avge	Best	5wl	10wM
Test																		
All First	2	2	0	68	37	34.00	-	-	1	-	42	16	87	0	-		-	-
1-day Int																		
NatWest																		
B&H																		
Refuge	4	4	0	22	18	5.50	-	-	-	-	32	0	166	8	20.75	4-49	-	

Career Performances

	M	Inns	NO	Runs	HS	Avge	100s	50s	Ct	St	Balls	Runs	Wkts	Avge	Best	5wl	10wM
Test																	
All First	2	2	0	68	37	34.00	-	-	1	-	252	87	0	-		-	-
1-day Int																	
NatWest																	
B&H																	
Refuge	4	4	0	22	18	5.50	-	-	-	-	192	166	8	20.75	4-49	-	

McDERMOTT, C. J.   Yorkshire

Name: Craig John McDermott
Role: Right-hand bat, right-arm fast-medium bowler
Born: 14 May 1965, Ipswich, Queensland, Australia
Test debut: 1984-85
Tests: 31
One-Day Internationals: 69
1st-Class 50s scored: 4
1st-Class 5 w. in innings: 24
1st-Class 10 w. in match: 2
1st-Class catches: 33
Strike rate: (career 50.90)
Overseas tours: Australia U19 to England 1983; Australia to England 1985; New Zealand 1985-86; India 1986-87; Pakistan 1988-89; West Indies 1990-91
Overseas teams played for: Queensland, Australia
Extras: First overseas player to be signed to play for Yorkshire
Best batting: 74 Queensland v Western Australia, Perth 1990-91
Best bowling: 8-44 Queensland v Tasmania, Brisbane 1989-90

Career Performances

	M	Inns	NO	Runs	HS	Avge	100s	50s	Ct	St	Balls	Runs	Wkts	Avge	Best	5wI	10wM
Test	31	43	4	424	42 *	10.87	-	-	8	-	6770	3659	122	29.99	8-97	6	1
All First	108	134	22	1882	74	16.80	-	4	33	-	21429	11513	421	27.34	8-44	24	2
1-day Int	69	47	11	329	37	9.13	-	-	17	-	3735	2738	102	26.84	5-44	1	
NatWest																	
B&H																	
Refuge																	

McEWAN, S. M.   Durham

Name: Steven Michael McEwan
Role: Right-hand bat, right-arm
fast-medium bowler
Born: 5 May 1962, Worcester
Height: 6ft 1in **Weight:** 13st 7lbs
Nickname: IG, Macca
County debut: 1985 (Worcestershire)
County cap: 1989 (Worcestershire)
50 wickets in a season: 1
1st-Class 50s scored: 1
1st-Class 5 w. in innings: 3
1st-Class catches: 17
Place in batting averages: (1990 207th
av. 23.42)
Place in bowling averages: (1990 36th
av. 31.28)
Strike rate: (career 55.06)
Parents: Michael James and Valerie
Jeanette
Wife and date of marriage: Debbie,
30 September 1989
Family links with cricket: Father and uncle played club cricket
Education: Worcester Royal Grammar School
Qualifications: 6 O-levels, 3 A-levels. Technician's certificate in building
Cricketers particularly admired: Richard Hadlee, Malcolm Marshall
Other sports followed: American football
Relaxations: Reading, golf, skittles, watching films
Extras: Took 10 wickets for 13 runs in an innings in 1983 for Worcester Nomads against Moreton-in-Marsh. Also broke school bowling record, 60 wickets, at Worcester RGS, 1982. Took hat-trick for Worcestershire v Leicestershire at Leicester, 1990. Released by Worcestershire at the end of the 1991 season and signed for Durham

Opinions on cricket: 'Second team games should be played on first-class grounds. It seems every year a new rule is introduced which is detrimental towards the bowler. It is probably only a matter of time before limited run-ups and the use of a tennis ball instead of a cricket ball.'

Best batting: 54 Worcestershire v Yorkshire, Worcester 1990
Best bowling: 6-34 Worcestershire v Leicestershire, Kidderminster 1989

1991 Season (no first team appearance)

Career Performances

	M	Inns	NO	Runs	HS	Avge	100s	50s	Ct	St	Balls	Runs	Wkts	Avge	Best	5wI	10wM
Test																	
All First	55	35	16	348	54	18.31	-	1	17	-	7654	4069	139	29.27	6-34	3	-
1-day Int																	
NatWest	2	1	0	6	6	6.00	-	-	-	-	84	66	3	22.00	3-51	-	
B&H	1	-	-	-	-	-	-	-	-	-	66	53	2	26.50	2-53	-	
Refuge	41	12	7	47	18 *	9.40	-	-	8	-	1420	1269	39	32.53	4-35	-	

MEDLYCOTT, K. T. Surrey

Name: Keith Thomas Medlycott
Role: Right-hand bat, slow left-arm bowler, slip fielder
Born: 12 May 1965, Whitechapel
Height: 5ft 11in **Weight:** 13st
Nickname: Medders
County debut: 1984
County cap: 1988
50 wickets in a season: 3
1st-Class 50s scored: 21
1st-Class 100s scored: 3
1st-Class 5 w. in innings: 18
1st-Class 10 w. in match: 6
1st-Class catches: 90
Place in batting averages: 157th av. 24.96 (1990 195th av. 25.62)
Place in bowling averages: 85th av. 34.75 (1990 90th av. 39.04)
Strike rate: 62.53 (career 63.03)
Parents: Thomas Alfred (deceased) and June Elizabeth
Marital status: Single
Family links with cricket: 'Father played club cricket for Colposa. Twin brother Paul

plays very occasionally.'

Education: Parmiters Grammar School; Wandsworth Comprehensive

Qualifications: 2 O-levels

Overseas tours: England to West Indies 1989-90; England A to Pakistan 1990-91

Overseas teams played for: Natal B 1988-89

Cricketers particularly admired: Tom Medlycott, David Ward – 'always plays with a smile.'

Other sports followed: Rugby, football

Relaxations: 'Sport in general.'

Extras: Scored 100 on debut (117* v Cambridge University) in 1984. Took first hat-trick of career against Hampshire 2nd XI, 1988. Capped in last game of season, against Kent. First bowler to take 50 wickets in 1990 season. Spent season on Lord's ground staff. Offered a contract by Northamptonshire in 1984. Directed to Surrey by Micky Stewart

Opinions on cricket: 'We should have four-day cricket. The TCCB should pay groundsmen instead of the clubs, and then sack the bad ones!'

Best batting: 153 Surrey v Kent, The Oval 1987

Best bowling: 8-52 Surrey v Sussex, Hove 1988

1991 Season

	M	Inns	NO	Runs	HS	Avge	100s	50s	Ct	St	O	M	Runs	Wkts	Avge	Best	5wl	10wM
Test																		
All First	19	27	2	624	109	24.96	1	4	6	-	510.4	115	1703	49	34.75	6-98	2	1
1-day Int																		
NatWest																		
B&H																		
Refuge	2	1	0	9	9	9.00	-	-	2	-								

Career Performances

	M	Inns	NO	Runs	HS	Avge	100s	50s	Ct	St	Balls	Runs	Wkts	Avge	Best	5wl	10wM
Test																	
All First	141	180	38	3684	153	25.94	3	21	90	-	22504	11517	357	32.26	8-52	18	6
1-day Int																	
NatWest	5	4	2	65	38	32.50	-	-	2	-	300	185	2	92.50	1-45	-	
B&H	6	3	0	14	11	4.66	-	-	2	-	291	235	7	33.57	3-48	-	
Refuge	43	29	7	300	44 *	13.63	-	-	11	-	1104	962	40	24.05	4-18	-	

139. For which Australian state does Yorkshire's Craig McDermott play?

MENDIS, G. D.   Lancashire

Name: Gehan Dixon Mendis
Role: Right-hand opening bat
Born: 24 April 1955, Colombo, Ceylon
Height: 5ft 8in **Weight:** 11st
Nickname: Mendo, Dix
County debut: 1974 (Sussex), 1986 (Lancs)
County cap: 1980 (Sussex), 1986 (Lancs)
1000 runs in a season: 12
1st-Class 50s scored: 101
1st-Class 100s scored: 40
1st-Class 200s scored: 3
1st-Class catches: 140
1st-Class stumpings: 1
One-Day 50s: 39
One-Day 100s: 8
Place in batting averages: 73rd av. 36.68
(1990 41st av. 53.48)
Parents: Sam Dixon Charles and Sonia
Marcelle (both deceased)
Children: Hayley, 11 December 1982; Josh, 26 November 1989
Education: St Thomas College, Mount Lavinia, Sri Lanka; Brighton, Hove & Sussex
Grammar School; Bede College, Durham University
Qualifications: BEd Mathematics, Durham; NCA coaching certificate
Cricketers particularly admired: Barry Richards, Richard Hadlee
Other sports followed: Formula One motor racing
Relaxations: Music, 'getting away from cricket.'
Extras: Turned down invitations to play for Sri Lanka in order to be free to be chosen for
England. Left Sussex at end of 1985 to join Lancashire. Played table tennis for Sussex at
junior level
Opinions on cricket: 'None, any more, as cricketers have not much say in the running of
the game. Sign of old age, I guess!'
Best batting: 209* Sussex v Somerset, Hove 1984
Best bowling: 1-65 Sussex v Yorkshire, Hove 1985

---

140. Who topped the first-class batting averages last season for
Middlesex?

141. Of which legendary fast bowler was it said that his knuckles
sometimes touched the pitch on his follow-through?

1991 Season

	M	Inns	NO	Runs	HS	Avge	100s	50s	Ct	St	O	M	Runs	Wkts	Avge	Best	5wI	10wM
Test																		
All First	23	43	5	1394	127 *	36.68	4	3	8	-								
1-day Int																		
NatWest	2	2	0	55	50	27.50	-	1	1	-								
B&H	7	7	1	366	125 *	61.00	1	2	4	-								
Refuge	14	14	0	344	79	24.57	-	1	3	-								

Career Performances

	M	Inns	NO	Runs	HS	Avge	100s	50s	Ct	St	Balls	Runs	Wkts	Avge	Best	5wl	10wM
Test																	
All First	343	601	60	20192	209 *	37.32	40	101	140	1	177	158	1	158.00	1-65	-	-
1-day Int																	
NatWest	40	40	4	1414	141 *	39.27	3	8	8	-							
B&H	68	68	3	1978	125 *	30.43	2	8	23	-							
Refuge	190	185	15	4679	125 *	27.52	3	23	50	-							

MERRICK, T. A.   Kent

Name: Tyrone Anthony Merrick
Role: Right-hand bat, right-arm
fast-medium bowler
Born: 10 June 1963, Antigua
Height: 6ft
County debut: 1987 (Warwicks),
1990 (Kent)
County cap: 1988 (Warwicks)
50 wickets in a season: 3
1st-Class 50s scored: 2
1st-Class 5 w. in innings: 15
1st-Class 10 w. in match: 2
1st-Class catches: 30
One-Day 50s: 1
Place in batting averages: 246th av. 12.00
(1990 271st av. 11.00)
Place in bowling averages: 44th av. 29.29
(1990 23rd av. 28.70)
Strike rate: 53.01 (career 47.61)
Children: Anthea, 6 January 1987
Education: All Saints Primary and Secondary Schools
Jobs outside cricket: Physical Education teacher

Overseas tours: West Indies YC to England 1982; West Indies B to Zimbabwe 1986
Overseas teams played for: Leeward Islands 1982-89
Cricketers particularly admired: Andy Roberts, Eldine Baptiste
Other sports followed: Soccer, lawn tennis
Relaxations: Listening to music
Extras: Played for Rawtenstall in Lancashire League 1985 and 1986. Released by Warwickshire at end of 1989 season. Released by Kent at the end of 1991 season
Best batting: 74* Warwickshire v Gloucestershire, Edgbaston 1987
Best bowling: 7-45 Warwickshire v Lancashire, Edgbaston 1987

1991 Season

	M	Inns	NO	Runs	HS	Avge	100s	50s	Ct	St	O	M	Runs	Wkts	Avge	Best	5wl	10wM
Test																		
All First	19	23	6	204	36	12.00	-	-	4	-	539	101	1787	61	29.29	7-99	1	-
1-day Int																		
NatWest	2	1	0	0	0	0.00	-	-	2	-	21	4	74	3	24.66	3-27	-	
B&H	5	3	2	26	22 *	26.00	-	-	1	-	50	2	207	6	34.50	2-31	-	
Refuge	12	6	4	23	13 *	11.50	-	-	-	-	89.2	3	463	6	77.16	1-16	-	

Career Performances

	M	Inns	NO	Runs	HS	Avge	100s	50s	Ct	St	Balls	Runs	Wkts	Avge	Best	5wl	10wM
Test																	
All First	88	111	23	1265	74 *	14.37	-	2	30	-	14807	7918	311	25.46	7-45	15	2
1-day Int																	
NatWest	4	3	0	15	13	5.00	-	-	2	-	252	113	6	18.83	3-27	-	
B&H	14	9	4	68	22 *	13.60	-	-	3	-	712	410	13	31.53	4-24	-	
Refuge	41	21	9	181	59	15.08	-	1	4	-	1820	1325	46	28.80	4-24	-	

142. For which county did Chris Lewis play last season?

METCALFE, A. A. *Yorkshire*

Name: Ashley Anthony Metcalfe
Role: Right-hand opening bat, off-break
bowler, county vice-captain
Born: 25 December 1963, Horsforth, Leeds
Height: 5ft 9¹/₂in **Weight:** 11st 7lbs
County debut: 1983
County cap: 1986
1000 runs in a season: 6
1st-Class 50s scored: 46
1st-Class 100s scored: 23
1st-Class 200s scored: 1
1st-Class catches: 62
One-Day 50s: 32
One-Day 100s: 4
Place in batting averages: 119th av. 29.51
(1990 46th av. 51.17)
Parents: Tony and Ann
Wife and date of marriage: Diane,
20 April 1986

Children: Zoe, 18 July 1990
Family links with cricket: Father played in local league; father-in-law Ray Illingworth
(Yorkshire and England)
Education: Ladderbanks Middle School; Bradford Grammar School; University College,
London
Qualifications: 9 O-levels, 3 A-levels, NCA coaching certificate
Career outside cricket: 'Metcalfe & Sidebottom Associates – Sports Promotion
Company.'
Off-season: 'Working for Yorkshire CCC on the commercial side, chasing sponsorship
and advertising.'
Overseas teams played for: Orange Free State 1988-89
Cricketers particularly admired: Barry Richards, Doug Padgett, Don Wilson, Arnie
Sidebottom, Pete Hartley, Paul Jarvis
Other sports followed: Most, particularly golf
Relaxations: 'Relaxing at home with my family.'
Extras: Made 122 on debut v Nottinghamshire at Park Avenue in 1983, the youngest ever
Yorkshire player to do so and it was the highest ever score by a Yorkshireman on debut.
Reached 2000 runs for the season in the last match of the 1990 season with 194* and 107
v Nottinghamshire at Trent Bridge
Opinions on cricket: 'Nice to see South Africa return to the international scene.'
Best batting: 216* Yorkshire v Middlesex, Headingley 1988
Best bowling: 2-18 Yorkshire v Warwickshire, Scarborough 1987

1991 Season

	M	Inns	NO	Runs	HS	Avge	100s	50s	Ct	St	O	M	Runs	Wkts	Avge	Best	5wI	10wM
Test																		
All First	24	43	2	1210	123	29.51	2	6	12	-	3	0	23	0	-	-	-	-
1-day Int																		
NatWest	1	1	0	8	8	8.00	-	-	-	-								
B&H	6	6	1	350	114	70.00	1	2	1	-								
Refuge	16	16	0	540	116	33.75	1	2	3	-								

Career Performances

	M	Inns	NO	Runs	HS	Avge	100s	50s	Ct	St	Balls	Runs	Wkts	Avge	Best	5wI	10wM
Test																	
All First	165	288	17	9683	216 *	35.73	23	46	62	-	392	316	4	79.00	2-18	-	-
1-day Int																	
NatWest	16	16	3	592	127 *	45.53	1	4	3	-	42	44	2	22.00	2-44	-	
B&H	27	27	4	1198	114	52.08	1	8	7	-							
Refuge	109	108	2	2944	116	27.77	2	20	27	-							

METSON, C. P. — Glamorgan

Name: Colin Peter Metson
Role: Right-hand bat, wicket-keeper
Born: 2 July 1963, Cuffley, Herts
Height: 5ft 5in **Weight:** 10st 7lbs
Nickname: Meto, Dempster
County debut: 1981 (Middlesex), 1987 (Glamorgan)
County cap: 1987 (Glamorgan)
1st-Class 50s scored: 6
1st-Class catches: 338
1st-Class stumpings: 25
Place in batting averages: 168th av. 23.60 (1990 246th av. 16.00)
Parents: Denis Alwyn and Jean Mary
Wife and date of marriage: Stephanie Leslie Astrid, 13 October 1991
Family links with cricket: Father played club cricket. Brother plays for Winchmore Hill CC
Education: Stanborough School, Welwyn Garden City; Enfield Grammar School; Durham University
Qualifications: 10 O-levels, 5 A-levels,

BA (Hons) Economic History, advanced cricket coach
Career outside cricket: Setting up cricket coaching clinics in Adelaide and involved in corporate hospitality
Off-season: 'Getting married, having a honeymoon, living in Cardiff, walking Smudge.'
Overseas teams played for: Payneham, Adelaide 1986-88; Rostrevor Old Boys, Adelaide 1988-91
Cricketers particularly admired: Bob Taylor, Mike Brearley, Viv Richards
Other sports followed: Football, American football, golf
Relaxations: 'Daily Telegraph crossword, taking Steph out for a good meal, drinking good wine.'
Extras: Young Wicket-keeper of the Year 1981. Played for England YC v India 1981. Captain Durham University 1984, losing finalists in UAU competition. Left Middlesex at end of 1986 season. Holds the Glamorgan record for most catches in an innings (7)
Opinions on cricket: 'Cricket should market itself better. Introduce four-day cricket. Give players time to practice. Look to play floodlit cricket. Clubs should help players staying at home to find work.'
Best batting: 96 Middlesex v Gloucestershire, Uxbridge 1984

1991 Season

	M	Inns	NO	Runs	HS	Avge	100s	50s	Ct	St	O	M	Runs	Wkts	Avge	Best	5wl	10wM
Test																		
All First	24	26	3	543	84	23.60	-	2	73	3								
1-day Int																		
NatWest	3	1	0	9	9	9.00	-	-	3	-								
B&H	1	1	0	0	0	0.00	-	-	-	-								
Refuge	15	10	4	97	20	16.16	-	-	12	2								

Career Performances

	M	Inns	NO	Runs	HS	Avge	100s	50s	Ct	St	Balls	Runs	Wkts	Avge	Best	5wl	10wM
Test																	
All First	143	184	40	2564	96	17.80	-	6	338	25							
1-day Int																	
NatWest	13	6	1	28	9	5.60	-	-	11	-							
B&H	20	13	1	124	23	10.33	-	-	10	2							
Refuge	87	56	28	451	30*	16.10	-	-	77	21							

143. Who took 8 for 53 against Essex on his 20th birthday last season?

MIDDLETON, T. C. Hampshire

Name: Tony Charles Middleton
Role: Right-hand bat, slow left-arm bowler
Born: 1 February 1964, Winchester
Height: 5ft 11in **Weight:** 11st
Nickname: Roo, Midders, TC
County debut: 1984
County cap: 1990
1000 runs in a season: 1
1st-Class 50s scored: 11
1st-Class 100s scored: 11
1st-Class catches: 40
One-Day 50s: 5
Place in batting averages: 117th av. 29.79
(1990 62nd av. 47.61)
Parents: Peter and Molly
Wife and date of marriage: Sherralyn,
23 September 1989
Family links with cricket: Brother plays
local club cricket in Hampshire
Education: Weeke Infants and Junior Schools; Montgomery of Alamein Comprehensive;
Peter Symonds Sixth Form College, Winchester
Qualifications: 1 A-level, 5 O-levels
Cricketers particularly admired: Barry Richards, Gordon Greenidge
Other sports followed: Football, rugby union, badminton, squash
Relaxations: Watching and playing other sports, gardening, real ale pubs
Extras: Played for England Schools 1982. Scored six consecutive 100s for Hampshire in
May 1990: 104 & 144 v Somerset II; 121 v Yorkshire II; 100 & 124 v Leics II; 104* for
1st XI v Essex. Scored 78 in NatWest final 1991, his first appearance in the competition
Opinions on cricket: 'Four-day matches in the County Championship would produce
better Test players and, played on good wickets, it would provide more interesting cricket
for spectators. Unfortunately it would reduce vital income for clubs. Perhaps a better
compromise could be reached in the future.'
Best batting: 127 Hampshire v Kent, Canterbury 1990
Best bowling: 2-41 Hampshire v Kent, Canterbury 1991

144. Who topped the first-class batting averages last season
for Nottinghamshire?

1991 Season

	M	Inns	NO	Runs	HS	Avge	100s	50s	Ct	St	O	M	Runs	Wkts	Avge	Best	5wI	10wM
Test																		
All First	18	31	2	864	102	29.79	1	3	15	-	12	2	77	3	25.66	2-41	-	-
1-day Int																		
NatWest	1	1	0	78	78	78.00	-	1	-	-								
B&H	4	4	0	156	60	39.00	-	2	3	-								
Refuge	6	6	0	162	56	27.00	-	1	-	-								

Career Performances

	M	Inns	NO	Runs	HS	Avge	100s	50s	Ct	St	Balls	Runs	Wkts	Avge	Best	5wI	10wM
Test																	
All First	54	90	9	2742	127	33.85	6	11	40	-	174	180	5	36.00	2-41	-	-
1-day Int																	
NatWest	1	1	0	78	78	78.00	-	1	-	-							
B&H	4	4	0	156	60	39.00	-	2	3	-							
Refuge	9	8	1	238	72	34.00	-	2	2	-							

MILBURN, E. T.   Gloucestershire

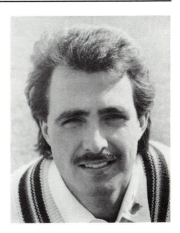

Name: Edward Thomas Milburn
Role: Right-hand bat, right-arm medium-fast bowler
Born: 15 September 1967, Nuneaton
Height: 6ft 1in **Weight:** 12st
Nickname: Ed
County debut: 1987 (Warwicks), 1990 (Gloucs)
1st-Class catches: 2
Family links with cricket: 'My father has always loved the game.'
Education: Bablake School, Coventry; King Edward VI College, Nuneaton
Qualifications: 1 A-level, 8 O-levels
Cricketers particularly admired: Richard Hadlee
Other sports followed: Golf, squash
Relaxations: Reading science fiction novels
Extras: Released by Warwickshire at end of 1988 season. Taken on to Gloucestershire staff in 1990 after playing for Leicestershire and Gloucestershire 2nd XIs in 1989. Released by Gloucestershire at the end of 1991 season

Best batting: 35 Gloucestershire v Indians, Bristol 1990
Best bowling: 3-43 Gloucestershire v Indians, Bristol 1990

1991 Season

	M	Inns	NO	Runs	HS	Avge	100s	50s	Ct	St	O	M	Runs	Wkts	Avge	Best	5wI	10wM
Test																		
All First	1	0	0	0	0	-	-	-	-	-	7	1	29	0	-	-	-	-
1-day Int																		
NatWest																		
B&H																		
Refuge	3	3	0	34	21	11.33	-	-	1	-								

Career Performances

	M	Inns	NO	Runs	HS	Avge	100s	50s	Ct	St	Balls	Runs	Wkts	Avge	Best	5wI	10wM
Test																	
All First	6	8	4	86	35	21.50	-	-	2	-	453	307	5	61.40	3-43	-	-
1-day Int																	
NatWest																	
B&H	1	0	0	0	0	-	-	-	-	-	30	23	1	23.00	1-23	-	
Refuge	9	5	2	43	21	14.33	-	-	2	-	144	163	3	54.33	2-34	-	

MILLNS, D. J. Leicestershire

Name: David James Millns
Role: Left-hand bat, right-arm fast medium bowler, slip fielder
Born: 27 February 1965, Mansfield
Height: 6ft 3in **Weight:** 14st 7lbs
Nickname: Bert, KK, Rocket Man
County debut: 1988 (Notts), 1990 (Leics)
County cap: 1991
50 wickets in a season: 1
1st-Class 5 w. in innings: 5
1st-Class 10 w. in match: 1
1st-Class catches: 18
Place in batting averages: 198th av. 19.12
Place in bowling averages: 56th av. 31.06 (1990 3rd av. 21.35)
Strike rate: 52.39 (career 52.25)
Parents: Bernard and Brenda
Marital status: Single
Family links with cricket: Nottinghamshire's

Andy Pick is brother-in-law. Great Uncle Richard played against the Australians for Saskatoon University, Canada in 1932 and bowled Don Bradman. Grandfather had ten brothers who all played in the same chapel team. Father played in club cricket and Notts Over 50s. Brother Paul plays for Clipstone WCC

Education: Samuel Barlow Junior; Garibaldi Comprehensive

Qualifications: 9 CSEs; qualified coach

Career outside cricket: Worked for British Coal for three years as linesman on survey staff

Off-season: 'Resting, buying a house and improving my golf.'

Overseas teams played for: Uitenhage, Port Elizabeth, South Africa 1988-89; Birkenhead, Auckland 1989-91

Cricketers particularly admired: Ian Botham, Clive Rice

Other sports followed: Football, American football, Formula One motor racing, golf, rugby (Leicester Tigers)

Injuries: Colour blindness – 'only saw one green one all season'

Relaxations: Walking brother's dog in Sherwood Forest, eating out, cinema, 'trying to beat James "Faldo" Whitaker and Phil "Woosnam" Whitticase at golf

Extras: Asked to be released by Nottinghamshire at the end of 1989 season and joined Leicestershire in 1990. Finished third in national bowling averages in 1990. Britannic Assurance Player of the Month in August 1991 after taking 9-37 against Derbyshire, the best Leicestershire figures since George Geary's 10-18 against Glamorgan in 1929

Opinions on cricket: 'Would like to see a greater input from players on how the current game should be structured. It is time over rates were sorted out. 18.5 overs per hour is too many, 17 would be a lot more practical. Fining the players is not the answer.'

Best batting: 44 Leicestershire v Middlesex, Uxbridge 1991

Best bowling: 9-37 Leicestershire v Derbyshire, Derby 1991

1991 Season

	M	Inns	NO	Runs	HS	Avge	100s	50s	Ct	St	O	M	Runs	Wkts	Avge	Best	5wI	10wM
Test																		
All First	20	24	8	306	44	19.12	-	-	9	-	550.1	95	1957	63	31.06	9-37	3	1
1-day Int																		
NatWest	2	0	0	0	0	-	-	-	-	-	21	4	87	2	43.50	2-27	-	
B&H	3	1	1	11	11 *	-	-	-	1	-	23	3	101	1	101.00	1-25	-	
Refuge	12	6	2	59	20 *	14.75	-	-	4	-	77	2	352	8	44.00	2-20	-	

Career Performances

	M	Inns	NO	Runs	HS	Avge	100s	50s	Ct	St	Balls	Runs	Wkts	Avge	Best	5wI	10wM
Test																	
All First	44	49	19	365	44	12.16	-	-	18	-	6323	3701	121	30.58	9-37	5	1
1-day Int																	
NatWest	2	0	0	0	0	-	-	-	-	-	126	87	2	43.50	2-27	-	
B&H	3	1	1	11	11 *	-	-	-	1	-	138	101	1	101.00	1-25	-	
Refuge	22	9	4	59	20 *	11.80	-	-	6	-	810	718	17	42.23	2-20	-	

MOLES, A. J.
Warwickshire

Name: Andrew James Moles
Role: Right-hand opening bat, right-arm medium bowler
Born: 12 February 1961, Solihull
Height: 5ft 10in **Weight:** 'Above average'
Nickname: Moler
County debut: 1986
County cap: 1987
1000 runs in a season: 4
1st-Class 50s scored: 49
1st-Class 100s scored: 21
1st-Class 200s scored: 3
1st-Class catches: 98
One-Day 50s: 19
One-Day 100s: 1
Place in batting averages: 90th av. 33.67
(1990 56th av. 48.78)
Parents: Stuart Francis and Gillian Margaret
Wife and date of marriage: Jacquie, 17 December 1988
Children: Daniel
Family links with cricket: Brother plays club cricket
Education: Finham Park Comprehensive, Coventry; Henley College of Further Education; Butts College of Further Education
Qualifications: 3 O-levels, 4 CSEs, Toolmaker/Standard Room Inspector City & Guilds
Career outside cricket: Host, and sell corporate hospitality
Overseas teams played for: Griqualand West, South Africa 1986-88
Cricketers particularly admired: Dennis Amiss, Fred Gardner, Tom Moody
Other sports followed: Football, golf
Relaxations: Playing golf and spending time with family
Opinions on cricket: 'We should play 17 four-day matches.'
Best batting: 230* Griqualand West v Northern Transvaal B, Verwoerdburg 1988-89
Best bowling: 3-21 Warwickshire v Oxford University, The Parks 1987

1991 Season

	M	Inns	NO	Runs	HS	Avge	100s	50s	Ct	St	O	M	Runs	Wkts	Avge	Best	5wI	10wM
Test																		
All First	22	39	2	1246	133	33.67	1	10	10	-	33	13	65	1	65.00	1-14	-	-
1-day Int																		
NatWest	4	4	1	109	62 *	36.33	-	1	1	-								
B&H	5	5	0	166	65	33.20	-	2	4	-	4	1	19	1	19.00	1-19	-	
Refuge	13	12	1	385	93 *	35.00	-	3	6	-	4	0	24	0	-	-	-	

Career Performances

	M	Inns	NO	Runs	HS	Avge	100s	50s	Ct	St	Balls	Runs	Wkts	Avge	Best	5wI	10wM
Test																	
All First	140	253	27	9364	230 *	41.43	21	49	98	-	2988	1582	34	46.52	3-21	-	-
1-day Int																	
NatWest	17	17	1	506	127	31.62	1	3	4	-	90	81	0	-	-	-	
B&H	20	19	0	594	72	31.26	-	7	5	-	210	170	3	56.66	1-11	-	
Refuge	53	49	3	1242	93 *	27.00	-	9	15	-	402	382	7	54.57	2-24	-	

MONTGOMERIE, R. R.   Northamptonshire

Name: Richard Robert Montgomerie
Role: Right-hand opening bat, right-arm off-break bowler
Born: 3 July 1971, Rugby
Height: 5ft 10½in **Weight:** 12 st
County debut: 1991
1st-Class 50s scored: 4
1st-Class catches: 9
Place in batting averages: 133rd av. 28.09
Parents: Robert and Gillian
Marital status: Single
Family links with cricket: Father captained Oxfordshire
Education: Rugby School; Worcester College, Oxford University
Qualifications: 12 O-levels, 4 A-levels
Off-season: 'Doing a lot of chemistry!'
Overseas tours: Oxford University to Namibia 199
Cricketers particularly admired: Mick Norman, David Gower, Allan Lamb, Allan Border, Graham Gooch 'and many others'
Other sports followed: All sports, particularly hockey, rackets and real tennis
Relaxations: Playing sports – hockey, rackets, real tennis, squash, tennis etc
Extras: Scored 50s (both not out) in both innings of 1991 Varsity match. Oxford rackets blue 1990
Opinions on cricket: 'I think the introduction of the one bouncer per over per batsman rule is an odd decision. There is too much cricket during the county season. Inevitably players will not perform to the high standards that should be expected of them if they play nearly every day for 4½ months.'
Best batting: 88 Oxford University v Hampshire, The Parks 1991

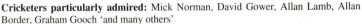

1991 Season

	M	Inns	NO	Runs	HS	Avge	100s	50s	Ct	St	O	M	Runs	Wkts	Avge	Best	5wI	10wM
Test																		
All First	9	13	2	309	88	28.09	-	4	9	-								
1-day Int																		
NatWest																		
B&H																		
Refuge																		

Career Performances

	M	Inns	NO	Runs	HS	Avge	100s	50s	Ct	St	Balls	Runs	Wkts	Avge	Best	5wI	10wM
Test																	
All First	9	13	2	309	88	28.09	-	4	9	-							
1-day Int																	
NatWest																	
B&H																	
Refuge																	

MOODY, T. M.   Worcestershire

Name: Thomas Masson Moody
Role: Right-hand bat, right-arm medium bowler
Born: 2 October 1965, Adelaide
Height: 6ft 6in
County debut: 1990 (Warwicks) 1991 (Worcestershire)
County cap: 1990 (Warwicks) 1991 (Worcestershire)
Test debut: 1989-90
Tests: 4
One-Day Internationals: 13
1000 runs in a season: 2
1st-Class 50s scored: 32
1st-Class 100s scored: 24
1st-Class 200s scored: 2
1st-Class 5 w. in innings: 1
1st-Class 10 w. in match: 1
1st-Class catches: 75
One-Day 50s: 15
Place in batting averages: 9th av. 62.90 (1990 3rd av. 89.46)
Off-season: Playing cricket in Australia

Overseas tours: Australia to England 1989
Overseas teams played for: Western Australia 1985-91
Extras: Scored 150s in both innings of 1988-89 Sheffield Shield Final for Western Australia v Queensland; hit a century against Warwickshire during Australia's 1989 tour – signed on a one-year contract for 1990. Hit centuries in first three first-class matches for Warwickshire, and seven in first eight matches – a unique achievement. Scored the fastest ever first-class century v Glamorgan in 26 minutes – taking advantage of deliberate declaration bowling. Reached 1000 first-class runs in first season of county cricket in only 12 innings – another record. Released by Warwickshire at the end of the 1990 season after they had chosen Allan Donald as their one overseas player. Signed by Worcestershire for 1991 when Graeme Hick was no longer considered an overseas player
Best batting: 210 Worcestershire v Warwickshire, Worcester 1991
Best bowling: 7-43 Western Australia v Victoria, Perth 1990-91

1991 Season

	M	Inns	NO	Runs	HS	Avge	100s	50s	Ct	St	O	M	Runs	Wkts	Avge	Best	5wl	10wM
Test																		
All First	22	34	4	1887	210	62.90	6	9	36	-	26.4	11	47	1	47.00	1-19	-	-
1-day Int																		
NatWest	2	2	1	79	42 *	79.00	-	-	1	-								
B&H	7	7	2	382	110 *	76.40	2	2	2	-	6	0	22	2	11.00	2-22	-	
Refuge	17	16	2	926	160	66.14	4	5	3	-	5	0	38	1	38.00	1-38	-	

Career Performances

	M	Inns	NO	Runs	HS	Avge	100s	50s	Ct	St	Balls	Runs	Wkts	Avge	Best	5wl	10wM
Test	4	6	0	234	106	39.00	1	1	3	-	234	53	1	53.00	1-23	-	-
All First	109	179	15	7822	210	47.69	24	32	75	-	4085	1761	51	34.52	7-43	1	1
1-day Int	13	13	2	281	89	25.54	-	2	3	-	102	81	1	81.00	1-21	-	
NatWest	4	4	1	188	58	62.66	-	2	3	-	61	41	1	41.00	1-7	-	
B&H	10	10	2	472	110 *	59.00	2	2	2	-	186	174	2	87.00	2-22	-	
Refuge	32	30	3	1308	160	48.44	4	9	8	-	363	353	7	50.42	2-42	-	

145. Which batsman has hit the most runs in a 5-match Test series?

MOORES, P.   Sussex

Name: Peter Moores
Role: Right-hand bat, wicket-keeper
Born: 18 December 1962, Macclesfield,
Cheshire
Height: 5ft 11¾in **Weight:** 13st
Nickname: Billy
County debut: 1983 (Worcs), 1985 (Sussex)
County cap: 1989
1st-Class 50s scored: 14
1st-Class 100s scored: 3
1st-Class catches: 238
1st-Class stumpings: 27
One-Day 50s: 1
Place in batting averages: 129th av. 28.56
(1990 214th av. 21.68)
Parents: Bernard and Winifred
Wife and date of marriage: Karen,
28 September 1989

Children: Karen Jane, 28 September 1989
Family links with cricket: Three brothers, Anthony, Stephen and Robert, all play club cricket
Education: King Edward VI School, Macclesfield
Qualifications: 7 O-levels, 3 A-levels. Advanced cricket coach
Career outside cricket: 'Spent two winters working for Britannia Building Society as an assistant research analyst.'
Off-season: Working for Sussex CCC
Overseas tours: Christians in Sport to India 1990; MCC to Namibia 1991; Leeward Islands 1992
Overseas teams played for: Orange Free State, South Africa 1988-89
Cricketers particularly admired: Bob Taylor, Alan Knott, Clive Lloyd
Other sports followed: Football, golf
Relaxations: Photography, golf, music and real ale
Extras: On the MCC ground staff in 1982 before joining Worcestershire in latter half of 1982 season. Joined Sussex in 1985
Opinions on cricket: 'The B&H should be spread over more of the season so more Championship cricket can be played early on. I am in favour of four-day cricket as it would give players a rest day each week and allow for more genuine results. This would only raise the quality of cricket played.'
Best batting: 116 Sussex v Somerset, Hove 1989

1991 Season

	M	Inns	NO	Runs	HS	Avge	100s	50s	Ct	St	O	M	Runs	Wkts	Avge	Best	5wI	10wM
Test																		
All First	23	28	3	714	102	28.56	1	6	56	6								
1-day Int																		
NatWest	2	2	0	30	26	15.00	-	-	2	-								
B&H	4	3	0	31	20	10.33	-	-	6	-								
Refuge	14	12	2	153	34	15.30	-	-	15	1								

Career Performances

	M	Inns	NO	Runs	HS	Avge	100s	50s	Ct	St	Balls	Runs	Wkts	Avge	Best	5wI	10wM
Test																	
All First	115	158	20	3082	116	22.33	3	14	238	27	12	16	0	-	-	-	-
1-day Int																	
NatWest	11	7	1	78	26	13.00	-	-	10	2							
B&H	13	9	1	165	76	20.62	-	1	13	2							
Refuge	73	49	17	397	34	12.40	-	-	65	17							

MORRIS, H.   Glamorgan

Name: Hugh Morris
Role: Left-hand bat, right-arm medium
bowler, slip fielder
Born: 5 October 1963, Cardiff
Height: 5ft 8in **Weight:** 12st 10lbs
Nickname: Banners, Banacek, H
County debut: 1981
County cap: 1986
Test debut: 1991
Tests: 3
1000 runs in a season: 5
1st-Class 50s scored: 53
1st-Class 100s scored: 24
1st-Class catches: 104
One-Day 50s: 21
One-Day 100s: 6
Place in batting averages: 22nd av. 53.02
(1990 34th av. 55.51)
Parents: Roger and Anne
Marital status: Single
Family links with cricket: Brother played for Glamorgan U19 and currently plays local
league cricket. Father played local club cricket

Education: Blundell's School; South Glamorgan Institute of HE
Qualifications: 9 O-levels, 3 A-levels, 1 AO-level, BA (Hons) in Physical Education, NCA coaching award
Career outside cricket: Journalism; Sales and Marketing
Off-season: Resting before touring with England A
Overseas tours: English Public Schoolboys to West Indies 1980-81; to Sri Lanka 1982-83; England A to Pakistan 1990-91; (called up to join England tour party in Australia); England A to Bermuda and West Indies 1991-92
Overseas teams played for: CBC Old Boys, Pretoria 1985-87
Cricketers particularly admired: Viv Richards, Ian Botham, Jimmy Cook
Other sports followed: Rugby, golf
Injuries: 'Fortunately I had an injury-free season.'
Relaxations: Music, watching movies, travelling and holiday at end of the season
Extras: Highest schoolboy cricket average in 1979 (89.71), 1981 (184.6) and 1982 (149.2). Captain of England U19 Schoolboys in 1981 and 1982. Played for England YC v West Indies 1982, and captain v Australia 1983. Played first-class rugby for Aberavon 1984-85 and South Glamorgan Institute, scoring over 150 points. Appointed youngest ever Glamorgan captain 1986, but resigned in 1989 to concentrate on batting. In 1990 scored most runs in a season by a Glamorgan player (2276) and hit most 100s (10). After missing selection for the tour of Australia, appointed captain for England A's tour of Pakistan; then, after Gooch had required a hand operation and England had lost the First Test to Australia, he flew out to join the senior tour until the England captain recovered
Best batting: 160* Glamorgan v Derbyshire, Cardiff 1990
Best bowling: 1-6 Glamorgan v Oxford University, The Parks 1987

1991 Season

	M	Inns	NO	Runs	HS	Avge	100s	50s	Ct	St	O	M	Runs	Wkts	Avge	Best	5wI	10wM
Test	3	6	0	115	44	19.16	-	-	3	-								
All First	23	41	7	1803	156 *	53.02	5	8	17	-								
1-day Int																		
NatWest	3	3	1	203	126 *	101.50	1	-	1	-								
B&H	4	4	0	43	36	10.75	-	-	-	-								
Refuge	13	13	0	433	75	33.30	-	3	6	-								

Career Performances

	M	Inns	NO	Runs	HS	Avge	100s	50s	Ct	St	Balls	Runs	Wkts	Avge	Best	5wI	10wM
Test	3	6	0	115	44	19.16	-	-	3	-							
All First	189	321	35	10539	160 *	36.85	24	53	104	-	319	323	2	161.50	1-6	-	-
1-day Int																	
NatWest	17	17	3	887	154 *	63.35	3	3	9	-							
B&H	27	27	2	685	143 *	27.40	3	2	11	-	12	14	1	14.00	1-14	-	
Refuge	99	97	8	2582	100	29.01	1	16	34	-							

MORRIS, J. E.   Derbyshire

Name: John Edward Morris
Role: Right-hand bat, right-arm medium
bowler, county vice-captain
Born: 1 April 1964, Crewe
Height: 5ft 10¹/₂in **Weight:** 13st 6lbs
Nickname: Animal
County debut: 1982
County cap: 1986
Test debut: 1990
Tests: 3
One-Day Internationals: 8
1000 runs in a season: 6
1st-Class 50s scored: 54
1st-Class 100s scored: 26
One-Day 50s: 18
One-Day 100s: 5
Place in batting averages: 52nd av. 41.11

(1990 38th av. 54.03)
1st-Class catches: 86
Parents: George (Eddie) and Jean
Wife and date of marriage: Sally, 30 September 1990
Family links with cricket: Father played for Crewe for many years as an opening bowler
Education: Shavington Comprehensive School; Dane Bank College of Further Education
Qualifications: O-levels
Career outside cricket: BMW car sales and promotion
Overseas tours: England to Australia 1990-91
Overseas teams played for: Griqualand West, South Africa 1988-89
Other sports followed: Athletics, motor racing, football, snooker
Relaxations: Movies, music, good food, fly-fishing
Extras: Youngest player to score a Sunday League 100
Best batting: 191 Derbyshire v Kent, Derby 1986
Best bowling: 1-13 Derbyshire v Yorkshire, Harrogate 1987

1991 Season

	M	Inns	NO	Runs	HS	Avge	100s	50s	Ct	St	O	M	Runs	Wkts	Avge	Best	5wI	10wM
Test																		
All First	21	36	2	1398	131	41.11	2	8	8	-	2	0	30	0	-	-	-	-
1-day Int																		
NatWest																		
B&H	4	4	0	89	71	22.25	-	1	1	-	4	0	14	0	-	-	-	-
Refuge	11	11	0	277	51	25.18	-	1	2	-	0.3	0	7	0	-	-	-	-

Career Performances

	M	Inns	NO	Runs	HS	Avge	100s	50s	Ct	St	Balls	Runs	Wkts	Avge	Best	5wI	10wM
Test	3	5	2	71	32	23.66	-	-	3	-							
All First	195	326	26	11448	191	38.16	26	54	86	-	723	740	4	185.00	1-13	-	-
1-day Int	8	8	1	167	63 *	23.85	-	1	2	-							
NatWest	16	15	3	350	94 *	29.16	-	2	5	-							
B&H	35	31	3	694	123	24.78	1	3	8	-	24	14	0	-		-	-
Refuge	120	114	8	2965	134	27.97	4	12	22	-	3	7	0	-		-	-

MORTENSEN, O. H   Derbyshire

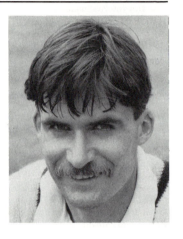

Name: Ole Henrik Mortensen
Role: Right-hand bat, right-arm
fast-medium bowler
Born: 29 January 1958, Vejle, Denmark
Height: 6ft 4in **Weight:** 14st 2lbs
Nickname: Stan, Blood-axe, The Great Dane
County debut: 1983
County cap: 1986
50 wickets in a season: 3
1st-Class 50s scored: 1
1st-Class 5 w. in innings: 15
1st-Class 10 w. in match: 1
1st-Class catches: 40
Place in bowling averages: 16th av. 23.86
(1990 5th av. 22.42)
Strike rate: 57.84 (career 52.01)
Parents: Willy and Inge
Wife: Jette Jepmond
Children: Julie Jepmond, 30 August
1982 and Emilia
Family links with cricket: 'My brother, Michael, is a very talented cricketer but gave the game up to concentrate on tennis, he has played in the Davis Cup for Denmark.'
Education: Brondbyoster School; Avedore College of Higher Education, Copenhagen
Career outside cricket: Working for Australian sports camps in Melbourne and for the Victoria Cricket Association
Off-season: 'Back in Melbourne for my seventh season with Brighton CC, a record in the league. Brighton care the second oldest club in Australia and celebrate their 150th anniversary in 1992-93.'
Overseas tours: Denmark to East Africa, England, Scotland, Wales, Ireland and Holland
Overseas clubs played for: Ellerslie, Auckland 1983-84; Brighton, Melbourne 1984-1992

Cricketers particularly admired: 'Anyone who is successful at first-class and Test level over a number of years.'

Other sports played: Tennis, golf, football, Australian Rules football

Injuries: Hamstring – 'as they say "no pain, no gain"! Keep going!'

Relaxations: Collecting stamps (only Danish) and coins, reading books about wine, sleeping in in the morning, reading newspapers

Extras: *Derbyshire's Dane* by Peter Hargreaves, published 1984. Played for Denmark in the ICC Trophy. Most economical bowler in Refuge League 1990. Played for Rest of the World XI v Australian XI in Melbourne 1990 (organised by Lord's Taverners of Australia). The only Dane at present playing first-class cricket in England. Plays as honorary Englishman under EEC regulations, i.e. not classified as overseas player

Opinions on cricket: 'I am worried about the greenhouse effect on the greatest team game in the world. Where will the moisture come from if it is never going to rain again in the cricket season. With more water shortage players may be asked not to take a shower after the day's play. Bring back Gene Kelly and " I'm playing in the rain"! Four-day cricket should be played at the beginning of the season. A minimum 100 overs per day is plenty.'

Best batting: 74* Derbyshire v Yorkshire, Chesterfield 1987

Best bowling: 6-27 Derbyshire v Yorkshire, Sheffield 1983

1991 Season

	M	Inns	NO	Runs	HS	Avge	100s	50s	Ct	St	O	M	Runs	Wkts	Avge	Best	5wI	10wM
Test																		
All First	19	17	9	32	8	4.00	-	-	5	-	559.1	143	1384	58	23.86	6-101	2	-
1-day Int																		
NatWest																		
B&H	4	2	1	6	4 *	6.00	-	-	-	-	40	10	115	6	19.16	2-16	-	
Refuge	10	5	5	13	7 *	-	-	-	3	-	80	7	317	12	26.41	3-29	-	

Career Performances

	M	Inns	NO	Runs	HS	Avge	100s	50s	Ct	St	Balls	Runs	Wkts	Avge	Best	5wI	10wM
Test																	
All First	130	146	79	592	74 *	8.83	-	1	40	-	20183	8878	388	22.88	6-27	15	1
1-day Int																	
NatWest	13	10	6	24	11	6.00	-	-	6	-	882	390	26	15.00	6-14	2	
B&H	31	9	5	14	4 *	3.50	-	-	2	-	1850	912	43	21.20	3-17	-	
Refuge	113	42	31	80	11	7.27	-	-	14	-	4983	3008	112	26.85	4-10	-	

MOXON, M. D.   Yorkshire

Name: Martyn Douglas Moxon
Role: Right-hand bat, right-arm medium
bowler, slip fielder, county captain
Born: 4 May 1960, Barnsley
Height: 6ft 1in **Weight:** 13st 7lbs
Nickname: Frog
County debut: 1981
County cap: 1984
Test debut: 1986
Tests: 10
One-Day Internationals: 8
1000 runs in a season: 8
1st-Class 50s scored: 75
1st-Class 100s scored: 28
1st-Class 200s scored: 2
1st-Class catches: 176
One-Day 50s: 32
One-Day 100s: 6

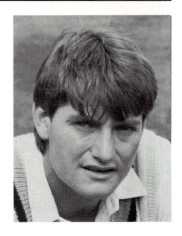

Place in batting averages: 36th av. 46.36
(1990 59th av. 48.02)
Parents: Audrey and Derek (deceased)
Wife and date of marriage: Sue, October 1985
Children: Charlotte Louise, 13 March 1990
Family links with cricket: Father and grandfather played local league cricket
Education: Holgate Grammar School, Barnsley
Qualifications: 8 O-levels, 3 A-levels, HNC in Business Studies, NCA coaching award
Off-season: Captaining England A tour to Bermuda and West Indies
Overseas tours: England to India and Australia 1984-85; Australia and New Zealand
1987-88; England B to Sri Lanka 1985-86; England A to Bermuda and West Indies 1991-
92
Overseas teams played for: Griqualand West, South Africa 1982-83 and 1983-84
Cricketers particularly admired: Viv Richards
Other sports followed: Football (supporter of Barnsley FC) and golf
Injuries: Hip problem – missed two weeks
Relaxations: Listening to most types of music, having a drink with friends
Extras: Captained Yorkshire Schools U15, North of England U15 and Yorkshire Senior
Schools. Played for Wombwell Cricket Lovers' Society U18 side. First Yorkshire player
to make centuries in his first two Championship games in Yorkshire, 116 v Essex at
Headingley (on debut) and 111 v Derbyshire at Sheffield, and scored 153 in his first innings
in a Roses Match. Picked for Lord's Test of 1984 v West Indies, but had to withdraw
through injury and had to wait until 1986 to make Test debut. Appointed Yorkshire captain
in 1990. Appointed captain of England A team to tour Bermuda and West Indies 1991-92.

Wombwell Cricket Lovers' Society Cricketer of the Year 1991
Best batting: 218* Yorkshire v Sussex, Eastbourne 1990
Best bowling: 3-24 Yorkshire v Hampshire, Southampton 1989

1991 Season

	M	Inns	NO	Runs	HS	Avge	100s	50s	Ct	St	O	M	Runs	Wkts	Avge	Best	5wI	10wM
Test																		
All First	21	37	1	1669	200	46.36	3	12	17	-	11	2	27	2	13.50	1-10	-	-
1-day Int																		
NatWest	1	1	0	2	2	2.00	-	-	1	-								
B&H	6	6	1	370	141 *	74.00	1	2	5	-	13	0	61	5	12.20	5-31	1	
Refuge	14	14	2	561	129 *	46.75	2	3	6	-	11.3	0	55	1	55.00	1-34	-	

Career Performances

	M	Inns	NO	Runs	HS	Avge	100s	50s	Ct	St	Balls	Runs	Wkts	Avge	Best	5wI	10wM
Test	10	17	1	455	99	28.43	-	3	10	-	48	30	0	-	-	-	-
All First	217	373	26	13849	218 *	39.91	28	75	176	-	2608	1467	28	52.39	3-24	-	-
1-day Int	8	8	0	174	70	21.75	-	1	5	-							
NatWest	19	19	6	739	107 *	56.84	1	7	9	-	156	85	5	17.00	2-19	-	
B&H	35	35	5	1451	141 *	48.36	2	10	14	-	330	229	9	25.44	5-31	1	
Refuge	95	87	7	2649	129 *	33.11	3	14	30	-	887	793	17	46.64	3-29	-	

146. How many Tests did New Zealand play in England before winning their first, and when was that win?

147. When was the first live radio cricket commentary, and at what match?

MULLALLY, A. D.   Leicestershire

Name: Alan David Mullally
Role: Right-hand bat, left-arm fast-medium
bowler
Born: 12 July 1969, Southend
Height: 6ft 5in **Weight:** 13st 5lb
Nickname: Spider
County debut: 1988 (Hampshire),
1990 (Leics)
1st-Class catches: 9
Place in bowling averages: (1990 79th
av. 38.05)
Strike rate: (career 85.96)
Parents: Michael and Ann
Marital status: Single
Education: Cannington High, Perth,
Australia
Qualifications: Radio technician
Off-season: Playing cricket in Australia
Overseas teams played for:
Western Australia
Cricketers particularly admired: Dennis Lillee, Wayne Andrews, Neil Mullally
Other sports followed: Hockey, hurling, Australian Rules
Injuries: Missed most of 1991 season with hip problem but pronounced fit for 1992
Relaxations: 'Music (UB40 etc), pubs, beaches – especially North Cottesloe.'
Extras: English-qualified as he was born in Southend, he made his first-class debut for
Western Australia in the 1987-88 Sheffield Shield final, and played one match for
Hampshire in 1988. Joined Leicestershire for 1990 season
Opinions on cricket: 'Too much cricket is played. Reduce the number of playing days and
the stupid over-rate fines.'
Best batting: 34 Western Australia v Tasmania, Perth 1989-90
Best bowling: 4-59 Leicestershire v Yorkshire, Sheffield 1990

1991 Season

	M	Inns	NO	Runs	HS	Avge	100s	50s	Ct	St	O	M	Runs	Wkts	Avge	Best	5wI	10wM
Test																		
All First	2	0	0	0	0	-	-	-	-	-	37.4	10	99	1	99.00	1-35	-	-
1-day Int																		
NatWest																		
B&H	3	2	0	6	5	3.00	-	-	-	-	33	2	134	1	134.00	1-45	-	
Refuge	2	0	0	0	0	-	-	-	2	-	16	1	50	4	12.50	2-19	-	

Career Performances

	M	Inns	NO	Runs	HS	Avge	100s	50s	Ct	St	Balls	Runs	Wkts	Avge	Best	5wI	10wM
Test																	
All First	38	32	11	196	34	9.33	-	-	9	-	6699	3216	77	41.76	4-59	-	-
1-day Int																	
NatWest	1	0	0	0	0	-	-	-	-	-	72	55	2	27.50	2-55	-	
B&H	6	2	0	6	5	3.00	-	-	-	-	324	209	3	69.66	1-28	-	
Refuge	16	6	3	26	10 *	8.66	-	-	4	-	679	481	16	30.06	2-19	-	

MUNTON, T. A. Warwickshire

Name: Timothy Alan Munton
Role: Right-hand bat, right-arm fast-medium
bowler
Born: 30 July 1965, Melton Mowbray
Height: 6ft 6in **Weight:** 15st 7lbs
Nickname: Harry, Herman
County debut: 1985
County cap: 1990
50 wickets in a season: 3
1st-Class 5 w. in innings: 12
1st-Class 10 w. in match: 2
1st-Class catches: 9
Place in batting averages: 240th av. 13.29
Place in bowling averages: 26th av. 25.52
(1990 25th av. 28.89)
Strike rate: 56.97 (career 58.68)
Parents: Alan and Brenda
Wife and date of marriage: Helen,
20 September 1986
Children: Camilla, 13 August 1988
Education: Sarson High School, King Edward VII Upper School, Melton Mowbray
Qualifications: 8 O-levels, 1 A-level; NCA coaching certificate
Career outside cricket: Brewery salesman
Off-season: Touring with England A
Overseas tours: England A to Pakistan 1990-91; Bermuda and West Indies 1991-92
Cricketers particularly admired: Richard Hadlee
Other sports followed: Basketball, soccer
Relaxations: 'Playing basketball, spending time with my family.'
Extras: Appeared for Leicestershire 2nd XI 1982-84. Second highest wicket-taker in 1990
with 78. Called into England A squad to tour Bermuda and West Indies when Dermot
Reeve replaced the injured Angus Fraser on the senior tour. Was voted Warwickshire

Player of the Season 1991

Opinions on cricket: 'The four-day game is a must. Coloured clothing should be introduced for Sunday cricket.'

Best batting: 38 Warwickshire v Yorkshire, Scarborough 1987

Best bowling: 8-89 Warwickshire v Middlesex, Edgbaston 1991

1991 Season

	M	Inns	NO	Runs	HS	Avge	100s	50s	Ct	St	O	M	Runs	Wkts	Avge	Best	5wI	10wM
Test																		
All First	23	25	8	226	31	13.29	-	-	14	-	693.1	184	1863	73	25.52	8-89	5	2
1-day Int																		
NatWest	4	2	0	6	5	3.00	-	-	2	-	41	7	111	3	37.00	2-42	-	
B&H	5	3	1	18	10	9.00	-	-	1	-	51.4	5	187	9	20.77	4-35	-	
Refuge	13	3	3	13	10 *	-	-	-	2	-	90	6	333	13	25.61	5-28	1	

Career Performances

	M	Inns	NO	Runs	HS	Avge	100s	50s	Ct	St	Balls		Runs	Wkts	Avge	Best	5wI	10wM
Test																		
All First	124	125	49	700	38	9.21	-	-	42	-	19728		8810	337	26.14	8-89	12	2
1-day Int																		
NatWest	14	5	3	8	5	4.00	-	-	2	-	784		425	14	30.35	3-36	-	
B&H	20	10	6	41	13	10.25	-	-	5	-	1240		724	25	28.96	4-35	-	
Refuge	76	21	18	63	10 *	21.00	-	-	12	-	3176		2095	72	29.09	5-23	2	

MURPHY, A. J.   Surrey

Name: Anthony John Murphy

Role: Right-hand bat, right-arm medium bowler

Born: 6 August 1962, Manchester

Height: 5ft 11in **Weight:** '14st-ish'

Nickname: Headless, Murph

County debut: 1985 (Lancs), 1989 (Surrey)

50 wickets in a season: 1

1st-Class 5 w. in innings: 5

1st-Class catches: 12

Place in bowling averages: 129th av. 47.62 (1990 113th av. 45.56)

Strike rate: 93.71 (career 71.93)

Parents: John Desmond and Elizabeth Catherine

Marital status: Single

Family links with cricket: Brother plays club cricket; 'distant cousin's grandfather ex-captain of Southern Ireland.'

Education: Xaverian College, Manchester; Swansea University

Qualifications: 9 O-levels, 4 A-levels
Career outside cricket: 'Trying to establish one in commercial property business.'
Off-season: Playing golf, travelling abroad and coaching in Argentina
Overseas tours: MCCA U25 to Kenya 1986; Lancashire to Jamaica 1986 and 1987; Surrey to Sharjah and Barbados 1989; Sharjah 1990; Barbados and Lanzarote 1991
Overseas teams played for: Central Districts, New Zealand 1985-86
Cricketers particularly admired: Clive Lloyd, Michael Holding, Rehan Alikhan
Other sports followed: American football, wrestling - 'any sort really'
Injuries: 'Several niggles but nothing too serious.'
Relaxations: Annoying batsmen/coaches, heavy rock music, loft conversions

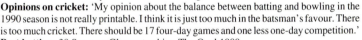

Extras: 'I have too many theories about bowling.'
Opinions on cricket: 'My opinion about the balance between batting and bowling in the 1990 season is not really printable. I think it is just too much in the batsman's favour. There is too much cricket. There should be 17 four-day games and one less one-day competition.'
Best batting: 38 Surrey v Gloucestershire, The Oval 1989
Best bowling: 6-97 Surrey v Derbyshire, Derby 1989

1991 Season

	M	Inns	NO	Runs	HS	Avge	100s	50s	Ct	St	O	M	Runs	Wkts	Avge	Best	5wl	10wM
Test																		
All First	19	20	8	71	18	5.91	-	-	4	-	546.4	118	1667	35	47.62	5-63	1	-
1-day Int																		
NatWest	4	2	2	1	1 *	-	-	-	-	-	40.2	5	158	3	52.66	1-27	-	
B&H	4	2	1	1	1	1.00	-	-	-	-	41	4	151	4	37.75	2-23	-	
Refuge	13	3	3	6	5 *	-	-	-	1	-	97	7	444	18	24.66	3-15	-	

Career Performances

	M	Inns	NO	Runs	HS	Avge	100s	50s	Ct	St	Balls	Runs	Wkts	Avge	Best	5wl	10wM
Test																	
All First	67	66	26	180	38	4.50	-	-	12	-	11725	6310	163	38.71	6-97	5	-
1-day Int																	
NatWest	8	2	2	1	1 *	-	-	-	-	-	524	338	8	42.25	2-34	-	
B&H	10	6	3	6	5 *	2.00	-	-	-	-	582	385	8	48.12	2-23	-	
Refuge	38	9	5	12	5 *	3.00	-	-	4	-	1632	1247	50	24.94	4-22	-	

NEALE, P. A. Worcestershire

Name: Phillip Anthony Neale
Role: Right-hand bat
Born: 5 June 1954, Scunthorpe
Height: 5ft 11in **Weight:** 12st 5lbs
Nickname: Phil
County debut: 1975
County cap: 1978
Benefit: 1988 (£153,005)
1000 runs in a season: 8
1st-Class 50s scored: 88
1st-Class 100s scored: 28
1st-Class catches: 134
One-Day 50s: 32
One-Day 100s: 2
Place in batting averages: 159th av. 24.64
(1990 82nd av. 44.36)
Parents: Geoff and Margaret
Wife and date of marriage: Christine,
26 September 1976
Children: Kelly Joanne, 9 November 1979; Craig Andrew, 11 February 1982
Education: Frederick Gough Grammar School, Scunthorpe; John Leggot Sixth Form College, Scunthorpe; Leeds University
Qualifications: 10 O-levels, 2 A-levels, BA (Hons) Russian. Preliminary football and cricket coaching awards
Career outside cricket: 'Phil Neale Tours Ltd – sports tours around the world for cricket, rugby and golf, specialising in Zimbabwe.'
Cricketers particularly admired: Basil D'Oliveira, Norman Gifford, Alan Ormrod
Other sports followed: Most sports – mainly via TV
Relaxations: 'Reading, spending time with my family, trying to play golf.'
Extras: Played for Lincolnshire 1973-74. Captain of Worcestershire 1983-91. Professional footballer with Lincoln City until 1985. Celebrated his benefit season by captaining Worcestershire to a County Championship and Sunday League double in 1988. Autobiography *A Double Life* published in 1990
Best batting: 167 Worcestershire v Sussex, Kidderminster 1988
Best bowling: 1-15 Worcestershire v Derbyshire, Worcester 1976

---

148. Which Englishman has hit most runs in a 5-match Test series?

1991 Season

	M	Inns	NO	Runs	HS	Avge	100s	50s	Ct	St	O	M	Runs	Wkts	Avge	Best	5wI	10wM
Test																		
All First	14	21	4	419	69 *	24.64	-	1	5	-	17.5	1	86	1	86.00	1-81	-	-
1-day Int																		
NatWest	2	1	0	8	8	8.00	-	-	-	-								
B&H	7	5	3	159	52 *	79.50	-	1	6	-								
Refuge	11	8	4	139	39	34.75	-	-	3	-								

Career Performances

	M	Inns	NO	Runs	HS	Avge	100s	50s	Ct	St	Balls	Runs	Wkts	Avge	Best	5wI	10wM
Test																	
All First	352	568	93	17366	167	36.56	28	89	134	-	472	369	2	184.50	1-15	-	-
1-day Int																	
NatWest	36	31	3	952	98	34.00	-	6	11	-							
B&H	70	63	10	1675	128	31.60	1	10	19	-							
Refuge	228	208	51	4596	102	29.27	1	16	60	-	50	50	2	25.00	2-46	-	

NEWELL, M.   Nottinghamshire

Name: Michael Newell
Role: Right-hand opening bat, leg-break bowler, occasional wicket-keeper, short leg
Born: 25 February 1965, Blackburn
Height: 5ft 8in **Weight:** 11st
Nickname: Sam, Tricky, Mott, Merrick
County debut: 1984
County cap: 1987
1000 runs in a season: 1
1st-Class 50s scored: 24
1st-Class 100s scored: 6
1st-Class 200s scored: 1
1st-Class catches: 90
1st-Class stumpings: 1
One-Day 50s: 4
One-Day 100s: 1
Place in batting averages: (1990 138th av. 34.04)
Parents: Barry and Janet
Wife and date of marriage: Jayne, 23 September 1989
Family links with cricket: Father chairman of Notts Unity CC. Brother Paul plays for Loughborough University

Education: West Bridgford Comprehensive
Qualifications: 8 O-levels, 3 A-levels. NCA advanced coach
Cricketers particularly admired: Chris Scott
Other sports followed: Watches rugby union and football, horse racing
Injuries: 'Dented pride!'
Relaxations: Good films, music and drinking at the Trent Bridge Inn
Extras: Carried his bat through the Nottinghamshire innings v Warwickshire, scoring 10 out of Nottinghamshire's 44
Best batting: 203* Nottinghamshire v Derbyshire, Derby 1987
Best bowling: 2-38 Nottinghamshire v Sri Lankans, Trent Bridge 1988

1991 Season

	M	Inns	NO	Runs	HS	Avge	100s	50s	Ct	St	O	M	Runs	Wkts	Avge	Best	5wI	10wM
Test																		
All First	1	1	0	91	91	91.00	-	1	-	-								
1-day Int																		
NatWest																		
B&H	1	1	0	18	18	18.00	-	-	-	-								
Refuge	1	1	0	12	12	12.00	-	-	-	-								

Career Performances

	M	Inns	NO	Runs	HS	Avge	100s	50s	Ct	St	Balls	Runs	Wkts	Avge	Best	5wI	10wM
Test																	
All First	100	175	24	4561	203 *	30.20	6	24	90	1	363	282	7	40.28	2-38	-	-
1-day Int																	
NatWest	5	5	0	136	60	27.20	-	1	3	-	6	10	0	-		-	-
B&H	10	10	1	205	39	22.77	-	-	2	-							
Refuge	25	22	4	621	109 *	34.50	1	3	8	-							

149. Who topped the first-class batting averages last season for Somerset?

NEWPORT, P. J.   Worcestershire

Name: Philip John Newport
Role: Right-hand bat, right-arm fast-medium bowler, outfielder
Born: 11 October 1962, High Wycombe
Height: 6ft 2in **Weight:** 13st 7lbs
Nickname: Schnozz, Barney Rubble
County debut: 1982
County cap: 1986
Test debut: 1988
Tests: 3
50 wickets in a season: 4
1st-Class 50s scored: 9
1st-Class 5 w. in innings: 23
1st-Class 10 w. in match: 3
1st-Class catches: 50
Place in batting averages: 191st av. 20.76 (1990 130th av. 35.33)
Place in bowling averages: 67th av. 32.42 (1990 37th av. 31.76)64.78 (career 51.87)
Strike rate: 59.65 (career 49.20)
Parents: John and Sheila Diana
Wife and date of marriage: Christine, 26 October 1985
Children: Nathan, 10 May 1989
Family links with cricket: 'Father was a good club cricketer, my younger brother Stewart plays for Octopus CC.'
Education: Royal Grammar School, High Wycombe; Portsmouth Polytechnic
Qualifications: 8 O-levels, 3 A-levels, BA (Hons) Geography, basic coaching qualification
Overseas tours: Selected for cancelled England tour to India 1988-89; England A to Pakistan 1990-91
Overseas teams played for: Boland, South Africa 1987-88
Cricketers particularly admired: John Lever, Graeme Pollock
Other sports followed: American football, soccer, athletics
Relaxations: Cinema, eating out
Extras: Had trial as schoolboy for Southampton FC. Played cricket for NAYC England Schoolboys 1981 and for Buckinghamshire in Minor Counties Championship in 1981 and 1982
Best batting: 98 Worcestershire v New Zealand, Worcester 1990
Best bowling: 8-52 Worcestershire v Middlesex, Lord's 1988

1991 Season

	M	Inns	NO	Runs	HS	Avge	100s	50s	Ct	St	O	M	Runs	Wkts	Avge	Best	5wI	10wM
Test																		
All First	25	26	9	353	48	20.76	-	-	4	-	712.4	138	2140	66	32.42	4-27	-	-
1-day Int																		
NatWest	1	0	0	0	0	-	-	-	-	-								
B&H	6	1	0	2	2	2.00	-	-	4	-	66	5	242	7	34.57	2-36	-	
Refuge	16	4	3	31	17 *	31.00	-	-	7	-	106.2	1	576	10	57.60	2-43	-	

Career Performances

	M	Inns	NO	Runs	HS	Avge	100s	50s	Ct	St	Balls	Runs	Wkts	Avge	Best	5wI	10wM
Test	3	5	1	110	40 *	27.50	-	-	1	-	669	417	10	41.70	4-87	-	-
All First	172	187	60	3253	98	25.61	-	9	50	-	25936	13987	500	27.97	8-52	23	3
1-day Int																	
NatWest	17	8	2	60	25	10.00	-	-	-	-	890	500	17	29.41	4-46	-	
B&H	29	17	4	129	28	9.92	-	-	8	-	1872	962	39	24.66	5-22	1	
Refuge	93	42	17	295	26 *	11.80	-	-	23	-	3340	2557	83	30.80	4-18	-	

NICHOLAS, M. C. J.   Hampshire

Name: Mark Charles Jefford Nicholas
Role: Right-hand bat, 'I think I bowl, but no-one else does', county captain
Born: 29 September 1957, London
Height: 6ft **Weight:** 12st 5lbs
Nickname: Skip, Dougie, Cappy
County debut: 1978
County cap: 1982
Benefit: 1991
1000 runs in a season: 7
1st-Class 50s scored: 60
1st-Class 100s scored: 29
1st-Class 200s scored: 1
1st-Class 5 w. in innings: 2
1st-Class catches: 186
One-Day 50s: 33
One-Day 100s: 1
Place in batting averages: 113th av. 30.59
(1990 128th av. 35.80)
Parents: Anne
Marital status: Single
Family links with cricket: Grandfather (F.W.H.) played for Essex as batsman and wicket-

keeper and toured with MCC. Father played for Navy
Education: Fernden Prep School; Bradfield College
Qualifications: 9 O-levels, 3 A-levels
Career outside cricket: 'Not at the moment – haven't time.'
Off-season: Completing benefit year. Journalism in Australia and caddying at golf tournaments in the Far East and Australasia
Overseas tours: English Counties XI to Zimbabwe 1984-85; captain of England B to Sri Lanka 1985-86; captain of England A to Zimbabwe and Kenya 1989-90
Cricketers particularly admired: Barry Richards, John Snow, Mike Brearley
Other sports followed: Most – football, golf, fives, squash
Injuries: Broken knuckle and finger - missed NatWest final
Relaxations: Theatre, music, golf, going out to dinner.
Extras: Hampshire captain since 1985 but missed Hampshire's first NatWest final after having his knuckle and finger broken a few days earlier by a delivery from Waqar Younis in the Championship game between the two NatWest finalists
Opinions on cricket: 'Do anything to encourage spin-bowling - uncover pitches, change the bowler's follow through laws, i.e. 5ft and 3in either side of stumps – anything but we must have variety. Change Sunday league rules, better still abandon it.'
Best batting: 206* Hampshire v Oxford University, The Parks 1982
Best bowling: 6-37 Hampshire v Somerset, Southampton 1989

1991 Season

	M	Inns	NO	Runs	HS	Avge	100s	50s	Ct	St	O	M	Runs	Wkts	Avge	Best	5wI	10wM
Test																		
All First	22	37	10	826	107 *	30.59	1	5	10	-	67.5	6	288	4	72.00	3-25	-	-
1-day Int																		
NatWest	4	1	1	24	24 *	-	-	-	2	-	2	0	9	0	-	-	-	
B&H	5	4	2	87	50	43.50	-	1	-	-	4	0	27	2	13.50	2-27	-	
Refuge	16	15	4	462	65 *	42.00	-	3	4	-	5	0	42	0	-	-	-	

Career Performances

	M	Inns	NO	Runs	HS	Avge	100s	50s	Ct	St	Balls	Runs	Wkts	Avge	Best	5wI	10wM
Test																	
All First	300	494	71	13949	206 *	32.97	29	60	186	-	5630	3107	70	44.38	6-37	2	-
1-day Int																	
NatWest	37	33	5	870	71	31.07	-	6	13	-	512	341	9	37.88	2-39	-	
B&H	51	46	6	978	74	24.45	-	4	17	-	1020	759	24	31.62	4-34	-	
Refuge	172	156	27	3625	108	28.10	1	23	53	-	1873	1751	59	29.67	4-30	-	

NIXON, P. A. Leicestershire

Name: Paul Andrew Nixon
Role: Left-hand bat, wicket-keeper
Born: 21 October 1970, Carlisle
Height: 6ft **Weight:** 12st 7lbs
Nickname: Nico
County debut: 1989
1st-Class catches: 69
1st-Class stumpings: 4
Place in batting averages: (1990 183rd
av. 27.40)
Parents: Brian and Sylvia
Marital status: Single
Family links with cricket: 'Grandfather
and father played local league cricket for
Edenhall CC and Penrith in the North
Lancashire League. Mum made teas.'
Education: Langwathby Primary,
Ullswater High
Qualifications: 2 O-levels, 6 CSEs, NCA
cricket coaching certificate
Jobs outside cricket: Working on father's farm
Cricketers particularly admired: Allan Knott, Bob Taylor, David Gower, Viv Richards
Other sports followed: Football (Carlisle and Spurs FCs), golf, rugby, basketball
Relaxations: Music, eating out
Extras: Played for England U15, Minor Counties for Cumberland at 16, MCC Young Pro
in 1988. Took eight catches in debut match v Warwickshire at Hinckley in 1989
Opinions on cricket: 'Second XI cricket should be played on first-class grounds as much
as possible and there should be more four-day matches.'
Best batting: 46 Leicestershire v Surrey, The Oval 1990

1991 Season

	M	Inns	NO	Runs	HS	Avge	100s	50s	Ct	St	O	M	Runs	Wkts	Avge	Best	5wI	10wM
Test																		
All First	4	4	1	54	31	18.00	-	-	8	1								
1-day Int																		
NatWest																		
B&H																		
Refuge	2	2	0	22	17	11.00	-	-	3	-								

	M	Inns	NO	Runs	HS	Avge	100s	50s	Ct	St	Balls	Runs	Wkts	Avge	Best	5wI	10wM
Test																	
All First	29	34	12	552	46	25.09	-	-	69	4							
1-day Int																	
NatWest	1	1	0	12	12	12.00	-	-	1	-							
B&H																	
Refuge	19	11	3	62	17	7.75	-	-	19	1							

NOON, W. M. Northamptonshire

Name: Wayne Michael Noon
Role: Right-hand bat, wicket-keeper
Born: 5 February 1971, Grimsby
Height: 5ft 9¹/₂in **Weight:** 11st 10lbs
Nickname: Spoon Head, Noonie
County debut: 1988 (one-day),
1989 (first-class)
1st-Class catches: 19
1st-Class stumpings: 2
Place in batting averages: 234th av. 13.71
Parents: Trafford and Rosemary
Marital status: Single
Education: Caistor Grammar School
Qualifications: 5 O-levels
Career outside cricket: Duck farmer
Off-season: Working for Kookaburra
Overseas tours: Lincolnshire U14 to
Pakistan 1984; England YC to Australia
1989-90

Overseas teams played for: Burnside West, Christchurch, New Zealand 1990-91
Cricketers particularly admired: Ian Botham, Alan Knott, Jack Russell
Other sports followed: Football (Lincoln City)
Injuries: Right-hand little finger – missed two weeks
Relaxations: 'Having a day's break from cricket and having a quiet beer.'
Extras: Played for England YC v New Zealand 1989; captain v Australia 1989-90 and
Pakistan 1990. Was the 1000th player to appear in the Sunday league competition
Opinions on cricket: 'I think the tea interval should be the same length as lunch and that
the cricket season should last seven months instead of six, playing the same amount of
cricket.'
Best batting: 37 Northamptonshire v Australians, Northampton 1989

1991 Season

	M	Inns	NO	Runs	HS	Avge	100s	50s	Ct	St	O	M	Runs	Wkts	Avge	Best	5wl	10wM
Test																		
All First	6	9	2	96	36	13.71	-	-	11	-								
1-day Int																		
NatWest																		
B&H																		
Refuge	4	2	1	12	8 *	12.00	-	-	3	1								

Career Performances

	M	Inns	NO	Runs	HS	Avge	100s	50s	Ct	St	Balls	Runs	Wkts	Avge	Best	5wl	10wM
Test																	
All First	10	14	2	139	37	11.58	-	-	19	2							
1-day Int																	
NatWest																	
B&H	1	0	0	0	0	-	-	-	-	-							
Refuge	10	8	2	60	21	10.00	-	-	7	1							

NORTH, J. A. Sussex

Name: John Andrew North
Role: Right-hand bat, right-arm medium-fast bowler, outfielder
Born: 19 November 1970, Slindon
Height: 5ft 11in **Weight:** 12st 4lbs
Nickname: Ollie
County debut: 1990
1st-Class 50s scored: 1
1st-Class catches: 1
Place in batting averages: 170th av. 23.28
Place in bowling averages: 48th av. 29.85
Strike rate: 46.95 (career 55.30)
Parents: John Allan and Margaret Anne
Marital status: Single
Family links with cricket: Brother Mark played county schoolboy cricket
Education: Bishop Luffa Comprehensive School; Slindon College
Qualifications: 10 O-levels, 2 A-levels
Off-season: Tours to Zimbabwe and South Africa, 'in Newburgh Arms, Slindon in between.'
Overseas tours: Buckingham Cavaliers to Cape Town, South Africa 1989 and 1992;

Sussex Martlets to Zimbabwe 1991
Overseas teams played for: University St Heliers, Auckland 1989-90
Cricketers particularly admired: Tony Dodemaide, Waqar Younis, Viv Richards
Other sports followed: 'Any sport without horses or rackets.'
Injuries: Chipped vertebrae of the spine after colliding with boundary boards
Relaxations: 'Films, eating out, away trips.'
Extras: Played for ESCA U15 and U17, NAYC and England YC v Pakistan 1990
Opinions on cricket: 'Politics and sport should not mix. Tea intervals should be extended. Too much cricket crammed into a six-month season.'
Best batting: 63* Sussex v Hampshire, Hove 1991
Best bowling: 4-47 Sussex v Sri Lankans, Hove 1991

1991 Season

	M	Inns	NO	Runs	HS	Avge	100s	50s	Ct	St	O	M	Runs	Wkts	Avge	Best	5wl	10wM
Test																		
All First	7	8	1	163	63 *	23.28	-	1	1	-	156.3	26	597	20	29.85	4-47	-	-
1-day Int																		
NatWest																		
B&H	4	3	0	44	22	14.66	-	-	-	-	41	1	208	4	52.00	2-80	-	
Refuge	6	6	1	50	18	10.00	-	-	5	-	27	1	162	8	20.25	3-29	-	

Career Performances

	M	Inns	NO	Runs	HS	Avge	100s	50s	Ct	St	Balls	Runs	Wkts	Avge	Best	5wl	10wM
Test																	
All First	11	13	2	204	63 *	18.54	-	1	2	-	1438	833	26	32.03	4-47	-	-
1-day Int																	
NatWest																	
B&H	5	3	0	44	22	14.66	-	-	-	-	294	256	5	51.20	2-80	-	
Refuge	8	8	2	66	18	11.00	-	-	6	-	210	207	10	20.70	3-29	-	

---

150. Who took 200 wickets for Yorkshire in his first full season, and in which year?

O'GORMAN, T. J. G. Derbyshire

Name: Timothy Joseph Gerard O'Gorman
Role: Right-hand bat, off-break bowler
Born: 15 May 1967, Woking
Height: 6ft 1in **Weight:** 11st 7lbs
County debut: 1987
1000 runs in a season: 1
1st-Class 50s scored: 9
1st-Class 100s scored: 5
1st-Class catches: 34
Place in batting averages: 138th av. 27.90
(1990 103rd av. 40.72)
Parents: Brian and Kathleen
Marital status: Single
Family links with cricket: Grandfather Joe O'Gorman played for Surrey; father played for Nigeria, for Sussex 2nd XI and Middlesex 2nd XI
Education: St George's College, Weybridge; St Chad's College, Durham University; College of Law, Guildford
Qualifications: 12 O-levels, 3 A-levels; BA (Hons) Law; Law Society finals
Career outside cricket: Solicitor
Off-season: In New Zealand
Overseas tours: Troubadours to Argentina and Brazil
Overseas teams played for: Alexandra, Zimbabwe
Cricketers particularly admired: David Gower, Greg Chappell, Richard Hadlee
Other sports followed: Tennis, golf, hockey, rugby
Relaxations: Arts, theatre, music, reading
Extras: Surrey Young Cricketer of the Year 1984. Captained Surrey Young Cricketers for three years. Trials for England schoolboys at hockey
Best batting: 148 Derbyshire v Lancashire, Old Trafford 1991
Best bowling: 1-17 Derbyshire v Surrey, Derby 1991

1991 Season

	M	Inns	NO	Runs	HS	Avge	100s	50s	Ct	St	O	M	Runs	Wkts	Avge	Best	5wI	10wM
Test																		
All First	25	44	4	1116	148	27.90	2	4	21	-	15	0	59	1	59.00	1-17	-	-
1-day Int																		
NatWest																		
B&H	4	3	1	78	49	39.00	-	-	1	-	1	0	1	0	-		-	-
Refuge	16	15	2	293	49 *	22.53	-	-	7	-								

Career Performances

	M	Inns	NO	Runs	HS	Avge	100s	50s	Ct	St	Balls	Runs	Wkts	Avge	Best	5wI	10wM
Test																	
All First	47	83	8	2197	148	29.29	5	9	34	-	90	59	1	59.00	1-17	-	-
1-day Int																	
NatWest																	
B&H	11	10	1	203	49	22.55	-	-	3	-	6	1	0	-		-	-
Refuge	29	28	6	478	49 *	21.72	-	-	7	-							

ORRELL, T. M. Lancashire

Name: Timothy Michael Orrell
Role: Right-hand bat, right-arm medium bowler
Born: 25 November 1967, Prestwich, Manchester
Height: 6ft **Weight:** 14st 10lbs
County debut: 1991
1st-Class catches: 0
Parents: Anne
Marital status: Single
Education: Bury Church High School; Stand College, Whitefield; Salford University
Qualifications: Degree in Engineering Metallurgy
Off-season: 'Doing odd jobs.'
Overseas tours: Represented ACT, Australia on a tour to Tasmania 1991
Overseas teams played for: South Canberra 1990-91
Cricketers particularly admired: Carl Hooper
Other sports followed: Football, tennis, 'anything exciting'
Injuries: Bruised fingers and short-leg injuries
Extras: Played for Combined Universities in 1990
Best batting: 16 Lancashire v Oxford University, The Parks 1991

151. Who captained the 1978 Pakistanis in England?

1991 Season

	M	Inns	NO	Runs	HS	Avge	100s	50s	Ct	St	O	M	Runs	Wkts	Avge	Best	5wI	10wM
Test																		
All First	1	2	0	21	16	10.50	-	-	-	-								
1-day Int																		
NatWest																		
B&H																		
Refuge																		

Career Performances

	M	Inns	NO	Runs	HS	Avge	100s	50s	Ct	St	Balls	Runs	Wkts	Avge	Best	5wI	10wM
Test																	
All First	1	2	0	21	16	10.50	-	-	-	-							
1-day Int																	
NatWest																	
B&H	2	2	0	15	15	7.50	-	-	1	-							
Refuge																	

OSTLER, D. P.   Warwickshire

Name: Dominic Piers Ostler
Role: Right-hand bat, right-arm medium bowler
Born: 15 July 1970, Solihull
Height: 6ft 3in
County debut: 1990
County cap: 1991
1000 runs in a season: 1
1st-Class 50s scored: 15
1st-Class 100s scored: 1
1st-Class catches: 30
Place in batting averages: 72nd av. 36.68 (1990 167th av. 30.00)
Marital status: Single
Education: Princethorpe College, Solihull Technical College
Extras: Warwickshire 2nd XI debut in 1989; played club cricket for Moseley in the Birmingham League; member of Warwickshire U19 side that won ESSO National Festival in 1988 and 1989
Best batting: 120* Warwickshire v Kent, Tunbridge Wells 1991

1991 Season

	M	Inns	NO	Runs	HS	Avge	100s	50s	Ct	St	O	M	Runs	Wkts	Avge	Best	5wI	10wM
Test																		
All First	22	40	5	1284	120 *	36.68	1	10	21	-	2	1	7	0	-	-	-	-
1-day Int																		
NatWest	4	3	1	47	34 *	23.50	-	-	-	-								
B&H	5	5	0	100	45	20.00	-	-	2	-								
Refuge	14	11	2	253	62 *	28.11	-	2	2	-								

Career Performances

	M	Inns	NO	Runs	HS	Avge	100s	50s	Ct	St	Balls	Runs	Wkts	Avge	Best	5wI	10wM
Test																	
All First	33	59	7	1794	120 *	34.50	1	15	30	-	12	7	0	-	-	-	-
1-day Int																	
NatWest	5	4	1	51	34 *	17.00	-	-	-	-							
B&H	5	5	0	100	45	20.00	-	-	2	-							
Refuge	21	17	4	350	62 *	26.92	-	2	5	-							

PARKER, P. W. G.   Durham

Name: Paul William Giles Parker
Role: Right-hand bat, leg-break bowler, cover fielder
Born: 15 January 1956, Bulawayo, Rhodesia
Height: 5ft 10½in **Weight:** 12st
Nickname: Porky, Polly
County debut: 1976 (Sussex)
County cap: 1979 (Sussex)
Benefit: 1988 (£59,400)
Test debut: 1981
Tests: 1
1000 runs in a season: 8
1st-Class 50s scored: 78
1st-Class 100s scored: 41
1st-Class 200s scored: 1
1st-Class catches: 228
One-Day 50s: 50
One-Day 100s: 6
Place in batting averages: 162nd av. 24.28 (1990 65th av. 46.90)
Parents: Anthony John and Margaret Edna
Wife and date of marriage: Teresa, 25 January 1980

Children: James William Ralph, 6 November 1980; Jocelyn Elizabeth, 10 September 1984

Family links with cricket: Father played for Essex 2nd XI. Uncle, David Green, played for Northamptonshire and Worcestershire. Two brothers, Guy and Rupert, 'very keen and active cricketers'. Father wrote *The Village Cricket Match* and was sports editor of ITN

Education: Collyer's Grammar School; St Catharine's College, Cambridge

Qualifications: MA (Cantab.)

Career outside cricket: 'Have set up own cricket-based company.'

Overseas teams played for: Natal, South Africa 1980-81

Cricketers particularly admired: Ken Barrington, Jimmy Cook

Other sports followed: Rugby union and to a lesser extent golf and tennis

Injuries: Poisoned left elbow

Relaxations: Reading, crosswords, bridge, music

Extras: Cambridge Blue at cricket and was selected for Varsity rugby match in 1977 but had to withdraw through injury. Was first reserve for England on Australia tour 1979-80. Appointed captain of Sussex 1988. Left Sussex at the end of 1991 season to join Durham

Opinions on cricket: 'The amount of cricket we play leads to stereotyped cricket ad cricketers and a mediocrity in standards. From the players point of view a balanced Championship of 17 four-day games should be introduced, with perhaps the number of limited-overs games reduced as well.'

Best batting: 215 Cambridge University v Essex, Fenner's 1976

Best bowling: 2-21 Sussex v Surrey, Guildford 1984

1991 Season

	M	Inns	NO	Runs	HS	Avge	100s	50s	Ct	St	O	M	Runs	Wkts	Avge	Best	5wI	10wM
Test																		
All First	16	26	1	607	111	24.28	1	3	8	-	2	0	10	0	-		-	-	-
1-day Int																		
NatWest	2	2	0	29	17	14.50	-	-	2	-								
B&H	3	3	0	123	87	41.00	-	1	1	-								
Refuge	11	11	0	307	104	27.90	1	1	5	-								

Career Performances

	M	Inns	NO	Runs	HS	Avge	100s	50s	Ct	St	Balls	Runs	Wkts	Avge	Best	5wI	10wM
Test	1	2	0	13	13	6.50	-	-	-	-							
All First	332	566	76	17164	215	35.02	41	78	228	-	965	668	11	60.72	2-21	-	-
1-day Int																	
NatWest	37	37	6	1157	109	37.32	1	9	8	-	12	17	1	17.00	1-10	-	
B&H	63	63	6	1561	87	27.38	-	11	16	-	8	6	2	3.00	2-3	-	
Refuge	193	181	24	4776	121 *	30.42	5	30	80	-	39	38	2	19.00	1-2	-	

PARKS, R. J. Hampshire

Name: Robert James Parks
Role: Right-hand bat, wicket-keeper
Born: 15 June 1959, Cuckfield, Sussex
Height: 5ft 7³/₄in **Weight:** 10st 7lbs
Nickname: Bobby
County debut: 1980
County cap: 1982
Benefit: 1992
1st-Class 50s scored: 14
1st-Class catches: 617
1st-Class stumpings: 70
Place in batting averages: (1990 224th
av. 19.63)
Parents: James and Irene
Wife and date of marriage: Amanda,
30 January 1982
Family links with cricket: Father, Jim
Parks, played for Sussex and England,
as did grandfather, J.H. Parks. Uncle,
H.W. Parks, also played for Sussex

Education: Eastbourne Grammar School; Southampton College of Higher Education
Qualifications: 9 O-levels, 1 A-level, OND and HND in Business Studies
Career outside cricket: Training as an accountant
Off-season: Preparing for his benefit year
Overseas tours: English Counties XI to Zimbabwe 1985
Cricketers particularly admired: Bob Taylor, Jeff Dujon
Other sports followed: Football (Tottenham Hotspur)
Relaxations: Interested in most sports, regular theatre-goer
Extras: Broke the Hampshire record for the number of dismissals in a match, v Derbyshire,
1982 (10 catches). One of the four wicket-keepers used by England v New Zealand at
Lord's, 1986 (after injury to Bruce French)
Opinions on cricket: 'There is no doubt that cricketers are asked to play too many games
in the domestic season thus reducing their motivation and their enjoyment of the game.'
Best batting: 89 Hampshire v Cambridge University, Fenner's 1984

152. Who won the first World Cup, and when was it held?

153. Who scored the only first-class quadruple century in England
this century?

	M	Inns	NO	Runs	HS	Avge	100s	50s	Ct	St	O	M	Runs	Wkts	Avge	Best	5wI	10wM
Test																		
All First																		
1-day Int																		
NatWest																		
B&H																		
Refuge	3	2	0	14	8	7.00	-	-	1	-								

Career Performances

	M	Inns	NO	Runs	HS	Avge	100s	50s	Ct	St	Balls	Runs	Wkts	Avge	Best	5wl	10wM
Test																	
All First	248	274	79	3775	89	19.35	-	14	617	70	189	166	0	-	-	-	-
1-day Int																	
NatWest	31	14	6	133	27 *	16.62	-	-	38	8							
B&H	46	27	11	190	23 *	11.87	-	-	57	6							
Refuge	157	62	29	594	38 *	18.00	-	-	154	29							

PARSONS, G. J. — Leicestershire

Name: Gordon James Parsons
Role: Left-hand bat, right-arm medium bowler, outfielder
Born: 17 October 1959, Slough
Height: 6ft 1in **Weight:** 13st 7lbs
Nickname: Bullhead, head of semtex and ' too many others to mention (non-complimentary)'
County debut: 1978 (Leics), 1986 (Warwicks)
County cap: 1984 (Leics), 1987 (Warwicks)
50 wickets in a season: 2
1st-Class 50s scored: 22
1st-Class 5 w. in innings: 16
1st-Class 10 w. in match: 1
1st-Class catches: 72
One-Day 50s: 1
Place in batting averages: (1990 268th av. 11.20)
Place in bowling averages: (1990 16th av. 27.51)
Strike rate: (career 58.77)

Parents: Dave and Evelyn
Wife and date of marriage: Hester Sophia, 8 February 1991
Family links with cricket: Father played club cricket , brother-in-law captains Orange Free State in South Africa
Education: Woodside County Secondary School, Slough
Qualifications: 6 O-levels
Off-season: Playing for Orange Free State in the Currie Cup
Overseas tours: ESCA to India 1977-78; Derrick Robbins XI to Australasia 1980; Leicestershire to Zimbabwe 1981
Overseas teams played for: Maharaja's, Sri Lanka 1979-81; Boland, South Africa 1982-84; Griqualand West 1984-86; Orange Free State 1987-92
Cricketers particularly admired: Dennis Lillee, Malcolm Marshall, Justin Benson, David Gower, Richard Hadlee, Graham Lloyd
Other sports followed: Golf, football (Reading) – 'they need all the support they can get'
Injuries: Two right shoulder operations, one in Feb '91 the other in June, also ruptured right bicep. Missed all but the last few weeks of the season – 'got to know Rob Stenner, our physio, very well!'
Extras: Played for Leicester 2nd XI since 1976 and for Buckinghamshire in 1977. Left Leicestershire after 1985 season and joined Warwickshire. Capped by Warwickshire while in plaster and on crutches. Released at end of 1988 season and returned to his old county. Justin Benson was best man at his wedding, 'contradiction in terms, though it is!'
Opinions on cricket: 'Looking forward to the English crowd reacting to coloured clothing and a white ball – excellent for Sunday cricket. Still feel that 18$\frac{1}{2}$ overs per hour is too high as a bowling rate.'
Best batting: 76 Boland v Western Province B, Cape Town 1984-85
Best bowling: 9-72 Boland v Transvaal B, Johannesburg 1984-85

1991 Season

	M	Inns	NO	Runs	HS	Avge	100s	50s	Ct	St	O	M	Runs	Wkts	Avge	Best	5wI	10wM
Test																		
All First	2	4	1	78	63	26.00	-	1	-	-	40	10	116	3	38.66	2-44	-	-
1-day Int																		
NatWest																		
B&H																		
Refuge	2	1	0	9	9	9.00	-	-	1	-	13	0	51	2	25.50	2-28	-	

> 154. When was South Africa's last Test series before their international ban, and what was the result of the series?

Career Performances

	M	Inns	NO	Runs	HS	Avge	100s	50s	Ct	St	Balls	Runs	Wkts	Avge	Best	5wI	10wM
Test																	
All First	246	327	75	4787	76	18.99	-	22	72	-	33917	17481	567	30.83	9-72	16	1
1-day Int																	
NatWest	20	12	3	121	23	13.44	-	-	4	-	1171	755	16	47.18	2-11	-	
B&H	42	21	9	252	63 *	21.00	-	1	10	-	2265	1340	48	27.91	4-12	-	
Refuge	127	71	23	577	26 *	12.02	-	-	17	-	4988	3766	114	33.03	4-19	-	

PATEL, M. M. Kent

Name: Minal Mahesh Patel
Role: Right-hand bat, left-arm spinner
Born: 7 August 1970, Bombay, India
Height: 5ft 9in **Weight:** 9st 7lbs
Nickname: Min
County debut: 1989
1st-Class 5 w. in innings: 2
1st-Class 10 w. in match: 1
1st-Class catches: 5
Place in batting averages: (1990 253rd av. 14.85)
Place in bowling averages: 89th av. 35.23 (1990 109th av. 41.80)
Strike rate: 84.46 (career 86.67)
Parents: Mahesh and Aruna
Marital status: Single
Family links with cricket: Father played good club cricket in India, Africa and England
Education: Dartford Grammar School; Erith College of Technology; Manchester Polytechnic
Qualifications: 6 O-levels, 3 A-levels
Off-season: 'Finishing my Economics degree and DJ-ing in Manchester.'
Overseas tours: Dartford GS to Barbados 1988
Cricketers particularly admired: Bishen Bedi, Derek Underwood, Sunil Gavaskar
Other sports followed: 'All except anything to do with horses!'
Relaxations: Listening to soul and dance music, playing snooker
Extras: Played for ESCA 1988, 1989, and NCA England South 1989. Kent League Young Player of the Year 1987, playing for Blackheath CC. First six overs in NatWest Trophy were maidens
Opinions on cricket: 'The Championship should be 17 four-day games.'

Best batting: 43 Kent v Leicestershire, Leicester 1991
Best bowling: 6-57 Kent v Leicestershire, Dartford 1990

1991 Season

	M	Inns	NO	Runs	HS	Avge	100s	50s	Ct	St	O	M	Runs	Wkts	Avge	Best	5wI	10wM
Test																		
All First	5	7	2	76	43	15.20	-	-	2	-	183.2	43	458	13	35.23	3-33	-	-
1-day Int																		
NatWest																		
B&H																		
Refuge																		

Career Performances

	M	Inns	NO	Runs	HS	Avge	100s	50s	Ct	St	Balls	Runs	Wkts	Avge	Best	5wI	10wM
Test																	
All First	15	20	7	183	43	14.07	-	-	5	-	2947	1328	34	39.05	6-57	2	1
1-day Int																	
NatWest	1	0	0	0	0	-	-	-	-	-	72	29	2	14.50	2-29	-	
B&H																	
Refuge																	

PENBERTHY, A. L. Northamptonshire

Name: Anthony Leonard Penberthy
Role: Left-hand bat, right-arm medium
bowler
Born: 1 September 1969, Troon, Cornwall
Height: 6ft 1in **Weight:** 11st 10lbs
Nickname: Berth, Penbers, After
County debut: 1989
1st-Class 50s scored: 4
1st-Class 100s scored: 1
1st-Class catches: 18
Place in batting averages: 220th av. 15.50
(1990 156th av. 31.07)
Place in bowling averages: 101st av. 37.00
(1990 62nd av. 35.95)
Strike rate: 69.73 (career 64.50)
Parents: Gerald and Wendy
Marital status: Single
Family links with cricket: Father
played in local leagues in Cornwall and

is now a qualified umpire instructor
Education: Troon County Primary; Camborne Comprehensive
Qualifications: 3 O-levels, 3 CSEs, coaching certificate
Off-season: Working back home in Cornwall
Cricketers particularly admired: Ian Botham, David Gower, Geoff Boycott, Dennis Lillee, Viv Richards, Eldine Baptiste
Other sports followed: Football, snooker, rugby, golf
Injuries: Septic tonsil, pulled internal oblique muscle
Relaxations: Listening to music, watching videos and comedy programmes
Extras: Had trials for Plymouth Argyle at football but came to Northampton for cricket trials instead. Took wicket with first ball in first-class cricket, Mark Taylor caught behind June 1989. Played for England YC v New Zealand 1989. Made first first-class 100 of 1990 season
Opinions on cricket: 'Too much one-day cricket. Lunch and tea intervals should be longer. 17 four-day matches. Over-rate fines too strict.'
Best batting: 101* Northamptonshire v Cambridge University, Fenner's 1990
Best bowling: 4-91 Northamptonshire v Warwickshire, Northampton 1990

1991 Season

	M	Inns	NO	Runs	HS	Avge	100s	50s	Ct	St	O	M	Runs	Wkts	Avge	Best	5wI	10wM
Test																		
All First	12	15	3	186	52	15.50	-	1	6	-	174.2	29	555	15	37.00	3-37	-	-
1-day Int																		
NatWest																		
B&H	2	1	0	3	3	3.00	-	-	-	-	17	3	65	2	32.50	2-22	-	
Refuge	8	3	2	69	41 *	69.00	-	-	2	-	32	2	165	5	33.00	2-20	-	

Career Performances

	M	Inns	NO	Runs	HS	Avge	100s	50s	Ct	St	Balls	Runs	Wkts	Avge	Best	5wI	10wM
Test																	
All First	28	40	6	696	101 *	20.47	1	4	18	-	2580	1508	40	37.70	4-91	-	-
1-day Int																	
NatWest																	
B&H	3	2	0	13	10	6.50	-	-	-	-	102	65	2	32.50	2-22	-	
Refuge	15	9	3	125	41 *	20.83	-	-	6	-	354	339	10	33.90	3-26	-	

PENN, C.   Kent

Name: Christopher Penn
Role: Left-hand bat, right-arm medium
bowler
Born: 19 June 1963, Dover
Height: 6ft 1in **Weight:** 13st-14st 7lbs
Nickname: Penny, Gazza
County debut: 1982
County cap: 1987
50 wickets in a season: 2
1st-Class 50s scored: 6
1st-Class 100s scored: 1
1st-Class 5 w. in innings: 12
1st-Class catches: 51
Place in batting averages: 209th av. 17.27
Place in bowling averages: 25th av. 25.44
(1990 138th av. 57.81)
Strike rate: 49.53 (career 60.34)
Parents: Reg and Brenda
Wife and date of marriage: Caroline Ann,
22 March 1986

Children: Matthew Thomas, 14 October 1987; David Thomas 30 March 1990
Family links with cricket: Father played club cricket for Dover CC for 26 years; mother
made the teas
Education: River Primary School; Dover Grammar School and 'Royal Oak, River'
Qualifications: 9 O-levels, 3 A-levels
Career outside cricket: Financial planning consultant. Lumberjack during storms. Also
worked for Avis and promotes cricket for Bromley Council
Off-season: 'Difficult problem for pro cricketer – probably coaching in Kent for the
county and working in cricket development for Bromley Council.'
Overseas tours: NCA South of England U19 to Denmark 1981; Whitbread Scholarship
to Australia 1982-83
Overseas teams played for: Koh-i-Noor Crescents, Johannesburg 1981-82, 1983-84
(part); West Perth, Australia 1982-83; Johannesburg Municipals 1983-84 (part);
Witwatersrand University, Johannesburg 1984-85; Green Point, Cape Town 1990-91
Cricketers particularly admired: Alan Knott, Dennis Lillee, Malcolm Marshall, 'plus
those I learnt from – my father, Colin Page, Brian Luckhurst, Graham Johnson, Barney
Lock, Darryll Foster'
Other sports followed: Football (Dover FC) and all sports except horse racing
Injuries: 'Niggles created by overuse and travel'
Relaxations: Music, art and art history, Indian food, local sport, keeping fit
Extras: Played for Young England and England Schools. Took hat-trick in first 2nd XI
match v Middlesex when 16 years old. Coached for Transvaal Cricket Council in the

Johannesburg townships during the early 80s. Kent Player of the Year 1988
Opinions on cricket: 'Same opinions for the last 10 years, so have things changed that much? We still have the same gripes. Do players opinions count for much?'
Best batting: 115 Kent v Lancashire, Old Trafford 1984
Best bowling: 7-70 Kent v Middlesex, Lord's 1988

1991 Season

	M	Inns	NO	Runs	HS	Avge	100s	50s	Ct	St	O	M	Runs	Wkts	Avge	Best	5wI	10wM
Test																		
All First	18	22	4	311	52	17.27	-	1	6	-	429.4	82	1323	52	25.44	5-43	3	-
1-day Int																		
NatWest	2	1	1	20	20 *	-	-	-	-	-	18	4	69	2	34.50	1-14	-	
B&H																		
Refuge	1	0	0	0	0	-	-	-	1	-	6	0	56	1	56.00	1-56	-	

Career Performances

	M	Inns	NO	Runs	HS	Avge	100s	50s	Ct	St	Balls	Runs	Wkts	Avge	Best	5wI	10wM
Test																	
All First	116	136	34	1959	115	19.20	1	6	51	-	16775	9016	278	32.43	7-70	12	-
1-day Int																	
NatWest	8	4	1	28	20 *	9.33	-	-	1	-	480	249	10	24.90	3-30	-	
B&H	23	15	7	97	24 *	12.12	-	-	3	-	1212	780	25	31.20	4-34	-	
Refuge	61	33	9	231	40	9.62	-	-	15	-	2383	1956	62	31.54	4-15	-	

155. What current Test umpire hit a century on his own Test debut?

PICK, R. A.　　　　　　　　　　Nottinghamshire

Name: Robert Andrew Pick
Role: Left-hand bat, right-arm fast-medium
bowler, gully fielder
Born: 19 November 1963, Nottingham
Height: 5ft 10in **Weight:** 13st
Nickname: Dad
County debut: 1983
County cap: 1987
50 wickets in a season: 3
1st-Class 50s scored: 2
1st-Class 5 w. in innings: 11
1st-Class 10 w. in match: 3
1st-Class catches: 31
Place in batting averages: 243rd av. 12.90
(1990 219th av. 20.40)
Place in bowling averages: 55th av. 31.04
(1990 43rd av. 32.49)
Strike rate: 58.26 (career 58.45)
Parents: Bob and Lillian

Wife and date of marriage: Jennie Ruth, 8 April 1989
Family links with cricket: Father, uncles and cousins all play local cricket; David Millns
is brother-in-law
Education: Alderman Derbyshire Comprehensive; High Pavement College
Qualifications: 7 O-levels, 1 A-level, coaching qualification
Off-season: Touring with England A
Overseas tours: England A to Pakistan 1990-91; Bermuda and West Indies 1991-92
Overseas teams played for: Wellington, New Zealand 1989-90
Cricketers particularly admired: Bob White, Mike Hendrick, Mike Harris, Franklyn
Stephenson
Other sports followed: Ice-hockey, soccer and American football
Relaxations: 'As much fishing as possible and listening to a wide range of music; eating
and drinking; going to the pictures.'
Extras: Played for England YC v Australia 1983. Played soccer for Nottingham Schoolboys
Opinions on cricket: 'Coloured clothing should be introduced for all one-day cricket.'
Best batting: 63 Nottinghamshire v Warwickshire, Nuneaton 1985
Best bowling: 7-128 Nottinghamshire v Leicestershire, Leicester 1990

---

156. Who is the only player to have scored a first-class century in each
innings, and take 5 wickets in each innings of the same match?

1991 Season

	M	Inns	NO	Runs	HS	Avge	100s	50s	Ct	St	O	M	Runs	Wkts	Avge	Best	5wI	10wM
Test																		
All First	23	16	5	142	46	12.90	-	-	7	-	650.4	117	2080	67	31.04	5-17	3	-
1-day Int																		
NatWest	3	1		0	*	-	-	-	1	-	30	4	111	4	27.75	3-41	-	
B&H	2	1		25	*	-	-	-	-	-	22	1	97	2	48.50	1-36	-	
Refuge	10	1		2	*	-	-	-	1	-	75	2	308	9	34.22	2-27	-	

Career Performances

	M	Inns	NO	Runs	HS	Avge	100s	50s	Ct	St	Balls	Runs	Wkts	Avge	Best	5wI	10wM
Test																	
All First	126	119	34	1272	63	14.96	-	2	31	-	18753	10512	328	32.04	7-128	11	3
1-day Int																	
NatWest	19	11	9	72	34 *	36.00	-	-	4	-	1243	769	29	26.51	5-22	1	
B&H	26	10	6	42	25 *	10.50	-	-	3	-	1581	1101	35	31.45	4-42	-	
Refuge	72	24	12	132	24	11.00	-	-	12	-	3068	2570	83	30.96	4-25	-	

PICKLES, C. S.　　　　　Yorkshire

Name: Christopher Stephen Pickles
Role: Right-hand bat, right-arm medium bowler
Born: 30 January 1966, Cleckheaton
Height: 6ft 1in **Weight:** 13st 6lbs
Nickname: Pick, Oke Koke
County debut: 1985
1st-Class 50s scored: 7
1st-Class catches: 22
Place in batting averages: 180th av. 21.84 (1990 136th av. 34.14)
Place in bowling averages: (1990 108th av. 41.53)
Strike rate: (career 82.89)
Parents: Ronnie and Christine
Wife and date of marriage: Janet, 22 October 1988
Children: Samantha, 10 October 1989
Family links with cricket: Father still plays in the Densbury League
Education: Whitcliffe Mount Comprehensive
Qualifications: Qualified cricket coach

Career outside cricket: Working for Heckmondwike FB Ltd, carpet manufacturers
Off-season: as above
Overseas tours: NCA U19 to Bermuda 1985; Yorkshire to Barbados 1990
Overseas teams played for: Whangerai, New Zealand 1988-89
Cricketers particularly admired: Malcolm Marshall, Viv Richards, Graham Gooch, Robin Smith
Other sports followed: Ruby union (Cleckheaton RFC)
Relaxations: Following rugby union and 'going out for a pint'
Extras: Made debut for Northamptonshire 2nd XI as a batsman and scored 100, made debut for Yorkshire 2nd XI as a bowler and took five wickets
Opinions on cricket: 'Should play four-day cricket with three 2-hour sessions per day. There is too much county cricket played and not enough time spent on fixture planning, with teams sometimes having to travel from one end of the country and then back again, when it could have been arranged as mini tours to distant areas. Players should not qualify as English until they have played county cricket for at least seven years.'
Best batting: 66 Yorkshire v Somerset, Taunton 1989
Best bowling: 4-92 Yorkshire v Northamptonshire, Northampton 1989

1991 Season

	M	Inns	NO	Runs	HS	Avge	100s	50s	Ct	St	O	M	Runs	Wkts	Avge	Best	5wI	10wM
Test																		
All First	11	16	3	284	51	21.84	-	2	2	-	138	19	468	6	78.00	2-8	-	-
1-day Int																		
NatWest	1	1	0	12	12	12.00	-	-	1	-	10.3	2	30	1	30.00	1-30	-	
B&H	1	0	0	0	0	-	-	-	-	-	11	0	49	2	24.50	2-49	-	
Refuge	11	9	4	78	30 *	15.60	-	-	6	-	63	0	361	14	25.78	3-12	-	

Career Performances

	M	Inns	NO	Runs	HS	Avge	100s	50s	Ct	St	Balls	Runs	Wkts	Avge	Best	5wI	10wM
Test																	
All First	52	67	20	1205	66	25.63	-	7	22	-	5720	3251	69	47.11	4-92	-	-
1-day Int																	
NatWest	2	2	0	15	12	7.50	-	-	1	-	135	71	2	35.50	1-30	-	
B&H	6	3	1	22	13 *	11.00	-	-	1	-	360	219	3	73.00	2-49	-	
Refuge	46	29	13	179	30 *	11.18	-	-	18	-	1804	1553	48	32.35	4-36	-	

157. Who topped the first-class batting averages last season for Sussex?

PIERSON, A. R. K.   Warwickshire

Name: Adrian Roger Kirshaw Pierson
Role: Right-hand bat, off-break bowler
Born: 21 July 1963, Enfield, Middlesex
Height: 6ft 4½in **Weight:** 12st
Nickname: Skirlog, Stick
County debut: 1985
1st-Class 5 w. in innings: 3
1st-Class catches: 17
Place in bowling averages: (1990 83rd av. 38.60)
Strike rate: (career 81.12)
Parents: Patrick Blake Kirshaw and Patricia Margaret
Wife and date of marriage: Helen Marjella, 29 September 1990
Education: Lochinver House Primary; Kent College, Canterbury; Hatfield Polytechnic
Qualifications: 8 O-levels, 2 A-levels, NCA senior coach
Cricketers particularly admired: John Emburey, Phil Edmonds, Tony Greig
Other sports followed: All sports 'except horse racing'
Relaxations: Music, driving, reading, golf, hockey, chess
Extras: On Lord's ground staff 1984-85. Had a shoulder operation while in Zimbabwe in 1989-90
Opinions on cricket: 'Make the game more commercial with coloured clothing and clear team sponsor logos, etc and be more accommodating towards public opinion. For example, make the bad light law less ambiguous. Keep the present pitches but return to something like the old ball.'
Best batting: 42* Warwickshire v Northamptonshire, Northampton 1986
Best bowling: 6-82 Warwickshire v Derbyshire, Nuneaton 1989

1991 Season

	M	Inns	NO	Runs	HS	Avge	100s	50s	Ct	St	O	M	Runs	Wkts	Avge	Best	5wI	10wM
Test																		
All First	5	6	4	55	35	27.50	-	-	1	-	73	11	279	4	69.75	3-45	-	-
1-day Int																		
NatWest																		
B&H	1	1	1	3	3*	-	-	-	-	-	2	0	7	0	-	-	-	-
Refuge	3	0	0	0	0	-	-	-	-	-	16	1	91	2	45.50	1-35	-	

Career Performances

	M	Inns	NO	Runs	HS	Avge	100s	50s	Ct	St	Balls	Runs	Wkts	Avge	Best	5wI	10wM
Test																	
All First	57	64	29	427	42 *	12.20	-	-	17	-	6896	3753	85	44.15	6-82	3	-
1-day Int																	
NatWest	5	1	1	1	1 *	-	-	-	2	-	318	160	4	40.00	3-20	-	
B&H	9	7	3	22	11	5.50	-	-	2	-	480	265	6	44.16	3-34	-	
Refuge	33	16	8	79	21 *	9.87	-	-	14	-	1232	987	22	44.86	3-21	-	

PIGOTT, A. C. S. Sussex

Name: Anthony Charles Shackleton Pigott
Role: Right-hand bat, right-arm fast bowler, slip fielder
Born: 4 June 1958, London
Height: 6ft 1in **Weight:** 13st
Nickname: Lester
County debut: 1978
County cap: 1982
Benefit: 1991
Test debut: 1983-84
Tests: 1
50 wickets in a season: 5
1st-Class 50s scored: 19
1st-Class 100s scored: 1
1st-Class 5 w. in innings: 23
1st-Class 10 w. in match: 1
1st-Class catches: 110
One-Day 50s: 2
Place in batting averages: 199th av. 18.82
(1990 228th av. 18.79)
Place in bowling averages: 109th av. 38.94 (1990 70th av. 36.98)
Strike rate: 74.05 (career 54.63)
Parents: Tom and Juliet
Marital status: Divorced
Children: Elliot Sebastian, 15 March 1983
Family links with cricket: Father captained village side, mother played at school 'and claims I got my cricket ability from her'
Education: Harrow School
Qualifications: 5 O-levels, 2 A-levels; junior coaching certificate
Career outside cricket: Owner of squash club at County Ground, Hove
Off-season: Finishing benefit year, touring with MCC to Leewards, at squash club

Overseas tours: Part of England tour to New Zealand 1983-84; MCC to Leeward Islands 1992

Overseas teams played for: Wellington, New Zealand 1982-83 and 1983-84

Cricketers particularly admired: Ian Botham, Geoff Arnold, John Snow, Mike Gatting

Other sports followed: Squash, soccer, golf, rugby

Injuries: 'Surprisingly none'

Relaxations: 'Full time job organising benefit'

Extras: Public Schools Racquets champion 1975. First three wickets in first-class cricket were a hat-trick. Had operation on back, April 1981, missing most of season, and was told by a specialist he would never play cricket again. Postponed wedding to make Test debut when called into England party on tour of New Zealand. Originally going to Somerset for 1984 season, but remained with Sussex. Was diagnosed as a diabetic after he lost 11lbs in two weeks in 1987, but recovered to take 74 wickets in 1988 season

Opinions on cricket: 'We should start playing total four-day cricket.'

Best batting: 104* Sussex v Warwickshire, Edgbaston 1986

Best bowling: 7-74 Sussex v Northamptonshire, Eastbourne 1982

1991 Season

	M	Inns	NO	Runs	HS	Avge	100s	50s	Ct	St	O	M	Runs	Wkts	Avge	Best	5wI	10wM
Test																		
All First	19	22	5	320	65	18.82	-	1	5	-	444.2	98	1402	36	38.94	5-37	1	-
1-day Int																		
NatWest	2	2	0	7	7	3.50	-	-	-	-	19.5	1	65	3	21.66	2-25	-	
B&H	4	3	0	47	29	15.66	-	-	3	-	41.4	4	175	5	35.00	3-29	-	
Refuge	15	14	3	73	14	6.63	-	-	5	-	95.5	2	461	27	17.07	5-30	1	

Career Performances

	M	Inns	NO	Runs	HS	Avge	100s	50s	Ct	St	Balls	Runs	Wkts	Avge	Best	5wI	10wM
Test	1	2	1	12	8 *	12.00	-	-	-	-	102	75	2	37.50	2-75	-	-
All First	217	263	56	4261	104 *	20.58	1	19	110	-	31306	17363	573	30.30	7-74	23	1
1-day Int																	
NatWest	21	11	0	160	53	14.54	-	1	6	-	1101	661	24	27.54	3-4	-	
B&H	34	23	8	222	49 *	14.80	-	-	14	-	1840	1277	43	29.69	3-29	-	
Refuge	134	79	28	938	51 *	18.39	-	1	46	-	5322	4322	205	21.08	5-24	3	

158. Who did Northamptonshire sign last season as a replacement for Curtly Ambrose?

PIPER, K. J. Warwickshire

Name: Keith John Piper
Role: Right-hand bat, wicket-keeper
Born: 18 December 1969
Height: 5ft 6in **Weight:** 10st 7lbs
Nickname: Tubbsy, Geeser
County debut: 1989
1st-Class 50s scored: 2
1st-Class 100s scored: 1
1st-Class catches: 114
1st-Class stumpings: 5
Place in batting averages: 205th av. 17.50
(1990 208th av. 23.05)
Parents: John and Charlotte
Marital status: Single
Family links with cricket: 'Dad plays
club cricket in Leicester.'
Education: Seven Sisters Junior;
Somerset Senior
Qualifications: Cricket senior coaching
award, basketball coaching award, volleyball
coaching award
Career outside cricket: Working in a warehouse
Off-season: Keeping fit and working
Overseas tours: Haringey Cricket College to Barbados 1986; Trinidad 1987; Jamaica
1988; Warwickshire to La Manga 1989; St Lucia 1990
Overseas teams played for: Desmond Haynes's XI, Barbados v Haringey Cricket College
Cricketers particularly admired: Jack Russell, John Morris, Dermot
Reeve, Paul Smith, Viv Richards, Desmond Haynes
Other sports followed: Snooker, football, squash, shooting, indoor cricket
Injuries: Bad knee
Relaxations: Indoor cricket, music, television, sleeping
Extras: London Young Cricketer of the Year, 1989
Opinions on cricket: 'I think day-night matches should be introduced.'
Best batting: 111 Warwickshire v Somerset, Edgbaston 1990

159. Which teams contested the 1991 Britannic Assurance Challenge?

160. Who has taken the most first-class hat-tricks, and how many?

1991 Season

	M	Inns	NO	Runs	HS	Avge	100s	50s	Ct	St	O	M	Runs	Wkts	Avge	Best	5wI	10wM
Test																		
All First	16	23	3	349	55	17.45	-	1	48	-								
1-day Int																		
NatWest	3	1	0	1	1	1.00	-	-	4	-								
B&H	4	4	2	35	11 *	17.50	-	-	5	-								
Refuge	9	4	3	17	15 *	17.00	-	-	7	3								

Career Performances

	M	Inns	NO	Runs	HS	Avge	100s	50s	Ct	St	Balls		Runs	Wkts	Avge	Best	5wI	10wM
Test																		
All First	44	59	6	1018	111	19.20	1	2	114	5								
1-day Int																		
NatWest	4	1	0	1	1	1.00	-	-	5	-								
B&H	4	4	2	35	11 *	17.50	-	-	5	-								
Refuge	25	14	6	103	30	12.87	-	-	13	7								

POLLARD, P. Nottinghamshire

Name: Paul Pollard
Role: Left-hand bat, right-arm medium bowler
Born: 24 September 1968, Carlton, Nottinghamshire
Height: 5ft 10in **Weight:** 12st
Nickname: Polly
County debut: 1987
1000 runs in a season: 2
1st-Class 50s scored: 11
1st-Class 100s scored: 6
1st-Class catches: 55
One-Day 50s scored: 5
One-Day 100s scored: 2
Place in batting averages: 92nd av. 33.02 (1990 216th av. 21.30)
Parents: Eric and Mary
Education: Gedling Comprehensive
Cricketers particularly admired: Clive Rice, Graeme Pollock, Richard Hadlee, David Gower
Other sports followed: Ice-hockey, golf, football, snooker

Relaxations: Watching videos, playing golf, 'spending time with my girlfriend'
Extras: Made debut for Nottinghamshire 2nd XI in 1985. Worked in Nottinghamshire CCC office on a Youth Training Scheme. Shared stands of 222 and 282 with Tim Robinson v Kent 1988. Youngest player to reach 1000 runs for Nottinghamshire
Best batting: 153 Nottinghamshire v Cambridge University, Fenner's 1989
Best bowling: 1-46 Nottinghamshire v Derbyshire, Derby 1991

1991 Season

	M	Inns	NO	Runs	HS	Avge	100s	50s	Ct	St	O	M	Runs	Wkts	Avge	Best	5wI	10wM
Test																		
All First	23	41	3	1255	145	33.02	3	4	21	-	23.5	8	75	1	75.00	1-46	-	-
1-day Int																		
NatWest	1	1	0	6	6	6.00	-	-	-	-								
B&H																		
Refuge	7	6	2	268	73	67.00	-	4	2	-								

Career Performances

	M	Inns	NO	Runs	HS	Avge	100s	50s	Ct	St	Balls	Runs	Wkts	Avge	Best	5wI	10wM
Test																	
All First	62	110	4	3156	153	29.77	6	11	55	-	154	80	1	80.00	1-46	-	-
1-day Int																	
NatWest	3	3	0	33	23	11.00	-	-	-	-							
B&H	8	8	0	110	77	13.75	-	1	3	-							
Refuge	28	26	3	784	123 *	34.08	2	4	8	-							

161. Who was Herbert Sutcliffe's opening partner for England immediately after the retirement of Sir Jack Hobbs?

162. What is the nickname of David Lawrence?

POOLEY, J. C.   Middlesex

Name: Jason Cavin Pooley
Role: Left-hand bat, right-arm slow bowler
Born: 8 August 1969, Hammersmith
Height: 6ft **Weight:** 13st 4lbs
County debut: 1989
1st-Class 50s scored: 2
1st-Class catches: 9
One-Day 100s: 1
Place in batting averages: 197th av. 19.38
Parents: Dave and Kath
Marital status: Single
Family links with cricket: Father and older
brother play club cricket. Younger brother
Gregg plays for Middlesex YC and
Middlesex 2nd XI
Education: Acton High School
Career outside cricket: Carpenter
Off-season: Playing in Australia for
Western Suburbs
Overseas teams played for: St George's, Sydney 1988-89
Cricketers particularly admired: David Gower, Mike Gatting, Clive Radley
Other sports followed: Horse racing and football (Portsmouth)
Relaxations: Watching all sports and listening to music
Extras: Won Rapid Cricketline 2nd XI Player of the Year in 1989, his first year on the
Middlesex staff
Opinions on cricket: 'All Championship matches should be four-day games.'
Best batting: 88 Middlesex v Derbyshire, Lord's 1991

1991 Season

	M	Inns	NO	Runs	HS	Avge	100s	50s	Ct	St	O	M	Runs	Wkts	Avge	Best	5wl	10wM
Test																		
All First	12	21	0	407	88	19.38	-	2	8	-								
1-day Int																		
NatWest																		
B&H	3	3	0	11	8	3.66	-	-	-	-								
Refuge	4	4	0	185	109	46.25	1	-	-	-								

Career Performances

	M	Inns	NO	Runs	HS	Avge	100s	50s	Ct	St	Balls	Runs	Wkts	Avge	Best	5wI	10wM
Test																	
All First	14	24	0	442	88	18.41	-	2	9	-	12	11	0	-	-	-	-
1-day Int																	
NatWest																	
B&H	3	3	0	11	8	3.66	-	-	-	-							
Refuge	5	5	0	191	109	38.20	1	-	-	-							

POTTER, L. Leicestershire

Name: Laurie Potter
Role: Right-hand bat, slow left-arm bowler, slip fielder
Born: 7 November 1962, Bexley Heath, Kent
Height: 6ft 1in **Weight:** 14st
Nickname: Pottsie
County debut: 1981 (Kent), 1986 (Leics)
County cap: 1988 (Leics)
1000 runs in a season: 3
1st-Class 50s scored: 45
1st-Class 100s scored: 7
1st-Class catches: 168
One-Day 50s: 15
One-Day 100s: 2
Place in batting averages: 107th av. 31.12 (1990 151st av. 32.72)
Place in bowling averages: 130th av. 47.78
Strike rate: 98.00 (career 82.24)
Parents: Ronald Henry Ernest and Audrey Megan
Wife and date of marriage: Helen Louise, October 1989
Children: Michael Laurie, 14 March 1990
Family links with cricket: Father-in-law FM Turner is Kent 2nd XI scorer
Education: Kelmscott Senior High School, Perth, Western Australia
Qualifications: Australian leaving exams
Off-season: 'Coaching in Leicester schools and at home with wife and son.'
Overseas tours: With Australian U19 team to Pakistan 1981
Overseas teams played for: West Perth, Australia; Griqualand West, South Africa 1984-85 and 1985-86 as captain; Orange Free State 1987-88
Other sports followed: Most – especially hockey
Relaxations: Home and family; following sport

Extras: Captained Australia U19 team to Pakistan 1981. Captained England YC v India 1981. Parents emigrated to Australia when he was 4. His mother wrote to Kent in 1978 asking for trial for him. Decided to leave Kent after 1985 season and joined Leicestershire. Youth Development Officer for Leicestershire CCC

Opinions on cricket: 'Lovely game.'

Best batting: 165* Griqualand West v Border, East London 1984-85

Best bowling: 4-52 Griqualand West v Boland, Stellenbosch 1985-86

1991 Season

	M	Inns	NO	Runs	HS	Avge	100s	50s	Ct	St	O	M	Runs	Wkts	Avge	Best	5wI	10wM
Test																		
All First	24	37	4	1027	89	31.12	-	7	21	-	457.2	105	1338	28	47.78	4-116	-	-
1-day Int																		
NatWest	2	2	1	82	57	82.00	-	1	-	-	6	1	32	1	32.00	1-32	-	
B&H	4	4	1	65	54	21.66	-	1	1	-	9	0	42	0	-	-	-	
Refuge	14	14	4	374	59	37.40	-	2	4	-	11	0	74	1	74.00	1-37	-	

Career Performances

	M	Inns	NO	Runs	HS	Avge	100s	50s	Ct	St	Balls	Runs	Wkts	Avge	Best	5wI	10wM
Test																	
All First	188	301	36	7789	165 *	29.39	7	45	168	-	10363	5046	126	40.04	4-52	-	-
1-day Int																	
NatWest	12	12	2	288	57	28.80	-	1	3	-	222	131	3	43.66	1-28	-	
B&H	27	25	4	534	112	25.42	1	1	9	-	426	295	5	59.00	2-70	-	
Refuge	111	108	13	2390	105	25.15	1	13	43	-	805	669	26	25.73	4-9	-	

163. Who captained the 1979 Indians in England?

PRICHARD, P. J.   Essex

Name: Paul John Prichard
Role: Right-hand bat,cover/mid-wicket
fielder
Born: 7 January 1965, Brentwood
Height: 5ft 10in **Weight:** 12st 7lbs
Nickname: Pablo, Middies
County debut: 1984
County cap: 1986
1000 runs in a season: 4
1st-Class 50s scored: 48
1st-Class 100s scored: 12
1st-Class 200s scored: 1
1st-Class catches: 107
One-Day 50s: 13
One-Day 100s: 2
Place in batting averages: 76th av. 36.25
(1990 57th av. 48.51)
Parents: John and Margaret

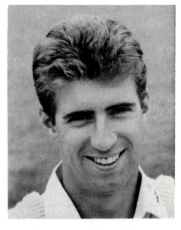

Marital status: Engaged to Jo-Anne
Family links with cricket: Father played club cricket in Essex
Education: Brentwood County High School
Qualifications: NCA senior coaching award
Off-season: Playing and coaching for Waverley CC, Sydney, Australia
Overseas teams played for: VOB Cavaliers, Cape Town 1981-82; Sutherland, Sydney
1984-87; Waverley, Sydney 1987-92
Cricketers particularly admired: Malcolm Marshall, Allan Border and all at Essex
Other sports followed: Golf, football (West Ham)
Injuries: Muscle spasms in lower back
Relaxations: Golf, listening to music (The Clash, Some Have Fins, Kitchens of Distinction,
Waterboys), Sydney beaches
Extras: Shared county record second wicket partnership of 403 with Graham Gooch v
Leicestershire in 1990
Opinions on cricket: '1991 was a much more even contest between bat and ball, mainly
due to the slight reworking of the rule regarding wicket preparation. But I would like to see
the groundsman being allowed the opportunity to make the ball turn earlier in the game
especially in three-day matches. '
Best batting: 245 Essex v Leicestershire, Chelmsford 1990
Best bowling: 1-28 Essex v Hampshire, Chelmsford 1991

1991 Season

	M	Inns	NO	Runs	HS	Avge	100s	50s	Ct	St	O	M	Runs	Wkts	Avge	Best	5wI	10wM
Test																		
All First	24	38	7	1124	190	36.25	4	3	19	-	13.3	0	158	1	158.00	1-28	-	-
1-day Int																		
NatWest	3	3	1	38	27 *	19.00	-	-	1	-								
B&H	6	6	1	111	38	22.20	-	-	3	-								
Refuge	13	11	1	248	54 *	24.80	-	1	7	-								

Career Performances

	M	Inns	NO	Runs	HS	Avge	100s	50s	Ct	St	Balls	Runs	Wkts	Avge	Best	5wI	10wM
Test																	
All First	171	268	34	8125	245	34.72	12	48	107	-	199	309	1	309.00	1-28	-	-
1-day Int																	
NatWest	15	14	2	363	94	30.25	-	2	6	-							
B&H	33	31	7	832	107	34.66	1	4	8	-							
Refuge	90	75	8	1607	103 *	23.98	1	7	23	-							

PRINGLE, D. R. Essex

Name: Derek Raymond Pringle
Role: Right-hand bat, right-arm fast-medium bowler, county vice-captain
Born: 18 September 1958, Nairobi
Height: 6ft 5in **Weight:** 16st 7lbs
Nickname: Del-Boy, Ralphy, Deltoid
County debut: 1978
County cap: 1982
Benefit: 1992
Test debut: 1982
Tests: 25
One-Day Internationals: 29
50 wickets in a season: 6
1st-Class 50s scored: 40
1st-Class 100s scored: 8
1st-Class 5 w. in innings: 24
1st-Class 10 w. in match: 3
1st-Class catches: 136
One-Day 50s: 26
Place in batting averages: 46th av. 43.35
(1990 137th av. 34.07)
Place in bowling averages: 37th av. 27.83 (1990 27th av. 29.23)

406

Strike rate: 68.14 (career 58.55)
Parents: Donald James (deceased) and Doris May
Marital status: Single
Family links with cricket: Father represented Kenya and East Africa (played in World Cup 1975)
Education: St Mary's School, Nairobi; Felsted School, Essex; Cambridge University (Fitzwilliam College)
Qualifications: 8 O-levels, 3 A-levels, MA Cantab.
Off-season: Preparing for benefit in 1992
Overseas tours: With England Schools to India 1978-79; England to Australia and New Zealand 1982-83; England B tour to Sri Lanka 1985-86; England A to Zimbabwe and Kenya 1990-91; England to New Zealand 1991-92
Cricketers particularly admired: Keith Fletcher ('now that he has retired'), Joel Garner
Other sports followed: Rugby union, football (Manchester United)
Relaxations: 'Getting into the wealth of largely unheard music that exists outside most playlists e.g. American Music Club, Soft Boys, The Minutemen, R.E.M., Misfits, Mid Miles Davis, X, Sunnyboys, Half Japanese. I read the Monday Telegraph every fortnight during the season for the above.'
Extras: Took all ten wickets for Nairobi Schools U13^1/$_2$ v Up Country Schools U13^1/$_2$. Captain of Cambridge University in 1982 (Blue 1979-82). Extra in 'Chariots of Fire'. 'Once went shark hunting with Chris Smith of Hampshire (a recklessly brave fellow) in the Maldive Islands.'
Opinions on cricket: 'If four-day cricket will allow more days off in order to mentally prepare oneself for each match, then I'm all for it. Uncovered wickets don't suit our batsmen so scrap that idea. Inception of up-to-date technologies in order to reduce umpiring errors, as there is too much at stake to merely grin and accept bad decisions, i.e. anything to aid the umpires who are now in a very high-pressure situation.'
Best batting: 128 Essex v Kent, Chelmsford 1988
Best bowling: 7-18 Essex v Glamorgan, Swansea 1989

1991 Season

	M	Inns	NO	Runs	HS	Avge	100s	50s	Ct	St	O	M	Runs	Wkts	Avge	Best	5wI	10wM
Test	4	7	0	128	45	18.28	-	-	1	-	128.1	33	322	12	26.83	5-100	1	-
All First	19	21	7	607	78 *	43.35	-	4	9	-	533.5	145	1308	47	27.83	5-70	2	-
1-day Int	3	1	0	1	1	1.00	-	-	1	-	27	2	130	2	65.00	2-52	-	
NatWest	3	2	0	21	19	10.50	-	-	1	-	34	3	127	7	18.14	3-21	-	
B&H	6	5	2	77	36 *	25.66	-	-	1	-	56.2	6	191	12	15.91	5-51	1	
Refuge	10	8	2	176	51 *	29.33	-	1	3	-	62.4	2	301	12	25.08	3-43	-	

164. Who topped the first-class batting averages last season for Warwickshire?

Career Performances

	M	Inns	NO	Runs	HS	Avge	100s	50s	Ct	St	Balls	Runs	Wkts	Avge	Best	5wl	10wM
Test	25	43	3	640	63	16.00	-	1	8	-	4519	2129	60	35.48	5-95	3	-
All First	260	360	68	8061	128	27.60	8	40	136	-	39409	17651	673	26.22	7-18	24	3
1-day Int	29	22	9	370	49 *	28.46	-	-	8	-	1601	1209	25	48.36	3-21	-	
NatWest	28	24	5	483	80 *	25.42	-	3	11	-	1649	888	37	24.00	5-12	2	
B&H	67	56	13	1386	77 *	32.23	-	13	16	-	3846	2314	97	23.85	5-35	2	
Refuge	128	97	23	2016	81 *	27.24	-	10	38	-	5071	4031	153	26.34	5-41	1	

PRINGLE, N. J.   Somerset

Name: Nicholas John Pringle
Role: Right-hand bat, right-arm medium bowler
Born: 20 September 1966, Weymouth, Dorset
Height: 5ft 11in **Weight:** 12st
Nickname: Pring
County debut: 1986
1st-Class 50s scored: 3
1st-Class catches: 15
Parents: Marion and Guy Pease
Marital status: Single
Education: Priorswood Comprehensive, Taunton; Taunton School
Qualifications: 8 O-levels, 1 A-level, NCA coaching award
Overseas tours: Taunton School to Sri Lanka 1983
Overseas teams played for: Mossman, Sydney 1986-87
Cricketers particularly admired: Martin Crowe, Richard Hadlee, Viv Richards, Greg Chappell
Other sports followed: Rugby, American football, anything except horse racing
Relaxations: Reading, watching videos and sport
Extras: On Lord's groundstaff before being called up by Somerset in 1986. Released by Somerset at the end of the 1991 season
Best batting: 79 Somerset v Warwickshire, Edgbaston 1987
Best bowling: 2-38 Somerset v Glamorgan, Weston-super-Mare 1987

1991 Season

	M	Inns	NO	Runs	HS	Avge	100s	50s	Ct	St	O	M	Runs	Wkts	Avge	Best	5wI	10wM
Test																		
All First	2	4	0	45	20	11.25	-	-	1	-								
1-day Int																		
NatWest																		
B&H																		
Refuge	2	2	0	8	7	4.00	-	-	-	-								

Career Performances

	M	Inns	NO	Runs	HS	Avge	100s	50s	Ct	St	Balls	Runs	Wkts	Avge	Best	5wI	10wM
Test																	
All First	27	48	6	707	79	16.83	-	3	15	-	852	551	5	110.20	2-35	-	-
1-day Int																	
NatWest	1	1	0	17	17	17.00	-	-	1	-							
B&H																	
Refuge	11	9	1	80	22	10.00	-	-	3	-	30	28	0	-	-	-	-

RADFORD, N. V.   Worcestershire

Name: Neal Victor Radford
Role: Right-hand bat, right-arm
fast-medium bowler, gully fielder
Born: 7 June 1957, Luanshya, Zambia
Height: 5ft 11in **Weight:** 12st 8lbs
Nickname: Radiz, Vic
County debut: 1980 (Lancs), 1985 (Worcs)
County cap: 1985 (Worcs)
Test debut: 1986
Tests: 3
One-Day Internationals: 6
50 wickets in a season: 5
1st-Class 50s scored: 5
1st-Class 5 w. in innings: 41
1st-Class 10 w. in match: 6
1st-Class catches: 117
Place in batting averages: 218th 15.70
(1990 239th av. 16.85)
Place in bowling averages: 48th av. 29.63
(1990 152nd av. 66.38)
Strike rate: 56.63 (career 49.40)
Parents: Victor Reginald and Edith Joyce

Wife: Lynne
Children: Luke Anthony, 20 November 1988; Josh Deckland 12 February 1990
Family links with cricket: Brother Wayne pro for Gowerton (SWCA) and Glamorgan 2nd XI. Also played for Orange Free State in Currie Cup
Education: Athlone Boys High School, Johannesburg
Qualifications: Matriculation and university entrance. NCA advanced coach
Overseas teams played for: Transvaal 1979-89
Overseas tours: With England to New Zealand and Australia 1987-88
Cricketers particularly admired: Vincent van der Bijl
Other sports followed: All sports
Injuries: 'A knee injury in May meant that I couldn't play in all the matches as I would have liked, but it made for an enjoyable rest!'
Relaxations: Music, TV, films
Extras: Only bowler to take 100 first-class wickets in 1985. First player to 100 wickets in 1987. Took most first-class wickets both years. One of Wisden's Five Cricketers of the Year, 1985. The Cricketers' Association Cricketer of the Year 1985
Opinions on cricket: 'We play too much cricket! A cut down will result in better standards all round. Have a day off for travelling as the majority of injuries and stiffness are caused by travelling hundreds of miles immediately after matches. I do feel as a professional working person, one should be entitled to accept work where one so desires.'
Best batting: 76* Lancashire v Derbyshire, Blackpool 1981
Best bowling: 9-70 Worcestershire v Somerset, Worcestershire 1986

1991 Season

	M	Inns	NO	Runs	HS	Avge	100s	50s	Ct	St	O	M	Runs	Wkts	Avge	Best	5wI	10wM
Test																		
All First	17	16	6	157	45	15.70	-	-	4	-	434.1	92	1363	46	29.63	7-43	2	-
1-day Int																		
NatWest	2	1		15	*	-	-	-	-	-	22	4	54	7	7.71	7-19	1	
B&H	6	1		25	*	-	-	-	2	-	61.5	13	244	16	15.25	3-22	-	
Refuge	16	4	2	38	20 *	19.00	-	-	7	-	108	3	571	25	22.84	5-42	1	

Career Performances

	M	Inns	NO	Runs	HS	Avge	100s	50s	Ct	St	Balls	Runs	Wkts	Avge	Best	5wI	10wM
Test	3	4	1	21	12 *	7.00	-	-	-	-	678	351	4	87.75	2-131	-	-
All First	235	234	55	2879	76 *	16.08	-	5	117	-	41628	21799	840	25.95	9-70	41	6
1-day Int	6	3	2	0	*	0.00	-	-	2	-	348	230	2	115.00	1-32	-	
NatWest	26	13	4	105	37	11.66	-	-	10	-	1488	769	36	21.36	7-19	1	
B&H	38	23	12	318	40	28.90	-	-	10	-	2174	1302	61	21.34	4-25	-	
Refuge	118	66	30	686	48 *	19.05	-	-	30	-	4718	3592	164	21.90	5-32	2	

RAMPRAKASH, M. R.   Middlesex

Name: Mark Ravindra Ramprakash
Role: Right-hand bat
Born: 5 September 1969, Bushey, Herts
Height: 5ft 9in **Weight:** 11st 10lbs
Nickname: Ramps, Axe
County debut: 1987
County cap: 1990
Test debut: 1991
Tests: 6
1000 runs in a season: 3
1st-Class 50s scored: 25
1st-Class 100s scored: 9
1st-Class catches: 34
One-Day 50s: 10
One-Day 100s scored: 3
Place in batting averages: 71st av. 36.68
(1990 58th av. 48.15)

Parents: Deo and Jennifer
Marital status: Single
Family links with cricket: Father played club cricket in Guyana
Education: Gayton High School; Harrow Weald Sixth Form College
Qualifications: 6 O-levels; 2 A-levels
Off-season: 'Break from cricket, a bit of training' then touring with England
Overseas tours: England YC to Sri Lanka 1987 and Australia for Youth World Cup 1988; England A to Pakistan 1990-91; England to New Zealand 1991-92
Overseas teams played for: Nairobi Jafferys, Kenya 1988; North Melbourne 1989
Cricketers particularly admired: 'All the great all-rounders.'
Other sports followed: Snooker, tennis, football
Injuries: Elbow – 'couldn't throw', rib intercostals
Relaxations: 'I enjoy playing snooker with friends even though I am hopeless: it helps me concentrate in the same way I try to do when batting, i.e. not to have a rush of blood.'
Extras: Won Best U15 Schoolboy of 1985 awarded by Cricket Society. Best Young Cricketer 1986. Did not begin to play cricket until he was nine years old. Made debut for Middlesex aged 17. Played for Bessborough CC at age 13. Played for ESCA U15 v Public Schools, 1984. Played in NCA Guernsey Festival Tournament and scored 204*. Played for England YC v Sri Lanka 1987 and New Zealand 1989. Played for Middlesex 2nd XI aged 16. In 1987 played for Stanmore CC and made 186* on his debut. Man of the Match in Middlesex's NatWest Trophy Final win 1988, on his debut in the competition. Cricket Society's Most Promising Player of the Year 1988.
Opinions on cricket: '1. There should be no limit on bouncers, it should be up to the umpires to interpret the law regarding intimidation. 2. County cricket does not encourage quick bowling, you can't bowl quick every day for 6 months. 3. There should be 17 four-

411

day matches in the Championship.'
Best batting: 158 England A v Sri Lanka A 1990-91
Best bowling: 1-0 Middlesex v Northamptonshire, Uxbridge 1991

1991 Season

	M	Inns	NO	Runs	HS	Avge	100s	50s	Ct	St	O	M	Runs	Wkts	Avge	Best	5wI	10wM
Test	6	10	0	210	29	21.00	-	-	4	-								
All First	21	36	4	1174	119	36.68	2	7	6	-	19	3	88	1	88.00	1-0	-	-
1-day Int	2	2	2	6	6*	-	-	-	-	-								
NatWest	2	2	0	57	32	28.50	-	-	-	-	13	1	46	2	23.00	2-15	-	
B&H	4	4	1	120	78*	40.00	-	1	3	-								
Refuge	8	8	2	382	111*	63.66	1	3	3	-	12	0	71	2	35.50	2-32	-	

Career Performances

	M	Inns	NO	Runs	HS	Avge	100s	50s	Ct	St	Balls	Runs	Wkts	Avge	Best	5wI	10wM
Test	6	10	0	210	29	21.00	-	-	4	-							
All First	88	146	26	4759	158	39.65	9	25	34	-	798	466	5	93.20	1-0	-	-
1-day Int	2	2	2	6	6*	-	-	-	-	-							
NatWest	12	11	0	346	104	31.45	1	1	2	-	102	60	2	30.00	2-15	-	
B&H	13	13	2	246	78*	22.36	-	1	5	-							
Refuge	48	46	11	1485	147*	42.42	2	8	16	-	99	96	3	32.00	2-32	-	

RANDALL, D. W. Nottinghamshire

Name: Derek William Randall
Role: Right-hand bat, cover fielder
Born: 24 February 1951, Retford, Nottinghamshire
Height: 5ft 8½in **Weight:** 11st
Nickname: Arkle, Rags
County debut: 1972
County cap: 1973
Benefit: 1983 (£42,000)
Test debut: 1976-77
Tests: 47
One-Day Internationals: 49
1000 runs in a season: 13
1st-Class 50s scored: 154
1st-Class 100s scored: 51
1st-Class 200s scored: 3
1st-Class catches: 344
One-Day 50s: 69

One-Day 100s: 6
Place in batting averages: 10th av. 62.68 (1990 126th av. 36.55)
Parents: Frederick and Mavis
Wife and date of marriage: Elizabeth, September 1973
Children: Simon, June 1977
Family links with cricket: Father played local cricket – 'tried to bowl fast off a long run and off the wrong foot too!'
Education: Sir Frederick Milner Secondary Modern School, Retford
Qualifications: ONC mechanical engineering, mechanical draughtsman
Overseas tours: England to India, Sri Lanka and Australia 1976-77; Pakistan and New Zealand 1977-78; Australia 1978-79; Australia and India 1979-80; Australia and New Zealand 1982-83; New Zealand and Pakistan 1983-84; England B to Sri Lanka 1985-86
Cricketers particularly admired: Sir Gary Sobers, Tom Graveney ('boyhood idol'), Reg Simpson
Other sports followed: Football, squash, golf
Relaxations: Listening to varied selection of tapes. Family man
Extras: Before joining Nottinghamshire staff, played for Retford CC in the Basset-law League, and helped in Championship wins of 1968 and 1969. Scored 174 in Centenary Test v Australia 1976-77. One of *Wisden's* Five Cricketers of the Year, 1978
Best batting: 237 Nottinghamshire v Derbyshire, Trent Bridge 1988
Best bowling: 3-15 Nottinghamshire v MCC, Lord's 1982

1991 Season

	M	Inns	NO	Runs	HS	Avge	100s	50s	Ct	St	O	M	Runs	Wkts	Avge	Best	5wI	10wM
Test																		
All First	22	34	9	1567	143 *	62.68	5	5	15	-	4	0	19	1	19.00	1-19	-	-
1-day Int																		
NatWest	3	3	0	166	95	55.33	-	1	-	-								
B&H	4	4	0	189	86	47.25	-	2	5	-								
Refuge	17	17	1	718	83 *	44.87	-	5	4	-								

Career Performances

	M	Inns	NO	Runs	HS	Avge	100s	50s	Ct	St	Balls	Runs	Wkts	Avge	Best	5wI	10wM
Test	47	79	5	2470	174	33.37	7	12	31	-	16	3	0	-		-	-
All First	464	788	78	27294	237	38.44	51	154	344	-	481	405	13	31.15	3-15	-	-
1-day Int	49	45	5	1067	88	26.67	-	5	25	-	2	2	1	2.00	1-2	-	
NatWest	40	40	5	1109	149 *	31.68	1	7	11	-	12	23	0	-		-	-
B&H	93	90	12	2647	103 *	33.93	2	17	42	-	17	5	0	-		-	-
Refuge	248	232	33	6647	123	33.40	3	40	68	-	5	9	0	-		-	-

RATCLIFFE, J. D.   Warwickshire

Name: Jason David Ratcliffe
Role: Right-hand opening bat, right-arm
medium bowler, slip fielder
Born: 19 June 1969, Solihull
Height: 6ft 3in **Weight:** 13st 7lbs
Nickname: Ratters, Roland
County debut: 1988
County cap: 1989
1st-Class 50s scored: 13
1st-Class 100s scored: 1
1st-Class catches: 29
One-Day 50s: 1
Place in batting averages: 102nd av. 31.76
(1990 179th av. 27.85)
Parents: David and Sheila
Marital status: Single
Family links with cricket: Father
(D.P. Ratcliffe) played for Warwickshire
1956-62

Education: Meadow Green Primary School; Sharmans Cross Secondary School; Solihull
Sixth Form College
Qualifications: 6 O-levels; NCA advanced cricket coach
Off-season: Playing cricket in Australia
Overseas teams played for: West End, Kimberley, South Africa 1987-88; Belmont,
Newcastle, NSW 1990-91
Cricketers particularly admired: Geoff Boycott, Dennis Amiss
Other sports followed: Football (Birmingham City) and most other sports
Relaxations: Music, reading, eating out.
Opinions on cricket: 'In favour of 17 four-day matches.'
Best batting: 127* Warwickshire v Cambridge University, Fenner's 1989
Best bowling: 1-15 Warwickshire v Yorkshire, Headingley 1989

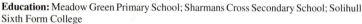

1991 Season

	M	Inns	NO	Runs	HS	Avge	100s	50s	Ct	St	O	M	Runs	Wkts	Avge	Best	5wI	10wM
Test																		
All First	17	31	1	953	94	31.76	-	8	15	-	3	1	14	0	-	-	-	-
1-day Int																		
NatWest	2	2	1	94	68 *	94.00	-	1	-	-								
B&H	1	1	0	29	29	29.00	-	-	-	-								
Refuge	1	1	0	1	1	1.00	-	-	-	-								

Career Performances

	M	Inns	NO	Runs	HS	Avge	100s	50s	Ct	St	Balls	Runs	Wkts	Avge	Best	5wI	10wM
Test																	
All First	46	86	8	2335	127 *	29.93	1	13	29	-	180	96	1	96.00	1-15	-	-
1-day Int																	
NatWest	3	3	1	153	68 *	76.50	-	2	-	-							
B&H	1	1	0	29	29	29.00	-	-	-	-							
Refuge	6	5	1	48	37	12.00	-	-	1	-	55	58	2	29.00	1-8	-	

REEVE, D. A. Warwickshire

Name: Dermot Alexander Reeve
Role: Right-hand bat, right-arm
fast-medium bowler, county vice-captain
Born: 2 April 1963, Hong Kong
Height: 6ft **Weight:** 12st
Nickname: Legend, Motte
County debut: 1983 (Sussex),
1988 (Warwicks)
County cap: 1986 (Sussex),
1989 (Warwicks)
One-Day Internationals: 1
1000 runs in a season: 2
50 wickets in a season: 2
1st-Class 50s scored: 34
1st-Class 100s scored: 5
1st-Class 200s scored: 1
1st-Class 5 w. in innings: 6
1st-Class catches: 110
One-Day 50s: 6
Place in batting averages: 27th av. 48.46 (1990 36th av. 54.30)
Place in bowling averages: 7th av. 21.26 (1990 22nd av. 28.48)
Strike rate: 53.62 (career 62.48)
Parents: Alexander James and Monica
Wife and date of marriage: Julie, 20 December 1986
Children: Emily Kaye, 14 September 1988
Family links with cricket: Father was captain of his school XI, brother Mark is an improving club cricketer
Education: King George V School, Kowloon, Hong Kong
Qualifications: 7 O-levels
Career outside cricket: Operations manager for Employment Agency
Off-season: Touring with England

Overseas tours: England to New Zealand 1991-92

Cricketers particularly admired: Wasim Akram, Waqar Younis, Jimmy Cook, Tim Munton, John Barclay

Other sports followed: Football (Man Utd), Aussie Rules

Relaxations: Music, videos, swimming, Perth beaches, Italian food

Extras: Formerly on Lord's ground staff. Represented Hong Kong in the ICC Trophy competition June 1982. Hong Kong Cricketer of the Year 1980-81. Hong Kong's Cricket Sports Personality of the Year 1981. Man of the Match in 1986 NatWest Final for Sussex and 1989 Final for Warwickshire. Twice Western Australian CA Cricketer of the Year. Originally selected for England A tour to Bermuda and West Indies 1991-92 but promoted to senior tour to New Zealand when Angus Fraser was ruled out by injury.

Opinions on cricket: 'Four-day cricket on covered wickets and 100 overs a day. More One-Day Internationals in England. Over-rate fines too strict. I would also like to see coloured clothing for Sunday cricket.'

Best batting: 202* Warwickshire v Northamptonshire, Northampton 1990

Best bowling: 7-37 Sussex v Lancashire, Lytham 1987

1991 Season

	M	Inns	NO	Runs	HS	Avge	100s	50s	Ct	St	O	M	Runs	Wkts	Avge	Best	5wI	10wM
Test																		
All First	20	33	7	1260	99 *	48.46	-	14	9	-	402.1	117	957	45	21.26	6-73	1	-
1-day Int	1	0	0	0	0	-	-	-	-	-	11	1	43	0	-	-	-	-
NatWest	4	3	1	89	57 *	44.50	-	1	5	-	35.5	7	101	3	33.66	2-19	-	
B&H	5	5	0	124	80	24.80	-	1	3	-	51.5	0	233	10	23.30	4-43	-	
Refuge	13	10	1	260	100	28.88	1	-	2	-	70.1	2	352	11	32.00	4-18	-	

Career Performances

	M	Inns	NO	Runs	HS	Avge	100s	50s	Ct	St	Balls	Runs	Wkts	Avge	Best	5wI	10wM
Test																	
All First	166	212	57	5445	202 *	35.12	5	34	110	-	21996	9538	352	27.09	7-37	6	-
1-day Int	1	0	0	0	0	-	-	-	-	-	66	43	0	-	-	-	-
NatWest	24	18	8	312	57 *	31.20	-	1	10	-	1378	651	23	28.30	4-20	-	
B&H	29	24	8	337	80	21.06	-	1	5	-	1479	1075	32	33.59	4-42	-	
Refuge	113	75	21	1292	100	23.92	1	4	32	-	3915	3089	111	27.82	5-23	1	

RHODES, S. J.   Worcestershire

Name: Steven John Rhodes
Role: Right-hand bat, wicket-keeper,
county vice-captain
Born: 17 June 1964, Bradford
Height: 5ft 9in **Weight:** 11st 11lbs
Nickname: Wilf, Bumpy
County debut: 1981 (Yorks), 1985 (Worcs)
County cap: 1988 (Worcs)
One-Day Internationals: 3
1st-Class 50s scored: 28
1st-Class 100s scored: 1
1st-Class catches: 444
1st-Class stumpings: 52
One-Day 50s: 2
One-Day 100s: 1
Place in batting averages: 82nd av. 34.88
(1990 81st av. 44.80)
Parents: Bill and Norma
Marital status: Single
Family links with cricket: Father played for Nottinghamshire 1959-64
Education: Bradford Moor Junior School; Lapage St Middle; Carlton-Bolling
Comprehensive, Bradford
Qualifications: 4 O-levels, coaching certificate
Off-season: On standby for England A tour to Bermuda and West Indies
Overseas tours: England B to Sri Lanka 1986-86; picked for cancelled England tour of
India 1988-89; England A to Zimbabwe and Kenya 1989-90; Pakistan 1990-91
Overseas teams played for: Past Bros, Bundaberg, Queensland; Avis Vogeltown, New
Plymouth, NZ
Cricketers particularly admired: Alan Knott, Bob Taylor, Graeme Hick, Richard Hadlee,
Jimmy Cook
Other sports followed: Rugby league
Injuries: Groin strain – missed two weeks early in the season
Relaxations: Tropical fish, golf
Extras: England YC v Australia in 1983. Youngest wicket-keeper to play for Yorkshire.
Record for most victims in an innings for Young England. Released by Yorkshire to join
Worcestershire at end of 1984 season. One of four players put on standby as reserves for
1992 World Cup squad
Opinions on cricket: 'County cricket is draining the enthusiasm out of pro cricketers,
particularly young players. This is due to the weight of cricket played in our domestic
season. My format for English cricket would be as follows: 17 four-day games (alternating
home and away each season), one 55 over competition (incl. zonal qualifiers) with a final
in September, 17 Sunday league games of 50 overs. By doing away with one cup it gives

players time which is much needed to keep standards high – quality not quantity. Hopefully this formula would make England the top cricketing nation.'

Best batting: 108 Worcestershire v Derbyshire, Derby 1988

1991 Season

	M	Inns	NO	Runs	HS	Avge	100s	50s	Ct	St	O	M	Runs	Wkts	Avge	Best	5wI	10wM
Test																		
All First	24	33	6	942	90	34.88	-	8	54	8	1	0	30	0	-		-	-
1-day Int																		
NatWest	2	2	0	51	41	25.50	-	-	-	-								
B&H	7	3	1	34	13 *	17.00	-	-	10	1								
Refuge	16	7	2	164	105	32.80	1	-	3	4								

Career Performances

	M	Inns	NO	Runs	HS	Avge	100s	50s	Ct	St	Balls	Runs	Wkts	Avge	Best	5wI	10wM
Test																	
All First	184	235	76	5044	108	31.72	1	28	444	52	6	30	0	-		-	-
1-day Int	3	2	1	9	8	9.00	-	-	3	-							
NatWest	24	17	6	205	61	18.63	-	1	25	4							
B&H	36	26	6	377	51 *	18.85	-	1	45	6							
Refuge	112	71	17	1208	105	22.37	1	-	105	29							

RICHARDS, I. V. A. Glamorgan

Name: Isaac Vivian Alexander Richards
Role: Right-hand bat, off-break bowler
Born: 7 March 1952, St John's, Antigua
Height: 5ft 11in **Weight:** 13st 7lbs
Nickname: Smokey, Vivvy, Master Blaster
County debut: 1974 (Somerset), 1990 (Glamorgan)
County cap: 1974 (Somerset), 1990 (Glamorgan)
Benefit: 1982 (£56,440)
Test debut: 1974
Tests: 121
One-Day Internationals: 187
1000 runs in a season: 13
1st-Class 50s scored: 151
1st-Class 100s scored: 111
1st-Class 200s scored: 7
1st-Class 5 w. in innings: 1

1st-Class catches: 430
1st-Class stumpings: 1
One-Day 50s: 97
One-Day 100s: 23
Place in batting averages: 14th av. 58.35 (1990 20th av. 61.95)
Parents: Malcolm and Gratel
Wife and date of marriage: Miriam, 24 March 1981
Children: Matara, Mali
Family links with cricket: Father played for Antigua as an all-rounder. Half-brother Donald played for Antigua and Leeward Islands and brother Mervyn played for Antigua
Education: St John's Boys School and Antigua Grammar School
Overseas tours: West Indies to India, Sri Lanka and Pakistan 1974-75; Australia 1975-76; England 1976; Australia 1979-80; England 1980; Pakistan 1980-81; Australia 1981-82; India 1983-84; England 1984; Australia 1984-85; Pakistan and New Zealand 1986-87; India 1987-88; England 1988; Australia 1988-89; England 1991
Overseas teams played for: Combined Islands and Leeward Islands since 1971-72; Queensland 1976-77
Other sports followed: Football, basketball, squash. Played football for Antigua and once had a trial with Bath City FC
Relaxations: Listening to music
Extras: 'I remain a religious person to the delight of my parents. I pray every night before going to sleep; occasionally I pray for success on the field.' Helps to sponsor young sportsmen in Antigua. 'Sounds mad but I am not a travelling man – I hate it in the air. Planes terrify me.' Captain of West Indies 1986-91. Released by Somerset at end of 1986 and played for Rishton in Lancashire League in 1987. Became first West Indian to hit 100 first-class 100s in 1988-89. Signed two-year contract with Glamorgan in 1989 but unable to play at all in his first season due to injury. Made his debut for Glamorgan in 1990 and has signed a further two-year contract for 1992 and 1993. Retired from Test cricket after The Oval Test against England in 1991. Published his autobiography *Hitting Across the Line* in 1991 and an official video biography of the same title was released in 1992
Best batting: 322 Somerset v Warwickshire, Taunton 1985
Best bowling: 5-88 West Indians v Queensland, Brisbane 1981-82

1991 Season

	M	Inns	NO	Runs	HS	Avge	100s	50s	Ct	St	O	M	Runs	Wkts	Avge	Best	5wI	10wM
Test	5	8	1	376	80	53.71	-	5	4	-	5	1	6	0	-	-	-	-
All First	12	18	4	817	131	58.35	1	6	9	-	47	9	161	2	80.50	1-32	-	-
1-day Int	3	3	0	145	78	48.33	-	1	1	-								
NatWest																		
B&H																		
Refuge																		

Career Performances

	M	Inns	NO	Runs	HS	Avge	100s	50s	Ct	St	Balls	Runs	Wkts	Avge	Best	5wI	10wM
Test	121	182	12	8540	291	50.23	24	45	122	-	5170	1964	32	61.37	2-17	-	-
All First	476	741	56	34255	322	50.00	111	151	430	1	15035	9801	219	44.75	5-88	1	-
1-day Int	187	167	24	6721	189 *	47.00	11	45	101	-	5644	4228	118	35.83	6-41	2	
NatWest	34	34	4	1410	139 *	47.00	4	7	16	-	967	592	20	29.60	3-15	-	
B&H	48	44	6	1499	132 *	39.44	1	10	21	-	712	425	12	35.41	3-38	-	
Refuge	158	153	17	5235	126 *	38.49	7	35	70	-	2741	2189	84	26.06	6-24	1	

RIPLEY, D. Northamptonshire

Name: David Ripley
Role: Right-hand bat, wicket-keeper
Born: 13 September 1966, Leeds
Height: 5ft 11in **Weight:** 11st 7lbs
Nickname: Rips, Spud, Sheridan
County debut: 1984
County cap: 1987
1st-Class 50s scored: 5
1st-Class 100s scored: 4
1st-Class catches: 305
1st-Class stumpings: 50
Place in batting averages: 122nd av. 29.18
(1990 169th av. 29.81)
Parents: Arthur and Brenda
Wife and date of marriage: Jackie,
24 September 1988
Children: Joe David 11 October 1989
Education: Woodlesford Primary;
Royds High, Leeds
Qualifications: 5 O-levels, NCA senior coaching award
Career outside cricket: Director of Gard Sports, Northampton
Off-season: Working in the shop, as above
Overseas tours: England YC to West Indies 1984-85
Cricketers particularly admired: Alan Knott, Bob Taylor, Clive Radley, Ian Botham, Dennis Lillee
Other sports followed: Soccer (Leeds United) and rugby league (Castleford), golf
Injuries: Back muscle – missed two weeks
Relaxations: Music, eating out, golf
Extras: Finished top of wicket-keepers' dismissals list for 1988 with 87 victims
Opinions on cricket: 'I would like to see 17 four-day games and the introduction of coloured clothing for the Sunday league.'

Best batting: 134* Northamptonshire v Yorkshire, Scarborough 1986
Best bowling: 2-89 Northamptonshire v Essex, Ilford 1987

1991 Season

	M	Inns	NO	Runs	HS	Avge	100s	50s	Ct	St	O	M	Runs	Wkts	Avge	Best	5wI	10wM
Test																		
All First	20	25	9	467	53 *	29.18	-	1	41	2								
1-day Int																		
NatWest	4	2	1	13	10 *	13.00	-	-	3	-								
B&H	5	3	2	47	36 *	47.00	-	-	7	1								
Refuge	13	7	2	57	14	11.40	-	-	8	-								

Career Performances

	M	Inns	NO	Runs	HS	Avge	100s	50s	Ct	St	Balls	Runs	Wkts	Avge	Best	5wI	10wM
Test																	
All First	155	196	47	3349	134 *	22.47	4	5	305	50	54	89	2	44.50	2-89	-	-
1-day Int																	
NatWest	24	15	6	108	27 *	12.00	-	-	23	2							
B&H	29	20	8	274	36 *	22.83	-	-	29	4							
Refuge	86	52	23	461	36 *	15.89	-	-	51	10							

ROBERTS, A. R.   Northamptonshire

Name: Andrew Richard Roberts
Role: Right-hand bat, leg-spin bowler
Born: 16 April 1971, Kettering
Height: 5ft 6in **Weight:** 10st 2lbs
Nickname: Reggie
County debut: 1989
1st-Class 5 w. in innings: 1
1st-Class catches: 9
Place in batting averages: 54th av. 40.66
Place in bowling averages: 94th av. 35.62
Strike rate: 68.65 (career 75.67)
Parents: David and Shirley
Marital status: Single
Family links with cricket: Father (Dave)
played a few games for Northants 2nd XI and
brother Tim won the Lord's Taverners
Award for U13 in 1991
Education: Bishop Stopford
Comprehensive, Kettering

Qualifications: 3 O-levels, 5 CSEs
Career outside cricket: 'Anything going!'
Off-season: Working and starting a carpentry course at college in the evenings
Overseas teams played for: Woolston Working Men's Club, Christchurch, New Zealand 1989-91
Cricketers particularly admired: Richard Williams, Wayne Larkins, Dennis Lillee
Other sports followed: Rugby and golf
Relaxations: 'Music, sleeping, eating, a good pint!'
Extras: Played for England YC v Pakistan 1990
Opinions on cricket: 'In favour of uncovered wickets, which would produce better technique and more exciting cricket.'
Best batting: 48 Northamptonshire v Gloucestershire, Bristol 1991
Best bowling: 6-72 Northamptonshire v Lancashire, Lytham 1991

1991 Season

	M	Inns	NO	Runs	HS	Avge	100s	50s	Ct	St	O	M	Runs	Wkts	Avge	Best	5wI	10wM
Test																		
All First	14	15	9	244	48	40.66	-	-	7	-	331.5	72	1032	29	35.58	6-72	1	-
1-day Int																		
NatWest																			
B&H																			
Refuge	4	1	0	14	14	14.00	-	-	1	-	21	0	118	6	19.66	3-26	-	

Career Performances

	M	Inns	NO	Runs	HS	Avge	100s	50s	Ct	St	Balls	Runs	Wkts	Avge	Best	5wI	10wM
Test																	
All First	18	21	10	271	48	24.63	-	-	9	-	2573	1396	34	41.05	6-72	1	-
1-day Int																	
NatWest																	
B&H																	
Refuge	4	1	0	14	14	14.00	-	-	1	-	126	118	6	19.66	3-26	-	

ROBERTS, B.   Derbyshire

Name: Bruce Roberts
Role: Right-hand bat, right-arm medium bowler, slip fielder
Born: 30 May 1962, Lusaka, Zambia
Height: 6ft 1in **Weight:** 14st
County debut: 1984
County cap: 1986
1000 runs in a season: 3
1st-Class 50s scored: 40

1st-Class 100s scored: 13
1st-Class 5 w. in innings: 1
1st-Class catches: 166
1st-Class stumpings: 1
One-Day 50s: 17
One-Day 100s: 2
Place in batting averages: (1990 129th av. 35.74)
Parents: Arthur William and Sara Ann
Wife: Ingrid
Family links with cricket: Father played for Country Districts
Education: Ruzawi, Peterhouse, and Prince Edward, Zimbabwe
Qualifications: O-levels, coaching qualifications
Career outside cricket: Working in family sports shop
Overseas teams played for: Transvaal 1982-89

Cricketers particularly admired: Allan Border, Clive Rice
Other sports followed: Rugby and most other sports
Relaxations: 'Family, watching a good programme on TV, stamps and computers.'
Best batting: 184 Derbyshire v Sussex, Chesterfield 1987
Best bowling: 5-68 Transvaal B v Northern Transvaal B, Johannesburg 1986-87

1991 Season

	M	Inns	NO	Runs	HS	Avge	100s	50s	Ct	St	O	M	Runs	Wkts	Avge	Best	5wI	10wM
Test																		
All First	1	2	2	80	44 *	-	-	-	1	-								
1-day Int																		
NatWest																		
B&H	4	3	0	75	49	25.00	-	-	2	-	13	1	69	2	34.50	1-11	-	
Refuge	5	5	0	44	15	8.80	-	-	1	-	10	1	61	2	30.50	1-27	-	

Career Performances

	M	Inns	NO	Runs	HS	Avge	100s	50s	Ct	St	Balls	Runs	Wkts	Avge	Best	5wI	10wM
Test																	
All First	205	333	34	9182	184	30.70	13	40	166	1	5389	2948	89	33.12	5-68	1	-
1-day Int																	
NatWest	15	14	3	342	64 *	31.09	-	3	10	-	138	104	2	52.00	2-73	-	
B&H	36	31	7	791	100	32.95	1	3	14	1	337	270	7	38.57	2-47	-	
Refuge	107	94	17	2247	101 *	29.18	1	11	38	-	898	979	43	22.76	4-29	-	

ROBERTS, M. L. Glamorgan

Name: Martin Leonard Roberts
Role: Right-hand bat, wicket-keeper, 'net bowler'
Born: 12 April 1966, Helston, Cornwall
Height: 5ft 11in **Weight:** 11st 8lbs
Nickname: Henry, Chicken, Saddlebags
County debut: 1985
1st-Class catches: 16
1st-Class stumpings: 4
Parents: Leonard and Marianne
Wife and date of marriage: Sue, 20 September 1986
Children: Christopher, 18 May 1989
Family links with cricket: Brother Kevin plays for Helston; father also used to play; uncle Graham was ex-Chelsea, Spurs and Rangers footballer
Education: Helston Comprehensive School

Qualifications: 5 O-levels; qualified cricket coach; OND in Hotel Administration/Catering
Career outside cricket: Coaching, also helps on voluntary basis at local Citizen's Advice Centre
Off-season: 'Looking for a new job either in the Cornwall police or in the catering trade.'
Overseas tours: Glamorgan to Trinidad 1990; Zimbabwe 1991
Cricketers particularly admired: Bob Taylor, John Steele, Dean Conway ('Glamorgan physio who is brilliant at tuning players up mentally'), Philip North, Colin Metson
Other sports followed: Football, power lifting, 'spoofing'
Injuries: 'Brain disorder on hearing of my release by Glamorgan! Plus usual wicket-keeper's day to day finger disorders.'
Relaxations: 'Eating out, buying beers for the boys, putting houses on the market (offers of £39,000 gratefully received) swimming, aerobics.'
Extras: Awarded 2nd XI Player of the Year 1989. Released by Glamorgan at the end of the 1991 season and 'open to offers'
Opinions on cricket: 'Not enough attention is paid by players to their mental preparation. It is just as important as physical fitness. Glamorgan are lucky to have a physio who is also a brilliant hypnotherapist and gee-er up for the boys. Four-day cricket is a must.'
Best batting: 25 Glamorgan v Sri Lanka, Ebbw Vale 1990

---

165. Which Englishman has hit most Test runs in a calendar year?

1991 Season

	M	Inns	NO	Runs	HS	Avge	100s	50s	Ct	St	O	M	Runs	Wkts	Avge	Best	5wI	10wM
Test																		
All First	1	0	0	0	0	-	-	-	1	2								
1-day Int																		
NatWest																		
B&H	3	3	1	2	1 *	1.00	-	-	2	-								
Refuge	1	0	0	0	0	-	-	-	1	-								

Career Performances

	M	Inns	NO	Runs	HS	Avge	100s	50s	Ct	St	Balls	Runs	Wkts	Avge	Best	5wI	10wM
Test																	
All First	10	10	2	100	25	12.50	-	-	16	4							
1-day Int																	
NatWest																	
B&H	3	3	1	2	1 *	1.00	-	-	2	-							
Refuge	4	3	3	19	12 *	-	-	-	2	-							

ROBINSON, J. D. Surrey

Name: Jonathan David Robinson
Role: Left-hand bat, right-arm medium
bowler
Born: 3 August 1966, Epsom, Surrey
Height: 5ft 10½in **Weight:** 12st 4lbs
Nickname: Robbo, Johnny Yamamoto
County debut: 1988
1st-Class 50s: 3
1st-Class catches: 4
One-Day 50s: 2
Place in batting averages: (1990 235th
av. 17.50)
Parents: Peter and Wendy
Marital status: Single
Family links with cricket: Father played
for Cambridge University and Esher CC;
'Mother bowled at me in the garden!'
Education: Danes Hill Preparatory School;
Lancing College; West Sussex Institute of
Higher Education
Qualifications: 6 O-levels, 3 A-levels, BA degree in Sports Studies, cricket coaching
award

Cricketers particularly admired: Ian Botham, David Gower, Robin Smith
Other sports followed: Rugby, squash, soccer, horse racing (brother Michael is a trainer)
Relaxations: Theatre, restaurants, TV, music, pubs, all sports, cinema, clubs, friends, travel
Extras: Did a major study at college about the commercialisation of cricket
Opinions on cricket: 'Four-day Championship matches can only be beneficial to English cricket, as a build-up to Test cricket. One-day matches, however, are a lot of fun to play in and for spectators.'
Best batting: 79 Surrey v Lancashire, Old Trafford 1991
Best bowling: 2-37 Surrey v Leicestershire, Leicester 1989

1991 Season

	M	Inns	NO	Runs	HS	Avge	100s	50s	Ct	St	O	M	Runs	Wkts	Avge	Best	5wI	10wM
Test																		
All First	4	6	1	186	79	37.20	-	2	-	-	28	3	110	2	55.00	1-18	-	-
1-day Int																		
NatWest	4	3	1	50	47	25.00	-	-	-	-	40	4	152	4	38.00	3-46	-	
B&H	3	3	0	77	38	25.66	-	-	2	-	19.2	3	60	3	20.00	2-31	-	
Refuge	15	13	3	253	55 *	25.30	-	2	4	-	88.1	3	402	9	44.66	2-32	-	

Career Performances

	M	Inns	NO	Runs	HS	Avge	100s	50s	Ct	St	Balls	Runs	Wkts	Avge	Best	5wI	10wM
Test																	
All First	22	32	5	591	79	21.88	-	3	4	-	1361	811	15	54.06	2-37	-	-
1-day Int																	
NatWest	4	3	1	50	47	25.00	-	-	-	-	240	152	4	38.00	3-46	-	
B&H	5	5	1	79	38	19.75	-	-	3	-	182	101	5	20.20	2-31	-	
Refuge	30	26	6	364	55 *	18.20	-	2	7	-	825	674	11	61.27	2-32	-	

166. Who was the last Englishman to hit a century on his Test debut?

ROBINSON, M. A.   Yorkshire

Name: Mark Andrew Robinson
Role: Right-hand bat, right-arm
fast-medium bowler
Born: 23 November 1966, Hull
Height: 6ft 3in **Weight:** 12st 12lbs
Nickname: Smokey, Coddy
County debut: 1987 (Northamptonshire),
1991 (Yorkshire)
County cap: 1990 (Northamptonshire)
1st-Class catches: 18
Place in bowling averages: 134th av. 49.64
(1990 119th av. 47.22)
Strike rate: 99.88 (career 72.84)
Parents: Joan Margaret and Malcolm
Marital status: Single
Family links with cricket: Maternal
grandfather an established local cricketer.
Father was hostile cricketer in back garden
Education: Fifth Avenue Primary;
Endike Junior High; Hull Grammar School
Qualifications: 6 O-levels, 2 A-levels, 1st NCA cricket coaching award
Overseas teams played for: Canterbury, New Zealand 1988-89
Cricketers particularly admired: Dennis Lillee, Richard Hadlee, Winston Davis, Neil
Foster, Mike Gatting, John Emburey
Other sports followed: Hull City FC ('The Tigers'), and all sports
Relaxations: Cinema, soap operas, reading, music, hot baths
Extras: Took hat-trick with first three balls of innings in Yorkshire League, playing for
Hull v Doncaster. First player to win Yorkshire U19 Bowler of the Season Award in two
successive years. Northamptonshire Uncapped Player of the Year 1989. Endured a world
record 11 innings without scoring a run during 1990 season
Best batting: 19* Northamptonshire v Essex, Chelmsford 1988
Best bowling: 4-19 Northamptonshire v Glamorgan, Wellingborough 1988

1991 Season

	M	Inns	NO	Runs	HS	Avge	100s	50s	Ct	St	O	M	Runs	Wkts	Avge	Best	5wl	10wM
Test																		
All First	17	13	4	17	8	1.88	-	-	4	-	416.1	85	1241	25	49.64	3-43	-	-
1-day Int																		
NatWest																			
B&H	3	1	1	1	1*	-	-	-	-	-	31	3	128	4	32.00	2-43	-	
Refuge	10	2	1	4	2*	4.00	-	-	1	-	64.5	3	349	11	31.72	4-33	-	

	M	Inns	NO	Runs	HS	Avge	100s	50s	Ct	St	Balls	Runs	Wkts	Avge	Best	5wl	10wM
Test																	
All First	82	81	36	89	19 *	1.97	-	-	18	-	12820	6434	176	36.55	4-19	-	-
1-day Int																	
NatWest	7	3	2	3	3 *	3.00	-	-	2	-	478	268	14	19.14	4-32	-	
B&H	12	4	3	2	1 *	2.00	-	-	-	3	682	414	13	31.84	3-20	-	
Refuge	42	13	4	7	2 *	0.77	-	-	5	-	1735	1466	33	44.42	4-33	-	

ROBINSON, P. E. *Yorkshire*

Name: Phillip Edward Robinson
Role: Right-hand middle-order bat, left-arm 'deccy' bowler
Born: 3 August 1963, Keighley
Height: 5ft 9in **Weight:** 13st 2lbs
Nickname: Billy, Red, Hare Krishna
County debut: 1984
County cap: 1988
1000 runs in a season: 3
1st-Class 50s scored: 44
1st-Class 100s scored: 7
1st-Class catches: 96
One-Day 50s: 14
Place in batting averages: 65th av. 38.02 (1990 88th av. 43.81)
Parents: Keith and Lesley
Wife and date of marriage: Jane, 19 September 1986
Family links with cricket: Brother Richard at Yorkshire Cricket Academy, mother secretary of local club, father umpires in Bradford League and elder brother plays in the same league
Education: Long Lee Primary; Hartington Middle; Greenhead Comprehensive
Qualifications: 2 O-levels
Off-season: Playing overseas
Overseas teams played for: Southlands and Lower Hutt, both in New Zealand
Cricketers particularly admired: Geoff Boycott, Richard Hadlee, Michael Holding
Relaxations: Watching TV, reading about warfare
Extras: Scored the highest score by a Yorkshire 2nd XI player when he made 233 in 1983. Scored most runs by an overseas player in the Auckland Cricket League for Eden Roskill 1989-90. Scored the fastest televised 50 in the Sunday league (19 balls) against Derbyshire at Chesterfield 1991. Released by Yorkshire at his own request at the end of the 1991 season

Opinions on cricket: 'Coloured clothing will be good from a spectator's point of view on a Sunday. The fixtures need sorting out. There is far too much travelling between games.'
Best batting: 189 Yorkshire v Lancashire, Scarborough 1991
Best bowling: 1-10 Yorkshire v Somerset, Scarborough 1990

1991 Season

	M	Inns	NO	Runs	HS	Avge	100s	50s	Ct	St	O	M	Runs	Wkts	Avge	Best	5wI	10wM
Test																		
All First	24	41	7	1293	189	38.02	2	8	20	-	10	1	49	0	-	-	-	-
1-day Int																		
NatWest	1	1	0	40	40	40.00	-	-	-	-								
B&H	6	5	1	92	43	23.00	-	-	3	-								
Refuge	16	15	3	301	64	25.08	-	2	9	-								

Career Performances

	M	Inns	NO	Runs	HS	Avge	100s	50s	Ct	St	Balls	Runs	Wkts	Avge	Best	5wI	10wM
Test																	
All First	132	217	31	6668	189	35.84	7	44	96	-	209	238	1	238.00	1-10	-	-
1-day Int																	
NatWest	8	5	0	113	66	22.60	-	1	3	-							
B&H	22	18	3	431	73 *	28.73	-	2	7	-							
Refuge	104	100	12	2194	78 *	24.93	-	11	37	-							

ROBINSON, R. T.   Nottinghamshire

Name: Robert Timothy Robinson
Role: Right-hand opening bat, right-arm bowler, county captain
Born: 21 November 1958, Sutton-in-Ashfield, Nottinghamshire
Height: 6ft **Weight:** 12st 4lbs
Nickname: Robbo
County debut: 1978
County cap: 1983
Benefit: 1992
Test debut: 1984-85
Tests: 29
One-Day Internationals: 26
1000 runs in a season: 9
1st-Class 50s scored: 92
1st-Class 100s scored: 42
1st-Class 200s scored: 2

1st-Class catches: 186
One-Day 50s: 45
One-Day 100s: 8
Place in batting averages: 16th av. 57.69 (1990 89th av. 43.67)
Parents: Eddy and Christine
Wife and date of marriage: Patricia, 2 November 1985
Children: Philip Thomas; Alex James
Family links with cricket: Father, uncle, cousin and brother all played local cricket.
Education: Dunstable Grammar School; High Pavement College, Nottingham; Sheffield University
Qualifications: Degree in Accountancy and Financial Management
Off-season: Running his own sports shop, planning his benefit year, after-dinner speaking
Overseas tours: England to India and Australia 1984-85; West Indies 1985-86; World Cup, India, New Zealand 1987-88; unofficial English team to South Africa 1989-90
Cricketers particularly admired: Geoffrey Boycott
Other sports followed: Soccer, rugby
Injuries: Muscle spasms in back
Relaxations: Spending time with family
Extras: Played for Northamptonshire 2nd XI in 1974-75 and for Nottinghamshire 2nd XI in 1977. Had soccer trials with Portsmouth, Chelsea and QPR. One of *Wisden's* Five Cricketers of the Year, 1985. Banned from Test cricket for joining 1990 tour of South Africa
Opinions on cricket: 'There should be a four-day County Championship.'
Best batting: 220* Nottinghamshire v Yorkshire, Trent Bridge 1990
Best bowling: 1-22 Nottinghamshire v Northamptonshire, Northampton 1982

1991 Season

	M	Inns	NO	Runs	HS	Avge	100s	50s	Ct	St	O	M	Runs	Wkts	Avge	Best	5wI	10wM
Test																		
All First	22	37	8	1673	180	57.69	3	10	18	-	8	0	39	1	39.00	1-30	-	-
1-day Int																		
NatWest	3	3	0	197	124	65.66	1	-	1	-								
B&H	4	4	0	239	116	59.75	1	1	1	-								
Refuge	16	16	4	278	35	23.16	-	-	6	-								

Career Performances

	M	Inns	NO	Runs	HS	Avge	100s	50s	Ct	St	Balls	Runs	Wkts	Avge	Best	5wI	10wM
Test	29	49	5	1601	175	36.38	4	6	8	-	6	0	0	-	-	-	-
All First	293	511	66	18662	220 *	41.93	42	92	186	-	234	250	3	83.33	1-22	-	-
1-day Int	26	26	0	597	83	22.96	-	3	6	-							
NatWest	29	29	2	1203	139	44.55	2	5	12	-							
B&H	57	56	7	2024	120	41.30	3	14	15	-							
Refuge	156	152	20	4209	116	31.88	3	23	54	-							

ROBSON, A. G. Surrey

Name: Andrew George Robson
Role: Right-hand bat, right-arm
fast-medium bowler
Born: 27 April 1971, Boldon,
Tyne and Wear
Height: 6ft 1in **Weight:** 13st
Nickname: George, Geordie
County debut: 1991
1st-Class catches: 0
Parents: George William and Cynthia
Marital status: Single
Family links with cricket: Father plays for
Boldon 3rd XI and is a selector, mother is an
avid cricket watcher and scorer
Education: Whitburn Comprehensive
School, Tyne and Wear
Qualifications: 2 O-levels
Off-season: 'Training hard for next season.'
Overseas tours: England U19 to Australia
1989-90
Cricketers particularly admired: Waqar Younis, Malcolm Marshall, Ian Botham – 'also
learnt a lot from Geoff Arnold'
Other sports followed: Boxing, horse racing, football
Injuries: Ankle injury
Relaxations: Watching boxing videos, eating out and socialising
Extras: Joined MCC groundstaff in 1989, signed for Surrey in June 1989. Released by
Surrey at the end of the 1991 season
Opinions on cricket: 'There should be 17 four-day games.'
Best batting: 3 Surrey v Kent, The Oval 1991
Best bowling: 1-72 Surrey v Kent, The Oval 1991

1991 Season

	M	Inns	NO	Runs	HS	Avge	100s	50s	Ct	St	O	M	Runs	Wkts	Avge	Best	5wI	10wM
Test																		
All First	2	3	0	3	3	1.00	-	-	-	-	39	14	103	1	103.00	1-72	-	-
1-day Int																		
NatWest																		
B&H																		
Refuge	3	0	0	0	0	-	-	-	-	-	24	0	128	7	18.28	3-42	-	

Career Performances

	M	Inns	NO	Runs	HS	Avge	100s	50s	Ct	St	Balls	Runs	Wkts	Avge	Best	5wI	10wM
Test																	
All First	2	3	0	3	3	1.00	-	-	-	-	234	103	1	103.00	1-72	-	-
1-day Int																	
NatWest																	
B&H																	
Refuge	4	0	0	0	0	-	-	-	-	-	186	165	8	20.62	3-42	-	

ROEBUCK, P. M.   Somerset

Name: Peter Michael Roebuck
Role: Right-hand bat, right-arm
'fast off-break bowler', slip fielder
Born: 6 March 1956, Oxford
Height: 'am slowly shrinking' **Weight:** 'a
few pounds more since the benefit'
Nickname: Professor
County debut: 1974
County cap: 1978
Benefit: 1990
1000 runs in a season: 9
1st-Class 50s scored: 93
1st-Class 100s scored: 33
1st-Class 200s scored: 2
1st-Class 5 w. in innings: 1
1st-Class catches: 162
One-Day 50s: 36
One-Day 100s: 5
Place in batting averages: 100th av. 32.03
(1990 53rd av. 49.30)
Parents: James and Elizabeth
Marital status: Single
Family links with cricket: Mother and sister both played for Oxford University Ladies.
Younger brother Paul played for Glamorgan
Education: Park School, Bath; Millfield School; Emmanuel College, Cambridge University
Qualifications: 1st Class Hons degree in law
Career outside cricket: 'Interested in writing, education, politics, travel and pontificating;
might run a Catholic school.'
Off-season: In Australia
Overseas tours: 'None apart from England to Holland, 1989.'
Cricketers particularly admired: Keith Fletcher

Other sports followed: 'Not synchronised swimming – I follow Bath Rugby (since 12 years of age) and Somerset cricket.'

Relaxations: 'Reading Massie, Kuderan, Marquez and lots of other people I won't mention as it might be bad for the image.'

Extras: Cambridge Blue 1975-77. Youngest Minor County cricketer, playing for Somerset 2nd XI at age of 13. Books published include: *Slice of Cricket, It Never Rains, It Sort of Clicks, Great Innings* and *From Sammy to Jimmy* for which he won the Wombwell Cricket Lovers' Society award for Cricket Writer of the Year 1991. Writes for *Sunday Times* and 'anyone else who asks'. Somerset captain 1986 to 1988. One of *Wisden's* Five Cricketers of the Year, 1988. Retired from county cricket at the end of the 1991 season

Opinions on cricket: 'Don't like insipid pitches or soft balls. Supposed to be a contest between bat and ball not an orgy.'

Best batting: 221* Somerset v Nottinghamshire, Trent Bridge 1986

Best bowling: 6-50 Cambridge University v Kent, Canterbury 1977

1991 Season

	M	Inns	NO	Runs	HS	Avge	100s	50s	Ct	St	O	M	Runs	Wkts	Avge	Best	5wI	10wM
Test																		
All First	17	29	3	833	101	32.03	1	5	4	-	130	33	315	9	35.00	3-10	-	-
1-day Int																		
NatWest	3	3	1	99	63 *	49.50	-	1	2	-	14	0	62	1	62.00	1-43	-	
B&H	4	4	0	74	61	18.50	-	1	-	-	13	0	63	0	-	-	-	
Refuge	9	7	0	152	45	21.71	-	-	2	-	49.4	3	236	11	21.45	4-11	-	

Career Performances

	M	Inns	NO	Runs	HS	Avge	100s	50s	Ct	St	Balls	Runs	Wkts	Avge	Best	5wI	10wM
Test																	
All First	335	552	81	17552	221 *	37.26	33	93	162	-	7606	3540	72	49.16	6-50	1	-
1-day Int																	
NatWest	38	38	3	1087	102	31.05	1	4	10	-	176	139	3	46.33	1-21	-	
B&H	68	64	6	1671	120	28.81	3	9	28	-	302	217	8	27.12	2-13	-	
Refuge	180	166	23	4191	105	29.30	1	23	33	-	707	618	28	22.07	4-11	-	

ROMAINES, P. W. Gloucestershire

Name: Paul William Romaines
Role: Right-hand opening bat, off-break bowler
Born: 25 December 1955, Bishop Auckland, Co Durham
Height: 6ft **Weight:** 12st 8lbs
Nickname: Canny, Human
County debut: 1975 (Northants), 1982 (Gloucs)
County cap: 1983 (Gloucs)
Benefit: 1991
1000 runs in a season: 3
1st-Class 50s scored: 41
1st-Class 100s scored: 13
1st-Class catches: 68
One-Day 50s: 20
One-Day 100s: 2
Place in batting averages: (1990 149th av. 32.77)

Parents: George and Freda
Wife and date of marriage: Julie Anne, 1979
Children: Claire Louise
Family links with cricket: Father played local cricket and is still an avid watcher. Grandfather, W. R. Romaines, represented Durham in Minor Counties cricket, and played v Australia in 1926
Education: Leeholme School, Bishop Auckland
Qualifications: 8 O-levels, NCA qualified coach
Career outside cricket: Commercial manager for Durham CCC
Off-season: Working towards the successful launching of Durham as a first-class county in 1992
Overseas teams played for: Griqualand West, South Africa 1984-85
Cricketers particularly admired: Zaheer Abbas, Graham Gooch, Clive Radley, Gordon Greenidge
Other sports followed: Athletics, squash, golf, soccer
Relaxations: 'Listening to music, having a good pint, antiques, people, writing letters, good conversation.'
Extras: Debut for Northamptonshire 1975. Played Minor County cricket with Durham 1977-81. Joined Gloucestershire in 1982. Retired from first-class cricket at the end of the 1991 season and joined Durham as commercial manager
Best batting: 186 Gloucestershire v Warwickshire, Nuneaton 1982
Best bowling: 3-42 Gloucestershire v Surrey, The Oval 1985

1991 Season

	M	Inns	NO	Runs	HS	Avge	100s	50s	Ct	St	O	M	Runs	Wkts	Avge	Best	5wI	10wM
Test																		
All First	3	5	0	35	28	7.00	-	-	1	-								
1-day Int																		
NatWest																		
B&H	1	1	0	22	22	22.00	-	-	1	-								
Refuge	6	4	2	47	27 *	23.50	-	-	1	-								

Career Performances

	M	Inns	NO	Runs	HS	Avge	100s	50s	Ct	St	Balls	Runs	Wkts	Avge	Best	5wI	10wM
Test																	
All First	173	309	23	8120	186	28.39	13	41	68	-	257	247	4	61.75	3-42	-	-
1-day Int																	
NatWest	16	16	2	400	82	28.57	-	3	3	-							
B&H	23	21	1	685	125	34.25	1	4	8	-							
Refuge	116	106	13	2546	105	27.37	1	13	24	-							

ROSE, G. D.   Somerset

Name: Graham David Rose
Role: Right-hand bat, right-arm
fast-medium bowler
Born: 12 April 1964, Tottenham
Height: 6ft 5in **Weight:** 14st 10lbs
Nickname: Hagar
County debut: 1985 (Middlesex),
1987 (Somerset)
County cap: 1988 (Somerset)
1000 runs in a season: 1
50 wickets in a season: 2
1st-Class 50s scored: 14
1st-Class 100s scored: 2
1st-Class 5 w. in innings: 4
1st-Class catches: 46
One-Day 50s: 6
One-Day 100s: 2
Place in batting averages: 83rd av. 34.70
(1990 33rd av. 55.55)
Place in bowling averages: 122nd av. 43.00 (1990 69th av. 36.81)
Strike rate: 77.52 (career 56.99)
Parents: William and Edna

Wife and date of marriage: Teresa Julie, 19 September 1987
Children: Georgina Charlotte, 6 December 1990
Family links with cricket: Father and brothers have played club cricket
Education: Northumberland Park School, Tottenham
Qualifications: 6 O-levels, 4 A-levels. NCA coaching certificate
Off-season: Working for Somerset County Council
Overseas teams played for: Carey Park, Bunbury, Western Australia 1984-85; Freemantle, Perth 1986-87; Paarl, Cape Town
Cricketers particularly admired: Wayne Daniel, Richard Hadlee, Jimmy Cook
Other sports followed: Football (Tottenham Hotspur), golf
Injuries: Back – Left sacroiliac joint
Relaxations: Wine, food, gardening and 'generally relaxing with my wife and daughter'
Extras: Played for England YC v Australia 1983. Took 6 wickets for 41 on Middlesex debut. Joined Somerset for 1987 season and scored 95 on debut. Completed double of 1000 runs and 50 wickets in first-class cricket in 1990 and scored fastest recorded 100s in NatWest Trophy (v Devon) and Sunday League (v Glamorgan)
Opinions on cricket: 'I am in favour of the Championship consisting solely of four-day games. Not only would it produce a fairer contest but it would also raise the standard of county cricket, and as a result the Test team, by allowing the best team to win more often with less of this horse-trading between captains on the final morning. It would also give the players a little extra time between games to avoid fatigue of mind and body.'
Best batting: 106 Somerset v Gloucestershire, Bristol 1991
Best bowling: 6-41 Middlesex v Worcestershire, Worcester 1985

1991 Season

	M	Inns	NO	Runs	HS	Avge	100s	50s	Ct	St	O	M	Runs	Wkts	Avge	Best	5wl	10wM
Test																		
All First	15	20	3	590	106	34.70	2	2	8	-	323	53	1075	25	43.00	4-77	-	-
1-day Int																		
NatWest	2	1	0	3	3	3.00	-	-	-	-	7	0	40	0	-		-	-
B&H	4	4	0	37	23	9.25	-	-	-	-	38.5	2	172	3	57.33	2-48	-	
Refuge	12	12	2	160	59	16.00	-	2	2	-	54.1	0	290	9	32.22	2-21	-	

Career Performances

	M	Inns	NO	Runs	HS	Avge	100s	50s	Ct	St	Balls	Runs	Wkts	Avge	Best	5wl	10wM
Test																	
All First	100	125	32	2796	106	30.06	2	14	46	-	13450	7090	236	30.04	6-41	4	-
1-day Int																	
NatWest	7	6	0	166	110	27.66	1	-	2	-	323	194	5	38.80	2-30	-	
B&H	26	20	3	317	64	18.64	-	1	5	-	1483	1005	31	32.41	4-37	-	
Refuge	78	65	11	1292	148	23.92	1	5	23	-	3026	2309	78	29.60	4-28	-	

ROSEBERRY, M. A. Middlesex

Name: Michael Anthony Roseberry
Role: Right-hand bat, right-arm occasional off-break and swing bowler, close-to-wicket fielder
Born: 28 November 1966, Houghton-le-Spring, Sunderland
Height: 6ft **Weight:** 14st
Nickname: Zorro
County debut: 1985
County cap: 1990
1000 runs in a season: 2
1st-Class 50s scored: 28
1st-Class 100s scored: 6
1st-Class catches: 69
One-Day 50s scored: 11
One-Day 100s scored: 1
Place in batting averages: 68th av. 37.77
(1990 107th av. 39.82)

Parents: Matthew and Jean
Wife and date of marriage: Helen Louise, 22 February 1991
Family links with cricket: Uncle, Peter Wyness, played for Royal Navy; brother Andrew has joined Leicester
Education: Tonstall Preparatory School; Durham School
Qualifications: 5 O-levels, 1 A-level, advanced cricket coach
Off-season: In Australia
Overseas tours: England YC to West Indies 1985
Cricketers particularly admired: Desmond Haynes, Geoff Boycott
Other sports followed: Football, rugby, 'I tend to follow and take part in most.'
Relaxations: 'I love eating out with Helen, listening to music, going out to a pub.'
Extras: Won Lord's Taverners/MCC Cricketer of the Year 1983. Won Cricket Society's Award for Best Young Cricketer of the Year 1984 and also twice won Cricket Society award for best all-rounder in schools cricket. Played in Durham League as a professional while still at school. At age 16, playing for Durham School v St Bees, he hit 216 in 160 minutes
Opinions on cricket: 'Championship cricket should be all four days with teams still encouraged to be positive. Coloured clothing and more razzmatazz in Sunday games.'
Best batting: 135 Middlesex v Essex, Ilford 1990
Best bowling: 1-1 Middlesex v Sussex, Hove 1988

1991 Season

	M	Inns	NO	Runs	HS	Avge	100s	50s	Ct	St	O	M	Runs	Wkts	Avge	Best	5wI	10wM
Test																		
All First	24	44	4	1511	123 *	37.77	2	8	19	-	14	1	63	0	-	-	-	-
1-day Int																		
NatWest	2	2	0	50	44	25.00	-	-	2	-	2	0	20	0	-	-	-	-
B&H	1	0	0	0	0	-												
Refuge	14	14	1	383	106 *	29.46	1	2	7	-								

Career Performances

	M	Inns	NO	Runs	HS	Avge	100s	50s	Ct	St	Balls	Runs	Wkts	Avge	Best	5wI	10wM
Test																	
All First	95	160	20	4738	135	33.84	6	28	69	-	405	311	4	77.75	1-1	-	-
1-day Int																	
NatWest	9	9	0	229	48	25.44	-	-	3	-	12	20	0	-	-	-
B&H	8	6	0	81	38	13.50	-	-	1	-							
Refuge	52	50	4	1437	106 *	31.23	1	11	17	-							

RUSSELL, R. C.   Gloucestershire

Name: Robert Charles Russell
Role: Left-hand bat, wicket-keeper
Born: 15 August 1963, Stroud
Height: 5ft 8½in **Weight:** 9st 8lbs
Nickname: Jack
County debut: 1981
County cap: 1985
Test debut: 1988
Tests: 25
One-Day Internationals: 26
1st-Class 50s scored: 24
1st-Class 100s scored: 4
1st-Class catches: 505
1st-Class stumpings: 80
One-Day 50s: 6
One-Day 100s: 1
Place in batting averages: 172nd av. 23.22
(1990 119th av. 37.81)
Parents: John and Jennifer
Wife and date of marriage: Aileen Ann, 6 March 1985
Children: Stepson, Marcus Anthony; Elizabeth Ann, March 1988; Victoria, 1989; Charles David 1991

Education: Uplands County Primary School; Archway Comprehensive School
Qualifications: 7 O-levels, 2 A-levels
Career outside cricket: Professional artist – Jack Russell Art, c/o Gloucestershire CCC
Off-season: 'Playing for my country as much as possible!'
Overseas tours: England to Pakistan 1987-88; to India and West Indies 1989-90; Australia 1990-91; New Zealand 1991-92
Cricketers particularly admired: Alan Knott, Bob Taylor
Other sports followed: Football ('a Spurs supporter, but only on television'), snooker
Relaxations: Drawing, sketching, painting (oil and watercolour). Watching comedy, Rory Bremner and Phil Cool especially
Extras: Spotted at age 9 by Gloucestershire coach, Graham Wiltshire. Record for most dismissals in a match on first-class debut: 8 (7 caught, 1 stumped) for Gloucestershire v Sri Lankans at Bristol, 1981. Youngest Gloucestershire wicket-keeper (17 years 307 days). Represented England YC v West Indies in 1982. Hat-trick of catches v Surrey at The Oval 1986. Had a three-week exhibition of his drawings in Bristol 1988 and published a book of his work entitled *A Cricketer's Art*. Co-author with Christopher Martin-Jenkins of *Sketches of a Season*, published in 1989. Was chosen as England's Man of the Test Series, England v Australia 1989. Commissioned by Dean of Gloucester to do a drawing of Gloucester Cathedral to raise funds for 900th Anniversary. Still turns out for his original club, Stroud CC, whenever he can. Runs six miles a day to keep fit and drinks up to 20 cups of tea a day. One of *Wisden's* Five Cricketers of the Year, 1990
Best batting: 128* England v Australia, Old Trafford 1989
Best bowling: 1-4 Gloucestershire v West Indians, Bristol 1991

1991 Season

	M	Inns	NO	Runs	HS	Avge	100s	50s	Ct	St	O	M	Runs	Wkts	Avge	Best	5wI	10wM
Test	5	9	1	102	46	12.75	-	-	8	-								
All First	20	32	5	627	111	23.22	1	2	48	4	1.2	0	14	1	14.00	1-4	-	-
1-day Int	3	1	0	1	1	1.00	-	-	4	-								
NatWest	2	2	0	48	25	24.00	-	-	5	1								
B&H	4	4	1	85	51	28.33	-	1	4	-								
Refuge	11	11	1	214	42	21.40	-	-	15	1								

Career Performances

	M	Inns	NO	Runs	HS	Avge	100s	50s	Ct	St	Balls	Runs	Wkts	Avge	Best	5wI	10wM
Test	25	40	7	869	128 *	26.33	1	3	66	6							
All First	224	309	68	6107	128 *	25.34	4	24	505	80	21	33	1	33.00	1-4	-	-
1-day Int	26	19	6	261	50	20.07	-	1	26	5							
NatWest	25	15	4	248	42 *	22.54	-	-	26	7							
B&H	38	25	8	343	51	20.17	-	1	37	7							
Refuge	115	79	20	1312	108	22.23	1	4	94	21							

SALIM MALIK   Essex

Name: Salim Malik
Role: Right-hand bat, right-arm medium
bowler
Born: 16 April 1963, Lahore, Pakistan
Height: 5ft 9in
County debut: 1991
County cap: 1991
Test debut: 1981-82
Tests: 63
One-Day Internationals: 125
1000 runs in a season: 1
1st-Class 50s scored: 53
1st-Class 100s scored: 28
1st-Class 200s scored: 1
1st-Class catches: 117
One-Day 50s: 26
One-Day 100s: 4
Place in batting averages: 4th av. 73.03
Place in bowling averages: 60th av. 31.53
Strike rate: 47.33 (career 53.96)
Education: Government College, Lahore
Off-season: Playing for Pakistan
Overseas tours: Pakistan U23 to Sri Lanka 1984-85; Pakistan to Australia 1981-82;
England 1982; India 1983-84; Australia 1983-84; New Zealand 1984-85; Sri Lanka 1985-86; India 1986-87; England 1987; West Indies 1987-88; New Zealand 1988-89; Australia 1989-90
Overseas teams played for: Lahore; Habib Bank
Best batting: 215 Essex v Leicestershire, Ilford 1991
Best bowling: 5-19 Habib Bank v Karachi, Karachi 1985-86

1991 Season

	M	Inns	NO	Runs	HS	Avge	100s	50s	Ct	St	O	M	Runs	Wkts	Avge	Best	5wI	10wM
Test																		
All First	24	36	9	1972	215	73.03	6	8	25	-	118.2	10	473	15	31.53	3-26	-	-
1-day Int																		
NatWest	3	3	1	55	26	27.50	-	-	4	-	6	0	34	0	-		-	-
B&H	6	6	2	217	90 *	54.25	-	2	1	-	2	0	7	1	7.00	1-7	-	
Refuge	11	11	1	451	89	45.10	-	3	6	-	18.2	1	71	1	71.00	1-25	-	

Career Performances

	M	Inns	NO	Runs	HS	Avge	100s	50s	Ct	St	Balls	Runs	Wkts	Avge	Best	5wI	10wM
Test	63	90	16	3146	119 *	42.51	8	18	46	-	260	106	5	21.20	1-3	-	-
All First	170	261	40	10435	215	47.21	28	53	117	-	2860	1621	53	30.58	5-19	2	-
1-day Int	125	117	15	3407	102	33.40	4	21	40	-	530	468	13	36.00	5-35	1	
NatWest	3	3	1	55	26	27.50	-	-	4	-	36	34	0	-	-	-	-
B&H	6	6	2	217	90 *	54.25	-	2	1	-	12	7	1	7.00	1-7	-	
Refuge	11	11	1	451	89	45.10	-	3	6	-	110	71	1	71.00	1-25	-	

SALISBURY, I. D. K. Sussex

Name: Ian David Kenneth Salisbury
Role: Right-hand bat, right-arm leg-spinner
Born: 2 January 1970, Northampton
Height: 5ft 11in **Weight:** 12st
Nickname: Budgie
County debut: 1989
County cap: 1991
1st-Class 50s scored: 1
1st-Class 5 w. in innings: 3
1st-Class catches: 34
Place in batting averages: 230th av. 14.46
(1990 202nd av.24.07)
Place in bowling averages: 118th av. 41.68
(1990 129th av. 49.40)
Strike rate: 79.79 (career 88.90)
Parents: Dave and Margaret
Marital status: Single
Family links with cricket: 'Dad is
vice-president of my first club, Brixworth.'
Education: Moulton Comprehensive, Northampton
Qualifications: 7 O-levels; NCA coaching certificate
Off-season: Touring with England A
Overseas tours: England A to Pakistan 1990-91; Bermuda and West Indies 1991-92
Cricketers particularly admired: Desmond Haynes, Viv Richards, Richard Blakey,
Richie Benaud and all of Sussex CCC
Other sports followed: 'All sports.'
Relaxations: Music and socialising
Opinions on cricket: 'Four-day cricket must be introduced. We should have at least a day
off a week, so travelling can be much safer, rather than driving straight after a game.'
Best batting: 68 Sussex v Derbyshire, Hove 1990
Best bowling: 5-32 Sussex v Worcestershire, Worcester 1990

1991 Season

	M	Inns	NO	Runs	HS	Avge	100s	50s	Ct	St	O	M	Runs	Wkts	Avge	Best	5wI	10wM
Test																		
All First	22	21	8	188	34	14.46	-	-	12	-	638.2	148	2001	48	41.68	5-40	1	-
1-day Int																		
NatWest	2	2	1	18	14 *	18.00	-	-	-	-	21	1	76	2	38.00	1-36	-	
B&H	4	3	1	32	17 *	16.00	-	-	2	-	41	3	149	6	24.83	3-40	-	
Refuge	15	9	2	61	23	8.71	-	-	2	-	82.1	4	399	10	39.90	3-10	-	

Career Performances

	M	Inns	NO	Runs	HS	Avge	100s	50s	Ct	St	Balls	Runs	Wkts	Avge	Best	5wI	10wM
Test																	
All First	56	58	23	565	68	16.14	-	1	34	-	9775	5264	109	48.29	5-32	3	-
1-day Int																	
NatWest	4	3	2	20	14 *	20.00	-	-	1	-	228	142	2	71.00	1-36	-	
B&H	6	4	1	34	17 *	11.33	-	-	2	-	348	241	7	34.42	3-40	-	
Refuge	29	15	5	90	23	9.00	-	-	6	-	937	785	22	35.68	3-10	-	

SARGEANT, N. F. Surrey

Name: Neil Fredrick Sargeant
Role: Right-hand bat, wicket-keeper
Born: 8 November 1965, Hammersmith
Height: 5ft 7in **Weight:** 10st 7lbs
Nickname: Sarge, Bilko, Dusty
County debut: 1989
1st-Class catches: 56
1st-Class stumpings: 10
Place in batting averages: 214th av. 16.29
Parents: Barry and Christine
Marital status: Single
Education: Grange Primary School; Whitmore High School
Qualifications: 2 O-levels
Cricketers particularly admired:
Alan Knott, Bob Taylor, Ray Jennings
Other sports followed: Football, golf, horse racing
Relaxations: Horse racing, music
Extras: Played football for Tottenham Hotspur Youth Team
Best batting: 49 Surrey v Lancashire, Old Trafford 1991
Best bowling: 1-88 Surrey v Gloucestershire, Guildford 1991

1991 Season

	M	Inns	NO	Runs	HS	Avge	100s	50s	Ct	St	O	M	Runs	Wkts	Avge	Best	5wl	10wM
Test																		
All First	21	28	4	391	49	16.29	-	-	46	8	5	0	88	1	88.00	1-88	-	-
1-day Int																		
NatWest																		
B&H																		
Refuge	2	1	1	13	13 *	-	-	-	-	1	-							

Career Performances

	M	Inns	NO	Runs	HS	Avge	100s	50s	Ct	St	Balls	Runs	Wkts	Avge	Best	5wl	10wM
Test																	
All First	27	33	5	436	49	15.57	-	-	56	10	30	88	1	88.00	1-88	-	-
1-day Int																	
NatWest																	
B&H																	
Refuge	4	2	1	35	22	35.00	-	-	4	-							

SAXELBY, M.   Nottinghamshire

Name: Mark Saxelby
Role: Left-hand bat, right-arm medium bowler
Born: 4 January 1969, Newark
Height: 6ft 3in **Weight:** 14st 7lbs
Nickname: Sax
County debut: 1989
1st-Class 50s scored: 2
1st-Class catches: 3
One-Day 50s: 1
Place in batting averages: 213th av. 16.55
(1990 163rd av. 30.45)
Parents: George Kenneth and Hilda Margaret
Marital status: Single
Family links with cricket: Brother played for Nottinghamshire; father played local cricket
Education: Nottingham High School
Qualifications: 7 O-levels, 2 A-levels
Career outside cricket: Lab technician
Cricketers particularly admired: Richard Hadlee, Derek Randall

Other sports followed: Rugby Union and League, football, American football
Relaxations: 'Good pubs, cinema, watching most sports.'
Opinions on cricket: 'Put the seam back on the ball fast. You're killing bowlers off. These flat pitches do nothing for the game. I would like to see more four-day cricket. Captains have become so adept at contrived finishes that spectators are bored.'
Best batting: 73 Nottinghamshire v Cambridge University, Fenner's 1990
Best bowling: 3-41 Nottinghamshire v Derbyshire, Derby 1991

1991 Season

	M	Inns	NO	Runs	HS	Avge	100s	50s	Ct	St	O	M	Runs	Wkts	Avge	Best	5wI	10wM
Test																		
All First	7	10	1	149	44	16.55	-	-	-	-	97.2	17	423	4	105.75	3-41	-	-
1-day Int																		
NatWest	2	2	1	42	36	42.00	-	-	1	-	18.4	1	90	3	30.00	2-42	-	
B&H	3	2	0	37	32	18.50	-	-	-	-	26	1	118	1	118.00	1-36	-	
Refuge	17	13	1	208	55	17.33	-	1	4	-	108	3	516	18	28.66	4-29	-	

Career Performances

	M	Inns	NO	Runs	HS	Avge	100s	50s	Ct	St	Balls	Runs	Wkts	Avge	Best	5wI	10wM
Test																	
All First	16	27	6	520	73	24.76	-	2	3	-	1050	743	9	82.55	3-41	-	-
1-day Int																	
NatWest	3	3	1	83	41	41.50	-	-	2	-	112	90	3	30.00	2-42	-	
B&H	4	3	0	37	32	12.33	-	-	-	-	156	118	1	118.00	1-36	-	
Refuge	28	22	3	396	55	20.84	-	1	9	-	888	775	24	32.29	4-29	-	

SCOTT, C. W.   Durham

Name: Christopher Wilmot Scott
Role: Right-hand bat, wicket-keeper
Born: 23 January 1964, Lincoln
Height: 5ft 8in **Weight:** 11st
Nickname: George
County debut: 1981 (Nottinghamshire)
County cap: 1988 (Nottinghamshire)
1st-Class 50s scored: 5
1st-Class catches: 135
1st-Class stumpings: 9
Parents: Kenneth and Kathleen
Wife and date of marriage: Jacqui, 18 March 1989
Family links with cricket: Father and two brothers all played for Collingham
Education: Robert Pattinson Comprehensive, North Hykeham, Lincoln

Qualifications: 4 O-levels, 2 CSEs, coaching certificate
Career outside cricket: Coaching, farming
Off-season: Working for the British Sugar Corporation, Newark
Overseas teams played for: Poverty Bay, New Zealand 1983-84; Queensland University 1985-86, 1987-89
Cricketers particularly admired: 'Ian Botham above all, but many others.'
Other sports followed: Rugby union
Extras: One of the youngest players to make Championship debut for Nottinghamshire – 17 years 157 days. Broke the Nottinghamshire record for most catches in a match with 10 against Derbyshire in 1988. Left Nottinghamshire at the end of the 1991 season to join Durham

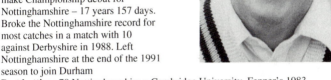

Best batting: 78 Nottinghamshire v Cambridge University, Fenner's 1983

1991 Season

	M	Inns	NO	Runs	HS	Avge	100s	50s	Ct	St	O	M	Runs	Wkts	Avge	Best	5wI	10wM
Test																		
All First	2	0	0	0	0	-	-	-	3	-								
1-day Int																		
NatWest																		
B&H																		
Refuge																		

Career Performances

	M	Inns	NO	Runs	HS	Avge	100s	50s	Ct	St	Balls	Runs	Wkts	Avge	Best	5wI	10wM
Test																	
All First	63	72	18	1263	78	23.38	-	5	135	9	6	10	0	-	-	-	-
1-day Int																	
NatWest	3	0	0	0	0	-	-	-	4	-							
B&H	4	3	1	28	18	14.00	-	-	1	-							
Refuge	25	11	4	95	26	13.57	-	-	21	1							

SCOTT, R. J.   Gloucestershire

Name: Richard James Scott
Role: Left-hand bat, right-arm medium bowler
Born: 2 November 1963, Bournemouth
Height: 5ft 11in **Weight:** 14st 'and a bit'
Nickname: SOS
County debut: 1986 (Hants), 1991 (Gloucs)
1st-Class 50s scored: 8
1st-Class 100s scored: 3
1st-Class catches: 26
One-Day 50s: 10
One-Day 100s: 1
Place in batting averages: 152nd av. 25.69
(1990 232nd av. 18.00)
Place in bowling averages: 112th av. 40.93
Strike rate: 76.00 (career 75.95)
Parents: Andy and Anne

Wife and date of marriage: Julie,
27 September 1991
Family links with cricket: Father and two brothers played for Dorset League side Colehill
Education: Queen Elizabeth School, Wimborne
Qualifications: 2 O-levels, CSEs, coaching award
Off-season: Coaching and playing in Perth, Western Australia
Overseas teams played for: South Perth, Western Australia 1989-92
Cricketers particularly admired: Malcolm Marshall, Robin Smith, Simon O'Donnell
Other sports followed: Golf, football, rugby
Injuries: Infected in-growing toenail
Relaxations: Playing golf, pub life
Extras: Played Minor Counties cricket for Dorset since 1981. Represented Minor Counties Cricket Association in 1985. Scored century on Gloucestershire debut
Opinions on cricket: 'Four-day game a revelation. Best side will always win Championship.'
Best batting: 127 Gloucestershire v Worcestershire, Worcester 1991
Best bowling: 3-43 Gloucestershire v Sussex, Hove 1991

---

167. Who holds the record for most catches in one first-class match, and how many (excluding wicket-keepers)?

1991 Season

	M	Inns	NO	Runs	HS	Avge	100s	50s	Ct	St	O	M	Runs	Wkts	Avge	Best	5wI	10wM
Test																		
All First	20	34	1	848	127	25.69	2	3	6	-	199	40	614	15	40.93	3-43	-	-
1-day Int																		
NatWest	2	2	0	11	11	5.50	-	-	-	-	22.2	3	54	6	9.00	4-22	-	
B&H	4	4	0	99	46	24.75	-	-	-	-	16.5	0	81	1	81.00	1-42	-	
Refuge	14	14	1	376	77	28.92	-	3	-	-	62	2	303	8	37.87	2-26	-	

Career Performances

	M	Inns	NO	Runs	HS	Avge	100s	50s	Ct	St	Balls	Runs	Wkts	Avge	Best	5wI	10wM
Test																	
All First	47	80	5	1765	127	23.53	3	8	26	-	1573	871	20	43.55	3-43	-	-
1-day Int																	
NatWest	5	4	0	33	22	8.25	-	-	-	-	134	54	6	9.00	4-22	-	
B&H	10	10	0	317	69	31.70	-	2	-	-	167	137	1	137.00	1-42	-	
Refuge	43	41	3	1100	116 *	28.94	1	8	7	-	556	474	14	33.85	2-8	-	

SEYMOUR, A. C. H.   Worcestershire

Name: Adam Charles Hilton Seymour
Role: Left-hand bat, right-arm medium bowler
Born: 7 December 1967, Royston, Cambridgeshire
Height: 6ft 3in **Weight:** 13st 7lbs
County debut: 1988 (Essex)
1st-Class 50s scored: 4
1st-Class 100s scored: 1
1st-Class catches: 8
Place in batting averages: 105th av. 31.35
Parents: Roger and Julie
Marital status: Single
Education: Millfield School
Career outside cricket: 'Work for father in his pub.'
Off-season: Playing cricket overseas
Overseas tours: Millfield School to Barbados 1987
Cricketers particularly admired: Graham Gooch, Neil Foster, Keith Fletcher
Other sports followed: Football, rugby, golf, American football
Relaxations: Eating out at Indian restaurants

Extras: First played for Essex 2nd XI in 1984, aged 16. In 1989 was the county's leading batsman in second team cricket. Left Essex at the end of the 1991 season to join Worcs
Best batting: 157 Essex v Glamorgan, Cardiff 1991

1991 Season

	M	Inns	NO	Runs	HS	Avge	100s	50s	Ct	St	O	M	Runs	Wkts	Avge	Best	5wl	10wM
Test																		
All First	10	18	1	533	157	31.35	1	3	7	-	4	0	27	0	-	-	-	-
1-day Int																		
NatWest	1	1	0	0	0	0.00	-	-	1	-								
B&H																		
Refuge	5	4	0	46	25	11.50	-	-	1	-								

Career Performances

	M	Inns	NO	Runs	HS	Avge	100s	50s	Ct	St	Balls	Runs	Wkts	Avge	Best	5wl	10wM
Test																	
All First	14	24	4	697	157	34.85	1	4	8	-	24	27	0	-	-	-	-
1-day Int																	
NatWest	1	1	0	0	0	0.00	-	-	1	-							
B&H																	
Refuge	5	4	0	46	25	11.50	-	-	1	-							

SHAHID, N. Essex

Name: Nadeem Shahid
Role: Right-hand bat, right-arm leg-spinner
Born: 23 April 1969, Karachi
Height: 6ft **Weight:** 11st 7lbs
Nickname: Prince, Biryani II, Nads
County debut: 1989
1000 runs in a season: 1
1st-Class 50s scored: 8
1st-Class 100s scored: 1
1st-Class catches: 34
Place in batting averages: 202nd av. 18.37
(1990 74th av. 45.59)
Parents: Ahmed and Salma
Marital status: Single
Family links with cricket: Brother plays in the local league
Education: Stoke High; Northgate High; Ipswich School; Plymouth Polytechnic

Qualifications: 6 O-levels, 1 A-level; coaching certificate
Cricketers particularly admired: Abdul Qadir, Ian Botham and John Garnham (of Copdock CC)
Overseas teams played for: Gosnells, Perth, Western Australia 1990-91
Other sports followed: Golf, badminton, tennis, golf, football and rugby
Relaxations: 'Listening to music, dining out, going to the cinema.'
Extras: Youngest Suffolk player aged 17. Played for HMC, MCC Schools, ESCA U19, NCA Young Cricketers (Lord's and International Youth tournament in Belfast), and at every level for Suffolk. TSB Young Player of the Year 1986, winner of *The Daily Telegraph* bowling award 1987 and 1988, and Cricket Society's All-rounder of the Year, 1988
Opinions on cricket: 'Old Reader balls should be re-introduced for the 1991 season in order to improve the imbalance between bat and ball. Captains should play more attacking cricket and perhaps be prepared to lose in order to win – setting reasonable targets rather than killing the game.'
Best batting: 125 Essex v Lancashire, Colchester 1990
Best bowling: 3-91 Essex v Surrey, The Oval 1990

1991 Season

	M	Inns	NO	Runs	HS	Avge	100s	50s	Ct	St	O	M	Runs	Wkts	Avge	Best	5wI	10wM
Test																		
All First	8	9	1	147	83	18.37	-	1	6	-								
1-day Int																		
NatWest	1	0	0	0	0	-	-	-	1	-								
B&H	6	4	0	51	42	12.75	-	-	1	-								
Refuge	11	6	1	103	36	20.60	-	-	3	-								

Career Performances

	M	Inns	NO	Runs	HS	Avge	100s	50s	Ct	St	Balls	Runs	Wkts	Avge	Best	5wI	10wM
Test																	
All First	34	47	10	1405	125	37.97	1	8	34	-	1155	780	15	52.00	3-91	-	-
1-day Int																	
NatWest	1	0	0	0	0	-	-	-	1	-							
B&H	6	4	0	51	42	12.75	-	-	1	-							
Refuge	18	11	2	193	36	21.44	-	-	5	-							

168. Which team holds the record for the most runs in a single first-class innings, against whom and in what season?

SHARP, K.   Yorkshire

Name: Kevin Sharp
Role: Left-hand bat, off-break bowler
Born: 6 April 1959, Leeds
Height: 5ft 9in **Weight:** 12st 7lbs
Nickname: Lambsy, Poodle
County debut: 1976
County cap: 1982
Benefit: 1991
1000 runs in a season: 1
1st-Class 50s scored: 47
1st-Class 100s scored: 14
1st-Class catches: 107
One-Day 50s: 27
One-Day 100s: 3
Place in batting averages: (1990 108th
av. 39.75)
Parents: Gordon and Joyce
Wife and date of marriage: Karen,
1 October 1983

Children: Amy Lauren, 28 December 1985; Nicholas Richard, 21 October 1989
Family links with cricket: Father played with Woodhouse in Leeds League for many years. Younger brother David now playing local cricket
Education: Abbey Grange C of E High School, Leeds
Qualifications: CSE Grade I Religious Education. Coaching award
Career outside cricket: Working for Credit Collections UK Ltd
Off-season: Finishing of benefit year
Overseas teams played for: Griqualand West, South Africa 1981-84
Cricketers particularly admired: Richard Hadlee, Malcolm Marshall
Other sports followed: Snooker, soccer, golf, squash
Relaxations: Decorating and maintaining the house
Extras: Scored 260* for England YC v West Indies 1977 – a record score for England in Youth Tests
Opinions on cricket: 'Too much continuous cricket. Because of travelling and playing every day I believe cricket is not up to the standard it could be. There should be more time between matches to allow players to prepare properly.'
Best batting: 181 Yorkshire v Gloucestershire, Harrogate 1986
Best bowling: 2-13 Yorkshire v Glamorgan, Bradford 1984

---

169. Who caught most catches in his first-class career (excluding wicket-keepers)?

1991 Season

	M	Inns	NO	Runs	HS	Avge	100s	50s	Ct	St	O	M	Runs	Wkts	Avge	Best	5wI	10wM
Test																		
All First																		
1-day Int																		
NatWest																		
B&H	1	1	0	0	0	0.00	-	-	-	-								
Refuge	2	2	0	78	41	39.00	-	-	1	-								

Career Performances

	M	Inns	NO	Runs	HS	Avge	100s	50s	Ct	St	Balls	Runs	Wkts	Avge	Best	5wI	10wM
Test																	
All First	218	361	38	9962	181	30.84	14	47	107	-	1262	887	12	73.91	2-13	-	-
1-day Int																	
NatWest	17	13	2	228	50	20.72	-	1	6	-	60	47	4	11.75	4-40	-	
B&H	45	40	3	1073	105 *	29.00	1	6	15	-							
Refuge	141	135	13	3393	114	27.81	2	20	44	-	1	1	0	-	-	-	-

SHARP, M. A.   Lancashire

Name: Marcus Anthony Sharp
Role: Left-hand bat, right-arm medium bowler, fine-leg specialist
Born: 1 June 1970, Oxford
Height: 6ft 6^1/$_2$in **Weight:** 14st
Nickname: Van Basten, Sherpa, Marco
County debut: 1991
1st-Class catches: 0
Parents: Robin and Cynthia
Marital status: 'Not even close'
Family links with cricket: 'Dad bowls nagging seamers for Clitheroe, My uncle Malcolm played one Test for Uganda.'
Education: Clitheroe Royal Grammar School; Edgehill College of Higher Education (Ormskirk)
Qualifications: 8 O-levels, 3 A-levels
Off-season: Final year at college
Overseas tours: Lancs to Mombasa 1990-91
Overseas teams played for: Old Selbournians, East London, South Africa 1988-89
Cricketers particularly admired: David Gower, Malcolm Marshall, Bob Ratcliffe (my first coach)

Other sports followed: Football (Blackburn Rovers) 'and everything else bar swimming'
Injuries: Thigh strain and shin splints
Relaxations: Music, books 'and the Waggon and Horses'
Opinions on cricket: 'Longer tea interval. Bowlers of my pace should be allowed to bowl off 19 yards. Pitches should offer less assistance to the batsmen so reducing the need for contrived results.'
Best bowling: 1-21 Lancashire v Oxford University, The Parks 1991

1991 Season

	M	Inns	NO	Runs	HS	Avge	100s	50s	Ct	St	O	M	Runs	Wkts	Avge	Best	5wI	10wM
Test																		
All First	1	0	0	0	0	-	-	-	-	-	15	7	21	1	21.00	1-21	-	-
1-day Int																		
NatWest																			
B&H																			
Refuge																			

Career Performances

	M	Inns	NO	Runs	HS	Avge	100s	50s	Ct	St	Balls	Runs	Wkts	Avge	Best	5wI	10wM
Test																	
All First	1	0	0	0	0	-	-	-	-	-	90	21	1	21.00	1-21	-	-
1-day Int																	
NatWest																	
B&H																	
Refuge																	

SHASTRI, R. J.   Glamorgan

Name: Ravishankar Jayadritha Shastri
Role: Right-hand bat, slow left-arm bowler
Born: 27 May 1962, Bombay, India
Height: 6ft 3½in **Weight:** 13st 1lb
Nickname: Shas
County debut: 1987
County cap: 1988
Test debut: 1980-81
Tests: 73
One-Day Internationals: 128
1000 runs in a season: 2
1st-Class 50s scored: 50
1st-Class 100s scored: 29
1st-Class 5 w. in innings: 16

1st-Class 10 w. in match: 3
1st-Class catches: 127
One-Day 50s: 28
One-Day 100s: 4
Place in batting averages: 28th av. 48.17
Place in bowling averages: 13th av. 23.35
Strike rate: 59.58 (career 82.18)
Parents: Jayadritha and Lakshmi
Marital status: Single
Education: Don Bosco High School,
Bombay; Bombay University
Qualifications: Bachelor of Commerce
Career outside cricket: Public relations
executive
Off-season: Playing for India
Overseas teams played for: Bombay
Overseas tours: Young India to Sri Lanka
1980; England 1981; India to New Zealand
1980-81; England 1982; Pakistan 1982-83;

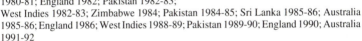

West Indies 1982-83; Zimbabwe 1984; Pakistan 1984-85; Sri Lanka 1985-86; Australia
1985-86; England 1986; West Indies 1988-89; Pakistan 1989-90; England 1990; Australia
1991-92
Cricketers particularly admired: Imran Khan, Viv Richards, Richard Hadlee, Gundappa
Vishwanath, Gary Sobers, Gordon Greenidge
Other sports followed: Tennis, athletics
Relaxations: Watching sport, films, music
Extras: Has batted at every number for India except No 11. Hit 6 sixes in an over off Tank
Raj on his way to 200 in 113 minutes and off 123 deliveries – the fastest double century
in first-class cricket
Best batting: 200* Bombay v Baroda, Bombay 1984-85
Best bowling: 9-101 Bombay v Rest of India, Indore 1981-82

1991 Season

	M	Inns	NO	Runs	HS	Avge	100s	50s	Ct	St	O	M	Runs	Wkts	Avge	Best	5wI	10wM
Test																		
All First	22	32	9	1108	133 *	48.17	2	7	9	-	307.5	88	724	31	23.35	5-71	1	-
1-day Int																		
NatWest	2	2	0	51	26	25.50	-	-	2	-	12	0	60	2	30.00	2-60	-	
B&H	3	3	1	161	138 *	80.50	1	-	1	-	32	1	124	2	62.00	1-40	-	
Refuge	13	13	2	342	90 *	31.09	-	2	3	-	51	1	241	7	34.42	3-26	-	

	M	Inns	NO	Runs	HS	Avge	100s	50s	Ct	St	Balls	Runs	Wkts	Avge	Best	5wI	10wM
Test	73	110	14	3460	157	36.04	10	12	36	-	15103	5914	143	41.35	5-75	2	-
All First	221	318	54	11650	217	44.12	29	50	127	-	40108	15684	466	33.65	9-101	16	3
1-day Int	128	106	19	2567	102	29.50	3	15	35	-	5810	4068	115	35.37	4-38	-	
NatWest	9	9	2	208	59 *	29.71	-	1	4	-	421	224	14	16.00	5-13	1	
B&H	15	14	3	362	138 *	32.90	1	1	6	-	888	538	6	89.66	1-17	-	
Refuge	50	49	9	1415	92	35.37	-	11	11	-	1542	1152	31	37.18	3-26	-	

SHINE, K. J. Hampshire

Name: Kevin James Shine
Role: Right-hand bat, right-arm
fast-medium bowler
Born: 22 February 1969, Bracknell,
Berkshire
Height: 6ft 3in **Weight:** 13st 11lbs
Nickname: Shirley, Ealham, Don, Shoe
County debut: 1989
1st-Class 5 w. in innings: 2
1st-Class catches: 3
Place in bowling averages: 106th av. 38.26
(1990 93rd av. 39.42)
Strike rate: 54.28 (career 58.12)
Parents: Joe and Clair
Marital status: Single
Education: Winnerish County Primary;
Maiden Erlegh Comprehensive
Qualifications: 5 O-levels, gave up
A-levels to pursue a cricket career

Off-season: 'Having a complete rest from cricket and beginning my training to get even fitter, stronger and more mobile.'
Overseas teams played for: Merewether, Newcastle, NSW 1990-91
Cricketers particularly admired: Malcolm Marshall, Cardigan Connor ('the fittest cricketer in the country'), Peter Sainsbury, Allan Donald ('the fastest I've ever seen')
Other sports followed: Football, basketball, athletics
Relaxations: 'Driving, relaxing with my girlfriend, going to the cinema.'
Opinions on cricket: 'The balls and pitches are still far too much in favour of the batsmen, thus giving them god-like status for the number of runs they score. Give the bowler a decent ball and an encouraging pitch and the contest would then be between mortals again.'
Best batting: 26* Hampshire v Middlesex, Lord's 1989
Best bowling: 5-43 Hampshire v Worcestershire, Portsmouth 1991

1991 Season

	M	Inns	NO	Runs	HS	Avge	100s	50s	Ct	St	O	M	Runs	Wkts	Avge	Best	5wl	10wM
Test																		
All First	16	18	8	92	25	9.20	-	-	2	-	343.5	48	1454	38	38.26	5-43	2	-
1-day Int																		
NatWest																		
B&H																		
Refuge	4	1	1	2	2*	-	-	-	-	-	27	0	102	5	20.40	2-35	-

Career Performances

	M	Inns	NO	Runs	HS	Avge	100s	50s	Ct	St	Balls	Runs	Wkts	Avge	Best	5wl	10wM
Test																	
All First	25	21	10	145	26*	13.18	-	-	3	-	3197	2094	55	38.07	5-43	2	-
1-day Int																	
NatWest																	
B&H	4	1	0	0	0	0.00	-	-	-	-	194	167	4	41.75	4-68	-
Refuge	4	1	1	2	2*	-	-	-	-	-	162	102	5	20.40	2-35	-

SIDEBOTTOM, A.   Yorkshire

Name: Arnold Sidebottom
Role: Right-hand bat, right-arm fast-medium bowler, outfielder
Born: 1 April 1954, Barnsley
Height: 6ft 2in **Weight:** 13st 10lbs
Nickname: Woofer, Red Setter, Arnie
County debut: 1973
County cap: 1980
Benefit: 1988 (£103,240)
Test debut: 1985
Tests: 1
50 wickets in a season: 4
1st-Class 50s scored: 13
1st-Class 100s scored: 1
1st-Class 5 w. in innings: 23
1st-Class 10 w. in match: 3
1st-Class catches: 63
One-Day 50s: 1
Parents: Jack and Florence
Wife and date of marriage: Gillian, 17 June 1977
Children: Ryan Jay, 1978; Dale, 1980
Family links with cricket: Father good cricketer

Education: Barnsley Broadway Grammar School
Career outside cricket: Professional footballer with Manchester United for five years, Huddersfield Town for two years and Halifax Town
Overseas teams played for: Orange Free State 1981-84
Overseas tours: Rebel England team to South Africa 1981-82
Cricketers particularly admired: Steve Oldham, David Bairstow, Graham Stevenson
Other sports followed: Most sports
Relaxations: Watching television, horse racing, playing with sons
Extras: Banned from Test cricket for three years for joining rebel team to South Africa in 1982. Injured toe during Test debut in 1985 and not picked for England again. Yorkshire Player of the Year 1989. Retired at the end of 1991 season due to persistent knee trouble and signed to play for Holmfirth in the Huddersfield League in 1992
Best batting: 124 Yorkshire v Glamorgan, Cardiff 1977
Best bowling: 8-72 Yorkshire v Leicestershire, Middlesbrough 1986

1991 Season

	M	Inns	NO	Runs	HS	Avge	100s	50s	Ct	St	O	M	Runs	Wkts	Avge	Best	5wl	10wM
Test																		
All First	1	1	1	18	18 *	-	-	-	1	-	11	4	26	1	26.00	1-26	-	-
1-day Int																		
NatWest																			
B&H	3	0	0	0	0	-	-	-	1	-	31	11	52	4	13.00	4-19	-	
Refuge	4	4	2	24	10	12.00	-	-	1	-	32	0	115	2	57.50	1-25	-	

Career Performances

	M	Inns	NO	Runs	HS	Avge	100s	50s	Ct	St	Balls	Runs	Wkts	Avge	Best	5wl	10wM
Test	1	1	0	2	2	2.00	-	-	-	-	112	65	1	65.00	1-65	-	-
All First	228	263	62	4508	124	22.42	1	13	63	-	30663	14558	596	24.42	8-72	23	3
1-day Int																	
NatWest	25	16	5	192	45	17.45	-	-	9	-	1506	699	37	18.89	5-27	1	
B&H	52	27	9	246	32	13.66	-	-	13	-	2981	1580	72	21.94	5-27	1	
Refuge	156	86	33	835	52 *	15.75	-	1	29	-	6502	4561	149	30.61	4-22	-	

170. In what year did Sri Lanka play their first Test, against whom and where?

SLADDIN, R. W.   Derbyshire

Name: Richard William Sladdin
Role: Right-hand bat, slow left-arm bowler
Born: 8 January 1969, Halifax
Height: 5ft 11in **Weight:** 12st 4lbs
Nickname: Slads, Boris
County debut: 1991
1st-Class 5 w. in innings: 1
1st-Class catches: 6
Place in bowling averages: 94th av. 35.74
Strike rate: 81.96
Parents: Raymond and Elsie
Marital status: Single
Family links with cricket: Father watches a
lot of club cricket, eldest brother Nigel plays
club cricket
Education: Sowerby Bridge High School
Qualification: 5 O-levels, 1 A-level
Career outside cricket: Trainee accountant
Off-season: Playing cricket in New Zealand

Cricketers particularly admired: Richard Hadlee, Derek Underwood, Abdul Qadir
Other sports followed: Football (Leeds United) and most other sports
Relaxations: Music, travelling, fishing, eating and drinking, clubs
Extras: Played for ESCA U19 in 1988 and 1989
Best batting: 18 Derbyshire v Essex, Chelmsford 1991
Best bowling: 5-186 Derbyshire v Essex, Chelmsford 1991

1991 Season

	M	Inns	NO	Runs	HS	Avge	100s	50s	Ct	St	O	M	Runs	Wkts	Avge	Best	5wI	10wM
Test																		
All First	8	9	4	68	18	13.60	-	-	6	-	368.5	101	965	27	35.74	5-186	1	-
1-day Int																		
NatWest																		
B&H																		
Refuge																		

> 171. Who topped the first-class batting averages last season
> for Yorkshire?

Career Performances

	M	Inns	NO	Runs	HS	Avge	100s	50s	Ct	St	Balls	Runs	Wkts	Avge	Best	5wI	10wM
Test																	
All First	8	9	4	68	18	13.60	-	-	6	-	2213	965	27	35.74	5-186	1	-
1-day Int																	
NatWest																	
B&H																	
Refuge																	

SMALL, G. C.   Warwickshire

Name: Gladstone Cleophas Small
Role: Right-hand bat, right-arm
fast-medium bowler
Born: 18 October 1961, St George,
Barbados
Height: 5ft 11st **Weight:** 12st
Nickname: Gladys
County debut: 1980
County cap: 1982
Test debut: 1986
Tests: 17
One-Day Internationals: 46
50 wickets in a season: 6
1st-Class 50s scored: 7
1st-Class 5 w. in innings: 27
1st-Class 10 w. in match: 2
1st-Class catches: 77
Place in batting averages: 211th av. 16.81
(1990 244th av. 16.44)
Place in bowling averages: 50th av. 29.93
(1990 72nd av. 37.18)
Strike rate: 66.40 (career 57.21)
Parents: Chelston and Gladys
Wife: Lois
Children: Zak
Family links with cricket: Cousin, Milton Small, toured England with West Indies in
1984
Education: Moseley School; Hall Green Technical College, Birmingham
Qualifications: 2 O-levels
Overseas tours: England YC to New Zealand 1979-80; England to Australia 1986-87;
World Cup 1987; India and West Indies 1989-90; Australia 1990-91

Overseas teams played for: South Australia 1985-86

Cricketers particularly admired: Dennis Lillee, Malcolm Marshall, Richard Hadlee, Bob Willis

Other sports followed: Athletics, golf, tennis, soccer

Relaxations: 'Playing a round of golf; listening to music and relaxing with my wife.'

Extras: Was called up for England Test squad v Pakistan at Edgbaston, July 1982, but did not play. Bowled 18-ball over v Middlesex in August 1982, with 11 no balls. Grandfather watched him take eight wickets in the Barbados Test v West Indies in 1989-90 on his return to the land of his birth. Was Andy Lloyd's best man

Opinions on cricket: 'The introduction of four-day Championship cricket will improve the first-class game: teams will have to bowl out the opposition twice instead of relying on contrived results. We should play on hard, fast and true wickets that would be beneficial to both batsmen and bowlers.'

Best batting: 70 Warwickshire v Lancashire, Old Trafford 1988

Best bowling: 7-15 Warwickshire v Nottinghamshire, Edgbaston 1988

1991 Season

	M	Inns	NO	Runs	HS	Avge	100s	50s	Ct	St	O	M	Runs	Wkts	Avge	Best	5wl	10wM
Test																		
All First	20	29	7	370	58	16.81	-	1	5	-	498	126	1347	45	29.93	4-36	-	-
1-day Int																		
NatWest	4	2	0	5	3	2.50	-	-	-	-	45	13	111	6	18.50	3-28	-	
B&H	4	3	0	5	2	1.66	-	-	1	-	44	2	193	1	193.00	1-55	-	
Refuge	10	3	0	4	3	1.33	-	-	3	-	65	3	322	10	32.20	2-25	-	

Career Performances

	M	Inns	NO	Runs	HS	Avge	100s	50s	Ct	St	Balls	Runs	Wkts	Avge	Best	5wl	10wM
Test	17	24	7	263	59	15.47	-	1	9	-	3927	1871	55	34.01	5-48	2	-
All First	255	334	76	3852	70	14.93	-	7	77	-	41192	20494	720	28.46	7-15	27	2
1-day Int	46	23	9	93	18 *	6.64	-	-	6	-	2504	1741	51	34.13	4-31	-	
NatWest	30	18	6	148	33	12.33	-	-	4	-	1801	940	34	27.64	3-22	-	
B&H	44	28	6	131	22	5.95	-	-	9	-	2492	1525	53	28.77	4-22	-	
Refuge	128	62	19	308	40 *	7.16	-	-	29	-	5469	4147	168	24.68	5-29	2	

> 172. Who played in a Test match whilst still a pupil at an English school?

SMITH, A. M.   Gloucestershire

Name: Andrew Michael Smith
Role: Right-hand bat, left-arm medium bowler
Born: 1 October 1967, Dewsbury, West Yorks
Height: 5ft 9in **Weight:** 11st 7lbs
Nickname: Smudge, Turbo, Dodo ('or anything else that Bill Athey thinks of')
County debut: 1991
1st-Class catches: 0
Place in bowling averages: 78th av. 33.89
Strike rate: 64.20
Parents: Hugh and Margaret
Marital status: Single
Family links with cricket: Father and brother both played good club cricket in Yorkshire
Education: Queen Elizabeth Grammar School, Wakefield; Exeter University
Qualification: BA (Hons) French and German
Off-season: Coaching and playing cricket in Nelson, New Zealand
Overseas tours: Bradford Junior Cricket League to Barbados: 1986; Exeter University to Barbados 1987
Overseas teams played for: Waimea, New Zealand 1990
Cricketers particularly admired: Richard Hadlee, Desmond Haynes, Eddie Milburn, Jack Russell
Other sports followed: Football (Leeds United), golf, table tennis
Relaxations: Playing golf, travel, reading, sleeping
Extras: Played for ESCA U19, NAYC and represented Combined Universities in 1988 and 1990
Opinions on cricket: 'Introduction of four-day cricket on suitable wickets would be beneficial. Too much cricket is played. Worn-out seamers get little chance to recuperate and consequently injuries occur.'
Best batting: 22 Gloucestershire v Warwickshire, Edgbaston 1991
Best bowling: 4-41 Gloucestershire v Leicestershire, Hinckley 1991

---

173. Who captained the 1981 Australians in England?

1991 Season

	M	Inns	NO	Runs	HS	Avge	100s	50s	Ct	St	O	M	Runs	Wkts	Avge	Best	5wI	10wM
Test																		
All First	14	13	2	60	22	5.45	-	-	-	-	310.2	55	983	29	33.89	4-41	-	-
1-day Int																		
NatWest	2	0	0	0	0	-	-	-	-	-	16	2	63	2	31.50	1-14	-	
B&H	4	3	2	12	8	12.00	-	-	1	-	33	2	95	2	47.50	1-30	-	
Refuge	13	7	6	27	15 *	27.00	-	-	3	-	66.4	2	378	15	25.20	3-16	-	

Career Performances

	M	Inns	NO	Runs	HS	Avge	100s	50s	Ct	St	Balls	Runs	Wkts	Avge	Best	5wI	10wM
Test																	
All First	14	13	2	60	22	5.45	-	-	-	-	1862	983	29	33.89	4-41	-	-
1-day Int																	
NatWest	2	0	0	0	0	-	-	-	-	-	96	63	2	31.50	1-14	-	
B&H	4	3	2	12	8	12.00	-	-	1	-	198	95	2	47.50	1-30	-	
Refuge	13	7	6	27	15 *	27.00	-	-	3	-	400	378	15	25.20	3-16	-	

SMITH, B. F.   Leicestershire

Name: Benjamin Francis Smith
Role: Right-hand bat, right-arm medium
bowler
Born: 3 April 1972, Corby
Height: 5ft 8in **Weight:** 9st 7lbs
Nickname: Gadget, Smudge
County debut: 1990
1st-Class 50s scored: 3
1st-Class catches: 4
Place in batting averages: 69th av. 37.44
Parents: Janet and Keith
Marital status: Single
Family links with cricket: Both
uncles played for ESCA, father played for
Northamptonshire Schools
Education: Tugby Primary; Kibworth High;
Robert Smyth, Market Harborough
Qualifications: 8 GCSEs, ESB distinction
Overseas tours: England YC to New Zealand
1990-91
Overseas teams played for: Alexandria, Zimbabwe
Cricketers particularly admired: Paul Parker

Other sports followed: Tennis, football, golf
Relaxations: Listening to music, playing golf
Extras: Played tennis for Leicestershire aged 12
Best batting: 71 Leicestershire v Worcestershire, Worcester 1991
Best bowling: 1-5 Leicestershire v Essex, Ilford 1991

1991 Season

	M	Inns	NO	Runs	HS	Avge	100s	50s	Ct	St	O	M	Runs	Wkts	Avge	Best	5wI	10wM
Test																		
All First	15	23	5	674	71	37.44	-	3	3	-	13	2	91	1	91.00	1-5	-	-
1-day Int																		
NatWest	2	1	0	6	6	6.00	-	-	-	-								
B&H																		
Refuge	12	12	3	226	33	25.11	-	-	2	-	3	0	15	0	-		-	-

Career Performances

	M	Inns	NO	Runs	HS	Avge	100s	50s	Ct	St	Balls	Runs	Wkts	Avge	Best	5wI	10wM
Test																	
All First	17	25	6	693	71	36.47	-	3	4	-	78	91	1	91.00	1-5	-	-
1-day Int																	
NatWest	2	1	0	6	6	6.00	-	-	-	-							
B&H																	
Refuge	16	16	3	281	33	21.61	-	-	2	-	18	15	0	-		-	-

SMITH, C. L.   Hampshire

Name: Christopher Lyall Smith
Role: Right-hand bat, off-spin bowler
Born: 15 October 1958, Durban, South Africa
Height: 5ft 11in **Weight:** 13st 10lbs
Nickname: Kippy
County debut: 1979 (Glamorgan), 1980 (Hampshire)
County cap: 1981 (Hampshire)
Benefit: 1990 (£181,679)
Test debut: 1983
Tests: 8
One-Day Internationals: 4
1000 runs in a season: 10
1st-Class 50s scored: 88
1st-Class 100s scored: 47
1st-Class 200s scored: 2
1st-Class 5 w. in innings: 1

1st-Class catches: 176
One-Day 50s: 39
One-Day 100s: 11
Place in batting averages: 7th av. 64.70
(1990 22nd av. 60.83)
Parents: John Arnold and Joy Lyall
Wife and date of marriage: Julie Owen,
August 1989
Children: Haley, 1991
Family links with cricket: Grandfather,
Vernon Lyall Shearer, played for Natal;
brother Robin plays for Hampshire and
England
Education: Northlands High School,
Durban, South Africa
Qualifications: Matriculation (2 A-level
equivalents)
Career outside cricket: Marketing manager,
Western Australia Cricket Association
Overseas tours: England to New Zealand and Pakistan 1983-84; England B to Sri Lanka
1985-86
Overseas teams played for: Natal (debut 1978)
Cricketers particularly admired: Barry Richards, Grayson Heath (coach in S. Africa)
Other sports followed: Watches football (Southampton FC), squash, golf
Relaxations: 'Walking with my dog or lying on the beach, swimming, listening to music.'
Extras: Made debut for Glamorgan in 1979. Played for Gorseinon in South Wales League
in 1979. Made Hampshire debut 1980. Captained Hampshire 2nd XI in 1981. Became
eligible to play for England in 1983. One of *Wisden's* Five Cricketers of the Year, 1983.
Left Hampshire towards the end of the 1991 season to take up his appointment with the
Western Australia Cricket Association in Perth
Opinions on cricket: 'Still feel the game is undersold and that too few clubs employ
successful, proven, get-up-and-go marketing managers. Welcome four-day cricket as it
should help to produce more potential Test players.'
Best batting: 217 Hampshire v Warwickshire, Edgbaston 1987
Best bowling: 5-69 Hampshire v Sussex, Southampton 1988

1991 Season

	M	Inns	NO	Runs	HS	Avge	100s	50s	Ct	St	O	M	Runs	Wkts	Avge	Best	5wI	10wM
Test																		
All First	16	27	3	1553	200	64.70	6	7	4	-	19	3	63	0	-		-	-	-
1-day Int																		
NatWest	4	3	1	194	105 *	97.00	1	1	1	-								
B&H	5	5	2	413	142	137.66	2	2	1	-								
Refuge	8	8	0	397	114	49.62	1	2	3	-								

Career Performances

	M	Inns	NO	Runs	HS	Avge	100s	50s	Ct	St	Balls	Runs	Wkts	Avge	Best	5wI	10wM
Test	8	14	1	392	91	30.15	-	2	5	-	102	39	3	13.00	2-31	-	-
All First	269	466	60	18028	217	44.40	47	88	176	-	4457	2685	50	53.70	5-69	1	-
1-day Int	4	4	0	109	70	27.25	-	1	-	-	36	28	2	14.00	2-8	-	
NatWest	32	31	5	1431	159	55.03	7	4	10	-	90	59	5	11.80	3-32	-	
B&H	38	34	7	1265	154 *	46.85	3	7	10	-	6	2	0	-	-	-	
Refuge	126	116	22	3567	114	37.94	1	27	17	-	21	10	2	5.00	2-3	-	

SMITH, D. M. Sussex

Name: David Mark Smith
Role: Left-hand bat, right-arm medium
bowler
Born: 9 January 1956, Balham
Height: 6ft 4in **Weight:** 16st
County debut: 1973 (Surrey), 1984 (Worcs),
1989 (Sussex)
County cap: 1980 (Surrey), 1984 (Worcs),
1989 (Sussex)
Test debut: 1985-86
Tests: 2
One-Day Internationals: 2
1000 runs in a season: 6
1st-Class 50s scored: 64
1st-Class 100s scored: 25
1st-Class catches: 171
One-Day 50s: 32
One-Day 100s: 5
Place in batting averages: 47th av. 42.69
(1990 197th av. 25.21)
Parents: Dennis and Tina
Wife and date of marriage: Jacqui, 7 January 1977
Children: Sarah-Jane Louise, 4 April 1982
Family links with cricket: Father played cricket for the BBC
Education: Battersea Grammar School
Qualifications: 3 O-levels
Career outside cricket: Company director
Off-season: Working for my company
Overseas tours: England to West Indies 1985-86; joined tour to West Indies 1989-90 as
a replacement for Graham Gooch
Overseas teams played for: Universals, Harare, Zimbabwe

Cricketers particularly admired: John Edrich, Clive Lloyd, Graham Gooch
Other sports followed: Football (Charlton Athletic), golf
Injuries: Broken left thumb twice, broken left little finger, 'otherwise fit as a fiddle'
Relaxations: Motor racing – 'keen to race at Le Mans and any other world series sports car event'
Extras: Played for Surrey 2nd XI in 1972. Was not retained after 1977 but was re-instated in 1978. Sacked by Surrey during 1983 season and joined Worcestershire in 1984. Rejoined Surrey in 1987, but released by Surrey at end of 1988 season. Joined Sussex for 1989. Called up as a replacement for England's tour of West Indies in 1989-90 – played in one match before breaking his thumb. Joined Sussex for 1989 season
Opinions on cricket: 'There is too much cricket played. Flat wickets and seamless balls do not make for good cricket. There should be more four-day cricket. I dislike listening to ex-cricketers rubbishing today's players.'
Best batting: 189* Worcestershire v Kent, Worcester 1984
Best bowling: 3-40 Surrey v Sussex, The Oval 1976

1991 Season

	M	Inns	NO	Runs	HS	Avge	100s	50s	Ct	St	O	M	Runs	Wkts	Avge	Best	5wI	10wM
Test																		
All First	20	35	6	1238	126*	42.69	2	8	14	-	2	0	15	0	-		-	-
1-day Int																		
NatWest	2	2	0	102	62	51.00	-	1	1	-								
B&H	4	4	0	209	102	52.25	1	1	2	-								
Refuge	5	5	0	208	78	41.60	-	1	3	-								

Career Performances

	M	Inns	NO	Runs	HS	Avge	100s	50s	Ct	St	Balls	Runs	Wkts	Avge	Best	5wI	10wM
Test	2	4	0	80	47	20.00	-	-	-	-							
All First	278	443	85	13061	189*	36.48	25	64	171	-	2773	1556	30	51.86	3-40	-	-
1-day Int	2	2	1	15	10*	15.00	-	-	-	-							
NatWest	33	32	6	1304	109	50.15	2	10	10	-	186	118	4	29.50	3-39	-	
B&H	63	59	9	1817	126	36.34	3	8	35	-	336	266	8	33.25	4-29	-	
Refuge	155	142	27	3230	87*	28.08	-	14	48	-	749	606	12	50.50	2-21	-	

174. What is the lowest score by a first-class county in one innings?

SMITH, G. Warwickshire

Name: Gareth Smith
Role: Right-hand bat, left-arm fast-medium bowler, specialist third man/fine leg
Born: 20 July 1966, Jarrow, County Durham
Height: 6ft 1¹/₂in **Weight:** 12st 7lbs
Nickname: Efty
County debut: 1986 (Northants), 1990 (Warwicks)
1st-Class 5 w. in innings: 1
1st-Class catches: 3
Parents: John and Patricia
Wife and date of marriage:
Katharine Jane, 6 October 1990
Family links with cricket: 'Father was, and still is, a magnificent back-garden bowler/batsman'
Education: Boldon Comprehensive School; South Tyneside College
Qualifications: 6 O-levels, BTec ONC/OND in Computer Studies

Career outside cricket: Computer operator/programmer, database analyst – 'anything in the field of computers'
Off-season: Working as a database analyst/marketing analyst at Misco (UK), Wellingborough
Overseas teams played for: Belgrano, Argentina 1986-87; Uitenhage, Eastern Province, South Africa 1987-88
Cricketers particularly admired: Tim Munton , Dermot Reeve, Allan Donald, Bob Carter, Wayne Larkins
Other sports followed: Football, athletics, golf, tennis – 'anything but snooker!'
Injuries: Thigh strains (x 2), sore shin/knee
Relaxations: Reading, golf, theatre, listening to all kinds of music (but mainly Kate Bush and Bon Jovi), having a pint of lager
Extras: Took part in relay run via all first-class county grounds to raise money for leukaemia research. Took wicket of Sunil Gavaskar with second ball in first-class cricket. Realised a lifelong ambition to play in a Lord's final (playing for Walsall against Teddington in the National Knockout). Released by Warwickshire at the end of the 1991 season.
Opinions on cricket: 'I would like to put on record that during my seven years as a pro at Northants and Warwicks I met a lot of good friends – thanks lads!'
Best batting: 30 Warwickshire v Sussex, Eastbourne 1990
Best bowling: 6-72 Northamptonshire v Sussex, Hove 1987

Career Performances

	M	Inns	NO	Runs	HS	Avge	100s	50s	Ct	St	Balls	Runs	Wkts	Avge	Best	5wI	10wM
Test																	
All First	10	11	2	90	30	10.00	-	-	3	-	1073	633	21	30.14	6-72	1	-
1-day Int																	
NatWest																	
B&H																	
Refuge	5	1	0	5	5	5.00	-	-	-	-	132	145	4	36.25	2-20	-	

SMITH, I. Durham

Name: Ian Smith
Role: Right-hand bat, right-arm medium bowler
Born: 11 March 1967, Consett, Co.Durham
Height: 6ft 3in **Weight:** 14st 5lbs
Nickname: Smudga, Cyril, Gilbert
County debut: 1985
1st-Class 50s scored: 5
1st-Class 100s scored: 3
1st-Class catches: 24
One-Day 50s: 2
Place in batting averages: 179th av. 22.27
(1990 102nd av. 41.00)
Parents: Jim and Mary
Marital status: Single
Family links with cricket: Father NCA Coach, brother played in League cricket. 'No relation to Chris, Robin, David, Neil, Paul, Gareth, etc, etc.'
Education: Ryton Comprehensive
Qualifications: 4 O-levels, CSE; studying for Open University degree in Social Psychology
Overseas tours: England YC to West Indies 1985
Cricketers particularly admired: Ian Botham, Mike Fatkin, Viv Richards
Other sports followed: Football, table tennis
Relaxations: Music, wine, theatre, golf
Extras: Glamorgan Young Player of the Year 1989. Offered terms by several football clubs. Released by Glamorgan at the end of the 1991 season and signed to play for Durham in 1992
Opinions on cricket: 'Can't believe that four-day cricket wasn't introduced for 1991. It's

by far the best form of cricket, particularly with wickets and balls as they were in 1990.'
Best batting: 116 Glamorgan v Kent, Canterbury 1989
Best bowling: 3-48 Glamorgan v Hampshire, Cardiff 1989

1991 Season

	M	Inns	NO	Runs	HS	Avge	100s	50s	Ct	St	O	M	Runs	Wkts	Avge	Best	5wI	10wM
Test																		
All First	10	13	2	245	47	22.27	-	-	7	-	42.1	8	156	4	39.00	1-7	-	-
1-day Int																		
NatWest	2	0	0	0	0	-	-	-	1	-	9	0	60	3	20.00	3-60	-	
B&H	4	4	0	90	51	22.50	-	1	1	-	10	0	69	1	69.00	1-51	-	
Refuge	11	11	3	244	41	30.50	-	-	3	-	28	0	158	4	39.50	2-35	-	

Career Performances

	M	Inns	NO	Runs	HS	Avge	100s	50s	Ct	St	Balls	Runs	Wkts	Avge	Best	5wI	10wM
Test																	
All First	62	81	13	1674	116	24.61	3	5	24	-	3712	2450	52	47.11	3-48	-	-
1-day Int																	
NatWest	5	3	0	60	33	20.00	-	-	2	-	150	123	5	24.60	3-60	-	
B&H	12	11	0	137	51	12.45	-	1	2	-	144	138	2	69.00	1-21	-	
Refuge	45	44	11	729	56 *	22.09	-	1	13	-	744	673	18	37.38	3-22	-	

SMITH, N. M. K.   Warwickshire

Name: Neil Michael Knight Smith
Role: Right-hand bat, off-spin bowler
Born: 27 July 1967, Solihull
Height: 6ft **Weight:** 12st 10lbs
Nickname: Gurt
County debut: 1987
1st-Class 50s scored: 3
1st-Class 100s scored: 1
1st-Class catches: 7
Place in batting averages: 116th av. 29.85
(1990 160th av. 30.83)
Parents: Mike (M.J.K.) and Diana
Marital status: Single
Family links with cricket: Father
captained Warwickshire and England
Education: Warwick School
Qualifications: 3 O-levels (Maths, English,
French); cricket coach Grade 1

Off-season: 'Earning as much money as I can.'
Overseas teams played for: Phoenix, Perth, Western Australia 1988-89
Cricketers particularly admired: David Gower, Allan Border
Other sports followed: Rugby
Relaxations: Sport and music
Opinions on cricket: 'I am in favour of a four-day Championship.'
Best batting: 161 Warwickshire v Yorkshire, Headingley 1989
Best bowling: 3-50 Warwickshire v Northamptonshire, Edgbaston 1991

1991 Season

	M	Inns	NO	Runs	HS	Avge	100s	50s	Ct	St	O	M	Runs	Wkts	Avge	Best	5wl	10wM
Test																		
All First	5	9	2	209	70	29.85	-	2	-	-	111	32	321	8	40.12	3-50	-	-
1-day Int																		
NatWest	2	2	0	38	38	19.00	-	-	-	-	13	1	37	2	18.50	1-17	-	
B&H	1	1	0	23	23	23.00	-	-	-	-	4	0	32	0	-	-	-	
Refuge	11	8	4	127	39	31.75	-	-	4	-	53.3	0	268	10	26.80	3-52	-	

Career Performances

	M	Inns	NO	Runs	HS	Avge	100s	50s	Ct	St	Balls	Runs	Wkts	Avge	Best	5wl	10wM
Test																	
All First	27	39	7	886	161	27.68	1	3	7	-	2799	1455	30	48.50	3-50	-	-
1-day Int																	
NatWest	6	6	2	121	52	30.25	-	1	1	-	192	117	4	29.25	1-6	-	
B&H	4	3	1	64	30 *	32.00	-	-	1	-	114	95	1	95.00	1-43	-	
Refuge	40	27	7	324	39	16.20	-	-	11	-	1188	1065	28	38.03	3-36	-	

175. Who was the first bowler to take 400 Test wickets, and when did he reach that total?

SMITH, P. A. Warwickshire

Name: Paul Andrew Smith
Role: Right-hand bat, right-arm
fast-medium bowler
Born: 15 April 1964, Newcastle-on-Tyne
Height: 6ft 2in **Weight:** 12st
Nickname: Smithy, Jim
County debut: 1982
County cap: 1986
1000 runs in a season: 2
1st-Class 50s scored: 44
1st-Class 100s scored: 4
1st-Class 5 w. in innings: 3
1st-Class catches: 47
One-Day 50s: 9
Place in batting averages: 1199th av. 18.68
(1990 53rd av. 32.50)
Place in bowling averages: 82nd av. 34.20
(1990 10th av. 24.85)
Strike rate: 62.86 (career 56.54)
Parents: Ken and Joy
Wife and date of marriage: Caroline, 31 July 1987
Children: Oliver James, 5 February 1988
Family links with cricket: Father played for Leicestershire. Both brothers played for Warwickshire
Education: Heaton Grammar School, Newcastle
Qualifications: 5 O-levels
Career outside cricket: Worked for *Birmingham Post and Mail* for three winters; restoring classic cars
Off-season: 'Somewhere in South Africa.'
Overseas teams played for: Played in South Africa 1982-83, South America 1983-84 and Australia 1984-85
Cricketers particularly admired: Ian Botham, Dennis Amiss, Tim Munton
Other sports followed: Most
Injuries: Broken left hand
Relaxations: Reading, gardening, American cars
Extras: Along with Andy Moles set a new world record for most consecutive opening partnerships of over 50. In 1989, scored 140 v Worcestershire, during which scored 100 out of partnership of 123 with Dermot Reeve and took a hat-trick against Northamptonshire. In 1990 took a hat-trick against Sussex, bowling in Tim Munton's boots – two sizes too big
Opinions on cricket: 'All for four-day cricket. B&H and NatWest should be played on Saturdays to attract bigger crowds. Coloured clothing on Sundays is a good idea.'
Best batting: 140 Warwickshire v Worcestershire, Worcester 1989

Best bowling: 5-28 Warwickshire v Gloucestershire, Edgbaston 1991

1991 Season

	M	Inns	NO	Runs	HS	Avge	100s	50s	Ct	St	O	M	Runs	Wkts	Avge	Best	5wI	10wM
Test																		
All First	14	23	1	411	68	18.68	-	2	2	-	157.1	31	513	15	34.20	5-28	1	-
1-day Int																		
NatWest	4	3	1	42	26	21.00	-	-	1	-	35.2	3	116	3	38.66	2-24	-	
B&H	5	5	0	62	34	12.40	-	-	1	-	28	3	108	4	27.00	3-28	-	
Refuge	13	10	0	252	75	25.20	-	1	2	-	77.3	1	404	21	19.23	4-21	-	

Career Performances

	M	Inns	NO	Runs	HS	Avge	100s	50s	Ct	St	Balls	Runs	Wkts	Avge	Best	5wI	10wM
Test																	
All First	173	282	33	6945	140	27.89	4	44	47	-	11196	7336	198	37.05	5-28	3	-
1-day Int																	
NatWest	21	20	3	343	79	20.17	-	2	1	-	858	548	20	27.40	3-10	-	
B&H	33	31	4	517	74	19.14	-	1	5	-	860	604	19	31.78	3-28	-	
Refuge	112	97	19	1912	93 *	24.51	-	6	23	-	2844	2539	81	31.34	4-21	-	

SMITH, R. A. Hampshire

Name: Robin Arnold Smith
Role: Right-hand bat, slip fielder
Born: 13 September 1963, Durban, South Africa
Height: 5ft 11¾in **Weight:** 14st 7lbs
Nickname: The Judge
County debut: 1982
County cap: 1985
Test debut: 1988
Tests: 28
One-Day Internationals: 31
1000 runs in a season: 6
1st-Class 50s scored: 69
1st-Class 100s scored: 31
1st-Class 200s scored: 1
1st-Class catches: 134
One-Day 50s: 32
One-Day 100s: 10
Place in batting averages: 19th av. 53.73
(1990 15th av. 66.09)

Parents: John Arnold and Joy Lyall
Wife and date of marriage: Katherine, 21 September 1988
Children: Harrison, December 1990
Family links with cricket: Grandfather played for Natal in Currie Cup. Brother Chris played for Hampshire and England
Education: Northlands Boys High, Durban
Qualifications: 'Highly qualified.'
Career outside cricket: Director of Holt and Haskell Ltd, cricket equipment specialists
Off-season: Touring with England
Overseas tours: England to India and West Indies 1989-90; Australia 1990-91; New Zealand 1991-92
Overseas teams played for: Natal 1980-84
Cricketers particularly admired: Malcolm Marshall, Graeme Hick, Graham Gooch. 'I learnt most from brother Chris, Barry Richards and Grayson Heath, my coach in South Africa.'
Other sports followed: Soccer, athletics, most sports
Injuries: Broken right index finger
Relaxations: 'Reading Sidney Sheldon novels, trout fishing, siestas, keeping fit and spending as much time as possible with my lovely wife.'
Extras: Played rugby for Natal Schools and for Romsey RFC as a full-back. Held nineteen school athletics records and two South African schools records in shot put and 100-metre hurdles. One of *Wisden*'s Five Cricketers of the Year, 1990. First child was born while he was on tour in Australia last winter
Opinions on cricket: 'I think four-day cricket so far has been a great success. I think the standard of umpiring in England is of a very high quality in comparison to umpiring in other parts of the world.'
Best batting: 209* Hampshire v Essex, Southampton 1987
Best bowling: 2-11 Hampshire v Surrey, Southampton 1985

1991 Season

	M	Inns	NO	Runs	HS	Avge	100s	50s	Ct	St	O	M	Runs	Wkts	Avge	Best	5wl	10wM
Test	5	9	3	483	148 *	80.50	2	3	3	-								
All First	16	30	4	1397	148 *	53.73	3	11	15	-	18	3	97	3	32.33	2-20	-	-
1-day Int																		
NatWest	5	5	3	331	79 *	165.50	-	4	-	-								
B&H	1	1	0	35	35	35.00	-	-	1	-								
Refuge	7	6	0	117	75	19.50	-	1	2	-								

176. What current English county player was appointed coach to Zimbabwe for the 1992 World Cup?

Career Performances

	M	Inns	NO	Runs	HS	Avge	100s	50s	Ct	St	Balls	Runs	Wkts	Avge	Best	5wI	10wM
Test	28	53	13	2118	148 *	52.95	6	15	14	-							
All First	206	352	65	12993	209 *	45.27	31	69	134	-	803	617	12	51.41	2-11	-	-
1-day Int	31	30	3	933	128	34.55	2	5	11	-							
NatWest	23	23	6	1128	125 *	66.35	2	6	16	-	17	13	2	6.50	2-13	-	
B&H	26	25	7	999	155 *	55.50	2	4	12	-	6	2	0	-	-	-	-
Refuge	84	79	10	2592	131	37.56	4	17	42	-							

SPEAK, N. J. Lancashire

Name: Nicholas Jason Speak
Role: Right-hand opening bat, off-spin bowler
Born: 21 October 1966, Manchester
Height: 6ft **Weight:** 11st 7lbs
Nickname: Twenty, Vision, Pod
County debut: 1986-87 in Jamaica
1st-Class 50s scored: 6
1st-Class 100s scored: 2
1st-Class catches: 17
One-Day 50s: 1
Place in batting averages: 132nd av. 28.13
(1990 76th av. 45.44)
Parents: John and Irene
Marital status: Single
Family links with cricket: Father was league professional in Lancashire and Yorkshire
Education: Parrs Wood High School and Sixth Form College
Qualifications: 6 O-levels; NCA coaching certificate
Cricketers particularly admired: Martin Crowe, Dexter Fitton, Neil Fairbrother
Other sports followed: Most sports – Manchester City FC
Relaxations: 'Sharing a lager with Graham Lloyd and discussing the finer points of the game. Indian food and red wine.'
Opinions on cricket: 'To see Holland reach Test level, along with Zimbabwe. More under-25 county cricket. Tea should be 10 minutes longer.'
Best batting: 153 Lancashire v Surrey, Old Trafford 1991
Best bowling: 1-0 Lancashire v Warwickshire, Old Trafford 1991

1991 Season

	M	Inns	NO	Runs	HS	Avge	100s	50s	Ct	St	O	M	Runs	Wkts	Avge	Best	5wI	10wM
Test																		
All First	18	33	3	844	153	28.13	1	2	8	-	0.1	0	0	1	0.00	1-0	-	-
1-day Int																		
NatWest																		
B&H	1	0	0	0	0	-	-	-	-	-								
Refuge	7	5	2	155	94 *	51.66	-	1	3	-								

Career Performances

	M	Inns	NO	Runs	HS	Avge	100s	50s	Ct	St	Balls	Runs	Wkts	Avge	Best	5wI	10wM
Test																	
All First	31	56	4	1488	153	28.61	2	6	17	-	31	26	2	13.00	1-0	-	-
1-day Int																	
NatWest																		
B&H	1	0	0	0	0	-	-	-	-	-							
Refuge	8	6	2	168	94 *	42.00	-	1	3	-							

SPEIGHT, M. P.   Sussex

Name: Martin Peter Speight
Role: Right-hand bat,
wicket-keeper/short leg
Born: 24 October 1967, Walsall
Height: 5ft 10½in **Weight:** 12st
Nickname: Sprog, Hoover, Ginger,
Professor, Ronald
County debut: 1986
County cap: 1991
1st-Class 50s scored: 23
1st-Class 100s scored: 3
1st-Class catches: 42
One-Day 50s: 6
One-Day 100s: 1
Place in batting averages: 57th av. 39.68
(1990 106th av. 40.44)
Parents: Peter John and Valerie
Marital status: Single
Education: Hassocks Infants School;
The Windmills School, Hassocks;
Hurstpierpoint College Junior and Senior Schools; Durham University (St Chad's College)
Qualifications: 13 O-levels, 3 A-levels; BA (Hons) (Archaeology/Ancient History)

Career outside cricket: Painting – landscapes/cricket grounds, painter and decorator
Off-season: Coaching, playing and painting in Wellington, New Zealand
Overseas tours: NCA U19 to Bermuda 1986; England YC tour to Sri Lanka 1987
Overseas teams played for: Karori, Wellington, New Zealand 1989-90; Wellington CC, 1989-90; Victoria University of Wellington 1990-92
Cricketers particularly admired: Viv Richards
Other sports followed: Golf, football, hockey, squash, horse racing
Injuries: Strained hamstring (April), back spasm (June), fractured rib (August)
Relaxations: TV and radio, art and painting
Extras: Member of Durham University UAU winning side 1987; played for Combined Universities in B&H Cup 1987 and 1988; Member of Durham University's men's hockey team to Barbados 1988. Sussex CCC's Most Promising Player, 1989. Painted an oil painting of the maiden first-class game at Arundel Castle between Sussex and Hampshire which was later auctioned to raise £1200 for the Sussex YC tour to India 1990-91. Limited edition has also been printed and sold. Has done paintings of Hove, Southampton and The Oval for the Benefits of Messrs Pigott, Parks and Greig
Opinions on cricket: 'Too much cricket played.'
Best batting: 149 Sussex v Cambridge University, Hove 1991
Best bowling: 1-2 Sussex v Middlesex, Hove 1988

1991 Season

	M	Inns	NO	Runs	HS	Avge	100s	50s	Ct	St	O	M	Runs	Wkts	Avge	Best	5wI	10wM
Test																		
All First	14	20	1	754	149	39.68	1	5	6	-								
1-day Int																		
NatWest	2	2	0	68	48	34.00	-	-	-	-								
B&H	3	3	0	42	35	14.00	-	-	-	-								
Refuge	11	11	1	295	106 *	29.50	1	-	5	-								

Career Performances

	M	Inns	NO	Runs	HS	Avge	100s	50s	Ct	St	Balls	Runs	Wkts	Avge	Best	5wI	10wM
Test																	
All First	60	97	10	2984	149	34.29	3	23	42	-	3	2	1	2.00	1-2	-	-
1-day Int																	
NatWest	6	5	0	127	48	25.40	-	-	2	-							
B&H	20	18	0	463	83	25.72	-	2	11	1							
Refuge	42	35	3	971	106 *	30.34	1	4	14	-							

Name: Neil Alan Stanley
Role: Right-hand bat, right-arm off-break
bowler
Born: 16 May 1968, Bedford
Height: 6ft 3in **Weight:** 14st 8lbs
Nickname: Giz, Swampy, Stanners
County debut: 1988
1st-Class 50s: 6
1st-Class 100s: 1
1st-Class catches: 5
Place in batting averages: 78th av. 36.15
Parents: Jack and Julie
Marital status: Single
Education: Bedford Modern School
Qualifications: 7 O-levels, NCA senior
coaching award
Career outside cricket: Chicken farmer,
postman
Off-season: Working in Northampton
Overseas tours: Bedford Modern to Barbados
1983; Young England to Youth World Cup, Australia 1988
Overseas teams played for: Sydenham, Christchurch, New Zealand 1989-90
Cricketers particularly admired: Ian Botham, Wayne Larkins
Other sports followed: Snooker, golf, football
Relaxations: 'Listening to Sigue Sigue Sputnik and other loud bands. Clint Eastwood
films and a good pint of bitter.'
Extras: Played for England Indoor cricket team v Australia in ManuLife Test series, 1990.
Missed entire 90 season due to two cracked vertebrae, operated on in March 1990
Opinions on cricket: 'Clubs should make more effort to find winter employment in the
UK for young players. 2nd team games should be played on main first-class grounds. Tea
interval should be longer.'
Best batting: 132 Northamptonshire v Lancashire, Lytham 1991

1991 Season

	M	Inns	NO	Runs	HS	Avge	100s	50s	Ct	St	O	M	Runs	Wkts	Avge	Best	5wI	10wM
Test																		
All First	8	13	0	470	132	36.15	1	2	5	-	10	2	19	0	-	-	-	-
1-day Int																		
NatWest																			
B&H																			
Refuge																			

Career Performances

	M	Inns	NO	Runs	HS	Avge	100s	50s	Ct	St	Balls	Runs	Wkts	Avge	Best	5wI	10wM
Test																	
All First	19	31	2	920	132	31.72	1	6	9	-	60	19	0	-		-	-	-
1-day Int																	
NatWest																	
B&H	3	2	0	13	8	6.50	-	-	1	-	6	3	1	3.00	1-3	-	
Refuge	9	8	3	78	18	15.60	-	-	2	-							

STANWORTH, J. Lancashire

Name: John Stanworth
Role: Right-hand bat, wicket-keeper
Born: 30 September 1960
Height: 5ft 10in **Weight:** 10st 10lbs
Nickname: Stany, Ming, Stanno, Big Ears
County debut: 1983
1st-Class catches: 56
1st-Class stumpings: 9
Parents: Bob and Freda
Wife and date of marriage: Dianne,
22 March 1986
Children: Scott and Katie (twins),
6 November 1988
Family links with cricket: Father played
club cricket
Education: Chadderton Grammar School;
Padgate College
Qualifications: BEd degree
Career outside cricket: PE teacher,
cricket coach

Off-season: Co-ordinating the Royal Insurance scheme (a coaching scheme for youngsters between 11 and 16)
Overseas tours: British Colleges to West Indies 1981
Overseas teams played for: Norths, Queensland 1978
Cricketers particularly admired: Alan Knott and Bob Taylor ('simply the best I've seen'), Gary Yates 'for his wholehearted approach'
Other sports followed: Rugby, football (Oldham)
Relaxations: 'Reading about Tony Murphy (ex-Lancashire, now Surrey), his interests and relaxations in *The Cricketers' Who's Who*.'
Extras: 2nd XI captain since 1988. 'Ran pre-season training at the club until the lads became fed up.'

Opinions on cricket: 'The *quantity* of county cricket played in this country is too high and as a result quite often the *quality* produced isn't all that it might be. As I get older I strongly believe that the lunch and especially the tea interval should be lengthened.'
Best batting: 50* Lancashire v Gloucestershire, Bristol 1985

1991 Season

	M	Inns	NO	Runs	HS	Avge	100s	50s	Ct	St	O	M	Runs	Wkts	Avge	Best	5wI	10wM
Test																		
All First	2	0	0	0	0	-	-	-	2	1								
1-day Int																		
NatWest																		
B&H																		
Refuge																		

Career Performances

	M	Inns	NO	Runs	HS	Avge	100s	50s	Ct	St	Balls	Runs	Wkts	Avge	Best	5wI	10wM
Test																	
All First	39	38	11	236	50 *	8.74	-	1	56	9							
1-day Int																	
NatWest	4	1	0	0	0	0.00	-	-	6	1							
B&H	6	3	2	17	8 *	17.00	-	-	4	-							
Refuge	16	4	2	7	4 *	3.50	-	-	10	1							

177. Who topped the first-class batting averages last season for Worcestershire?

STEMP, R. D.   Worcestershire

Name: Richard David Stemp
Role: Slow left-arm bowler
Born: 11 December 1967, Edgbaston
Height: 6ft **Weight:** 12st 4lbs
Nickname: Stempy, Stempez, Stench
County debut: 1990
1st-Class catches: 1
Place in bowling averages: 21st av. 25.00
Strike rate: 60.76 (career 72.38)
Parents: Arnold and Rita Homer
Marital status: Single
Family links with cricket: Father played
Birmingham League cricket for Old Hill
Education: Britannia High School,
Rowley Regis
Qualifications: NCA coaching award
Off-season: ' Hopefully in South Africa,
otherwise winter job in England.'
Overseas teams played for: Pretoria
Technikon 1988-89

Other sports followed: Indoor cricket, Australian Rules and American football
Relaxations: Ornithology, reading, driving, music.
Extras: Played for England Indoor cricket team v Australia in ManuLife Test series, 1990
Best batting: 15* Worcestershire v Nottinghamshire, Worcester 1991
Best bowling: 4-62 Worcestershire v Yorkshire, Headingley 1991

1991 Season

	M	Inns	NO	Runs	HS	Avge	100s	50s	Ct	St	O	M	Runs	Wkts	Avge	Best	5wI	10wM
Test																		
All First	9	8	5	30	15 *	10.00	-	-	-	-	172.1	43	425	17	25.00	4-62	-	-
1-day Int																		
NatWest																		
B&H																		
Refuge	4	0	0	0	0	-	-	-	2	-	22	1	89	5	17.80	3-18	-	

---

178. Who are the only two men to have hit over 300 runs in
their first Test?

Career Performances

	M	Inns	NO	Runs	HS	Avge	100s	50s	Ct	St	Balls	Runs	Wkts	Avge	Best	5wl	10wM
Test																	
All First	11	10	7	33	15 *	11.00	-	-	1	-	1303	548	18	30.44	4-62	-	-
1-day Int																	
NatWest																		
B&H	1	0	0	0	0	-	-	-	-	-	48	38	0	-		-	-
Refuge	6	2	1	4	3 *	4.00	-	-	3	-	204	154	5	30.80	3-18	-	

STEPHENSON, F. D. Sussex

Name: Franklyn Dacosta Stephenson
Role: Right-hand bat, right-arm fast bowler
Born: 8 April 1959, St James, Barbados
Height: 6ft 3½in **Weight:** 13st 7lbs
Nickname: Cookie
County debut: 1982 (Gloucs), 1988 (Notts)
County cap: 1988 (Notts)
1000 runs in a season: 1
50 wickets in a season: 4
1st-Class 50s scored: 22
1st-Class 100s scored: 4
1st-Class 5 w. in innings: 29
1st-Class 10 w. in match: 7
1st-Class catches: 49
One-Day 50s: 4
Place in batting averages: 187th av. 21.15
(1990 174th av. 28.82)
Place in bowling averages: 28th av. 25.76
(1990 86th av. 38.85)

Strike rate: 54.93 (career 46.95)
Parents: Leonard Young and Violet Stevenson
Wife and date of marriage: Julia, 2 April 1981
Children: Amanda, 20 October 1981; Orissa, 6 September 1983; Tamara, 1 November 1990
Education: St John Baptist Mixed School; Samuel Jackson Prescod Polytechnic
Qualifications: School leaving certificate
Career outside cricket: Professional golfer
Off-season: 'Cricketing, golfing and training.' Playing in South Africa
Overseas tours: With West Indies U19 to England 1978; rebel West Indies team to South Africa 1982-83 and 1983-84
Overseas teams played for: Tasmania 1981-82; Barbados 1981-82 and 1989-90; Orange

Free State 1991-92

Cricketers particularly admired: Sir Garfield Sobers, Sylvester Clarke, Collis King, Richard Hadlee

Other sports followed: All

Injuries: Sore toe 'flat-wicket-itis'

Relaxations: Watching sport on television, listening to music, spending time with family

Extras: Played League cricket for Littleborough in the Central Lancashire League in 1979, Royton in 1980 (100 wickets and 621 runs), Rawtenstall in 1981 and 1982 (100+ wickets and 500+ runs both years). Hit 165 for Barbados in 1982 having been sent in as night-watchman. Took 10 wickets in match on debut for Tasmania. In 1988 did the double when he scored 1018 runs and took 125 wickets in first-class cricket. Britannic Assurance Player of the Year, 1988. One of *Wisden's* Five Cricketers of the Year, 1988. Now again eligible to play for West Indies, having been banned for playing in South Africa. Left Nottinghamshire at the end of the 1991 season and signed to play for Sussex in 1992

Opinions on cricket: 'I would like to see the county game a more even contest between bat and ball. Players should remember that spectators attend three/four-day games to be entertained and not to be bored to tears.'

Best batting: 165 Barbados v Leeward Islands, Basseterre 1981-82

Best bowling: 8-47 Nottinghamshire v Essex, Trent Bridge 1989

1991 Season

	M	Inns	NO	Runs	HS	Avge	100s	50s	Ct	St	O	M	Runs	Wkts	Avge	Best	5wI	10wM
Test																		
All First	22	27	7	423	58	21.15	-	1	6	-	719.1	158	2010	78	25.76	5-27	4	-
1-day Int																		
NatWest	3	2	0	8	7	4.00	-	-	-	-	29	0	99	2	49.50	1-10	-	
B&H	4	3	1	19	14	9.50	-	-	1	-	37	9	135	7	19.28	5-30	1	
Refuge	17	11	3	164	36 *	20.50	-	-	3	-	129.2	11	525	32	16.40	5-31	1	

Career Performances

	M	Inns	NO	Runs	HS	Avge	100s	50s	Ct	St	Balls	Runs	Wkts	Avge	Best	5wI	10wM
Test																	
All First	118	181	24	3998	165	25.46	4	22	49	-	22144	11021	471	23.39	8-47	29	7
1-day Int																	
NatWest	11	7	1	81	29	13.50	-	-	1	-	684	335	11	30.45	2-17	-	
B&H	21	18	6	317	98 *	26.41	-	2	3	-	1214	680	32	21.25	5-30	1	
Refuge	71	56	13	892	69	20.74	-	1	16	-	3205	2290	115	19.91	5-31	1	

STEPHENSON, J. P. Essex

Name: John Patrick Stephenson
Role: Right-hand opening bat, right-arm medium bowler
Born: 14 March 1965, Stebbing, Essex
Height: 6ft ¹/₂in **Weight:** 13st
Nickname: Stan, Arnie Schmurdlenburglar
County debut: 1985
County cap: 1989
Test debut: 1989
Tests: 1
1000 runs in a season: 3
1st-Class 50s scored: 40
1st-Class 100s scored: 12
1st-Class 200s scored: 1
1st-Class catches: 68
One-Day 50s: 12
One-Day 100s: 2
Place in batting averages: 70th av. 37.39 (1990 30th av. 57.18)
Place in bowling averages: 14th av. 23.47
Strike rate: 37.64 (career 67.12)
Parents: Pat and Eve
Marital status: 'Will never marry'
Family links with cricket: Father was member of Rugby Meteors Cricketer Cup winning side in 1973. Three brothers played in Felsted 1st XI; Guy played for Essex 2nd XI and now plays for Teddington
Education: Felsted Prep School; Felsted Senior School; Durham University
Qualifications: 7 O-levels, 3 A-levels; BA General Arts (Dunelm)
Off-season: Playing in Queensland on the Gold Coast and touring with England A
Overseas tours: ESCA U19 to Zimbabwe 1982-83; England A to Kenya and Zimbabwe and Kenya 1989-90; Bermuda and West Indies 1991-92
Overseas teams played for: Fitzroy, Melbourne 1982-83, 1987-88; Boland, South Africa 1988-89; Gold Coast Dolphins and Bond University, Australia 1990-91
Cricketers particularly admired: Brian Hardie
Relaxations: 'Listening to vinyl, eg. Pylon, Yo La Tengo, Chickasaw Mudd Puppies, Young Fresh Fellows, Mark Eitzel, Blue Aeroplanes, Fleshtones, The Nits.'
Extras: Awarded 2nd XI cap in 1984 when leading run-scorer with Essex 2nd XI. Essex Young Player of the Year, 1985. Captained Durham University to victory in UAU Competition 1986 and captain of Combined Universities team 1987 in the first year that it was drawn from all universities. Called up to replace the injured Michael Atherton on England A tour to Bermuda and West Indies 1991-92
Opinions on cricket: 'There are too many theory men around. Cricket is all confidence.

That is the only common denominator to success.'
Best batting: 202* Essex v Somerset, Bath 1990
Best bowling: 4-30 Essex v Cambridge University, Fenner's 1991

1991 Season

	M	Inns	NO	Runs	HS	Avge	100s	50s	Ct	St	O	M	Runs	Wkts	Avge	Best	5wI	10wM
Test																		
All First	25	41	3	1421	116	37.39	3	8	8	-	106.4	19	399	17	23.47	4-30	-	-
1-day Int																		
NatWest	3	3	0	117	59	39.00	-	2	-	-	6	0	36	0	-		-	-
B&H	6	6	0	349	142	58.16	1	2	4	-	11	0	57	1	57.00	1-17	-	
Refuge	14	13	0	399	67	30.69	-	3	7	-	51	2	194	13	14.92	4-17	-	

Career Performances

	M	Inns	NO	Runs	HS	Avge	100s	50s	Ct	St	Balls	Runs	Wkts	Avge	Best	5wI	10wM
Test	1	2	0	36	25	18.00	-	-	-	-							
All First	129	219	24	7161	202*	36.72	12	40	68	-	3155	1789	47	38.06	4-30	-	-
1-day Int																	
NatWest	10	9	1	259	59	32.37	-	3	1	-	84	82	1	82.00	1-24	-	
B&H	22	17	2	645	142	43.00	1	4	6	-	498	338	16	21.12	3-22	-	
Refuge	66	53	8	1110	109	24.66	1	5	28	-	932	691	28	24.67	4-17	-	

STEWART, A. J. Surrey

Name: Alec James Stewart
Role: Right-hand bat, wicket-keeper, county captain
Born: 8 April 1963, Merton
Nickname: Stewie
Height: 5ft 11in **Weight:** 12st
County debut: 1981
County cap: 1985
Test debut: 1989-90
Tests: 14
One-Day Internationals: 23
1000 runs in a season: 6
1st-Class 50s scored: 64
1st-Class 100s scored: 18
1st-Class 200s scored: 1
1st-Class catches: 243
1st-Class stumpings: 6
One-Day 50s: 31

One-Day 100s: 5
Place in batting averages: 42nd av. 44.65 (1990 93rd av. 42.78)
Parents: Michael and Sheila
Wife and date of marriage: Lynn, 28 September 1991
Family links with cricket: Father played for England (1962-64) and Surrey (1954 -72). Brother Neil captains Malden Wanderers CC
Education: Tiffin Boys School
Qualifications: 4 O-levels
Off-season: Touring with England
Overseas tours: England to India (Nehru Cup) 1989; West Indies 1989-90; Australia 1990-91; New Zealand 1991-92
Overseas teams played for: Midland Guildford 1981-89
Cricketers particularly admired: Geoff Arnold, Kevin Gartrell, Tony Mann, Graham Monkhouse
Other sports followed: Football (Chelsea) and all sports
Relaxations: 'Eating out, listening to Neil Kendrick, watching Ray Alikhan bat.'
Opinions on cricket: 'Four-day cricket is a must.'
Best batting: 206* Surrey v Essex, The Oval 1989
Best bowling: 1-7 Surrey v Lancashire, Old Trafford 1989

1991 Season

	M	Inns	NO	Runs	HS	Avge	100s	50s	Ct	St	O	M	Runs	Wkts	Avge	Best	5wI	10wM
Test	2	4	2	225	113 *	112.50	1	-	4	-								
All First	19	34	8	1161	113 *	44.65	2	6	24	-	7	0	34	0	-	-	-	-
1-day Int																		
NatWest	4	4	1	206	76 *	68.66	-	2	6	-								
B&H	4	4	1	195	110 *	65.00	1	1	3	-								
Refuge	13	12	1	341	84 *	31.00	-	4	13	1								

Career Performances

	M	Inns	NO	Runs	HS	Avge	100s	50s	Ct	St	Balls	Runs	Wkts	Avge	Best	5wI	10wM
Test	14	27	3	766	113 *	31.91	1	3	19	-							
All First	196	323	39	10824	206 *	38.11	18	64	243	6	353	329	3	109.66	1-7	-	
1-day Int	23	21	3	497	61	27.61	-	2	11	-							
NatWest	21	19	3	754	107 *	47.12	1	5	14	-							
B&H	29	29	4	922	110 *	36.88	1	7	10	2							
Refuge	109	99	9	2554	125	28.37	3	17	65	5	4	8	0	-	-	-	

SUCH, P. M. Essex

Name: Peter Mark Such
Role: Right-hand bat, off-spin bowler
Born: 12 June 1964, Helensburgh, Scotland
Height: 6ft **Weight:** 11st 7lbs
Nickname: Suchy
County debut: 1982 (Notts), 1987 (Leics), 1990 (Essex)
County cap: 1991
1st-Class 5 w. in innings: 6
1st-Class catches: 44
Place in bowling averages: 35th av. 27.44 (1990 60th av. 35.75)
Strike rate: 65.32 (career 68.29)
Parents: John and Margaret
Marital status: Single
Family links with cricket: Father and brother village cricketers
Education: Lantern Lane Primary School; Harry Carlton Comprehensive, East Leake, Notts
Qualifications: 9 O-levels, 3 A-levels, advanced cricket coach
Off-season: Playing and coaching in Bulawayo, Zimbabwe
Overseas teams played for: Kempton Park, South Africa 1982-83; Bathurst, Australia 1985-86; Matabeleland, Zimbabwe 1989-90
Cricketers particularly admired: Bob White, Eddie Hemmings, Graham Gooch, John Childs
Other sports followed: American football
Relaxations: Listening to music, watching movies, playing golf and hockey, gardening
Extras: Played for England YC v Australia 1983. Played for TCCB XI v New Zealand, 1985. Left Nottinghamshire at end of 1986 season. Joined Leicestershire in 1987 and released at the end of 1989. Signed by Essex for 1990. Played in one-day games for England A v Sri Lanka 1991
Opinions on cricket: 'The balance has tipped too far in favour of batsmen. Wickets need pace and bounce to encourage batsmen but the bowlers have to have a chance with a small amount of sideways movement. Both green and flat wickets produce boring cricket.'
Best batting: 27 Essex v Middlesex, Ilford 1990
Best bowling: 6-123 Nottinghamshire v Kent, Trent Bridge 1983

---

179. Which Test players were known as 'Willy Po' and 'Willy Wo'?

1991 Season

	M	Inns	NO	Runs	HS	Avge	100s	50s	Ct	St	O	M	Runs	Wkts	Avge	Best	5wI	10wM
Test																		
All First	14	6	4	31	23 *	15.50	-	-	3	-	370.1	101	933	34	27.44	3-7	-	-
1-day Int																		
NatWest	3	1	1	0	0 *	-	-	-	-	-	36	2	102	5	20.40	2-29	-	
B&H	6	2	1	5	4	5.00	-	-	1	-	58	4	232	4	58.00	2-52	-	
Refuge	13	3	3	4	2 *	-	-	-	2	-	86	3	423	13	32.53	4-30	-	

Career Performances

	M	Inns	NO	Runs	HS	Avge	100s	50s	Ct	St	Balls	Runs	Wkts	Avge	Best	5wI	10wM
Test																	
All First	117	92	37	202	27	3.67	-	-	44	-	17825	8019	261	30.72	6-123	6	-
1-day Int																	
NatWest	3	1	1	0	0 *	-	-	-	-	-	216	102	5	20.40	2-29	-	
B&H	10	2	1	5	4	5.00	-	-	1	-	612	418	9	46.44	3-50	-	
Refuge	28	7	5	17	8 *	8.50	-	-	8	-	1038	937	23	40.73	4-30	-	

SWALLOW, I. G.   Somerset

Name: Ian Geoffrey Swallow
Role: Right-hand bat, off-break bowler, cover or slip fielder
Born: 18 December 1962, Barnsley
Height: 5ft 7in **Weight:** 10st
Nickname: Chicken, Swal
County debut: 1983 (Yorks), 1990 (Somerset)
1st-Class 50s scored: 2
1st-Class 100s scored: 1
1st-Class 5 w. in innings: 1
1st-Class catches: 43
Place in batting averages: (1990 230th av. 18.70)
Place in bowling averages: (1990 148th av. 63.94)
Strike rate: (career 105.85)
Parents: Geoffrey and Joyce
Marital status: Single
Family links with cricket: Father and brother both played for Elsecar Village CC
Education: Hayland Kirk Comprehensive School, Balk; Barnsley Technical College
Qualifications: 3 O-levels

Cricketers particularly admired: Viv Richards, John Emburey
Other sports followed: Barnsley FC, all sports, 'play for fun.'
Relaxations: Sports in general
Extras: Took hat-trick v Warwickshire 2nd XI 1984. Figures: 4-3-2-4. Released by Yorkshire at end of 1989 season and joined Somerset for 1990. Released by Somerset at the end of the 1991 season
Best batting: 114 Yorkshire v MCC, Scarborough 1987
Best bowling: 7-95 Yorkshire v Nottinghamshire, Trent Bridge 1987

1991 Season

	M	Inns	NO	Runs	HS	Avge	100s	50s	Ct	St	O	M	Runs	Wkts	Avge	Best	5wI	10wM
Test																		
All First	4	5	3	67	41*	33.50	-	-	3	-	100.1	16	354	8	44.25	3-43	-	-
1-day Int																		
NatWest																		
B&H	3	2	0	5	3	2.50	-	-	1	-	24	1	111	2	55.50	1-31	-	
Refuge	1	1	1	4	4*	-	-	-	-	-	3	0	16	0	-	-	-	-

Career Performances

	M	Inns	NO	Runs	HS	Avge	100s	50s	Ct	St	Balls	Runs	Wkts	Avge	Best	5wI	10wM
Test																	
All First	88	104	28	1550	114	20.39	1	2	43	-	11221	5798	106	54.69	7-95	1	-
1-day Int																	
NatWest	4	1	1	17	17*	-	-	-	1	-	102	85	0	-	-	-	-
B&H	13	8	2	49	18	8.16	-	-	8	-	635	469	8	58.62	2-32	-	
Refuge	17	10	6	83	31	20.75	-	-	1	-	456	412	6	68.66	2-44	-	

180. Which county's colours are Oxford blue, Cambridge blue and gold?

Name: Steven Antony Sylvester
Role: Right-hand bat, left-arm fast-medium bowler
Born: 26 September 1968, Chalfont St Giles, Bucks
Height: 5ft 11in **Weight:** 12st 5lbs
Nickname: Silvers
County debut: 1991
1st-Class catches: 1
Parents: Ormond Alexander and Jennifer Irene
Marital status: Single
Family links with cricket: Father has played cricket all his life, both in St Vincent, West Indies and in England for Marlow Park and Maidenhead & Bray
Education: Wellesbourne School; The Buckinghamshire College; University of London, Goldsmith's College
Qualifications: 7 O-levels, 3 A-levels, BSc (Hons) in Psychology
Career outside cricket: 'Yet to be discovered...'
Off-season: Training hard at both fitness and technique
Cricketers particularly admired: Angus Fraser, Ian Bishop, Curtly Ambrose, John Lever and Gordon Greenidge
Other sports followed: Football, judo
Injuries: Strained hamstring
Relaxations: Work-outs at local fitness studio, reading anything to do with sports psychology
Extras: Played cricket and football for Buckinghamshire
Opinions on cricket: 'I believe the new ruling on one bouncer per over will give the batsman a slight advantage. While something has to be done about intimidatory bowling, I am not sure that restricting the bowler's use of the bouncer is the right way to do it. I feel batsmen will remain untested by the short-pitched delivery.'
Best batting: 0 Middlesex v Glamorgan, Cardiff 1991

---

181. Who has taken the most Test wickets for England in one match?

1991 Season

	M	Inns	NO	Runs	HS	Avge	100s	50s	Ct	St	O	M	Runs	Wkts	Avge	Best	5wI	10wM
Test																		
All First	1	1	0	0	0	0.00	-	-	1	-	20	2	98	0	-	-	-	-
1-day Int																		
NatWest																		
B&H																		
Refuge																		

Career Performances

	M	Inns	NO	Runs	HS	Avge	100s	50s	Ct	St	Balls	Runs	Wkts	Avge	Best	5wI	10wM
Test																		
All First	1	1	0	0	0	0.00	-	-	1	-	120	98	0	-	-	-	-	
1-day Int																		
NatWest																		
B&H																		
Refuge																		

TAVARE, C. J.   Somerset

Name: Christopher James Tavare
Role: Right-hand bat, off-break bowler, slip fielder, county captain
Born: 27 October 1954, Orpington
Height: 6ft 1½in **Weight:** 12st 12lbs
Nickname: Tav, Rowdy
County debut: 1974 (Kent), 1989 (Somerset)
County cap: 1978 (Kent), 1989 (Somerset)
Benefit: 1988 (£92,318) (Kent)
Test debut: 1980
Tests: 31
One-Day Internationals: 29
1000 runs in a season: 15
1st-Class 50s scored: 130
1st-Class 100s scored: 44
1st-Class 200s scored: 1
1st-Class catches: 381
One-Day 50s: 63
One-Day 100s: 13
Place in batting averages: 21st av. 53.86 (1990 25th av. 58.50)
Parents: Andrew and June
Wife and date of marriage: Vanessa, 22 March 1980

Family links with cricket: Father, Uncle Jack Tavare, and Uncle Derrick Attwood, all played school and club cricket. Elder brother Stephen and younger brother Jeremy also both play

Education: Sevenoaks School; Oxford University

Qualifications: Zoology degree

Off-season: Studying for a Diploma in Management

Overseas tours: England to India and Sri Lanka 1981-82; Australia and New Zealand 1982-83; New Zealand and Pakistan 1983-84

Other sports followed: 'Take an interest in most sports, especially American football in winter.'

Relaxations: Music, zoology, films, gardening, woodwork, golf

Extras: Played for England Schools v India at Birmingham in 1973, scoring 124*. Oxford University cricket Blue 1975-77. Whitbread Scholarship to Perth, Australia, 1978-79. Suffers from asthma and hay-fever. Captain of Kent 1983-84. Rejected Kent's offer of a new contract for 1989 and joined Somerset as vice-captain. Appointed Somerset captain for 1990 after retirement of Vic Marks

Best batting: 219 Somerset v Sussex, Hove 1990

Best bowling: 1-3 Kent v Hampshire, Canterbury 1986

1991 Season

	M	Inns	NO	Runs	HS	Avge	100s	50s	Ct	St	O	M	Runs	Wkts	Avge	Best	5wI	10wM
Test																		
All First	23	37	7	1601	183	53.36	5	7	20	-								
1-day Int																		
NatWest	3	3	0	127	59	42.33	-	1	3	-								
B&H	4	4	0	139	53	34.75	-	1	2	-								
Refuge	15	15	2	542	75*	41.69	-	5	7	-								

Career Performances

	M	Inns	NO	Runs	HS	Avge	100s	50s	Ct	St	Balls	Runs	Wkts	Avge	Best	5wI	10wM
Test	31	56	2	1755	149	32.50	2	12	20	-	30	11	0	-	-	-	-
All First	397	660	72	23120	219	39.32	44	130	381	-	769	687	5	137.40	1-3	-	-
1-day Int	29	28	2	720	83*	27.69	-	4	7	-	12	3	0	-	-	-	
NatWest	35	35	7	1494	162*	53.35	4	8	18	-							
B&H	87	86	8	2596	143	33.28	2	16	50	-							
Refuge	204	202	27	5721	136*	32.69	7	35	77	-							

TAYLOR, C. W.   Middlesex

Name: Charles William Taylor
Role: Left-hand bat, left-arm seam bowler
Born: 12 August 1966, Banbury,
Oxfordshire
Height: 6ft 5¹/₂in **Weight:** 14st
Nickname: Farmer, Seth
County debut: 1990
1st-Class 5 w. in innings: 1
1st-Class catches: 2
Place in bowling averages: 31st av. 26.66
Strike rate: 49.00 (career 48.70)
Parents: Richard and Ann
Marital status: Single
Family links with cricket: Brother plays
for Banbury, father played village cricket
for Sandford St Martin
Education: Spendlove Comprehensive
School, Charlbury; Banbury Technical
College
Qualifications: City and Guilds Certificate in agriculture; 1 O-level
Career outside cricket: Agriculture
Off-season: Working on the family farm plus a holiday in Australia
Overseas teams played for: Cricketers Club, New South Wales 1988-89
Cricketers particularly admired: Richard Hadlee, David Gower, Paul Tew ('my first
club captain')
Other sports followed: National Hunt racing, most sports
Injuries: Back injury
Relaxations: Golf, game shooting
Extras: Returned figures of 5 for 33 in second first-class match as Middlesex gained an
important win on the way to the 1990 Championship title
Best batting: 21 Middlesex v Kent, Lord's 1991
Best bowling: 5-33 Middlesex v Yorkshire, Headingley 1990

1991 Season

	M	Inns	NO	Runs	HS	Avge	100s	50s	Ct	St	O	M	Runs	Wkts	Avge	Best	5wI	10wM
Test																		
All First	7	5	0	59	21	11.80	-	-	2	-	147	29	480	18	26.66	3-35	-	-
1-day Int																		
NatWest																		
B&H																		
Refuge	5	1	0	3	3	3.00	-	-	4	-	27.2	0	153	3	51.00	1-14	-	

	M	Inns	NO	Runs	HS	Avge	100s	50s	Ct	St	Balls	Runs	Wkts	Avge	Best	5wl	10wM
Test																	
All First	9	7	1	72	21	12.00	-	-	2	-	1169	619	24	25.79	5-33	1	-
1-day Int																	
NatWest																		
B&H																		
Refuge	5	1	0	3	3	3.00	-	-	4	-	164	153	3	51.00	1-14	-	

TAYLOR, J. P.   Northamptonshire

Name: Jonathan Paul Taylor
Role: Left-hand bat, left-arm
fast-medium bowler
Born: 8 August 1964, Ashby-de-la-Zouch,
Leicestershire
Height: 6ft 2in **Weight:** 13st
Nickname: Roadie ('as in roadrunner'), JP
County debut: 1988 (Derbyshire),
1991 (Northamptonshire)
1st-Class 5 w. in innings: 1
1st-Class catches: 7
Place in bowling averages: 79th av. 34.07
Strike rate: 65.62 (career 70.00)
Parents: Derek and Janet
Marital status: Engaged to Elaine
Family links with cricket: Father and
brother played local league cricket
Education: Pingle School, Swadlincote
Qualifications: 6 O-levels, NCA coaching
certificate

Career outside cricket: Electrical retail management
Off-season: Coaching in Australia
Overseas teams played for: Papakura, New Zealand 1984-85; Napier High School Old
Boys, New Zealand 1985-86; North Kalgoorlie, Australia 1990-91
Cricketers particularly admired: Bob Taylor, John Lever
Other sports followed: Soccer and rugby
Relaxations: Basketball, squash, swimming, watching videos
Extras: Spent four seasons on the staff at Derbyshire 1984-87. Played Minor Counties for
Staffordshire 1989-90.
Best batting: 11
Best bowling: 5-42 Northamptonshire v Leicestershire, Northampton 1991

1991 Season

	M	Inns	NO	Runs	HS	Avge	100s	50s	Ct	St	O	M	Runs	Wkts	Avge	Best	5wI	10wM
Test																		
All First	13	11	4	22	5 *	3.14	-	-	4	-	295.2	50	920	27	34.07	5-42	1	-
1-day Int																		
NatWest	4	1	1	3	3 *	-	-	-	1	-	42	6	132	8	16.50	2-11	-	
B&H	4	2	2	2	1 *	-	-	-	1	-	42	9	106	4	26.50	2-30	-	
Refuge	10	5	2	24	16	8.00	-	-	1	-	74	7	301	15	20.06	2-18	-	

Career Performances

	M	Inns	NO	Runs	HS	Avge	100s	50s	Ct	St	Balls		Runs	Wkts	Avge	Best	5wI	10wM
Test																		
All First	20	18	6	51	11	4.25	-	-	7	-	2590		1407	37	38.02	5-42	1	-
1-day Int																		
NatWest	6	3	1	17	9	8.50	-	-	1	-	396		280	8	35.00	2-11	-	
B&H	4	2	2	2	1 *	-	-	-	1	-	252		106	4	26.50	2-30	-	
Refuge	16	8	2	29	16	4.83	-	-	2	-	684		517	23	22.47	3-14	-	

TAYLOR, N. R.   Kent

Name: Neil Royston Taylor
Role: Right-hand bat, off-break bowler
Born: 21 July 1959, Farnborough, Kent
Height: 6ft 1in **Weight:** 14st 7lbs
Nickname: Map
County debut: 1979
County cap: 1982
Benefit: 1991
1000 runs in a season: 8
1st-Class 50s scored: 63
1st-Class 100s scored: 37
1st-Class 200s scored: 2
1st-Class catches: 133
One-Day 50s: 28
One-Day 100s: 5
Place in batting averages: 17th av. 56.53
(1990 21st av. 61.84)
Parents: Leonard and Audrey
Wife and date of marriage: Jane Claire,
25 September 1982
Children: Amy Louise, 7 November 1985; Lauren, 21 July 1988
Family links with cricket: Brother Colin played for Kent U19 Father played club cricket

Education: Cray Valley Technical High School
Qualifications: 8 O-levels, 2 A-levels, NCA coaching certificate
Off-season: Coaching and organizing benefit year in 1992
Overseas tours: With England Schools Team to India 1977-78
Cricketers particularly admired: Chris Tavare, Mark Benson and Robin Smith
Other sports followed: Rugby union, golf
Injuries: Badly bruised thumb during the last month of the season
Relaxations: 'Reading Wilbur Smith, Frederick Forsyth and cricket autobiographies, listening to music.'
Extras: Made 110 on debut for Kent CCC v Sri Lanka, 1979. Won four Man of the Match awards in first five matches. Scored three successive centuries in the B&H. Played for England B v Pakistan, 1982. Fielded twice as 12th man for England v India in 1982 and West Indies in 1988, both matches at The Oval. Provides a weekly contribution to Radio Kent through the summer
Opinions on cricket: 'Perhaps the groundsmen could be employed by the TCCB, so that they do not feel pressured by their county club. They can then produce their best pitches, instead of inferior ones!'
Best batting: 204 Kent v Surrey, Canterbury 1990
Best bowling: 2-20 Kent v Somerset, Canterbury 1985

1991 Season

	M	Inns	NO	Runs	HS	Avge	100s	50s	Ct	St	O	M	Runs	Wkts	Avge	Best	5wl	10wM
Test																		
All First	23	36	4	1806	203 *	56.43	7	7	14	-	3	0	26	0	-	-	-	-
1-day Int																		
NatWest	2	2	0	46	44	23.00	-	-	-	-								
B&H	5	5	1	230	110	57.50	1	1	2	-								
Refuge	14	14	1	467	82 *	35.92	-	4	1	-								

Career Performances

	M	Inns	NO	Runs	HS	Avge	100s	50s	Ct	St	Balls	Runs	Wkts	Avge	Best	5wl	10wM
Test																	
All First	243	415	54	14115	204	39.10	37	63	133	-	1575	891	16	55.68	2-20	-	-
1-day Int																	
NatWest	20	20	1	452	85	23.78	-	2	5	-	95	48	3	16.00	3-29	-	
B&H	42	39	2	1600	137	43.24	5	7	8	-	12	5	0	-	-	-	
Refuge	110	107	9	3006	95	30.67	-	19	30	-							

TENNANT, L.   Essex

Name: Lloyd Tennant
Role: Right-hand bat, right-arm medium
bowler, outfielder
Born: 9 April 1968, Walsall
Height: 5ft 11in **Weight:** 13st
Nickname: Charmaine
County debut: 1986 (Leicestershire)
1st-Class catches: 1
Place in batting averages: 219th av. 15.66
Place in bowling averages: 70th av. 32.75
Strike rate: 49.30 (career 53.20)
Parents: Dennis and Jean
Marital status: Single
Family links with cricket: Father played
club cricket as an opening bowler
Education: Shelfield Comprehensive,
Pelsall
Qualifications: 8 CSEs
Off-season: Working for GBG Fences Ltd
Overseas tours: England U19 to Sri Lanka
1986-87
Cricketers particularly admired: Ian Botham, Malcolm Marshall
Other sports followed: Football mainly, but all other sports as well
Relaxations: Listening to music, watching TV, playing football
Extras: Moved from Leicestershire to Essex at the end of the 1991 season
Opinions on cricket: 'Politics should be kept out of the game.'
Best batting: 23* Leicestershire v Sussex, Hove 1991
Best bowling: 4-54 Leicestershire v Cambridge University, Fenner's 1991

1991 Season

	M	Inns	NO	Runs	HS	Avge	100s	50s	Ct	St	O	M	Runs	Wkts	Avge	Best	5wI	10wM
Test																		
All First	6	9	3	94	23*	15.66	-	-	-	-	99	20	393	12	32.75	4-54	-	-
1-day Int																		
NatWest																		
B&H																		
Refuge	2	1	0	0	0	0.00	-	-	-	-	9	0	56	0	-	-	-	-

Career Performances

	M	Inns	NO	Runs	HS	Avge	100s	50s	Ct	St	Balls	Runs	Wkts	Avge	Best	5wI	10wM
Test																	
All First	10	13	5	110	23 *	13.75	-	-	1	-	798	503	15	33.53	4-54	-	-
1-day Int																	
NatWest																	
B&H																	
Refuge	16	8	5	44	17 *	14.66	-	-	4	-	540	410	11	37.27	3-25	-	

TERRY, V. P. Hampshire

Name: Vivian Paul Terry
Role: Right-hand bat, right-arm medium bowler, slip and outfielder
Born: 14 January 1959, Osnabruck, West Germany
Height: 6ft **Weight:** 13st 6lbs
County debut: 1978
County cap: 1983
Test debut: 1984
Tests: 2
1000 runs in a season: 8
1st-Class 50s scored: 64
1st-Class 100s scored: 24
1st-Class catches: 243
One-Day 50s: 35
One-Day 100s: 9
Place in batting averages: 62nd av. 38.87 (1990 97th av. 41.62)
Parents: Charles Michael and Patricia Mary
Wife and date of marriage: Bernadette, 4 June 1986
Children: Siobhan Catherine, 13 September 1987; Sean Paul, 1 August 1991
Education: Durlston Court, Hampshire; Millfield School, Somerset
Qualifications: 8 O-levels, 1 A-level, advanced cricket coach
Off-season: Playing and coaching in Perth, Western Australia
Overseas tours: ESCA to India 1977-78; English Counties to Zimbabwe 1985
Cricketers particularly admired: Gordon Greenidge, Chris Smith, Viv Richards, Barry Richards, Malcolm Marshall, Gary Sobers
Other sports followed: Most sports – golf, squash, football
Injuries: Hamstring and neck injuries
Relaxations: Music, sport
Opinions on cricket: 'Not enough done to ease pressures on cricketers during the winter.

We are expected to reach April at a level of fitness and skill but always in our own time.'
Best batting: 190 Hampshire v Sri Lankans, Southampton 1988

1991 Season

	M	Inns	NO	Runs	HS	Avge	100s	50s	Ct	St	O	M	Runs	Wkts	Avge	Best	5wI	10wM
Test																		
All First	20	35	3	1244	171	38.87	2	7	24	-								
1-day Int																		
NatWest	5	5	2	209	62 *	69.66	-	1	4	-								
B&H	1	1	0	10	10	10.00	-	-	-	-								
Refuge	15	14	1	408	123	31.38	1	1	5	-								

Career Performances

	M	Inns	NO	Runs	HS	Avge	100s	50s	Ct	St	Balls	Runs	Wkts	Avge	Best	5wI	10wM
Test	2	3	0	16	8	5.33	-	-	2	-							
All First	216	362	36	11515	190	35.32	24	64	243	-	95	58	0	-		-	-	-
1-day Int																	
NatWest	32	30	3	1135	165 *	42.03	2	8	13	-							
B&H	40	40	3	1375	134	37.16	2	9	16	-							
Refuge	156	142	17	3865	142	30.92	5	18	80	-							

THOMAS, J. G.   Northamptonshire

Name: John Gregory Thomas
Role: Right-hand bat, right-arm fast bowler
Born: 12 August 1960, Trebanos, Swansea
Height: 6ft 3in **Weight:** 14st
Nickname: Blodwen
County debut: 1979 (Glamorgan),
1989 (Northamptonshire)
County cap: 1986 (Glamorgan)
1991 (Northamptonshire)
Test debut: 1985-86
Tests: 5
One-Day Internationals: 3
50 wickets in a season: 1
1st-Class 50s scored: 7
1st-Class 100s scored: 2
1st-Class 5 w. in innings: 18
1st-Class 10 w. in match: 1
1st-Class catches: 74
Place in batting averages: 176th av. 22.88

(1990 252nd av. 15.20)
Place in bowling averages: 75th av. 33.46 (1990 101st av. 40.37)
Strike rate: 59.71 (career 53.09)
Parents: Illtyd and Margaret
Marital status: Single
Family links with cricket: Father played village cricket
Education: Cwmtawe Comprehensive School; South Glamorgan Institute of Higher Education
Qualifications: Qualified teacher, advanced cricket coach
Overseas tours: England to West Indies 1985-86; unofficial English team to South Africa 1989-90
Overseas teams played for: Border 1983-87; Eastern Province 1987-89
Relaxations: Any sport, music
Extras: Having never hit a first-class century before, hit two in August 1988. Signed for Northamptonshire in 1989. Banned from Test cricket for joining tour to South Africa in 1989-90. Career best bowling figures against his old county in 1990. Retired at the end of the 1991 season after problems with arthritis in his left hip
Best batting: 110 Glamorgan v Warwickshire, Edgbaston 1988
Best bowling: 7-75 Northamptonshire v Glamorgan, Northampton 1990

1991 Season

	M	Inns	NO	Runs	HS	Avge	100s	50s	Ct	St	O	M	Runs	Wkts	Avge	Best	5wI	10wM
Test																		
All First	12	12	3	206	64	22.88	-	1	3	-	278.4	40	937	28	33.46	5-62	2	-
1-day Int																		
NatWest																			
B&H	5	4	1	19	9	6.33	-	-	-	-	49.3	5	173	9	19.22	5-29	1	
Refuge	7	3	1	69	34	34.50	-	-	2	-	39	0	209	6	34.83	2-20	-	

Career Performances

	M	Inns	NO	Runs	HS	Avge	100s	50s	Ct	St	Balls	Runs	Wkts	Avge	Best	5wI	10wM
Test	5	10	4	83	31 *	13.83	-	-	-	-	774	504	10	50.40	4-70	-	-
All First	192	253	45	3419	110	16.43	2	7	74	-	27874	16303	525	31.05	7-75	18	1
1-day Int	3	3	2	1	1 *	1.00	-	-	-	-	156	144	3	48.00	2-59	-	
NatWest	14	11	3	151	34	18.87	-	-	4	-	707	427	18	23.72	5-17	1	
B&H	36	27	3	216	32	9.00	-	-	5	-	1961	1273	48	26.52	5-29	1	
Refuge	101	79	18	761	37	12.47	-	-	19	-	3949	3182	120	26.51	5-38	1	

THORPE, G. P.   Surrey

Name: Graham Paul Thorpe
Role: Left-hand bat, right-arm medium
bowler, slip and cover fielder
Born: 1 August 1969, Farnham
Height: 5ft 10in **Weight:** 11st 10lbs
Nickname: Chalky
County debut: 1988
County cap: 1991
1000 runs in a season: 2
1st-Class 50s scored: 20
1st-Class 100s scored: 7
1st-Class catches: 39
One-Day 50s: 13
One-Day 100s: 1
Place in batting averages: 50th av. 41.48
(1990 182nd av. 27.63)
Parents: Geoff and Toni
Marital status: Single
Family links with cricket: Both brothers
play for Farnham, father also plays cricket and mother is 'professional scorer'
Education: Weydon Comprehensive; Farnham Sixth Form College
Qualifications: 6 O-levels, PE Diploma
Off-season: Touring with England A
Overseas tours: England A to Zimbabwe and Kenya 1989-90; Pakistan 1990-91; Bermuda
and West Indies 1991-92
Cricketers particularly admired: Viv Richards, Grahame Clinton, David Gower
Other sports followed: Football, tennis
Relaxations: Eating Chinese food, swimming, sunbathing and spending time with
girlfriend
Extras: Played England Schools cricket U15 and U19 and England Schools football U18
Opinions on cricket: 'There should be 17 four-day matches, with two limited-overs
competitions.'
Best batting: 177 Surrey v Sussex, The Oval 1991
Best bowling: 2-31 Surrey v Essex, The Oval 1989

---

182. Which member of the 1991 England Rugby World Cup team has
played first-class cricket?

1991 Season

	M	Inns	NO	Runs	HS	Avge	100s	50s	Ct	St	O	M	Runs	Wkts	Avge	Best	5wI	10wM
Test																		
All First	23	38	9	1203	177	41.48	4	4	8	-	64	10	242	4	60.50	2-48	-	-
1-day Int																		
NatWest	4	4	1	138	93	46.00	-	1	1	-	0.1	0	0	0	-		-	-
B&H	4	4	0	112	41	28.00	-	-	1	-	8	0	35	0	-		-	-
Refuge	15	13	2	431	115 *	39.18	1	3	2	-	12	0	78	3	26.00	3-21	-	

Career Performances

	M	Inns	NO	Runs	HS	Avge	100s	50s	Ct	St	Balls	Runs	Wkts	Avge	Best	5wI	10wM
Test																	
All First	68	109	22	3529	177	40.56	7	20	39	-	1122	659	13	50.69	2-31	-	-
1-day Int																	
NatWest	9	9	2	252	93	36.00	-	2	3	-	13	12	0	-		-	-
B&H	10	10	1	223	50 *	24.77	-	1	2	-	156	115	4	28.75	3-35	-	
Refuge	44	41	6	1309	115 *	37.40	1	10	10	-	198	203	5	40.60	3-21	-	

THRELFALL, P. W. Sussex

Name: Philip Walter Threlfall
Role: Right-hand bat, right-arm medium-fast bowler
Born: 11 February 1967, Barrow-in-Furness
Height: 6ft 3in
County debut: 1988
1st-Class catches: 0
Education: Barrow-in-Furness Grammar School; Parkview School
Extras: Played Warwicks 2nd XI 1984 and Minor Counties cricket for Cumberland in 1987. Released by Sussex at the end of the 1991 season
Best bowling: 3-45 Sussex v Sri Lanka, Hove 1990

1991 Season

	M	Inns	NO	Runs	HS	Avge	100s	50s	Ct	St	O	M	Runs	Wkts	Avge	Best	5wl	10wM
Test																		
All First	1	0	0	0	0	-	-	-	-	-	4	1	10	2	5.00	2-10	-	-
1-day Int																		
NatWest																		
B&H																		
Refuge																		

Career Performances

	M	Inns	NO	Runs	HS	Avge	100s	50s	Ct	St	Balls	Runs	Wkts	Avge	Best	5wl	10wM
Test																	
All First	3	0	0	0	0	-	-	-	-	-	276	130	7	18.57	3-45	-	-
1-day Int																	
NatWest																	
B&H																	
Refuge																	

TITCHARD, S. P.   Lancashire

Name: Stephen Paul Titchard
Role: Right-hand bat, right-arm medium bowler
Born: 17 December 1967, Warrington, Cheshire
Height: 6ft 3in **Weight:** 15st 2lbs ('approx')
Nickname: Titch, Stainy, Tyrone
County debut: 1990
1st-Class 50s: 3
1st-Class 100s: 1
1st-Class catches: 8
Parents: Alan and Margaret
Marital status: Single
Family links with cricket: Father, uncle and two brothers have played for Grappenhall 1st XI in the Manchester Association League
Education: Lymm County High School, Priestley College
Qualifications: 3 O-levels
Off-season: Playing cricket in Australia
Cricketers particularly admired: Dennis Amiss, Geoff Trim ('formerly Lancs CCC,

who helped me with my early development')
Other sports followed: Football (Manchester City) and rugby league (Warrington)
Relaxations: Snooker and golf
Opinions on cricket: 'Four-day cricket is worthwhile as it gives players greater opportunity to play their natural game – although when fielding at short leg it can seem a very long time!'
Best batting: 135 Lancashire v Nottinghamshire, Old Trafford 1991

1991 Season

	M	Inns	NO	Runs	HS	Avge	100s	50s	Ct	St	O	M	Runs	Wkts	Avge	Best	5wI	10wM
Test																		
All First	8	15	1	546	135	39.00	1	2	8	-								
1-day Int																		
NatWest																		
B&H																		
Refuge	1	1	0	13	13	13.00	-	-	-	-								

Career Performances

	M	Inns	NO	Runs	HS	Avge	100s	50s	Ct	St	Balls	Runs	Wkts	Avge	Best	5wI	10wM
Test																	
All First	11	20	1	675	135	35.52	1	3	8	-							
1-day Int																	
NatWest																	
B&H																	
Refuge	1	1	0	13	13	13.00	-	-	-	-							

183. Which current England cricketer holds the record for the earliest first-class century of any English season, and what was the date?

TOLLEY, C. M. Worcestershire

Name: Christopher Mark Tolley
Role: Right-hand bat, left-arm medium
bowler
Born: 30 December 1967, Kidderminster
Height: 5ft 9in **Weight:** 11st
Nickname: Treefrog, Red dog
County debut: 1989
1st-Class catches: 7
One-Day 50s scored: 2
Place in batting averages: 165th av. 24.00
Place in bowling averages: 11th av. 22.94
Strike rate: 53.66 (career 77.50)
Parents: Ray and Liz
Marital status: Single
Family links with cricket: Father played
local league; brother Richard plays in the
Birmingham League
Education: Oldswinford Primary School;
Redhill Comprehensive School;
King Edward VI College, Stourbridge; Loughborough University
Qualifications: 9 O-levels, 3 A-levels, BSc in PE Sports Science & Recreation Management
Off-season: Teaching PE at Chase School, Malvern
Overseas tours: British Universities Sports Federation tour to Barbados October 1989
Cricketers particularly admired: Ian Botham, Richard Hadlee, Graeme Hick
Other sports followed: Football, athletics, hockey
Injuries: Shoulder strain
Relaxations: Watching TV, eating out
Extras: Played for ESCA U19 in 1986 and for the Combined Universities in the B&H Cup
Opinions on cricket: 'There is too much cricket played during the season. Players do not
have time to prepare physically or mentally for each individual game.'
Best batting: 37 Worcestershire v Kent, Worcester 1989
Best bowling: 4-69 Worcestershire v Sri Lankans, Worcester 1991

1991 Season

	M	Inns	NO	Runs	HS	Avge	100s	50s	Ct	St	O	M	Runs	Wkts	Avge	Best	5wl	10wM
Test																		
All First	8	10	4	144	36	24.00	-	-	3	-	161	39	413	18	22.94	4-69	-	-
1-day Int																		
NatWest																		
B&H																		
Refuge	4	0	0	0	0	-	-	-	2	-	14	0	107	2	53.50	1-23	-	

Career Performances

	M	Inns	NO	Runs	HS	Avge	100s	50s	Ct	St	Balls	Runs	Wkts	Avge	Best	5wl	10wM
Test																	
All First	20	22	7	343	37	22.86	-	-	7	-	1956	915	24	38.12	4-69	-	-
1-day Int																	
NatWest	1	0	0	0	0	-	-	-	-	-	36	32	0	-		-	-
B&H	9	8	1	201	77	28.71	-	2	3	-	522	336	4	84.00	1-12	-	
Refuge	9	2	1	2	1 *	2.00	-	-	3	-	246	190	5	38.00	1-18	-	

TOPLEY, T. D.   Essex

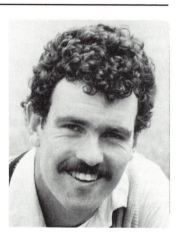

Name: Thomas Donald Topley
Role: Right-hand bat, right-arm
medium-fast bowler
Born: 25 February 1964, Canterbury
Height: 6ft 3in **Weight:** 13st 5lbs
Nickname: Toppers, Wimble, Jack, Tetley,
Luther
County debut: 1985 (Surrey), 1985
(Essex)
County cap: 1988 (Essex)
50 wickets in a season: 3
1st-Class 50s scored: 4
1st-Class 5 w. in innings: 14
1st-Class 10 w. in match: 2
1st-Class catches: 59
Place in batting averages: 186th av. 21.33
Place in bowling averages: 66th av. 32.12
(1990 41st av. 32.40)
Strike rate: 54.38 (career 51.44)
Parents: Tom (deceased) and Rhoda
Marital status: Single
Family links with cricket: Brother Peter played for Kent (1972-76)
Education: Royal Hospital School, Holbrook, Suffolk
Qualifications: 6 O-levels, NCA advanced coach
Career outside cricket: Coaching
Off-season: In Zimbabwe as their national coach, and on to Australia and New Zealand
for the World Cup
Overseas tours: Benefit tour to Barbados 1986
Overseas teams played for: Noodsburg and Midlands, Natal 1985-86; Roodeport City,
Transvaal 1986-87; Griqualand West, South Africa 1987-88; Harare Sports Club, Zimbabwe
1990-91

Cricketers particularly admired: Richard Hadlee, Graham Gooch, Ian Botham
Other sports followed: Rugby, soccer, badminton and all other ball sports
Injuries: 'Perpetual shin soreness and problems to left leg.'
Relaxations: Photography and travel and 'arguing/discussions with D.Pringle and N.Foster'
Extras: Spent three years prior to joining Essex on the MCC Young Professionals at Lord's. As 12th man held famous one-handed 'catch' for England v West Indies at Lord's in 1984, stepping over the boundary in taking it. Also played for Norfolk (1982-84) and Surrey
Opinions on cricket: 'Bring back higher seam ball as current ball v bat contest is boring and one-sided. Produce a ball that encourages swing bowling. Abolish fines on over-rates and reduce the amount of cricket we play.'
Best batting: 66 Essex v Yorkshire, Headingley 1987
Best bowling: 7-75 Essex v Derbyshire, Chesterfield 1988

1991 Season

	M	Inns	NO	Runs	HS	Avge	100s	50s	Ct	St	O	M	Runs	Wkts	Avge	Best	5wI	10wM
Test																		
All First	20	19	4	320	50 *	21.33	-	2	15	-	498.3	86	1767	55	32.12	5-58	3	-
1-day Int																		
NatWest	3	1	0	7	7	7.00	-	-	-	-	34	6	103	6	17.16	3-38	-	
B&H	3	2	1	7	6 *	7.00	-	-	1	-	28	4	124	4	31.00	4-41	-	
Refuge	14	6	2	50	38 *	12.50	-	-	2	-	95.5	5	469	20	23.45	3-29	-	

Career Performances

	M	Inns	NO	Runs	HS	Avge	100s	50s	Ct	St	Balls	Runs	Wkts	Avge	Best	5wI	10wM
Test																	
All First	100	113	26	1436	66	16.50	-	4	59	-	16822	8694	327	26.58	7-75	14	2
1-day Int																	
NatWest	11	4	1	32	15 *	10.66	-	-	2	-	680	389	18	21.61	4-21	-	
B&H	21	5	4	26	10 *	26.00	-	-	6	-	1236	697	29	24.03	4-22	-	
Refuge	72	34	11	182	38 *	7.91	-	-	9	-	3022	2287	90	25.41	6-33	2	

184. Who captained the 1983 New Zealanders in England?

TOWNSEND, G. T. J. Somerset

Name: Gareth Terence John Townsend
Role: Right-hand opening batsman
Born: 28 June 1968, Tiverton, Devon
Height: 6ft **Weight:** 11st 7lbs
Nickname: Gobbler, Winscombe,
Thunder Bat
County debut: 1990
1st-Class 50s scored: 1
1st-Class catches: 6
Parents: Terry and Sheila
Marital status: Single
Family links with cricket: 'Father played
before giving up time to help me with my
career; older brother David played
Devon Schools cricket and club cricket,
other brother Graeme is secretary of his
club side.'
Education: Tiverton Comprehensive
School and Birmingham University
Qualifications: 7 O-levels, 4 A-levels, BA (Hons) General Studies
Career outside cricket: 'Unsure.'
Off-season: Playing cricket in Sydney, Australia
Overseas teams played for: Hawks, Perth, Western Australia 1989-90; Waverley, Sydney
1991-92
Cricketers particularly admired: Gordon Greenidge, Jimmy Cook, Peter Roebuck
Other sports followed: Golf and rugby
Relaxations: 'Playing golf and socialising with mates.'
Extras: Scored 85 and 115* on 2nd XI debut v Hampshire in 1987
Opinions on cricket: 'Good to see South Africa competing in the World Cup, though I feel
that the situation is by no means settled in South Africa which may lead to further
repercussions affecting their future in world cricket.'
Best batting: 53 Somerset v Sri Lankans, Taunton 1991

1991 Season

	M	Inns	NO	Runs	HS	Avge	100s	50s	Ct	St	O	M	Runs	Wkts	Avge	Best	5wI	10wM
Test																		
All First	3	5	0	121	53	24.20	-	1	3	-								
1-day Int																		
NatWest																		
B&H																		
Refuge	2	2	0	54	27	27.00	-	-	1	-								

Career Performances

	M	Inns	NO	Runs	HS	Avge	100s	50s	Ct	St	Balls	Runs	Wkts	Avge	Best	5wI	10wM
Test																	
All First	5	9	1	142	53	17.75	-	1	6	-							
1-day Int																	
NatWest																	
B&H																	
Refuge	2	2	0	54	27	27.00	-	-	1	-							

TREMLETT, T. M.   Hampshire

Name: Timothy Maurice Tremlett
Role: Right-hand bat, right-arm medium bowler
Born: 26 July 1956, Wellington, Somerset
Height: 6ft 2in **Weight:** 13st 7lbs
Nickname: Hurricane, Trooper, R2
County debut: 1976
County cap: 1983
50 wickets in a season: 4
1st-Class 50s scored: 18
1st-Class 100s scored: 1
1st-Class 5 w. in innings: 11
Place in bowling averages: (1990 91st av. 39.30)
Strike rate: (career 58.97)
Parents: Maurice Fletcher and Melina May
Wife and date of marriage: Carolyn Patricia, 28 September 1979
Children: Christopher Timothy, 2 September 1981; Alastair Jonathan, 1 February 1983; Benjamin Paul, 2 May 1984
Family links with cricket: Father played for Somerset and for England against West Indies in the West Indies 1947-48. Captained Somerset 1958-60. Younger brother plays local club cricket for Deanery CC
Education: Bellemoor Secondary Modern; Richard Taunton Sixth Form College
Qualifications: 5 O-levels, 1 A-level. Advanced coaching certificate
Career outside cricket: Head Coach/Cricket Administrator for Hampshire CCC
Overseas tours: English Counties tour to Zimbabwe 1985; England B to Sri Lanka 1985-86
Cricketers particularly admired: Vincent van der Bijl, Mike Hendrick, Malcolm Marshall, Richard Hadlee

Other sports followed: Golf, table tennis, squash, swimming, badminton
Relaxations: Collecting cricket books and records, gardening, cinema
Opinions on cricket: 'With ever increasing numbers of top-class cricketers withdrawing from international fixtures, the cricketing authorities must begin to reduce the amount of cricket played in this country, especially one-day cricket. With the emphasis still geared towards one-day matches, specialists are still outnumbered heavily by bits-and-pieces performers, with young spin-bowlers particularly at a disadvantage. To ensure that the highest standards are maintained, the structure of English first-class cricket is in further need of streamlining.'
Best batting: 102* Hampshire v Somerset, Taunton 1985
Best bowling: 6-53 Hampshire v Somerset, Weston-super-Mare 1987

1991 Season

	M	Inns	NO	Runs	HS	Avge	100s	50s	Ct	St	O	M	Runs	Wkts	Avge	Best	5wI	10wM
Test																		
All First	1	1	0	2	2	2.00	-	-	-	-	10	3	39	1	39.00	1-39	-	-
1-day Int																		
NatWest																		
B&H																		
Refuge	3	2	1	13	8	13.00	-	-	-	-	22.1	0	90	2	45.00	1-27	-	

Career Performances

	M	Inns	NO	Runs	HS	Avge	100s	50s	Ct	St	Balls	Runs	Wkts	Avge	Best	5wI	10wM
Test																	
All First	207	250	66	3864	102 *	21.00	1	18	73	-	26540	10798	450	23.99	6-53	11	-
1-day Int																	
NatWest	23	13	4	142	43 *	15.77	-	-	4	-	1280	697	28	24.89	4-38	-	
B&H	36	25	10	213	36 *	14.20	-	-	6	-	1955	1063	46	23.10	4-30	-	
Refuge	141	60	27	375	35	11.36	-	-	26	-	5759	4412	178	24.78	5-28	1	

185. Whose nickname is 'Macko'?

TRUMP, H. R. J.   Somerset

Name: Harvey Russell John Trump
Role: Right-hand bat, off-spin bowler,
gully/slip fielder
Born: 11 October 1968, Taunton
Height: 6ft 2in **Weight:** 13st 7lbs
Nickname: Trumpy, Club foot
County debut: 1988
50 wickets in a season: 1
1st-Class 5 w. in innings: 4
1st-Class catches: 28
Place in batting averages: 251st av. 10.80
Place in bowling averages: 117th av. 41.43
Strike rate: 74.94 (career 81.87)
Wife and date of marriage: Nicola,
26 October 1991
Family links with cricket: Father played
for Somerset 2nd XI and captained Devon
Education: Edgarley Hall (Millfield Jnr
School); Millfield School; Chester College
of Higher Education
Qualifications: 6 O-levels, 2 A-levels, BA (Hons) Grade 2 Level 1
Career outside cricket: Teacher at Stamford School, Lincolnshire
Off-season: Teaching history and coaching cricket, hockey and rugby
Overseas tours: England YC to Sri Lanka 1987; to Australia for Junior World Cup 1988
Cricketers particularly admired: David Graveney, John Emburey, Mike Gatting, Viv
Richards
Other sports followed: Hockey, rugby and most other sports
Relaxations: Reading, walking, eating out, watching sport
Extras: Played county hockey for Somerset U19. Qualified lifeguard, attaining bronze
medallion life-saving award. Preliminary teacher of disabled swimming certificate. "He's
the best fielder off his own bowling I've ever seen" – David Graveney, 1991
Opinions on cricket: 'Something has got to be done about the seam on the ball. Over-rates
need to be looked at and adjusted appropriately. It is vitally important for youngsters to
have a good grounding at junior levels in two- and three-day, cricket not just one-day.'
Best batting: 48 Somerset v Hampshire, Taunton 1988
Best bowling: 6-48 Somerset v Worcestershire, Weston-super-Mare, 1991

186. Who was Hampshire's first-choice wicket-keeeper in 1991?

1991 Season

	M	Inns	NO	Runs	HS	Avge	100s	50s	Ct	St	O	M	Runs	Wkts	Avge	Best	5wI	10wM
Test																		
All First	18	17	7	108	30 *	10.80	-	-	12	-	637.2	111	2113	51	41.43	6-48	4	-
1-day Int																		
NatWest	1	1	0	1	1	1.00	-	-	-	-	6	0	33	0	-		-	-
B&H																		
Refuge	7	2	1	21	19	21.00	-	-	3	-	54	1	277	7	39.57	2-31	-	

Career Performances

	M	Inns	NO	Runs	HS	Avge	100s	50s	Ct	St	Balls	Runs	Wkts	Avge	Best	5wl	10wM
Test																	
All First	48	48	11	275	48	7.43	-	-	28	-	8924	4454	109	40.86	6-48	4	-
1-day Int																	
NatWest	3	2	0	1	1	0.50	-	-	1	-	162	106	2	53.00	2-44	-	
B&H																	
Refuge	20	6	1	27	19	5.40	-	-	4	-	828	651	17	38.29	2-23	-	

TUFNELL, P. C. R.   Middlesex

Name: Philip Clive Roderick Tufnell
Role: Right-hand bat, slow left-arm spinner
Born: 29 April 1966, Hadley Wood, Hertfordshire
Height: 6ft **Weight:** 12st 7lbs
Nickname: The Cat
County debut: 1986
County cap: 1990
Test debut: 1990-91
Tests: 6
One-Day Internationals: 9
50 wickets in a season: 3
1st-Class 5 w. in innings: 15
1st-Class 10 w. in match: 1
1st-Class catches: 43
Place in batting averages: 249th av. 11.66 (1990 213th av. 21.76)
Place in bowling averages: 23rd av. 25.21 (1990 58th av. 35.60)
Strike rate: 61.61 (career 74.06)
Parents: Sylvia and Alan

Marital status: Divorced
Education: Highgate School; Southgate School
Qualifications: O-level in Art; City & Guilds Silversmithing
Career outside cricket: 'Silversmith, cabbie, builder's dogsbody'
Off-season: 'Sleeping' then touring with England
Overseas tours: England U19 to West Indies 1985; England to Australia 1990-91; New Zealand 1991-92
Overseas teams played for: Queensland University, Australia
Cricketers particularly admired: Jason Pooley
Other sports followed: American football
Injuries: Knee injury
Relaxations: Sleeping
Extras: MCC Young Cricketer of the Year 1984. Middlesex Uncapped Bowler of the Year 1987. Was originally a seam bowler and gave up cricket for three years in his mid-teens
Opinions on cricket: 'Drier wickets and four-day games.'
Best batting: 37 Middlesex v Yorkshire, Headingley 1990
Best bowling: 7-116 Middlesex v Hampshire, Lord's 1991

1991 Season

	M	Inns	NO	Runs	HS	Avge	100s	50s	Ct	St	O	M	Runs	Wkts	Avge	Best	5wl	10wM
Test	2	2	0	2	2	1.00	-	-	1	-	102	25	292	12	24.33	6-25	2	-
All First	22	24	6	210	34	11.66	-	-	9	-	903.4	254	2219	88	25.21	7-116	7	1
1-day Int																		
NatWest	1	1	0	8	8	8.00	-	-	-	-	12	2	29	1	29.00	1-29	-	
B&H	4	3	1	19	18	9.50	-	-	1	-	39	0	187	4	46.75	3-50	-	
Refuge	1	0	0	0	0	-	-	-	-	-	8	0	28	3	9.33	3-28	-	

Career Performances

	M	Inns	NO	Runs	HS	Avge	100s	50s	Ct	St	Balls	Runs	Wkts	Avge	Best	5wl	10wM
Test	6	8	4	15	8	3.75	-	-	2	-	1452	637	21	30.33	6-25	3	-
All First	93	94	34	657	37	10.95	-	-	43	-	22664	9826	306	32.11	7-116	15	1
1-day Int	9	5	4	10	5 *	10.00	-	-	3	-	498	347	9	38.55	3-40	-	
NatWest	4	1	0	8	8	8.00	-	-	2	-	288	130	7	18.57	3-29	-	
B&H	6	4	2	26	18	13.00	-	-	1	-	342	265	5	53.00	3-50	-	
Refuge	8	2	2	13	13 *	-	-	-	-	-	330	276	6	46.00	3-28	-	

TURNER, I. J.   Hampshire

Name: Ian John Turner
Role: Right-hand bat, slow left-arm bowler
Born: 18 July 1968, Denmead
Height: 6ft 1in **Weight:** 13st 7lbs
Nickname: Turns, Bunsen, Jet & Trunky,
Mr Angry
County debut: 1989
1st-Class catches: 5
Place in batting averages: 229th av. 14.50
Place in bowling averages: 126th av. 45.50
Strike rate: 102.35 (career 93.81)
Parents: Robert and Sheila
Marital status: Single
Family links with cricket: Father plays for
Hambledon CC
Education: Cowplain Comprehensive
School; South Downs College
Qualifications: 7 CSEs, pass in BTec
General Diploma in Business Studies
Career outside cricket: Bank clerk

Off-season: Four months in Argentina
Overseas teams played for: Waverley, Sydney 1989-90
Cricketers particularly admired: Phil Edmonds
Other sports followed: Football – 'mainly Liverpool but look at local scores.'
Relaxations: Listening to music, sleeping
Opinions on cricket: 'State of pitches in 2nd XI cricket is inadequate. There should be more four-day cricket.'
Best batting: 39* Hampshire v Glamorgan, Swansea 1991
Best bowling: 4-28 Hampshire v Derbyshire, Chesterfield 1991

1991 Season

	M	Inns	NO	Runs	HS	Avge	100s	50s	Ct	St	O	M	Runs	Wkts	Avge	Best	5wl	10wM
Test																		
All First	8	10	4	87	39 *	14.50	-	-	3	-	238.5	65	637	14	45.50	4-28	-	-
1-day Int																		
NatWest																		
B&H																		
Refuge																		

	M	Inns	NO	Runs	HS	Avge	100s	50s	Ct	St	Balls	Runs	Wkts	Avge	Best	5wl	10wM
Test																	
All First	14	15	6	111	39 *	12.33	-	-	5	-	2533	1109	27	41.07	4-28	-	-
1-day Int																	
NatWest																	
B&H																	
Refuge																	

TURNER, R. J. Somerset

Name: Robert Julian Turner
Role: Right-hand bat, wicket-keeper
Born: 25 November 1967, Worcestershire
Height: 6ft 2in **Weight:** 13st 7lbs
Nickname: Noddy, Clockwork, Bungalow, Teflon, Iron Gloves, RJ, Turns
County debut: 1991
1st-Class 50s scored: 3
1st-Class catches: 36
1st-Class stumpings: 12
Place in batting averages: 142nd av. 27.66
Parents: Derek Edward and Doris Lilian
Marital status: Single
Family links with cricket: Brother Simon played for Somerset (1984-85) as a wicket-keeper and is now captain of Weston-super-Mare. Other brother Richard also plays for Weston-super-Mare 1st team and father is chairman of the club

Education: Uphill Primary School; Broadoak School, Weston-super-Mare; Millfield School, Cambridge University
Qualifications: Honours Degree in Engineering and Diploma in Computer Science
Career outside cricket: 'Sponsored by Rolls Royce plc whilst at university, but now open to suggestions.'
Off-season: Playing cricket in Perth, Western Australia and 'spending plenty of time on Scarborough beach'
Overseas tours: Combined Universities to Barbados 1989
Overseas teams played for: Claremont-Nedlands, Perth, Western Australia 1991-92
Cricketers particularly admired: Andy Brassington, Stuart Turner, and Paul Sadler and Chris Snorton (both of Weston-super-Mare)
Other sports followed: Nearly all sports - 'play hockey, golf, squash and badminton'

Injuries: Broken thumb while batting against Northamptonshire – unable to play for Combined Universities in the B&H Cup
Relaxations: Photography, meeting friends for a quiet beer, playing the piano, reading, sleeping, eating curries, watching 'Neighbours'
Extras: Captain of Cambridge University and Combined Universities 1991
Opinions on cricket: 'The three-day game seems to induce too many contrived situations; the four-day game is a greater test of actual cricketing ability (if played on a good cricket wicket) and more interesting to spectators.'
Best batting: 69* Cambridge University v Middlesex, Fenner's 1991

1991 Season

	M	Inns	NO	Runs	HS	Avge	100s	50s	Ct	St	O	M	Runs	Wkts	Avge	Best	5wI	10wM
Test																		
All First	9	13	4	249	69 *	27.66	-	1	12	1								
1-day Int																		
NatWest																		
B&H																		
Refuge																		

Career Performances

	M	Inns	NO	Runs	HS	Avge	100s	50s	Ct	St	Balls	Runs	Wkts	Avge	Best	5wI	10wM
Test																	
All First	34	54	9	959	69 *	21.31	-	3	36	12							
1-day Int																	
NatWest																	
B&H	4	4	3	49	25 *	49.00	-	-	2	1							
Refuge																	

TWOSE, R. G.   Warwickshire

Name: Roger Graham Twose
Role: Left-hand bat, right-arm fast-medium bowler
Born: 17 April 1968, Torquay ('in a car!')
Height: 6ft **Weight:** 14st
Nickname: Twosey, Buffalo
County debut: 1989
1st-Class 50s scored: 6
1st-Class catches: 10
One-Day 50s: 1
Place in batting averages: (1990 188th av. 26.77)
Parents: Paul and Patricia
Marital status: Single

Family links with cricket: Father played for Devon, brother Richard plays for Devon. Uncles – Roger Tolchard (Leicestershire and England) and Jeff Tolchard (Leicestershire)
Education: Wolborough Hill, Newton Abbot, Devon; King's College, Taunton
Qualifications: 7 O-levels, 2 A-levels, NCA coaching certificate
Off-season: Playing in New Zealand
Overseas teams played for: Northern Districts, New Zealand 1989-90; Central Districts, New Zealand 1991-92
Cricketers particularly admired: Giles Barber, Rick Pickard, Ken Rogers
Other sports followed: Chess, bridge and billiards
Relaxations: Playing golf
Extras: 'Once took all ten wickets in an innings whilst playing in New Zealand: a feat I plan to reproduce in first-class cricket!'

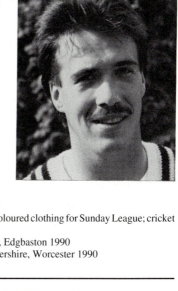

Opinions on cricket: '17 four-day matches; coloured clothing for Sunday League; cricket under floodlights.'
Best batting: 64* Warwickshire v Sri Lanka, Edgbaston 1990
Best bowling: 1-10 Warwickshire v Worcestershire, Worcester 1990

1991 Season

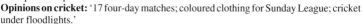

	M	Inns	NO	Runs	HS	Avge	100s	50s	Ct	St	O	M	Runs	Wkts	Avge	Best	5wI	10wM
Test																		
All First	2	2	1	42	41	42.00	-	-	-	-	9	0	27	1	27.00	1-27	-	-
1-day Int																		
NatWest																		
B&H	1	1	0	5	5	5.00	-	-	-	-								
Refuge	5	3	2	27	26 *	27.00	-	-	2	-	8	0	49	0	-		-	-

Career Performances

	M	Inns	NO	Runs	HS	Avge	100s	50s	Ct	St	Balls	Runs	Wkts	Avge	Best	5wI	10wM
Test																	
All First	21	36	7	819	64 *	28.24	-	6	10	-	869	499	7	71.28	1-10	-	-
1-day Int																	
NatWest	3	3	0	66	56	22.00	-	1	2	-	120	79	2	39.50	1-31	-	
B&H	4	3	0	24	17	8.00	-	-	2	-	18	16	0	-		-	
Refuge	26	18	5	219	40	16.84	-	-	5	-	466	422	11	38.36	2-11	-	

Name: Shaun David Udal
Role: Right-hand bat, off-spin bowler,
field in the deep
Born: 18 March 1969, Farnborough
Height: 6ft 3in **Weight:** 13st 6lbs
Nickname: Uffers, Prawn
County debut: 1989
1st-Class catches: 2
Place in bowling averages: (1990 104th
av. 40.90)
Strike rate: (career 67.87)
Parents: Robin and Mary
Marital status: Single
Family links with cricket: Father played
for Surrey Colts and is still playing club
cricket for Camberley after 41 years, brother
plays for Camberley 1st XI
Education: Tower Hill Infant and
Junior Schools; Cove Comprehensive
School

Qualifications: 8 CSEs, qualified print finisher
Career outside cricket: Printing trade
Off-season: Working at Omega Print Finishers in Camberley
Overseas teams played for: Hamilton Wickham, Newcastle, NSW 1990
Cricketers particularly admired: Ian Botham, Malcolm Marshall, Robin Smith, Nick
Hawkins ('club cricketer who has helped me in my career')
Other sports followed: 'Watch a lot of football and mostly see Aldershot's home games
although they don't play a lot of football!'
Injuries: 'Hernia affected me from July onwards. I was OK for one-day games only. Had
operation on September 17th.'
Relaxations: 'Spending time with my wife Emma, generally being with my friends and
family. Eating at nice restaurants and enjoying a few beers at Camberley CC.'
Extras: Has taken two hat-tricks in club cricket, and scored a double hundred in a 40-over
club game. Man of the Match on NatWest debut against Berkshire 1991
Opinions on cricket: 'We play far too much cricket in general, not only one-day stuff, and
this is affecting players' performances over the season. The fixtures were also arranged
poorly this season with teams sometimes travelling considerable distance between the 2nd
and 3rd days of a Championship match, just to play a Refuge game. This must be rectified
in the near future. The balance between bat and ball seemed to be better this year.'
Best batting: 28* Hampshire v Surrey, Southampton 1990
Best bowling: 4-139 Hampshire v Sri Lanka, Southampton 1990

1991 Season

	M	Inns	NO	Runs	HS	Avge	100s	50s	Ct	St	O	M	Runs	Wkts	Avge	Best	5wI	10wM
Test																		
All First	1	1	0	0	0	0.00	-	-	-	-	22	3	117	2	58.50	2-117	-	-
1-day Int																		
NatWest	5	0	0	0	0	-	-	-	2	-	50	3	191	6	31.83	3-47	-	
B&H	5	2	0	10	9	5.00	-	-	2	-	55	9	189	9	21.00	3-41	-	
Refuge	16	7	3	66	23	16.50	-	-	4	-	119.2	6	594	17	34.94	3-40	-	

Career Performances

	M	Inns	NO	Runs	HS	Avge	100s	50s	Ct	St	Balls	Runs	Wkts	Avge	Best	5wI	10wM
Test																	
All First	9	7	2	79	28 *	15.80	-	-	2	-	1629	1038	24	43.25	4-139	-	-
1-day Int																	
NatWest	5	0	0	0	0	-	-	-	2	-	300	191	6	31.83	3-47	-	
B&H	5	2	0	10	9	5.00	-	-	2	-	330	189	9	21.00	3-41	-	
Refuge	19	8	4	68	23	17.00	-	-	5	-	836	686	21	32.66	3-40	-	

VAN TROOST, A. P.   Somerset

Name: Adrianus Pelrus van Troost
Role: Right-hand bat, right-arm
medium-fast bowler
Born: 2 October 1972, Schiedam, Holland
Height: 6ft 7in **Weight:** 13st
Nickname: Flappie, Rooster
County debut: 1991
1st-Class catches: 1
Parents: Aad and Anneke
Marital status: Single
Family links with cricket: Father plays for
Excelsior CC in Holland, brother plays for
Excelsior and Holland U23. Grandfather
played for Excelsior and Holland
Education: Spieringshoek College,
Schiedam
Qualifications: Finished Havo schooling
Overseas tours: Unibind XI to Zimbabwe
1989; Holland to Dubai and Namibia 1990;
Holland U19 to Canada 1991
Overseas teams played for: Excelsior, Holland 1979-91
Cricketers particularly admired: Richard Hadlee, Ian Botham, Malcolm Marshall

517

Other sports followed: Football, tennis and most other sports
Injuries: Foot injury
Relaxations: Films, music, visiting pubs
Extras: Played for Holland at the age of 16. Third Dutch national to play professional cricket
Opinions on cricket: 'I really think Holland should be admitted to the B& H Cup or the NatWest Trophy.'
Best batting: 0* Somerset v Kent, Taunton 1991
Best bowling: 2-25 Somerset v Kent, Taunton 1991

1991 Season

	M	Inns	NO	Runs	HS	Avge	100s	50s	Ct	St	O	M	Runs	Wkts	Avge	Best	5wI	10wM
Test																		
All First	4	1	1	0	0*	-	-	-	-	1	-	86.4	12	267	6	44.50	2-25	-	-
1-day Int																			
NatWest																			
B&H																			
Refuge																			

Career Performances

	M	Inns	NO	Runs	HS	Avge	100s	50s	Ct	St	Balls	Runs	Wkts	Avge	Best	5wI	10wM
Test																	
All First	4	1	1	0	0*	-	-	-	1	-	520	267	6	44.50	2-25	-	-
1-day Int																	
NatWest																	
B&H																	
Refuge																	

WALKER, A.   Northamptonshire

Name: Alan Walker
Role: Left-hand bat, right-arm fast-medium bowler
Born: 7 July 1962, Emley, near Huddersfield
Height: 5ft 11in **Weight:** 12st 7lbs
Nickname: Wacky
County debut: 1983
County cap: 1987
1st-Class 5 w. in innings: 2
1st-Class catches: 37
Strike rate: (career 60.05)
Parents: Malcolm and Enid
Marital status: Engaged to Julie

Education: Emley Junior School; Kirkburton Middle School; Shelley High School

Qualifications: 2 O-levels, 4 CSEs, qualified coal-face worker

Career outside cricket: Miner, also worked in iron foundry

Off-season: Building work

Overseas tours: NYCA North U19 to Denmark

Overseas teams played for: Uitenhage, South Africa 1984-85 and 1987-88

Cricketers particularly admired: Dennis Lillee, Richard Hadlee

Other sports followed: Football (Huddersfield Town and Emley), rugby league (Wakefield Trinity)

Relaxations: DIY, drinking, gardening

Best batting: 41* Northamptonshire v Warwickshire, Edgbaston 1987
Best bowling: 6-50 Northamptonshire v Lancashire, Northampton 1986

1991 Season

	M	Inns	NO	Runs	HS	Avge	100s	50s	Ct	St	O	M	Runs	Wkts	Avge	Best	5wI	10wM
Test																		
All First	4	4	1	35	13	11.66	-	-	2	-	103	20	296	6	49.33	3-84	-	-
1-day Int																		
NatWest	4	1	0	11	11	11.00	-	-	-	-	42	6	129	4	32.25	2-39	-	
B&H	1	1	1	0	0*	-	-	-	-	-	9	1	33	1	33.00	1-33	-	
Refuge	14	4	0	17	6	4.25	-	-	6	-	98.5	8	335	12	27.91	2-7	-	

Career Performances

	M	Inns	NO	Runs	HS	Avge	100s	50s	Ct	St	Balls	Runs	Wkts	Avge	Best	5wI	10wM
Test																	
All First	94	89	45	624	41*	14.18	-	-	37	-	13093	6757	218	30.99	6-50	2	-
1-day Int																	
NatWest	16	4	1	22	11	7.33	-	-	3	-	928	511	19	26.89	4-7	-	
B&H	23	8	5	35	15*	11.66	-	-	6	-	1225	891	24	37.12	4-46	-	
Refuge	83	18	8	73	13	7.30	-	-	22	-	3301	2379	96	24.78	4-21	-	

WALSH, C. A. Gloucestershire

Name: Courtney Andrew Walsh
Role: Right-hand bat, right-arm fast bowler
Born: 30 October 1962, Kingston, Jamaica
Height: 6ft 5¹/₂in **Weight:** 14st 7lbs
Nickname: Mark, Walshy, Cuddy
County debut: 1984
County cap: 1985
Test debut: 1984-85
Tests: 50
One-Day Internationals: 96
50 wickets in a season: 5
1st-Class 50s scored: 5
1st-Class 5 w. in innings: 44
1st-Class 10 w. in match: 9
1st-Class catches: 58
Place in batting averages: (1990 184th
av. 27.29)
Place in bowling averages: 61st av. 31.55
(1990 19th av. 28.08)

Strike rate: 67.20 (career 48.12)
Parents: Eric and Joan Wollaston
Marital status: Single
Education: Excelsior High School
Qualifications: GCE and CXL
Off-season: Playing in the West Indies
Overseas tours: West Indies YC to Zimbabwe 1983; West Indies to England 1984; Australia 1984-85; Pakistan, Australia and New Zealand 1986-87; India (World Cup) 1987-88; England 1988; Australia 1988-89; Pakistan 1990-91; England 1991
Overseas teams played for: Jamaica 1981-91
Cricketers particularly admired: Michael Holding, Viv Richards, Lawrence Rowe, Richard Hadlee, Clive Lloyd, Imran Khan
Other sports followed: Basketball, track and field events
Relaxations: Swimming, reading and listening to music
Extras: Took record 10-43 in Jamaican school cricket in 1979. On tour, he has the reputation as an insatiable collector of souvenirs. David Graveney, when captaining Gloucestershire, reckoned Walsh was the 'best old-ball bowler in the world'. One of *Wisden's* Five Cricketers of the Year, 1986. Took hat-trick for West Indies v Australia in 1988-89
Best batting: 63* Gloucestershire v Yorkshire, Cheltenham 1990
Best bowling: 9-72 Gloucestershire v Somerset, Bristol 1986

1991 Season

	M	Inns	NO	Runs	HS	Avge	100s	50s	Ct	St	O	M	Runs	Wkts	Avge	Best	5wI	10wM
Test	5	7	0	66	18	9.42	-	-	-	-	187	42	493	15	32.86	4-64	-	-
All First	11	8	1	66	18	9.42	-	-	-	-	324.5	75	915	29	31.55	4-39	-	-
1-day Int	3	3	2	30	29 *	30.00	-	-	-	-	33	1	140	2	70.00	2-34	-	
NatWest																		
B&H																		
Refuge																		

Career Performances

	M	Inns	NO	Runs	HS	Avge	100s	50s	Ct	St	Balls	Runs	Wkts	Avge	Best	5wI	10wM
Test	50	67	22	437	30 *	9.71	-	-	6	-	9820	4342	174	24.95	6-62	5	1
All First	225	267	67	2560	63 *	12.80	-	5	58	-	40760	20059	847	23.68	9-72	44	9
1-day Int	96	33	14	166	29 *	8.73	-	-	13	-	5115	3326	108	30.79	5-1	1	
NatWest	13	8	3	63	25 *	12.60	-	-	1	-	816	451	25	18.04	6-21	1	
B&H	17	10	3	74	28	10.57	-	-	-	-	999	574	19	30.21	2-19	-	
Refuge	64	34	7	261	35	9.66	-	-	12	-	2595	1765	84	21.01	4-19	-	

WAQAR YOUNIS   Surrey

Name: Waqar Younis
Role: Right-hand bat, right-arm fast bowler
Born: 16 November 1971, Burewala,
Punjab
Height: 5ft 11in **Weight:** 12st
Nickname: Wicky
County debut: 1990
County cap: 1990
Test debut: 1989-90
Tests: 11
One-Day Internationals: 31
50 wickets in a season: 2
1st-Class 50s scored: 1
1st-Class 5 w. in innings: 26
1st-Class 10 w. in match: 8
1st-Class catches: 17
Place in batting averages: 227th av. 14.75
Place in bowling averages: 1st av. 14.65
(1990 7th av. 23.80)
Strike rate: 30.90 (career 35.43)
Marital status: Single
Education: Pakistani College, Sharjah; Sadiq Public School, Burewala

Qualifications: Studying law
Off-season: Playing for Pakistan
Overseas tours: Pakistan to India, Australia and Sharjah 1989-90
Overseas teams played for: United Bank
Cricketers particularly admired: Imran Khan, Wasim Akram, Geoff Arnold, Alec Stewart
Other sports followed: Football, badminton, squash
Relaxations: 'Sleeping and family get-togethers.'
Extras: Made Test debut for Pakistan v India aged 17, taking 4 for 80 at Karachi. Signed by Surrey during 1990 season on recommendation of Imran Khan, who had first seen him bowling on TV. Made county debut in B&H quarter-final v Lancashire. Martin Crowe described his bowling during Pakistan's series with New Zealand as the best display of fast bowling he had ever seen. The Cricketers' Association Cricketer of the Year 1991
Opinions on cricket: 'In favour of 17 four-day matches in County Championship. There should be no over-rate fines.'
Best batting: 51 United Bank v PIA, Lahore 1989-90
Best bowling: 7-73 Surrey v Warwickshire, The Oval 1990

1991 Season

	M	Inns	NO	Runs	HS	Avge	100s	50s	Ct	St	O	M	Runs	Wkts	Avge	Best	5wl	10wM
Test																		
All First	18	20	8	177	31	14.75	-	-	4	-	582	112	1656	113	14.65	7-87	13	3
1-day Int																		
NatWest	4	2	0	30	26	15.00	-	-	-	-	44.3	5	171	13	13.15	5-40	1	
B&H	4	3	2	8	5 *	8.00	-	-	1	-	35.4	2	140	4	35.00	3-29	-	
Refuge	12	6	1	10	8	2.00	-	-	2	-	88.4	8	371	21	17.66	4-21	-	

Career Performances

	M	Inns	NO	Runs	HS	Avge	100s	50s	Ct	St	Balls	Runs	Wkts	Avge	Best	5wl	10wM
Test	11	13	2	69	18	6.27	-	-	1	-	2249	1072	55	19.49	7-76	5	-
All First	67	67	26	532	51	12.97	-	1	17	-	11689	6069	302	20.09	7-64	26	8
1-day Int	31	10	6	40	20 *	10.00	-	-	3	-	1410	905	59	15.33	6-26	5	
NatWest	6	2	0	30	26	15.00	-	-	-	-	411	233	18	12.94	5-40	1	
B&H	5	4	2	12	5 *	6.00	-	-	1	-	280	195	6	32.50	3-29	-	
Refuge	24	8	3	11	8	2.20	-	-	5	-	1026	767	52	14.75	5-26	1	

187. What have Martyn Moxon and Bruce French in common?

WARD, D. M. Surrey

Name: David Mark Ward
Role: Right-hand bat, right-arm off-spin bowler, occasional wicket-keeper
Born: 10 February 1961, Croydon, South London
Height: 6ft 1in **Weight:** 14st
Nickname: Cocker, Wardy, Jaws, Gnasher, Fat Boy, Piano Man
County debut: 1985
County cap: 1990
1000 runs in a season: 2
1st-Class 50s scored: 21
1st-Class 100s scored: 11
1st-Class 200s scored: 2
1st-Class catches: 97
1st-Class stumpings: 3
One-Day 50s: 15
One-Day 100s: 1
Place in batting averages: 55th av. 40.35

(1990 5th av. 76.74)
Parents: Tom and Dora
Marital status: Single
Family links with cricket: 'Uncle (John Goodey) local legend with Banstead and Temple Bar CC.'
Education: Haling Manor High School; Croydon Technical College
Qualifications: 2 O-levels, Advanced City and Guilds in Carpentry and Joinery
Career outside cricket: Mortgage expert (Home Owners Advisory Service), carpenter
Off-season: Playing in Australia
Overseas tours: Surrey to Barbados 1984, 1989, 1991; Lancashire to Mombasa 1990
Overseas teams played for: Caulfield, Melbourne 1984-87; Sunshine, Melbourne 1988-89; Perth, Western Australia 1990-91
Cricketers particularly admired: Robert Thompson (brother of 'Candles' Thompson) of Sturt CC, Adelaide, Geoff Howarth, Grahame Clinton
Other sports followed: Greyhound racing
Injuries: Toothache
Relaxations: 'Eating Chinese meal on an away trip with Keith Medlycott (when he pays)'
Extras: First Surrey batsman since John Edrich to score 2000 runs in a season in 1990 and shared county record stand of 413 for third wicket with Darren Bicknell v Kent at Canterbury
Best batting: 263 Surrey v Kent, Canterbury 1990
Best bowling: 2-66 Surrey v Gloucestershire, Guildford 1991

1991 Season

	M	Inns	NO	Runs	HS	Avge	100s	50s	Ct	St	O	M	Runs	Wkts	Avge	Best	5wI	10wM
Test																		
All First	23	40	6	1372	151	40.35	1	10	10	-	7.5	0	66	2	33.00	2-66	-	-
1-day Int																		
NatWest	4	4	0	164	62	41.00	-	2	-	-								
B&H	4	4	0	120	46	30.00	-	-	-	-								
Refuge	15	14	1	268	56	20.61	-	3	6	-								

Career Performances

	M	Inns	NO	Runs	HS	Avge	100s	50s	Ct	St	Balls	Runs	Wkts	Avge	Best	5wI	10wM
Test																	
All First	103	162	25	5551	263	40.51	11	21	97	3	83	97	2	48.50	2-66	-	-
1-day Int																	
NatWest	13	12	0	406	97	33.83	-	4	7	-							
B&H	18	16	2	311	46 *	22.21	-	-	7	2							
Refuge	92	82	14	1736	102 *	25.52	1	11	45	1							

WARD, M. J. P.   Lancashire

Name: Michael John Paul Ward
Role: Right-hand bat, right-arm off-spin bowler
Born: 12 September 1971, Oldham
Height: 5ft 11in **Weight:** 12st 5lb
Nickname: Wardster
County debut: 1991
1st-Class catches: 0
Parents: David and Gillian
Marital status: Single
Family links with cricket: Father played for Manchester Association
Education: Manchester Grammar School; Cardiff Institute of Higher Education
Qualifications: 9 GCSEs, 3 A-levels
Career outside cricket: Student
Off-season: Studying for BA (Hons) Sport and Human Movement
Overseas teams played for: Nambour and Queensland U19 1990-91
Cricketers particularly admired: Michael Atherton, Viv Richards, Dexter Fitton
Other sports followed: Football (Bolton Wanderers)

Relaxations: Listening to music, following sport in general

1991 Season

	M	Inns	NO	Runs	HS	Avge	100s	50s	Ct	St	O	M	Runs	Wkts	Avge	Best	5wI	10wM
Test																		
All First	1	0	0	0	0	-	-	-	-	-	2	0	6	0	-	-	-	-
1-day Int																		
NatWest																		
B&H																		
Refuge																		

Career Performances

	M	Inns	NO	Runs	HS	Avge	100s	50s	Ct	St	Balls		Runs	Wkts	Avge	Best	5wI	10wM
Test																		
All First	1	0	0	0	0	-	-	-	-	-	12		6	0	-	-	-	-
1-day Int																		
NatWest																		
B&H																		
Refuge																		

WARD, T. R. Kent

Name: Trevor Robert Ward
Role: Right-hand bat, off-spin bowler
Born: 18 January 1968, Farningham, Kent
Height: 5ft 11in **Weight:** 12st 9lbs
Nickname: Wardy, Chikka
County debut: 1986
County cap: 1989
1000 runs in a season: 1
1st-Class 50s scored: 23
1st-Class 100s scored: 8
1st-Class 200s scored: 1
1st-Class catches: 46
One-Day 50s: 11
Place in batting averages: 35th av. 46.65
(1990 155th av. 31.96)
Parents: Robert Henry and Hazel Ann
Wife and date of marriage: Sarah Ann,
29 September 1990
Education: Anthony Roper County
Primary; Hextable Comprehensive

Qualifications: 7 O-levels
Off-season: Coaching
Overseas tours: NCA to Bermuda 1985; England YC to Sri Lanka 1987; Australia for Youth World Cup 1988
Overseas teams played for: Scarborough, Perth, Western Australia 1986-87
Cricketers particularly admired: Ian Botham, Graham Gooch, Robin Smith
Other sports followed: Most sports
Injuries: Shoulder injury
Relaxations: Fishing
Opinions on cricket: 'Four-day cricket has been proved this season to be a good thing, with matches running their course without contrived results.'
Best batting: 235* Kent v Middlesex, Canterbury 1991
Best bowling: 2-48 Kent v Worcestershire, Canterbury 1990

1991 Season

	M	Inns	NO	Runs	HS	Avge	100s	50s	Ct	St	O	M	Runs	Wkts	Avge	Best	5wI	10wM
Test																		
All First	22	34	2	1493	235 *	46.65	5	6	10	-	17	4	40	1	40.00	1-20	-	-
1-day Int																		
NatWest	2	2	0	75	55	37.50	-	1	-	-								
B&H	5	5	0	165	87	33.00	-	1	2	-								
Refuge	14	14	2	347	62 *	28.91	-	3	5	-								

Career Performances

	M	Inns	NO	Runs	HS	Avge	100s	50s	Ct	St	Balls	Runs	Wkts	Avge	Best	5wI	10wM
Test																	
All First	72	123	9	4035	235 *	35.39	8	23	46	-	695	426	6	71.00	2-48	-	-
1-day Int																	
NatWest	7	7	0	258	83	36.85	-	2	-	-	72	58	1	58.00	1-58	-	
B&H	15	15	2	474	94	36.46	-	3	4	-	12	10	0	-	-	-	
Refuge	45	45	2	1015	80	23.60	-	6	7	-	222	176	5	35.20	3-20	-	

188. In which town are the administrative headquarters of Durham CCC?

WARNER, A. E.   Derbyshire

Name: Allan Esmond Warner
Role: Right-hand bat, right-arm fast bowler,
outfielder
Born: 12 May 1959, Birmingham
Height: 5ft 8in **Weight:** 10st
Nickname: Esis
County debut: 1982 (Worcs),
1985 (Derbys)
County cap: 1987 (Derbys)
1st-Class 50s scored: 13
1st-Class 5 w. in innings: 2
1st-Class catches: 36
One-Day 50s: 2
Place in batting averages: 194th av. 19.52
Place in bowling averages: 71st av. 32.83
(1990 100th av. 40.30)

Strike rate: 72.43 (career 63.84)
Parents: Edgar and Sarah
Children: Alvin, 6 September 1980
Education: Tabernacle School, St Kitts,
West Indies
Qualifications: CSE Maths
Cricketers particularly admired: Malcolm Marshall, Michael Holding
Other sports followed: Football, boxing and athletics
Relaxations: Watching movies, music (soul, reggae and calypso)
Extras: Released by Worcestershire at end of 1984 and joined Derbyshire
Best batting: 91 Derbyshire v Leicestershire, Chesterfield 1986
Best bowling: 5-27 Worcestershire v Glamorgan, Worcester 1984

1991 Season

	M	Inns	NO	Runs	HS	Avge	100s	50s	Ct	St	O	M	Runs	Wkts	Avge	Best	5wl	10wM
Test																		
All First	17	24	3	410	53	19.52	-	2	4	-	446.4	101	1215	37	32.83	4-42	-	-
1-day Int																		
NatWest																		
B&H	4	4	2	39	35 *	19.50	-	-	-	-	37.3	6	130	4	32.50	2-57	-	
Refuge	11	10	2	189	51	23.62	-	1	4	-	76.5	2	429	12	35.75	3-38	-	

	M	Inns	NO	Runs	HS	Avge	100s	50s	Ct	St	Balls	Runs	Wkts	Avge	Best	5wI	10wM
Test																	
All First	146	206	38	2954	91	17.58	-	13	36	-	18963	9703	297	32.67	5-27	2	-
1-day Int																	
NatWest	11	7	1	67	32	11.16	-	-	-	-	657	438	13	33.69	4-39	-	
B&H	36	23	8	169	35 *	11.26	-	-	4	-	1925	1302	50	26.04	4-36	-	
Refuge	105	75	18	856	68	15.01	-	2	18	-	4092	3596	115	31.27	5-39	1	

WASIM AKRAM   Lancashire

Name: Wasim Akram
Role: Left-hand bat, left-arm
fast-medium bowler
Born: 3 June 1966, Lahore, Pakistan
Height: 6ft 3in **Weight:** 12st 7lbs
County debut: 1988
County cap: 1989
Test debut: 1984-85
Tests: 37
One-Day Internationals: 99
50 wickets in a season: 2
1st-Class 50s scored: 9
1st-Class 100s scored: 3
1st-Class 5 w. in innings: 28
1st-Class 10 w. in match: 5
1st-Class catches: 34
One-Day 50s: 4
Place in batting averages: 140th av. 27.70
(1990 263rd av. 12.27)
Place in bowling averages: 10th av. 22.33 (1990 96th av. 40.00)
Strike rate: 46.01 (career 58.21)
Education: Islamia College
Off-season: Playing for Pakistan
Overseas tours: Pakistan U23 to Sri Lanka 1984-85; Pakistan to New Zealand 1984-85;
Sri Lanka 1985-86; India 1986-87; England 1987; West Indies 1987-88; Australia 1989-90
Overseas teams played for: PACO 1984-86; Lahore Whites 1985-86
Extras: His second first-class match was playing for Pakistan on tour in New Zealand.
Imran Khan wrote of him: 'I have great faith in Wasim Akram. I think he will become a
great all-rounder, as long as he realises how much hard work is required. As a bowler he
is extremely gifted, and has it in him to be the best left-armer since Alan Davidson.' Hit

maiden Test 100 v Australia 1989-90 during stand of 191 with Imran Khan
Best batting: 123 Pakistan v Australia, Adelaide 1989-90
Best bowling: 7-42 World XI v MCC, Scarborough 1989

1991 Season

	M	Inns	NO	Runs	HS	Avge	100s	50s	Ct	St	O	M	Runs	Wkts	Avge	Best	5wI	10wM
Test																		
All First	14	19	2	471	122	27.70	1	1	5	-	429.3	99	1251	56	22.33	6-66	7	1
1-day Int																		
NatWest	2	2	1	40	29	40.00	-	-	-	-	23.3	2	86	4	21.50	3-40	-	
B&H	6	4	2	71	45 *	35.50	-	-	-	-	61	5	246	11	22.36	4-18	-	
Refuge	16	13	4	179	38	19.88	-	-	2	-	117.5	1	620	13	47.69	2-30	-	

Career Performances

	M	Inns	NO	Runs	HS	Avge	100s	50s	Ct	St	Balls	Runs	Wkts	Avge	Best	5wI	10wM
Test	37	46	7	766	123	19.64	1	3	12	-	8126	3427	142	24.13	6-62	9	
All First	103	134	20	2525	123	22.14	3	9	34	-	19587	8553	360	23.75	7-42	28	5
1-day Int	99	70	14	776	86	13.85	-	1	19	-	4941	3131	133	23.54	5-21	2	
NatWest	12	10	2	129	29	16.12	-	-	3	-	736	447	20	22.35	4-27	-	
B&H	17	14	4	277	52	27.70	-	1	1	-	1066	670	33	20.30	5-27	1	
Refuge	54	42	11	746	56	24.06	-	2	9	-	2304	1758	74	23.75	4-19	-	

WATKIN, S. L.   Glamorgan

Name: Steven Llewellyn Watkin
Role: Right-hand bat, right-arm
fast-medium bowler
Born: 13 September 1964, Duffryn,
Rhondda, nr Port Talbot
Height: 6ft 3in **Weight:** 12st 8lbs
Nickname: Watty, Banger
County debut: 1986
County cap: 1989
Test debut: 1991
Tests: 2
50 wickets in a season: 3
1st-Class 5 w. in innings: 15
1st-Class 10 w. in match: 3
1st-Class catches: 18
Place in batting averages: 245th av. 12.36
(1990 272nd av. 11.00)
Place in bowling averages: 47th av. 29.39

(1990 92nd av. 39.30)
Strike rate: 59.09 (career 60.51)
Parents: John and Sandra
Marital status: Single
Family links with cricket: 'Brother plays local cricket.'
Education: Cymer Afan Comprehensive; Swansea College of Further Education; South Glamorgan Institute of Higher Education
Qualifications: 8 O-levels, 2 A-levels, BA (Hons) in Human Movement Studies
Overseas tours: British Colleges to West Indies 1987; England A to Kenya and Zimbabwe 1989-90; Pakistan and Sri Lanka 1990-91
Overseas teams played for: Potchefstroom University, South Africa 1987-88
Cricketers particularly admired: Richard Hadlee, Dennis Lillee, Ian Botham
Other sports followed: All sports except horse racing
Relaxations: Watching TV, music, DIY, motor mechanics, 'a quiet pint'
Extras: Joint-highest wicket-taker in 1989 with 94 wickets. Sister Lynda has played for Great Britain at hockey
Opinions on cricket: 'Four-day cricket must replace three-day. Travelling must be cut down for the sake of safety.'
Best batting: 31 Glamorgan v Leicestershire, Leicester 1989
Best bowling: 8-59 Glamorgan v Warwickshire, Edgbaston 1988

1991 Season

	M	Inns	NO	Runs	HS	Avge	100s	50s	Ct	St	O	M	Runs	Wkts	Avge	Best	5wI	10wM
Test	2	3	0	8	6	2.66	-	-	-	-	36	4	153	5	30.60	3-38	-	-
All First	22	19	8	136	25 *	12.36	-	-	2	-	728.5	155	2175	74	29.39	6-55	4	-
1-day Int																		
NatWest	3	1	1	5	5 *	-	-	-	1	-	36	2	116	4	29.00	2-40	-	
B&H	4	3	1	25	15	12.50	-	-	-	-	44	7	190	5	38.00	3-28	-	
Refuge	12	7	1	55	31 *	9.16	-	-	1	-	83	4	382	16	23.87	3-30	-	

Career Performances

	M	Inns	NO	Runs	HS	Avge	100s	50s	Ct	St	Balls	Runs	Wkts	Avge	Best	5wI	10wM
Test	2	3	0	8	6	2.66	-	-	-	-	216	153	5	30.60	3-38	-	-
All First	92	95	28	585	31	8.73	-	-	18	-	18225	9193	301	30.54	8-59	15	3
1-day Int																	
NatWest	8	3	3	13	6 *	-	-	-	1	-	534	258	11	23.45	3-18	-	
B&H	13	11	6	48	15	9.60	-	-	1	-	759	499	10	49.90	3-28	-	
Refuge	46	20	6	144	31 *	10.28	-	-	8	-	1819	1485	54	27.50	5-23	1	

WATKINSON, M.   Lancashire

Name: Michael Watkinson
Role: Right-hand bat, right-arm medium or off-break bowler
Born: 1 August 1961, Westhoughton
Height: 6ft 1½in **Weight:** 13st
Nickname: Winker
County debut: 1982
County cap: 1987
50 wickets in a season: 3
1st-Class 50s scored: 32
1st-Class 100s scored: 3
1st-Class 5 w. in innings: 17
1st-Class catches: 89
One-Day 50s: 10
Place in batting averages: 161st av. 24.45 (1990 127th av. 35.90)
Place in bowling averages: 113th av. 41.00 (1990 48th av. 33.57)
Strike rate: 71.24 (career 64.69)

Parents: Albert and Marian
Wife and date of marriage: Susan, 12 April 1986
Children: Charlotte, 24 February 1989; Liam 27 July 1991
Education: Rivington and Blackrod High School, Horwich
Qualifications: 8 O-levels, HTC Civil Engineering
Career outside cricket: Draughtsman
Off-season: Working as an estimator with William Hare Ltd, Bolton
Cricketers particularly admired: Clive Lloyd, Imran Khan
Other sports followed: Football
Extras: Played for Cheshire in Minor Counties, and NatWest Trophy (v Middlesex) 1982. Man of the Match in the first ever Refuge Cup Final 1988 and in 1990 B&H Cup Final 1990
Best batting: 138 Lancashire v Yorkshire, Old Trafford 1990
Best bowling: 7-25 Lancashire v Sussex, Lytham 1987

1991 Season

	M	Inns	NO	Runs	HS	Avge	100s	50s	Ct	St	O	M	Runs	Wkts	Avge	Best	5wI	10wM
Test																		
All First	21	35	4	758	114*	24.45	1	3	8	-	629.2	116	2173	53	41.00	4-45	-	-
1-day Int																		
NatWest	2	2	0	12	7	6.00	-	-	-	-	22	7	72	3	24.00	2-10	-	
B&H	5	5	3	94	32*	47.00	-	-	1	-	54.4	4	221	12	18.41	5-49	1	
Refuge	17	14	0	315	83	22.50	-	2	5	-	122	1	644	22	29.27	3-27	-	

Career Performances

	M	Inns	NO	Runs	HS	Avge	100s	50s	Ct	St	Balls	Runs	Wkts	Avge	Best	5wl	10wM
Test																	
All First	180	267	35	5710	138	24.61	3	32	89	-	25489	13308	394	33.77	7-25	17	
1-day Int																	
NatWest	26	21	5	419	90	26.18	-	3	7	-	1583	1027	25	41.08	3-14	-	
B&H	44	30	7	468	70 *	20.34	-	2	8	-	2283	1584	53	29.88	5-49	1	
Refuge	132	104	32	1667	83	23.15	-	5	27	-	5229	4233	141	30.02	5-46	1	

WAUGH, M. E. Essex

Name: Mark Edward Waugh
Role: Right-hand bat, right-arm medium pace bowler
Born: 2 June 1965, Canterbury, New South Wales
Height: 6ft **Weight:** 13st 7lbs
County debut: 1988
County cap: 1989
Test debut: 1990-91
Tests: 7
One-Day Internationals: 23
1000 runs in a season: 2
1st-Class 50s scored: 35
1st-Class 100s scored: 28
1st-Class 200s scored: 3
1st-Class 5 w. in innings: 1
1st-Class catches: 111
One-Day 50s: 11
One-Day 100s: 3
Place in batting averages: (1990 6th av. 76.74)
Place in bowling averages: (1990 149th av. 64.25)
Strike rate: 95.50 (career 69.72)
Parents: Rodger and Beverley
Marital status: Single
Family links with cricket: Uncle a 1st Grade cricketer in Sydney for Bankstown/ Canterbury. Twin brother Steve plays for Australia and played for Somerset in 1988. Younger brother Dean played in Bolton League with Astley Bridge in 1989 and made debut for NSW in 1990-91
Education: East Hills Boys High School
Qualifications: Higher School Certificate, cricket coach
Off-season: Playing cricket for New South Wales

Overseas teams played for: New South Wales 1985-92
Cricketers particularly admired: 'Allan Border for his guts and determination, Doug Walters for his ability and sportsmanship, Greg Chappell – pure class.'
Other sports followed: 'Any – but mainly golf, football and horse racing.'
Relaxations: 'Sleeping, eating and gambling.'
Extras: Steve and Mark are only twins to score hundreds in the same innings of a first-class match and to both play international cricket. Chosen as New South Wales Cricketer of the Year, 1988 and Sheffield Shield Cricketer of the Year, jointly with D. Tazelaar of Queensland. First batsman to score a century on his Sunday League debut. Signed again by Essex for 1992 to replace Salim Malik who is likely to be touring England with Pakistan
Opinions on cricket: 'Too much cricket is played.'
Best batting: 229 New South Wales v Western Australia, Perth 1990-91
Best bowling: 5-37 Essex v Northamptonshire, Northampton 1990

Did not play for Essex in 1991

Career Performances

	M	Inns	NO	Runs	HS	Avge	100s	50s	Ct	St	Balls	Runs	Wkts	Avge	Best	5wI	10wM
Test	7	11	2	554	139 *	61.55	2	2	11	-	426	209	8	26.12	4-80	-	-
All First	111	175	26	8210	229 *	55.10	28	33	111	-	5069	2953	76	38.85	5-37	1	-
1-day Int	23	22	2	477	67	23.85	-	2	11	-	459	337	20	16.85	4-37	-	
NatWest	3	2	0	47	47	23.50	-	-	1	-	30	17	0	-	-	-	
B&H	12	10	1	302	93	33.55	-	2	4	-	48	45	1	45.00	1.25	-	
Refuge	36	35	6	1201	112 *	41.41	3	7	14	-	511	493	16	30.81	3-37	-	

189. Who captained the 1984 Sri Lankans in England?

WEEKES, P. N. Middlesex

Name: Paul Nicholas Weekes
Role: Left-hand bat, right-arm off-break
bowler
Born: 8 July 1969, Hackney
Height: 5ft 11in **Weight:** 11st 4lbs
Nickname: Weekesy, Twiddles
County debut: 1990
1st-Class 50s scored: 3
1st-Class catches: 8
Place in batting averages: 158th av. 24.90
Parents: Robert and Carol
Marital status: Single
Family links with cricket: Father
played club cricket
Education: Homerton House Secondary
School, Hackney; Hackney College
Qualifications: NCA cricket coach
Career outside cricket: Coaching cricket
in the inner city schools
Off-season: Coaching for the Middlesex Youth Trust
Overseas teams played for: Newcastle University, NSW, Australia 1989; Sunrise, Zimbabwe 1990
Cricketers particularly admired: David Gower, Richie Richardson
Other sports followed: Boxing – 'middle and heavyweight especially'
Relaxations: Dancing and listening to music
Extras: Scored 50 in first innings for both 2nd and 1st teams
Opinions on cricket: 'There should be more entertainment for the spectators during lunch intervals, i.e. competitions for throwing distances and bowling speeds.'
Best batting: 86 Middlesex v Surrey, The Oval 1991
Best bowling: 3-57 Middlesex v Worcestershire, Worcester 1991

1991 Season

	M	Inns	NO	Runs	HS	Avge	100s	50s	Ct	St	O	M	Runs	Wkts	Avge	Best	5wI	10wM
Test																		
All First	6	11	1	249	86	24.90	-	2	5	-	56.4	12	188	7	26.85	3-57	-	-
1-day Int																		
NatWest	1	1	0	7	7	7.00	-	-	-	-	12	1	30	1	30.00	1-30	-	
B&H	1	1	0	0	0	0.00	-	-	1	-								
Refuge	13	9	2	115	32 *	16.42	-	-	6	-	70.2	2	373	9	41.44	3-27	-	

Career Performances

	M	Inns	NO	Runs	HS	Avge	100s	50s	Ct	St	Balls	Runs	Wkts	Avge	Best	5wl	10wM
Test																	
All First	9	14	1	324	86	24.92	-	3	8	-	820	452	11	41.09	3-57	-	-
1-day Int																	
NatWest	1	1	0	7	7	7.00	-	-	-	-	72	30	1	30.00	1-30	-	
B&H	2	1	0	0	0	0.00	-	-	1	-	42	27	0	-	-	-	
Refuge	16	10	3	144	32 *	20.57	-	-	8	-	518	465	11	42.27	3-27	-	

WELLS, A. P. Sussex

Name: Alan Peter Wells
Role: Right-hand bat, right-arm medium
bowler, county captain
Born: 2 October 1961, Newhaven
Height: 6ft **Weight:** 12st 4lbs
Nickname: Morph, Bomber
County debut: 1981
County cap: 1986
1000 runs in a season: 6
1st-Class 50s scored: 55
1st-Class 100s scored: 21
1st-Class 200s scored: 1
1st-Class catches: 107
One-Day 50s: 26
Place in batting averages: 12th 59.46
(1990 91st av. 43.54)
Parents: Ernest William Charles and
Eunice Mae

Wife and date of marriage:
Melanie Elizabeth, 26 September 1987
Children: Luke William Peter 29 December 1990
Family links with cricket: Father played for many years for local club. Eldest brother Ray
plays club cricket. Brother Colin plays for Sussex
Education: Tideway Comprehensive, Newhaven
Qualifications: 5 O-levels, NCA coaching certificate
Career outside cricket: Family packaging business
Off-season: Running the business (as above) with brother Colin
Overseas tours: Unofficial England team to South Africa 1989-90
Overseas teams played for: Border, South Africa 1981-82
Injuries: Broken toe, 'Waqar'd' – missed one game
Relaxations: Listening to music, eating out, drinking in country pubs, cooking

Extras: Played for England YC v India 1981. Banned from Test cricket for joining tour of South Africa. Scored a century in each of his first two matches as acting captain and won both matches
Best batting: 253* Sussex v Yorkshire, Middlesbrough 1991
Best bowling: 3-67 Sussex v Worcestershire, Worcester 1987

1991 Season

	M	Inns	NO	Runs	HS	Avge	100s	50s	Ct	St	O	M	Runs	Wkts	Avge	Best	5wI	10wM
Test																		
All First	22	36	6	1784	253 *	59.46	7	5	7	-	5	1	21	1	21.00	1-21	-	-
1-day Int																		
NatWest	2	2	0	48	40	24.00	-	-	-	-								
B&H	4	4	1	96	66	32.00	-	1	1	-								
Refuge	13	13	0	289	58	22.23	-	1	4	-								

Career Performances

	M	Inns	NO	Runs	HS	Avge	100s	50s	Ct	St	Balls	Runs	Wkts	Avge	Best	5wI	10wM
Test																	
All First	212	351	59	11016	253 *	37.72	21	55	107	-	787	596	9	66.22	3-67	-	-
1-day Int																	
NatWest	21	19	4	454	86 *	30.26	-	4	8	-	6	1	0	-		-	-
B&H	37	34	3	884	74	28.51	-	7	9	-	60	72	3	24.00	1-17	-	
Refuge	140	126	14	2867	98	25.59	-	15	34	-	62	69	4	17.25	1-0	-	

190. Who topped the first-class batting averages last season for Surrey?

WELLS, C. M. Sussex

Name: Colin Mark Wells
Role: Right-hand bat, right-arm medium bowler
Born: 3 March 1960, Newhaven
Height: 6ft **Weight:** 13st
Nickname: Bomber, Dougie
County debut: 1979
County cap: 1982
Benefit: 1993
One-Day Internationals: 2
1000 runs in a season: 6
50 wickets in a season: 2
1st-Class 50s scored: 58
1st-Class 100s scored: 20
1st-Class 200s scored: 1
1st-Class 5 w. in innings: 7
1st-Class catches: 85
One-Day 50s: 23
One-Day 100s: 4
Place in batting averages: 91st av. 33.53 (1990 145th av. 33.32)
Place in bowling averages: 95th av. 35.77 (1990 154th av. 72.76)
Strike rate: 76.88 (career 72.72)
Parents: Ernest William Charles and Eunice Mae
Wife and date of marriage: Celia, 25 September 1982
Children: Jessica Louise, 2 October 1987
Family links with cricket: Father, Billy, had trials for Sussex and played for Sussex Cricket Association. Eldest brother Ray plays club cricket and youngest brother Alan plays for Sussex
Education: Tideway Comprehensive School, Newhaven
Qualifications: 9 O-levels, 2 CSEs, 1 A-level, intermediate coaching certificate
Overseas tours: England to Sharjah 1985
Overseas teams played for: Border 1980-81; Western Province 1984-85
Other sports followed: Football, rugby, hockey, basketball, tennis, table tennis
Relaxations: Sea-angling, philately, listening to music
Extras: Played in three John Player League matches in 1978. Was recommended to Sussex by former Sussex player, Ian Thomson. Vice-captain since 1988
Opinions on cricket: 'Should play four-day cricket as soon as possible. Strongly believe that we cram in too much cricket, which must have a detrimental effect on all, especially the fast bowlers, particularly long term.'
Best batting: 203 Sussex v Hampshire, Hove 1984
Best bowling: 7-42 Sussex v Derbyshire, Derby 1991

1991 Season

	M	Inns	NO	Runs	HS	Avge	100s	50s	Ct	St	O	M	Runs	Wkts	Avge	Best	5wI	10wM
Test																		
All First	14	21	6	503	76	33.53	-	3	3	-	230.4	62	644	18	35.77	7-42	1	-
1-day Int																		
NatWest	2	2	0	11	11	5.50	-	-	-	-	21	3	55	4	13.75	3-16	-	
B&H																		
Refuge	9	8	2	128	34 *	21.33	-	-	1	-	53	0	228	1	228.00	1-31	-	

Career Performances

	M	Inns	NO	Runs	HS	Avge	100s	50s	Ct	St	Balls	Runs	Wkts	Avge	Best	5wI	10wM
Test																	
All First	270	429	68	12070	203	33.43	20	58	85	-	27780	13087	382	34.25	7-42	7	-
1-day Int	2	2	0	22	11	11.00	-	-	-	-							
NatWest	29	24	3	426	76	20.28	-	1	7	-	1318	625	17	36.76	3-16	-	
B&H	46	45	5	1253	117	31.32	3	4	13	-	1632	1049	33	31.78	4-21	-	
Refuge	172	157	23	3549	104 *	26.48	1	18	35	-	5671	3530	113	31.23	4-15	-	

WELLS, V. J. Leicestershire

Name: Vincent John Wells
Role: Right-hand bat, right-arm medium
pace bowler, occasional wicket-keeper
Born: 6 August 1965, Dartford
Height: 6ft **Weight:** 13st
Nickname: Wellsy, Vinny
County debut: 1987 (Kent)
1st-Class 50s scored: 3
1st-Class 5 w. in innings: 1
1st-Class catches: 11
Place in batting averages: (1990 206th
av. 23.46)
Place in bowling averages: (1990 4th
av. 21.41)
Strike rate: (career 45.22)
Parents: Pat and Jack
Wife and date of marriage: Deborah
Louise, 14 October 1989
Family links with cricket: Brother plays
league cricket in Kent
Education: Downs School, Dartford; Sir William Nottidge School, Whitstable
Qualifications: 1 O-level, 8 CSEs, coaching certificate

Off-season: Working for brother-in-law's mailing house, Macdonald Mailing
Overseas teams played for: Parnell, Auckland 1986; Avendale, Cape Town 1987-89, 1990-91
Cricketers particularly admired: David Gower, Robin Smith, Ian Botham
Other sports followed: Most sports except horse racing
Injuries: No injuries but missed four weeks due to pneumonia
Relaxations: 'Eating out with my wife, keeping fit, watching sport.'
Extras: Was a schoolboy footballer with Leyton Orient. Scored 100* on NatWest debut v Oxfordshire. Left Kent at the end of 1991 season to join Leicestershire
Opinions on cricket: 'All 2nd XI cricket should be played on first-class grounds. County Championship should be all four-day matches.'
Best batting: 58 Kent v Hampshire, Bournemouth 1990
                58 Kent v Oxford University, The Parks 1991
Best bowling: 5-43 Kent v Leicestershire, Leicester 1990

1991 Season

	M	Inns	NO	Runs	HS	Avge	100s	50s	Ct	St	O	M	Runs	Wkts	Avge	Best	5wI	10wM
Test																		
All First	3	4	0	87	58	21.75	-	1	1	-	22.4	8	45	4	11.25	3-21	-	-
1-day Int																		
NatWest																		
B&H	2	2	0	32	25	16.00	-	-	2	-								
Refuge	1	1	0	8	8	8.00	-	-	-	-								

Career Performances

	M	Inns	NO	Runs	HS	Avge	100s	50s	Ct	St	Balls	Runs	Wkts	Avge	Best	5wI	10wM
Test																	
All First	14	25	1	482	58	20.08	-	3	11	-	814	414	18	23.00	5-43	1	-
1-day Int																	
NatWest	1	1	1	100	100*	-	1	-	-	-							
B&H	4	3	1	47	25	23.50	-	-	2	-	42	33	0	-	-	-	-
Refuge	10	6	2	56	16	14.00	-	-	5	-	138	73	7	10.42	3-17	-	-

191. Which current county players have scored a century against each county but their own?

WESTON, M. J.   Worcestershire

Name: Martin John Weston
Role: Right-hand bat, right-arm medium bowler
Born: 8 April 1959, Worcester
Height: 6ft 1in **Weight:** 14st
Nickname: Spaghetti
County debut: 1979
County cap: 1986
1000 runs in a season: 1
1st-Class 50s scored: 26
1st-Class 100s scored: 3
1st-Class catches: 72
One-Day 50s: 15
One-Day 100s: 1
Place in batting averages: (1990 274th av. 10.00)
Parents: John Franklyn and Sheila Margaret
Marital status: Single
Family links with cricket: 'Father was a pretty useful all-rounder for the British Waterways team.'
Education: St George's C of E Junior; Samuel Southall Secondary Modern, – 'and Worcester's Pavilion Bar!'
Qualifications: City & Guilds and Advanced Crafts in Bricklaying
Career outside cricket: Midland Finance
Off-season: Holiday, golf 'and, hopefully, Midland Finance'
Cricketers particularly admired: Andy Moles, Gordon Lord, Ian Botham, Peter Scudamore
Other sports followed: Horse racing, football
Injuries: 'Lack of injuries to other people affected my cricket this season!'
Relaxations: Horse racing, walking, golf, watching sport from settee
Opinions on cricket: 'Four-day cricket is a must. Certain one-day games should be played in coloured clothing, with a white ball.'
Best batting: 145* Worcestershire v Northamptonshire, Worcester 1984
Best bowling: 4-24 Worcestershire v Warwickshire, Edgbaston 1988

---

192. Who is the 1992 captain of Nottinghamshire?

1991 Season

	M	Inns	NO	Runs	HS	Avge	100s	50s	Ct	St	O	M	Runs	Wkts	Avge	Best	5wl	10wM
Test																		
All First	3	3	0	15	9	5.00	-	-	1	-	12	2	52	1	52.00	1-27	-	-
1-day Int																		
NatWest																		
B&H	1	1	0	30	30	30.00	-	-	-	-	11	0	41	1	41.00	1-41	-	
Refuge	17	11	4	162	51	23.14	-	1	4	-	113.1	4	437	10	43.70	2-25	-	

Career Performances

	M	Inns	NO	Runs	HS	Avge	100s	50s	Ct	St	Balls	Runs	Wkts	Avge	Best	5wl	10wM
Test																	
All First	152	242	20	5294	145 *	23.84	3	26	72	-	6325	3050	79	38.60	4-24	-	-
1-day Int																	
NatWest	20	20	4	571	98	35.68	-	2	7	-	650	410	10	41.00	4-30	-	
B&H	34	34	2	744	99 *	23.25	-	5	8	-	643	387	13	29.76	2-27	-	
Refuge	135	114	19	1942	109	20.44	1	8	29	-	3580	2494	77	32.39	4-11	-	

WESTON, W. P. C.   Worcestershire

Name: William Philip Christopher Weston
Role: Left-hand bat, left-arm medium bowler
Born: 16 June 1973, Durham
Height: 6ft 3in
County debut: 1991
1st-Class catches: 0
Family links with cricket: Father played cricket for Durham and rugby for England
Education: Durham School
Qualifications: O-levels, A-Levels
Overseas tours: England U19 to New Zealand 1990-91; Pakistan 1991-92
Extras: Played for England U19 v Australia 1991, scoring a century in the 3rd Test. Appointed captain of England U19 for their tour to Pakistan 1991-92. Told by Keble College, Oxford that he would not be accepted if he decided to tour he chose to sacrifice his place at Oxford. Played for Northants 2nd XI and Worcestershire 2nd XI in 1989
Best batting: 15 Worcestershire v Nottinghamshire, Trent Bridge 1991

1991 Season

	M	Inns	NO	Runs	HS	Avge	100s	50s	Ct	St	O	M	Runs	Wkts	Avge	Best	5wI	10wM
Test																		
All First	2	3	0	28	15	9.33	-	-	-	-								
1-day Int																		
NatWest																		
B&H																		
Refuge																		

Career Performances

	M	Inns	NO	Runs	HS	Avge	100s	50s	Ct	St	Balls	Runs	Wkts	Avge	Best	5wI	10wM
Test																	
All First	2	3	0	28	15	9.33	-	-	-	-							
1-day Int																	
NatWest																	
B&H																	
Refuge																	

WHITAKER, J. J.   Leicestershire

Name: John James Whitaker
Role: Right-hand bat, off-break bowler,
county vice-captain
Born: 5 May 1962, Skipton, Yorkshire
Height: 6ft **Weight:** 13st
County debut: 1983
County cap: 1986
Test debut: 1986-87
Tests: 1
One-Day Internationals: 2
1000 runs in a season: 8
1st-Class 50s scored: 57
1st-Class 100s scored: 24
1st-Class 200s scored: 1
1st-Class catches: 129
One-Day 50s: 22
One-Day 100s: 4
Place in batting averages: 66th av. 37.91
(1990 77th av. 45.30)
Parents: John and Anne
Family links with cricket: Father plays club cricket for Skipton
Education: Uppingham School

Qualifications: 7 O-levels
Overseas tours: England to Australia 1986-87; England A to Zimbabwe and Kenya 1989-90
Cricketers particularly admired: Geoff Boycott, Dennis Amiss
Other sports followed: Football, hockey, tennis, Leicester Tigers rugby
Relaxations: Discos, music, reading, eating out
Extras: One of *Wisden's* Five Cricketers of the Year, 1986
Opinions on cricket: 'There is too much first-class cricket.'
Best batting: 200* Leicestershire v Nottinghamshire, Leicester 1986
Best bowling: 1-41 Leicestershire v Essex, Leicester 1986

1991 Season

	M	Inns	NO	Runs	HS		Avge	100s	50s	Ct	St	O	M	Runs	Wkts	Avge	Best	5wI	10wM
Test																			
All First	23	37	3	1289	105		37.91	1	8	13	-	1	0	14	0	-		-	-
1-day Int																			
NatWest	2	2	1	133	94	*	133.00	-	1	-	-								
B&H	4	4	0	187	100		46.75	1	1	-	-								
Refuge	14	14	0	550	88		39.28	-	4	6	-								

Career Performances

	M	Inns	NO	Runs	HS		Avge	100s	50s	Ct	St	Balls	Runs	Wkts	Avge	Best	5wI	10wM
Test	1	1	0	11	11		11.00	-	-	1	-							
All First	203	323	40	11173	200	*	39.48	24	57	129	-	128	182	1	182.00	1-41	-	-
1-day Int	2	2	1	48	44	*	48.00	-	-	1	-							
NatWest	16	16	1	636	155		42.40	1	2	1	-	24	9	0	-		-	-
B&H	33	30	2	775	100		27.67	1	2	4	-							
Refuge	110	100	11	3003	132		33.74	2	18	27	-	2	4	0	-		-	-

193. Whose nickname is 'Arkle'?

Name: Craig White
Role: Right-hand bat, off-spin bowler, cover fielder
Born: 16 December 1969, Morley, Yorkshire
Height: 6ft **Weight:** 12st
Nickname: Chalkey, Leathers, Pineapple Head
County debut: 1990
1st-Class 5 w. in innings: 1
1st-Class catches: 5
Place in batting averages: (1990 256th av. 14.11)
Place in bowling averages: (1990 115th av. 46.76)
Strike rate: (career 73.38)
Parents: Fred Emsley and Cynthia Anne
Marital status: Single
Family links with cricket: Father played with Pudsey St Lawrence
Education: Kennington Primary; Flora Hill High School and Bendigo Senior High School (Victoria, Australia)
Off-season: 'I'll always travel back to Australia to play in Victoria.'
Overseas tours: Australian YC to West Indies 1990
Overseas teams played for: Victoria (debut 1990-91)
Cricketers particularly admired: Allan Border, Dean Jones, David Gower, Martyn Moxon
Other sports followed: Australian Rules football
Relaxations: Holidaying at Surfers Paradise in Queensland, mountain bike riding
Extras: Recommended to Yorkshire CCC by Victorian Cricket Academy. Eligible to play for Yorkshire as he was born in the county. 'Fred Trueman and I are the only Yorkshire players to debut in the 1sts before the 2nds.'
Best batting: 38 Yorkshire v Northamptonshire, Northampton 1990
Best bowling: 5-74 Yorkshire v Surrey, Harrogate 1990

---

194. Who is the present groundsman at The Oval, and has been for the last 17 years?

1991 Season

	M	Inns	NO	Runs	HS	Avge	100s	50s	Ct	St	O	M	Runs	Wkts	Avge	Best	5wI	10wM
Test																		
All First																		
1-day Int																		
NatWest																		
B&H																		
Refuge	3	3	0	49	37	16.33	-	-	1	-								

Career Performances

	M	Inns	NO	Runs	HS	Avge	100s	50s	Ct	St	Balls	Runs	Wkts	Avge	Best	5wI	10wM
Test																	
All First	12	13	2	155	38	14.09	-	-	5	-	1122	678	15	45.20	5-74	1	-
1-day Int																	
NatWest																	
B&H	3	2	1	18	17 *	18.00	-	-	1	-	54	31	1	31.00	1-31	-	
Refuge	9	6	3	125	37	41.66	-	-	3	-	145	165	5	33.00	2-49	-	

WHITE, G. W. Somerset

Name: Giles William White
Role: Right-hand bat, leg-spin bowler
Born: 23 March 1972
Height: 5ft 11in **Weight:** 12st
Nickname: Chalkey, Mophead, Mooner
County debut: 1991
1st-Class catches: 0
Parents: John and Christina
Marital status: Single
Family links with cricket: Father played club cricket
Education: Exeter Cathedral School; Millfield School; Loughborough University
Qualifications: 8 GCSEs, 2 A-levels
Off-season: Starting at Loughborough University
Overseas teams played for: Waverley, Sydney 1990-91
Cricketers particularly admired: Peter Roebuck, Viv Richards, Ian Botham
Other sports followed: Football, rugby, tennis
Relaxations: Travelling, playing tennis

Extras: Made debut for Devon aged 16. Played for Devon in Holt Cup final at Lord's 1991. Represented England Schools U15

Opinions on cricket: 'More four-day cricket where results don't have to be manufactured.'

Best batting: 42 Somerset v Sri Lanka, Taunton 1991

Best bowling: 1-30 Somerset v Sri Lanka, Taunton 1991

1991 Season

	M	Inns	NO	Runs	HS	Avge	100s	50s	Ct	St	O	M	Runs	Wkts	Avge	Best	5wl	10wM
Test																		
All First	1	1	0	42	42	42.00	-	-	-	-	6	1	30	1	30.00	1-30	-	-
1-day Int																		
NatWest																		
B&H																		
Refuge																		

Career Performances

	M	Inns	NO	Runs	HS	Avge	100s	50s	Ct	St	Balls	Runs	Wkts	Avge	Best	5wl	10wM
Test																	
All First	1	1	0	42	42	42.00	-	-	-	-	36	30	1	30.00	1-30	-	-
1-day Int																	
NatWest																	
B&H																	
Refuge																	

WHITTICASE, P.   Leicestershire

Name: Philip Whitticase
Role: Right-hand bat, wicket-keeper
Born: 15 March 1965, Wythall, Birmingham
Height: 5ft 8in **Weight:** 11st
Nickname: Jasper, Tracy, Boggy, Rat
County debut: 1984
County cap: 1987
1st-Class 50s scored: 15
1st-Class 100s scored: 1
1st-Class catches: 284
1st-Class stumpings: 12
Place in batting averages: 110th av. 31.00
Parents: Larry Gordon and Ann
Marital status: Single
Family links with cricket: Grandfather and father played local club cricket (both were wicket-keepers)

Education: Belle Vue Junior and Middle School; Buckpool Secondary; Crestwood Comprehensive
Qualifications: 5 O-levels, 4 CSEs, senior coaching certificate
Off-season: Coaching cricket in Leicester and teaching PE at a prep school
Overseas teams played for: South Bunbury, Western Australia 1983-85
Cricketers particularly admired: Bob Taylor, Alan Knott, Dennis Amiss
Other sports followed: Football, rugby
Relaxations: Playing soccer, watching rugby and 'a good night out'
Extras: Played schoolboy football for Birmingham City. Was Derek Underwood's last first-class victim
Opinions on cricket: 'I would like to see all four-day cricket, with 102 overs every day.

This would leave the weekends to play one-day cricket which would be better from a spectator's point of view.'
Best batting: 114* Leicestershire v Hampshire, Bournemouth

1991 Season

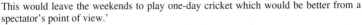

	M	Inns	NO	Runs	HS	Avge	100s	50s	Ct	St	O	M	Runs	Wkts	Avge	Best	5wI	10wM
Test																		
All First	20	25	5	620	114 *	31.00	1	4	44	3								
1-day Int																		
NatWest	2	0	0	0	0	-	-	-	2	-								
B&H	4	3	1	67	34 *	33.50	-	-	1	1								
Refuge	13	12	3	108	24	12.00	-	-	7	-								

Career Performances

	M	Inns	NO	Runs	HS	Avge	100s	50s	Ct	St	Balls	Runs	Wkts	Avge	Best	5wI	10wM
Test																	
All First	121	159	36	2901	114 *	23.58	1	15	284	12	5	7	0	-	-	-	-
1-day Int																	
NatWest	13	6	1	67	32	13.40	-	-	14	-							
B&H	22	15	6	284	45	31.55	-	-	24	2							
Refuge	64	41	8	378	38	11.45	-	-	55	4							

WIGHAM, G.   Durham

Name: Gary Wigham
Role: Right-hand bat, right-arm fast-medium bowler
Born: 2 March 1973, Bishop Auckland
Height: 6ft 7in **Weight:** 16st
Nickname: Wiggy
Parents: Margaret and Barry
Marital status: Single
Education: Bishop Auckland Barrington Comprehensive
Qualifications: 4 CSE
Off-season: Playing cricket in New Zealand
Overseas teams played for: Riccarton, Christchurch 1991-92
Cricketers particularly admired: Ian Botham, Chris Broad
Other sports followed: Football
Relaxations: Music, watching cricket videos
Extras: Was on the MCC groundstaff in 1991

No appearance in first-class cricket or any one-day competition

WILKINSON, C. W.   Leicestershire

Name: Craig William Wilkinson
Role: Right-hand bat, right-arm medium bowler
Born: 19 March 1963, Rochdale
Height: 6ft ½in **Weight:** 12st 2lbs
Nickname: Digger, Liquor
County debut: 1991
1st-Class catches: 7
Place in batting averages: 244th av. 12.54
Place in bowling averages: 125th av. 43.87
Strike rate: 82.17
Parents: William Arthur and Patricia
Marital status: Single
Family links with cricket: Uncle, Peter Blackburn, played Lancashire League cricket
Education: Carnamah District High School; Scotch College, Perth, Western Australia
Career outside cricket: 'Various entrepreneurial activities'
Off-season: Playing cricket in Australia

Overseas teams played for: Mount Lawley, Perth, Western Australia 1987-92
Cricketers particu larly admired: Terry Alderman, Malcolm Marshall, Stephen Davies, John Maguire
Other sports followed: Australian Rules football, golf
Injuries: Strained ligament in knee
Relaxations: Golf, loud music, playing guitar
Extras: 'Disappointed my impersonation of James Whitaker fielding was mistaken for a three-toed sloth!' Played for Sussex 2nd XI in 1987
Opinions on cricket: 'Should be more four-day games.'
Best batting:
41 Leicestershire v Nottinghamshire, Trent Bridge 1991
Best bowling:
4-59 Leicestershire v Derbyshire, Derby 1991

1991 Season

	M	Inns	NO	Runs	HS	Avge	100s	50s	Ct	St	O	M	Runs	Wkts	Avge	Best	5wI	10wM
Test																		
All First	14	13	2	138	41	12.54	-	-	7	-	315	64	1009	23	43.87	4-59	-	-
1-day Int																		
NatWest	2	0	0	0	0	-	-	-	-	-	16.5	5	62	3	20.66	3-16	-	
B&H	3	2	2	28	19 *	-	-	-	2	-	31	3	130	3	43.33	3-46	-	
Refuge	13	6	5	52	35 *	52.00	-	-	3	-	88.3	1	437	10	43.70	2-31	-	

Career Performances

	M	Inns	NO	Runs	HS	Avge	100s	50s	Ct	St	Balls	Runs	Wkts	Avge	Best	5wI	10wM
Test																	
All First	14	13	2	138	41	12.54	-	-	7	-	1890	1009	23	43.87	4-59	-	-
1-day Int																	
NatWest	2	0	0	0	0	-	-	-	-	-	101	62	3	20.66	3-16	-	
B&H	3	2	2	28	19 *	-	-	-	2	-	186	130	3	43.33	3-46	-	
Refuge	13	6	5	52	35 *	52.00	-	-	3	-	531	437	10	43.70	2-31	-	

WILLEY, P.   Leicestershire

Name: Peter Willey
Role: Right-hand bat, off-break bowler
Born: 6 December 1949, Sedgefield,
Co Durham
Height: 6ft 1in **Weight:** 13st
Nickname: Chin, Will
County debut: 1966 (Northants),
1984 (Leics)
County cap: 1971 (Northants), 1984 (Leics)
Benefit: 1981 (£31,400)
Test debut: 1976
Tests: 26
One-Day Internationals: 26
1000 runs in a season: 10
50 wickets in a season: 2
1st-Class 50s scored: 101
1st-Class 100s scored: 44
1st-Class 200s scored: 1
1st-Class 5 w. in innings: 26
1st-Class 10 w. in match: 3
1st-Class catches: 235
One-Day 50s: 63
One-Day 100s: 9

Place in batting averages: 212th av. 16.69 (1990 140th av. 33.82)
Place in bowling averages: (1990 120th av. 47.43)
Strike rate: (career 77.55)
Parents: Oswald and Maisie
Wife and date of marriage: Charmaine, 23 September 1971
Children: Heather Jane, 11 September 1985
Family links with cricket: Father played local club cricket in County Durham
Education: Secondary School, Seaham, County Durham
Overseas tours: England to Australia and India 1979-80; West Indies 1980-81 and 1985-86; with unofficial England XI to South Africa 1981-82
Overseas teams played for: Eastern Province, South Africa 1982-85
Cricketers particularly admired: Bishen Bedi, Geoffrey Boycott
Other sports followed: Football, golf, rugby
Relaxations: Reading, taking Irish Setter for long walks and shooting, gardening
Extras: With Wayne Larkins, received 2016 pints of beer (seven barrels) from a brewery in Northampton as a reward for their efforts in Australia with England in 1979-80. Youngest player ever to play for Northamptonshire CCC at 16 years 180 days v Cambridge U in 1966. Banned from Test cricket for three years for joining England rebel tour of South Africa in 1982. Left Northamptonshire at end of 1983 and moved to Leicestershire as vice-

captain. Appointed Leicestershire captain for 1987, but resigned after only one season. Released by Leicestershire at the end of the 1991 season to play for Northumberland in 1992. Appointed to the first-class umpires reserve list for 1992

Opinions on cricket: 'Good pitches is the only way to get good cricketers. Four-day cricket won't make people better cricketers. Young players have things made too easy for them.'

Best batting: 227 Northamptonshire v Somerset, Northampton 1976
Best bowling: 7-37 Northamptonshire v Oxford University, The Parks 1975

1991 Season

	M	Inns	NO	Runs	HS	Avge	100s	50s	Ct	St	O	M	Runs	Wkts	Avge	Best	5wI	10wM
Test																		
All First	12	18	5	217	42 *	16.69	-	-	6	-	157.4	36	441	5	88.20	2-15	-	-
1-day Int																		
NatWest	2	2	0	34	28	17.00	-	-	-	-	19	3	56	0	-		-	-
B&H	4	4	0	69	36	17.25	-	-	-	-	36.5	4	111	2	55.50	1-29	-	
Refuge	10	9	1	153	31	19.12	-	-	2	-	60	2	238	8	29.75	4-17	-	

Career Performances

	M	Inns	NO	Runs	HS	Avge	100s	50s	Ct	St	Balls	Runs	Wkts	Avge	Best	5wI	10wM
Test	26	50	6	1184	102 *	26.90	2	5	3	-	1091	456	7	65.14	2-73	-	-
All First	559	918	121	24361	227	30.56	44	101	235	-	58633	23400	756	30.95	7-37	26	3
1-day Int	26	24	1	538	64	23.39	-	5	4	-	1031	659	13	50.69	3-33	-	
NatWest	50	49	7	1513	154	36.02	2	9	13	-	2919	1513	35	43.22	3-33	-	
B&H	73	67	11	1758	88 *	31.39	-	14	19	-	3794	1772	46	38.52	3-12	-	
Refuge	278	265	20	6506	107	26.55	7	35	83	-	9410	6405	234	27.37	4-17	-	

195. Who topped the first-class batting averages last season for Leicestershire?

WILLIAMS, N. F. Middlesex

Name: Neil Fitzgerald Williams
Role: Right-hand bat, right-arm
fast-medium bowler
Born: 2 July 1962, Hopewell, St Vincent,
West Indies
Height: 5ft 11in **Weight:** 11st 7lbs
Nickname: Joe
County debut: 1982
County cap: 1984
Test debut: 1990
Tests: 1
50 wickets in a season: 3
1st-Class 50s scored: 11
1st-Class 5 w. in innings: 13
1st-Class 10 w. in match: 1
1st-Class catches: 42
Place in batting averages: 228th av. 14.62
(1990 215th av. 21.33)

Place in bowling averages: 92nd av. 35.48
(1990 29th av. 29.96)
Strike rate: 67.00 (career 54.72)
Parents: Alexander and Aldreta
Marital status: Single
Family links with cricket: 'Uncle Joe was 12th man for St Vincent and played 1st
Division cricket.'
Education: Cane End Primary School, St Vincent; Acland Burghley School, Tufnell Park
Qualifications: School Leaver's Certificate, 6 O-levels, 1 A-level
Off-season: Playing in the West Indies
Overseas tours: English Counties to Zimbabwe 1985
Overseas teams played for: Windward Islands 1982-83 and 1989-90; Tasmania 1983-84
Cricketers particularly admired: Viv Richards, Andy Roberts, Michael Holding, Dennis
Lillee, Malcolm Marshall, Lawrence Rowe
Other sports followed: Most
Relaxations: Reggae, soca, soul, cinema
Extras: Was on stand-by for England in New Zealand and Pakistan 1983-84. Test debut
v India at The Oval in 1990
Best batting: 77 Middlesex v Warwickshire, Edgbaston 1991
Best bowling: 7-55 English Counties XI v Zimbabwe, Harare 1984-85

1991 Season

	M	Inns	NO	Runs	HS	Avge	100s	50s	Ct	St	O	M	Runs	Wkts	Avge	Best	5wI	10wM
Test																		
All First	18	27	3	351	77	14.62	-	1	5	-	524.5	99	1668	47	35.48	5-89	1	-
1-day Int																		
NatWest	2	2	0	9	6	4.50	-	-	1	-	12	2	43	1	43.00	1-11	-	--
B&H	4	3	0	10	6	3.33	-	-	1	-	44	8	123	5	24.60	2-19	-	
Refuge	12	5	2	48	27	16.00	-	-	6	-	83	2	408	8	51.00	1-24	-	

Career Performances

	M	Inns	NO	Runs	HS	Avge	100s	50s	Ct	St	Balls	Runs	Wkts	Avge	Best	5wI	10wM
Test	1	1	0	38	38	38.00	-	-	-	-	246	148	2	74.00	2-148	-	-
All First	176	207	43	3320	77	20.24	-	11	42	-	24849	13552	457	29.65	7-55	13	1
1-day Int																	
NatWest	17	9	3	45	10	7.50	-	-	3	-	853	563	14	40.21	4-36	-	
B&H	43	24	5	219	29 *	11.52	-	-	4	-	2267	1405	44	31.93	3-16	-	
Refuge	94	44	16	425	43	15.17	-	-	20	-	3873	2970	105	28.28	4-39	-	

WILLIAMS, R. C.   Gloucestershire

Name: Ricardo Cecil Williams
Role: Right-hand bat, right-arm fast-medium bowler
Born: 7 February 1968, Camberwell, London
Height: 5ft 10in **Weight:** 11st
Nickname: Raw Deal, Tricky Ricky, Gus
County debut: 1991
1st-Class catches: 0
Parents: Wilfred Harry Williams and Cecile Yvonne Jordan
Marital status: Single
Education: Haringey College; Ellerslie Secondary School, Barbados; Haringey Cricket College
Qualifications: 3 O-levels, NCA coaching award
Off-season: Playing in Australia
Overseas tours: Haringey Cricket College to Jamaica 1988,1989,1990
Overseas teams played for: Geelong City, Victoria, Australia 1991-92
Cricketers particularly admired: Malcolm Marshall, Viv Richards, Richie Richardson, Jimmy Cook, Gordon Greenidge, Jack Russell, David Lawrence

553

Other sports followed: Football, tennis, volleyball, basketball, athletics, baseball
Relaxations: Listening to music, buying clothes, relaxing with friends, watching videos
Opinions on cricket: 'Prepare faster wickets for batsmen and bowlers to compete on in both 1st and 2nd XIs.'
Best batting: 13 Gloucestershire v Derbyshire, Gloucester 1991
Best bowling: 1-81 Gloucestershire v Derbyshire, Gloucester 1991

1991 Season

	M	Inns	NO	Runs	HS	Avge	100s	50s	Ct	St	O	M	Runs	Wkts	Avge	Best	5wI	10wM
Test																		
All First	1	2	0	13	13	6.50	-	-	-	-	26	4	81	1	81.00	1-81	-	-
1-day Int																		
NatWest																		
B&H																		
Refuge																		

Career Performances

	M	Inns	NO	Runs	HS	Avge	100s	50s	Ct	St	Balls	Runs	Wkts	Avge	Best	5wI	10wM
Test																	
All First	1	2	0	13	13	6.50	-	-	-	-	156	81	1	81.00	1-81	-	-
1-day Int																	
NatWest																	
B&H																	
Refuge																	

196. Who captained the 1986 New Zealanders in England?

WILLIAMS, R. C. J.   Gloucestershire

Name: Richard Charles James Williams
Role: Left-hand bat, wicket-keeper
Born: 8 August 1969, Bristol
Height: 5ft 9in **Weight:** 10st 5lbs
Nickname: Reggie
County debut: 1990
1st-Class 50s scored: 2
1st-Class catches: 45
1st-Class stumpings: 7
Parents: Michael and Angela
Marital status: Single
Family links with cricket: Father played
local club cricket
Education: Clifton College
Preparatory School, Millfield School
Off-season: 'Working for a temping
agency.'
Cricketers particularly admired: Andy
Brassington, Jack Russell, Alan Knott,
Graham Wiltshire, Eddie Barlow ' and all of the senior players at Gloucestershire'
Other sports followed: Football, hockey, squash, windsurfing
Relaxations: Listening to music, watching and playing sport
Best batting: 55* Gloucestershire v Derbyshire, Gloucester 1991

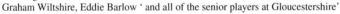

1991 Season

	M	Inns	NO	Runs	HS	Avge	100s	50s	Ct	St	O	M	Runs	Wkts	Avge	Best	5wI	10wM
Test																		
All First	10	12	2	95	55*	9.50	-	1	18	3								
1-day Int																		
NatWest																		
B&H																		
Refuge	2	0	0	0	0	-	-	-	-	-								

Career Performances

	M	Inns	NO	Runs	HS	Avge	100s	50s	Ct	St	Balls	Runs	Wkts	Avge	Best	5wI	10wM
Test																	
All First	18	20	6	227	55*	16.21	-	2	45	7							
1-day Int																	
NatWest																	
B&H																	
Refuge	6	0	0	0	0	-	-	-	5	-							

WILLIAMS, R. G.   Northamptonshire

Name: Richard Grenville Williams
Role: Right-hand bat, off-break bowler
Born: 10 August 1957, Bangor, Wales
Height: 5ft 6in **Weight:** 12st
Nickname: Chippy
County debut: 1974
County cap: 1979
Benefit: 1989 (£100,053)
1000 runs in a season: 6
1st-Class 50s scored: 55
1st-Class 100s scored: 18
1st-Class 5 w. in innings: 9
1st-Class catches: 99
One-Day 50s: 22
Place in batting averages: 136th av. 28.00
(1990 185th av. 26.95)
Place in bowling averages:
(1990 85th av. 38.83)
Strike rate: (career 72.12)
Parents: Gordon and Rhianwen
Wife and date of marriage: Helen Laura, 24 April 1982
Children: Bryn Reece, 3 October 1991
Family links with cricket: Father played for Caernarvonshire and North Wales
Education: Ellesmere Port Grammar School
Career outside cricket: Qualified carpenter (self-employed)
Off-season: Working – carpentry and joinery
Overseas tours: England YC to West Indies 1976; English Counties to Zimbabwe 1985
Other sports followed: Golf
Injuries: Pulled calf and knee injury
Relaxations: Fly fishing, shooting, fly tying
Extras: Debut for 2nd XI in 1972 aged 14 years 11 months. Made maiden century in 1979 and then scored four centuries in five innings. Hat-trick v Gloucestershire, at Northampton 1980. Was first player to score a century against the 1980 West Indies touring team. Was stand-by for England tour to India 1981-82
Best batting: 175* Northamptonshire v Leicestershire, Leicester 1980
Best bowling: 7-73 Northamptonshire v Cambridge University, Fenner's 1980

---

197. Who is the 1992 captain of Sussex?

1991 Season

	M	Inns	NO	Runs	HS	Avge	100s	50s	Ct	St	O	M	Runs	Wkts	Avge	Best	5wI	10wM
Test																		
All First	8	11	3	224	101 *	28.00	1	-	1	-	91.3	19	259	4	64.75	2-29	-	-
1-day Int																		
NatWest	3	2	0	7	6	3.50	-	-	3	-	36	4	99	2	49.50	2-34	-	
B&H	4	4	2	96	29	48.00	-	-	1	-	33	2	109	2	54.50	1-31	-	
Refuge	12	7	4	141	66 *	47.00	-	1	3	-	70	0	360	12	30.00	2-22	-	

Career Performances

	M	Inns	NO	Runs	HS	Avge	100s	50s	Ct	St	Balls	Runs	Wkts	Avge	Best	5wI	10wM
Test																	
All First	282	444	65	11788	175 *	31.10	18	55	99	-	26830	12639	372	33.97	7-73	9	-
1-day Int																	
NatWest	36	32	6	567	94	21.80	-	2	13	-	1512	844	35	24.11	4-10	-	
B&H	51	42	11	1012	83	32.64	-	7	10	-	1560	935	29	32.24	4-41	-	
Refuge	169	139	28	2611	82	23.52	-	13	44	-	3266	2676	91	29.40	5-30	1	

WOOD, J.   Durham

Name: John Wood
Role: Right-hand bat, right-arm fast-medium bowler
Born: 22 July 1970, Wakefield
Height: 6ft 2¹/₂in **Weight:** 16st
Nickname: Angry
Parents: Brian and Anne
Marital status: Single
Education: Crofton High School; Wakefield District College; Leeds Polytechnic
Qualifications: HND in Electrical and Electronic Engineering
Career outside cricket: Electrical and Electronic Engineering
Off-season: Working for West Riding Home Securities in Wakefield
Overseas teams played for: Griqualand West Cricket Union, South Africa 1990-91
Cricketers particularly admired: Ian Botham, David Gower, Richard Hadlee
Other sports followed: Rugby union, football
Injuries: Shin splints

Relaxations: Golf
Extras: Has been playing in the Bradford League. Made his debut for Durham in 1991

1991 Season

	M	Inns	NO	Runs	HS	Avge	100s	50s	Ct	St	O	M	Runs	Wkts	Avge	Best	5wI	10wM
Test																		
All First																		
1-day Int																		
NatWest	1	1	0	1	1	1.00	-	-	-	-	10	0	82	0	-		-	-
B&H																		
Refuge																		

Career Performances

	M	Inns	NO	Runs	HS	Avge	100s	50s	Ct	St	Balls	Runs	Wkts	Avge	Best	5wI	10wM
Test																	
All First																	
1-day Int																	
NatWest	1	1	0	1	1	1.00	-	-	-	-	60	82	0	-		-	-
B&H																	
Refuge																	

WOOD, J. R.   Hampshire

Name: Julian Ross Wood
Role: Left-hand bat, right-arm medium bowler
Born: 21 November 1968, Winchester, Hampshire
Height: 5ft 8in **Weight:** 13st 6lbs
Nickname: Woody, Bamba 'and many more'
County debut: 1989
1st-Class 50s scored: 4
One-Day 50s: 3
1st-Class catches: 7
Parents: Ross and Susan Keysell
Marital status: Single
Family links with cricket: Father NCA coach, Minor Counties umpire, and also played in local league
Education: St Barts Prep School; Priors Court School; Leighton Park School

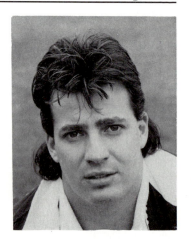

Qualifications: 3 O-levels, NCA coach (Grade 1)

Career outside cricket: 'Various jobs – sheep farming, timber work, sports master, contract cleaning.'

Off-season: 'Improving my batting technique and getting fit for the coming season.'

Overseas tours: Berkshire U19 to Sri Lanka 1987; MCC YC to Hong Kong 1988; Hampshire to Barbados 1990

Overseas teams played for: Newcastle City, Sydney 1989-91

Cricketers particularly admired: Ian Botham ('for his never-say-die attitude'), Robin and Chris Smith ('for their dedication'), Viv Richards ('for the way he makes world-class bowlers look so average')

Other sports followed: Football (Manchester United) and all other sports

Relaxations: 'Good pubs and restaurants, good beer, listening to music, watching videos, spending time with my lovely girlfriend Heather.'

Extras: Hit first ball in first-class cricket for four as he scored 65 on debut v Sussex. England Schools U15, U19. MCC Young Professionals groundstaff. Hampshire Young Player of the Year, 1989. Won first Man of the Match award in B&H Cup against Minor Counties 1991. Hit 40 sixes in the 2nd XI Championship 1991

Opinions on cricket: 'I would like to see floodlit day/night games introduced with coloured clothing and names printed on shirts. I do not agree with the one bouncer per over rule, some players like myself benefit from short-pitched bowling. It is generally thought by most cricketers that four-day Championship games will enhance the profession.'

Best batting: 96 Hampshire v Northamptonshire, Northampton 1989

Best bowling: 1-5 Hampshire v Sussex, Southampton 1989

1991 Season

	M	Inns	NO	Runs	HS	Avge	100s	50s	Ct	St	O	M	Runs	Wkts	Avge	Best	5wI	10wM
Test																		
All First	2	2	0	25	25	12.50	-	-	-	-	6	0	17	0	-	-	-	-
1-day Int																		
NatWest																		
B&H	4	4	1	90	70 *	30.00	-	1	3	-								
Refuge	11	10	0	204	54	20.40	-	1	2	-								

Career Performances

	M	Inns	NO	Runs	HS	Avge	100s	50s	Ct	St	Balls	Runs	Wkts	Avge	Best	5wI	10wM
Test																	
All First	16	22	2	641	96	32.05	-	4	7	-	63	38	1	38.00	1-5	-	-
1-day Int																	
NatWest	2	1	1	3	3 *	-	-	-	-	-							
B&H	5	5	2	133	70 *	44.33	-	1	3	-							
Refuge	17	15	0	312	66	20.80	-	2	4	-							

WREN, T. N.   Kent

Name: Timothy Neil Wren
Role: Right-hand bat, left-arm
medium bowler
Born: 26 March 1970, Folkestone
Height: 6ft 3in **Weight:** 15st
Nickname: The Bear, Grizzly
County debut: 1989 (one-day), 1990
(first-class)
1st-Class catches: 2
Parents: James and Gillian
Marital status: Single
Family links with cricket: Father
and played local cricket so did brother 'who
has just staged a remarkable comeback'
Education: Lyminge Primary;
Harvey Grammar School, Folkestone
Qualifications: 6 O-levels; NCA coaching
certificate
Off-season: 'Getting fit and training for the
1992 season.'
Overseas teams played for: Universals, Zimbabwe 1989-90
Cricketers particularly admired: Graham Kersey, Ian Botham, Richard
Hadlee
Other sports followed: Any sports
Relaxations: Good movies, eating out, music and socialising
Extras: First played for Kent 2nd XI in 1987, aged 17
Opinions on cricket: ' Too much cricket played, not enough time to work on bad habits.
Second team cricket, if it is to be a proving ground for young cricketers, should be played
on first-class grounds (no club wickets) under first-class conditions.'
Best batting: 16 Kent v Essex, Canterbury 1990
Best bowling: 3-14 Kent v Oxford University, The Parks 1991

1991 Season

	M	Inns	NO	Runs	HS	Avge	100s	50s	Ct	St	O	M	Runs	Wkts	Avge	Best	5wI	10wM
Test																		
All First	1	0	0	0	0	-	-	-	-	-	19.3	3	48	4	12.00	3-14	-	-
1-day Int																		
NatWest																		
B&H																		
Refuge	1	1	1	0	0 *	-	-	-	-	-	5	0	33	1	33.00	1-33	-	

Career Performances

	M	Inns	NO	Runs	HS	Avge	100s	50s	Ct	St	Balls	Runs	Wkts	Avge	Best	5wl	10wM
Test																	
All First	6	5	2	23	16	7.66	-	-	2	-	849	537	10	53.70	3-14	-	-
1-day Int																	
NatWest																	
B&H																	
Refuge	3	1	1	0	0 *	-	-	-	-	-	-	111	105	3	35.00	1-31	-	

WRIGHT, A. J. Gloucestershire

Name: Anthony John Wright
Role: Right-hand bat, off-break bowler, county captain
Born: 27 July 1962, Stevenage, Hertfordshire
Height: 6ft **Weight:** 14st
Nickname: Billy, Horace
County debut: 1982
County cap: 1987
1000 runs in a season: 4
1st-Class 50s scored: 46
1st-Class 100s scored: 11
1st-Class catches: 129
One-Day 50s: 24
Place in batting averages: 38th av. 45.60 (1990 192nd av. 26.02)
Parents: Michael and Patricia
Wife and date of marriage: Rachel, 21 December 1986
Children: Hannah, 3 April 1988
Education: Alleyn's School, Stevenage
Qualifications: 6 O-levels
Cricketers particularly admired: Viv Richards, Ian Botham, Malcolm Marshall, Jack Russell
Other sports followed: All sports except motor racing
Relaxations: Eating out, reading, playing golf
Extras: Appointed captain of Gloucestershire for 1990
Best batting: 161 Gloucestershire v Glamorgan, Bristol 1987
Best bowling: 1-16 Gloucestershire v Yorkshire, Harrogate 1989

1991 Season

	M	Inns	NO	Runs	HS	Avge	100s	50s	Ct	St	O	M	Runs	Wkts	Avge	Best	5wI	10wM
Test																		
All First	25	41	6	1596	120	45.60	3	10	19	-	0.3	0	4	0	-	-	-	-
1-day Int																		
NatWest	2	2	0	67	56	33.50	-	1	-	-								
B&H	4	4	0	175	81	43.75	-	1	-	-								
Refuge	15	14	1	414	71	31.84	-	3	3	-								

Career Performances

	M	Inns	NO	Runs	HS	Avge	100s	50s	Ct	St	Balls	Runs	Wkts	Avge	Best	5wI	10wM
Test																	
All First	186	319	23	8565	161	28.93	11	46	129	-	62	41	1	41.00	1-16	-	-
1-day Int																	
NatWest	17	16	0	606	92	37.87	-	7	4	-							
B&H	26	23	0	643	97	27.95	-	4	4	-							
Refuge	101	93	11	1984	81	24.19	-	13	39	-	26	22	0	-	-	-

YATES, G.   Lancashire

Name: Gary Yates
Role: Right-hand bat, off-spin bowler
Born: 20 September 1967,
Ashton-under-Lyne
Height: 6ft 1in **Weight:** 12st 11lbs
Nickname: Yugo, Pearly, Backyard, Zippy
County debut: 1990
1st-Class 100s scored: 2
1st-Class catches: 10
Place in batting averages: 163rd av. 24.23
Place in bowling averages: 141st av. 61.74
Strike rate: 114.38 (career 116.61)
Parents: Alan and Patricia
Marital status: Single
Family links with cricket: Father played in
Lancashire Leagues
Education: Manchester Grammar School
Qualifications: 6 O-levels,
Australian Coaching Council coach
Career outside cricket: Coaching cricket in Brisbane
Off-season: Playing in Brisbane
Overseas tours: Lancs to Tasmania and Western Australia 1990; Western Australia 1991

Overseas teams played for: South Barwon, Geelong, Australia 1987-88; Johnsonville, Wellington, New Zealand 1989-90; Western Suburbs, Brisbane 1991-92

Cricketers particularly admired: Michael Atherton, Ian Botham, Viv Richards

Other sports followed: All sports, especially football, golf, motor rallying

Relaxations: Playing golf, watching football and good films

Extras: Played for Worcestershire 2nd XI in 1987; made debut for Lancashire 2nd XI in 1988 and taken on to county staff in 1990; scored century on Championship debut v Nottinghamshire at Trent Bridge

Opinions on cricket: 'Would like to see a Championship of four-day cricket only.'

Best batting: 106 Lancashire v Nottinghamshire, Trent Bridge 1990

Best bowling: 4-94 Lancashire v Sri Lanka, Old Trafford 1990

1991 Season

	M	Inns	NO	Runs	HS	Avge	100s	50s	Ct	St	O	M	Runs	Wkts	Avge	Best	5wI	10wM
Test																		
All First	20	26	13	315	100 *	24.23	1	-	9	-	591	117	1914	31	61.74	3-39	-	-
1-day Int																		
NatWest																		
B&H	3	0	0	0	0	-	-	-	1	-	22	3	85	2	42.50	2-50	-	
Refuge	4	0	0	0	0	-	-	-	-	-	20	1	125	2	62.50	2-45	-	

Career Performances

	M	Inns	NO	Runs	HS	Avge	100s	50s	Ct	St	Balls	Runs	Wkts	Avge	Best	5wI	10wM
Test																	
All First	25	30	15	480	106	32.00	2	-	10	-	4548	2334	39	59.84	4-94	-	-
1-day Int																	
NatWest																	
B&H	3	0	0	0	0	-	-	-	1	-	132	85	2	42.50	2-50	-	
Refuge	4	0	0	0	0	-	-	-	-	-	120	125	2	62.50	2-45	-	

THE UMPIRES

ADAMS, P.

Name: Paul Adams
Born: 22 December 1949, London
Height: 6ft **Weight:** 12st
Appointed to 1st-class list: On the reserve list for 1992
Parents: George (deceased) and Mary
Education: The Campion School, Hornchurch, Essex; Nottingham University
Qualifications: Honours Degree in Russian
Career outside cricket:
Deputy Headmaster, St Ignatius College, Enfield
Off-season: Teaching
Other sports followed: Rugby union and 'the usual East End devotion to West Ham'
Relaxations: Crosswords, reading – 'and anything to do with cricket, whatsoever!'

Extras: Keen club cricketer with Ilford Catholic CC and then Brentwood CC in the Essex league ('left-arm seamer but not quick enough!'). Played in the 1971 UAU final at Trent Bridge. Began umpiring seriously in 1982 'in order to stay with the best level of cricket possible – the writing was on the wall as far as my playing was concerned.' Has umpired County 2nd XI cricket since 1985 and has been on the Minor Counties list since 1987. Travelled as umpire on the Club Cricket Conference tour of Hong Kong and Australia in 1991
Opinions on cricket: 'Not only the best game in the world, but also one which has enabled me to meet some of the nicest people. Good manners still prevail – at least, most of the time!'

Did not play first-class cricket

BALDERSTONE, J. C.

Name: John Christopher Balderstone
Role: Right-hand opening bat, slow
left-arm bowler
Born: 16 November 1940, Huddersfield
Height: 6ft 1in **Weight:** 12st 10lbs
Nickname: Baldy
Appointed to 1st-class list: 1988
Appointed to Test panel: Stand-by
umpire in 1991
Counties: Yorkshire, Leicestershire
County debut: 1961 (Yorks); 1971 (Leics)
County cap: 1973 (Leics)
Test debut: 1976
Tests: 2
1000 runs in a season: 11
1st-Class 50s scored: 102
1st-Class 100s scored: 32
1st-Class 5 w. in innings: 5
One-Day 50s: 32
One-Day 100s: 5
1st-Class catches: 210

Parents: Frank and Jennie (deceased)
Education: Paddock County School, Huddersfield
Qualifications: Advanced cricket coach, soccer coach
Career outside cricket: Former professional footballer, sales representative for various products, cricket and soccer coach
Off-season: Coaching cricket
Cricketing superstitions or habits: 'Grew out of superstitions a long time ago, in the harsh reality of professional cricket and soccer. They don't help when the ball is whistling around your ears!'
Other sports followed: Soccer – Huddersfield Town, Carlisle United, Doncaster Rovers and Queen of the South
Cricketers particularly admired: Willie Watson and Ray Illingworth
Relaxations: Golf
Best batting: 181* Leicestershire v Gloucestershire, Leicester 1984
Best bowling: 6-25 Leicestershire v Hampshire, Southampton 1978

First-Class Career Performances

	M	Inns	NO	Runs	HS	Avge	100s	Ct	St	Runs	Wkts	Avge	Best	5wI	10wM
Test	2	4	0	39	35	9.75	-	-	1	80	1	80.00	1-80	-	-
All First	390	619	61	19034	181 *	34.11	32	210	-	8160	310	26.32	6-25	5	-

BIRD, H. D.

Name: Harold Dennis Bird, MBE
Role: Right-hand opening bat
Born: 19 April 1933, Barnsley
Height: 5ft 10in **Weight:** 12st
Nickname: Dickie
Appointed to 1st-class list: 1969
Appointed to Test panel: 1972
Tests umpired: 47
One-Day Internationals umpired: 79
Counties: Yorkshire, Leicestershire
County debut: 1956 (Yorks); 1960 (Leics)
County cap: 1960 (Leics)
1000 runs in a season: 1
1st-Class 50s scored: 14
1st-Class 100s scored: 2
1st-Class catches: 20
Parents: James Harold and Ethel
Marital status: Bachelor
Education: Raley School, Barnsley
Qualifications: MCC advanced cricket coach
Career outside cricket: 'Cricket is my life.'
Off-season: After-dinner speaking

Cricketing superstitions or habits: Twitch of the shoulders, wears distinctive white cap
Other sports followed: Football
Cricketers particularly admired: Sir Garfield Sobers, Dennis Lillee, Viv Richards
Cricketers particularly learnt from: Sir Gubby Allen, Johnny Wardle
Relaxations: Listening to recordings of Barbra Streisand and Diana Ross
Extras: Has umpired 126 international matches to date. Has umpired three World Cup finals at Lord's (1975,1979,1983). Also umpired at the World Cup in India in 1987. Umpired the Queen's Silver Jubilee Test, England v Australia 1977, the Centenary Test, England v Australia 1980 and the MCC Bi-Centenary Test, England v Rest of the World 1987. In 1982 he umpired the Women's World Cup final in Christchurch, New Zealand. During the mid-1980s he umpired several times in the various competitions staged at Sharjah, UAE. To date he has umpired 32 Cup finals all over the world, as well as the finals of other cricket events such as The Best All-rounder in the World, The Best Batsman in the World and the World Double Wicket competition. In 1977 he was voted Yorkshire Personality of the Year. He is the author of three bestselling books, Not Out, That's Out and From the Pavilion End. Despite lucrative offers to join the 'Packer circus' and to visit South Africa with rebel tours, he remained loyal to the TCCB and to the established game on which he had been brought up in Yorkshire and which had given him so much in life. In June 1986 he was made a Member of the Most Excellent Order of the British Empire (MBE) in the Queen's Birthday Honours List

Opinions on cricket: 'The greatest game in the world. A game to be enjoyed by young and old. I have consistently advocated playing through all light unless the umpires are convinced that there is genuine physical danger to the batsman.'

Best batting: 181* Yorkshire v Glamorgan, Bradford 1959

First-Class Career Performances

	M	Inns	NO	Runs	HS	Avge	100s	Ct	St	Runs	Wkts	Avge	Best	5wl	10wM
Test															
All First	93	170	10	3314	181 *	20.71	2	28	-	22	0	-	-	-	-

BOND, J. D.

Name: John David Bond
Role: Right-hand bat
Born: 6 May 1932, Kearsley, Lancashire
Nickname: Jackie
Appointed to 1st-class list: 1988
Counties: Lancashire, Nottinghamshire
County debut: 1955 (Lancashire);
1974 (Nottinghamshire)
County cap: 1961 (Lancashire)
1000 runs in a season: 2
1st-Class 50s scored: 54
1st-Class 100s scored: 14
1st-Class catches: 223
Education: Bolton School
Extras: Captain of Lancashire 1968-1972,
during which time Lancashire won
the Gillette Cup three years in succession,
1970,1971,1972, and the John Player
Sunday League in 1969 and 1970. He

moved to Nottinghamshire in 1974 and was a Test selector in the same year. He was appointed Cricket Manager at Lancashire CCC in 1980 and held the position until 1986
Best batting: 157 Lancashire v Hampshire, Old Trafford 1962

First-Class Career Performances

	M	Inns	NO	Runs	HS	Avge	100s	Ct	St	Runs	Wkts	Avge	Best	5wl	10wM
Test															
All First	362	548	80	12125	157	25.90	14	222	-	69	0	-	-	-	-

BURGESS, G. I.

Name: Graham Iefvion Burgess
Role: Right-hand bat, right-arm
medium bowler
Born: 5 May 1943,
Glastonbury, Somerset
Appointed to 1st-class list: 1991
County: Somerset
County debut: 1966
County cap: 1968
Testimonial: 1977
1st-Class 100s scored: 2
1st-Class 5 w. in innings: 18
1st-Class 10 w. in match: 2
1st-Class catches: 120
Education: Millfield School
Extras: Played Minor Counties cricket
for Wiltshire 1981-82 and for
Cambridgeshire 1983-84
Best batting: 129 Somerset v Gloucestershire,
Taunton 1973
Best bowling: 7-43 Somerset v Oxford University, The Parks 1975

First-Class Career Performances

	M	Inns	NO	Runs	HS	Avge	100s	Ct	St	Runs	Wkts	Avge	Best	5wI	10wM
Test															
All First	252	414	37	7129	129	18.90	2	120	-	13543	474	28.57	7-43	18	2

198. Who does Denis Compton say are the two fastest England bowlers he ever saw?

CLARKSON, A.

Name: Anthony Clarkson
Role: Right-hand opening bat,
right-arm off-break bowler
Born: 5 September 1939
Height: 5ft 11in **Weight:** 14st 3lbs
Appointed to 1st-class list: On reserve list
for 1992
County: Somerset
County debut: 1963
County cap: 1969
1000 runs in a season: 2
1st-Class 100s scored: 2
1st-Class catches: 52
Parents: Joseph Newton and Clarrie
Marital status: Divorced – now engaged
to Cheryl
Children: André Anthony Joseph
(aged 27); Chantal Mirielle (24);
Pierre Anthony Henri (22) -
'French connection via ex-wife!'

Education: Harrogate Grammar School; Bradford Technical College; Brunel Technical
College, Bristol
Career outside cricket: Civil engineering – Harrogate Borough, Ripon City, Torquay
Borough, Bath City, Yorkshire Water
Off-season: 'Trying to set up a business in architectural and civil engineering design.'
Other sports followed: Rugby, preferably league
Cricketers particularly admired: Barry Richards, 'as the complete batsman', Brian
Close, 'for leadership and guts on the field, Tom Cartwright, 'for ability and fairness.'
Relaxations: Golf, garden, DIY, watching rugby league
Extras: The first English player to score a century in the Sunday league, Greg Chappell
had scored an earlier one
Best batting: 131 Somerset v Northamptonshire, Northampton 1969
Best bowling: 3-51 Somerset v Essex, Yeovil 1967

First-Class Career Performances

	M	Inns	NO	Runs	HS	Avge	100s	Ct	St	Runs	Wkts	Avge	Best	5wI	10wM
Test															
All First	110	189	12	4458	131	25.18	2	52	-	367	13	28.23	3-51	-	-

CONSTANT, D. J.

Name: David John Constant
Role: Left-hand bat, slow left-arm bowler
Born: 9 November 1941,
Bradford-on-Avon, Wiltshire
Nickname: Connie
Appointed to 1st-class list: 1969
Appointed to Test panel: 1971
Tests umpired: 36
One-Day Internationals umpired: 27
Counties: Kent, Leicestershire
County debut: 1961 (Kent);
1965 (Leicestershire)
1st-Class 50s scored: 6
1st-Class catches: 33
Extras: County bowls player for
Gloucestershire 1984-86
Best batting:
80 Leicestershire v Gloucestershire,
Bristol 1966

First-Class Career Performances

	M	Inns	NO	Runs	HS	Avge	100s	Ct	St	Runs	Wkts	Avge	Best	5wI	10wM
Test															
All First	61	93	14	1517	80	19.20	-	33	-	36	1	36.00	1-28	-	-

199. Who flew 50 bombing missions over Germany in the Second World War, won the DSO and DFC and has two sons who played for England?

DUDLESTON, B.

Name: Barry Dudleston
Role: Right-hand opening bat, slow
left-arm bowler, occasional wicket-keeper
Born: 16 July 1945, Bebington, Cheshire
Height: 5ft 9in **Weight:** 13st
Nickname: Danny, Dapper
Appointed to 1st-class list: 1984
Appointed to Test panel: 1991
Tests umpired: 1
Counties: Leicestershire, Gloucestershire
County debut: 1966 (Leics); 1981 (Gloucs)
County cap: 1969 (Leics)
Benefit: 1980 (£25,000)
1000 runs in a season: 8
1st-Class 100s scored: 32
1st-Class 200s scored: 1
One-Day 50s: 21
One-Day 100s: 4
1st-Class catches: 234
Parents: Percy and Dorothy Vera
Marital status: Divorced
Children: Sharon Louise, 29 October 1968; Matthew Barry 12 September 1988
Education: Stockport School
Qualifications: O-levels, junior coaching certificate, Shell marketing exams
Career outside cricket: Managing Director of Sunsport Tours
Off-season: Organising and hosting sports tours
Other sports followed: Most
Cricketers particularly admired: Gary Sobers, Tom Graveney
Cricketers particularly learnt from: Vinoo Mankad
Relaxations: TV, bridge, wine, golf
Extras: Played for England U25. Suffered badly from broken fingers, broke fingers on the same hand three times in 1978. Played for Rhodesia in the Currie Cup 1976-80
Opinions on cricket: 'It is still the greatest test of skill and character – beautiful to watch when played well. Am worried about the declining standards of behaviour.'
Best batting: 202 Leicestershire v Derbyshire, Leicester 1979
Best bowling: 4-6 Leicestershire v Surrey, Leicester 1972

First-Class Career Performances

	M	Inns	NO	Runs	HS	Avge	100s	Ct	St	Runs	Wkts	Avge	Best	5wI	10wM
Test															
All First	295	501	47	14747	202	32.48	32	234	7	1365	47	29.04	4-6	-	-

FAWKNER-CORBETT, Dr D.

Name: Dr David Fawkner-Corbett
Born: 10 January 1946,
Swanwick, Hampshire
Height: 6ft ¹/₂in **Weight:** 13st 8lbs
Nickname: Doc, DFC
Appointed to 1st-class list: On the
reserve list since 1990
Parents: Peter (deceased) and Phyllis
Wife: Marion
Children: Sara, Paul, Clare and Emma
Education: Portsmouth Grammar School;
St Thomas's Hospital Medical School
Career outside cricket:
General practitioner
Off-season: Working in Medicine
Other sports followed: Hockey,
rugby union
Relaxations: Fell-walking, DIY, eating
out, country pubs with real ale
Extras: First umpired in village cricket at the age of 12. Minor Counties umpire since 1978

Did not play first-class cricket

HAMPSHIRE, J. H.

Name: John Harry Hampshire
Role: Right-hand bat
Born: 10 February 1941,
Thurnscoe, Yorkshire
Appointed to 1st-class list: 1985
Appointed to Test panel: 1989
Tests umpired: 9
One-Day Internationals umpired: 4
Counties: Yorkshire, Derbyshire
County debut: 1961 (Yorkshire);
1982 (Derbyshire)
County cap: 1963 (Yorkshire);
1982 (Derbyshire)
Benefit: 1976
Test debut: 1969
Tests: 8
1000 runs in a season: 15
1st-Class 50s scored: 142
1st-Class 100s scored: 53
1st-Class catches: 445
1st-Class 5 w. in innings: 1
One-Day 50s: 39
One-Day 100s: 7
Parents: Jack and Vera
Wife: Judy
Children: Ian and Paul
Family links with cricket: Father (J.) and brother (A.W.) both played for Yorkshire.
Extras: Captained Yorkshire 1979-80. Played for Tasmania 1967-69 and 1977-79. Scored a century (107) in his first Test match, against West Indies at Lord's 1969
Best batting: 183* Yorkshire v Surrey, Hove 1971
Best bowling: 7-52 Yorkshire v Glamorgan, Cardiff 1963

First-Class Career Performances

	M	Inns	NO	Runs	HS	Avge	100s	Ct	St	Runs	Wkts	Avge	Best	5wI	10wM
Test	8	16	1	405	107	26.86	1	9	-						
All First	577	924	112	28059	183 *	34.55	43	445	-	1637	30	54.56	7-52	2	-

HARRIS, J. H.

Name: John Humphrey Harris
Role: Left-hand bat, right-arm
fast-medium bowler
Born: 13 February 1936, Taunton
Appointed to 1st-class list: 1983
County: Somerset
County debut: 1952
1st-Class catches: 6
Extras: Made his debut for Somerset
aged 16 years 99 days. Played Minor
Counties cricket for Suffolk (1960-62)
and Devon (1975)
Best batting:
41 Somerset v Worcestershire,
Taunton 1957
Best bowling:
3-29 Somerset v Worcestershire,
Bristol 1959

First-Class Career Performances

	M	Inns	NO	Runs	HS	Avge	100s	Ct	St	Runs	Wkts	Avge	Best	5wI	10wM
Test															
All First	15	18	4	154	41	11.00	-	6	-	609	19	32.05	3.29	-	-

HARRIS, M. J.

Name: Michael John Harris
Role: Right-hand bat, leg-break bowler, wicket-keeper
Born: 25 May 1944,
St Just-in-Roseland, Cornwall
Height: 6ft 1in **Weight:** 16st
Nickname: Pasty
Appointed to 1st-class list: On reserve list since 1988
Counties: Middlesex, Nottinghamshire
County debut: 1964 (Middx); 1969 (Notts)
County cap: 1967 (Middx); 1970 (Notts)
1000 runs in a season: 11
1st-Class 50s scored: 98
1st-Class 100s scored: 41
1st-Class 200s scored: 1
1st-Class catches: 322
Parents: Richard and Winnie
Wife and date of marriage: Danielle Ruth, 10 September 1969
Children: Jodie, Richard
Education: Gerrans Comprehensive
Qualifications: MCC advanced coach, SRA squash coach
Career outside cricket: Sports teacher, Stowe School
Other sports followed: Squash, golf
Cricketing superstitions or habits: Left boot and pad go on first
Cricketers particularly admired: Gary Sobers, Clive Rice
Cricketers particularly learnt from: Eric Russell (Middlesex)
Relaxations: 'A nice lager.'
Extras: Played for Eastern Province in the Currie Cup (1971-72) and for Wellington in the Shell Shield (1975-76). Scored nine centuries in 1971 to equal Nottinghamshire county record, scoring two centuries in a match twice and totalling 2238 for the season at an average of 50.86. Also shared Middlesex record 1st wicket partnership (312) with Eric Russell v Pakistanis at Lord's in 1967
Best batting: 201* Nottinghamshire v Glamorgan, Trent Bridge 1973
Best bowling: 4-16 Nottinghamshire v Warwickshire, Trent Bridge 1969

First-Class Career Performances

	M	Inns	NO	Runs	HS	Avge	100s	Ct	St	Runs	Wkts	Avge	Best	5wI	10wM
Test															
All First	344	581	58	19196	201 *	36.70	41	288	14	3459	79	43.78	4-16	-	-

HOLDER, J. W.

Name: John Wakefield Holder
Role: Right-hand bat, right-arm
fast-medium bowler
Born: 19 March 1945,
St George, Barbados
Height: 6ft **Weight:** 13st
Nickname: Benson
Appointed to 1st-class list: 1983
Appointed to Test panel: 1988
Tests umpired: 10
One-Day Internationals umpired: 8
County: Hampshire
County debut: 1968
50 wickets in a season: 1
1st-Class 5 w. in innings: 5
1st-Class 10 w. in match: 1
1st-Class catches: 12
Parents: Charles and Carnetta
Wife: Glenda
Children: Christopher 1968; Nigel 1970
Family links with cricket: Both sons have played for Royston in the Central Lancashire
League
Education: St Giles Boys School; Combermere High School, Barbados
Qualifications: 3 O-levels, MCC advanced cricket coach
Career outside cricket: Financial consultant
Off-season: Working as a financial consultant for Albany Life
Other sports followed: Football (Manchester United)
Cricketers particularly admired: Garfield Sobers, Richard Hadlee
Cricketers particularly learnt from: Encouraged by Everton Weekes as a schoolboy
Extras: Recorded best bowling figures in Rothmans International Cavaliers cricket
matches – 6-7 for Hampshire Cavaliers at Tichbourne Park in 1968. Played professional
league cricket in Yorkshire and Lancashire (1974-82). Took one first-class hat-trick,
Hampshire v Kent 1972, 'but finished with 3-100!'
Best batting: 33 Hampshire v Sussex, Hove 1971
Best bowling: 7-79 Hampshire v Gloucestershire, Gloucester 1972

First-Class Career Performances

	M	Inns	NO	Runs	HS	Avge	100s	Ct	St	Runs	Wkts	Avge	Best	5wI	10wM
Test															
All First	47	49	14	374	33	10.68	-	12	-	3415	139	24.56	7-79	5	1

HOLDER, V. A.

Name: Vanburn Alonza Holder
Role: Right-hand bat, right-arm
fast-medium bowler
Born: 8 October 1945,
St Michael, Barbados
Nickname: Van
Appointed to 1st-class list: 1992
County: Worcestershire
County debut: 1968
County cap: 1970
Test debut: 1969
Tests: 40
1st-Class 50s scored: 4
1st-Class 100s scored: 1
1st-Class 5 w. in innings: 38
1st-Class 10 w. in match: 3
1st-Class catches: 98
Overseas tours: West Indies to England
1969, 1973, 1976; to India Sri Lanka and

Pakistan 1974-75; Australia 1975-76; India and Sri Lanka 1978-79 (as vice-captain)
Extras: Made his debut for Barbados in the Shell Shield competition in 1966-67.
Best batting: 122 Barbados v Trinidad, Bridgetown 1973-74
Best bowling: 7-40 Worcestershire v Glamorgan, Cardiff 1974

First-Class Career Performances

	M	Inns	NO	Runs	HS	Avge	100s	Ct	St	Runs	Wkts	Avge	Best	5wI	10wM
Test	40	59	11	682	42	14.20	-	16	-	3627	109	33.27	6-28	3	-
All First	311	354	81	3559	122	13.03	1	98	-	23183	948	24.45	7-40	38	3

JONES, A. A.

Name: Alan Arthur Jones
Role: Right-hand bat, right-arm
fast-medium bowler
Born: 9 December 1947, Horley, Surrey
Height: 6ft 3in **Weight:** 14st
Nickname: Jonah
Appointed to 1st-class list: 1985
Counties: Sussex, Somerset,
Middlesex, Glamorgan
County debut: 1966 (Sussex);
1970 (Somerset); 1976 (Middlesex);
1980 (Glamorgan)
County cap: 1972 (Somerset);
1976 (Middlesex); 1980 (Glamorgan)
50 wickets in a season: 4
1st-Class 5 w. in innings: 23
1st-Class 10 w. in match: 3
1st-Class catches: 50
Parents: Leslie and Hazel
Marital status: Married
Education: St John's College, Horsham
Qualifications: 5 O-levels, MCC Advanced Coach, NCA Staff Coach
Career outside cricket: 'None at present'
Off-season: 'Generally enjoying life'
Overseas teams played for: Northern Transvaal 1972-73; Orange Free State 1976-77
Other sports followed: All sports
Cricketers particularly admired: Tom Cartwright
Cricketers particularly learnt from: Mike Brearley
Relaxations: Golf
Opinions on cricket: 'I would like to see the return of uncovered wickets in first-class
cricket.'
Best batting: 33 Middlesex v Kent, Canterbury 1978
Best bowling: 9-51 Somerset v Sussex, Hove 1976

First-Class Career Performances

	M	Inns	NO	Runs	HS	Avge	100s	Ct	St	Runs	Wkts	Avge	Best	5wI	10wM
Test															
All First	214	216	68	799	33	5-39	-	50	-	15414	549	28.07	9-51	23	3

JULIAN, R.

Name: Raymond Julian
Role: Right-hand bat, wicket-keeper
Born: 23 August 1936,
Cosby, Leicestershire
Height: 5ft 11in **Weight:** 13st
Nickname: Julie
Appointed to 1st-class list: 1972
County: Leicestershire
County debut: 1953
County cap: 1961
1st-Class 50s scored: 2
1st-Class catches: 382
1st-Class stumpings: 39
Parents: George Ernest and Doris
Children:
Peter Raymond, 1 February 1958;
John Kelvin, 13 October 1960;
David Andrew, 15 October 1963;
Paul Anthony, 22 September 1967
Education: Wigston Secondary Modern
Career outside cricket: Cricket coach, painter, gardener
Cricketing superstitions or habits: Always put left shoe on first
Other sports followed: All sports. Played goalkeeper at football. First-class football referee for 15 years. Linesman on Southern League. Refereed one FA Cup fixture
Cricketers particularly admired: Gary Sobers, Keith Andrew
Cricketers particularly learnt from: Tony Lock, Willie Watson, Keith Andrew, Maurice Hallam
Relaxations: Gardening, holidays, travelling
Extras: Youngest player to make debut for Leicestershire (aged 15 years). Gave 8 lbw decisions in succession, Glamorgan v Sussex at Cardiff 1986. Played for the Army 1955-57. Has umpired three B&H semi-finals and one Gillette Cup semi-final. Took 6 catches in an innings, Leicestershire v Northants, Kettering 1965. Has been stand-by umpire for two Test matches
Opinions on cricket: 'Enjoy all cricket – believe in four-day cricket.'
Best batting: 51 Leicestershire v Worcestershire, Worcester 1962

First-Class Career Performances

	M	Inns	NO	Runs	HS	Avge	100s	Ct	St	Runs	Wkts	Avge	Best	5wI	10wM
Test															
All First	192	288	23	2581	51	9.73	-	381	40						

KITCHEN, M. J.

Name: Mervyn John Kitchen
Role: Left-hand bat, right-arm medium bowler
Born: 1 August 1940, Nailsea, Somerset
Appointed to 1st-class list: 1982
Appointed to Test panel: 1990
Tests umpired: 3
One-Day Internationals umpired: 3
County: Somerset
County debut: 1960
County cap: 1966
Testimonial: 1973
1000 runs in a season: 7
1st-Class 50s scored: 68
1st-Class 100s scored: 17
1st-Class catches: 157
One-Day 50s: 22
One-Day 100s: 1
Education: Blackwell Secondary Modern, Nailsea
Best batting: 189 Somerset v Pakistan, Taunton 1967

First-Class Career Performances

	M	Inns	NO	Runs	HS	Avge	100s	Ct	St	Runs	Wkts	Avge	Best	5wI	10wM
Test															
All First	354	612	32	15230	189	26.25	17	157	-	109	2	54.50	1-4	-	-

LEADBEATER, B.

Name: Barrie Leadbeater
Role: Right-hand opening bat, right-arm medium bowler, slip fielder
Born: 14 August 1943, Leeds
Height: 6ft **Weight:** 13st
Nickname: Leady
Appointed to 1st-class list: 1981
County: Yorkshire
County debut: 1966
County cap: 1969
Benefit: 1980 (joint benefit with G.A. Cope)
1st-Class 50s scored: 27
1st-Class 100s scored: 1
1st-Class catches: 82
One-Day 50s: 11
Parents: Ronnie (deceased) and Nellie
Wife and date of marriage: Jacqueline, 18 September 1971
Children: Richard Barrie, 23 November 1972; Michael Spencer, 21 March 1976; Daniel Mark Ronnie, 19 June 1981
Education: Brownhill County Primary; Harehills Secondary Modern, Leeds
Qualifications: 2 O-levels
Career outside cricket: Coach, driver
Overseas tours: Duke of Norfolk's XI to West Indies 1970
Overseas teams played for: Johannesburg Municipals 1978-79
Other sports followed: Rugby union, most other sports
Cricketers particularly admired: Colin Cowdrey, Clive Rice, Richard Hadlee, Gary Sobers, Michael Holding
Cricketers learnt from: Brian Close, Willie Watson, Arthur Mitchell, Maurice Leyland
Relaxations: Family, car maintenance, DIY, music
Opinions on cricket: 'Disappointed in players who lack self-control and professional pride and set bad examples to young players and public alike. Public should be regularly and properly informed during stoppages in play. Stoppages for bad light cause more frustration for public, players and, not least, umpires and a change in regulations may be needed soon if the game is to retain its support and credibility.'
Best batting: 140* Yorkshire v Hampshire, Portsmouth 1976

First-Class Career Performances

	M	Inns	NO	Runs	HS	Avge	100s	Ct	St	Runs	Wkts	Avge	Best	5wI	10wM
Test															
All First	147	241	29	5373	140 *	25.34	1	82	-	5	1	5.00	1-1	-	-

MEYER, B. J.

Name: Barrie John Meyer
Role: Right-hand bat, wicket-keeper
Born: 21 August 1931, Bournemouth
Height: 5ft 10¹/₂in **Weight:** 12st 5lbs
Nickname: BJ
Appointed to 1st-class list: 1973
Appointed to Test panel: 1978
Tests umpired: 23
One-Day Internationals umpired: 21
County: Gloucestershire
County debut: 1957
County cap: 1958
Benefit: 1971
1st-Class 50s scored: 11
1st-Class catches: 707
1st-Class stumpings: 118
Parents: Deceased
Wife and date of marriage: Gillian,
4 September 1965

Children: Stephen Barrie; Christopher John; Adrian Michael
Education: Boscombe Secondary School, Bournemouth
Career outside cricket: Salesman
Off-season: Coaching and umpiring in South Africa
Other sports followed: Golf (handicap 8), football (was a pro-footballer for Bristol Rovers, Plymouth Argyle, Newport County and Bristol City)
Cricketers particularly learnt from: Andy Wilson and Sonny Avery (coaches for Gloucestershire)
Relaxations: Golf, music, reading
Best batting: 63 (3 times) Gloucestershire v Indians, Cheltenham 1959; Gloucestershire v Oxford University, Bristol 1962; Gloucestershire v Sussex, Bristol 1964

First-Class Career Performances

	M	Inns	NO	Runs	HS	Avge	100s	Ct	St	Runs	Wkts	Avge	Best	5wI	10wM
Test															
All First	406	569	191	5367	63	14.19	-	707	118						

OSLEAR, D. O.

Name: Donald Osmund Oslear
Role: Right-hand bat, right-arm medium bowler
Born: 3 March 1929, Cleethorpes, Lincolnshire
Height: 6ft **Weight:** 14st 7lbs
Appointed to 1st-class list: 1975
Appointed to Test panel: 1980
Tests umpired: 5
One-Day Internationals umpired: 14
Parents: John Osmund and Violet Maude
Education: Elliston Street Senior School, Cleethorpes
Career outside cricket: Wholesale fish distribution, Grimsby
Off-season: 'In Sri Lanka helping their umpires and administrators to enhance their knowledge of the Laws of Cricket and standing in their four-day domestic tournament.'
Other sports followed: Professional soccer, ice hockey – 'I watch most sports.'
Cricketers particularly admired: Jimmy Cook, Garth Le Roux
Relaxations: Study of the Laws of Cricket and first-class playing regulations
Extras: Has umpired 4 one-day internationals in Zimbabwe
Opinions on cricket: 'One of the best things in recent years is the fact that South Africa will be playing again at the highest level. The worst thing will be the introduction of an independent panel of umpires.'

Did not play first-class cricket

PALMER, K. E.

Name: Kenneth Ernest Palmer
Role: Right-hand bat, right-arm
fast-medium bowler
Born: 22 April 1937, Winchester
Height: 5ft 10in **Weight:** 13st
Nickname: Pedlar
Appointed to 1st-class list: 1972
Appointed to Test panel: 1978
Tests umpired: 19
One-Day Internationals umpired: 8
County: Somerset
County debut: 1955
County cap: 1958
Testimonial: 1968
Test debut: 1965
Tests: 1
1000 runs in a season: 1
50 wickets in a season: 6
1st-Class 50s scored: 27
1st-Class 100s scored: 2
1st-Class 5 w. in innings: 46
1st-Class 10 w. in match: 5
1st-Class catches: 156
Parents: Harry and Cecilia

Wife and date of marriage: Wife deceased
Children: Gary Vincent, 6 September 1961
Education: Southbroom Secondary Modern, Devizes
Off-season: Decorating and gardening at home
Overseas tours: Commonwealth XI to Pakistan 1962; International Cavaliers to West Indies 1963-64
Other sports followed: Football and squash
Cricketers particularly admired: Gary Sobers, Richard Hadlee, Viv Richards, David Gower, Michael Holding, Malcolm Marshall
Cricketers particularly learnt from: Father and Maurice Tremlett
Relaxations: Car enthusiast
Extras: Called into Test side while coaching in South Africa 1964-65. Umpired two Benson and Hedges finals and two NatWest finals. Twice on World Cup panel in England. Won Carling Single Wicket Competition 1961. Did the 'double' in 1961 (114 wickets, 1036 runs). With Bill Alley holds the Somerset record for 6th wicket partnership.
Best batting: 125* Somerset v Northamptonshire, Northampton 1961
Best bowling: 9-57 Somerset v Nottinghamshire, Trent Bridge 1963

First-Class Career Performances

	M	Inns	NO	Runs	HS	Avge	100s	Ct	St	Runs	Wkts	Avge	Best	5wl	10wM
Test	1	1	0	10	10	10.00	-	-	-	189	1	189.00	1-113	-	-
All First	314	481	105	7771	125 *	20.66	2	156	-	18485	866	21.34	9-57	46	5

PALMER, R.

Name: Roy Palmer
Role: Right-hand bat, right-arm
fast-medium bowler
Born: 12 July 1942, Devizes, Wiltshire
Appointed to 1st-class list: 1980
County: Somerset
County debut: 1965
50 wickets in a season: 1
1st-Class 50s scored: 1
1st-Class 5 w. in innings: 4
1st-Class catches: 25
Family links with cricket: Brother of
Ken Palmer, Test umpire and former
Somerset player, nephew Gary also
played for Somerset
Education: Southbroom Secondary
Modern, Devizes
Best batting:
84 Somerset v Leicestershire, Taunton 1967
Best bowling: 6-45 Somerset v Middlesex, Lord's 1967

First-Class Career Performances

	M	Inns	NO	Runs	HS	Avge	100s	Ct	St	Runs	Wkts	Avge	Best	5wl	10wM
Test															
All First	74	110	32	1037	84	13.29	-	25	-	5439	172	31.62	6-45	4	-

PLEWS, N. T.

Name: Nigel Trevor Plews
Role: Right-hand opening bat
Born: 5 September 1934, Nottingham
Height: 6ft 6½in **Weight:** 16st 8lbs
Appointed to 1st-class list: 1982
Appointed to Test panel: 1988
Tests umpired: 5
One-Day Internationals umpired: 4
Parents: Deceased
Wife and date of marriage:
Margaret, 1956
Children: Elaine, 1961; Douglas, 1964
Education: Mundella Grammar School,
Nottingham
Qualifications: School Certificate in
Commercial Subjects, RSA Advanced
Book-keeping
Career outside cricket: Nottingham City
Police for 25 years (Det Sgt in Fraud Squad)

Off-season: Employed by Touche Ross, Chartered Accountants, in insolvency work, as
every year since 1980
Other sports played: Table tennis, swimming, soccer
Other sports followed: Rugby union
Relaxations: Hill-walking, reading, travel
Extras: Played local league and club cricket in Nottingham. Toured as umpire with MCC
to Namibia 1991

Did not play first-class cricket

SHARP, G.

Name: George Sharp
Role: Right-hand bat, wicket-keeper
Born: 12 March 1950,
Hartlepool, County Durham
Height: 5ft 11in **Weight:** 15st
Nickname: Blunt, Razor, Sharpie
Appointed to 1st-class list: 1992
County: Northamptonshire
County debut: 1967
County cap: 1972
1st-Class catches: 565
1st-Class stumpings: 90
Parents: George and Grace
Wife: Audrey
Children: Gareth (aged 7)
Off-season: Working in Sales
Other sports followed: Most ball games
Cricketers particularly admired: Alan
Knott, Bob Taylor, Keith Andrew
Relaxations: Golf
Best batting: 98 Northamptonshire v Yorkshire, Northampton 1983

First-Class Career Performances

	M	Inns	NO	Runs	HS	Avge	100s	Ct	St	Runs	Wkts	Avge	Best	5wI	10wM
Test															
All First	306	396	81	6254	98	19.85	-	565	90	70	1	70.00	1-47	-	-

SHEPHERD, D. R.

Name: David Robert Shepherd
Role: Right-hand bat, right-arm
medium bowler
Born: 27 December 1940,
Bideford, Devon
Height: 5ft 10in **Weight:** 16st
Nickname: Shep
Appointed to 1st-class list: 1981
Appointed to Test panel: 1985
Tests umpired: 13
One-Day Internationals umpired: 'over 40'
County: Gloucestershire
County debut: 1965
County cap: 1969
Benefit: 1978 (joint benefit with J. Davey)
1000 runs in a season: 2
1st-Class 50s scored: 55
1st-Class 100s scored: 12
1st-Class catches: 95
One-Day 50s: 18
One-Day 100s: 2
Parents: Herbert and Doris (both deceased)
Marital status: Single
Education: Barnstable Grammar School; St Luke's College, Exeter
Career outside cricket: Teacher
Off-season: Assisting brother in local post office/newsagent. Umpiring World Cup in Australia/New Zealand
Cricketing superstitions or habits: 111 (Nelson!)
Other sports followed: Rugby, soccer, most ball sports
Cricketers particularly admired: Gary Sobers, Mike Procter
Relaxations: All sports, philately, TV
Extras: Played Minor Counties cricket for Devon 1959-64. Only Gloucestershire player to score a century on his first-class debut. Umpired the MCC Bi-Centenary Test, England v Rest of the World, at Lord's in 1987
Best batting: 153 Gloucestershire v Middlesex, Bristol 1968

First-Class Career Performances

	M	Inns	NO	Runs	HS	Avge	100s	Ct	St	Runs	Wkts	Avge	Best	5wl	10wM
Test															
All First	282	476	40	10672	153	24.47	12	95	-	106	2	53.00	1-1	-	-

STICKLEY, G. A.

Name: Gerald Albert Stickley
Role: Right-hand bat, wicket-keeper
Born: 24 September 1938, Birmingham
Height: 5ft 9¹/₂in **Weight:** 12st 6lbs
Appointed to 1st-class list: 1992
Parents: Albert and Dora (both deceased)
Wife: Janet
Children: Mark (aged 29), Diane (27),
Alan (21)
Education: Grammar school,
West Midlands
Career outside cricket: British Telecom
engineer; local government officer
(Social Services Dept)
Off-season: Employed by
Dorset County Council
Other sports followed: Soccer,
table tennis, golf
Cricketers particularly admired:
Jimmy Cook

Relaxations: Listening to music, especially jazz, reading
Opinions on cricket: 'Cricket should be entertaining with more thought given to the
paying spectator.'

Did not play first-class cricket

TOLCHARD, R. C.

Name: Raymond Charles Tolchard
Role: Left-hand bat, right-arm
medium bowler
Born: 13 October 1953, Torquay, Devon
Height: 5ft 10¹/₂in **Weight:** 13st
Appointed to 1st-class list: 1991
Wife: Sharon
Children: Samuel Thomas, 1989;
Sophie Jane 1991
Parents: Tom and Dorothy
Family links with cricket: Brother J.G.
played for Devon and Leicestershire,
and brother R.G. played for Devon,
Leicestershire and England
Education: Malvern College, Worcs
Career outside cricket: Hotel manager,
owns hairdressing salon in partnership
with his wife
Off-season: 'Baby-sitting!'
Other sports followed: Bowls (father and grandmother played bowls for England,
Cricketers particularly learnt from: 'My two brothers, Roger and Jeff.'
Relaxations: Indoor bowls
Extras: Played Minor Counties cricket for Devon 1975-84 (cap 1977). Played for
Leicestershire 2nd XI in 1977 and represented Minor Counties (South) in the B&H Cup
in 1979. Scored 100 against Durham in 1978 to win play-off for the Minor Counties
Championship for Devon

Did not play first-class cricket

---

200. Who scored 237 and took 12 wickets in the same match in 1891?

WHITE, R. A.

Name: Robert Arthur White
Role: Left-hand bat, off-break bowler
Born: 6 October 1936, Fulham
Height: 5ft 9½in **Weight:** 12st 4lbs
Nickname: Knocker
Appointed to 1st-class list: 1982
Counties: Middlesex, Nottinghamshire
County debut: 1958 (Middlesex);
1966 (Nottinghamshire)
County cap: 1963 (Middlesex);
1966 (Nottinghamshire)
Benefit: 1974
1000 runs in a season: 1
50 wickets in a season: 2
1st-Class 50s scored: 50
1st-Class 100s scored: 5
1st-Class 5 w. in innings: 28
1st-Class 10 w. in match: 4
1st-Class catches: 190
Wife: Janice
Children: Robin and Vanessa
Education: Chiswick Grammar School
Qualifications: Matriculation
Career outside cricket: Self-employed salesman
Other sports followed: All sports – soccer, ice-hockey and horse racing in particular
Cricketers particularly admired: 'Garfield Sobers more than anyone else.'
Cricketers particularly learnt from: 'I tried to learn from everyone I encountered.'
Relaxations: Theatre-going
Extras: Made independent coaching trips to South Africa, 1959, 1960, 1966, 1967, 1968.
Together with M.J. Smedley broke the Nottinghamshire record for a 6th wicket partnership
with 204 v Surrey at The Oval 1966
Opinions on cricket: 'Too controversial to go into print.'
Best batting: 116* Nottinghamshire v Surrey, The Oval 1967
Best bowling: 7-41 Nottinghamshire v Derbyshire, Ilkeston 1971

First-Class Career Performances

	M	Inns	NO	Runs	HS	Avge	100s	Ct	St	Runs	Wkts	Avge	Best	5wI	10wM
Test															
All First	413	642	105	12452	116 *	23.18	5	190	-	21138	693	30.50	7-41	28	4

WHITEHEAD, A. G. T.

Name: Alan Geoffrey Thomas Whitehead
Role: Left-hand bat,
slow left-arm bowler
Born: 28 October 1940,
Butleigh, Somerset
Appointed to 1st-class list: 1970
Appointed to Test panel: 1982
Tests umpired: 5
County: Somerset
County debut: 1957
1st-Class 5 w. in innings: 3
1st-Class catches: 20
Best batting: 15 Somerset v Hampshire,
Southampton 1959
Best bowling: 6-74 Somerset v Sussex,
Eastbourne 1959

First-Class Career Performances

	M	Inns	NO	Runs	HS	Avge	100s	Ct	St	Runs	Wkts	Avge	Best	5wI	10wM
Test															
All First	38	49	25	137	15	5.70	-	20	-	2306	67	34.41	6-74	3	-

WIGHT, P. B.

Name: Peter Bernard Wight
Role: Right-hand bat, off-break bowler
Born: 25 June 1930,
Georgetown, British Guiana
Height: 5ft 10in **Weight:** 11st
Nickname: Flipper
Appointed to 1st-class list: 1966
County: Somerset
County debut: 1953
County cap: 1954
Benefit: 1963
1000 runs in a season: 10

1st-Class 50s scored: 207
1st-Class 100s scored: 26
1st-Class 200s scored: 2
1st-Class 5 w. in innings: 1
1st-Class catches: 204
Parents: Henry DeLisle and Mary Matilda
Wife and date of marriage: Joyce,
26 January 1957
Children: Paul Anthony and Anne-Marie
Family links with cricket: Three brothers
played for British Guiana
and one, G.L., played for the West Indies
Education: St Stanislaus College
Career outside cricket: Owns his own
indoor cricket school
Off-season: Coaching and running his
indoor school
Other sports followed: Football, hockey,
squash, skittles, 'all ball games'
Cricketers particularly admired: Alec Bedser,
Gary Sobers, Peter May, Ken Barrington, Tony Lock, Everton Weekes, Frank Worrell
Relaxations: Gardening, all kinds of sport
Extras: Has coached in East Africa and New Zealand. 'Encouraged in cricket by my father
and brothers – Arnold, Norman and Leslie.'
Opinions on cricket: 'A game to be played and enjoyed by all. I am proud to be President
of Somerset Wanderers Ladies Cricket Club.'
Best batting: 222 Somerset v Kent, Taunton 1959
Best bowling: 6-29 Somerset v Derbyshire, Chesterfield 1957

First-Class Career Performances

	M	Inns	NO	Runs	HS	Avge	100s	Ct	St	Runs	Wkts	Avge	Best	5wI	10wM
Test															
All First	333	590	53	17773	222 *	33.09	28	204	-	2262	68	33.26	6-29	1	-

WILLEY, P.

Appointed to 1st-class list: On reserve list for 1992
(see player's entry on page 550)

BRITANNIC ASSURANCE CHAMPIONSHIP

Final Table

		P	W	L	D	T	Bt	Bl	Pts
1	Essex (2)	22	11	5	6	0	69	67	312
2	Warwickshire (5)	22	11	4	7	0	58	65	299
3	Derbyshire (12)	22	9	5	8	0	46	68	258
4	Notts (13)	22	7	5	10	0	64	69	245
5	Surrey (9)	22	8	6	8	0	47	66	241
6	Worcestershire (4)	22	6	4	12	0	54	59	209
	Kent (16)	22	6	3	12	1	50	55	209
8	Lancashire (6)	22	6	9	7	0	60	49	205
9	Hampshire (3)	22	5	7	10	0	57	56	193
10	Northants (11)	22	5	6	11	0	55	54	189
11	Sussex (17)	22	4	3	14	1	57	60	189
12	Glamorgan (8)	22	5	5	12	0	50	57	187
13	Gloucestershire (13)	22	5	10	7	0	42	53	175
14	Yorkshire (10)	22	4	6	12	0	58	37	159
15	Middlesex (1)	22	3	9	10	0	48	63	159
16	Leicestershire (7)	22	3	8	11	0	46	53	147
17	Somerset (15)	22	2	5	15	0	66	45	143

1990 positions shown in brackets

BENSON & HEDGES CUP

Winners: Worcestershire
Runners-up: Lancashire
Losing semi-finalists: Essex and Yorkshire

NATWEST TROPHY

Winners: Hampshire
Runners-up: Surrey
Losing semi-finalists: Warwickshire and Northamptonshire

REFUGE ASSURANCE LEAGUE

Final Table

		P	W	L	T	NR	Away Wins	Pts	Run Rate	Runs	Balls
1	Notts (4)	16	13	3	0	0	7	52	83.47	3040	3642
2	Lancashire (2)	16	12	3	0	1	8	50	89.78	2908	3239
3	Northants (17)	16	10	4	0	2	3	44	86.26	2826	3276
4	Worcs (10)	16	9	4	1	2	4	42	95.16	3206	3369
5	Warwicks (14)	16	8	4	1	3	4	40	82.53	2339	2834
6	Essex (12)	16	7	4	1	4	1	38	84.41	2541	3010
7	Yorkshire (6)	16	9	7	0	0	4	36	86.38	3116	3607
8	Surrey (7)	16	7	7	0	2	5	32	81.94	2764	3373
9	Somerset (8)	16	7	7	0	2	4	32	80.85	2771	3427
10	Kent (11)	16	6	8	1	1	2	28	87.46	3020	3453
11	Middlesex (3)	16	6	9	0	1	4	26	79.15	2756	3482
12	Gloucs (9)	16	5	9	0	2	4	24	77.68	2541	3271
13	Sussex (13)	16	5	9	0	2	3	24	81.42	2625	3224
14	Leics (16)	16	5	10	0	1	3	22	78.29	2676	3418
15	Derbyshire (1)	16	5	11	0	0	2	20	84.38	2930	3472
16	Glamorgan (15)	16	4	10	0	2	1	20	82.61	3026	3663
17	Hampshire (5)	16	3	12	0	1	1	14	79.24	2802	3536

1990 positions shown in brackets

REFUGE ASSURANCE CUP

Winners: Lancashire
Runners-up: Worcestershire
Losing semi-finalists: Northamptonshire and Nottinghamshire

1991 AVERAGES (all first-class matches)

BATTING AVERAGES - Including fielding
Qualifying requirements : 6 completed innings and averages over 30.00

Name	Matches	Inns	NO	Runs	HS	Avge	100s	50s	Ct	St
C.L.Hooper	16	25	9	1501	196	93.81	5	8	20	-
S.J.Cook	24	42	8	2755	210 *	81.02	11	8	16	-
M.W.Gatting	22	39	11	2057	215 *	73.46	8	6	14	-
Salim Malik	24	36	9	1972	215	73.03	6	8	25	-
G.A.Gooch	20	31	4	1911	259	70.77	6	6	22	-
R.B.Richardson	15	26	5	1403	135 *	66.81	6	6	14	-
C.L.Smith	16	27	3	1553	200	64.70	6	7	4	-
D.A.Leatherdale	5	6	0	379	157	63.16	1	2	4	-
T.M.Moody	22	34	4	1887	210	62.90	6	9	37	-
D.W.Randall	22	34	9	1567	143 *	62.68	5	5	15	-
M.P.Maynard	23	36	6	1803	243	60.10	7	5	18	-
A.P.Wells	22	36	6	1784	253 *	59.46	7	5	7	-
M.Azharuddin	22	39	5	2016	212	59.29	7	10	24	-
I.V.A.Richards	12	18	4	817	131	58.35	1	6	9	-
G.J.Turner	8	8	2	349	101 *	58.16	1	2	1	-
R.T.Robinson	22	37	8	1673	180	57.69	3	10	18	-
N.R.Taylor	23	36	4	1806	203 *	56.43	7	7	14	-
N.Hussain	25	33	8	1354	196	54.16	3	8	38	-
R.A.Smith	16	30	4	1397	148 *	53.73	3	11	15	-
S.T.Jayasuriya	6	11	2	482	100 *	53.55	1	3	-	-
C.J.Tavare	23	37	7	1601	183	53.36	5	7	20	-
H.Morris	23	41	7	1803	156 *	53.02	5	8	17	-
C.B.Lambert	7	13	2	551	116	50.09	1	4	5	-
B.C.Broad	21	38	3	1739	166	49.68	5	7	9	-
N.V.Knight	7	10	1	441	101 *	49.00	1	3	5	-
P.Johnson	23	37	7	1454	124	48.46	3	11	12	-
D.A.Reeve	20	33	7	1260	99 *	48.46	-	14	19	-
R.J.Shastri	22	32	9	1108	133 *	48.17	2	7	9	-
M.R.Benson	20	30	2	1329	257	47.46	4	6	9	-
D.J.Bicknell	24	42	2	1888	151	47.20	5	9	11	-
K.D.James	24	37	10	1274	134 *	47.18	2	6	9	-
A.Fordham	24	42	3	1840	165	47.17	4	9	8	-
J.P.Crawley	12	20	2	849	130	47.16	1	8	13	-
M.A.Garnham	25	29	8	986	123	46.95	3	5	62	-
T.R.Ward	22	34	2	1493	235 *	46.65	5	6	10	-
M.D.Moxon	21	37	1	1669	200	46.36	3	12	17	-
N.H.Fairbrother	19	29	6	1064	121	46.26	5	3	19	-

Name	Matches	Inns	NO	Runs	HS	Avge	100s	50s	Ct	St
A.J.Wright	25	41	6	1596	120	45.60	3	10	19	-
A.R.Butcher	23	39	2	1677	147	45.32	4	13	13	-
C.W.J.Athey	25	40	6	1522	127	44.76	5	9	18	-
T.S.Curtis	25	40	3	1653	248	44.67	3	9	15	-
A.J.Stewart	19	34	8	1161	113 *	44.65	2	6	24	-
D.Byas	24	41	6	1557	153	44.48	5	2	21	-
R.J.Harden	24	39	8	1355	134	43.71	3	9	21	-
I.T.Botham	13	21	3	785	161	43.61	2	4	12	-
D.R.Pringle	19	21	7	607	78 *	43.35	-	4	9	-
D.M.Smith	20	35	6	1238	126 *	42.69	2	8	14	-
D.L.Haynes	13	22	5	721	151	42.41	1	4	4	-
A.M.Hooper	7	12	1	458	125	41.63	1	2	-	-
G.P.Thorpe	23	38	9	1203	177	41.48	4	4	8	-
A.Dale	17	26	5	869	140	41.38	1	5	8	-
J.E.Morris	21	36	2	1398	131	41.11	2	8	8	-
M.A.Atherton	14	23	3	820	138	41.00	3	2	10	-
A.R.Roberts	14	15	9	244	48	40.66	-	-	7	-
D.M.Ward	23	40	6	1372	151	40.35	1	10	10	-
P.J.L.Dujon	11	14	3	439	142 *	39.90	1	2	21	-
M.P.Speight	14	20	1	754	149	39.68	1	5	6	-
R.J.Bailey	21	36	5	1224	117	39.48	1	11	10	-
G.R.Cowdrey	22	34	4	1175	114	39.16	3	5	17	-
N.E.Briers	24	43	5	1485	160	39.07	4	7	18	-
S.P.Titchard	8	15	1	546	135	39.00	1	2	8	-
V.P.Terry	20	35	3	1244	171	38.87	2	7	24	-
A.J.Lamb	19	30	2	1081	194	38.60	3	5	21	-
P.V.Simmons	15	28	1	1031	136	38.18	3	4	13	-
P.E.Robinson	24	41	7	1293	189	38.02	2	8	20	-
J.J.Whitaker	23	37	3	1289	105	37.91	1	8	14	-
K.J.Barnett	24	39	2	1399	217	37.81	2	9	25	-
M.A.Roseberry	24	44	4	1511	123 *	37.77	2	8	20	-
B.F.Smith	15	23	5	674	71	37.44	-	3	3	-
J.P.Stephenson	25	41	3	1421	116	37.39	3	8	7	-
M.R.Ramprakash	21	36	4	1174	119	36.68	2	7	6	-
D.P.Ostler	22	40	5	1284	120 *	36.68	1	10	21	-
G.D.Mendis	23	43	5	1394	127 *	36.68	4	3	8	-
W.Larkins	9	16	6	365	75	36.50	-	2	6	-
N.J.Lenham	19	33	3	1091	193	36.36	3	4	11	-
P.J.Prichard	24	38	7	1124	190	36.25	4	3	19	-
S.A.Kellett	24	40	5	1266	125 *	36.17	2	8	19	-
N.A.Stanley	8	13	0	470	132	36.15	1	2	5	-
J.D.R.Benson	9	12	1	393	133 *	35.72	1	1	9	-
P.D.Bowler	24	44	3	1458	104 *	35.56	2	11	15	-
B.T.P.Donelan	13	15	5	353	61	35.30	-	2	3	-

Name	Matches	Inns	NO	Runs	HS	Avge	100s	50s	Ct	St
S.J.Rhodes	24	33	6	942	90	34.88	-	8	54	8
G.D.Rose	15	20	3	590	106	34.70	2	2	8	-
D.I.Gower	23	38	5	1142	80 *	34.60	-	8	13	-
K.M.Curran	21	31	7	828	89 *	34.50	-	6	12	-
C.C.Lewis	16	20	2	621	73	34.50	-	4	9	-
K.R.Brown	24	41	6	1184	143 *	33.82	1	6	36	-
A.N.Hayhurst	19	32	5	910	172 *	33.70	3	1	5	-
S.A.Marsh	23	32	5	910	113 *	33.70	2	5	66	4
A.J.Moles	22	39	2	1246	133	33.67	1	10	10	-
C.M.Wells	14	21	6	503	76	33.53	-	3	3	-
P.Pollard	23	41	3	1255	145	33.02	3	4	21	-
P.A.De Silva	5	7	1	198	57 *	33.00	-	1	4	-
R.I.Alikhan	19	34	2	1055	96 *	32.96	-	8	10	-
P.N.Hepworth	23	38	4	1119	115	32.91	2	4	19	-
G.A.Hick	22	36	2	1119	186	32.91	3	5	25	-
W.K.Hegg	22	32	8	784	97	32.66	-	3	43	3
T.A.Lloyd	21	35	2	1076	97	32.60	-	10	10	-
D.S.B.P.Kuruppu	7	12	0	389	86	32.41	-	4	3	-
P.M.Roebuck	17	29	3	833	101	32.03	1	5	4	-
M.W.Alleyne	25	40	5	1121	165	32.02	1	6	12	1
J.D.Ratcliffe	17	31	1	953	94	31.76	-	8	15	-
M.V.Fleming	20	32	3	917	116	31.62	2	6	14	-
C.J.Adams	15	24	2	691	134	31.40	2	1	15	-
A.C.Seymour	10	18	1	533	157	31.35	1	3	7	-
T.J.Boon	22	40	2	1185	108	31.18	2	6	11	-
L.Potter	24	37	4	1027	89	31.12	-	7	21	-
U.C.Hathurusinghe	6	11	1	311	74 *	31.10	-	3	2	-
N.D.Burns	23	34	8	808	108	31.07	1	4	35	8
P.Whitticase	20	25	5	620	114 *	31.00	1	4	44	3
S.R.Lampitt	22	23	6	523	93	30.76	-	4	6	-
G.Fowler	19	33	2	953	113	30.74	2	3	2	-
M.C.J.Nicholas	22	37	10	826	107 *	30.59	1	5	10	-
K.Greenfield	9	14	1	394	127 *	30.30	2	1	15	-
M.A.Crawley	11	13	4	272	112	30.22	1	-	14	-
N.M.K.Smith	5	9	2	209	70	29.85	-	2	-	-
T.C.Middleton	18	31	2	864	102	29.79	1	3	15	-
G.D.Hodgson	23	39	2	1101	105	29.75	1	7	8	-
A.A.Metcalfe	24	43	2	1210	123	29.51	2	6	12	-
R.J.Bartlett	5	7	1	177	71	29.50	-	1	3	-
A.P.Gurusinha	6	10	0	292	98	29.20	-	1	2	-
D.Ripley	20	25	9	467	53 *	29.18	-	1	41	2
J.R.Ayling	10	14	3	321	58	29.18	-	2	3	-
M.A.Feltham	13	18	5	375	69 *	28.84	-	1	4	-
S.P.James	11	19	3	461	70	28.81	-	2	8	-

Name	Matches	Inns	NO	Runs	HS	Avge	100s	50s	Ct	St
P.Carrick	21	32	9	662	67	28.78	-	4	3	-
A.I.C.Dodemaide	20	30	9	602	100 *	28.66	1	1	8	-
J.W.Hall	15	26	2	686	117 *	28.58	1	4	8	-
P.Moores	23	28	3	714	102	28.56	1	6	56	5
I.J.F.Hutchinson	14	24	1	656	125	28.52	2	2	14	-
N.A.Foster	22	22	4	513	107 *	28.50	1	1	11	-
N.J.Speak	18	33	3	844	153	28.13	1	2	8	-
R.R.Montgomerie	9	13	2	309	88	28.09	-	4	9	-
E.A.E.Baptiste	18	22	1	589	80	28.04	-	4	9	-
A.N Aymes	24	30	7	644	53	28.00	-	2	51	2
R.G.Williams	8	11	3	224	101 *	28.00	1	-	1	-
D.Gough	13	14	3	307	72	27.90	-	2	3	-
T.J.G.O'Gorman	25	44	4	1116	148	27.90	2	4	21	-
K.H.Macleay	15	21	6	417	63	27.80	-	2	5	-
Wasim Akram	14	19	2	471	122	27.70	1	1	5	-
J.W.Lloyds	24	35	6	803	71 *	27.69	-	8	21	-
R.J.Turner	9	13	4	249	69 *	27.66	-	1	12	1
G.D.Lloyd	18	30	0	829	96	27.63	-	6	11	-
A.L.Logie	12	17	1	433	78	27.06	-	3	7	-
D.B.D'Oliveira	17	24	2	586	237	26.63	1	1	21	-
S.C.Goldsmith	16	26	3	610	127	26.52	1	2	2	-
Asif Din	15	27	1	685	140	26.34	2	1	9	-
K.P.Evans	15	18	7	289	56 *	26.27	-	1	6	-
I.D.Austin	12	16	4	315	101 *	26.25	1	1	4	-
R.P.Lefebvre	16	18	4	366	100	26.14	1	1	6	-
R.J.Blakey	24	38	2	941	196	26.13	1	6	40	5
R.J.Scott	20	34	1	848	127	25.69	2	3	6	-
D.J.Capel	22	33	2	792	100	25.54	1	7	9	-
C.P.Ramanayake	6	8	2	152	41 *	25.33	-	-	1	-
C.Gupte	8	9	1	200	55 *	25.00	-	1	2	-
G.Lovell	9	13	3	250	49	25.00	-	-	6	-
K.T.Medlycott	19	27	2	624	109	24.96	1	4	6	-
P.N.Weekes	6	11	1	249	86	24.90	-	2	5	-
P.A.Neale	14	21	4	419	69 *	24.64	-	1	5	-
B.C.Lara	9	14	0	344	93	24.57	-	3	9	-
M.Watkinson	21	35	4	758	114 *	24.45	1	3	8	-
P.W.G.Parker	16	26	1	607	111	24.28	1	3	8	-
G.Yates	20	26	13	315	100 *	24.23	1	-	8	-
P.Bent	8	13	1	288	100 *	24.00	1	1	3	-
C.M.Tolley	8	10	4	144	36	24.00	-	-	3	-

BOWLING AVERAGES
Qualifying requirements : 10 wickets taken and average below 35.00

Name	Overs	Mdns	Runs	Wkts	Avge	Best	5wI	10wM
Waqar Younis	582	112	1656	113	14.65	7-87	13	3
C.E.L.Ambrose	390	122	869	51	17.03	6-52	3	-
P.W.Jarvis	95	26	235	12	19.58	4-28	-	-
A.A.Donald	522.3	91	1634	83	19.68	6-69	8	2
M.A.Ealham	118.1	24	354	17	20.82	5-39	2	-
N.A.Foster	757.2	185	2138	102	20.96	8-99	7	1
D.A.Reeve	402.1	117	957	45	21.26	6-73	1	-
N.M.Kendrick	105	26	262	12	21.83	5-54	2	1
G.R.Dilley	305.2	62	823	37	22.24	5-91	1	-
Wasim Akram	429.3	99	1251	56	22.33	6-66	7	1
C.M.Tolley	161	39	413	18	22.94	4-69	-	-
N.A.Mallender	349.5	76	969	42	23.07	6-43	3	-
R.J.Shastri	307.5	88	724	31	23.35	5-71	1	-
J.P.Stephenson	106.4	19	399	17	23.47	4-30	-	-
J.R.Ayling	211.1	49	595	25	23.80	4-47	-	-
O.H.Mortensen	559.1	143	1384	58	23.86	6-101	2	-
D.V.Lawrence	515.1	79	1790	74	24.18	6-67	4	1
P.A.J.DeFreitas	657.1	173	1780	73	24.38	7-70	3	-
I.T.Botham	351.1	73	1077	44	24.47	7-54	3	-
K.J.Barnett	211.1	47	496	20	24.80	6-28	1	-
R.D.Stemp	172.1	43	425	17	25.00	4-62	-	-
K.M.Curran	436.2	110	1204	48	25.08	5-60	1	-
P.C.R.Tufnell	903.4	254	2219	88	25.21	7-116	7	1
C.C.Lewis	471.4	127	1213	48	25.27	6-111	3	-
C.Penn	429.4	82	1323	52	25.44	5-43	3	-
T.A.Munton	693.1	184	1863	73	25.52	8-89	5	2
D.G.Cork	494.3	84	1460	57	25.61	8-53	1	1
F.D.Stephenson	719.1	158	2010	78	25.76	5-27	4	1
M.D.Marshall	282.1	57	782	30	26.06	4-33	-	-
R.J.Ratnayake	137.3	15	447	17	26.29	6-97	2	-
C.W.Taylor	147	29	480	18	26.66	3-35	-	-
C.L.Hooper	336.2	71	837	31	27.00	5-94	1	-
A.P.Igglesden	471	94	1351	50	27.02	5-36	1	-
S.R.Barwick	317.5	86	767	28	27.39	4-46	-	-
P.M.Such	370.1	101	933	34	27.44	3-7	-	-
M.J.Gerrard	131.5	20	415	15	27.66	6-40	1	1
D.R.Pringle	533.5	145	1308	47	27.83	5-70	2	-
M.P.Bicknell	470.5	118	1256	45	27.91	7-52	1	-
B.P.Patterson	287.3	68	912	32	28.50	5-81	2	-
P.Carrick	701.2	231	1748	61	28.65	5-13	2	-
M.Frost	533.2	90	1868	65	28.73	7-99	1	1

E.A.E.Baptiste	529.2	122	1443	50	28.86	7-95	3	-
D.R.Gilbert	648.5	137	1865	64	29.14	8-55	1	-
T.A.Merrick	539	101	1787	61	29.29	7-99	1	-
J.H.Childs	751.1	248	1907	65	29.33	6-61	4	-
S.R.Lampitt	503.4	84	1643	56	29.33	5-70	4	-
S.L.Watkin	728.5	155	2175	74	29.39	6-55	4	-
N.V.Radford	434.1	92	1363	46	29.63	7-43	2	-
J.A.North	156.3	26	597	20	29.85	4-47	-	-
G.C.Small	498	126	1347	45	29.93	4-36	-	-
M.J.McCague	153.3	23	481	16	30.06	6-88	1	-
A.I.C.Dodemaide	579	116	1637	54	30.31	5-130	1	-
M.C.J.Ball	186	36	582	19	30.63	5-128	1	-
M.A.Feltham	349.5	57	1075	35	30.71	4-36	-	-
R.A.Pick	650.4	117	2080	67	31.04	5-17	3	-
D.J.Millns	550.1	95	1957	63	31.06	9-37	3	1
Aqib Javed	510.1	84	1656	53	31.24	6-91	3	-
S.J.W.Andrew	399.3	74	1352	43	31.44	4-38	-	-
R.M.Ellison	484.1	102	1480	47	31.48	7-33	2	-
Salim Malik	118.2	10	473	15	31.53	3-26	-	-
C.A.Walsh	324.5	75	915	29	31.55	4-39	-	-
J.N.Maguire	786	168	2437	77	31.64	7-57	4	-
J.A.Afford	670.3	207	1817	57	31.87	4-44	-	-
J.E.Emburey	906.3	246	2170	68	31.91	7-71	1	-
K.P.Evans	425	89	1278	40	31.95	5-52	2	-
T.D.Topley	498.3	86	1767	55	32.12	5-58	3	-
P.J.Newport	712.4	138	2140	66	32.42	4-27	-	-
D.J.Foster	223.5	35	814	25	32.56	6-84	1	-
P.J.Bakker	239.3	65	655	20	32.75	4-66	-	-
L.Tennant	99	20	393	12	32.75	4-54	-	-
A.E.Warner	446.4	101	1215	37	32.83	4-42	-	-
A.A.Barnett	107.4	23	329	10	32.90	4-119	-	-
K.D.James	442.5	99	1354	41	33.02	4-32	-	-
P.N.Hepworth	119.2	20	463	14	33.07	3-51	-	-
J.G.Thomas	278.4	40	937	28	33.46	5-62	2	-
S.C.Goldsmith	187	32	607	18	33.72	3-42	-	-
H.A.G.Anthony	223.3	30	878	26	33.76	3-28	-	-
A.M.Smith	310.2	55	983	29	33.89	4-41	-	-
J.P.Taylor	295.2	50	920	27	34.07	5-42	1	-
N.G.Cowans	542.1	144	1500	44	34.09	4-42	-	-
B.T.P.Donelan	426.3	112	1162	34	34.17	6-62	2	1
P.A.Smith	157.1	31	513	15	34.20	5-28	1	-
A.N.Jones	527.2	74	1918	56	34.25	5-46	2	-
D.E.Malcolm	388.5	53	1451	42	34.54	5-45	1	-
K.T.Medlycott	510.4	115	1703	49	34.75	6-98	2	1
K.H.Macleay	284.3	54	872	25	34.88	3-40	-	-

ANSWERS TO QUIZ

1. Richie Richardson
2. Martyn Moxon
3. David Graveney
4. Martyn Moxon
5. Not a single Derbyshire player scored a first-class century for his county.
6. Geoff Cook
7. Salim Malik
8. Neil Fairbrother
9. Essex
10. Hampshire
11. Hugh Morris
12. Worcestershire
13. Nottinghamshire
14. Basil D'Oliveira
15. Phil Carrick
16. Staffordshire
17. Carl Hooper
18. Waqar Younis
19. Oxfordshire
20. Barry Wood
21. *From Sammy to Jimmy*
22. Colin Metson of Glamorgan
23. Mohammad Azharuddin
24. Graham Gooch, 259 for Essex v Middlesex
25. Chris Adams
26. Nawab of Pataudi
27. Sidath Wettimuny
28. Bob Cottam
29. Neil Foster
30. Somerset
31. Hampshire
32. Trevor Jesty
33. Yorkshire
34. Ravi Shastri
35. Carl Hooper, 28
36. Waqar Younis and Neil Foster
37. Steve Marsh for Kent against Middlesex
38. David Lawrence
39. Kent and Middlesex
40. 1981
41. 1985
42. 1988
43. Tony Middleton
44. Chris Cowdrey
45. Viv Richards
46. Barbados, Desmond Haynes
47. Lance Gibbs, 309
48. Herbert Sutcliffe
49. Mark Ealham
50. Mark Nicholas
51. Alan Butcher
52. Tony Wright
53. Salim Malik
54. He performed the hat trick twice in the same match
55. Wilfred Rhodes, 23
56. Commentator Don Mosey
57. Eastern Province
58. Clive Rice
59. H.K. Foster (1901-10), Norman Gifford (1971-80) and Phil Neale (1982-91)
60. Neil Lenham
61. Wasim Akram
62. J.C. 'Farmer' White
63. Douglas Vivian Parson
64. Frank Worrell
65. Don Wilson
66. Jack Russell
67. The Nissan Shield
68. Angus Fraser
69. Batting for 72 minutes without scoring
70. Geoff Arnold
71. Frank Worrell, Clyde Walcott and Everton Weekes of the West Indies
72. Chris Lewis

73.	They all lived until over 90
74.	Brian Statham
75.	David Hookes
76.	Peter van der Merve
77.	Mike Gatting
78.	Yorkshire, 31
79.	Surrey
80.	David Gower
81.	They each scored a century in their Test debut for Australia
82.	Mark Waugh
83.	Allan Lamb
84.	5
85.	David Gower and John Morris
86.	Nawab of Pataudi
87.	Franklyn Stephenson
88.	Clive Radley
89.	True
90.	Gary Sobers 10, Viv Richards 8
91.	Paul Jarvis
92.	Neil Mallender
93.	Don Bradman, 201.50, Australia v South Africa 1931-32
94.	Jim Laker, 46 in 1956
95.	Warwick Armstrong
96.	Sunil Gavaskar
97.	Sir Richard Hadlee
98.	Waqar Younis
99.	Ian Botham
100.	Graham Dowling
101.	Rodney Marsh
102.	Tony Dodemaide
103.	Alan Knott
104.	Allan Border
105.	Jack Hobbs
106.	Martyn Moxon
107.	Ian Austin, 61 balls, Lancashire v Yorkshire, batting at No 10
108.	Allan Donald
109.	Ray Lindwall
110.	Orange Free State
111.	John Birch
112.	Intikhab Alam
113.	Chris Broad, with a century against Somerset
114.	Freddie Brown
115.	Ted Dexter
116.	Graham Dilley
117.	Gubby Allen
118.	Viv Richards
119.	Tony Wright
120.	Sir Richard Hadlee
121.	Sunil Gavaskar
122.	Javed Miandad
123.	Chris Smith
124.	Arjuna Ranatunga
125.	Rohan Kanhai
126.	Jack Hobbs
127.	Colin Cowdrey
128.	Neil Taylor
129.	Allan Border
130.	John Waite
131.	Michael Atherton
132.	Wilfred Rhodes of England, 52 years 165 days
133.	Mushtaq Mohammad, of Pakistan, 15 years 124 days
134.	James Southerton of England, 49 years 119 days
135.	Allan Lamb
136.	Bob Woolmer
137.	Melbourne Cricket Ground
138.	Greg Chappell
139.	Queensland
140.	Paul Downton
141.	Harold Larwood
142.	Leicestershire
143.	Dominic Cork
144.	Derek Randall
145.	Don Bradman, 974 runs, Australia v England 1930
146.	29, 1983
147.	1927, Essex v New Zealand at Leyton
148.	Wally Hammond, 905, England v Australia 1928-29
149.	Jimmy Cook

150.	Bob Appleyard, 1951
151.	Wasim Bari
152.	West Indies, 1975
153.	Graeme Hick, 405*, Worcestershire v Somerset 1988
154.	1970, South Africa beat Australia 4-0
155.	John Hampshire
156.	George Hirst, Yorkshire v Somerset at Bath in 1906
157.	Rodney Bunting
158.	Eldine Baptiste
159.	Essex and Victoria
160.	Doug Wright, 7
161.	Cyril Walters of Worcestershire
162.	Syd
163.	S. Venkataraghavan
164.	Piran Holloway
165.	Dennis Amiss, 1379 in 1974
166.	Frank Hayes, 106* v West Indies at The Oval 1973
167.	Wally Hammond, 10
168.	1107, Victoria v New South Wales 1926-27
169.	Frank Woolley
170.	1982, against England at Colombo
171.	Martyn Moxon
172.	Imran Khan, while at Royal Grammar School, Worcester
173.	Kim Hughes
174.	12, Northamptonshire v Gloucestershire 1907
175.	Sir Richard Hadlee, 1990
176.	Don Topley
177.	Tim Moody
178.	Lawrence Rowe, West Indies and R.E. Foster, England
179.	Ponsford and Woodfull of Australia
180.	Yorkshire
181.	Jim Laker, 19-90, England v Australia, Old Trafford, 1956
182.	Rob Andrew, former Captain of Cambridge University
183.	Michael Atherton, 13th April, 1991, Lancashire v Cambridge University
184.	Geoff Howarth
185.	Malcolm Marshall
186.	Adrian Aymes
187.	The same nickname, 'Frog'
188.	Houghton-le-Spring
189.	Duleep Mendis
190.	Darren Bicknell
191.	Chris Broad, Graham Gooch, Wayne Larkins, Mark Benson
192.	Tim Robinson
193.	Derek Randall
194.	Harry Brind
195.	Nigel Briers
196.	Jeremy Coney
197.	Alan Wells
198.	Ken Farnes and Frank Tyson
199.	A.B. 'Sandy' Greig, father of Tony and Ian
200.	George Giffen

INDEX OF PLAYERS BY COUNTY

DERBYSHIRE

ADAMS, C. J.
AZHARUDDIN, M. *
BARNETT, K. J.
BASE, S. J.
BISHOP, I. R.
BOWLER, P. D.
BROWN, A. M.
CORK, D. G.
FOLLEY, I.*
GOLDSMITH, S. C.
GRIFFITH, F. A.
JEAN-JACQUES, M.
KRIKKEN, K. M.G.
MAHER, B. J. M.
MALCOLM, D. E.
McCRAY, E.*
MORRIS, J. E.
MORTENSEN, O. H
O'GORMAN, T. J. G.
ROBERTS, B.*
SLADDIN, R.W.
WARNER, A. E.

DURHAM

BAINBRIDGE, P.
BERRY, P. J.
BLENKIRON, D. A.
BOTHAM, I. T.
BRIERS, M. P.
BROWN, G.K.
BROWN, S. J. E.
COOK, G.
DALEY, J.A.
FOTHERGILL, A. R.
GLENDENEN, J. D.
GRAVENEY, D. A.
HENDERSON, P. W.

HUGHES, S. P.
HUTTON, S.
JONES, D. M.
LARKINS, W.
McEWAN, S. M.
PARKER, P. W. G.
SCOTT, C.W.
SMITH, I
WIGHAM, G.
WOOD, J.

ESSEX

ANDREW, S. J. W.
BUTLER, K.A.
CHILDS, J. H.
EAST, D. E.*
FOSTER, N. A.
FRASER, A. G. J.
GARNHAM, M. A.
GOOCH, G. A.
HUSSAIN, N.
ILOTT, M. C.
KNIGHT, N.V.
LEWIS, J. J. B.
LOVELL, W.G.
PRICHARD, P. J.
PRINGLE, D. R.
SALIM MALIK*
SHAHID, N.
STEPHENSON, J. P.
SUCH, P. M.
TENNANT, L.
TOPLEY, T. D.
WAUGH, M. E.

GLAMORGAN

BARWICK, S. R.

BASTIEN, S.
BUTCHER, A. R.
CANN, M. J.*
COTTEY, P. A.
CROFT, R. D. B.
DALE, A.
DENNIS, S. J.*
DERRICK, J.*
FOSTER, D. J.
FROST, M.
HEMP, D.L.
HOLMES, G. C. *
JAMES, S. P.
KIRNON, S.
MAYNARD, M. P.
METSON, C. P.
MORRIS, H.
RICHARDS, I. V. A.
ROBERTS, M. L.*
SHASTRI, R.J.*
WATKIN, S. L.

GLOUCESTERSHIRE

ALLEYNE, M. W.
ATHEY, C. W. J.
BABINGTON, A. M.
BALL, M. C. J.
BARNES, S. N.*
BELL, R. M.*
DAVIES, M.
DAWSON, R.I.
DE LA PENA, J. M.
GERRARD, M. J.
GILBERT, D. R.*
HANCOCK, T. H. C.
HARDY, J. J. E.*
HINKS, S. G.
HODGSON, G. D.
HUNT, A.J.

605

LAWRENCE, D. V.
LLOYDS, J. W.*
MILBURN, E. T.*
ROMAINES, P. W.*
RUSSELL, R. C.
SCOTT, R. J.
SMITH, A.M.
WALSH, C. A.
WILLIAMS, R.C.
WILLIAMS, R. C. J.
WRIGHT, A. J.

HAMPSHIRE

AQIB JAVED*
AYLING, J. R.
AYMES, A. N.
BAKKER, P.-J.
CONNOR, C. A.
COX, R. M. F.
GOWER, D. I.
JAMES, K. D.
MARSHALL, M. D.
MARU, R. J.
MIDDLETON, T. C.
NICHOLAS, M. C. J.
PARKS, R. J.
SHINE, K. J.
SMITH, C. L.*
SMITH, R. A.
TERRY, V. P.
TREMLETT, T. M.
TURNER, I. J.
UDAL, S. D.
WOOD, J. R.

KENT

BENSON, M. R.
COWDREY, C. S.*
COWDREY, G. R.
DAVIS, R. P.
DOBSON, M. C.*

EALHAM, M. A.
ELLISON, R. M.
FLEMING, M. V.
HOOPER, C. L.
IGGLESDEN, A. P.
KELLEHER, D. J. M.*
KERSEY, G.J.
LLONG, N.J.
LONGLEY, J.I.
MARSH, S. A.
McCAGUE, M.J.
MERRICK, T. A.*
PATEL, M. M.
PENN, C.
TAYLOR, N. R.
WARD, T. R.
WREN, T. N.

LANCASHIRE

ALLOTT, P. W.
ATHERTON, M. A.
AUSTIN, I. D.
BARNETT, A. A.
CRAWLEY, J. P.
DEFREITAS, P. A. J.
FAIRBROTHER, N. H.
FITTON, J. D.
FLETCHER, S. D.
FOWLER, G.
HEGG, W. K.
HUGHES, D. P.
IRANI, R.
JACK, S.
JESTY, T. E.*
LLOYD, G. D.
MARTIN, P. J.
MENDIS, G. D.
ORRELL, T. M.*
SHARP, M. A.
SPEAK, N. J.
STANWORTH, J.
TITCHARD, S. P.
WARD, M. J. P.*

WASIM AKRAM*
WATKINSON, M.
YATES, G.

LEICESTERSHIRE

BENSON, J. D. R.
BOON, T. J.
BRIERS, N. E.
GIDLEY, M. I.
HEPWORTH, P. N.
MAGUIRE, J. N.
MARTYN, D. R.*
MILLNS, D. J.
MULLALLY, A. D.
NIXON, P. A.
PARSONS, G. J.
POTTER, L.
SMITH, B. F.
WELLS, V. J.
WHITAKER, J. J.
WHITTICASE, P.
WILKINSON, C.W.*
WILLEY, P.*

MIDDLESEX

BROWN, K. R.
COWANS, N. G.
DOWNTON, P. R.*
ELLCOCK, R. M.
EMBUREY, J. E.
FARBRACE, P.
FRASER, A. R. C.
GATTING, M. W.
HAYNES, D. L.
HEADLEY, D.W.
HUTCHINSON, I. J. F.
KEECH, M.
POOLEY, J. C.
RAMPRAKASH, M. R.
ROSEBERRY, M. A.
SYLVESTER, S. A.

TAYLOR, C. W.
TUFNELL, P. C. R.
WEEKES, P. N.
WILLIAMS, N. F.

NORTHAMPTONSHIRE

AMBROSE, C. E. L.
BAILEY, R. J.
BAPTISTE, E. A. E.*
CAPEL, D. J.
COOK, N. G. B.
CURRAN, K. M.
FELTON, N. A.
FORDHAM, A.
HUGHES, J. G.
LAMB, A. J.
LOYE, M.B.
MONTGOMERIE, R.R.
NOON, W. M.
PENBERTHY, A. L.
RIPLEY, D.
ROBERTS, A. R.
STANLEY, N. A.
TAYLOR, J. P.
THOMAS, J. G.*
WALKER, A.
WILLIAMS, R. G.

NOTTINGHAMSHIRE

AFFORD, J. A.
BROAD, B. C.
BROADLEY, V. J. P.
CAIRNS, C.
COOPER, K. E.
CRAWLEY, M. A.
EVANS, K. P.
FIELD-BUSS, M. G.
FRENCH, B. N.
HEMMINGS, E. E.
JOHNSON, P.
LEWIS, C. C.

MARTINDALE, D. J. R.*
NEWELL, M.
PICK, R. A.
POLLARD, P.
RANDALL, D. W.
ROBINSON, R. T.
SAXELBY, M.

SOMERSET

BARTLETT, R. J.
BEAL, D.
BURNS, N. D.
CADDICK, A. R.
CLEAL, M. W.*
COOK, S. J.*
FLETCHER, I.
HALLETT, J. C.
HARDEN, R. J.
HAYHURST, A. N.
LATHWELL, M. N.
LEFEBVRE, R. P.
MACLEAY, K.H.
MALLENDER, N. A.
PRINGLE, N. J.*
ROEBUCK, P. M.*
ROSE, G. D.
SWALLOW, I. G.*
TAVARE, C. J.
TOWNSEND, G. T. J.
TRUMP, H. R. J.
TURNER, R. J.
VAN TROOST, A. P.
WHITE, G. W.

SURREY

ALIKHAN, R. I.
BENJAMIN, J. E.
BICKNELL, D. J.
BICKNELL, M. P.
BOILING, J.
BROWN, A. D.

BULLEN, C.K.*
BUTCHER, M. A.
FELTHAM, M. A.
GREIG, I. A.
KENDRICK, N. M.
LYNCH, M. A.
MEDLYCOTT, K. T.
MURPHY, A. J.
ROBINSON, J. D.
ROBSON, A. G.*
SARGEANT, N. F.
STEWART, A. J.
THORPE, G. P.
WAQAR YOUNIS*
WARD, D. M.

SUSSEX

BUNTING, R. A.*
DODEMAIDE, A. I. C.*
DONELAN, B. T. P.
GIDDINS, E. S. H.
GOULD, I. J.*
GREENFIELD, K.
HALL, J. W.
HANLEY, R.
HANSFORD, A. R.*
JONES, A. N.
LENHAM, N. J.
MOORES, P.
NORTH, J. A.
PIGOTT, A. C. S.
SALISBURY, I. D. K.
SMITH, D. M.
SPEIGHT, M. P.
STEPHENSON, F. D.
THRELFALL, P. W.*
WELLS, A. P.
WELLS, C. M.

WARWICKSHIRE

ASIF DIN, M.
BOOTH, P. A.
BROWN, D. R.
BURNS, M.
DONALD, A. A.
GREEN, S. J.*
HOLLOWAY, P. C. L.
LLOYD, T. A.
MOLES, A. J.
MUNTON, T. A.
OSTLER, D. P.
PIERSON, A. R. K.*
PIPER, K. J.
RATCLIFFE, J. D.
REEVE, D. A.
SMALL, G. C.
SMITH, G.*
SMITH, N. M. K.
SMITH, P. A.
TWOSE, R. G.

WORCESTERSHIRE

BENT, P.*
BEVINS, S. R.
CURTIS, T. S.
DILLEY, G. R.
D'OLIVEIRA, D. B.
HAYNES, G. R.
HICK, G. A.
ILLINGWORTH, R. K.
LAMPITT, S. R.
LEATHERDALE, D. A.
LORD, G. J.*
MOODY, T. M.
NEALE, P. A.
NEWPORT, P. J.
RADFORD, N. V.
RHODES, S. J.
SEYMOUR, A. C.
STEMP, R. D.
TOLLEY, C. M.

WESTON, M. J.
WESTON, W.P.C.

YORKSHIRE

BATTY, J. D.
BLAKEY, R. J.
BROADHURST, M.
BYAS, D.
CARRICK, P.
CHAPMAN, C. A.
GOUGH, D.
GRAYSON, P. A.
HARTLEY, P. J.
HOUSEMAN, I. J.
JARVIS, P. W.
KELLETT, S. A.
McDERMOTT, C. J.
METCALFE, A. A.
MOXON, M. D.
PICKLES, C. S.
ROBINSON, M. A.
ROBINSON, P. E.*
SHARP, K.
SIDEBOTTOM, A.*

*denotes not registered for 1992 season. Where players are known to have moved in the off-season they are listed under their new county.